THE
OSCAR®
MOVIES

FOURTH EDITION

THE
OSCAR®
MOVIES

FOURTH EDITION

Roy Pickard

Facts On File

AN INFOBASE HOLDINGS COMPANY

THE OSCAR® MOVIES Fourth Edition

Copyright © 1994 Roy Pickard

Facts On File, Inc.
460 Park Avenue South
New York NY 10016
USA

Library of Congress Cataloging-in-Publication Data

Pickard, Roy.
The Oscar movies / Roy Pickard.
p.   cm.
Previous ed. published under title: The Oscar movies from A–Z.
Includes bibliographical references and index.
ISBN 0-8160-2709-9
1. Academy Awards (Motion pictures)   2. Motion pictures—Plots, themes, etc.   I. Pickard, Roy. Oscar movies from A–Z.   II. Title.
PN1993.92.P53   1993
791.43'079—dc20   93-8338

A British CIP catalogue record for this book is available from the British Library.

Facts On File books are available at special discounts when purchased in bulk quantities for businesses, associations, institutions or sales promotions. Please call our Special Sales Department in New York at 212/683-2244 or 800/322-8755.

Text design by Ellen Levine
Jacket design by Carla Weise
Composition by the Maple-Vail Book Manufacturing Group
Manufactured by R. R. Donnelley & Sons, Inc.
Printed in the United States of America

10 9 8 7 6 5 4 3 2 1

This book is printed on acid-free paper.

Dedicated to Joan and Claire (again) and the late Margaret Herrick, President of the Academy, who first enthused over this project and whose help, patience and frequent correspondence helped me bring this book to fruition.

Photo Acknowledgments

The pictures in this book were originally issued to publicize or promote films made or distributed by the following companies, to whom I gratefully offer acknowledgment: Allied Artists, American-International, Carolco, Castle Rock, Columbia, Walt Disney/Buena Vista, Eagle-Lion, Ealing Studies, EMI, Enigma, First National, Goldcrest, Goldwyn, GW Films, London Films, Lorimar, Metro-Goldwyn-Mayer, Monogram, Orion, Palace, Paramount, The Rank Organization, Renaissance Films, Republic, RKO/RKO Radio, Selznick, Touchstone, 20th Century-Fox, United Artists, Universal/Universal International, and Warner Brothers.

Contents

Photo Acknowledgments   vii

Introduction   xi

The Oscar Movies A–Z   1

Appendix 1: The Winners Year by Year   183

Appendix 2: Nominees Year by Year   192

Appendix 3: Oscar Record-Holders   221

Appendix 4: Documentary and Short
Subjects   226

Appendix 5: Oscar Winners at the Box
Office   238

Appendix 6: Directors Who Worked with Oscar-
Winning Actors   244

Appendix 7: Nominated Films That Lost   246

Appendix 8: Over 200 Great Films That Weren't
Nominated   249

Appendix 9: Memorial and Honorary
Awards   252

Appendix Ten: Oscar Night Hosts   259

Selected Bibliography   262

Index   263

Introduction

When I first compiled this book—this is the fourth edition, following those published in the late 1970s and during the 1980s—I made the observation that Oscar night was just about the only event that linked the Hollywood of old with the new Hollywood. Today, as many of us prepare, a trifle apprehensively, for what the rest of the 1990s have to offer us, this remains just as true as ever.

The kinds of films we watch may have changed beyond all recognition, but Oscar's glitz, razzmatazz, vulgarity, color and overkill are still there, and so are the excitement and fierce ambition that reveal themselves on every Academy Award night. As one noted American film director told me recently: "You may not agree with the idea—but if you're nominated and find yourself in a race you might as well try and win it!"

The critics haven't changed much either. Every February when the nominations are released, their knives come out as they give full expression to their cynicism and their vendettas. And when, six weeks later, the year's best are finally announced, the same critics invariably assert that those films and actors who won did so simply because they enjoyed the best publicity campaigns. All of which conveniently overlooks such previous deserving winners as *Casablanca, Gone With the Wind, All About Eve, On the Waterfront, The Apartment, Lawrence of Arabia, Midnight Cowboy, The Godfather, Patton, Annie Hall* and *One Flew Over the Cuckoo's Nest.*

It matters not a jot anyway. The critics, thankfully, pass very quickly into oblivion; the Oscars, courtesy of the Academy of Motion Picture Arts And Sciences, carry on regardless, each year recognizing the achievements of those men and women working before and behind the cameras.

This book is not intended to be a critical analysis of the Academy Awards or a film review book. Instead it is meant to serve as a tool for readers, providing the facts about the 600-plus feature films that have won Oscars since the awards were first introduced back in 1929. Its alphabetical format allows a researcher or buff to look up his or her own favorite film at a glance, see how many Oscars it won, and check on its story line, main credits, and other pertinent information, such as studio and running time. If a film's Oscar is of some particular significance, then that detail is highlighted and related to other films in the book. It's as simple as that.

The actual birth of the Academy of Motion Picture Arts and Sciences—the organization that each year hands out the Oscars—occurred on May 4, 1927 when 36 people from various areas of film production met to organize a non-profit-making corporation dedicated to the ideal of improving the artistic quality of the film medium. There were some impressive names among those first three dozen members: Douglas Fairbanks, who was the Academy's first president; actors Richard Barthelmess, Mary Pickford and Conrad Nagel; directors Fred Niblo, Raoul Walsh, Henry King and Frank Lloyd; studio executives Louis B. Mayer and Irving Thalberg; and art director Cedric Gibbons.

It was the last-named who was responsible for the design of Oscar himself. At a banquet at Hollywood's Biltmore Hotel, just after the formation of the Academy, he responded to a request for a symbol that would depict continuing progress in the industry and that was both militant and dynamic. His pencil quickly moved across the tablecloth in front of him, and in a few minutes the design for Oscar was complete—the figure of a man with a crusader's sword, standing on a reel of film.

The very first awards were presented at Hollywood's Roosevelt Hotel on May 16, 1929. Seven categories were honored: best film, direction, actor, actress, writing, cinematography and art direction. The presentations took roughly ten minutes.

The sound recording award was introduced two years later (1929/30), when Douglas Shearer won for MGM's *The Big House*. Awards for short subjects— cartoons, two-reeler comedies, and so on—were inaugurated in 1931/32.

The year 1934 saw the first editing award (to Conrad Nervig for *Eskimo*) and also the first honors for music, with Columbia's Grace Moore vehicle *One Night of Love* winning for best score and "The Continental" (featured in *The Gay Divorcee*) for best song.

Awards for supporting roles were first presented in 1937 (for performances in 1936), when Walter Brennan *(Come and Get It)* and Gale Sondergaard *(Anthony Adverse)* took the Oscars. The year 1939 saw the introduction of the first regular special effects awards and the first Oscar for color cinematography.

From 1940 on, cinematography and art direction awards were divided into color and black and white, as indeed were awards for costume design when they were introduced in 1948. After 1966, when only a handful of black and white films were still being made, the award reverted to a single category.

The most recent category to receive a regular award is that of makeup, which was introduced in 1981.

Over 5,000 members currently make up the Academy of Motion Picture Arts and Sciences. They include actors, directors, writers, cinematographers, sound recordists, musicians, and just about everyone else who helps to make a motion picture. Members of their own individual branch vote for the five nominees in their category. The full membership then votes in every catgory when the final balloting takes place. Only films that have played in the Los Angeles area for at least one week between January 1 and December 31 of the year in question are eligible for nomination.

As for Oscar himself? He weighs just eight pounds (although he feels much heavier), stands 13½ inches high, is made of 92.5 percent tin and 7.5 percent copper, and is coated with 14-carat gold. He was named "Oscar" by Margaret Herrick, late president of the Academy, who spotted a copy of the statuette on an executive's desk and exclaimed, "Why, he looks like my Uncle Oscar!" That was in 1931. Before that, the award was known simply, and rather less colorfully, as "The Statuette."

"The Statuette" or "Uncle Oscar" has been going strong ever since. Each year some 30 statuettes are produced by the Dodge Trophy Company of Crystal Lake, Illinois, all of them presented at the ceremonies in Hollywood the following spring. The value of the statuette is said to be $250, but to those who have won it over the past 65 years it was and is worth its weight in gold.

The names of those winners can all be found within the pages of this book—a volume in which such blockbusters as *Lawrence of Arabia* and *The Last Emperor* rub shoulders with minor films that have won solitary awards for sound effects or makeup. You'll also find Oscar record holders such as *Ben-Hur*, still the biggest-ever winner with 11 awards; *All About Eve*, the film with the most nominations (14); and *It Happened One Night*, *One Flew Over the Cuckoo's Nest* and *The Silence of the Lambs*, the only films to have won all five major Academy Awards.

I still believe that there is no other book quite like *The Oscar Movies*. There are other books on the Academy Awards, yes, but none that allows you to find, within seconds, an Oscar-winning film that is either 40 years old or was a winner just a year ago. Even if you require only a quick check to find out just how many Oscars a film has won, the stars beside a movie's title—one for each Oscar—provide an immediate answer. It is a book to take down from the shelf when you are searching for information or trying to settle an argument. I hope it proves as useful today as it did a decade ago.

—Roy Pickard

A

THE ABYSS (1989) ★

★ best visual effects John Bruno, Dennis Muren, Hoyt Yeatman & Dennis Skotak

The crew of an oil rig is called upon to rescue a nuclear submarine stranded two and a half miles down on the floor of the Caribbean. Also down there: strange luminous alien beings with miraculous powers. A blend of *Close Encounters of the Third Kind* (1977), and *20,000 Leagues Under the Sea* (1954), enhanced by a $60 million budget and stunning special effects.

A 20th Century-Fox Picture, directed by James Cameron. With Ed Harris, Mary Elizabeth Mastrantonio, Michael Biehn, Leo Burmester, Todd Graff, John Bedford Lloyd, J. C. Quinn, Kimberly Scott. 70 mm/DuArt color; prints by DeLuxe. 140 mins.

THE ACCIDENTAL TOURIST (1988)

★ best supporting actress Geena Davis

American travel writer William Hurt, separated from his wife Kathleen Turner after the death

William Hurt (center) with his new family Geena Davis and Robert Gorman in Lawrence Kasdan's *The Accidental Tourist* (Warner Bros., 1988). Davis was named best supporting actress of the year for her performance.

of their 12-year-old son, gets a new lease on life from a kooky young dog trainer who offers him romance and a fresh ongoing relationship. Hurt was nominated for many of his films in the 1980s, but not on this occasion. Geena Davis took the honors in the supporting category for her way with a wisecrack and her coaching of Hurt's scene-stealing corgi.

A Warner Bros. Picture, directed by Lawrence Kasdan. With William Hurt, Kathleen Turner, Geena Davis, Amy Wright, David Ogden Stiers, Ed Begley Jr., Bill Pullman, Robert Gorman, Bradley Mott. Technicolor. 121 mins.

THE ACCUSED (1988)   ★

★ best actress Jodie Foster

Waitress Jodie Foster, gang-raped in a seedy small-town bar, brings a court case against those who perpetrated the crime and also the drunken onlookers who encouraged it. A partly exploitative film—there is an explicit portrayal of Foster's humiliation—but one that also effec-

Jodie Foster, best actress of 1988 for her portrayal of a rape victim in *The Accused* (Paramount).

tively points out several important issues on rape. Foster's first Oscar (she won again three years later for *The Silence of the Lambs* after being nominated at the age of 12 for her young prostitute in Scorsese's *Taxi Driver* [1976]).

A Paramount Picture, directed by Jonathan Kaplan. With Kelly McGillis, Jodie Foster, Bernie Coulson, Leo Rossi, Ann Hearn, Carmen Argenziano, Steve Antin, Tom O'Brien. Technicolor. 111 mins.

THE ADVENTURES OF DON JUAN (1949)   ★

★ best color costume design Leah Rhodes, Travilla and Marjorie Best

Lavish Technicolor swashbuckler, set in 17th-century Spain, with Errol Flynn as the legendary lover saving Queen Viveca Lindfors from the evil machinations of the King's first minister, Robert Douglas.

A Warner Bros. Picture, directed by Vincent Sherman. With Errol Flynn, Viveca Lindfors, Robert Douglas, Alan Hale, Romney Brent, Ann Rutherford. Technicolor. 110 mins.

THE ADVENTURES OF ROBIN HOOD (1938)   ★ ★ ★

★ best art direction Carl Weyl
★ best editing Ralph Dawson
★ best music: original score Erich Wolfgang Korngold

The first Technicolor version of the Robin Hood legend, with Flynn dueling to the death with Basil Rathbone around the shadowy walls of Nottingham Castle. A silken Claude Rains adds a purring Prince John, a lovely Olivia de Havilland beauty and adoration. Along with *Captain Blood* (1935) the only swashbuckler ever to be nominated for the best picture award.

A Warner Bros. Picture, directed by Michael Curtiz & William Keighley. With Errol Flynn, Olivia de Havilland, Claude Rains, Basil Rathbone, Ian Hunter, Eugene Pallette, Alan Hale, Melville Cooper. Technicolor. 105 mins.

THE AFRICAN QUEEN (1951) ★

★ best actor Humphrey Bogart

Grizzled Canadian tug boat skipper Humphrey Bogart and spinster Katharine Hepburn make a treacherous journey down an African river during the eary days of World War I. Ahead of them: perilous rapids, leeches and a 100 ft. enemy gunboat. Based on the novel by C. S. Forester, and the film that earned Bogart his sole Academy Award. His other best actor nominations: Rick Blaine in *Casablanca* (1943); and Captain Queeg in *The Caine Mutiny* (1954).

A Romulus Film, directed by John Huston. With Humphrey Bogart, Katharine Hepburn, Robert Morley, Peter Bull, Theodore Bikel. Technicolor. 106 mins.

AIR FORCE (1943) ★

★ best editing George Amy

Howard Hawks' World War II account of the flight of a single flying fortress and her crew from takeoff in San Francisco on December 6, 1941, to the battles over the South Pacific.

A Warner Bros. Picture, directed by Howard Hawks. With John Garfield, John Ridgely, Gig Young, Arthur Kennedy, Charles Drake, Harry Carey, George Tobias. 124 mins.

AIRPORT (1970) ★

★ best supporting actress Helen Hayes

One of the most troublesome nights in movie aviation history, with all the runways of Lincoln International Airport snowed in by a blizzard and Van Heflin as a mad bomber blowing an airliner half to bits in mid-flight. Pilot Dean Martin brings 'em back alive, including aged stowaway Helen Hayes—the first actress to win a supporting award as well as a major acting Oscar. She won her first award in 1931 for *The Sin of Madelon Claudet*.

A Universal Picture, directed by George Seaton. With Burt Lancaster, Dean Martin, Jean Seberg, Jacqueline Bisset, George Kennedy, Helen Hayes, Van Heflin, Maureen Stapleton, Barry Nelson, Dana Wynter, Lloyd Nolan. Technicolor. 136 mins.

ALADDIN (1992) ★★

★ best original score Alan Menken
★ best original song "Whole New World" (Alan Menken, music; Tim Rice, lyrics)

Disney's first venture into the Arabian Nights, the oft-told tale of an endearing young thief-cum-street urchin whose life is changed by his love for a princess and by the genie that emerges from a magic lamp. The voice of Robin Williams brings style and gusto to the genie; composer Alan Menken brings his usual melodic touch to the score. His double Oscar win for music and song followed similar achievements for *The Little Mermaid* (1989) and *Beauty and the Beast* (1991), earning him a record six Oscars in only four years.

A Buena Vista release of a Walt Disney Pictures production. Directors: John Musker and Ron Clements. Voices by Scott Weinger, Robin Williams, Linda Larkin, Jonathan Freeman, Frank Welker, Gilbert Gottfried, Douglas Seale. Technicolor. 90 mins.

THE ALAMO (1960) ★

★ best sound Gordon E. Sawyer & Fred Hynes

The full story of how, in 1836, a handful of assorted Americans defended a broken-down mission against the full might of the Mexican Army. Wayne, besides directing, stars as Davy Crockett; Richard Widmark is Jim Bowie; Laurence Harvey is the commander of the mission, William Travis.

A United Artists Picture, directed by John Wayne. With John Wayne, Richard Widmark,

Laurence Harvey, Richard Boone, Frankie Avalon. Todd-AO/Technicolor. 192 mins.

ALEXANDER'S RAGTIME BAND (1938) ★

★ best music score Alfred Newman

Large-scale Fox show-biz epic covering the period 1911 to 1938. Plenty of three-way romance (Power, Faye, Ameche) and plenty of Irving Berlin melodies, the latter helping the film win its solitary Oscar. Songs include "Easter Parade," "Blue Skies," and "A Pretty Girl Is Like a Melody."

A 20th Century-Fox Picture, directed by Henry King. With Tyrone Power, Alice Faye, Don Ameche, Ethel Merman, Jack Haley, Jean Hersholt, Helen Westley, John Carradine. 105 mins.

ALICE DOESN'T LIVE HERE ANY MORE (1974) ★

★ best acress Ellen Burstyn

Ellen Burstyn as a widow with a teenage son trying to make an independent life for herself but finding out just how difficult it can be.

A Warner Bros. Picture, directed by Martin Scorsese. With Ellen Burstyn, Kris Kristofferson, Billy Green Bush, Diane Ladd, Lelia Goldoni, Lane Bradbury, Jodie Foster. Technicolor. 112 mins.

ALIEN (1979) ★

★ best visual effects H. R. Giger, Carlo Rambaldi, Brian Johnson, Nick Allder & Denys Aling

A variation on the "people trapped in a haunted house" type of movie, only this time the setting

Ian Holm and Sigourney Weaver in *Alien* (20th Century-Fox), winner of the award for best visual effects in 1979.

is outer space and the characters are the terrified crew of the spacecraft *Nostromo*. There is no ghost, just a constantly changing monster that bursts out of John Hurt's chest and devours the crew one by one—except Sigourney Weaver, who alone survives the terror.

A 20th Century-Fox Picture, directed by Ridley Scott. With Tom Skerritt, Sigourney Weaver, Veronica Cartwright, Harry Dean Stanton, John Hurt, Ian Holm, Yaphet Kotto, Helen Horton. Eastman Color, prints by DeLuxe. 117 mins.

ALIENS (1986)

★ best sound effects editing Don Sharpe
★ best visual effects Robert Skotak, Stan Winston, John Richardson & Suzanne Benson

Sigourney Weaver returns to the planet that gave birth to the alien fiend and finds bigger and better monsters incubating in the cocooned corpses of space colonists. A detachment of battle-hungry Marines do their best to help her out, but things prove no easier than they were in film number one. Weaver earned herself a best-actress nomination for her portrayal of Flight Officer Ripley. She was not nominated for the first movie.

A 20th Century-Fox Picture, directed by James Cameron. With Sigourney Weaver, Car-

Back to the monster planet! A desperate Sigourney Weaver and a wounded Michael Biehn after encountering the *Aliens* (20th Century-Fox, 1986).

rie Henn, Michael Biehn, Paul Reiser, Lance Henrriksen, Bill Paxton, William Hope, Jenette Goldstein. 70 mm. Eastman Color, prints by DeLuxe. 137 mins.

ALL ABOUT EVE (1950)

★ best film Darryl F. Zanuck (producer)
★ best direction Joseph L. Mankiewicz
★ best supporting actor George Sanders
★ best screenplay Joseph L. Mankiewicz
★ best b/w costume design Edith Head & Charles LeMaire
★ best sound recording W. D. Flick & Roger Heman

Backstage movie about New York's theater world, with Bette Davis at the peak of her powers as fading actress Margo Channing warning everybody that "it's going to be a bumpy night." Also on hand: Anne Baxter as her scheming understudy and critic George Sanders, cynically amused by the whole thing. Its 14 nominations make it the most nominated film in the history of the Academy.*

A 20th Century-Fox Picture, directed by Joseph L. Mankiewicz. With Bette Davis, Anne Baxter, George Sanders, Celeste Holm, Gary Merrill, Hugh Marlowe, Thelma Ritter, Marilyn Monroe. 138 mins.

ALL QUIET ON THE WESTERN FRONT (1929/30)   ★ ★

★ best film Carl Laemmle, Jr. (producer)
★ best direction Lewis Milestone

Wholly pacifist movie following the experiences of a group of German schoolboys who, in World War I, volunteer to serve their fatherland for death and glory only to find their romantic illusions shattered at the front.

---

* *Note: Gone With the Wind* (1939), *From Here to Eternity* (1953) and *Who's Afraid of Virginia Woolf?* (1966) all earned 13 nominations in their respective years.

Lewis Milestone's *All Quiet on the Western Front* (Universal), voted best picture of the year, 1929/30.

A Universal Picture, directed by Lewis Milestone. With Lew Ayres, Louis Wolheim, John Wray, Raymond Griffith, Slim Summerville, Russell Gleason. 140 mins.

ALL THAT JAZZ (1979)   ★★★★

★ best art direction Philip Rosenberg & Tony Walton
    set decoration Edward Stewart & Gary Brink
★ best costume design Albert Wolsky
★ best editing Alan Heim
★ best adaptation score Ralph Burns

Virtually a self-portrait by director Bob Fosse, following the last few months in the hectic life of a Broadway choreographer/film director (Roy Scheider) as he drinks himself into an early grave through a surfeit of work, sex and drugs. Not exactly an uplifting experience, but Fosse's musical numbers are exhilarating and the scenes of life behind the glamor of the Broadway stage uncomfortably realistic. Best-actor nominee Scheider lost to Dustin Hoffman (*Kramer vs. Kramer*) in the 1979 Oscar race.

A Columbia/20th Century-Fox Picture, directed by Bob Fosse. With Roy Scheider, Jessica Lange, Ann Reinking, Leland Palmer, Cliff Gorman, Ben Vereen, Erzsebet Foldi, Michael Tolan. Technicolor; prints by DeLuxe. 123 mins.

ALL THAT MONEY CAN BUY (1941)   ★

★ best music: scoring of a dramatic picture Bernard Herrmann

An adaptation of the Stephen Vincent Benet story "The Devil and Daniel Webster," a parallel of the Faust tale in a New Hampshire setting, with James Craig as a young farmer signing a contract with the Devil (Walter Huston) and selling his soul for a pot of gold. Composer Bernard Herrmann was also nominated in 1941 for his score for Orson Welles' *Citizen Kane* and subsequently for *Anna and the King of Siam* (1946), *Obsession* (1976) and *Taxi Driver* (1976). He was not nominated for his work on Alfred Hitchcock's *Psycho* (1960) or for any of the other seven films he scored for the director.

An RKO Picture, directed by William Dieterle. With Edward Arnold, Walter Huston, James Craig, Anne Shirley, Jane Darwell, Simone Simon, Gene Lockhart. 112 mins.

ALL THE KING'S MEN (1949)   ★★★

★ best film Robert Rossen (producer)
★ best actor Broderick Crawford
★ best supporting actress Mercedes McCambridge

The rise and fall of "hick" politician Willie Stark (Crawford), who becomes corrupted during his rise to power and ends up the ruthless self-styled dictator of his home state. Adapted from the Pulitzer Prize-winning novel by Robert Penn Warren, which, in turn, was based on the career of Huey "Kingfish" Long, the Louisiana presidential contender assassinated in the mid-1930s. Mercedes McCambridge's Oscar was for her debut performance as Crawford's vixenish campaign manager.

A Columbia Picture, directed by Robert Rossen. With Broderick Crawford, John Derek, Joanne Dru, John Ireland, Mercedes McCambridge, Shepperd Strudwick. 109 mins.

On the Watergate trail—Dustin Hoffman and Robert Redford in *All the President's Men* (Warner Bros.), winner of four Oscars in 1976.

ALL THE PRESIDENT'S MEN (1976) ★★★★

★ best supporting actor Jason Robards
★ best screenplay William Goldman
★ best art direction George Jenkins
    set decoration George Gaines
★ best sound Arthur Piantadosi, Les Fresholtz, Dick Alexander & Jim Webb

The Watergate scandal—as exposed by *Washington Post* reporters Bob Woodward (Robert Redford) and Carl Bernstein (Dustin Hoffman)—meticulously transferred to the screen by Alan Pakula and proving that politics, provided they are sensational enough, can be both a critical and box-office success. Jason Robards won his supporting Oscar for his portrait of *Washington Post* editor Ben Bradlee.

A Warner Bros, Picture, directed by Alan J. Pakula. With Dustin Hoffman, Robert Redford, Jack Warden, Martin Balsam, Hal Holbrook, Jason Robards, Jane Alexander, Meredith Baxter, Ned Beatty. Technicolor. 138 mins.

AMADEUS (1984) ★★★★★★★★

★ best film Saul Zaentz (producer)
★ best direction Milos Forman

★ best actor F. Murray Abraham
★ best screenplay Peter Shaffer
★ best art direction Patrizia Von Brandenstein
    set decoration Karel Cerny
★ best costume design Theodor Pistek
★ best sound Mark Berger, Tom Scott, Todd Boekelheide & Chris Newman
★ best makeup Paul LeBlanc & Dick Smith

Lavishly mounted, musically splendid version of Peter Shaffer's play about the rivalry between the youthful genius Wolfgang Amadeus Mozart and the Viennese court composer Antonio Salieri, whose insane jealousy (according to Shaffer) led him to plot Mozart's downfall and ultimately his death. Nominated for 11 Academy Awards, the film emerged with eight on Oscar night. Tom Hulce (Mozart) was the unluckiest man of the evening, losing out as best actor to F. Murray Abraham for his Salieri. Filmed by Milos Forman on location in Prague.

A Zaentz/Orion Picture, directed by Milos Forman. With F. Murray Abraham, Tom Hulce,

Milos Forman's *Amadeus* (Zaentz/Orion), winner of eight Oscars in 1984, including best film and best direction.

Elizabeth Berridge, Simon Callow, Roy Do-trice, Christine Ebersole, Jeffrey Jones, Charles Kay, Kenny Baker. Panavision/Technicolor. 70 mm. 160 mins.

AMARCORD (1974)   ★

★ best foreign language film Italy/France

Federico Fellini* reminisces about the people and day-to-day events that occurred in a small North Italian town under the fascists in the 1930s. Fellini's fourth foreign language film award—the others were *La Strada* (1956), *The Nights of Cabiria* (1957), and *8½* (1963).

F. C. Produzioni (Rome), P. E. C. F. (Paris), directed by Federico Fellini. With Pupella Maggio, Magali Noel, Armando Brancia, Ciccio Ingrassia, Nandino Orfei, Luigi Rossi. Technicolor 123 mins.

AMERICA, AMERICA (1963)   ★

★ best b/w art direction Gene Callahan

Elia Kazan's basically factual account of how his Greek immigrant uncle struggled to leave oppressed Turkey at the turn of the century and make the long journey to the promised land of America.

A Warner Bros. Picture, directed by Elia Kazan. With Stathis Giallelis, Frank Wolff,

---

* Fellini has never been named best director, despite being nominated on three occasions for *La Dolce Vita* (1961), *8½* (1963) and *Fellini Satyricon* (1970). He has also been nominated seven times for his screenplays: *Open City* (1946) with Sergio Amidei; *Paisan* (1949) with Roberto Rossellini; *La Strada* (1956) with Tullio Pinelli; *I Vitelloni* (1957) with Ennio Flaiano and Tullio Pinelli; *8½* (1963) with Ennio Flaiano, Tullio Pinelli and Brunello Rondi; *Amarcord* (1975) with Tonino Guerra; and *Fellini's Casanova* (1976) with Bernadino Zapponi. In 1993 he received a special honorary award for his contribution to the cinema.

Harry Davis, Elena Karam, Estelle Hemsley, Gregory Rozakis. 174 mins.

AN AMERICAN IN PARIS (1951)   ★★★★★★

★ best film Arthur Freed (producer)
★ best story & screenplay Alan Jay Lerner
★ best color cinematography Alfred Gilks & John Alton
★ best color art direction Cedric Gibbons & Preston Ames
    color set decoration Edwin B. Willis & Keogh Gleason
★ best color costume, design Orry-Kelly, Walter Plunkett & Irene Sharaff
★ best scoring of a musical Johnny Green & Saul Chaplin

Gershwin musical about a footloose American painter (Gene Kelly) pursuing delightful French girl Leslie Caron and being pursued by wealthy American art promoter Nina Foch in postwar Paris.

An MGM Picture, directed by Vincente Minnelli. With Gene Kelly, Leslie Caron, Oscar Levant, Georges Guetary, Nina Foch. Technicolor. 113 mins.

AN AMERICAN WEREWOLF IN LONDON (1981)   ★

★ best makeup Rick Baker

American youth David Naughton is attacked and bitten by a werewolf on a moor in the North of England and then goes on a rampage around London on the night of the full moon. Nurse Jenny Agutter provides him with love; Rick Baker provides him with Academy Award-winning makeup of sprouting hair, claws, etc. Part humorous, part scary movie; the very first to win in the best makeup category.

A Lycanthrope Picture for Polygram. Directed by John Landis. With David Naughton, Jenny Agutter, Griffin Dunne, John Woodvine, Brian Glover, Lila Kaye. Technicolor. 97 mins.

ANASTASIA (1956) ★

★ best actress Ingrid Bergman

Ingrid Bergman as an amnesiac refugee chosen by scheming conman Yul Brynner as the woman to be passed off as the last surviving daughter of Tsar Nicholas of Russia and his wife Alexandra. Bergman's second Oscar, her first having been won 12 years earlier for *Gaslight* (1944). In 1974 she also won as best supporting actress for *Murder on the Orient Express*.

A 20th Century-Fox Picture, directed by Anatole Litvak. With Ingrid Bergman, Yul Brynner, Helen Hayes, Akim Tamiroff, Martita Hunt, Felix Aylmer. CinemaScope/DeLuxe Color. 105 mins.

ANCHORS AWEIGH (1945) ★

★ best scoring of a musical Georgie Stoll

Kelly and Sinatra teamed for the first time as two sailors on shore leave in Hollywood. The film's highlight, however, is another teaming—Kelly and cartoon mouse Jerry, who dance together in a combined live-action animated sequence.

An MGM Picture, directed by George Sidney. With Gene Kelly, Frank Sinatra, Kathryn Grayson, Jose Iturbi, Dean Stockwell. Technicolor. 140 mins.

ANNA AND THE KING OF SIAM (1946) ★★

★ best b/w cinematography Arthur Miller
★ best b/w art direction Lyle Wheeler & William Darling
      b/w interior, decoration Thomas Little & Frank E. Hughes

The true story of a 19th-century British governess (Irene Dunne) who took on the job of tutor to the royal children of the King of Siam (Rex Harrison). Rodgers and Hammerstein's musical version of the story, *The King and I*, was a bigger award-winner when it was released ten years later.

A 20th Century-Fox Picture, directed by John Cromwell. With Irene Dunne, Rex Harrison, Linda Darnell, Lee J. Cobb, Gale Sondergaard. 128 mins.

ANNE OF THE THOUSAND DAYS (1969) ★

★ best costume design Margaret Furse

The love affair and tragic marriage of Henry VIII (Richard Burton) and the young Anne Boleyn (Genevieve Bujold), who failed to give him his much-desired male heir and ended up, as did several others, with her head on the executioner's block.

A Universal Picture, directed by Charles Jarrott. With Richard Burton, Genevieve Bujold, Irene Papas, Anthony Quayle, John Colicos, Michael Hordern. Panavision/Technicolor. 146 mins.

ANNIE GET YOUR GUN (1950) ★

★ best scoring of a musical Adolph Deutsch & Roger Edens

MGM version of Irving Berlin's musical stage hit about the rise to fame of backwoods sharpshooting gal Annie Oakley (Betty Hutton). Howard Keel co-stars as rival sharpshooter Frank Butler, Louis Calhern as Buffalo Bill.

An MGM Picture, directed by George Sidney. With Betty Hutton, Howard Keel, Louis Calhern, J. Carrol Naish, Edward Arnold, Keenan Wynn. Technicolor. 107 mins.

ANNIE HALL (1977) ★★★★

★ best film Charles H. Joffe (producer)
★ best direction Woody Allen
★ best actress Diane Keaton
★ best original screenplay Woody Allen & Marshall Brickman

Autobiographical comedy by Woody Allen that traces the on-and-off relationship between a TV nightclub comic (Allen) and a young singer (Diane Keaton) who meet, fall in love, quarrel, make up and finally split. Like Orson Welles for *Citizen Kane* (1941), Woody Allen* was nominated in three categories—acting, writing and direction. Welles emerged the victor in only the writing category; Allen won for writing and direction. No one has yet won in all three categories. The film marked the first time a studio had won the best picture award in three successive years, United Artists having won in 1975 for *One Flew Over the Cuckoo's Nest* and in 1976 for *Rocky*.

A United Artists Picture, directed by Woody Allen. With Woody Allen, Diane Keaton, Tony Roberts, Carol Kane, Paul Simon, Shelley Duvall, Janet Margolin. DeLuxe Color. 93 mins.

ANTHONY ADVERSE (1936)

★ best supporting actress Gale Sondergaard
★ best cinematography Tony Gaudio
★ best editing Ralph Dawson
★ best music score* Leo Forbstein

Fredric March as a young Napoleonic adventurer finding love and excitement wherever his travels take him—America, Cuba, Mexico, France, Africa. Adapted from the best-seller by Hervey Allen. Gale Sondergaard (she was the first winner in the supporting actress category)

---

* Woody Allen's nominations were actually not equal to those garnered by Orson Welles for *Citizen Kane* (1941); Welles received four nominations on his film debut, including one for being the producer of the best picture. Warren Beatty has subsequently earned four nominations—best producer, director, actor and screenplay—for his work on *Heaven Can Wait* (1978) and *Reds* (1981).
* Note: Erich Wolfgang Korngold composed the score for *Anthony Adverse* (1936) and by rights should have been awarded the Oscar. Leo Forbstein was only music director on the movie.

is featured as the friend and associate of Scottish-born merchant Edmund Gwenn.

A Warner Bros. Picture, directed by Mervyn LeRoy. With Fredric March, Olivia de Havilland, Anita Louise, Edmund Gwenn, Claude Rains, Donald Woods, Louis Hayward, Gale Sondergaard, Akim Tamiroff. 136 mins.

THE APARTMENT (1960)

★ best film Billy Wilder (producer)
★ best direction Billy Wilder
★ best story & screenplay Billy Wilder & I. A. L. Diamond

Insurance clerk Jack Lemmon has more than he can handle with would-be suicide Shirley MacLaine in Billy Wilder's *The Apartment*, best picture of 1960 and the last film photographed in black and white to be named best of its year.

★ best b/w art direction Alexander Trauner
b/w set decoration Edward G. Boyle
★ best editing Daniel Mandell

Billy Wilder's acid comedy about a young, stuck-in-the-groove insurance clerk (Jack Lemmon) who advances his prospects of promotion by lending his apartment to executives and their girlfriends. The last best-picture winner to be filmed in black-and-white.

A United Artists Picture, directed by Billy Wilder. With Jack Lemmon, Shirley MacLaine, Fred MacMurray, Ray Walston, David Lewis, Jack Kruschen, Joan Shawlee, Edie Adams. Panavision. 125 mins.

APOCALYPSE NOW (1979)   ★ ★

★ best cinematography Vittorio Storaro
★ best sound Walter Murch, Mark Berger, Richard Beggs & Nat Boxer

The most realistic account of the physical and psychological horrors of the Vietnam War; an updating of Conrad's *Heart of Darkness* about an army captain (Martin Sheen) who is ordered to hunt down a deranged American officer (Marlon Brando) operating in Cambodia with an army of guerrilla tribesmen. The long river journey to Brando's headquarters forms the core of a nightmare film that earned eight Oscar nominations (including best picture) but won in only two minor categories. The less ambitious and less expensive *Kramer vs. Kramer* scooped the main awards in 1979.

An Omni Zoetrope production/United Artists. Directed by Francis Ford Coppola. With Marlon Brando, Robert Duvall, Martin Sheen, Frederic Forrest, Albert Hall, Sam Bottoms, Larry Fishburne, Dennis Hopper, G. D. Spradlin, Harrison Ford. Technovision/Technicolor. 153 mins.

ARISE MY LOVE (1940)   ★

★ best original story Benjamin Glazer & John S. Toldy

Paramount wartime propaganda piece with Claudette Colbert involved with imprisoned flier Ray Milland in the latter days of the Spanish Civil War.

A Paramount Picture, directed by Mitchell Leisen. With Claudette Colbert, Ray Milland, Dennis O'Keefe, Walter Abel, Dick Purcell, George Zucco. 100 mins.

AROUND THE WORLD IN EIGHTY DAYS (1956)   ★ ★ ★ ★

★ best film Michael Todd (producer)
★ best screenplay: adapted James Poe, John Farrow & S. J. Perelman
★ best color cinematography Lionel Lindon
★ best editing Gene Ruggiero & Paul Weatherwax
★ best music score of a drama or comedy Victor Young

Can Jules Verne's staid, confident Englishman Phileas Fogg (David Niven) win his bet and go around the world in 80 days at the turn of the century? He can and does, in exactly that time and the equal of 165 screen minutes. Victor Young's Oscar (his only one after 19 nominations) was awarded posthumously, the composer having died just four months before the 1956 awards were presented.

Victim and assassin. Marlon Brando as Colonel Kurtz and Martin Sheen as Captain Willard in Francis Ford Coppola's *Apocalypse Now* (Omni Zoetrope/United Artists), a double Oscar winner in 1979.

A Todd-United Artists Picture, directed by Michael Anderson. With David Niven, Cantinflas, Robert Newton, Shirley MacLaine and all-star cast. Todd-AO/Eastman Color. 165 mins.

ARTHUR (1981)

★ best supporting actor John Gielgud
★ best song "Arthur's Theme" ("Best That You Can Do"), music and lyrics by Burt Bacharach, Carole Bayer Sager, Christopher Cross & Peter Allen

A 1930s-type comedy about a habitually drunken playboy (Dudley Moore) who will inherit a vast fortune if he marries equally wealthy Jill Eikenberry and modifies his scandalous life-style. Instead, he choose a less-than-wealthy shop-lifter, Liza Minnelli, and a more contented, if less than prosperous, future. John Gielgud's Oscar was for his portrait of Moore's discreet English butler, Hobson.

An Orion Picture (distributed by Warner Bros.), directed by Steve Gordon. With Dudley Moore, Liza Minnelli, John Gielgud, Geraldine Fitzgerald, Jill Eikenberry, Stephen Elliot, Ted Ross. Technicolor. 97 mins.

THE ASSAULT (1986) ★

★ best foreign language film Netherlands

Compelling drama about a World War II survivor who is forced to recall the traumatic events of his childhood and the incidents that led to the liquidation by the Nazis of his family and 40 hostages in January 1945. An indictment against all those who would forget the past, and the first Dutch picture to win an Academy Award as best foreign language film of its year. Made by veteran Dutch filmmaker Fons Rademakers.

A Cannon (Netherlands) Picture, directed by Fons Rademakers. With Derek De Lint, Marc Van Uchelen, Monique Van DeVen, John Kraaykamp, Huub Van Der Lubbe, Elly Weller, Ina Van Der Molen, Frans Vortman. Fujicolor. 148 mins.

THE AWFUL TRUTH (1937) ★

★ best direction Leo McCarey

Irene Dunne and Cary Grant, about to get divorced, find that they love each other after all, and ultimately link up again. Wild matrimonial farce expertly directed by McCarey, who snatched the director's prize from William Dieterle, maker of 1937's best picture, *The Life of Emile Zola*.

A Columbia Picture, directed by Leo McCarey. With Irene Dunne, Cary Grant, Ralph Bellamy, Alexander D'Arcy, Cecil Cunningham. 90 mins.

B

BABETTE'S FEAST (1987)

★ best foreign language film Denmark

A French exile (Stephane Audran) finds refuge with two elderly sisters in a fishing village in late 19th-century Denmark. After winning 10,000 francs in a French lottery she prepares a sumptuous banquet with her winnings and brings about an irrevocable change in their lives. A delightful, slightly ironic tale, full of philosophical undercurrents, derived from a story by Isak Dinesen. It became the first Danish film to win the foreign language award, triumphing over Louis Malle's much-admired *Au Revoir Les Enfants* (1987).

Panorama Film International, in cooperation with Nordisk Film & The Danish Film Institute. Directed by Gabriel Axel. With Stephane Audran, Jean-Philippe Lafont, Gudmar Wivesson, Jarl Kulle, Bibi Andersson, Hanne Stensgaard, Bodil Kjer. Eastman Color. 103 mins.

THE BACHELOR AND THE BOBBY-SOXER (1947)

★ best original screenplay Sidney Sheldon

RKO comedy of the late 1940s with artist-playboy Cary Grant finding himself an embarrassed knight-in-shining-armor to lovesick, 17-year-old Shirley Temple. Myrna Loy adds grace, elegance and common sense as a lady judge.

An RKO Picture, directed by Irving Reis. with Cary Grant, Myrna Loy, Shirley Temple, Rudy Vallee, Ray Collins, Harry Davenport. 95 mins.

BACK TO THE FUTURE (1985)

★ best sound effects editing Charles L. Campbell & Robert Rutledge

Time travel movie about a teenager (Michael J. Fox) who zips back to 1955, where he meets his parents as high schoolers and has to unite the two of them or cease to exist. His task is made more complicated when 17-year-old future mom develops a crush on him. Crazy inventor Christopher Lloyd is the one who sets the bizarre events in motion with his DeLorean Car Time Machine.

An Amblin Entertainment Picture for Universal, directed by Robert Zemeckis. With Michael J. Fox, Christopher Lloyd, Lea Thompson, Crispin Glover, Thomas F. Wilson, Claudia Wells, Marc McClure, Wendie Jo Sperber. 70 mm/Technicolor. 116 mins.

THE BAD AND THE BEAUTIFUL (1952) ★★★★★

★ best supporting actress Gloria Grahame
★ best screenplay Charles Schnee
★ best b/w cinematography Robert Surtees
★ best b/w art direction Cedric Gibbons & Edward Carfagno
      b/w set decoration Edwin B. Willis & Keogh Gleason
★ best b/w costume design Helen Rose

Ruthless Hollywood film producer Kirk Douglas reaches the top by double-crossing each of his three closest colleagues—hardworking young director Barry Sullivan, Pulitzer Prize–winning author Dick Powell and alcoholic star Lana Turner. Hard-hitting Hollywood movie said to be based partly on the career of David Selznick.

An MGM Picture, directed by Vincente Minnelli. With Lana Turner, Kirk Douglas, Walter Pidgeon, Dick Powell, Barry Sullivan, Gloria Grahame. 118 mins.

BAD GIRL (1931/32)

★ best direction Frank Borzage
★ best writing: adaptation Edwin Burke

Part melodrama, part comedy, spanning one year in the life of store clerk James Dunn and the girl he has to marry after they have spent one night together.

A Fox Picture, directed by Frank Borzage. With James Dunn, Sally Eilers, Minna Gombell, Frank Darien, William Pawley. 88 mins.

THE BAREFOOT CONTESSA (1954)   ★

★ best supporting actor Edmond O'Brien

Earthy Spanish flamenco dancer, discovered in a Madrid night club, becomes a major Hollywood star and then rejects the tinsel world she has conquered. Ava Gardner is the dancer, Bogie a cynical movie director, Edmond O'Brien (memorable) a high-powered, sweating press agent.

A United Artists Picture, directed by Joseph L. Mankiewicz. With Humphrey Bogart, Ava Gardner, Edmond O'Brien, Marius Goring, Valentina Cortese, Rossano Brazzi. Technicolor. 128 mins.

BARRY LYNDON (1975)   ★★★★

★ best cinematography John Alcott
★ best art direction Ken Adam & Roy Walker
      set decoration Vernon Dixon
★ best costume design Ulla-Britt Soderlund & Milena Canonero
★ best music scoring: adaptation Leonard Rosenman

The rise to power and eventual fall from grace of an amorous young Irish adventurer (Ryan O'Neal). Based on Thackeray's novel *The Memoirs of Barry Lyndon, Esq.* and set in 18th-century Ireland and Europe.

A Warner Bros. Picture, directed by Stanley Kubrick. With Ryan O'Neal, Marisa Berenson,

Patrick Magee, Hardy Kruger, Steven Berkoff, Gay Hamilton. Eastman Color. 187 mins.

BATMAN (1989)

★ best art direction Anton Furst
      set decoration Peter Young

A $40 million reworking of Bob Kane's comic strip, with the mysterious Caped Crusader (Michael Keaton) and the malevolent Joker (Jack Nicholson) pitting their wits against each other in a nightmarish Gotham City. An over-the-top Nicholson, complete with white face, green hair and perpetual grin, missed out at nomination time, but British designer Anton Furst won a deserved award for the visual splendors of his huge sets, reminiscent at times of those in Fritz Lang's *Metropolis* (1927).

A Warner Bros./Guber-Peters Company Production, directed by Tim Burton. With Michael Keaton, Jack Nicholson, Kim Basinger, Robert Wuhl, Pat Hingle, Billy Dee Williams, Michael Gough, Jack Palance, Jerry Hall, Tracey Walter. 70mm/Technicolor. 126 mins.

BATTLEGROUND (1949)   ★★

★ best story & screenplay Robert Pirosh
★ best b/w cinematography Paul C. Vogel

The Battle of the Bulge—the Germans' last great offensive of World War II—as experienced by the men of an American airborne infantry division in the bleak, snow-covered Ardennes near Bastogne.

An MGM Picture, directed by William A. Wellman. With Van Johnson, Ricardo Montalban, John Hodiak, George Murphy, Marshall Thompson. 118 mins.

BEAUTY AND THE BEAST (1991)

★ best original score Alan Menken
★ best original song "Beauty and the Beast" (Alan Menken, music; Howard Ashman, lyrics)

Disney's retelling of the oft-told fairy tale about a selfish prince who is cursed by a righteous witch and then confined to his castle as a beast until he can love and be loved in return. Close to the standards of the *Pinocchio/Bambi/Fantasia* era and the first animated feature to be nominated as best film of the year. Plenty of magical Disney moments—the prince's household staff being turned into candlesticks, teapots, clocks, etc.—and a pleasing Oscar-winning score by Alan Menken and Howard Ashman.

A Buena Vista release of a Walt Disney Pictures presentation in association with Silver Screen Partners IV. Directors: Gary Trousdale and Kirk Wise. Voices by Paige O'Hara, Robby Benson, Jerry Orbach, Angela Lansbury, Richard White, David Ogden Stiers, Jesse Corti. Technicolor. 85 mins.

BECKET (1964) ★

★ best screenplay Edward Anhalt

Film version of Anouilh's stage play *Becket* about the relationship between church and politics in 12th-century England and, more dramatically, the conflict between two men—the Norman King Henry II (Peter O'Toole) and his former Saxon companion (Richard Burton), later Archbishop of Canterbury.

A Paramount Picture, directed by Peter Glenville. With Richard Burton, Peter O'Toole, Sir Donald Wolfit, Sir John Gielgud, Martita Hunt. Panavision/Technicolor. 148 mins.

BEDKNOBS AND BROOMSTICKS (1971) ★

★ best special visual effects Danny Lee, Eustace Lycett & Alan Maley

Mary Poppins country revisited by Disney, with apprentice witch Angela Lansbury delighting the three evacuee children in her care by doing most of her traveling on a magic bedstead. The Oscar-winning special effects included a live action/animated football game in

Noboombu Land refereed by an unlucky David Tomlinson.

A Walt Disney Picture, directed by Robert Stevenson. With Angela Lansbury, David Tomlinson, Roddy McDowall, Sam Jaffe, John Ericson, Bruce Forsyth. Technicolor. 117 mins.

BEETLEJUICE (1988) ★

★ best makeup Ve Neill, Steve La Porte and Robert Short

A newly deceased couple return as ghosts to the house they love only to find it inhabited by an earthly pair who want to turn their town into a supernatural tourist attraction. Crazed spirit Michael Keaton, a kind of bio-exorcist who rids houses of infestations of the living, comes to their aid. Director Burton's bizarre visions of a rather quirky afterlife was a major factor in helping the film win its makeup award.

A Geffen Film Company Production (distributed by Warner Bros.), directed by Tim Burton. With Alec Baldwin, Geena Davis, Annie McEnroe, Maurice Page, Hugo Stanger, Michael Keaton, Rachel Mittelman, Catherine O'Hara. Technicolor. 92 mins.

BEING THERE (1979) ★

★ best supporting actor Melvyn Douglas

A satirical look at Washington political life, centering on an illiterate and naive gardener (Peter Sellers) who is hailed as a sage when he is let loose on the world after living a life of seclusion in the house of a benefactor. Based on the amiable fable of Jerzy Kosinski, the film earned Melvyn Douglas his second best-supporting-actor award (he won his first for *Hud* [1963]) for his portrait of an ailing financier. Sellers was nominated for best actor but lost to Dustin Hoffman for *Kramer vs. Kramer* (1979).

A Lorimar Film-Und Fernsproduktion GmbH Production/United Artists. Directed by Hal Ashby. With Peter Sellers, Shirley MacLaine, Melvyn Douglas, Jack Warden, Richard Dysart, Richard Basehart, Ruth Attaway, Dave Clennon. Metrocolor; prints by Technicolor. 130 mins.

THE BELLS OF ST. MARY'S (1945) ★

★ best sound recording Stephen Dunn

Leo McCarey's attempt to cash in on the success of *Going My Way* (1944). Bing Crosby again as a priest (Father Chuck), Ingrid Bergman as a tubercular nun—but, alas, no Barry Fitzgerald.

An RKO Picture, directed by Leo McCarey. With Bing Crosby, Ingrid Bergman, Henry Travers, Joan Carroll, Martha Sleeper. 126 mins.

BEN-HUR (1959) ★★★★★★★★★★★

★ best film Sam Zimbalist (producer)
★ best direction William Wyler
★ best actor Charlton Heston
★ best supporting actor Hugh Griffith
★ best color cinematography Robert Surtees
★ best color art direction William A. Horning & Edward Carfagno
       color set decoration Hugh Hunt
★ best color costume design Elizabeth Haffenden
★ best editing Ralph E. Winters & John D. Dunning
★ best sound Franklin E. Milton
★ best sound effects A. Arnold Gillespie
       visual effects Robert MacDonald
       audible effects Milo Lory
★ best music score of a drama or comedy Miklos Rozsa

An adaptation of General Lew Wallace's famous novel of how Christianity gradually made inroads into the pagan civilization of ancient Rome. Ends in a spectacular bloodbath in the chariot arena, with converted Christian Ben-Hur (Charlton Heston) defeating Roman commander and former boyhood friend Messala (Stephen Boyd) in one of the most spectacular screen races of all time. The only remake to win the best-picture award; its 11 Oscars make it the all-time Academy record holder.

An MGM Picture, directed by William Wyler. With Charlton Heston, Jack Hawkins, Hugh Griffith, Martha Scott, Cathy O'Donnell, Haya Hayareet, Stephen Boyd, Sam Jaffe, Finlay Currie. Camera 65/Panavision/Technicolor. 217 mins.

The spectacular chariot race from William Wyler's *Ben-Hur* (MGM), still the all-time Oscar champ, with 11 Academy Awards in 1959.

THE BEST YEARS OF OUR LIVES (1946) ★★★★★★★

- ★ best film Samuel Goldwyn (producer)
- ★ best direction William Wyler
- ★ best actor Fredric March
- ★ best supporting actor Harold Russell
- ★ best screenplay Robert E. Sherwood
- ★ best editing Daniel Mandell
- ★ best music score of a drama or comedy Hugo Friedhofer

Sam Goldwyn's classic about the problems facing three ex-servicemen—a sergeant (Fredric March), a captain (Dana Andrews) and a handless sailor (Harold Russell)—when they return to their hometown at the end of World War II.

A Sam Goldwyn Production (released through RKO Pictures), directed by William Wyler. With Myrna Loy, Fredric March, Dana Andrews, Teresa Wright, Virginia Mayo, Cathy O'Donnell, Hoagy Carmichael, Harold Russell. 172 mins.

THE BIG BROADCAST OF 1938 (1938) ★

- ★ best song "Thanks for the Memory" (Ralph Rainger, music; Leo Robin, lyrics)

Fourth in Paramount's series of musical revues of the 1930s, and famous for introducing the song that became Bob Hope's theme on his radio and TV shows.

A Paramount Picture, directed by Mitchell Leisen. With W. C. Fields, Martha Raye, Dorothy Lamour, Shirley Ross, Lynne Overman, Bob Hope, Ben Blue. 97 mins.

THE BIG COUNTRY (1958) ★

- ★ best supporting actor Burl Ives

Large-scale Western with two opposing landowners, wealthy Charles Bickford and patriarch Burl Ives, fighting over the grazing water known as Big Muddy. Stars Gregory Peck, Charlton Heston, Jean Simmons and Carroll Baker help settle the matter. The memorable music score by Jerome Moross was nominated but did not prove a winner, the Oscar going to Dimitri Tiomkin for *The Old Man and the Sea*.

A United Artists Picture, directed by William Wyler. With Gregory Peck, Jean Simmons, Carroll Baker, Charlton Heston, Burl Ives, Charles Bickford. Technirama/Technicolor. 165 mins.

THE BIG HOUSE (1929/30) ★★

- ★ best writing achievement Frances Marion
- ★ best sound recording Douglas Shearer

One of the toughest and most realistic of the early prison dramas, with Wallace Beery (in a role originally intended for Lon Chaney) as a condemned convict and Robert Montgomery as a cowardly informer. Shearer's sound recording Oscar was the first to be awarded in this category.

An MGM Picture, directed by George Hill. With Chester Morris, Wallace Beery, Lewis Stone, Robert Montgomery, Leila Hyams, George F. Marion. 88 mins.

BIRD (1988)

- ★ best sound Les Fresholtz, Dick Alexander, Vern Poore & Willie D. Burton

The life of saxophonist Charlie "Yardbird" Parker, whose playing revolutionized jazz in the 1940s and whose private life was wracked with self-destruction brought on by drug addiction and alcoholism. Forest Whitaker (Parker) was named best actor at the 1988 Cannes Film Festival but failed to win a nomination at Oscar time. Parker's own recordings were used throughout the film but mixed with newly recorded backing tracks.

A Warner Bros. Picture (A Malpaso Production), directed by Clint Eastwood. With Forest Whitaker, Diane Venora, Michael Zelniker, Samuel E. Wright, Keith David, Michael McGuire, James Handy. Technicolor. 160 mins.

THE BISHOP'S WIFE (1947)   ★

★ best sound recording Gordon Sawyer

Man-of-the-world angel (Cary Grant) comes to the aid of overworked bishop David Niven in answer to the latter's prayer for funds for a new city cathedral. Goldwyn whimsy; the bishop's wife of the title is Loretta Young.

A Sam Goldwyn Production (released through RKO Pictures), directed by Henry Koster. With Cary Grant, Loretta Young, David Niven, Monty Woolley, James Gleason, Gladys Cooper, Elsa Lanchester. 105 mins.

BLACK AND WHITE IN COLOR (1976)   ★

★ best foreign language film Ivory Coast

A satirical look at racism, colonialism and imperialism in Africa during World War I when a handful of Frenchmen find belatedly that they are at war with Germany and attack some Germans living in a nearby European community—both sides eventually relying on native armies to fight their respective "causes."

An Arthur Cohn Production/Societe Ivoirienne De Cinema, directed by Jean Jacques Annaud. With Jean Carmet, Jacques Dufilho, Catherine Rouvel, Jacques Spiesser, Dora Doll, Maurice Barrier. Eastman Color. 100 mins.

BLACK NARCISSUS (1947)   ★★

★ best color cinematography Jack Cardiff
★ best color art direction Alfred Junge
      set decoration Alfred Junge

Rumer Godden's story of five British nuns, led by Deborah Kerr, who set up a school and a hospital in the Himalayas. Historically important for its notable color designs and photography, both honored by the Academy.

An Archers Production, directed by Michael Powell and Emeric Pressburger. With Deborah Kerr, Sabu, David Farrar, Flora Robson, Esmond Knight, Jean Simmons, Kathleen Ryan. Technicolor. 100 mins.

BLACK ORPHEUS (1959)   ★

★ best foreign language film France/Italy

Updated version of the Orpheus legend, with the doomed lovers playing out their game of inevitable death amid the riotous pageantry of a carnival in Rio de Janiero. Superb color and bossa nova score.

Dispatfilm Paris, Gemma Cinematografica, directed by Marcel Camus. With Breno Mello, Marpessa Dawn, Lourdes De Oliveira, Lea Garcia. Eastman Color. 98 mins.

THE BLACK STALLION (1979)   ★

★ best sound effects editing Alan Splet

An American schoolboy (Kelly Reno), shipwrecked with an Arab stallion on an island off North Africa, befriends the animal and later trains him to become the fastest racehorse in America. A Carroll Ballard film, based on the 1941 best-seller by Walter Farley and featuring Mickey Rooney, who earned a supporting Oscar nomination for his portrait of a retired racehorse trainer. The movie's sound effects Oscar was a special achievement award.

An Omni Zoetrope Production, released by United Artists. Directed by Carroll Ballard. With Kelly Reno, Mickey Rooney, Teri Garr, Clarence Muse, Hoyt Axton, Michael Higgins. Technicolor. 117 mins.

THE BLACK SWAN (1942)   ★

★ best color cinematography Leon Shamroy

Pirate swashbuckler, based on the novel by Rafael Sabatini, with Tyrone Power as the athletic hero, George Sanders the red-bearded villain, and Laird Cregar the real-life reformed pirate Sir Henry Morgan. The film earned Leon Shamroy the first of his four Academy Awards for color cinematography, a record that still stands to this day. Shamroy's other wins: *Wilson* (1944), *Leave Her to Heaven* (1945), *Cleopatra* (1963).

A 20th Century-Fox Picture, directed by Henry King. With Tyrone Power, Maureen O'Hara, Laird Cregar, Thomas Mitchell, George Sanders, Anthony Quinn, George Zucco. Technicolor. 85 mins.

BLITHE SPIRIT (1946)   ★

★ best special effects Thomas Howard

An adaptation of Noel Coward's sophisticated stage play about a famous novelist (Rex Harrison) who finds his marriage to wife no. 2 (Constance Cummings) complicated by the return of his first wife's ghost (Kay Hammond). Not surprisingly, spiritualist Margaret Rutherford is the cause of all the trouble.

A Two Cities-Cineguild Picture, directed by David Lean. With Rex Harrison, Constance Cummings, Kay Hammond, Margaret Rutherford, Joyce Carey. Technicolor 97 mins.

BLOOD AND SAND (1941)   ★

★ best color cinematography Ernest Palmer & Ray Rennahan

Tyrone Power as an innocent young bullfighter involved with dangers not only inside but also outside the bullring—from Spanish aristocrat Rita Hayworth and childhood sweetheart Linda Darnell.

A 20th Century-Fox Picture, directed by Rouben Mamoulian. With Tyrone Power, Linda Darnell, Rita Hayworth, Alla Nazimova, Anthony Quinn, J. Carrol Naish, John Carradine, Laird Cregar. Technicolor. 124 mins.

BLOOD ON THE SUN (1945)   ★

★ best b/w art direction Wiard Ihnen
                interior decoration A. Roland Fields

American newsman James Cagney in Tokyo in the 1920s fighting a one-man campaign against Japanese militarists planning world conquest.

A United Artists Picture, directed by Frank Lloyd. With James Cagney, Sylvia Sidney,

Wallace Ford, Rosemary De Camp, Robert Armstrong, John Emery. 98 mins.

BLOSSOMS IN THE DUST (1941)   ★

★ best color art direction Cedric Gibbons & Urie McCleary
                interior decoration Edwin B. Willis

Greer Garson as Edna Gladney, the famous child welfare worker who founded a Texas orphanage after the loss of her own child and did much to remove the 19th-century social stigma from illegitimate children. Soap opera with a message, and the film that made Garson a superstar.

An MGM Picture, directed by Mervyn LeRoy. With Greer Garson, Walter Pidgeon, Felix Bressart, Marsha Hunt, Fay Holden, Samuel S. Hinds. Technicolor. 100 mins.

BODY AND SOUL (1947)   ★

★ best editing Francis Lyon & Robert Parrish

One of the half-dozen most famous boxing films of all time with John Garfield fighting his way up from the Lower East Side to middleweight champion of the world, only to find himself owned completely—"body and soul"—by the shady characters who run his seedy racket.

A United Artists Picture, directed by Robert Rossen. With John Garfield, Lili Palmer, Hazel Brooks, Anne Revere, William Conrad, Joseph Pevney, Canada Lee. 104 mins.

BONNIE AND CLYDE (1967)   ★★

★ best supporting actress Estelle Parsons
★ best color cinematography Burnett Guffey

The real-life exploits of Bonnie Parker (Faye Dunaway) and Clyde Barrow (Warren Beatty), who created a reign of terror and killed 18 people while robbing banks in the American Southwest of the early 1930s. Co-star Estelle Parsons won her Oscar for her portrayal of a preacher's daughter, the wife of Barrow's brother Buck (Gene Hackman).

A Warner Bros. Picture, directed by Arthur Penn. With Warren Beatty, Faye Dunaway, Michael J. Pollard, Gene Hackman, Estelle Parsons. Technicolor. 111 mins.

BORN FREE (1966)

★ best original music score John Barry
★ best song "Born Free" (John Barry, music; Don Black, lyrics)

The true story of Joy Adamson's life with Elsa, the tame lioness she raised from a cub in the African bush and then gradually reconditioned to her normal wildlife existence.

A Columbia Picture, directed by James Hill. With Virginia McKenna, Bill Travers, Geoffrey Keen. Panavision/Technicolor. 95 mins.

BORN ON THE FOURTH OF JULY (1989)   ★ ★

★ best direction Oliver Stone
★ best editing David Brenner & Joe Hutshing

Oliver Stone's second Vietnam movie, more ambitious than *Platoon* (1986), and telling the real-life story of Ron Kovic (Tom Cruise), who returns from the conflict an embittered paraplegic and then has to come to terms with the fact that the country for which he fought has no interest in him or in those like him. Stone's award for direction was his fourth Oscar. He won earlier for his screenplay for *Midnight Express* (1978) and his direction and screenplay for *Platoon*.

An Ixtlan Production for Universal, directed by Oliver Stone. With Tom Cruise, Willem Dafoe, Raymond J. Barry, Caroline Kava, Kyra Sedgwick, Bryan Larkin, Jerry Levine, Josh Evans, Frank Whaley, Tom Berenger. DeLuxe Color. 144 mins.

BORN YESTERDAY (1950)   ★

★ best actress Judy Holliday

Judy Holliday as *the* dumb blonde of all time, taken to Washington on a business trip by millionaire junk dealer Broderick Crawford and given a crash course in culture by literate young journalist William Holden. Based on the Broadway hit by Garson Kanin.

A Columbia Picture, directed by George Cukor. With Judy Holliday, William Holden, Broderick Crawford, Howard St. John, Frank Otto. 103 mins.

BOUND FOR GLORY (1976)

★ best cinematography Haskell Wexler
★ best adaptation music score Leonard Rosenman

The early career of Oklahoma-born folk singer Woody Guthrie, following him from his no-hope life in the depressed Southwest of the mid-1930s to California, where he successfully breaks into radio before eventually opting for a life on the open road. Based on Guthrie's autobiography and featuring David Carradine in the lead role.

A United Artists Picture, directed by Hal Ashby. With David Carradine, Ronny Cox, Melinda Dillon, Gail Strickland, John Lehne, Randy Quaid. Panavision/DeLuxe Color. 148 mins.

BOYS' TOWN (1938)   ★ ★

★ best actor Spencer Tracy
★ best original story Dore Schary & Eleanore Griffin

Spencer Tracy as Father Flanagan, the priest who helped create a community for delinquent teenage boys of every race and creed. His biggest problem? Mickey Rooney, as a tough, poker-playing, aggressive rebel. With his performance in this film Tracy became the first actor to win two best-acting Oscars, having also won the previous year for *Captains Courageous*.

An MGM Picture, directed by Norman Taurog. With Spencer Tracy, Mickey Rooney,

Henry Hull, Leslie Fenton, Addison Richards, Edward Norris. 96 mins.

BRAM STOKER'S DRACULA (1992)

- ★ best costume design Eiko Ishioka
- ★ best makeup Greg Cannom, Michele Burke & Matthew W. Mungle
- ★ best sound effects editing Tom C. McCarthy & David E. Stone

By far the most opulent—and sexually explicit—version of Stoker's vampire tale, with Gary Oldman as the 15th-century Vlad the Impaler finding in Winona Ryder a Victorian beauty with whom he can share his eternal life. A cinematic tour de force by Francis Ford Coppola, and the only version of the classic tale to be honored at Oscar time.

A Columbia release of an American Zoetrope/Osiris Films Production, directed by Francis Ford Coppola. With Gary Oldman, Winona Ryder, Anthony Hopkins, Keanu Reeves, Richard E. Grant, Cary Elwes, Bill Campbell, Sadie Frost, Tom Waits. Technicolor. 123 mins.

THE BRAVE ONE (1956) ★

- ★ best motion picture story Robert Rich*

A young boy adopts a bull as a pet and then travels all the way to Mexico City to try to prevent it from being put into the ring for a duel to the death with Mexico's greatest toreador.

An RKO Picture, directed by Irving Rapper. With Michael Ray, Rodolfo Hoyos, Elsa Cardenas, Carlos Navarro, Joi Lansing, Fermin Rivera. CinemaScope/Technicolor. 94 mins.

---

* *Note*: Robert Rich was a pseudonym for the blacklisted Dalton Trumbo, who received his award 20 years later, shortly before his death in 1976.

BREAKFAST AT TIFFANYS (1961) ★★

- ★ best music score of a drama or comedy Henry Mancini
- ★ best song "Moon River" (Henry Mancini, music; Johnny Mercer, lyrics)

The adventures of bizarre "supertramp" Holly Golightly (Audrey Hepburn) with struggling writer George Peppard in Manhattan. Adapted—and toned down—from Truman Capote's best-selling novella.

A Paramount Picture, directed by Blake Edwards. With Audrey Hepburn, George Peppard, Patricia Neal, Martin Balsam, Mickey Rooney, Buddy Ebsen, John McGiver. Technicolor. 115 mins.

BREAKING AWAY (1979) ★

- ★ best original screenplay Steve Tesich

One of the sleepers of the late 1970s, an old-fashioned tale of small-town America, concentrating on the lives of four Indiana teenagers as they embark uncertainly on their adult lives after leaving high school. The simmering class tensions between the four boys and the university students of the town finally come to a boil during a climactic bicycle race on campus. Winner for best original screenplay, though a little unlucky not to emerge with higher honors.

A 20th Century-Fox Picture, directed by Peter Yates. With Dennis Christopher, Dennis Quaid, Daniel Stern, Jackie Earle Haley, Barbara Barrie, Paul Dooley, Robyn Douglass, Hart Bochner, Amy Wright. DeLuxe Color. 101 mins.

BREAKING THE SOUND BARRIER (1952) ★

(Original U.K. title: *The Sound Barrier*)

- ★ best sound recording London Films Sound Dept.

David Lean's film about the human obsession with flying planes faster than the speed of sound.

Appropriately enough, it won the best sound recording award, although Ralph Richardson—as a ruthless aircraft design pioneer driven by his vision of conquering the unknown—should have been among the best-actor nominees. He wasn't, which was surprising considering the New York Film Critics' Circle had named him best actor of the year in their poll.

A London Films Production, directed by David Lean. With Ralph Richardson, Ann Todd, Nigel Patrick, John Justin, Dinah Sheridan, Joseph Tomelty, Denholm Elliott. 118 mins.

THE BRIDGE OF SAN LUIS REY (1928/29)   ★

★ best art direction Cedric Gibbons

A 1929 version (remade in 1944) of Thornton Wilder's Pulitzer Prize–winning novel—set in 18th-century Peru—about five people who meet their deaths when a rickety bridge collapses and hurtles them to their doom.

An MGM Picture, directed by Charles Brabin. With Lily Damita, Ernest Torrence, Raquel Torres, Don Alvarado, Duncan Renaldo, Henry B. Walthall. 10 reels.

THE BRIDGE ON THE RIVER KWAI (1957)   ★★★★★★★

★ best film Sam Spiegel (producer)
★ best direction David Lean
★ best actor Alec Guinness
★ best screenplay Pierre Boulle*
★ best cinematography Jack Hildyard
★ best editing Peter Taylor
★ best music scoring Malcolm Arnold

---

* *Note:* Despite the credit "screenplay by Pierre Boulle," the author of the original novel had nothing to do with the writing of the picture. The screenplay was written by two blacklisted American writers—Carl Foreman and Michael Wilson—both of whom were awarded posthumous Oscars (announced in 1985) for their work on the film.

Pierre Boulle's famous story—set in the jungles of Siam during World War II—about the construction by British POWs of a railway bridge on the murderous Bangkok–to–Rangoon railroad, and of its subsequent destruction by a small commando unit. Guinness plays the British colonel in charge of the bridge building. With this film David Lean became the first-ever British director to win an American Oscar.

A Columbia Picture, directed by David Lean. With William Holden, Alec Guinness, Jack Hawkins, Sessue Hayakawa, James Donald, Geoffrey Horne, Andre Morell. CinemaScope/Technicolor. 161 mins.

THE BRIDGES AT TOKO-RI (1955)   ★

★ best special effects Paramount Studios

James A. Michener tale of the Korean War, with jet pilots William Holden and Mickey Rooney performing heroically on a special mission against the communists. Grace Kelly is the wife who waits behind, Fredric March the admiral-in-chief. Notable special effects work in the climactic blowing up of the North Korean bridges and the aerial photography.

A Paramount Picture, directed by Mark Robson. With William Holden, Grace Kelly, Fredric March, Mickey Rooney, Robert Strauss, Charles McGraw. Vista Vision/Technicolor. 103 mins.

THE BROADWAY MELODY (1928/29)   ★

★ best film Harry Rapf (producer)

The very first MGM musical, with songs like "Wedding of the Painted Doll" (presented as a big two-color Technicolor production number), "Give My Regards to Broadway" and "You Were Meant for Me." Advertised with the words "All Talking, All Singing, All Dancing," it featured Charles King as an amorous songwriter who breaks up the show-biz sister act of Bessie Love and Anita Page.

An MGM Picture, directed by Harry Beaumont. With Bessie Love, Anita Page, Charles King, Jed Prouty, Kenneth Thompson, Mary Doran, Eddie Kane. Scenes in two-color Technicolor. 110 mins.

THE BROADWAY MELODY OF 1936 (1935) ★

★ best dance direction David Gould for the "I've Got a Feeling You're Fooling" number

The first of MGM's Broadway Melody series, with Eleanor Powell at the top of her dancing form and Jack Benny stealing the acting honors as a Walter Winchell-type columnist always panning things he doesn't like. Robert Taylor is featured as a young producer. David Gould was also named the same year for his work on *Folies Bergere*.

An MGM Picture, directed by Roy Del Ruth. With Jack Benny, Eleanor Powell, Robert Taylor, June Knight, Una Merkel, Buddy Ebsen. 118 mins.

BROKEN LANCE (1954) ★

★ best motion picture story Philip Yordan

Spencer Tracy as a beef baron of the prairies, Katy Jurado as his Indian wife, and Richard Widmark, Robert Wagner and Hugh O'Brian as his three sons. A *King Lear* of the West and a remake of Joseph Mankiewicz's *House of Strangers* (1949).

A 20th Century-Fox Picture, directed by Edward Dmytryk. With Spencer Tracy, Richard Widmark, Katy Jurado, Jean Peters, Hugh O'Brian, Earl Holliman. CinemaScope/DeLuxe Color. 96 mins.

THE BUDDY HOLLY STORY (1978) ★

★ best adaptation score Joe Renzetti

Typical old-style Hollywood musical biography, a mini *Glenn Miller Story* (1954) following the same rags-to-riches story line and climaxing in its hero's premature death in a plane crash. An impressive portrait of Buddy Holly by Gary Busey (Oscar nominated, best actor) with many famous Holly numbers on the soundtrack— "That'll Be the Day," "Words of Love," "Peggy Sue," etc.

An Innovasions-ECA Production, directed by Steve Rash. With Gary Busey, Don Stroud, Charles Martin Smith, Conrad Janis, William Jordan, Maria Richwine, Amy Johnston. CFI Color, prints by MGM. 114 mins.

BUGSY (1991)

★ best art direction Dennis Gassner
    set decoration Nancy Haigh
★ best costume design Albert Wolsky

Vivid re-creation of gangster Bugsy Siegel's life in Hollywood in the 1940s and his obsessions— with starlet Virginia Hill (Annette Bening) and with the building of the Flamingo hotel/casino complex in the remote desert township of Las Vegas just after World War II. Warren Beatty was nominated for his psychotic Bugsy, just as he had been for his Clyde Barrow in *Bonnie and Clyde* almost 25 years before, but Anthony Hopkins took the acting honors on Oscar night for his even-more-sinister killer Hannibal Lecter in *Silence of the Lambs*.

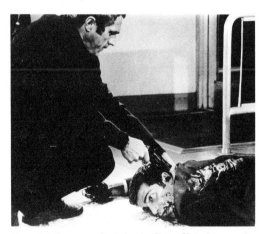

Steve McQueen and victim in Peter Yates' tense cop thriller *Bullitt* (Warner Bros.), winner of the best editing award in 1968.

Mulholland Productions/Baltimore Pictures for TriStar, directed by Barry Levinson. With Warren Beatty, Annette Bening, Harvey Keitel, Ben Kingsley, Elliott Gould, Joe Mantegna, Richard Sarafian, Bebe Neuwirth. Technicolor. 136 mins.

BULLITT (1968)   ★

★ best editing Frank P. Keller

Steve McQueen as a cop and Robert Vaughn as an opportunistic politician pursuing a well-organized underworld syndicate in the streets of San Francisco. High spot—and the main reason the film won the best editing award—the stunning car chase up and down the steep Frisco hills.

A Warner Bros. Picture, directed by Peter Yates. With Steve McQueen, Robert Vaughn, Jacqueline Bisset, Don Gordon, Robert Duvall, Simon Oakland, Norman Fell. Technicolor. 114 mins.

BUTCH CASSIDY AND THE SUNDANCE KID (1969)   ★ ★ ★

★ best story & screenplay William Goldman
★ best cinematography Conrad Hall
★ best original music score Burt Bacharach
★ best song "Raindrops Keep Fallin' On My Head" (Burt Bacharach, music; Hal David, lyrics)

The final years of two of the West's most legendary characters, who, around the turn of the century, operated out of a place called "Hole in the Wall" and finished their days less than gloriously in the dusty towns of Bolivia. New-

man is Cassidy, Robert Redford the Sundance Kid.

A 20th Century-Fox Picture, directed by George Roy Hill. With Paul Newman, Robert Redford, Katharine Ross, Strother Martin, Henry Jones, Jeff Corey, George Furth, Cloris Leachman. Panavision/DeLuxe Color. 110 mins.

BUTTERFIELD 8 (1960)

★ best actress Elizabeth Taylor

Elizabeth Taylor as a New York prostitute caught up with the socially prominent and very-much-married Laurence Harvey. From the novel by John O'Hara. The intriguing title is simply Taylor's telephone exchange, for those clients with the urge.

An MGM Picture, directed by Daniel Mann. With Elizabeth Taylor, Laurence Harvey, Eddie Fisher, Dina Merrill, Mildred Dunnock. Cinemascope/Metrocolor. 108 mins.

BUTTERFLIES ARE FREE (1972)

★ best supporting actress Eileen Heckart

Bittersweet love story about a feckless would-be actress (Goldie Hawn) and a blind young songwriter (Edward Albert) living in the same small apartment block. Adapted by Leonard Gershe from his own play and dominated by Eileen Heckart as Mr. Albert's overpowering ma.

A Columbia Picture, directed by Milton Katselas. With Goldie Hawn, Edward Albert, Eileen Heckart, Michael Glasser, Mike Warren. Eastman Color. 109 mins.

C

CABARET (1972) ★★★★★★★★

- ★ best direction Bob Fosse
- ★ best actress Liza Minnelli
- ★ best supporting actor Joel Grey
- ★ best cinematography Geoffrey Unsworth
- ★ best art direction Rolf Zehetbauer & Jurgen Kiebach
      set direction Herbert Strabl
- ★ best editing David Bretherton
- ★ best sound Robert Knudson & David Hildyard
- ★ best scoring: adaptation & original song score Ralph Burns

Sally Bowles' experiences as a nightclub singer in prewar Berlin just prior to the country's takeover by the Nazis. A musical version of John Van Druten's play, which, in turn, was based on the collected stories of Christopher Isherwood, entitled *Goodbye to Berlin*. Liza Minnelli is the "divinely decadent" Sally, Joel Grey the lurid MC of the nightclub where she works.

An Allied Artists Picture, directed by Bob Fosse. With Liza Minnelli, Michael York, Helmut Griem, Joel Grey, Fritz Weber, Marisa Berenson. Technicolor. 123 mins.

CACTUS FLOWER (1969) ★

- ★ best supporting actress Goldie Hawn

Broadway comedy-farce, set in Greenwich Village, and based on the misunderstandings among four people who eventually sort themselves out with the right partners. Walter Matthau is a good-time bachelor dentist, Ingrid Bergman his secretary, Goldie Hawn his kooky blonde girlfriend and Rick Lenz a struggling young writer with an apartment next door.

A Columbia Picture, directed by Gene Saks. With Walter Matthau, Ingrid Bergman, Goldie Hawn, Jack Weston, Rick Lenz. Technicolor. 104 mins.

CALAMITY JANE (1953)

- ★ best song "Secret Love" (Sammy Fain, music; Paul Francis Webster, lyrics)

Musical horse opera with an effervescent Doris Day clad in buckskin in the title role and Howard Keel as her deadshot singing lover Wild Bill Hickok. The Sammy Fain/Paul Francis Webster score included not only the Oscar-winning "Secret Love" but also "The Deadwood Stage," "The Black Hills of Dakota" and "I Just Blew In from the Windy City."

A Warner Bros. Picture, directed by David Butler. With Doris Day, Howard Keel, Allyn McLerie, Philip Carey, Dick Wesson. Technicolor. 101 mins.

CALIFORNIA SUITE (1978)

- ★ best supporting actress Maggie Smith*

Four lightweight playlets by Neil Simon, all set in the Beverly Hills Hotel in Los Angeles. Alan Alda, Jane Fonda, Michael Caine, Walter Matthau and Richard Pryor are among those who indulge in Simon's fun and games, although it is Maggie Smith as an English stage actress nominated for an Oscar who steals the proceedings.

---

* *Note:* Maggie Smith's award—she had previously won as best actress for *The Prime of Miss Jean Brodie* in 1969—made her the third performer to win in both the best-actress and best-supporting-actress categories. Helen Hayes (*The Sin of Madelon Claudet*, 1931; *Airport*, 1970) and Ingrid Bergman (*Gaslight*, 1944; *Anastasia*, 1956; *Murder on the Orient Express*, 1974) had both previously achieved this feat; Meryl Streep has since achieved it with her performances in *Kramer vs. Kramer* (1979) and *Sophie's Choice* (1982).

A Columbia Picture, directed by Herbert Ross. With Alan Alda, Michael Caine, Bill Cosby, Jane Fonda, Walter Matthau, Elaine May, Richard Pryor, Maggie Smith. Color. 103 mins.

CALL ME MADAM (1953)   ★

★ best scoring of a musical Alfred Newman

Irving Berlin's satirical musical about socialite Perle Mesta's life as a Washington hostess and ambassadress to Lichtenburg. Ethel Merman ("The Hostess with the Mostess") stars as the Mesta character.

A 20th Century-Fox Picture, directed by Walter Lang. With Ethel Merman, Donald O'Connor, Vera-Ellen, George Sanders, Billy DeWolfe, Helmut Dantine. Technicolor. 117 mins.

CAMELOT (1967)   ★ ★ ★

★ best color art direction John Truscott & Edward Carrere
    set decoration John W. Brown
★ best color costume design John Truscott
★ best music adaptation or treatment Alfred Newman & Ken Darby

Arthurian legend and the stirring, romantic events of the days of the Knights of the Round Table set to music by Frederick Loewe and Alan Jay Lerner. Richard Harris is Arthur, Vanessa Redgrave Guenevere, and Franco Nero, Lancelot du Lac. Based on T. H. White's *The Once and Future King*.

A Warner Bros. Picture, directed by Joshua Logan. With Richard Harris, Vanessa Redgrave, Franco Nero, David Hemmings, Lionel Jeffries, Laurence Naismith. Panavision 70/Technicolor. 181 mins.

THE CANDIDATE (1972)   ★

★ best story and screenplay Jeremy Larner

The fortunes of a young lawyer–civil rights worker (Robert Redford) who is gradually turned, against his better judgment, into a Kennedy-style U.S. senator by the party's campaign machine.

A Warner Bros. Picture, directed by Michael Ritchie. With Robert Redford, Peter Boyle, Don Porter, Allen Garfield, Karen Carlson, Melvyn Douglas. Technicolor. 110 mins.

CAPTAIN CAREY, U.S.A. (1950)

(U.K. title: *After Midnight*)

★ best song "Mona Lisa" (Ray Evans & Jay Livingston; music & lyrics)

Alan Ladd involved in obscure intrigue in postwar Italy. The Oscar-winning song (made famous by Nat King Cole) is now the only reason the film is remembered.

A Paramount Picture, directed by Mitchell Leisen. With Alan Ladd, Wanda Hendrix, Francis Lederer, Joseph Calleia, Celia Lovsky. 83 mins.

CAPTAINS COURAGEOUS (1937)   ★

★ best actor Spencer Tracy

The spoiled son of a business tycoon finds humility and learns life's important lessons the hard way during his voyage on a small fishing boat and through his acquaintance with an understanding Portuguese fisherman (Spencer Tracy). Freddie Bartholomew stars as the boy; from the Kipling novel of the same name.

An MGM Picture, directed by Victor Fleming. With Freddie Bartholomew, Spencer Tracy, Lionel Barrymore, Melvyn Douglas, Mickey Rooney, Charley Grapewin, John Carradine. 115 mins.

CASABLANCA (1943)   ★ ★ ★

★ best film Hal B. Wallis, (producer)
★ best direction Michael Curtiz
★ best written screenplay Julius J. Epstein, Philip G. Epstein & Howard Koch

One of the finest casts of all time sweats it out in the North African town of Casablanca—

"haven to the refugees fleeing persecution in Nazi Europe." Cynicism, intrigue, disillusionment, old love rekindled, and Humphrey Bogart as Rick ordering pianist Dooley Wilson to play "As Time Goes By."

A Warner Bros. Pictuure, directed by Michael Curtiz. With Humphrey Bogart, Ingrid Bergman, Paul Henreid, Claude Rains, Conrad Veidt, Sydney Greenstreet, Peter Lorre, S. Z. Sakall. 102 mins.

CAT BALLOU (1965) ★

★ best actor Lee Marvin

Rare Western parody, with Jane Fonda as a well-educated young lady who turns outlaw to avenge her father's death, and Lee Marvin as the whiskey-sodden, has-been gunfighter she employs to help her in her task.

A Columbia Picture, directed by Elliott Silverstein. With Jane Fonda, Lee Marvin, Michael Callan, Dwayne Hickman, Nat King Cole, Stubby Kaye. Technicolor. 96 mins.

CAVALCADE (1932/33) ★★★

★ best film Winfield Sheehan (producer)
★ best direction Frank Lloyd
★ best art direction William S. Darling

Noel Coward's famous panorama of English history observed from the point of view of one family as they live through the period from 1899 to World War I and its aftermath. Among the spectacular highlights: the celebrations at the Relief of Mafeking, the departure of the troops to the war, the Zeppelin raids, the sinking of the Titanic.

A Fox Picture, directed by Frank Lloyd. With Diana Wynyard, Clive Brook, Una O'Connor, Herbert Mundin, Beryl Mercer, Irene Browne, Tempe Pigott. 115 mins.

THE CHAMP (1931/32) ★★

★ best actor Wallace Beery
★ best original story Frances Marion

Wallace Beery splitting his Oscar with Fredric March (the only best-actor tie in the history of the Academy) as a drunken, broken-down boxer who makes a comeback for the sake of his idolizing young son, Jackie Cooper. March's award was for his performance in *Dr. Jekyll and Mr. Hyde* (1932).

An MGM Picture, directed by King Vidor. With Wallace Beery, Jackie Cooper, Irene Rich, Jesse Scott, Roscoe Ates, Hale Hamilton. 87 mins.

CHAMPION (1949)

★ best editing Harry Gerstad

Kirk Douglas in one of his early "heel" parts as a young middleweight who tramples over his crippled brother, wife, assorted girlfriends and long-suffering manager on the way to the top. The ferocious boxing scenes helped Gerstad win his Oscar for best editing.

A United Artists Picture, directed by Mark Robson. With Kirk Douglas, Marilyn Maxwell, Arthur Kennedy, Paul Stewart, Ruth Roman, Lola Albright. 99 mins.

THE CHARGE OF THE LIGHT BRIGADE (1936) ★

★ best assistant direction Jack Sullivan

Lavish $1,200,000 version of the famous charge by some 700 English cavalrymen—led on this occasion by Errol Flynn—against the Russian artillery in the Crimea in the 1850s.

A Warner Bros. Picture, directed by Michael Curtiz. With Errol Flynn, Olivia de Havilland, Patric Knowles, Henry Stephenson, Nigel Bruce, Donald Crisp, David Niven. 115 mins.

CHARIOTS OF FIRE (1981)

★ best film David Puttnam (producer)
★ best original screenplay Colin Welland
★ best costume design Milena Canonero
★ best original score Vangelis

The moving story of two British athletes, both outsiders and both running for a cause in the 1924 Olympics—Jewish Harold Abrahams, who

Ben Cross as Harold Abrahams in Hugh Hudson's drama of the 1924 Olympics, *Chariots of Fire* (Enigma/ 20th Century-Fox), voted best picture of 1981.

runs to overcome the prejudice he experiences at Cambridge University, and missionary's son Eric Liddell, who runs for the greater glory of God. A deserved but surprise best-picture winner in a year when most thought the major award would go to Warren Beatty's multi-nominated epic *Reds*. The first British best-picture winner since *Oliver!* in 1968.

An Enigma Production for 20th Century-Fox and Allied Stars (distributed in America by The Ladd Company/Warner Bros.). Directed by Hugh Hudson. With Ben Cross, Ian Charleson, Nigel Havers, Nicholas Farrell, Daniel Gerroll, Cheryl Campbell, Alice Krige, John Gielgud, Lindsay Anderson, Nigel Davenport, Ian Holm. Color. 121 mins.

CHARLY (1968)   ★

★ best actor Cliff Robertson

Provocative movie about a man with the mind of a child (Cliff Robertson) who becomes a genius virtually overnight after a brain operation, only to slip back into his original feeble-minded state. Claire Bloom co-stars as the ther-apist who has an affair with the transformed man during his brief period of normality and then helplessly watches his deterioration.

A Selmur-Robertson Associates Production, directed by Ralph Nelson. With Cliff Robertson, Claire Bloom, Leon Janney, Lilia Skala, Dick Van Patton, William Dwyer. Techniscope/Technicolor. 103 mins.

CHILDREN OF A LESSER GOD (1986)   ★

★ best actress Marlee Matlin

An attractive young woman, once the most gifted pupil at a school for the deaf, now works there as a cleaning woman. Unorthodox speech teacher William Hurt determines to find out why, and falls in love along the way. A weepie with a serious message, based on the stage play by Mark Medoff and earning deaf newcomer Marlee Matlin a unique Oscar as best actress. The film's director, Randa Haines, was the unluckiest at Oscar time. Her film was nominated for best picture but she failed to be nominated for best director.

A Paramount Picture, directed by Randa Haines. With William Hurt, Marlee Matlin,

Deaf actress Marlee Matlin, voted best of the year in 1986 for her performance in Randa Haines' *Children of a Lesser God* (Paramount).

Shootout in *Chinatown* (Paramount, 1974). Femme fatale Faye Dunaway at the climax of Polanski's private-eye thriller, scripted by Robert Towne, who was honored by the Academy for his screenplay.

Piper Laurie, Philip Holmes, Georgia Ann Cline, William D. Byrd, Frank Carter Jr., John Limnidis, Bob Hiltermann. Metrocolor. 119 mins.

CHINATOWN (1974) ★

★ best original screenplay Robert Towne

Many-layered private-eye thriller, with brash matrimonial investigator Jack Nicholson involved with corruption, mystery, double-cross and murder in 1937 Los Angeles. Faye Dunaway is the enigmatic femme fatale, John Huston the embodiment of smiling villainy, and, for a few seconds, Roman Polanski, a menacing little hood with a knife.

A Paramount Picture, directed by Roman Polanski. With Jack Nicholson, Faye Dunaway, John Huston, Perry Lopez, John Hillerman, Darrell Zwerling, Diane Ladd, Roman Polanski. Panavision/Technicolor. 131 mins.

CIMARRON (1930/31) ★ ★ ★

★ best film William LeBaron (producer)
★ best writing adaptation Howard Estabrook
★ best art direction Max Ree

Western epic by Edna Ferber about the development of the small Oklahoma town of Osage from its founding in the 1880s to its growth into a great modern industrial city. The first Western to win best film, it has since been matched by *Dances with Wolves* (1990) and *Unforgiven* (1992). The film's highlight: the frenzied land rush, in which the first settlers race in covered wagons and on horseback to claim their land. Other Westerns nominated for best picture: *In Old Arizona* (1928/29), *Stagecoach* (1939), *The Ox-Bow Incident* (1943), *High Noon* (1952), *Shane* (1953), *The Alamo* (1960), *How the West Was Won* (1963), and *Butch Cassidy and the Sundance Kid* (1969).

An RKO Picture, directed by Wesley Ruggles. With Richard Dix, Irene Dunne, Estelle Taylor, Nance O'Neil, William Collier, Jr., Roscoe Ates, George E. Stone. 130 mins.

CINEMA PARADISO (1989) ★

★ best foreign language film Italy

Magical, semiautobiographical picture set in a tiny Sicilian village during and after World War II in which a warm-hearted projectionist befriends a young boy and instructs him in the pleasures of the picture palace. A poignant love letter to the movies, filmed in the director's hometown, Bagheria.

A Cristaldifilm (Rome)/Films Ariane (Paris) production, directed by Giuseppe Tornatore.

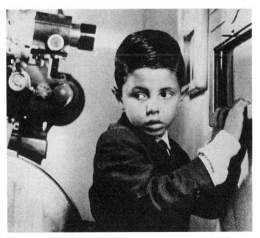

Learning about the movies. Salvatore Cascio in *Cinema Paradiso* (best foreign language film, Italy, 1989).

With Philippe Noiret, Jacques Perrin, Salvatore Cascio, Mario Leonardi, Agnese, Pupella Maggio, Antonella Attili. Color. 155 mins.

CITIZEN KANE (1941)   ★

★ best original screenplay Herman J. Mankiewicz & Orson Welles

The rise to power of an American newspaper tycoon (Orson Welles), told in flashback through interviews with people who were close to him in his lifetime. Closely based on the career of William Randolph Hearst and generally regarded as the greatest film ever made, but winner of only one Oscar—for writing. Its other eight nominations were for best film, direction, actor, cinematography (Gregg Toland), art direction, editing, sound and music.

An RKO Picture, directed by Orson Welles. With Orson Welles, Dorothy Comingore, Joseph Cotten, Everett Sloane, George Coulouris, Ray Collins, Ruth Warrick, Erskine Sanford, Agnes Moorehead, Paul Stewart. 119 mins.

CITY SLICKERS (1991)   ★

★ best supporting actor Jack Palance

A 39-year-old family man (Billy Crystal), suffering badly from a mid-life crisis, joins a couple of buddies on a two-week vacation on a cattle drive out West. A commercially successful comedy enlivened by the macabre comments and dry philosophy of Jack Palance as trail boss Curly. Palance was first nominated in 1952 for trying to murder Joan Crawford in *Sudden Fear*, and again in 1953 when he blasted poor Elisha Cook to bits in *Shane*.

Castle Rock Entertainment in association with Nelson Entertainment presentation of a Face production (Columbia). Directed by Ron Underwood. With Billy Crystal, Daniel Stern, Bruno Kirby, Patricia Wettig, Helen Slater, Jack Palance, Josh Mostel. Color: CFI. 114 mins.

Trail boss Jack Palance, Oscar winner as best supporting actor in the male menopause comedy *City Slickers* (Castle Rock Entertainment, 1991).

CLEOPATRA (1934)   ★

★ best cinematography Victor Milner

Restrained (for DeMille) account of the Cleopatra–Caesar–Antony story, with Claudette Colbert, Warren William and Henry Wilcoxon featured as the doomed trio.

A Paramount Picture, directed by Cecil B. DeMille. With Claudette Colbert, Warren William, Henry Wilcoxon, Gertrude Michael, Joseph Schildkraut. 95 mins.

CLEOPATRA (1963)   ★ ★ ★ ★

★ best color cinematography Leon Shamroy
★ best color art direction John DeCuir, Jack Martin Smith, Hilyard Brown, Herman Blumenthal, Elven Webb, Maurice Pelling & Boris Juraga

set decoration Walter M. Scott, Paul S. Fox & Ray Moyer
★ best color costume design Irene Sharaff, Vittorio Nino Novarese & Renie
★ best special effects Emil Kosa, Jr.

Multi-million-dollar version of two historic love affairs, the first between Caesar (Rex Harrison) and Cleopatra (Elizabeth Taylor), the second between the same lady and Marc Antony (Richard Burton). The film was described by its director, Joseph Mankiewicz, as being "conceived in a state of emergency," "shot in confusion" and "winding up in blind panic." Not surprisingly, at $37 million, it nearly bankrupted the Fox studio.

A 20th Century-Fox Picture, directed by Joseph L. Mankiewicz. With Elizabeth Taylor, Richard Burton, Rex Harrison, Pamela Brown, George Cole, Hume Cronyn, Cesare Danova, Kenneth Haigh, Roddy McDowall. Todd-AO/DeLuxe Color. 243 mins.

CLOSE ENCOUNTERS OF THE THIRD KIND (1977) ★★

★ best cinematography Vilmos Zsigmond
★ best sound effects editing Frank Warner*

UFO science fiction drama from the director of *Jaws* (1975), set in modern-day America and following the experiences of an electrical lineman (Richard Dreyfuss) and a distraught mother (Melinda Dillon) when the latter's small child is kidnapped from his home by extraterrestrial visitors. The film had outstanding special effects, but was outshone at Academy Awards time by seven-Oscar-winner *Star Wars*.

A Columbia Picture, directed by Steven Spielberg. With Richard Dreyfuss, François Truffaut, Teri Garr, Melinda Dillon, Bob Balaban, J. Patrick McNamara, Cary Guffey. Panavision/Metrocolor. 135 mins.

---

* *Note:* Frank Warner's Oscar for sound effects editing was a special achievement award.

CLOSELY WATCHED TRAINS (1967)

★ best foreign language film Czechoslovakia

The experiences—sad, funny and tender by turn—of a young apprentice railroad worker at a sleepy country station in wartime Czechoslovakia.

A Ceskoslovensky Film, Barrandov Studio Production, directed by Jiri Menzel. With Vaclav Neckar, Jitka Bendova, Vladimir Valenta, Josef Somr, Libuse Havelkova. 92 mins.

COAL MINER'S DAUGHTER (1980) ★

★ best actress Sissy Spacek

Moving bio-pic of Loretta Lynn, with Sissy Spacek doing wonders both dramatically and musically (she sings all her own songs) as the Appalachian mountain girl who was married at 13, the mother of four by the time she was 18, and went on to become the queen of country music. Tommy Lee Jones co-stars as Loretta's husband, Beverly D'Angelo as country star Patsy Cline.

A Universal Picture, directed by Michael Apted. With Sissy Spacek, Tommy Lee Jones, Levon Helm, Phyllis Boyens, William Sanderson, Beverly D'Angelo. Technicolor. 124 mins.

COCOON (1985)

★ best supporting actor Don Ameche
★ best visual effects Ken Ralston, Ralph McQuarrie, Scott Farrar & David Berry

The film for which the 77-year-old Don Ameche (never before nominated in a 49-year acting career) won his only Oscar—as one of three retired residents of a Florida retirement community who suddenly find themselves rejuvenated when they take a forbidden swim in the pool of an empty house. As usual in this kind of fantasy, aliens are behind it all. A big commercial success, one of the very few boasting an aging cast.

A 20th Century-Fox Picture (Fox-Zanuck-Brown Productions), directed by Ron Howard. With Don Ameche, Wilford Brimley, Hume Cronyn, Jack Gilford, Steve Guttenberg, Maureen Stapleton, Jessica Tandy, Gwen Verdon. DeLuxe Color. 117 mins.

THE COLOR OF MONEY (1986)   ★

★ best actor Paul Newman

Fast Eddie Felson (Newman), an ex-pool shark now a liquor salesman who banks young pool players, is lured back to the tables through a love–hate relationship with a flashy young pro-tégé (Cruise) who reminds him of himself in his earlier years. Directed by Martin Scorsese, the film earned Paul Newman an Oscar after a 28-year wait. His other nominations: *Cat on a Hot Tin Roof* (1958), *The Hustler* (1961), *Hud* (1963), *Cool Hand Luke* (1967), *Absence of Malice* (1981) and *The Verdict* (1982). Newman's win marked the first occasion that an actor earned an Oscar for repeating a role he had played previously. Newman first appeared as Felson in Robert Rossen's *The Hustler*.

A Touchstone Picture in association with Silver Screen Partners II (Buena Vista), directed by Martin Scorsese. With Paul Newman, Tom Cruise, Mary Elizabeth Mastrantonio, Helen Shaver, John Turturro, Bill Cobbs, Keith McCready, Robert Agins. Color by DeLuxe. 119 mins.

COME AND GET IT (1936)   ★

★ best supporting actor Walter Brennan

Edna Ferber tale of the Wisconsin lumber country and in particular of the life of lumber magnate Edward Arnold, who becomes a rival to his son for the daughter of a woman he knew years before. The first supporting actor winner, Walter Brennan, featured as Arnold's faithful Swedish buddy Swan Bostrom. Also up for

supporting Oscar nomination that year: Mischa Auer *(My Man Godfrey)*, Stuart Erwin *(Pigskin Parade)*, Basil Rathbone *(Romeo and Juliet)* and Akim Tamiroff *(The General Died at Dawn)*.

A Sam Goldwyn Production (released through United Artists), directed by Howard Hawks and William Wyler. With Edward Arnold, Joel McCrea, Frances Farmer, Walter Brennan, Andrea Leeds. 105 mins.

COME BACK LITTLE SHEBA (1952)   ★

★ best actress Shirley Booth

William Inge's study (based on his play) of a marriage dying from resignation. Shirley Booth, in her screen debut, plays the slovenly, middle-aged housewife living in a pathetic make-believe world and Burt Lancaster her husband, whose medical career was ruined years before when as a student he was forced to marry her.

A Paramount Picture, directed by Daniel Mann. With Burt Lancaster, Shirley Booth, Terry Moore, Richard Jaeckel, Philip Ober, Edwin Max. 99 mins.

COMING HOME (1978)   ★ ★ ★

★ best actor Jon Voight
★ best actress Jane Fonda
★ best original screenplay Waldo Salt & Robert C. Jones; Nancy Dowd (story)

Hal Ashby film about three people whose lives are affected by the Vietnam War—an American wife (Jane Fonda) who volunteers to work in a V.A. hospital; an embittered paraplegic (Jon Voight) she meets there; and her hawkish Marine husband (Bruce Dern), whose values change after his battle experiences. Set in 1968 and using many songs of the period (including several by The Beatles, Bob Dylan and Aretha Franklin), the film earned three Academy Awards but ran second for best-picture honors to the other big Vietnam film of the year, *The Deer Hunter*.

Best actress and best actor—Jane Fonda and disabled War veteran Jon Voight in the Vietnam rehabilitation drama *Coming Home* (United Artists, 1978).

A United Artists Picture, directed by Hal Ashby. With Jane Fonda, Jon Voight, Bruce Dern, Robert Carradine, Penelope Milford, Robert Ginty, Charles Cyphers, Teresa Hughes. DeLuxe Color. 128 mins.

COOL HAND LUKE (1967)　　★

★ best supporting actor George Kennedy

Modern chain-gang drama of the American South, with Paul Newman as the indomitable boss baiter who stubbornly refuses to buckle under and becomes a hero to his fellow convicts. George Kennedy's supporting Oscar was for his performance as Dragline—until Newman's arrival the uncrowned king of the chain-gang.
A Warner Bros. Picture, directed by Stuart Rosenberg. With Paul Newman, George Kennedy, J. D. Cannon, Lou Antonio, Robert Drivas, Strother Martin, Jo Van Fleet, Clifton James. Panavision/Technicolor. 127 mins.

COQUETTE (1928/29)　　★

★ best actress Mary Pickford

Mary Pickford's only Oscar role, as the heartless belle of a Southern town whose love affair with a crude mountaineer ends in tragedy. The song, "Coquette," used in the picture, was composed by Irving Berlin.

A United Artists Picture, directed by Sam Taylor. With Mary Pickford, John Mack Brown, Matt Moore, John Sainpolis, William Janney, Henry Kolker. 9 reels.

THE COUNTRY GIRL (1954)　　★★

★ best actress Grace Kelly
★ best screenplay George Seaton

Film version of Clifford Odets' poignant stage play about a faded, drunken stage star (Bing Crosby), his long-suffering wife (Grace Kelly) and the young Broadway director (William Holden) who tries to help the actor recover some of his lost eminence by casting him in a big comeback role.
A Paramount Picture, directed by George Seaton. With Bing Crosby, Grace Kelly, William Holden, Anthony Ross, Gene Reynolds. 104 mins.

COVER GIRL (1944)　　★

★ best scoring of a musical Morris Stoloff & Carmen Dragon

Rita Hayworth and Gene Kelly dancing together for the first and only time in Columbia's super backstage musical of the mid-1940s. Rita rises from Brooklyn singer to cover girl of *Van-*

The Country Girl: Grace Kelly's Oscar-winning role as the downtrodden wife of boozy stage performer Bing Crosby (Paramount, 1954).

ity magazine, dancer Kelly is the honest guy in her life, and Phil Silvers and Eve Arden provide the wisecracks. Numbers by Ira Gershwin and Jerome Kern include "Long Ago and Far Away."

A Columbia Picture, directed by Charles Vidor. With Gene Kelly, Rita Hayworth, Phil Silvers, Lee Bowman, Otto Kruger, Eve Arden. Technicolor. 107 mins.

THE COWBOY AND THE LADY (1938) ★

★ best sound recording Thomas T. Moulton

Typical 1930s comedy from the Goldwyn stable with aristocratic, fun-loving Merle Oberon falling for lanky rodeo star Gary Cooper.

A Sam Goldwyn Picture (released through United Artists), directed by H. C. Potter. With Gary Cooper, Merle Oberon, Patsy Kelly, Walter Brennan, Fuzzy Knight, Mabel Todd, Henry Kolker, Harry Davenport. 91 mins.

CRASH DIVE (1943) ★

★ best special effects Fred Sersen (photographic) Roger Heman (sound)

Technicolor war story centering on a submarine in the North Atlantic, with Tyrone Power as a specialist in naval warfare (both in PT boats and subs), Dana Andrews as the sub captain and Anne Baxter the girl they're both in love with.

A 20th Century-Fox Picture, directed by Archie Mayo. With Tyrone Power, Anne Baxter, Dana Andrews, James Gleason, Dame May Whitty, Henry Morgan. Technicolor. 105 mins.

CRIES AND WHISPERS (1973) ★

★ best cinematography Sven Nykvist

The haunting memories of a young woman (Harriet Andersson) dying in the house where she was born and being cared for by her devoted servant (Kari Sylwan) and her married sisters (Ingrid Thulin, Liv Ullmann).

A Cinematograph-Svenska Filminstitutet Film, directed by Ingmar Bergman. With Harriet Andersson, Kari Sylwan, Ingrid Thulin, Liv Ullmann, Erland Josephson, Henning Moritzen. Eastman Color. 91 mins.

CROMWELL (1970) ★

★ best costume design Nino Novarese

The rise of Oliver Cromwell, from Puritan squire and Member of Parliament, to dictator of 17th-century England. Richard Harris is the usurper, Alec Guinness the defiant Charles I.

A Columbia Picture, directed by Ken Hughes. With Richard Harris, Alec Guinness, Robert Morley, Dorothy Tutin, Frank Finlay, Timothy Dalton, Patrick Wymark, Patrick Magee. Panavision/Technicolor. 140 mins.

THE CRYING GAME (1992) ★

★ best original screenplay Neil Jordan

Troubled IRA man Stephen Rea, partly responsible for the kidnapping and death of a British soldier in Ireland, seeks out the dead man's girlfriend in London, where he discovers a few home truths not only about her but also about himself. One of the most disorienting "surprise" thrillers since Hitchcock's *Vertigo*, encompassing politics, race and sexuality, and earning Irish writer-director Neil Jordan his first Academy Award. The film also earned nominations in the best picture, director, actor, supporting actor and editing categories.

A Palace Pictures/Mirimax Production, directed by Neil Jordan. With Forest Whitaker, Miranda Richardson, Stephen Rea, Adrian Dunbar, Breffini McKenna, Joe Savino, Birdie Sweeney, Jaye Davidson, Jim Broadbent. In Color. 112 mins.

CYRANO DE BERGERAC (1950) ★

★ best actor Jose Ferrer

Jose Ferrer as the famous long-nosed 17th-century French swordsman-poet, who secretly worships his beautiful cousin Roxanne but disguises his passion in brilliant love letters written for a more suitably handsome suitor. A timeless tale of true love, honor and the shallow gift of beauty, made on a shoestring by the then newly formed Stanley Kramer production company. Based on the 1897 verse comedy by Edmond Rostand.

A United Artists Picture, directed by Michael Gordon. With Jose Ferrer, Mala Powers, William Prince, Morris Carnovsky, Ralph Clanton, Lloyd Corrigan. 112 mins.

CYRANO DE BERGERAC (1990) ★

★ best costume design Franca Squarciapino

The same story with an equally big-nosed Gerard Depardieu as Cyrano and the added pleasures of color, superb sets and costumes—which earned the film its only Academy Award. Depardieu perhaps came closest to achieving what no actor has yet accomplished in Oscar history—winning for best actor when a previous performer had already won for the same role. *Cyrano* was nominated for best foreign language film but lost to *Journey of Hope*.

Hachette Premiere Production, Orion Classics (France), directed by Jean-Paul Rappeneau. With Gerard Depardieu, Jacques Weber, Anne Brochet, Vincent Perez, Roland Bertin, Philippe Morier-Genoud, Philippe Volter, Josiane Stoleru. Panavision/In Color. 138 mins.

D

A DAMSEL IN DISTRESS (1937)   ★

★ best dance direction Hermes Pan for the "Fun House" number

Gershwin musical, set in London society, with Joan Fontaine as an heiress whom Fred Astaire mistakes for a chorus girl. Songs include "A Foggy Day in London Town" and "Nice Work If You Can Get It." The number "Fun House" for which Hermes Pan won his Oscar is an elaborate and inventive routine full of distorting mirrors, revolving drums, etc.

An RKO Picture, directed by George Stevens. With Fred Astaire, George Burns, Gracie Allen, Joan Fontaine, Reginald Gardiner, Ray Noble, Constance Collier. 100 mins.

DANCES WITH WOLVES (1990)   ★★★★★★★

★ best film Jim Wilson & Kevin Costner (producers)
★ best direction Kevin Costner
★ best screenplay Michael Blake
★ best cinematography Dean Semler
★ best editing Neil Travis
★ best original score John Barry
★ best sound Russell Williams II, Jeffrey Perkins, Bill W. Benton & Greg Watkins

The first Western since *Cimarron* (made almost 60 years earlier) to win for best picture; a combination of *Broken Arrow* (1950) and *Soldier Blue* (1970) with Kevin Costner as a disillusioned Civil War officer who opts for a life on the Western frontier and finds himself drawn into the fold of a Sioux Indian tribe that renames him Dances With Wolves. Costner's award for direction followed those earned by other actors-

Kevin Costner as Lieutenant Colonel Dunbar in *Dances With Wolves* (Tig Productions, 1990), winner of seven Oscars and the first Western to win as best picture since *Cimarron* some 60 years earlier.

turned-directors in the 1980s: Robert Redford *(Ordinary People)*; Warren Beatty *(Reds)*; and Richard Attenborough *(Gandhi).* The film received twelve nominations, the most since *Reds* nine years earlier.

Tig Productions/Orion. Directed by Kevin Costner. With Kevin Costner, Mary McDonnell, Graham Greene, Rodney A. Grant, Floyd Red Crow Westerman, Tantoo Cardinal, Robert Pastorelli, Charles Rocket. Panavision/DeLuxe Color. 180 mins.

DANGEROUS (1935)   ★

★ best actress Bette Davis

Bette Davis, in the first of her two Oscar-winning roles, as a once-famous Broadway actress who has fallen to the depths, and Franchot

Tone as the young architect who helps her rise from the gutter to a successful comeback. The film made Davis an international star and helped compensate for her missing out on the Oscar the year before for *Of Human Bondage*.

A Warner Bros. Picture, directed by Alfred E. Green. With Bette Davis, Franchot Tone, Margaret Lindsay, Alison Skipworth, John Eldredge, Dick Foran. 78 mins.

DANGEROUS LIAISONS (1988) ★★★

★ best screenplay (adaptation) Christopher Hampton
★ best art direction Stuart Craig
　　　　set decoration Gerard James
★ best costume design James Acheson

Notorious libertine Glenn Close ("I was born to dominate your sex and avenge my own") bets her male counterpart, the Vicomte de Valmont (John Malkovich), that he cannot seduce the virtuous Michelle Pfeiffer. He succeeds, but with tragic results. Sumptuously set, lavishly dressed version of the novel by Choderlos de Laclos, set just prior to the French Revolution. James Acheson's award for costumes followed his Oscar for *The Last Emperor* a year earlier.

A Warner Bros. Picture, directed by Stephen Frears. With Glenn Close, John Malkovich, Michelle Pfeiffer, Swoosie Kurtz, Keanu Reeves,

Intrigue and lust—the scheming Glenn Close and John Malkovich in Stephen Frears' *Dangerous Liaisons* (Warner Bros. 1988).

Mildred Natwick, Uma Thurman, Peter Capaldi. Eastman Color. 120 mins.

DANGEROUS MOVES (1984) ★

★ best foreign language film Switzerland

Soviet grand master Michel Piccoli takes on a young rival, now a defector and living in exile, in an international chess championship in Geneva. Obsessed with the game that occupies their lives, they find themselves being drawn into a larger game being played around them. An absorbing Cold War metaphor; the first Swiss film to win the foreign language award.

An Arthur Cohn Production, directed by Richard Dembo. With Michel Piccoli, Alexandre Arbatt, Liv Ullmann, Leslie Caron, Daniel Olbrychski, Michel Aumont, Serge Avedikian, Pierre Michael. Color. 110 mins.

THE DARK ANGEL (1935) ★

★ best art direction Richard Day

Goldwyn soap opera with Merle Oberon and Fredric March as a pair of lovers whose lives are almost destroyed when the latter is blinded in the trenches in World War I. Herbert Marshall co-stars as the other suitor for Miss Oberon's hand.

A Sam Goldwyn Picture (released through United Artists), directed by Sidney Franklin. With Fredric March, Merle Oberon, Herbert Marshall, Janet Beecher, John Halliday, Henrietta Crosman, Frieda Inescort. 105 mins.

DARLING (1965) ★★★

★ best actress Julie Christie
★ best story and screenplay Frederic Raphael
★ best b/w costume design Julie Harris

The career of a vain, man-eating fashion model (Julie Christie) who soars up the social scale by using all the men she comes in contact with—a young TV interviewer (Dirk Bogarde), a suave business executive (Laurence Harvey) and an Italian prince (Jose-Luis de Villalonga), who finally traps and frustrates her in a loveless marriage. A cold, hard look into the empty heart (and mind) of a girl living in London in the swinging sixties.

A Warner-Pathe-Anglo Amalgamated Picture, directed by John Schlesinger. With Dirk Bogarde, Laurence Harvey, Julie Christie, Roland Curram, Alex Scott, Basil Henson. 127 mins.

THE DAWN PATROL (1930/31)　　　★

★ best original story John Monk Saunders

Howard Hawks' first sound film, set in World War I and concerning the strains on inexperienced British fliers who live with almost certain death as they do daily battle above the trenches at the front line.

A Warner Bros. Picture, directed by Howard Hawks. With Richard Barthelmess, Douglas Fairbanks, Jr., Neil Hamilton, William Janney, James Finlayson. 95 mins.

DAY FOR NIGHT (1973)　　　★

★ best foreign language film France/Italy

A film within a film, with François Truffaut (as a fictional film director) beset with difficulties of all kinds—the love affairs and emotional problems of his international cast—as he works his way through his latest production.

Les Films Du Carosse-P.E.C.F.-P.I.C., directed by François Truffaut. With Jacqueline Bisset, Jean Pierre Leaud, François Truffaut, Valentina Cortese, Jean-Pierre Aumont. Technicolor. 116 mins.

DAYS OF HEAVEN (1978)　　　★

★ best cinematography Nestor Almendros

The tragic experiences of three young people— a poor industrial worker, his girlfriend and his kid sister—when they leave Chicago and make

a new life among the migrant workers in the Texas Panhandle. "Art for art's sake," but breathtakingly photographed by Nestor Almendros, whose images of bleak skies, wheatfields, and locust plagues, earned him a deserved Academy Award for cinematography.

A Paramount Picture, directed by Terrence Malick. With Richard Gere, Brooke Adams, Sam Shepard, Linda Manz, Robert Wilke, Jackie Shultis, Stuart Margolin. Metrocolor. 94 mins.

DAYS OF WINE AND ROSES (1962)　　　★

★ best song "Days of Wine and Roses" (Henry Mancini, music; Johnny Mercer, lyrics)

The harrowing account of two seemingly normal young people—a hard-pressed advertising executive (Jack Lemmon) and his wife (Lee Remick)—whose lives are shattered by drink as they sink deeper and deeper into alcoholism.

A Warner Bros. Picture, directed by Blake Edwards. With Jack Lemmon, Lee Remick, Charles Bickford, Jack Klugman, Alan Hewitt, Tom Palmer, Jack Albertson. 117 mins.

DEAD POETS SOCIETY (1989)　　　★

★ best original screenplay Tom Schulman

English teacher Robin Williams blazes his way into a boys' prep school in Vermont, inspiring his pupils with his exuberant philosophy of life and telling them to seize the day and make their lives extraordinary. A long way from Mr. Chips, but a puckish Williams managed a nomination, as did the film and the director, Peter Weir. Only Schulman triumphed with his original screenplay.

A Touchstone Picture, in association with Silver Screen Partners IV, Witt-Thomas Productions (distributed by Warner Bros.), directed by Peter Weir. With Robin Williams, Robert Sean Leonard, Ethan Hawke, Josh Charles, Gale Hansen, Dylan Kussman, Alle-

Seizing the day! Unorthodox English teacher Robin Williams inspires his delighted pupils in *Dead Poets Society* (Touchstone), winner for best original screenplay, 1989.

lon Ruggiero, Norman Lloyd. Metrocolor. 129 mins.

DEATH BECOMES HER (1992)   ★

★ best visual effects Ken Ralston, Doug Chiang, Doug Smythe & Tom Woodruff

Vain actress Meryl Streep and bitchy novelist Goldie Hawn vie for the love of superstar plastic surgeon Bruce Willis and then for something far more important—the secret of eternal life and youth. Isabella Rossellini is the kinky beauty who has the potion. The state-of-the-art effects include Streep's breasts moving up and then in, and Hawn parading around with an enormous see-through hole where her stomach used to be! A Universal Picture, directed by Robert Zemeckis. With Meryl Streep, Bruce Willis, Gol-

die Hawn, Isabella Rossellini, Ian Ogilvy, Adam Storke. DeLuxe Color. 103 mins.

DEATH ON THE NILE (1978)   ★

★ best costume design Anthony Powell

Murder on a riverboat during a honeymoon cruise down the River Nile. Similar in treatment to the earlier Agatha Christie opus *Murder on the Orient Express* (1974) but less stylish (costume design and Jack Cardiff's color work apart) than its predecessor. Peter Ustinov is Christie's Belgian sleuth Hercule Poirot; Bette Davis, Mia Farrow, Jon Finch and Maggie Smith are among the suspects.

An EMI Picture, directed by John Guillermin. With Peter Ustinov, Jane Birkin, Lois Chiles, Bette Davis, Mia Farrow, Jon Finch, Olivia Hussey, I. S. Johar, George Kennedy, Angela Lansbury, Simon MacCorkindale, David Niven, Maggie Smith, Jack Warden, Harry Andrews. Technicolor. 140 mins.

THE DEER HUNTER (1978)   ★★★★★

★ best film Barry Spikings, Michael Deeley, Michael Cimino & John Peverall (producers)
★ best direction Michael Cimino
★ best supporting actor Christopher Walken
★ best editing Peter Zinner
★ best sound Richard Portman, William McCaughey, Aaron Rochin, & Darrin Knight

A huge, sprawling movie about the effects of the Vietnam War on three young Pennsylvania steelworkers who leave their hometown for a tour of duty at the front. Only the strongest of the three (Robert De Niro) survives; the others (Christopher Walken and John Savage) are crushed physically and mentally by the war and torture at the hands of the Viet Cong. One of two Vietnam films to win as best picture, the other being *Platoon* in 1986.

An EMI Picture, directed by Michael Cimino. With Robert De Niro, John Cazale, John Savage, Christopher Walken, Meryl Streep,

Michael Cimino directs Robert De Niro in the 1978 best-picture winner, *The Deer Hunter* (EMI).

George Dzundza, Chuck Aspegren. Panavision/Technicolor. 182 mins.

THE DEFIANT ONES (1958)   ★★

★ best story & screenplay Nathan E. Douglas & Harold Jacob Smith
★ best cinematography Sam Leavitt

Two convicts, one white, one black, make their escape from a police van in the South but have to spend their short-lived freedom chained together by the wrist. Stanley Kramer's optimistic movie about racial tolerance, with Tony Curtis and Sidney Poitier as the two convicts.

A United Artists Picture, directed by Stanley Kramer. With Tony Curtis, Sidney Poitier, Theodore Bikel, Charles McGraw, Lon Chaney, Jr., King Donovan, Claude Akins. 97 mins.

DERSU UZALA (1975)   ★

★ best foreign language film Russia/Japan

Akira Kurosawa adventure, set at the turn of the century, centering on a Siberian trapper and a hunter-explorer who become inseparable friends while surveying the unexplored forests of eastern Siberia and the taiga.

Mosfilm, Moscow-Toho, Tokyo, directed by Akira Kurosawa. With Maxim Munzuk, Yuri Solomin. Color. 137 mins.

DESIGNING WOMAN (1957)   ★

★ best story & screenplay George Wells

Sportswriter Gregory Peck and successful dress designer Lauren Bacall find, after their marriage, unforeseen difficulties as they try to adapt to each other's friends and habits. Sophisticated updating of the 1942 hit *Woman of the Year*, which also won a writing Oscar.

An MGM Picture, directed by Vincente Minnelli. With Gregory Peck, Lauren Bacall, Dolores Gray, Sam Levene, Tom Helmore, Mickey Shaughnessy, Jesse White. Cinema-Scope/Metrocolor. 118 mins.

DESTINATION MOON (1950)   ★

★ best special effects Lee Zavitz & George Pal

The first of the big postwar science fiction movies, based on scientific knowledge of the time and showing how four men journey to the moon and back in an atomic rocket. Set designer Ernst Fegte's intriguing moonscapes helped win the film its special effects award.

An Eagle Lion Picture, directed by Irving Pichel. With John Archer, Warner Anderson, Tom Powers, Dick Wesson, Erin O'Brien Moore. Technicolor. 90 mins.

THE DIARY OF ANNE FRANK (1959)   ★★★

★ best supporting actress Shelley Winters
★ best b/w cinematography William C. Mellor
★ best b/w art direction Lyle R. Wheeler & George W. Davis
          set decoration Walter M. Scott & Stuart A. Reiss

The story of how in World War II two Jewish families and a garrulous old dentist lived in unbearably cramped conditions above an attic in an Amsterdam warehouse. The group was found by the Nazis just nine months before the liberation of Holland, and only the father of Anne Frank (the young girl through whose diary the world heard the story) survived.

A 20th Century-Fox Picture, directed by George Stevens. With Millie Perkins, Joseph Schildkraut, Shelley Winters, Richard Beymer, Gusti Huber, Lou Jacobi, Ed Wynn. CinemaScope. 170 mins.

DICK TRACY (1990)

- ★ best song "Sooner or Later" ("I Always Get My Man") (Stephen Sondheim, music & lyrics)
- ★ best art direction Richard Sylbert
        set decoration Rick Simpson
- ★ best makeup John Caglione, Jr. & Doug Drexler

Pop art version of Chester Gould's famous comic strip, with Warren Beatty—complete with lemon-colored trench coat and fedora—as the jut-jawed hero up against underworld boss Big Boy Caprice (Al Pacino) and double-crossing torch singer Breathless Mahoney (Madonna). Also on hand: Glenne Headly as Dick's dame Tess Trueheart, and assorted crooks Dustin Hoffman, Dick Van Dyke and James Caan, all of whom are hidden behind the exaggerated rubbery makeup of Messrs. Caglione and Drexler.

A Touchstone Picture (in association with Silver Screen Partners IV), directed by Warren Beatty. With Warren Beatty, Al Pacino, Charlie Korsmo, Michael Donovan O'Donnell, Jim Wilkey, William Forsythe, Glenne Headly, Madonna. 77mm/Technicolor. 105 mins.

DIRTY DANCING (1987)

- ★ best song "I've Had the Time of My Life" (Franke Previte, John Nicola, Donald Markowitz, music; Franke Previte, lyrics)

Femme fatale Madonna and All-American hero Warren Beatty in two scenes from *Dick Tracy* (Touchstone), Oscar winner in 1990 for best art direction, makeup and song.

A spoiled teenage girl learns a few lessons about life when she has an affair with a hot-blooded dance instructor at a Catskills resort hotel. Flashy camerawork, sexy choreography and any number of old songs on the sound track by Frankie Valli and The Four Seasons, The Ronettes, Otis Redding, et al. The Oscar-winning song was performed in the movie by Bill Medley and Jennifer Warnes.

A Vestron Picture, directed by Emile Ardolino. With Jennifer Grey, Patrick Swayze, Jerry Orbach, Cynthia Rhodes, Jack Weston, Jane Bruckner, Kelly Bishop, Lonny Price. Color. 100 mins.

THE DIRTY DOZEN (1967)   ★

★ best sound effects John Poyner

Twelve misfits, rapists, murderers and psychopaths are turned by Major Lee Marvin into a bloodthirsty commando group to perform a dangerous mission in World War II—proving themselves heroes in the process.

An MGM Picture, directed by Robert Aldrich. With Lee Marvin, Ernest Borgnine, Charles Bronson, John Cassavetes, Richard Jaeckel, Robert Ryan, Telly Savalas, Donald Sutherland, George Kennedy. 70mm Widescreen/Metrocolor. 150 mins.

THE DISCREET CHARM OF THE BOURGEOISIE (1972)   ★

★ best foreign language film France

Superficially the tale of the inability of six rich people to get through an elusive meal without interruption, but basically yet another blistering attack by the cinema's master anarchist, Luis Buñuel, on the stupidities of the world's bourgeoisie.

A Greenwich Film Production, directed by Luis Buñuel. With Fernando Rey, Delphine Seyrig, Stephane Audran, Bulle Ogier, Jean-Pierre Cassel, Paul Frankeur. Eastman Color. 105 mins.

DISRAELI (1929/30)   ★

★ best actor George Arliss

George Arliss' sound debut (at 61 years of age), recreating the role he played silently nine years earlier and becoming the first British actor, albeit in an American film, to win a best-actor Oscar. As Britain's wily Prime Minister Benjamin Disraeli he thwarts a group of Russian agents and at the same time raises money to purchase the Suez Canal.

A Warner Bros. Picture, directed by Alfred E. Green. With George Arliss, Joan Bennett, Florence Arliss, Anthony Bushell, David Torrence, Ivan Simpson, Doris Lloyd. 9 reels.

THE DIVINE LADY (1928/29)   ★

★ best direction Frank Lloyd

The story of the lowly born Emma Hamilton, who rises to a position of some distinction by marrying the British ambassador at the Court of Naples and then achieves considerable notoriety by falling in love with Britain's greatest hero, Horatio Nelson. Corinne Griffith is Emma, Victor Varconi is Nelson, and H. B. Warner is the luckless Sir William Hamilton.

A First National Picture, directed by Frank Lloyd. With Corinne Griffith, Victor Varconi, H. B. Warner, Ian Keith, William Conklin, Marie Dressler. 12 reels.

THE DIVORCEE (1929/30)   ★

★ best actress Norma Shearer

Norma Shearer's Oscar-winning role and the first of several wayward wives she was to play on the screen in subsequent years. In this film she plays one of the first liberated women—a woman who discards her newspaperman husband (Chester Morris) when she discovers he's been cheating on her, emulates his sexual freedom and finally takes him back.

An MGM Picture, directed by Robert Z. Leonard. With Norma Shearer, Chester Morris, Conrad Nagel, Robert Montgomery, Florence Eldridge, Helene Millard. 9 reels.

DIVORCE ITALIAN STYLE (1962) ★

★ best story & screenplay Ennio De Concini, Alfredo Giannetti & Pietro Germi

Black comedy about the vanishing Sicilian aristocracy, with Marcello Mastroianni as an impoverished Sicilian nobleman finding that the only way he can court his beautiful young cousin is by murdering his amiable but demanding wife.

A Lux-Vides-Galatea Picture (Italy), directed by Pietro Germi. With Marcello Mastroianni, Daniella Rocca, Stefania Sandrelli, Leopoldo Trieste. 104 mins.

DOCTOR DOLITTLE (1967) ★★

★ best song "Talk to the Animals" (Leslie Bricusse, music & lyrics)
★ best special visual effects L. B. Abbott

Musical version of Hugh Lofting's stories, with Rex Harrison as the irascible Dr. John Dolittle (taught some 500 animal dialects by his sagacious parrot) off in search of the elusive Great Pink Sea Snail.

A 20th Century-Fox Picture, directed by Richard Fleischer. With Rex Harrison, Samantha Eggar, Anthony Newley, Richard Attenborough, Peter Bull. Todd-AO/DeLuxe Color. 152 mins.

DOCTOR ZHIVAGO (1965) ★★★★★

★ best screenplay from another medium Robert Bolt
★ best color cinematography Freddie Young
★ best color art direction John Box & Terry Marsh
  set decoration Dario Simoni
★ best color costume design Phyllis Dalton
★ best music score Maurice Jarre

Julie Christie's Lara taking revenge on her lover Rod Steiger in David Lean's 1965 epic *Doctor Zhivago* (MGM).

Idealist Russian doctor-poet (Omar Sharif), in sympathy with the ideals of the Revolution, finds himself unable to adjust to the new society when the Revolution finally occurs. Boris Pasternak's classic statement of the liberal bourgeois position, set in the revolutionary period and hinging on the doomed romance between Zhivago and his beautiful mistress Lara (Julie Christie).

An MGM Picture, directed by David Lean. With Omar Sharif, Julie Christie, Geraldine Chaplin, Tom Courtenay, Alec Guinness, Siobhan McKenna, Ralph Richardson, Rod Steiger, Rita Tushingham. Panavision/Metrocolor. 197 mins.

DODSWORTH (1936) ★

★ best art direction Richard Day

Midwestern industrialist Sam Dodsworth (Walter Huston), married to an immature and restless wife, finds a new set of values on a trip to the Continent, where an American widow teaches him to appreciate the traditions of Europe. William Wyler's version of the novel by Sinclair Lewis.

A Sam Goldwyn Picture (released through United Artists), directed by William Wyler. With Walter Huston, Ruth Chatterton, Paul Lukas, Mary Astor, David Niven, Maria Ouspenskaya. 90 mins.

DOG DAY AFTERNOON (1975)   ★

★ best original screenplay Frank Pierson

The story of three young men who hold up a Brooklyn bank in order to get money to finance a sex-change operation. Based on real-life characters and events that occurred in a Chase Manhattan bank in 1972 and starring Al Pacino, John Cazale and Gary Springer as the gay bank robbers.

A Warner Bros. Picture, directed by Sidney Lumet. With Al Pacino, John Cazale, Gary Springer, Sully Boyar, Penelope Allen, Beulah Garrick. Technicolor. 130 mins.

LA DOLCE VITA (1961)   ★

★ best b/w costume design Piero Gherardi

The film that created a world sensation in the early 1960s—a scorching look at the jet-set life in Rome (especially at the decadence of the moneyed classes) as seen through the eyes of scandal reporter Marcello Mastroianni.

Riama Film (Italy/France), directed by Federico Fellini. With Marcello Mastroianni, Yvonne Furneaux, Anouk Aimee, Anita Ekberg, Alain Cuny, Annibale Ninchi, Magali Noel, Lex Barker, Nadia Gray. 175 mins.

A DOUBLE LIFE (1947)   ★ ★

★ best actor Ronald Colman
★ best music score of a drama or comedy Miklos Rozsa

Schizophrenic actor Ronald Colman, obsessed with the role of Othello he is playing on the Broadway stage, finds he is playing the part in real life, even to the point where he commits murder. Colman's only Oscar, and a belated one at that. He had previously been nominated for *Bulldog Drummond* (1929/30) and *Random Harvest* (1942).

A Universal-International Picture, directed by George Cukor. With Ronald Colman, Signe Hasso, Edmond O'Brien, Shelley Winters, Ray Collins, Philip Loeb, Millard Mitchell. 103 mins.

THE DOVE (1927/28)   ★

★ best art direction William Cameron Menzies

Romantic melodrama with Norma Talmadge as a dance-hall girl ("The Dove" of the title) in love with gambler Gilbert Roland. Complicating things, and the third member of the eternal triangle, is wealthy caballero Noah Beery. Menzies was the first art director to win an Oscar, and was also named for his work on *The Tempest*, released the same year.

A United Artists picture, directed by Roland West. With Norma Talmadge, Noah Beery, Gilbert Roland, Eddie Borden, Harry Myers. 9 reels.

DRIVING MISS DAISY (1989)   ★ ★ ★ ★

★ best film Richard D. Zanuck & Lili Fini Zanuck (producers)
★ best actress Jessica Tandy
★ best screenplay adaptation Alfred Uhry
★ best makeup Manlio Rocchetti, Lyn Barber & Kevin Haney

Adaptation by Alfred Uhry of his Pulitzer Prize-winning play charting the 25-year relationship between an eccentric Southern matron (Jessica Tandy) and her faithful black chauffeur (Morgan Freeman). Bruce Beresford's omission from the list of director nominees marked only the third time that a film won for best picture without its director being nominated. Previous occasions: 1927/28, when William Wellman missed out for *Wings;* and 1931/32, when Edmund Goulding was overlooked for *Grand Hotel.* At 80 years and 10 months of age, Jessica Tandy became the oldest performer to win an Oscar, edging out George Burns, who was seven months younger when he won for *The Sunshine Boys* (1975). Morgan Freeman was nominated for best actor but lost to Daniel Day-Lewis for *My Left Foot.*

A Zanuck Company Production (distributed by Warner Bros.), directed by Bruce Beresford. With Morgan Freeman, Jessica Tandy, Dan Aykroyd, Patti Lupone, Esther Rolle, Joann Havrilla, William Hall, Jr., Alvin M. Sugerman. Color; prints by Technicolor. 99 mins.

DR. JEKYLL AND MR. HYDE (1931/32) ★

★ best actor Fredric March

The most successful of the many attempts to film Robert Louis Stevenson's nightmare tale of a Victorian doctor (March) who finds that by taking a special drug he can change into his other self—ruthless, cruel and bestial. Rose Hobart is the doctor's luckless fiancée, Miriam Hopkins the cockney slut who arouses Hyde. March's acting award was shared with Wallace Beery for *The Champ.*

A Paramount Picture, directed by Rouben Mamoulian. With Fredric March, Miriam Hopkins, Rose Hobart, Holmes Herbert, Edgar Norton, Halliwell Hobbes. 90 mins.

DUMBO (1941)

★ best scoring of a musical picture Frank Churchill & Oliver Wallace

Full-length cartoon by Walt Disney (his fifth) about a baby elephant who learns to fly by using his enormous ears as wings. Songs include "Casey Junior," "Baby Mine" and "When I See an Elephant Fly."

A Walt Disney Picture, released by RKO. Supervising director, Ben Sharpsteen. Voices by Edward Brophy, Herman Bing, Verna Felton, Sterling Holloway, Cliff Edwards. Technicolor. 64 mins.

E

EARTHQUAKE (1974)

- ★ best sound Ronald Pierce & Melvin Metcalfe, Sr.
- ★ best visual effects Frank Brendel, Albert Whitlock, & Glen Robinson*

The biggest earthquake film since *San Francisco* (1936), with not one but two tremors as a massive quake hits Los Angeles, the first destroying most of the city, the second bursting the Hollywood Dam. Heroic efforts by L.A. engineer Charlton Heston and cop George Kennedy prove to be in vain.

A Universal Picture, directed by Mark Robson. With Charlton Heston, Ava Gardner, George Kennedy, Lorne Greene, Genevieve Bujold, Richard Roundtree. Panavision/Sensurround/Technicolor. 123 mins.

EASTER PARADE (1948)

- ★ best scoring of a musical Johnny Green & Roger Edens

Technicolor musical with a plot right off the MGM conveyor belt, with Fred Astaire taking on chorus girl Judy Garland as his new dancing partner after clashing with ambitious Ann Miller. Set in the early 1920's and with Astaire's "Drum Crazy," Miller's "Shakin' the Blues Away" and the Astaire–Garland duet "We're a Couple of Swells" as the highlights.

An MGM Picture, directed by Charles Walters. With Fred Astaire, Judy Garland, Peter Lawford, Ann Miller, Dick Beavers, Jules

---

* *Note:* The Oscar for best visual effects was a special achievement award "for the realistic depiction of the devastation of Los Angeles by an earthquake."

Munshin, Clinton Sundberg. Technicolor. 103 mins.

EAST OF EDEN (1955)

- ★ best supporting actress Jo Van Fleet

Steinbeck's 20th-century allegory of the Cain and Abel story with rebellious James Dean and wholesome Richard Davalos as the two contrasted sons competing for the love of their patriarchal father Raymond Massey. Set in California in 1917 and co-starring Oscar winner Jo Van Fleet as the boys' mother who has broken free of her family and becomes the proprietress of a nearby brothel.

A Warner Bros. Picture, directed by Elia Kazan. With Julie Harris, James Dean, Raymond Massey, Richard Davalos, Burl Ives, Jo Van Fleet, Albert Dekker. CinemaScope/Warner Color. 115 mins.

8½ (1963)

- ★ best foreign language film Italy
- ★ best b/w costume design Piero Gherardi

The memories, fantasies and desires of an artistically exhausted Italian film director (based on Fellini himself), as he rests his mind and body at a spa and searches frantically for a story for his new film. A vivid piece of cinematic self-analysis.

An Angelo Rizzoli Picture, directed by Federico Fellini. With Marcello Mastroianni, Claudia Cardinale, Anouk Aimee, Sandra Milo, Rosella Falk, Barbara Steele, Guido Alberti. 135 mins.

ELMER GANTRY (1960)

- ★ best actor Burt Lancaster
- ★ best supporting actress Shirley Jones
- ★ best screenplay Richard Brooks

Burt Lancaster as Sinclair Lewis' whoring, whiskey-drinking salesman who joins up

Burt Lancaster in his Oscar-winning role as Sinclair Lewis' whiskey-drinking salesman *Elmer Gantry* (United Artists, 1960).

with evangelist Jean Simmons, exploits her tent-pitching revivalist group and unscrupulously turns it into big business. Based on Lewis' 1927 novel of the American Midwest; Shirley Jones' supporting Oscar was for her portrayal of Gantry's former girlfriend turned prostitute.

A United Artists Picture, directed by Richard Brooks. With Burt Lancaster, Jean Simmons, Arthur Kennedy, Shirley Jones, Dean Jagger, Patti Page, Edward Andrews, John McIntire. Eastman Color. 146 mins.

THE EMPIRE STRIKES BACK (1980)   ★ ★

★ best sound Bill Varney, Steve Maslow, Gregg Landaker & Peter Sutton
★ best visual effects Brian Johnson, Richard Edlund, Dennis Muren & Bruce Nicholson

The Rebel Alliance from *Star Wars* (1977)— Luke Skywalker, Han Solo, Princess Leia, et al.—back in action against the dark forces of the galactic empire led by Darth Vader. The same invigorating mixture as before, combining fairy tale with science fiction and introducing several new characters, notably Yoda, the wizened old master of "the force." The movie's Oscar for visual effects was a special achievement award.

A 20th Century-Fox Picture, directed by Irvin Kershner. With Mark Hamill, Harrison Ford, Carrie Fisher, Billy Dee Williams, Anthony Daniels, David Prowse, James Earl Jones, Peter Mayhew, Kenny Baker, Frank Oz, Alec Guinness. Panavision/Eastman Color. 124 mins.

THE ENEMY BELOW (1957)   ★

★ best special effects Walter Rossi

The futile waste of human life in wartime revealed in a gripping duel between the captains of an American destroyer and a German U-boat who play cat and mouse in the Atlantic in World War II. Robert Mitchum commands the destroyer, Curt Jurgens the sub. Notable underwater effects.

A 20th Century-Fox Picture, directed by Dick Powell. With Robert Mitchum, Curt Jurgens, Al Hedison, Theodore Bikel, Russell Collins, Kurt Kreuger. CinemaScope/DeLuxe Color. 98 mins.

ESKIMO (1934)   ★

★ best editing Conrad Nervig

Documentary feature about Eskimo life in the northernmost inhabited settlement in Alaska. Filmed on the spot by W. S. Van Dyke (who traveled with his technicians by whaling schooner to Alaska to get his footage) and edited into a magnificent whole by Conrad Nervig—the first editor to win an Oscar. The entire native cast spoke in the Eskimo tongue.

An MGM Picture, directed by W. S. Van Dyke from a script by John Lee Mahin. With a native cast headed by Mala. 117 mins.

E.T. THE EXTRA-TERRESTRIAL (1982) ★★★★

- ★ best sound Robert Knudson, Robert Glass, Don Digirolamo & Gene Cantamessa
- ★ best visual effects Carlo Rambaldi, Dennis Murren & Kenneth F. Smith
- ★ best sound effects editing Charles L. Campbell & Ben Burtt
- ★ best original score John Williams

A 10-year-old boy living in a Los Angeles suburb befriends an alien creature accidentally stranded near his home and then helps him return to his own planet. Still the highest-grossing movie of all time, with some moments of genuine Spielberg magic (e.g. an aerial bike ride across the face of the moon), but at Oscar time it was somewhat overshadowed by *Gandhi*, winning just four awards against the eight garnered by Attenborough's film.

A Universal Picture, directed by Steven Spielberg. With Dee Wallace, Henry Thomas, Peter Coyote, Robert MacNaughton, Drew Barrymore, K. C. Martel, Sean Frye, Tom Howell. 70 mm/DeLuxe Color; prints by Technicolor. 115 mins.

Ernest Gold, composer of the Oscar-winning score for Otto Preminger's *Exodus* (United Artists), filmed in Israel in 1960.

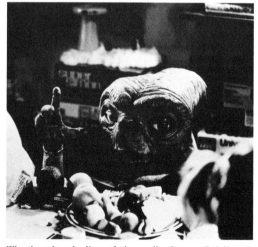

The best-loved alien of them all—Steven Spielberg's *E.T. The Extra-Terrestrial* (Universal, 1982). The film earned four Academy Awards, including one to John Williams for his music score.

EXODUS (1960)   ★

- ★ best music score of a drama or comedy Ernest Gold

The founding of the modern state of Israel in 1948, based partly on historical fact and partly on the fiction of the 600-page best-seller of the same name by Leon Uris. Ernest Gold's inspired score deservedly won the music award but, alas, sadly defeated Elmer Bernstein's music for *The Magnificent Seven*—an almost certain winner in any other year and one of the unluckiest music losers in the history of the awards.

A United Artists Picture, directed by Otto Preminger. With Paul Newman, Eva Marie Saint, Ralph Richardson, Peter Lawford, Lee J. Cobb, Sal Mineo, John Derek, Hugh Griffith. Super-Panavision 70/Technicolor. 213 mins.

THE EXORCIST (1973)

★ best screenplay William Peter Blatty
★ best sound Robert Knudson & Chris
   Newman

The only horror film to be nominated as best picture of the year—the story of a 12-year-old girl (Linda Blair), living in Washington with her actress mother (Ellen Burstyn), who sud-denly finds herself in the power of the Devil and unable to free herself from the horrors that possess her. Mercedes McCambridge (never seen) is the rasping, hoarsely mocking voice of Satan. Rarely has a sound track Oscar been so well deserved.

A Warner Bros. Picture, directed by William Friedkin. With Ellen Burstyn, Max Von Sydow, Lee J. Cobb, Kitty Winn, Jack MacGowran, Jason Miller, Linda Blair. Metrocolor. 122 mins.

F

THE FACTS OF LIFE (1960)   ★

★ best b/w costume design Edith Head & Edward Stevenson

Bob Hope–Lucille Ball comedy, in more serious vein than usual, with the comic pair starring as two middle-aged marrieds who, despite doing their utmost to make adultery succeed, find it just too much trouble. Don DeFore and Ruth Hussey co-star as the shelved partners.

A United Artist Picture, directed by Melvin Frank. With Bob Hope, Lucille Ball, Ruth Hussey, Don DeFore, Louis Nye, Philip Ober. 103 mins.

THE FAIR CO-ED (1927/28)   ★

★ best title writing Joseph Farnham

Silent American comedy-romance with John Mack Brown working his way through college as a basketball coach and Marion Davies as the girl who joins the team and becomes the star player. One of the three films to figure in the only title-writing Oscar given by the Academy, Farnham also winning that year for his work on *Laugh, Clown, Laugh* and *Telling the World*.

An MGM Picture, directed by Sam Wood. With Marion Davies, John Mack Brown, Jane Winton, Thelma Hill, Lillian Leighton. 7 reels.

FAME (1980)   ★★

★ best original score Michael Gore
★ best original song "Fame" (Michael Gore, music; Dean Pitchford, lyrics)

Realistic musical drama set against the background of Manhattan's High School for the Performing Arts and focusing on a group of talented youngsters from the day of their first audition to their graduation four years later. The first movie* to have two numbers nominated in the best-song category, "Out Here On My Own" also being up for the song award in 1980.

An MGM Picture, directed by Alan Parker. With Irene Cara, Lee Curreri, Laura Dean, Antonia Franceschi, Paul McCrane, Barry Miller, Gene Anthony Ray, Maureen Teefy. Metrocolor. 133 mins.

FANNY AND ALEXANDER (1983)   ★★★★

★ best foreign language film Sweden
★ best cinematography Sven Nykvist
★ best art direction Anna Asp
★ best costume design Marik Vos

Two years in the life of the affluent Ekdahl family in a provincial Swedish town at the beginning of the century, full of family crises, philanderings, quarrels, illicit liaisons—many of them seen through the eyes of a 10-year-old boy and his young sister Fanny. Ingmar Bergman's most optimistic and certainly most opulent film; the third made by the director to win as best foreign language film. The others: *The Virgin Spring* (1960) and *Through a Glass Darkly* (1961).

---

* Other movies that have since earned double or triple song nominations: *Flashdance* (1983)—"Flashdance . . . What a Feeling" and "Maniac"; *Yentl* (1983)—"Papa, Can You Hear Me?" and "The Way He Makes Me Feel"; *Footloose* (1984)—"Footloose" and "Let's Hear It for the Boy"; *White Nights* (1985)—"Say You, Say Me" and "Separate Lives"; *The Little Mermaid* (1989)—"Under the Sea" and "Kiss the Girl"; *Beauty and the Beast* (1991)—"Beauty and the Beast," "Belle" and "Be Our Guest"; *The Bodyguard* (1992)—"Run to You" and "Have Nothing"; and *Aladdin* (1992)—"Friend Like Me" and "Whole New World."

Cinematograph for The Swedish Film Institute/Swedish Television SVTI/Gaumont/Personafilm/Tobis Filmkunst. Directed by Ingmar Bergman. With Gunn Wallgren, Borje Ahlstedt, Christina Schollin, Bertil Guve, Pernilla Allwin, Gunnar Bjornstrand, Jan Malmsjo, Ewa Froeling, Erland Josephson, Harriet Andersson. Eastman Color. 189 mins. (Swedish TV transmission time: 300 mins.)

FANTASTIC VOYAGE (1966) ★★

★ best color art direction Jack Martin Smith & Dale Hennesy
    set decoration Walter M. Scott & Stuart A. Reiss
★ best special visual effects Art Cruickshank

Science fiction, set in the year 1995, about a four-man (and one woman) scientific team who are miniaturized to microbe size and travel by submarine into a patient's bloodstream. Their task? To perform a difficult brain operation and save the life of a Czech scientist who has vital secrets to tell.

A 20th Century-Fox Picture, directed by Richard Fleischer. With Stephen Boyd, Raquel Welch, Edmond O'Brien, Donald Pleasence, Arthur O'Connell, William Redfield, Arthur Kennedy. CinemaScope/DeLuxe Color. 100 mins.

A FAREWELL TO ARMS (1932/33) ★★

★ best cinematography Charles B. Lang, Jr.
★ best sound recording Harold C. Lewis

Ernest Hemingway's doomed romance between an American ambulance driver (Gary Cooper), wounded at the Italian front in World War I, and the English Red Cross nurse (Helen Hayes) who nurses him back to health. The first of Hemingway's novels to reach the screen.

A Paramount Picture, directed by Frank Borzage. With Helen Hayes, Gary Cooper, Adolphe Menjou, Mary Philips, Jack La Rue, Blanche Frederici. 78 mins.

THE FARMER'S DAUGHTER (1947) ★

★ best actress Loretta Young

Swedish maid Loretta Young, employed as a servant in the home of political matriarch Ethel Barrymore, quickly makes it big in Washington, winning not only a seat in Congress but a husband (Joseph Cotten) into the bargain. Cheerful comedy-drama that won Miss Young a somewhat surprising best-actress Oscar, other nominees that year being Joan Crawford (*Possessed*), Susan Hayward (*Smash Up*), Rosalind Russell (*Mourning Becomes Electra*) and Dorothy McGuire (*Gentleman's Agreement*).

An RKO Picture, directed by H. C. Potter. With Loretta Young, Joseph Cotten, Ethel Barrymore, Charles Bickford, Rose Hobart, Rhys Williams, Harry Davenport. 97 mins.

FATHER GOOSE (1964) ★

★ best story & screenplay Peter Stone & Frank Tarloff (screenplay), S. H. Barnett (story)

Unshaven, boozy beachcomber (Cary Grant), tricked by the Australian navy into reporting on Japanese plane and ship movements in World War II, suddenly finds himself having to share his isolated outpost with a gaggle of stranded schoolchildren and their frosty teacher, Leslie Caron.

A Universal Picture, directed by Ralph Nelson. With Cary Grant, Leslie Caron, Trevor Howard, Jack Good, Verina Greenlaw, Pip Sparke. Technicolor. 115 mins.

FELLINI'S CASANOVA (1976) ★

★ best costume design Danilo Donati

Federico Fellini's visual treat—a stylized and very personal vision of the life of the celebrated 18th-century lover. Donald Sutherland is featured in the lead.

A P.E.A.–Produzioni Europee Associate S.P.A. Production (Italy), directed by Federico

Fellini. With Donald Sutherland, Tina Aumont, Cicely Browne, Olimpia Carlisi, Adele Angela Lojodice. Eastman Color. 166 mins.

FIDDLER ON THE ROOF (1971) ★★★

- ★ best cinematography Oswald Morris
- ★ best sound Gordon K. McCallum & David Hildyard
- ★ best scoring: adaptation & original song score John Williams

The Sheldon Harnick/Jerry Bock stage musical about traditional Jewish life in a small prerevolutionary village in the Ukraine. Topol stars as the honest milkman Tevye, determined to find good husbands for his five daughters.

A United Artists Picture, directed by Norman Jewison. With Topol, Norma Crane, Leonard Frey, Molly Picon, Paul Mann. Panavision 70/Technicolor. 180 mins.

A FISH CALLED WANDA (1988) ★

- ★ best supporting actor Kevin Kline

An Anglo-American gang of crooks pulls off a multi-million-dollar diamond heist in London, then finds that the consequences are not quite what they expected. Barrister John Cleese comes off best, starting a new life in South America with sexy con artist Jamie Lee Curtis; Oscar-winning Kevin Kline fares worst, as a manic and insanely jealous weapons man who is run over by a steamroller. Veteran filmmaker Charles Crichton, who 37 years earlier made the rather gentler *The Lavender Hill Mob*, was nominated as best director for the first time at the age of 78.

Michael Palin undergoes torture from crazy Kevin Kline (best supporting actor, 1988) in Charles Crichton's black comedy *A Fish Called Wanda* (MGM).

A Prominent Features Picture for MGM, directed by Charles Crichton. With John Cleese, Jamie Lee Curtis, Kevin Kline, Michael Palin, Maria Aitken, Tom Georgeson, Patricia Hayes, Geoffrey Palmer. Technicolor. 108 minutes.

THE FISHER KING (1991) ★

★ best supporting actress Mercedes Ruehl

A former New York talk-show host (Jeff Bridges) and a zany, schizoid former medievalist (Robin Williams) decide to seek spiritual redemption by searching for the Holy Grail in the Big Apple. Visually inventive Terry Gilliam fantasy enlivened by some elaborate production designs and a sizzling performance from Mercedes Ruehl as Bridges' girlfriend-cum-video store owner.

A TriStar release of a Hill/Obst production, directed by Terry Gilliam. With Robin Williams, Jeff Bridges, Amanda Plummer, Mercedes Ruehl, Michael Jeter, Adam Bryant, Paul Lombardi, David Pierce, Ted Ross, Lara Harris. Technicolor. 137 mins.

FLASHDANCE (1983) ★

★ best song "Flashdance . . . What a Feeling" (Giorgio Moroder, music; Keith Forsey & Irene Cara, lyrics)

An object lesson in how to become a member of the Pittsburgh ballet company—work as a girl welder by day and perform exciting, sexy dance routines in a bar at night. Jennifer Beals does both and achieves her aim. A sleeper movie of the 1980s with several erotic disco numbers, many of which were doubled for Beals by Marine Jahan. Besides the Oscar-winning song, another song—"Maniac," with music and lyrics by Michael Sembello and Dennis Matkosky—was also nominated.

A Polygram Picture for Paramount, directed by Adrian Lyne. With Jennifer Beals, Michael Nouri, Lilia Skala, Sunny Johnson, Kyle T. Heffner, Lee Ving, Ron Karabarsos. Color by Movielab. 98mins.

Jeff Goldblum about to become *The Fly* (20th Century-Fox), David Cronenberg's horror chiller of 1986. The film received an Academy Award for its makeup.

THE FLY (1986) ★

★ best makeup Chris Walas & Stephan Dupuis

A scientist's experiment goes horribly wrong and he gradually turns into an enormous housefly, much to the distress of his faithful girlfriend when she gives him a big hug and knocks one of his ears off. A film with a high disgust quotient, although the makeup work is extraordinary. A long way from the original, made by Kurt Neumann in 1958 and starring Al Hedison and Vincent Price.

A Brooksfilms Picture for 20th Century-Fox, directed By David Cronenberg. With Jeff Goldblum, Geena Davis, John Getz, Joy Boushel, Les Carlson, George Chuvalo, Michael Copeman. DeLuxe Color. 96 mins.

FOLIES BERGERE (1935) ★

★ best dance direction Dave Gould for the "Straw Hat" number

Lavish musical with a double-identity plot, with Folies Bergere entertainer Maurice Chevalier impersonating a look-alike baron who finds his fortune suddenly in jeopardy. Dance director Gould was also named that year for his work on *The Broadway Melody of 1936*.

A 20th Century Picture, directed by Roy Del Ruth. With Maurice Chevalier, Merle Oberon,

Shyster lawyer Walter Matthau and "patient" Jack Lemmon in Billy Wilder's 1966 comedy *The Fortune Cookie* (United Artists). Matthau was named best supporting actor of the year for his performance.

Ann Sothern, Walter Byron, Lumsden Hare, Robert Grief, Eric Blore. 83 mins.

THE FORTUNE COOKIE (1966)   ★

(U.K. title: *Meet Whiplash Willie*)

★ best supporting actor Walter Matthau

TV cameraman Jack Lemmon, slightly injured when filming a football game, takes to his bed on the advice of his brother-in-law, shyster lawyer Walter Matthau, so they can cook up a million-dollar accident insurance claim against all concerned. A prime example of a major acting performance being slotted into the supporting category so that the performer would stand a better chance of winning an Oscar.

A United Artists Picture, directed by Billy Wilder. With Jack Lemmon, Walter Matthau,

Ron Rich, Cliff Osmond, Judi West, Lurene Tuttle. Panavision. 126 mins.

FOR WHOM THE BELL TOLLS (1943)   ★

★ best supporting actress Katina Paxinou

Hemingway's 1940 novel of the Spanish Civil War, with Gary Cooper (as an American schoolteacher) and Ingrid Bergman (as a tortured orphan girl) fighting for the Loyalists and trying to blow up a strategic bridge in a heavily guarded mountain pass. Katina Paxinou's Oscar-winning performance was for her fiery peasant leader, Pilar.

A Paramount Picture, directed by Sam Wood. With Gary Cooper, Ingrid Bergman, Akim Tamiroff, Arturo de Cordova, Vladimir Sokoloff, Katina Paxinou, Joseph Calleia. Technicolor. 170 mins.

A FREE SOUL (1930/31)   ★

★ best actor Lionel Barrymore

Modern gal Norma Shearer, brought up by her drunken lawyer father (Lionel Barrymore) to do exactly what she wants, finds that what she *does* want is a sordid love affair with Clark Gable, whom she discovers, too late, to be nothing more that a brutal underworld leader.

An MGM Picture, directed by Clarence Brown. With Norma Shearer, Lionel Barrymore, Clark Gable, Leslie Howard, James Gleason, Lucy Beaumont. 91 mins.

THE FRENCH CONNECTION (1971)   ★★★★★

★ best film Philip D'Antoni (producer)
★ best direction William Friedkin
★ best actor Gene Hackman
★ best screenplay Ernest Tidyman
★ best editing Jerry Greenberg

Gene Hackman, best actor of 1971 for his hard-nosed detective "Popeye" Doyle, in *The French Connection* (20th Century-Fox).

Based-on-fact thriller about two New York Narcotics Squad detectives (Gene Hackman and Roy Scheider) who play a long-shot hunch hoping to smash a $32 million dope smuggling ring. Highlight: A reckless car chase in which Hackman drives madly beneath an elevated subway line after a speeding train.

A 20th Century-Fox Picture, directed by William Friedkin. With Gene Hackman, Fernando Rey, Roy Scheider, Tony LoBianco, Marcel Bozzuffi, Frederic de Pasquale. DeLuxe Color. 104 mins.

FRENCHMAN'S CREEK (1945)   ★

★ best color art direction Hans Dreier & Ernst Fegte
                interior decoration Sam Comer

Lavish Daphne du Maurier romance about a young aristocratic Englishwoman (Joan Fontaine) who, when domiciled at her Cornish estate, finds herself involved with a handsome French pirate (Arturo de Cordova), who is plundering the Cornish coast. Set in the 17th century and among the most beautiful American color films of the 1940s.

A Paramount Picture, directed by Mitchell Leisen. With Joan Fontaine, Arturo de Cordova, Basil Rathbone, Nigel Bruce, Cecil Kellaway, Ralph Forbes. Technicolor. 113 mins.

FROM HERE TO ETERNITY (1953)   ★★★★★★★★

★ best film Buddy Adler (producer)
★ best direction Fred Zinnemann
★ best supporting actor Frank Sinatra
★ best supporting actress Donna Reed
★ best screenplay Daniel Taradash
★ best b/w cinematography Burnett Guffey
★ best sound recording John P. Livadary
★ best editing William Lyon

The novel they said "couldn't be filmed"—the sex lives and personal problems of the men of an American Army infantry outfit in Hawaii just prior to Pearl Harbor. The Oscar winners were in the supporting roles: Frank Sinatra as a cocky little G.I. and Donna Reed as a professional hostess "two steps up from the pavement." In the leads: Burt Lancaster as a tough company sergeant; Deborah Kerr as an unhappy army wife; and Montgomery Clift as the G.I. who refuses to box for the company's team because he once blinded a man in the ring. With its eight Oscars, the highest Academy Award winner since *Gone With the Wind* 14 years earlier.

A Columbia Picture, directed by Fred Zinnemann. With Burt Lancaster, Montgomery Clift, Deborah Kerr, Frank Sinatra, Donna Reed, Philip Ober, Mickey Shaughnessy, Ernest Borgnine. 118 mins.

FUNNY GIRL (1968)   ★

★ best actress Barbra Streisand

The story of musical comedy star Fanny Brice (Barbra Streisand), the determined little girl from New York's Lower East Side who makes it to stardom on Broadway but suffers in her private life and in her marriage to gambler Nick Arnstein (Omar Sharif). Streisand's film debut and an Oscar winner first time out. The number "Don't Rain on My Parade" is the film's musical tour-de-force. Streisand's best actress award was shared with Katharine Hepburn for *The Lion in Winter*, the only best-actress tie in Oscar history.

A Columbia Picture, directed by William Wyler. With Barbra Streisand, Omar Sharif, Kay Medford, Anne Francis, Walter Pidgeon, Lee Allen. Panavision 70/Technicolor. 147 mins.

A FUNNY THING HAPPENED ON THE WAY TO THE FORUM (1966) ★

★ best music: adaptation or treatment Ken Thorne

Send-up of slave life in first-century Rome, with moon-faced Zero Mostel as a slave bent on gaining his freedom, Phil Silvers as a fast-talking brothel owner, and a bevy of nubile, busty girls.

A United Artists Picture, directed by Richard Lester. With Zero Mostel, Phil Silvers, Jack Gilford, Buster Keaton, Michael Crawford, Annette Andre, Patricia Jessel, Michael Hordern. DeLuxe Color. 98 mins.

G

GANDHI
(1982) ★★★★★★★★

★ best film Richard Attenborough (producer)
★ best direction Richard Attenborough
★ best actor Ben Kingsley
★ best original screenplay John Briley
★ best cinematography Billy Williams & Ronnie Taylor

★ best art direction Stuart Craig & Bob Laing set decoration Michael Seirton
★ best costume design John Mollo & Ehanu Athaiya
★ best editing John Bloom

The film Richard Attenborough toiled over for more than 20 years—a sweeping account of the life and times of Mahatma Gandhi (Ben Kingsley), who struggled against imperialism all his life and eventually, after years of organizing peaceful resistance, ended British rule in India. Nominated for 11 Academy Awards, the film became the fifth British picture to be named the best of the year; with its eight awards it also became Britain's biggest-ever Oscar suc-

Richard Attenborough and Ben Kingsley surrounded by the Oscars won by the 1982 epic *Gandhi* (Columbia).

cess. Previous British winners: *Hamlet* (1948), *Tom Jones* (1963), *Oliver* (1968) and *Chariots of Fire* (1981).

An Indo-British Films Picture (distributed by Columbia), directed by Richard Attenborough. With Ben Kingsley, Candice Bergen, Edward Fox, John Gielgud, Trevor Howard, John Mills, Martin Sheen, Ian Charleson, Athol Fugard, Gunter Maria Halmer, Geraldine James, Saeed Jaffrey. Panavision/70mm/Technicolor. 188 mins.

THE GARDEN OF THE FINZI CONTINIS (1971) ★

★ best foreign language film Italy/West Germany

Vittorio de Sica's major work of his later period—the story of an unrequited love affair, set in the Mussolini-dominated Italy of 1938 and against the background of the country's decaying aristocratic Jewry.

A Documento Film, directed by Vittorio de Sica. With Dominique Sanda, Lino Capolicchio, Helmut Berger, Romolo Valli, Fabio Testi. Eastman Color. 95 mins.

GASLIGHT (1944) ★★

★ best actress Ingrid Bergman
★ best b/w art direction Cedric Gibbons & William Ferrari
          interior decoration Edwin B. Willis & Paul Huldschinsky

Handsome Charles Boyer, cast against type as a ruthless murderer, marries his victim's niece (Ingrid Bergman) and then tries to gain her inheritance by driving her slowly insane. Set mainly within the confines of an old Victorian house and based on the psychological stage melodrama by Patrick Hamilton. Joseph Cotten co-stars as a Scotland Yard man.

An MGM Picture, directed by George Cukor. With Charles Boyer, Ingrid Bergman, Joseph Cotten, Angela Lansbury, Dame May Whitty. 114 mins.

GATE OF HELL (1954)

★ best color costume design Sanzo Wada

Exotic tragedy, set in 12th-century Japan, about a married Japanese woman who finds herself loved not only by her husband but passionately and illicitly by a conquering Japanese warrior. The film earned a special award as the best foreign language picture of the year and was the first Japanese production to make use of a Western color process.

A Daiei Picture, directed by Teinosuke Kinugasa. With Kazuo Hasegawa, Machiko Kyo, Isao Yamagata, Yataro Kurokawa, Kotaro Bando. Eastman Color. 90 mins.

THE GAY DIVORCEE (1934) ★

★ best song "The Continental" (Con Conrad, music; Herb Magidson, lyrics)

The first musical in which Astaire and Rogers had the leading roles. Also the forerunner of things to come, with the usual mistaken identity plot (dancer Fred is suspected by Ginger of being the hired corespondent in her divorce suit) and the usual magnificent numbers— "Looking for a Needle in a Haystack," "Night and Day" and the climactic Oscar-winning routine, "The Continental," the first song to win an Academy Award.

An RKO Picture, directed by Mark Sandrich. With Fred Astaire, Ginger Rogers, Alice Brady, Edward Everett Horton, Erik Rhodes, Eric Blore. 107 mins.

GENTLEMAN'S AGREEMENT (1947) ★★★

★ best film Darryl F. Zanuck (producer)
★ best direction Elia Kazan
★ best supporting actress Celeste Holm

Journalist Gregory Peck, asked to write a series of magazine articles on anti-Semitism, passes himself off as a Jew for six weeks and finds his eyes opened by the many hidden prejudices around him. One of the first of Hollywood's

Gentleman's Agreement (20th Century-Fox), Elia Kazan's indictment of anti-Semitism in postwar America and winner of the best-picture Oscar for 1947. Pictured from left to right: Gregory Peck, Dorothy McGuire, Celeste Holm and John Garfield.

social-message pictures of the postwar period and released in the same year as *Crossfire*, which dealt with the same subject and was also nominated for best picture, but *Gentlemen's Agreement* ended up with the award.

A 20th Century-Fox Picture, directed by Elia Kazan. With Gregory Peck, Dorothy McGuire, John Garfield, Celeste Holm, Anne Revere, June Havoc, Albert Dekker, Jane Wyatt. 118 mins.

GET OUT YOUR HANDKERCHIEFS (1978)   ★

★ best foreign language film France/Belgium

Bertrand Blier comedy about the experiences of a bored and frustrated young Frenchwoman, first with a potential lover provided by her bewildered boyfriend and then with a 13-year-old innocent who finally turns her on. An affectionately made comedy of situation; the fourth French film to win the foreign language Oscar during the 1970s. The others: *The Discreet Charm of the Bourgeoisie* (1972), *Day for Night* (1973), and *Madame Rosa* (1977).

Les Films Ariane/CAPAC (Paris)/Belga Films/ SODEP (Brussels). Directed by Bertrand Blier. With Gerard Depardieu, Patrick Dewaere, Carole Laure, Riton, Michel Serrault. Eastman Color. 109 mins.

GHOST (1990)

★ best supporting actress Whoopi Goldberg
★ best original screenplay Bruce Joel Rubin

Young Manhattan banker Patrick Swayze is accidentally rubbed out by a mugger but remains on earth in a ghostly state to enlist the help of a medium to warn his former romantic partner (Demi Moore) that she too is in danger. A fantasy-thriller-romance all rolled into one and the surprise blockbuster hit of 1990. Whoopi Goldberg, as storefront psychic Oda Mae Brown, became the first black actress to win an Academy Award since Hattie McDaniel for *Gone With the Wind* some fifty years earlier.

A Paramount Picture, directed by Jerry Zucker. With Patrick Swayze, Demi Moore, Tony Goldwyn, Whoopi Goldberg, Stanley Lawrence, Christopher J. Keene, Susan Breslau, Martina Degnan. Technicolor. 127 mins.

GIANT (1956)

★ best direction George Stevens

George Stevens' massive chronicle of a Texas land-rich family, spanning several generations and showing how huge empires were built by beef and oil. Based on the novel by Edna Ferber, it proved to be James Dean's last film before his death in a car crash. Both Dean (as a ranch hand who becomes an oil millionaire) and Rock Hudson (as a stubborn, old-style Texas rancher) received acting nominations.

A Warner Bros. Picture, directed by George Stevens. With Elizabeth Taylor, Rock Hudson, James Dean, Jane Withers, Chill Wills, Mercedes McCambridge, Carroll Baker, Dennis Hopper. Warner Color. 198 mins.

GIGI (1958) ★★★★★★★★

★ best film Arthur Freed (producer)
★ best direction Vincente Minnelli
★ best screenplay Alan Jay Lerner
★ best color cinematography Joseph Ruttenberg
★ best color art direction William A. Horning & Preston Ames

James Dean's last role, as Jet Rink, the ranch hand turned oil millionaire in George Stevens' version of Edna Ferber's Texas epic *Giant* (Warner Bros., 1956).

set decoration Henry Grace & Keogh Gleason
★ best color costume design Cecil Beaton
★ best editing Adrienne Fazan
★ best scoring of a musical picture Andre Previn
★ best song "Gigi" (Frederick Loewe, music; Alan Jay Lerner, lyrics)

Colette's turn-of-the-century Parisian fairy tale about an innocent schoolgirl (Leslie Caron) who is carefully trained by her grandmother (Hermione Gingold) and aunt (Isabel Jeans) for the role of grand *cocotte*. An elegant musical that won awards in just about every category except acting and, at the time of its release, proved to be the biggest Oscar winner since the Academy was first formed 30 years earlier. The record lasted only 12 months. A year later, *Ben Hur* swept the board with 11 wins and has been the Oscar record holder ever since.

An MGM Picture, directed by Vincente Minnelli. With Leslie Caron, Maurice Chevalier, Louis Jourdan, Hermione Gingold, Eva Gabor, Jacques Bergerac, Isabel Jeans. CinemaScope/Metrocolor. 116 mins.

THE GLENN MILLER STORY (1954)   ★

★ best sound recording Leslie I. Carey

Biographical movie of 1940s bandleader Glenn Miller, an American trombonist who wanted to make music *his* way and who brought a new kind of sound to popular band music. A brilliant Harlem jam session featuring Louis Armstrong, Gene Krupa and other jazz stars is the film's highlight.

A Universal-International Picture, directed by Anthony Mann. With James Stewart, June Allyson, Henry Morgan, Charles Drake, George Tobias. Technicolor. 116 mins.

GLORY (1989)   ★★★

★ best supporting actor Denzel Washington
★ best cinematography Freddie Francis

★ best sound Donald O'Mitchell, Gregg C. Rudloff, Elliot Tyson & Russell Williams II

The story of the men of the 54th Massachusetts Regiment (the first black regiment to fight for the Union in the Civil War) and how an inexperienced white colonel was chosen to train and lead them. Denzel Washington's portrayal of a rebellious former slave who joins the thousand-strong outfit earned him the year's supporting actor award; cameraman Freddie Francis won his second Oscar some 29 years after winning his first for his work on *Sons and Lovers*. Washington's Oscar was only the second awarded to a black actor in a supporting role and followed the one presented to Louis Gossett, Jr. in *An Officer and a Gentleman* seven years earlier.

A Tri-Star Picture (distributed by Columbia Tri-Star), directed by Edward Zwick. With Matthew Broderick, Denzel Washington, Cary Elwes, Morgan Freeman, Jihmi Kennedy, Andre Braugher, John Finn, Donovan Leitch, Jane Alexander. Technicolor. 133 mins.

THE GODFATHER (1972)   ★★★

★ best film Albert S. Ruddy (producer)
★ best actor Marlon Brando
★ best screenplay Mario Puzo & Francis Ford Coppola

The gangster film of the contemporary cinema, a massive saga of honor, loyalty and brutal murder as the Corleone family of New York fights to keep its ascendancy over rival Mafia-type families trying to muscle in and take over. Marlon Brando won (and refused) his second Oscar for his Mafia chief Don Vito Corleone; Al Pacino (as the son who eventually succeeds to his throne), James Caan and Robert Duvall all earned supporting actor nominations. Along with its sequel, the only out-and-out gangster film ever to win the best-picture award.

A Paramount Picture, directed by Francis Ford Coppola. With Marlon Brando, Al Pacino, James Caan, Richard Castellano, Robert Duvall, Sterling Hayden, John Marley, Richard

A Don Corleone henchman is garrotted in Francis Ford Coppola's Mafia movie *The Godfather* (Paramount, 1972). The film won for best picture, best actor (Brando) and best screenplay.

Conte, Diane Keaton, Al Lettieri, Talia Shire, John Cazale. Technicolor. 175 mins.

THE GODFATHER PART II (1974)   ★★★★★★

- ★ best film Francis Ford Coppola (producer)
- ★ best direction Francis Ford Coppola
- ★ best supporting actor Robert De Niro
- ★ best screenplay adaptation Francis Ford Coppola & Mario Puzo
- ★ best art direction Dean Tavoularis & Angelo Graham
      set decoration George R. Nelson
- ★ best original dramatic score Nino Rota & Carmine Coppola

The continuing family saga, with a prelude showing how Brando's Don Vito character (played as a young man by Robert De Niro) arrived in the States from Sicily and attained his position of power, and also a sequel to Part I with Al Pacino carrying on his bloodthirsty reign. *The Godfather, Part II* marks the only occasion that a sequel has won the best-movie award. As in the first film, three of the year's supporting actor nominees came from the cast—De Niro, Michael V. Gazzo and Lee Strasberg.

A Paramount Picture, directed by Francis Ford Coppola. With Al Pacino, Robert Duvall, Diane Keaton, Robert De Niro, John Cazale, Talia Shire, Lee Strasberg, Michael V. Gazzo. Technicolor. 200 mins.

GOING MY WAY (1944)   ★★★★★★★

- ★ best film Leo McCarey (producer)
- ★ best direction Leo McCarey
- ★ best actor Bing Crosby
- ★ best supporting actor Barry Fitzgerald
- ★ best screenplay Frank Butler & Frank Cavett
- ★ best original story Leo McCarey
- ★ best song "Swinging on a Star" (James Van Heusen, music; Johnny Burke, lyrics)

Singing priest Bing Crosby turns a group of young Manhattan delinquents into a choir and tours the country with them to raise funds for the old mortgage-ridden church of St. Dominic's. Sentimental comedy made saltier by Barry Fitzgerald, who, as a vain, stubborn little priest of a poor parish, brings out all the pathos of old age. The New York Film Critics' Circle voted Fitzgerald best actor of the year. The Academy named Crosby best actor and Fitzgerald for the supporting award.

A Paramount Picture, directed by Leo McCarey. With Bing Crosby, Rise Stevens, Barry Fitzgerald, James Brown, Jean Heather, Eily Malyon. 130 mins.

GOLD DIGGERS OF 1935 (1935)   ★

- ★ best song "Lullaby of Broadway" (Harry Warren, music; Al Dubin, lyrics)

The movie that elevated dance director Busby Berkeley to full directorial status—a slight story of Dick Powell and Gloria Stuart finding romance in a swank New England summer hotel. The picture is memorable for its climactic number "Lullaby of Broadway," which is almost a film within a film, telling of the tragedy of life

Bing Crosby, Frank McHugh and Barry Fitzgerald in Leo McCarey's *Going My Way* (Paramount, 1944); with its seven Oscars, it was the most successful Academy Award film in the studio's history.

in a big city and breathtakingly performed by an army of Warner tap dancers.

A Warner Bros. Picture, directed by Busby Berkeley. With Dick Powell, Adolphe Menjou, Gloria Stuart, Alice Brady, Glenda Farrell, Frank McHugh. 95 mins.

GOLDFINGER (1964) ★

★ best sound effects Norman Wanstall

The third of the Bond sagas, with never a let-up as Bond drives his Aston Martin special, out-judoes Honor Blackman, escapes being cut in two by a laser, and fights Oddjob to the death in Fort Knox with a ticking atom bomb attached to his wrist. Gert Frobe co-stars as the title character and Harold Sakata is his lethal henchman, the hat-throwing Korean, Oddjob.

A United Artists Picture, directed by Guy Hamilton. With Sean Connery, Gert Frobe, Honor Blackman, Shirley Eaton, Tania Mallett, Harold Sakata, Bernard Lee. Technicolor. 108 mins.

GONE WITH THE WIND (1939) ★★★★★★★★

★ best film David O. Selznick (producer)
★ best direction Victor Fleming
★ best actress Vivien Leigh
★ best supporting actress Hattie McDaniel
★ best screenplay Sidney Howard

★ best color cinematography Ernest Haller & Ray Rennahan
★ best art direction Lyle Wheeler
★ best editing Hal C. Kern & James E. Newcom
★ Special award to William Cameron Menzies for outstanding achievement in the use of color for the enhancement of dramatic mood in *Gone With the Wind*.

The loves of tempestuous Southern belle Scarlett O'Hara during and after the Civil War. At the time of the 1939 Oscar awards the most honored film in the history of the Academy; its nine Oscars (including the first award for color photography and the first to a black performer, Hattie McDaniel) easily outstripped the five held by the previous record-holder, *It Happened One Night* (1934). Vivien Leigh as Scarlett also became the first British actress to be honored in the best-actress category. Two of those who surprisingly missed out were Clark Gable, whose Rhett Butler was defeated by Robert Donat's schoolteacher in *Goodbye, Mr. Chips*, and composer Max Steiner, whose memorable music score lost out to Herbert Stothart's music for *The Wizard of Oz*.

A Selznick International Picture (released through MGM), directed by Victor Fleming. With Vivien Leigh, Clark Gable, Leslie Howard, Olivia de Havilland, Hattie McDaniel, Thomas Mitchell. Technicolor. 219 mins.

Gable and Leigh as Rhett and Scarlett in the biggest Oscar-winner of the 1930s—*Gone With the Wind* (Selznick International/MGM, 1939).

Oscar winner Richard Dreyfuss with co-star Marsha Mason in the 1977 screen version of Neil Simon's comedy *The Goodbye Girl* (MGM/Warner Bros.).

THE GOODBYE GIRL (1977)   ★

★ best actor Richard Dreyfuss

Neil Simon comedy about a former dancer, Marsha Mason, who is forced to share her Manhattan apartment when she finds that her ex-lover has sublet their tenement home to aspiring young actor Richard Dreyfuss. Miss Mason's precocious 10-year-old daughter (Quinn Cummings) provides adolescent problems; Mr. Dreyfuss supplies initial hostility and eventual romance.

An MGM/Warner Bros. Picture, directed by Herbert Ross. With Richard Dreyfuss, Marsha Mason, Quinn Cummings, Paul Benedict, Barbara Rhoades, Theresa Merritt, Michael Shawn. Metrocolor. 110 mins.

GOODBYE, MR. CHIPS (1939)   ★

★ best actor Robert Donat

James Hilton's story of a schoolmaster (Robert Donat) whose strict adherence to the rules makes him an unpopular and lonely figure with the boys but whose marriage to a young actress (Greer Garson) transforms him into a warm, understanding person. Donat aged from 25 to 83 for his Oscar-winning performance—which incidentally robbed Clark Gable of what seemed like a certain Oscar for Rhett Butler the same year.

An MGM Picture, directed by Sam Wood. With Robert Donat, Greer Garson, Terry Kilburn, John Mills, Paul Von Henreid, Judith Furse, Lyn Harding. 114 mins.

THE GOOD EARTH (1937) ★★

★ best actress Luise Rainer
★ best cinematography Karl Freund

Pearl Buck's moving story about Chinese farming peasants (Paul Muni and Luise Rainer) fighting for survival in prerevolutionary China. Karl Freund's superb photography of the exterior production effects—storm, famine and a locust plague—earned him the only Oscar of his distinguished career. Rainer's acting award made her the first performer, male or female, to win two Academy Awards. She had won the previous year for her portrayal of Anna Held in *The Great Ziegfeld*.

An MGM Picture, directed by Sidney Franklin. With Paul Muni, Luise Rainer, Walter Connolly, Tillie Losch, Jessie Ralph, Charley Grapewin. 138 mins.

GOODFELLAS (1990) ★

★ best supporting actor Joe Pesci

Mafia gangster film about real-life hoodlum Henry Hill, who grew up in an Italian-American neighborhood in Brooklyn and who succeeded in achieving his boyhood dream—becoming a key member of the mob. A searing, bleak portrait of the Mafia at street level, with a frightening performance from Oscar winner Pesci as a psychotic Mafioso who gets his kicks from humiliating people and then killing them. Set in the mid-1950s and based on the book *Wise Guy* by Nicholas Pileggi.

A Warner Bros. Picture, directed by Martin Scorsese. With Robert De Niro, Ray Liotta, Joe Pesci, Lorraine Bracco, Paul Sorvino, Frank Sivero, Tony Darrow, Mike Starr, Frank Vincent. Technicolor. 145 mins.

THE GRADUATE (1967) ★

★ best direction Mike Nichols

Satirical 1960s comedy about a young college graduate (Dustin Hoffman) who returns home a hero to his middle-class parents and finds himself protesting against the values their world represents. In trying to find his own values he ends up having simultaneous affairs with a neighbor's neurotic wife (Anne Bancroft) and her daughter (Katharine Ross).

An Embassy Picture, directed by Mike Nichols. With Anne Bancroft, Dustin Hoffman, Katharine Ross, William Daniels, Murray Hamilton, Elizabeth Wilson. Panavision/Technicolor. 108 mins.

GRAND HOTEL (1931/32) ★

★ best picture Paul Bern (producer)

The first of MGM's glossy, all-star vehicles and the only one to win a best-picture Oscar. Based on Vicki Baum's successful novel and play, the film looks at life in a large luxury Berlin hotel and includes just about every major star on the MGM lot—among them Garbo as a mercurial ballerina, John Barrymore as an impoverished baron, Wallace Beery as a Prussian business tycoon, Joan Crawford as an ambitious hotel stenographer and Lionel Barrymore as a dying clerk out on a final spending spree.

An MGM Picture, directed by Edmund Goulding. With Greta Garbo, John Barrymore, Joan Crawford, Wallace Beery, Lionel Barrymore, Lewis Stone, Jean Hersholt. 112 mins.

GRAND PRIX (1966) ★★★

★ best editing Frederic Steinkamp, Henry Berman, Stewart Linder & Frank Santillo
★ best sound Franklin E. Milton
★ best sound effects Gordon Daniel

Formula One motor racing looked at in depth by John Frankenheimer in this story of four drivers—Garner, Montand, Bedford and Sabato—all out for the title of motor racing champion in a typical Grand Prix season. Superb special effects—use of split screen and multiple images, zooms into cars, helicopter shots, smashups, etc.

An MGM Picture, directed by John Frankenheimer. With James Garner, Eva Marie Saint, Yves Montand, Toshiro Mifune, Brian Bedford, Jessica Walter, Antonio Sabato. Cinerama & Super Panavision/Metrocolor. 179 mins.

THE GRAPES OF WRATH (1940) ★★

★ best direction John Ford
★ best supporting actress Jane Darwell

John Steinbeck's odyssey of the Joads, a family of Okies who are driven from their homestead in the Oklahoma dust bowl in the Depression and journey westward in a battered old Ford to the promised land of California. Henry Fonda (in his only Oscar-nominated role until he eventually won the award for *On Golden Pond* (1981) is featured as the restless son Tom Joad; Jane Darwell, in a heartbreaking performance, is his never-say-die Ma.

A 20th Century-Fox Picture, directed by John Ford. With Henry Fonda, Jane Darwell, John Carradine, Charles Grapewin, Dorris Bowden, Russell Simpson. 127 mins.

THE GREAT CARUSO (1951) ★

★ best sound recording Douglas Shearer

MGM's Technicolor rags-to-riches musical of lowly-born Neapolitan boy Enrico Caruso (Mario Lanza), who rises from street singer to world-famous tenor. The film made Lanza a star of the first magnitude, earned Metro a small fortune and, with its 27 songs and operatic excerpts, thoroughly deserved its sound award.

An MGM Picture, directed by Richard Thorpe. With Mario Lanza, Ann Blyth, Dorothy Kirsten, Jarmila Novotna, Richard Hageman, Carl Benton Reid, Eduard Franz. Technicolor. 109 mins.

The film that made Mario Lanza a star: MGM's *The Great Caruso*, an Oscar winner for the studio in 1951. Pictured here with Lanza: Dorothy Kirsten.

THE GREATEST SHOW ON EARTH (1952) ★★

★ best film Cecil B. DeMille (producer)
★ best motion picture story Frederic M. Frank. Theodore St. John & Frank Cavett

The only DeMille film to win the best picture award, and the only time the famous producer-director was honored with a creative Oscar, although in this case it was in the former capacity as producer of the best film. Mixed in with the Ringling Bros. & Barnum and Bailey Circus story is a romantic triangle—Heston, Hutton and Wilde—a clown (James Stewart) wanted for murder, and a real humdinger of a train wreck that lets loose all the animals on the circus train.

A Paramount Picture, directed by Cecil B. DeMille. With James Stewart, Betty Hutton, Cornel Wilde, Charlton Heston, Gloria Grahame, Dorothy Lamour, Emmett Kelly. Technicolor. 153 mins.

GREAT EXPECTATIONS (1947)   ★ ★

★ best b/w cinematography Guy Green
★ best b/w art direction John Bryan
           set decoration Wilfred Shingleton

Charles Dickens' novel about a young country blacksmith (John Mills) who becomes a gentleman in London society through the generosity of an unknown benefactor. Important in the history of the Awards in that together with *Black Narcissus* it marked the first time British films scooped all four Oscars in the photography and art direction categories.

A Cineguild-Rank Picture, directed by David Lean. With John Mills, Valerie Hobson, Bernard Miles, Francis L. Sullivan, Finlay Currie, Martita Hunt, Anthony Wager, Jean Simmons, Alec Guinness. 115 mins.

THE GREAT GATSBY (1974)   ★ ★

★ best costume design Theoni V. Aldredge
★ best original song score or scoring adaptation Nelson Riddle

The third film version of Scott Fitzgerald's classic 1920s novel of a mysterious racketeer, Jay Gatsby (Robert Redford), who buys a fabulous Long Island estate to be near the woman he loved and lost. Robert Redford stars as the poor little rich boy, Mia Farrow as his spoiled aristocratic ex-lover.

A Paramount Picture, directed by Jack Clayton. With Robert Redford, Mia Farrow, Bruce Dern, Karen Black, Scott Wilson, Sam Waterston, Lois Chiles. Eastman Color. 140 mins.

THE GREAT LIE (1941)   ★

★ best supporting actress Mary Astor

Unrestrained soap opera, Warners 1940s style, with Bette Davis in a maternal role for a change, raising George Brent's child—by fiery Mary Astor—as her own. For once Davis didn't have the acting awards sewn up and it was Astor, as Brent's spoiled first wife, who took the Oscar, albeit a supporting one.

A Warner Bros. Picture, directed by Edmund Goulding. With Bette Davis, George Brent, Mary Astor, Lucile Watson, Hattie McDaniel, Grant Mitchell, Jerome Cowan. 102 mins.

THE GREAT McGINTY (1940)   ★

★ best original screenplay Preston Sturges

Brian Donlevy, down-and-out and on the skids, gains the favor of crooked political boss Akim Tamiroff by voting 37 times in one day for the same candidate, thus taking the first steps towards the governor's mansion. Only when he attempts to go straight do things start to go wrong. Preston Sturges' first film as a writer-director and the only occasion on which he earned an Academy Award. He was subsequently nominated for his screenplays for *Hail the Conquering Hero* and *The Miracle of Morgan's Creek* (both 1944) but was never named for his direction.

A Paramount Picture, directed by Preston Sturges. With Brian Donlevy, Muriel Angelus, Akim Tamiroff, Allyn Joslyn, William Demarest, Louis Jean Heydt. 81 mins.

THE GREAT RACE (1965)   ★

★ best sound effects Tregoweth Brown

Slapstick, comic-strip kind of movie about an international car race from New York to Paris in the early 1900s. The three whose paths crisscross during the massive race are Tony Curtis as the handsome, daredevil hero; Natalie Wood as the heroine in distress; and Jack Lemmon as the sneering villain in malevolent black.

A Warner Bros. Picture, directed by Blake Edwards. With Tony Curtis, Jack Lemmon, Natalie Wood, Peter Falk, Keenan Wynn, Arthur O'Connell, Vivian Vance, Panavision/Technicolor. 150 mins.

THE GREAT WALTZ (1938)   ★

★ best cinematography Joseph Ruttenberg

Lavish MGM biography of Austrian composer Johann Strauss, with Parisian Fernand Gravet as the Waltz King. Joseph Ruttenberg's swirling cameras earned him the first of his four Oscars for cinematography, a record he shares with Leon Shamroy.

An MGM Picture, directed by Julien Duvivier. With Luise Rainer, Fernand Gravet, Miliza Korjus, Hugh Herbert, Lionel Atwill, Minna Gombell, Herman Bing, Sig Ruman, Henry Hull. 102 min.

THE GREAT ZIEGFELD (1936)   ★★★

★ best film Hunt Stromberg (producer)
★ best actress Luise Rainer
★ best dance direction Seymour Felix for the "A Pretty Girl Is Like a Melody" number

The story of American showman Florenz Ziegfeld (William Powell), charting his rise to fame and boasting some of the most lavish musical numbers ever put on the screen. The Oscar-winning "A Pretty Girl Is Like a Melody" sequence is set on a massive revolving set-piece shaped like a gigantic wedding cake and carrying hundreds of men, girls, costumes and props. Luise Rainer won her Oscar for her portrayal of Ziegfeld's first wife, Anna Held; Myrna Loy appeared as wife no. 2, Billie Burke.

An MGM Picture, directed by Robert Z. Leonard. With William Powell, Myrna Loy, Luise Rainer, Frank Morgan, Fanny Brice, Ray Bolger, Virginia Bruce, Nat Pendleton, Reginald Owen. 184 mins.

GREEN DOLPHIN STREET (1947)   ★

★ best special effects A. Arnold Gillespie & Warren Newcombe: visual Douglas Shearer & Michael Steinore: audible

Soap opera from the novel by Elizabeth Goudge, with two sisters (Lana Turner and Donna Reed) after the same man (Richard Hart) in 19th-century New Zealand. Native uprisings, earthquakes and tidal waves interfere with their plans.

An MGM Picture, directed by Victor Saville. With Lana Turner, Van Heflin, Donna Reed, Richard Hart, Frank Morgan, Edmund Gwenn, Dame May Whitty, Reginald Owen. 141 min.

GUESS WHO'S COMING TO DINNER (1967)   ★★

★ best actress Katharine Hepburn
★ best story & screenplay William Rose

Spencer Tracy as a liberal American father and Kate Hepburn as his equally progressive wife are brought face to face with their ideals as their one and only daughter brings home black Sidney Poitier and announces her intention to marry him. The ninth and last of the movies that Tracy and Hepburn made together, Tracy dying just a few days after shooting had ended.

A Columbia Picture, directed by Stanley Kramer. With Spencer Tracy, Katharine Hepburn, Sidney Poitier, Katharine Houghton, Cecil Kellaway, Beah Richards, Roy E. Glenn, Sr. Technicolor. 112 mins.

Katharine Hepburn and Spencer Tracy relaxing on the set of *Guess Who's Coming to Dinner* (Columbia, 1967), the last film the pair made together, and the one for which Hepburn won the second of her four Academy Awards. Tracy died shortly after filming was completed.

THE GUNS OF NAVARONE (1961) ★

★ best special effects Bill Warrington: visual
Vivian C. Greenham: audible

Alistair MacLean World War II adventure about a tough team of Allied saboteurs—Peck, Niven, Quinn, et al.—who make a daring raid on a Greek island, break into the fortress of Navarone and blow up the giant German guns hidden in a cave of solid rock.

A Columbia Picture, directed by J. Lee Thompson. With Gregory Peck, David Niven, Anthony Quayle, Anthony Quinn, Stanley Baker, Irene Papas, Gia Scala, James Darren, James Robertson Justice. CinemaScope/Eastman Color. 159 mins.

H

HAMLET (1948)   ★★★★

- ★ best film Laurence Olivier (producer)
- ★ best actor Laurence Olivier
- ★ best b/w art direction Roger K. Furse
        set decoration Carmen Dillon
- ★ best b/w costume design Roger K. Furse

Shakespeare's* great tragedy transformed and reduced (from 4½ hours to 2½) by Laurence Olivier, who both directed and starred as Hamlet, Prince of Denmark, who learns from a ghost that his father has been murdered and that his mother has married the murderer. The first wholly British film to be named best of the year. The black-and-white costume designs were also the first to be awarded an Oscar in that category; the first color costume design award went to Victor Fleming's epic *Joan of Arc*.

A Two Cities Picture, directed by Laurence Olivier. With Laurence Olivier, Eileen Herlie, Basil Sydney, Jean Simmons, Norman Wooland, Felix Aylmer. 155 mins.

HANNAH AND HER SISTERS (1986)   ★★★

- ★ best supporting actor Michael Caine
- ★ best supporting actress Dianne Wiest
- ★ best original screenplay Woody Allen

Apart from *Annie Hall* (1977), the only Woody Allen movie to be nominated for best picture—an affectionate family saga about three New

---

* *Note:* Four other films based on the works of Shakespeare have been nominated for best film: Warner Bros. *A Midsummer Night's Dream* (1935), MGM's *Romeo and Juliet* (1936), Olivier's *Henry V* (1946) and Zeffirelli's *Romeo and Juliet* (1968). None of them won.

Michael Caine, pictured with Mia Farrow, in his Oscar-winning performance (best supporting actor, 1986) in Woody Allen's *Hannah and Her Sisters* (Orion).

York sisters and their romantic ups and downs over a period of three years, starting with one annual Thanksgiving get-together and ending with another. Mia Farrow, Barbara Hershey and Dianne Wiest play the sisters. Wiest was honored by the Academy for her portrayal of a self-destructive neurotic who spends most of her time jumping between careers and men. Michael Caine, after best-actor nominations for *Alfie* (1966), *Sleuth* (1972) and *Educating Rita* (1983), earned his award for playing a husband whose mid-life crisis includes having an affair with his wife's beautiful sister (Hershey). Woody's second award for best screenplay (*Annie Hall* being the first).

An Orion Picture, directed by Woody Allen. With Woody Allen, Michael Caine, Mia Farrow, Carrie Fisher, Barbara Hershey, Lloyd Nolan, Maureen O'Sullivan, Daniel Stern, Max von Sydow, Dianne Wiest, Sam Waterston. Technicolor; prints by DeLuxe. 107 mins.

HARRY AND THE HENDERSONS (1987)   ★

- ★ best makeup Rick Baker

A Seattle family—Mom, Dad and two kids—adopt a huge, hairy Bigfoot-type monster they come across during a camping trip to the mountains but find all kinds of problems when they take him home to his new urban environment. For his creature effects Rick Baker became the first makeup artist to win two Oscars, having won his first six years earlier, when the award was first established, for *An American Werewolf in London*.

An Amblin Entertainment for Universal, directed by William Dear. With John Lithgow, Melinda Dillon, Margaret Langrick, Joshua Rudoy, Kevin Peter Hall, David Suchet, Lainie Kazan, Don Ameche, M. Emmet Walsh. DeLuxe Color. 111 mins.

HARRY AND TONTO (1974) ★

★ best actor Art Carney

The experiences, funny and sad by turn, of elderly widower Art Carney who, after being evicted from his West Side Manhattan apartment, travels across America with his cat Tonto to start a new life in California. Carney's best-actor award proved to be one of the major surprises of the 1970s, with the 56-year-old actor coming out ahead of such strong contenders as Albert Finney in *Murder on the Orient Express*, Dustin Hoffman in *Lenny*, Jack Nicholson in *Chinatown* and Al Pacino in *The Godfather Part II*.

A 20th Century-Fox Picture, directed by Paul Mazursky. With Art Carney, Ellen Burstyn, Chief Dan George, Geraldine Fitzgerald, Larry Hagman, Arthur Hunnicutt, DeLuxe Color. 115 mins.

HARVEY (1950) ★

★ best supporting actress Josephine Hull

James Stewart in one of his most famous roles as the gently eccentric Elwood P. Dowd, whose amiable life in a small American town with his friend Harvey, an invisible 6-ft. 4-in. white rabbit, causes considerable consternation to his sister and niece. Josephine Hull, as the sister who ends up spending some time in the mental

home she had intended for her brother, won the supporting actress award. Stewart received a nomination but lost out to Jose Ferrer's *Cyrano de Bergerac*.

A Universal International Picture, directed by Henry Koster. With James Stewart, Josephine Hull, Peggy Dow, Charles Drake, Cecil Kellaway, Victoria Horne, Jesse White. 103 mins.

THE HARVEY GIRLS (1946) ★

★ best song "On the Atchison, Topeka and Santa Fe" (Harry Warren, music; Johnny Mercer, lyrics)

Boisterous Judy Garland musical about the famous Fred Harvey traveling waitresses who brought clean living, chastity and clean tablecloths to the rough-and-tough towns of the pioneer Southwest. Famous mainly for the Oscar-winning Harry Warren/Johnny Mercer song.

An MGM Picture, directed by George Sidney. With Judy Garland, John Hodiak, Ray Bolger, Angela Lansbury, Preston Foster, Virginia O'Brien, Kenny Baker, Marjorie Main. Technicolor. 104 mins.

HEAVEN CAN WAIT (1978) ★

★ best art direction Paul Sylbert & Edwin O'Donovan
        set decoration George Gaines

Warren Beatty as a Los Angeles football player who is killed in a road accident before his time but is allowed to return to earth in the company of heavenly escort James Mason. A remake of the 1941 fantasy *Here Comes Mr. Jordan* (in which the unfortunate hero was a boxer) and nominated for nine Academy Awards. Winner of only one Oscar, however, losing out to the much-praised *The Deer Hunter* at the 1978 award ceremonies.

A Paramount Picture, directed by Warren Beatty and Buck Henry. With Warren Beatty, Julie Christie, James Mason, Jack Warden,

Charles Grodin, Dyan Cannon, Buck Henry. Movielab Color. 101 mins.

THE HEIRESS (1949) ★★★★

★ best actress Olivia de Havilland
★ best b/w art direction Harry Horner & John Meehan
              set decoration Emile Kuri
★ best b/w costume design Edith Head & Gile Steele
★ best scoring of a drama or comedy Aaron Copland

Adaptation of Henry James' "Washington Square," with Olivia de Havilland winning her second Oscar in four years as a plain spinster heiress who is wooed for her money by handsome fortune hunter Montgomery Clift. Ralph Richardson co-stars as the unfortunate girl's arrogant doctor father.

A Paramount Picture, directed by William Wyler. With Olivia de Havilland, Ralph Richardson, Montgomery Clift, Miriam Hopkins, Vanessa Brown, Betty Linley, Ray Collins. 115 mins.

HELLO DOLLY! (1969) ★★★

★ best art direction John DeCuir, Jack Martin Smith & Herman Blumenthal
              set decoration Walter M. Scott, George Hopkins, Raphael Bretton
★ best scoring of a musical Lennie Hayton & Lionel Newman
★ best sound Jack Solomon & Murray Spivak

Musical version of the Thornton Wilder play *The Matchmaker*, with Barbra Streisand as widowed Dolly Levi setting her sights on rich merchant Walter Matthau and conniving and singing her hardest until she gets him. Guest appearance of the late Louis Armstrong in the lavish title number.

A 20th Century-Fox Picture, directed by Gene Kelly. With Barbra Streisand, Walter Matthau, Michael Crawford, Louis Armstrong. Todd-AO/DeLuxe Color. 148 mins.

HELLO, FRISCO, HELLO (1943) ★

★ best song "You'll Never Know" (Harry Warren, music; Mack Gordon, lyrics)

The ups and downs of honky-tonk singer Alice Faye and saloon keeper John Payne on San Francisco's Barbary Coast at the turn of the century. Miss Faye suffers, Mr. Payne reaches Nob Hill and then comes down again. The song "You'll Never Know" continually links them together.

A 20th Century-Fox Picture, directed by Bruce Humberstone. With Alice Faye, John Payne, Jack Oakie, June Havoc, Lynn Bari, Laird Cregar, Ward Bond. Technicolor. 98 mins.

HENRY V (1989)

★ best costume design Phyllis Dalton

Realistic version of Shakespeare's celebrated play, with Kenneth Branagh offering a much harsher portrait of the warrior king than Olivier* some 45 years before but still seeking the same things out of life—the throne of France and Princess Katherine to go with it. Phyllis Dalton's costume designs earned the film its only Oscar; Branagh missed out on the main awards after being nominated for his direction and performance.

A Renaissance Film, in association with the BBC. Directed by Kenneth Branagh. With Kenneth Branagh, Derek Jacobi, Brian Blessed, Alec McCowen, Ian Holm, John Sessions, Richard Briers, Robert Stephens, Robbie Col-

---

*   *Note:* In 1946, Olivier's *Henry V* was nominated for best film and Olivier for his portrayal of the king. William Walton (music) and Paul Sheriff and Carmen Dillon (art direction) also received nominations. Olivier won a special award for "his outstanding achievement as actor, producer and director in bringing *Henry V* to the screen."

Emma Thompson and Kenneth Branagh in *Henry V* (Renaissance Films); winner for best costume design, 1989.

trane, Judi Dench, Paul Scofield, Emma Thompson. Eastman Color. 137 mins.

HERE COMES MR. JORDAN (1941)   ★★

- ★ best original story Harry Segall
- ★ best screenplay Sidney Buchman & Seton I. Miller

Heavenly messenger Edward Everett Horton makes a dreadful error and sends prizefighter Robert Montgomery up to heaven 50 years before his time—and just as Montgomery was set to win the world's boxing championship. The celestial powers must find a suitable body for the boxer to occupy on his return to earth. Remade in 1978 as *Heaven Can Wait*, which won an Oscar for best art direction and set decoration.

A Columbia Picture, directed by Alexander Hall. With Robert Montgomery, Evelyn Keyes, Claude Rains, Rita Johnson, Edward Everett Horton, James Gleason, John Emery. 93 mins.

HERE COMES THE GROOM (1951)   ★

- ★ best song "In the Cool, Cool, Cool of the Evening" (Hoagy Carmichael, music; Johnny Mercer, lyrics)

Roving reporter Bing Crosby, after sentimentally importing three French orphans to the States, finds he needs a wife to look after them and sets his sights on Jane Wyman even though she's already engaged to rich Bostonian Franchot Tone. Like many other movies, a film remembered primarily for a song, the Oscar-winning "In the Cool, Cool, Cool of the Evening."

A Paramount Picture, directed by Frank Capra. With Bing Crosby, Jane Wyman, Alexis Smith, Franchot Tone, James Barton, Robert Keith. 113 min.

THE HIGH AND THE MIGHTY (1954)   ★

- ★ best music score of a drama or comedy Dimitri Tiomkin

Almost a *Grand Hotel* of the air, with the passengers and crew of a Honolulu–to–San Francisco airliner finding themselves looking back over their lives as the plane runs into trouble. Based on the novel by Ernest Gann and full of nervous strains and tensions, even with pilots John Wayne and Robert Stack at the controls. Dimitri Tiomkin's music score was favored over that of Leonard Bernstein (*On the Waterfront*), which was also nominated that year.

A Warner Bros. Picture, directed by William A. Wellman. With John Wayne, Claire Trevor, Laraine Day, Robert Stack, Jan Sterling, Phil Harris, Robert Newton, David Brian, Paul Kelly, Sidney Blackmer. CinemaScope/Warner Color. 147 mins.

HIGH NOON (1952)   ★★★★

- ★ best actor Gary Cooper
- ★ best editing Elmo Williams & Harry Gerstad
- ★ best music score of a drama or comedy Dimitri Tiomkin
- ★ best song "High Noon" ("Do Not Forsake Me, Oh My Darlin' ") (Dimitri Tiomkin, music; Ned Washington, lyrics)

Gary Cooper winning his second Oscar as a retiring small-town marshal who is completely abandoned by the townspeople he has defended for so long, and left alone at noon to face a vengeful killer and his gang of outlaws. The choice of the New York Film Critics Circle as best of the year, the film lost to DeMille's *The Greatest Show on Earth* on Oscar night. Director Fred Zinnemann and screenwriter Carl Foreman were among the unlucky nominees.

A United Artists Picture, directed by Fred Zinnemann. With Gary Cooper, Katy Jurado, Thomas Mitchell, Lloyd Bridges, Grace Kelly, Otto Kruger, Lon Chaney, Jr. 85 mins.

THE HINDENBURG (1975)   ★ ★

★ best special visual effects* Albert Whitlock & Glen Robinson
★ best sound effects* Peter Berkos

The last transatlantic flight of the German airship Hindenburg before its destruction through sabotage above Lakehurst, New Jersey in April 1937. The film hinges on which of the star-studded passengers and crew is the saboteur, but its real appeal lies in the brilliant photography and special effects work.

A Universal Picture, directed by Robert Wise. With George C. Scott, Anne Bancroft, William Atherton, Roy Thinnes, Gig Young, Burgess Meredith. Panavision/Technicolor. 116 mins.

A HOLE IN THE HEAD (1959)   ★

★ best song "High Hopes" (James Van Heusen, music; Sammy Cahn, lyrics)

The emotional and business problems of small-time promoter-widower Frank Sinatra, who operates a fleabag hotel in Miami Beach. Among his problems—his 11-year-old son, a rich widow, and an older, more sensible brother (Edward G. Robinson) who bails him out from time to time. Sinatra's recording of the film's hit song, "High Hopes," earned more attention than his performance and became one of his biggest hits.

---

* *Note:* Both of the picture's Oscars were special achievement awards.

A United Artists Picture directed by Frank Capra. With Frank Sinatra, Edward G. Robinson, Eleanor Parker, Carolyn Jones, Thelma Ritter, Keenan Wynn. CinemaScope/DeLuxe Color. 120 mins.

HOLIDAY INN (1942)   ★

★ best song "White Christmas" (Irving Berlin, music & lyrics)

Fred Astaire and Bing Crosby in the first of the two films in which they starred together (they later appeared in *Blue Skies*) competing for the hand of blonde Marjorie Reynolds in a holiday nightclub converted from an old New England farm. Mainly a series of musical episodes, containing some of Berlin's most famous numbers, among them the Oscar-winning "White Christmas."

A Paramount Picture, directed by Mark Sandrich. With Bing Crosby, Fred Astaire, Marjorie Reynolds, Virginia Dale, Walter Abel, Louise Beavers, Irving Bacon. 101 mins.

THE HOSPITAL (1971)   ★

★ best story & screenplay Paddy Chayefsky

George C. Scott at the top of his form as a hospital Chief of Medicine who is almost at the end of his tether, both personally through the breakup of his 24-year marriage and professionally when he finds that a mad killer is loose in the hospital wards. The film earned Chayefsky the second of his three Academy Awards for screenwriting. He won his first in 1955 for *Marty* and his third and last for Sidney Lumet's *Network* (1976).

A United Artists Picture, directed by Arthur Hiller. With George C. Scott, Diana Rigg, Barnard Hughes, Nancy Marchand, Stephen Elliott. DeLuxe Color. 102 mins.

THE HOUSE ON 92ND STREET (1945)   ★

★ best original story Charles G. Booth

The last flight of the German airship *The Hindenburg* (Universal), Oscar winner in 1975 for visual and sound effects.

Semidocumentary movie—the first of several of its kind in the postwar period—showing how the FBI smashed an American-based spy ring which in 1941 was gaining access to the secrets of Process 97, code name for the atomic bomb.

A 20th Century-Fox Picture, directed by Henry Hathaway. With William Eythe, Lloyd Nolan, Signe Hasso, Gene Lockhart, Leo G. Carroll. 88 mins.

HOWARDS END (1992) ★★★

★ best actress Emma Thompson
★ best adapted screenplay Ruth Prawer Jhabvala

★ best art direction Luciana Arrighi
   set decoration Ian Whittaker

Meticulous Merchant–Ivory dramatization of the celebrated novel by E. M. Forster; an examination of Edwardian middle-class values and the unlikely marriage between no-nonsense businessman Henry Wilcox (Anthony Hopkins) and the free-spirited Margaret Schlegel (Emma Thompson), whose values are intellectual and humanitarian. At the heart of the story lies the inheritance of Howards End, a house that comes to stand ultimately for England and its future. Like *A Room with a View* (1986), the film earned three Academy Awards; Emma Thompson's

Oscar made her the first British star to be named best actress since Glenda Jackson won for *A Touch of Class* in 1973.

Merchant Ivory Productions/Sony Pictures Classics, directed by James Ivory. With Anthony Hopkins, Vanessa Redgrave, Helena Bonham Carter, Emma Thompson, James Wilby, Samuel West, Prunella Scales, Joseph Bennett. In color. 142 mins.

HOW GREEN WAS MY VALLEY (1941)   ★★★★★

★ best film Darryl F. Zanuck (producer)
★ best direction John Ford
★ best supporting actor Donald Crisp
★ best b/w cinematography Arthur Miller
★ best b/w art direction Richard Day & Nathan Juran
    interior decoration Thomas A. Little

Novelist Richard Llewellyn's remembrance of things past, about the life and slow disintegration of a coal-mining family living in a Welsh valley at the end of the last century. Donald Crisp's portrait of the head of the Morgan family earned him a supporting Oscar; art directors Richard Day and Nathan Juran earned theirs mainly for their magnificent set of the Welsh village with its cobbled streets, stone houses and colliery. The film won the best-picture Oscar in a vintage year when *Citizen Kane*, *The Maltese Falcon* and *The Little Foxes* were all up for the award.

A 20th Century-Fox Picture, directed by John Ford. With Walter Pidgeon, Maureen O'Hara, Donald Crisp, Anna Lee, Roddy McDowall, John Loder, Sara Allgood, Barry Fitzgerald. 118 mins.

HOW THE WEST WAS WON (1963)   ★★★

★ best story & screenplay James R. Webb
★ best editing Harold F. Kress
★ best sound Franklin E. Milton

The first story film in the Cinerama process; a superwestern tracing, through the lives of a single family, 50 years in the growth of the West from the early days of the pioneers of the Ohio River Valley to the days of the wagon trains, the gold rush, the building of the railroads, the outlaws and the final winning of the West.

An MGM Picture, directed by John Ford, Henry Hathaway and George Marshall. With Gregory Peck, James Stewart, Henry Fonda, Richard Widmark, Debbie Reynolds, Karl Malden, Carroll Baker, George Peppard, Robert Preston, Lee J. Cobb, Eli Wallach, John Wayne. Cinerama/Technicolor. 165 mins.

HUD (1963)   ★★★

★ best actress Patricia Neal
★ best supporting actor Melvyn Douglas
★ best b/w cinematography James Wong Howe

Drama of modern Texas, contrasting the enduring values of veteran rancher Melvyn Douglas with those of his rootless, amoral son (Paul Newman), whose idea of the new breed of cowboy is to make a buck as fast as he can and own a pink Cadillac convertible. Newman was perhaps unlucky not to gain an Oscar for his swaggering portrayal of a contemporary rebel; Patricia Neal, as the rancher's sexy housekeeper, and Melvyn Douglas were more fortunate.

A Paramount Picture, directed by Martin Ritt. With Paul Newman, Melvyn Douglas, Patricia Neal, Brandon de Wilde, Whit Bissell, John Ashley. 112 mins.

THE HUMAN COMEDY (1943)   ★

★ best original story William Saroyan

The lives of ordinary people living in a small California town in World War II, and the joys and sorrows they experience during the war years. Mickey Rooney stars as the Western Union messenger who has the unenviable task of delivering telegrams during a time when a telegram can only mean that someone has been killed or wounded overseas.

An MGM Picture, directed by Clarence Brown. With Mickey Rooney, James Craig, Frank Morgan, Fay Bainter, Marsha Hunt, Van Johnson, Donna Reed. 118 mins.

THE HUNT FOR RED OCTOBER (1990) ★

★ best sound effects editing Cecilia Hall & George Watters II

Pre-glasnost adventure drama about a renegade Soviet commander who defects to the States, taking his entire crew and his nuclear submarine with him, and then has the problem of convincing the Pentagon that he's on the level. A white-haired Sean Connery is the Russian who causes all the trouble; CIA analyst Alec Baldwin is the man who has to sort it all out. Based on the novel by Tom Clancy.

A Paramount Picture, directed by John McTiernan. With Sean Connery, Alec Baldwin, Scott Glenn, Sam Neill, James Earl Jones, Joss Ackland, Richard Jordan, Peter Firth, Tim Curry. 70mm. Panavision/Technicolor. 135 mins.

THE HURRICANE (1937) ★

★ best sound recording Thomas T. Moulton

Jon Hall and Dorothy Lamour as two South Sea islanders whose idyllic way of life is almost destroyed by the vindictive French governor of the islands. The hurricane of the title was the work of James Basevi, who would almost certainly have won an Oscar if the special effects awards had then been in existence (they didn't begin until 1939). As it was, it was the sound rather than the sight of the terrifying hurricane that brought an award to UA's sound department.

A Sam Goldwyn Production (released through United Artists), directed by John Ford. With Dorothy Lamour, Jon Hall, Mary Astor, C. Aubrey Smith, Thomas Mitchell, Raymond Massey, John Carradine. 110 mins.

THE HUSTLER (1961)

★ best b/w cinematography Eugene Shuftan
★ best b/w art direction Harry Horner
        set decoration Gene Callahan

Young pool shark "Fast Eddie" Felson (Paul Newman) cons a living in cheap poolrooms while waiting to take on—and take over from—reigning pool champ Minnesota Fats (Jackie Gleason). Derived from the novel by Walter Tevis and nominated for nine Oscars, the film was unlucky in being released the same year as the musical *West Side Story* and ended up with only camerawork and design awards. Newman was nominated for best actor; he eventually won when he reprised the role of Eddie Felson in Martin Scorsese's 1986 sequel, *The Color of Money*.

A 20th Century-Fox Picture, directed by Robert Rossen. With Paul Newman, Piper Laurie, George C. Scott, Jackie Gleason, Myron McCormick, Murray Hamilton. CinemaScope. 135 mins.

I

I'LL CRY TOMORROW (1955)   ★

★ best b/w costume design Helen Rose

Susan Hayward suffering almost as much as she did three years later in *I Want to Live*, as singer Lillian Roth, who slips from the top to skid row because of chronic alcoholism. Hayward, who sang her own songs, was recognized as best actress at the Cannes Film Festival; Hollywood gave her only a nomination, preferring Anna Magnani in *The Rose Tattoo* as the year's best.

An MGM Picture, directed by Daniel Mann. With Susan Hayward, Richard Conte, Eddie Albert, Jo Van Fleet, Don Taylor, Ray Danton, Margo. 117 mins.

INDIANA JONES AND THE LAST CRUSADE (1989)   ★

★ best sound effects editing Ben Burtt & Richard Hymns

Indy (Harrison Ford) and his old man (Sean Connery) in a tight spot in Steven Spielberg's *Indiana Jones and the Last Crusade* (Paramount), the winner for best sound effects editing in 1989.

Third and perhaps final adventure of the laconic, whip-cracking hero first introduced by Spielberg and George Lucas in *Raiders of the Lost Ark* (1981). Ingredients: more Nazis, hectic chases, a German castle and a hidden temple of the Holy Grail. Also on hand: Sean Connery as Indy's dad and River Phoenix as a teenage Indy.

A Lucasfilm for Paramount, directed by Steven Spielberg. With Harrison Ford, Sean Connery, Denholm Elliott, Alison Doody, John Rhys-Davies, Julian Glover, River Phoenix, Michael Byrne. 70mm/Eastman Color; prints by DeLuxe. 127 mins.

INDIANA JONES AND THE TEMPLE OF DOOM (1984)   ★

★ best visual effects Dennis Muren, Michael McAlister, Lorne Peterson & George Gibbs

Number two in the Indiana Jones series, with Harrison Ford teamed with an American songstress (Kate Capshaw) and a small Chinese orphan as they search for the sacred sankara stone in India. Actually a prequel to the first film, set in 1935 and boasting a superbly staged opening sequence in a Shanghai nightclub. A breakneck escape by underground railway was instrumental in helping the film win its award for visual effects.

A Lucasfilm for Paramount, directed by Steven Spielberg. With Harrison Ford, Kate Capshaw, Ke Huy Quan, Amrish Puri, Roshan Seth, Philip Stone, Roy Chiao, David Yip. 70 mm/Rank color; prints by DeLuxe. 117 mins.

INDOCHINE (1992)*   ★

★ best foreign language film France

* *Note:* Previous French winners of the foreign film award: *Mon Oncle* (1958), *Black Orpheus* (1959), *Sundays and Cybele* (1962), *A Man and a Woman* (1966), *The Discreet Charm of the Bourgeoisie* (1972), *Day for Night* (1973), *Madame Rosa* (1977) and *Get Out Your Handkerchiefs* (1978).

Lush epic set against the collapse of French colonialism in prewar Indochina and examining the relationship between a French plantation owner (Catherine Deneuve) and her adopted Vietnamese daughter when they both fall in love with the same man. Enhanced by the presence of two natural beauties—Deneuve and the southeast Asia landscape—this is the ninth French film to capture the foreign language award, equaling the record held by Italy, established with the release of *Mediterraneo* one year earlier.

Paradis Films & General D'Images/BAC Films/Orly Films/Cine Cinq. Directed by Regis Wargnier. With Catherine Deneuve, Vincent Perez, Linh Dan Pham, Jean Yanne, Dominique Blanc, Henri Marteau, Carlo Brandt. Color. 154 mins.

THE INFORMER (1935)   ★★★★

★ best direction John Ford
★ best actor Victor McLaglen
★ best screenplay Dudley Nichols
★ best music score Max Steiner

Liam O'Flaherty's novel of Dublin during the troubles, centering around a slow-witted Irish giant (McLaglen) who turns traitor and betrays a comrade to the police because he needs the money to go to America. A monumental performance from McLaglen as Gypo Nolan, and very atmospheric direction from John Ford, who here won the first of his four Academy Awards.

An RKO Picture, directed by John Ford. With Victor McLaglen, Heather Angel, Preston Foster, Margot Grahame, Wallace Ford, Una O'Connor. 91 mins.

INNERSPACE (1987)   ★

★ best visual effects Dennis Muren, William George, Harley Jessup & Kenneth Smith

Fantastic Voyage (1967) revisited, this time for laughs, as alcoholic test pilot Dennis Quaid is miniaturized until he is invisible to the naked eye and then accidentally injected into the rear end of hypochondriac supermarket clerk Martin Short. The net result: both are pursued by evil agents. The film's interior body sequences combined model work with actual microphotography of arteries and organs.

A Warner Bros. Picture (Amblin Entertainment), directed by Joe Dante. With Dennis Quaid, Martin Short, Meg Ryan, Kevin McCarthy, Fiona Lewis, Veron Wells, Robert Picardo, Wendy Schaal. Technicolor. 120 mins.

IN OLD ARIZONA (1928/29)   ★

★ best actor Warner Baxter

Warner Baxter as the caballero The Cisco Kid— a character played later by several other actors but here in Academy Award-winning style by Baxter, as he robs Wells Fargo, keeps one step ahead of the law and comes dangerously close to death as he becomes infatuated with a double-dealing Mexican girl, Dorothy Burgess.

A Fox Picture, directed by Raoul Walsh and Irving Cummings. With Edmund Lowe, Warner Baxter, Dorothy Burgess, J. Farrell MacDonald, Ivan Linow. 95 mins.

IN OLD CHICAGO (1937)   ★

★ best supporting actress Alice Brady
★ best assistant direction Robert Webb

Melodrama built around the great Chicago fire of 1871, with the special effects men winning the honors for their recreation of the fire—said to have burned on the Fox lot for three full days. The Oscar, however, went to Alice Brady for her portrayal of Mrs. O'Leary, whose three sons, Tyrone Power, Don Ameche and Tom Brown, find adventure and political opportunity in the city. Alice Faye, taking over the role from Jean Harlow, who had been cast for the film just prior to her death, provides the romantic interest.

A 20th Century-Fox Picture, directed by Henry King. With Tyrone Power, Alice Faye, Don Ameche, Alice Brady, Andy Devine, Brian Donlevy, Phyllis Brooks, Tom Brown. 110 mins.

INTERRUPTED MELODY (1955) ★

★ best story & screenplay William Ludwig & Sonya Levien

Another MGM movie of 1955 dealing with the comeback of a famous entertainer, this time Australian opera singer Marjorie Lawrence, who was stricken with polio at the height of her fame but courageously overcame her disability and made a triumphant return to the stage. Eileen Farrell dubbed eight arias for Eleanor Parker, who was nominated for an Academy Award for her performance but remained one of those actresses who were frequently on the verge of winning but never actually won an Oscar. She had been nominated previously for her performances in *Caged* (1950) and *Detective Story* (1951).

An MGM Picture, directed by Curtis Bernhardt. With Glenn Ford, Eleanor Parker, Roger Moore, Cecil Kellaway, Peter Leeds, Evelyn Ellis. CinemaScope/Eastman Color. 106 mins.

IN THE HEAT OF THE NIGHT (1967) ★★★★★

★ best film Walter Mirisch (producer)
★ best actor Rod Steiger
★ best screenplay Stirling Silliphant
★ best editing Hal Ashby
★ best sound Walter Goss

Quiet little movie which, like *Crossfire* some 20 years earlier, explored an important social problem—racial prejudice in the Deep South—through the form of a crime thriller. Rod Steiger stars as the thick-witted, small-town police chief who has to investigate a murder; Sidney Poitier is the black homicide expert from Philadelphia who is ordered to help the grudging Steiger find the suspect. The film won the best-picture award over the more favored contenders *Bonnie and Clyde* and *The Graduate*.

A United Artists Picture, directed by Norman Jewison. With Rod Steiger, Sidney Poitier, Warren Oates, Lee Grant, James Patterson,

Quentin Dean, Larry Gates. DeLuxe Color. 109 mins.

THE INVADERS (1942)

(Original U.K. title: *Forty Ninth Parallel*)

★ best original story Emeric Pressburger

War drama, heavily laced with propaganda, about the adventures of a group of Nazis when their submarine is sunk and they try to make it to safety across Canada. Chief Nazi is Eric Portman; assorted democrats include Leslie Howard, Laurence Olivier and Anton Walbrook. The story by Pressburger won the film its Oscar; more deserving might have been Vaughan Williams' beautiful music, which was not even among the best-music-score nominees.

An Ortus Film, directed by Michael Powell. With Leslie Howard, Raymond Massey, Laurence Olivier, Anton Walbrook, Eric Portman, Glynis Johns, Niall MacGinnis. 123 mins.

INVESTIGATION OF A CITIZEN ABOVE SUSPICION (1970) ★

★ best foreign language film Italy

Drama about a powerful Rome police chief who meddles in the investigation of a murder he has himself committed, perfectly sure in his own mind that, since he has been promoted to a high office in political intelligence, he is above the law.

A Vera Film, directed by Elio Petri. With Gian Maria Volonte, Florinda Bolkan, Salvo Randone, Gianni Santuccio, Arturo Dominici. Technicolor. 115 mins.

IRMA LA DOUCE (1963) ★

★ best scoring: adaptation or treatment Andre Previn

Billy Wilder's straight comedy of the Broadway musical hit, omitting the 16 numbers and concentrating solely on the relationship between a Parisian prostitute (Shirley MacLaine) and a gendarme (Jack Lemmon) who is so jealous in his love for her that he disguises himself as an English nobleman in order to keep her for himself.

A United Artists Picture, directed by Billy Wilder. With Jack Lemmon, Shirley MacLaine, Lou Jacobi, Bruce Yarnell, Herschel Bernardi, Hope Holiday, Joan Shawlee. Panavision/Technicolor. 147 mins.

IT HAPPENED ONE NIGHT (1934) ★★★★★

★ best film Harry Cohn (producer)
★ best direction Frank Capra
★ best actor Clark Gable
★ best actress Claudette Colbert
★ best writing adaptation Robert Riskin

The first, and until *One Flew Over the Cuckoo's Nest* (1975), only film to win all five major Academy Awards—a sleeper from Columbia Pictures (which had never won a best-picture award before) about a runaway heiress (Colbert) and a wandering journalist (Gable) who form a lasting relationship in their journey across country together. The movie earned Frank Capra the first of the three directorial awards he won in the 1930s. Capra still holds the record of being the only director to win three Oscars within a five-year span of filmmaking—for this film, *Mr. Deeds Goes to Town* (1936) and *You Can't Take It With You* (1938).

A Columbia Picture, directed by Frank Capra. With Claudette Colbert, Clark Gable, Walter Connolly, Roscoe Karns, Jameson Thomas, Alan Hale, Ward Bond. 105 mins.

IT'S A MAD, MAD, MAD, MAD WORLD (1963) ★

★ best sound effects Walter G. Elliott

Retiring police captain Spencer Tracy is determined to catch a group of crazies who are after a dead gangster's hidden treasure—and then makes off with the loot himself. Massive slapstick comedy with a cast of comedy greats involved in wild chases, car and plane crashes, etc.

A United Artists Picture, directed by Stanley Kramer. With Spencer Tracy, Milton Berle, Sid Caesar, Buddy Hackett, Ethel Merman, Mickey Rooney, Phil Silvers, Terry-Thomas, Dick Shawn, Jonathan Winters, Peter Falk, Jimmy Durante. Ultra Panavision/Technicolor. 190 mins.

I WANT TO LIVE (1958) ★

★ best actress Susan Hayward

Robert Wise's powerful indictment of capital punishment, with Susan Hayward at last winning her Oscar (she had four previous nominations) as the habitual petty criminal Barbara Graham, who went to the gas chamber in San Quentin on a charge of murder but who protested her innocence to the very end. Hayward's previous nominations: *Smash-Up, the Story of a Woman* (1947); *My Foolish Heart* (1949); *With a Song in My Heart* (1952); and *I'll Cry Tomorrow* (1955).

A United Artists Picture, directed by Robert Wise. With Susan Hayward, Simon Oakland, Virginia Vincent, Theodore Bikel, Wesley Lau, Philip Coolidge. 120 mins.

I WANTED WINGS (1941) ★

★ best special effects Farciot Edouart & Gordon Jennings (photographic), Louis Mesenkop (sound)

Wartime propaganda piece about three very different young men—Long Island playboy Ray Milland, garage mechanic William Holden and college athlete Wayne Morris—undergoing rigorous training for the Army Air Corps. A class "B" story given excitement in its time by special effects wizardry and aerial shots of planes flashing across the sky.

A Paramount Picture, directed by Mitchell Leisen. With Ray Milland, William Holden, Wayne Morris, Brian Donlevy, Constance Moore, Veronica Lake, Harry Davenport. 131 mins.

J

JAWS (1975) ★★★

★ best editing Verna Fields
★ best sound Robert Hoyt, Roger Heman, Earl Madery & John Carter
★ best original score John Williams

A trio of shark hunters puts out to sea in a ramshackle boat to track down the massive shark that has terrorized and killed vacationers along the beaches of a Long Island holiday resort. For a short period the number-one box-office attraction of all time, but a long way from an Oscar record holder, coming out way behind the year's top winner, *One Flew Over the Cuckoo's Nest*.

A Universal Picture, directed by Steven Spielberg. With Roy Scheider, Robert Shaw, Richard Dreyfuss, Lorraine Gary, Murray Hamilton, Carl Gottlieb. Panavision/Technicolor. 125 mins.

JEZEBEL (1938) ★★

★ best actress Bette Davis
★ best supporting actress Fay Bainter*

Romantic melodrama of New Orleans in the 1850s, with spoiled wealthy Southern belle

---

*   *Note:* Fay Bainter was also nominated as best actress in 1938 for her role in *White Banners*. Other actresses who have been nominated twice in the same year: Teresa Wright, nominated for best actress in 1942 for *The Pride of the Yankees* and winner for best supporting actress for *Mrs. Miniver*; Jessica Lange, nominated for best actress in 1982 for *Frances* and winner for best supporting actress for *Tootsie*; and Sigourney Weaver, who lost out on both of her nominations in 1988—best actress for *Gorillas in the Mist* and best supporting actress for *Working Girl*.

(Davis) finding through bitter experience that life is not all sweetness and light. Handsome young banker Henry Fonda and George Brent are the rivals for her affections, Fay Bainter her sympathetic aunt.

A Warner Bros, Picture, directed by William Wyler. With Bette Davis, Henry Fonda, George Brent, Donald Crisp, Fay Bainter, Margaret Lindsay, Henry O'Neill, John Litel. 100 mins.

JFK (1991) ★★

★ best cinematography Robert Richardson
★ best editing Joe Hutshing & Pietro Scalia

Not, as the title would indicate, a biography but an investigation into who killed the president, and why, in Dallas in November 1963. The answer, according to writer-director Oliver Stone, was that a combination of the CIA, some anti-Castro Cubans and the senior military command had Kennedy killed because he was proposing to pull out of Vietnam. Stone's Oscar-winning editors and their assistants brilliantly combined fictional material with newsreel footage and made the theorizing seem almost believable. Kevin Costner stars as District Attorney Jim Garrison; a host of actors appear in fleeting cameo roles—Jack Lemmon, Walter Matthau, Donald Sutherland, among others.

A Camelot Production/Warner Bros. Directed by Oliver Stone. With Kevin Costner, Gary Oldman, Sissy Spacek, Tommy Lee Jones, Laurie Metcalf, Michael Rooker, Jay O. Sanders, Sally Kirkland, Anthony Ramirez, Joe Pesci, Ed Asner. Panavision/Color: DuArt, prints by Technicolor. 189 mins.

JOAN OF ARC (1948) ★★

★ best color cinematography Joseph Valentine, William V. Skall & Winton C. Hoch
★ best color costume design Dorothy Jeakins & Karinska

Account of the life of the young French farmgirl (Ingrid Bergman) who, in 15th-century France, had religious visions when she was 13, went on to lead the French armies against the English

The assassination of John F. Kennedy as recreated by Oliver Stone in *JFK* (Warner Bros.); the film was named for its editing and cinematography in 1991.

and was eventually tried for sorcery and burned at the stake. The first film to win an award in the color costume category.

An RKO Picture, directed by Victor Fleming. With Ingrid Bergman, Jose Ferrer, Francis L. Sullivan, J. Carrol Naish, Ward Bond, Gene Lockhart. Technicolor. 145 mins.

Jane Wyman, best actress in 1948 for her portrayal of a deaf-mute farm girl in *Johnny Belinda* (Warner Bros.).

JOHNNY BELINDA (1948)   ★

★ best actress Jane Wyman

Deaf-mute farmgirl Jane Wyman, living in a remote Nova Scotia fishing community, is befriended and educated by kindly local doctor Lew Ayres after being raped by drunken seaman Stephen McNally. Wyman's Oscar was the film's only award, despite the fact that it was nominated in 12 categories.

A Warner Bros. Picture, directed by Jean Negulesco. With Jane Wyman, Lew Ayres, Charles Bickford, Agnes Moorehead, Stephen McNally, Jan Sterling, Rosalind Ivan. 102 mins.

JOHNNY EAGER (1942)   ★

★ best supporting actor Van Heflin

Robert Taylor stars as a paroled convict who runs a host of criminal activities on the side and gets together with good girl Lana Turner, stepdaughter of the DA who put Taylor away in the first place. Advertised as TNT ("Taylor 'n' Turner"), the film's most memorable performance came from Van Heflin as Taylor's drunken, cynical pal, a many-shaded portrayal that won Heflin an Oscar and made him a star in his own right.

An MGM Picture, directed by Mervyn LeRoy. With Robert Taylor, Lana Turner, Edward Arnold, Van Heflin, Robert Sterling, Patricia Dane, Glenda Farrell. 107 mins.

THE JOKER IS WILD (1957) ★

★ best song "All the Way" (James Van Heusen, music; Sammy Cahn, lyrics)

Frank Sinatra as Joe E. Lewis, an entertainer who started out as a promising young nightclub singer of the roaring twenties, had his vocal cords slashed when he fell afoul of mobsters, and then made an unlikely comeback as a humorist. Downbeat drama, with alcoholism and several women, among them Mitzi Gaynor and Jeanne Crain, adding further complications to Lewis' life.

A Paramount Picture, directed by Charles Vidor. With Frank Sinatra, Jeanne Crain, Mitzi Gaynor, Eddie Albert, Beverly Garland, Jackie Coogan, Barry Kelley, Ted de Corsia. Vista Vision. 126 mins.

THE JOLSON STORY (1946) ★ ★

★ best sound recording John Livadary
★ best scoring of a musical picture Morris Stoloff

Columbia Pictures' biography of the legendary vaudeville entertainer from his boyhood to his success on stage and in the early talkies. Jolson, who wanted to play himself in the movie, sings the songs and actor Larry Parks mimes all-time hits like "Swanee," "April Showers" and "Mammy." Evelyn Keyes is featured as Jolson's first wife, Ruby Keeler.

A Columbia Picture, directed by Alfred E. Green. With Larry Parks, Evelyn Keyes, William Demarest, Bill Goodwin, Ludwig Donath, Tamara Shayne, John Alexander. Technicolor. 128 mins.

JOURNEY OF HOPE (1990) ★

★ best foreign language film Switzerland

A hoped-for better life turns into a nightmare as a poverty-stricken refugee family discovers that no one wants or even cares about them when they make the long trek from southern Turkey to the promised and more bountiful land of Switzerland. A powerful and very moving portrait of human despair, based on a true story, and often controversial in its observations of European attitudes towards asylum seekers. A surprise Oscar winner of its year, it defeated the highly favored *Cyrano de Bergerac* in the foreign film category.

A Catpics/Condor Features Production, directed by Xavier Koller. With Necmettin Cobanoglu, Nur Surer, Emin Sivas, Erdine Akbas, Yaman Okay, Yasar Gner, Hseyin Mete. Color. 110 mins.

JUDGMENT AT NUREMBERG (1961) ★ ★

★ best actor Maximilian Schell
★ best screenplay Abby Mann

Just how guilty and responsible were the German people for Hitler's Third Reich? This gigantic movie attempts to answer the unanswerable as it follows the trial of four former Hitler judges in a Nuremberg court presided over by small-town American judge Spencer Tracy. Maximilian Schell won an Oscar for his fiercely nationalistic defense counsel, Tracy a best-actor nomination, and Judy Garland and Montgomery Clift supporting nominations for their Nazi victims of torture.

A United Artists Picture, directed by Stanley Kramer. With Spencer Tracy, Burt Lancaster, Richard Widmark, Marlene Dietrich, Maximilian Schell, Judy Garland, Montgomery Clift. 178 mins.

JULIA (1977)

★ best supporting actor Jason Robards
★ best supporting actress Vanessa Redgrave
★ best screenplay Alvin Sargent

The awakening in the 1930s of playwright Lillian Hellman (Jane Fonda) to the threat of Nazism through the persecution and final execution of her beloved childhood friend Julia (Vanessa Redgrave). A sensitive Fred Zinnemann film made with taste, style and elegance. Jason Robards as Hellman's lover, author Dashiell Hammett, won his second successive supporting Oscar, the only supporting performer to do so in the history of the Academy.

A 20th Century-Fox Picture, directed by Fred Zinnemann. With Jane Fonda, Vanessa Redgrave, Jason Robards, Maximilian Schell, Hal Holbrook, Rosemary Murphy. Technicolor; prints by DeLuxe. 117 mins.

JULIUS CAESAR (1953)

★ best b/w art direction Cedric Gibbons & Edward Carfagno
　　　　　　set decoration Edwin B. Willis & Hugh Hunt

Shakespeare's political thriller about the assassination of Julius Caesar in 44 B.C. Straight Shakespeare, acted with great power by Brando as Marc Antony and with intelligence and subtlety by James Mason as Brutus and John Gielgud as Cassius. Only Brando earned an Academy Award nomination, the best actor Oscar going to William Holden for *Stalag 17*.

An MGM Picture, directed by Joseph L. Mankiewicz. With James Mason, Marlon Brando, Louis Calhern, John Gielgud, Edmond O'Brien, Greer Garson, Deborah Kerr, George Macready. 121 mins.

K

KENTUCKY (1938)   ★

★ best supporting actor Walter Brennan

A story of rival horsebreeding families in the bluegrass country, with Loretta Young as the heroine of the hour, paying her family's debts by winning the Kentucky Derby. Walter Brennan collected his second supporting Oscar in three years as Loretta's uncle.

A 20th Century-Fox Picture, directed by David Butler. With Loretta Young, Richard Greene, Walter Brennan, Douglas Dumbrille, Karen Morley, Moroni Olsen. Technicolor. 95 mins.

KEY LARGO (1948)   ★

★ best supporting actress Claire Trevor

Gangster thriller with ex-bootlegger Edward G. Robinson and his hoods holding Bogie, Bacall and Lionel Barrymore hostage in a resort hotel on the stormy Florida Keys. The film's high spot is Claire Trevor's performance as a faded torch singer, a portrait in jaded alcoholism that deservedly won her the year's best supporting actress award.

A Warner Bros. Picture, directed by John Huston. With Humphrey Bogart, Edward G. Robinson, Lauren Bacall, Lionel Barrymore, Claire Trevor, Thomas Gomez. 101 mins.

THE KILLING FIELDS (1984)   ★★★

★ best supporting actor Haing S. Ngor
★ best cinematography Chris Menges
★ best editing Jim Clark

Epic hymn to friendship and courage, set during and after the fall of Phnom Penh, with

Haing S. Ngor, best supporting actor for his portrayal of Dith Pran in Roland Joffe's *The Killing Fields* (Goldcrest/Warner Bros., 1984).

Cambodian photographer Dith Pran escaping the torture of the Khmer Rouge and making a heroic trek back to freedom and a reunion with his long-time friend, *New York Times* reporter Sydney Schanberg. The 36-year-old Haing S. Ngor, a Cambodian doctor who lived through the turmoil, became the first nonprofessional to win an Academy Award since Harold Russell for *The Best Years of Our Lives* (1946).

Goldcrest Films And Television/An Enigma (First Casualty) Production/Warner Bros., directed by Roland Joffe. With Sam Waterston, Doctor Haing S. Ngor, John Malkovich, Julian Sands, Craig T. Nelson, Spalding Gray, Bill Paterson, Athol Fugard. Eastman Color. 142 mins.

THE KING AND I (1956)   ★★★★★

★ best actor Yul Brynner
★ best color art direction Lyle R. Wheeler & John DeCuir
            set decoration Walter M. Scott & Paul S. Fox
★ best color costume design Irene Sharaff
★ best sound recording Carl Faulkner

★ best scoring of a musical Alfred Newman & Ken Darby

The musical remake of *Anna and the King of Siam* (1946), with Yul Brynner as the stubborn Siamese king and Deborah Kerr as his children's spirited tutor. Music by Rodgers and Hammerstein. The Oscars, Brynner's apart, were mainly for the film's sumptuous production values.

A 20th Century-Fox Picture, directed by Walter Lang. With Deborah Kerr, Yul Brynner, Rita Moreno, Martin Benson, Terry Saunders, Rex Thompson, Carlos Rivas. CinemaScope/DeLuxe Color. 133 mins.

KING KONG (1976) ★

★ best special visual effects* Carlo Rambaldi, Glen Robinson & Frank Van Der Veer

Remake of the 1933 monster classic, with the 40-foot Kong once again being discovered on Skull Island and transported to civilization to be humiliated. Part of the film's "special effects" were performed by actor Rick Baker, including some of the close-ups in ape costume. The 1933 movie—incredibly—didn't win a single award or nomination.

A Dino De Laurentiis Corporation Picture, directed by John Guillermin. With Jeff Bridges, Charles Grodin, Jessica Lange, John Randolph, Rene Auberjonois, Julius Harris. Panavision/Metrocolor. 135 mins.

KING OF JAZZ (1929/30) ★

★ best art direction Herman Rosse

Universal's contribution to the musical revue type of movie produced by several of the top Hollywood studios at the advent of sound. Paul Whiteman and his band playing from atop a gigantic piano headlined the film, which boasted huge production numbers, two-color Technicolor sequences and somewhere in the huge

cast, The Rhythm Boys—a singing threesome, one of whom was Bing Crosby.

A Universal picture, directed by John Murray Anderson. With Paul Whiteman and His Orchestra, Jeanette Loff, Stanley Smith, The Rhythm Boys (Bing Crosby, Harry Barris and Al Rinker), The Brox Sisters, John Boles. Two-Color Technicolor sequences. 105 mins.

KING SOLOMON'S MINES (1950)

★ best color cinematography Robert Surtees
★ best editing Ralph E. Winters & Conrad A. Nervig

H. Rider Haggard's adventure story about the search by great white hunter Allan Quartermain (Stewart Granger) for a woman's missing explorer husband and for the famed diamond mines of darkest Africa guarded by the 7-foot Watusi tribe. Photographed on location by Robert Surtees, who caught all the different forms of African animal life—including a stampede—in his great camerawork.

An MGM Picture, directed by Compton Bennett and Andrew Marton. With Deborah Kerr, Stewart Granger, Richard Carlson, Hugo Haas, Lowell Gilmore. Technicolor. 102 mins.

KISS OF THE SPIDER WOMAN (1985) ★

★ best actor William Hurt

Two cellmates, one a left-wing journalist (Raul Julia), the other a homosexual window dresser (William Hurt), share a cell in a Latin American jail and eke out their existence and growing friendship by reliving exotic tales from old Technicolor Hollywood B movies. Hurt was originally set for the role of the political activist, but the two actors decided to switch parts just prior to shooting. Julia, somewhat unluckily, was not nominated in the best-actor category. The film was based on the celebrated novel by Manuel Puig.

HB Films, for Island Alive, in association with FilmDallas. Directed by Hector Babenco.

---

* *Note:* The Oscar for best special visual effects was a special achievement award.

With William Hurt, Raul Julia, Sonia Braga, Jose Lewgoy, Milton Goncalves, Miriam Pires, Nuno Leal Maia, Fernando Torres. In Color. 121 mins.

KITTY FOYLE (1940)　　★

★ best actress Ginger Rogers

Ginger Rogers proving that she was more than just Fred Astaire's dancing partner by winning a tear-stained Oscar as a girl from the wrong side of the tracks who falls in love with a handsome socialite but eventually finds true happiness with a man from her own level of society. Adapted by Dalton Trumbo from the novel by Christopher Morley.

An RKO Picture, directed by Sam Wood. With Ginger Rogers, Dennis Morgan, James Craig, Eduardo Ciannelli, Ernest Cossart, Gladys Cooper. 108 mins.

KLUTE (1971)　　★

★ best actress Jane Fonda

Kafkaesque thriller with Donald Sutherland as a private eye searching for a suburban husband last seen in New York City. Fonda is the call girl who once counted the husband among her clients.

A Warner Bros. Picture, directed by Alan J. Pakula. With Jane Fonda, Donald Sutherland, Charles Cioffi, Roy Scheider, Dorothy Tristan, Rita Gam. Panavision/Technicolor. 114 mins.

KRAMER VS. KRAMER (1979)　　★ ★ ★ ★ ★

★ best film Stanley R. Jaffe (producer)
★ best direction Robert Benton
★ best actor Dustin Hoffman
★ best supporting actress Meryl Streep
★ best screenplay Robert Benton

The top Oscar-winning film of 1979, with Dustin Hoffman as a young advertising executive who raises his seven-year-old son when his wife (Meryl Streep) deserts them. She returns months later and begins a court battle over custody of the boy. Hoffman earned the first of his two Academy Awards for his performance, winning again some nine years later for his autistic savant in Barry Levinson's *Rain Man*. Hoffman's other best actor nominations: *The Graduate* (1967), *Midnight Cowboy* (1969), *Lenny* (1974) and *Tootsie* (1982).

A Columbia Picture, directed by Robert Benton. With Dustin Hoffman, Meryl Streep, Jane Alexander, Justin Henry, Howard Duff, George Coe, Jobeth Williams. Technicolor. 105 mins.

L

LADY BE GOOD (1941) ★

★ best song "The Last Time I Saw Paris"
(Jerome Kern, music; Oscar Hammerstein
II, lyrics)

The ups and downs of married songwriters Ann
Sothern and Robert Young in America's Tin
Pan Alley. A slender plot, superb Gershwin
numbers (plus the Oscar-winning "The Last
Time I Saw Paris") and a lavish, Busby Berke-
ley-staged "Fascinating Rhythm" number with
Eleanor Powell and a massive chorus line.

An MGM Picture, directed by Norman Z.
McLeod. With Eleanor Powell, Ann Sothern,
Robert Young, Lionel Barrymore, John Carroll,
Red Skelton, Virginia O'Brien. 111 mins.

THE LAST COMMAND (1927/28) ★

★ best actor Emil Jannings

Emil Jannings as a one-time White Russian
general who flees the revolution and ends up as
an extra in Hollywood. The film was based on
an idea by Ernst Lubitsch and allowed a European performer to win the first best-actor
Oscar ever awarded, Jannings also being named
for his performance in *The Way of All Flesh*
released the same year. Jannings' competition
in that historic first year came from Richard
Barthelmess (*The Noose* and *The Patent Leather
Kid*) and Charles Chaplin (*The Circus*).

A Paramount Picture, directed by Josef Von
Sternberg. With Emil Jannings, Evelyn Brent,
William Powell, Nicholas Soussanin, Michael
Visaroff. 95 mins.

THE LAST EMPEROR (1987) ★★★★★★★★★

★ best film Jeremy Thomas (producer)
★ best direction Bernardo Bertolucci
★ best screenplay Mark Peploe & Bernardo
   Bertolucci
★ best cinematography Vittorio Storaro
★ best art direction Ferdinando Scarfiotti
      set decoration Bruno Cesari & Osvaldo
      Desideri
★ best costume design James Acheson
★ best editing Gabriella Cristiani
★ best sound Bill Rowe & Ivan Sharrock
★ best original score Ryuichi Sakamoto, David
   Byrne & Cong Su

Sumptuous Bertolucci epic inspired by the life
of Pu Yi, the last emperor of China, who was
crowned at the age of three, lived a cloistered
life in the Forbidden City, was deposed during
the revolution and ended his days happily as a
humble gardener. Along with *Ben-Hur* (11), *West
Side Story* (10), *Gigi* (9) and *Gone With the Wind*
(9) among the most honored films in Academy
history, and one of the few to win every award

John Lone as *The Last Emperor* (Columbia), directed by
Bernardo Bertolucci and winner of nine Academy Awards
in 1987, including best picture of the year.

for which it was nominated. The cast did not receive any Oscars or nominations, however.

Yanco Films (Beijing)/Tao Film (Rome), in association with Recorded Picture Company, AAA Sopro Films. Distributed by Columbia. Directed by Bernardo Bertolucci. With John Lone, Joan Chen, Peter O'Toole, Ying Ruocheng, Victor Wong, Dennis Dun, Ryuichi Sakamoto, Maggie Han, Ric Young. Technovision/Eastman Color. 163 mins.

THE LAST OF THE MOHICANS (1992) ★

★ best sound Chris Jenkins, Doug Hemphill, Mark Smith & Simon Kaye

Spectacular version of James Fenimore Cooper's adventure tale of the French and Indian Wars in 18th-century colonial America. Daniel Day-Lewis is the intrepid scout and hunter Hawkeye, the scene-stealing Wes Studi is the treacherous Mohawk Magua, who vows to tear out and eat a commanding officer's heart—and does! Filmed on location in the Blue Ridge and Great Smoky Mountains of North Carolina.

A 20th Century-Fox/Morgan Creek Picture, directed by Michael Mann. With Daniel Day-Lewis, Madeleine Stowe, Russell Means, Eric Schweig, Johdi May, Steven Waddington, Wes Studi. Scope. Deluxe Color. 122 mins.

THE LAST PICTURE SHOW (1971) ★ ★

★ best supporting actor Ben Johnson
★ best supporting actress Cloris Leachman

Study of day-to-day life in a bleak little Texas town in the early 1950s. From a cast filled mainly with young American unknowns, the two older members—Ben Johnson as the owner of the pool hall and the local movie house (the only entertainment in town) and Cloris Leachman as a neglected wife—emerged as the film's Oscar winners.

A Columbia Picture, directed by Peter Bogdanovich. With Timothy Bottoms, Jeff Bridges, Cybill Shepherd, Ben Johnson, Cloris Leachman, Ellen Burstyn, Eileen Brennan, Clu Gulager, Sam Bottoms. 118 mins.

LAUGH, CLOWN, LAUGH (1927/28) ★

★ best title writing Joseph Farnham

The near-tragic story of a clown (Lon Chaney) and his love for a young woman he adopted as a child who, in turn, is desired by wealthy nobleman Nils Asther. One of the three films to be awarded a title-writing Oscar (the others being *The Fair Co-ed* and *Telling the World*, both written by Farnham the same year) before sound finally took over in the late 1920s.

An MGM Picture, directed by Herbert Brenon. With Lon Chaney, Bernard Siegel, Loretta Young, Cissy Fitzgerald, Nils Asther, Gwen Lee. 8 reels.

LAURA (1944) ★

★ best b/w cinematography Joseph LaShelle

Mystery thriller about a detective's obsession with the portrait of a beautiful woman (Gene Tierney) whose violent death he is investigating. Prominent among the suspects: Vincent Price, Judith Anderson, and Clifton Webb as the cynical, acid-tongued New York columnist Waldo Lydecker. The latter was aced out of the supporting award by Barry Fitzgerald, who won for his priest in *Going My Way*.

A 20th Century-Fox Picture, directed by Otto Preminger. With Gene Tierney, Dana Andrews, Clifton Webb, Vincent Price, Judith Anderson. 88 mins.

THE LAVENDER HILL MOB (1952) ★

★ best story & screenplay T. E. B. Clarke

Meek little bank clerk Alec Guinness, sculptor associate Stanley Holloway and small-time crooks Sid James and Alfie Bass steal a million pounds worth of gold bullion, melt it down and smug-

Alec Guinness and Stanley Holloway, the brains behind *The Lavender Hill Mob* (Ealing, 1951). T. E. B. Clarke won an Academy Award for his story and screenplay.

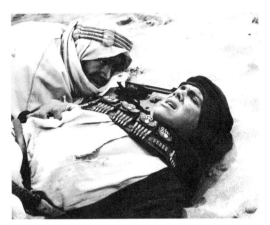

Peter O'Toole and Michel Ray in *Lawrence of Arabia* (Columbia), arguably David Lean's finest achievement and hailed as the first truly satisfying screen epic. Its Oscar tally in 1962? Seven, including awards for best film, direction and music score.

gle it out of the country in the form of miniature Eiffel Towers. First released in the UK in 1951 and the only Ealing comedy ever to be honored by the Academy. Other Oscar nominations for Ealing films: *Saraband for Dead Lovers* (art direction) and *Passport to Pimlico* (story and screenplay)—both 1949; *The Lavender Hill Mob* (Alec Guinness, for best actor) and *The Cruel Sea* (screenplay)—1953; and *The Ladykillers* (story and screenplay)—1956.

An Ealing Picture, directed by Charles Crichton. With Alec Guinness, Stanley Holloway, Sidney James, Alfie Bass, Marjorie Fielding, John Gregson, Clive Morton. 78 mins.

LAWRENCE OF ARABIA (1962) ★★★★★★★

★ best film Sam Spiegel (producer)
★ best direction David Lean
★ best color cinematography Freddie A. Young
★ best color art direction John Box & John Stoll
        set decoration Dario Simoni
★ best editing Anne Coates
★ best sounding recording John Cox
★ best original music score Maurice Jarre

The film that many called the first truly satisfying epic, combining on the one hand a spectacular look at two years of Lawrence's Arabian campaigns and on the other a deeper investigation into the complexities of Lawrence's character. Freddie Young's enormous desert vistas remain among the most beautiful ever put on the screen.

A Columbia Picture, directed by David Lean. With Peter O'Toole, Alec Guinness, Anthony Quinn, Jack Hawkins, Omar Sharif, Anthony Quayle, Claude Rains, Arthur Kennedy, Jose Ferrer, Donald Wolfit. Super Panavision 70/ Technicolor. 221 mins.

LEAVE HER TO HEAVEN (1945) ★

★ best color cinematography Leon Shamroy

Gene Tierney in her element—and in one of her best roles of the 1940s—as a femme fatale of the most demented kind, a murderously possessive wife who allows her husband's crippled brother to drown before her eyes, deliberately kills her own unborn child and finally takes poison in order to incriminate her half-sister

Jeanne Crain for the crime. Lurid but handsomely photographed.

A 20th Century-Fox Picture, directed by John M. Stahl. With Gene Tierney, Cornel Wilde, Jeanne Crain, Vincent Price, Mary Philips, Ray Collins, Gene Lockhart. Technicolor. 111 mins.

LES GIRLS (1957)   ★

★ best costume design Orry-Kelly

A smart, sophisticated film about an American hoofer (Kelly) who tours with his dancing act through Europe, falling in love with each of his dancing partners in turn—American Mitzi Gaynor, scatterbrained British dancer Kay Kendall and French beauty Taina Elg.

An MGM Picture, directed by George Cukor. With Gene Kelly, Mitzi Gaynor, Kay Kendall, Taina Elg, Jacques Bergerac, Leslie Phillips, Henry Daniell. CinemaScope/Metrocolor. 114 mins.

LET IT BE (1970)   ★

★ best original song score (music & lyrics by The Beatles)

Beatles documentary focusing on the group toward the end of their reign, providing an intimate view of the four as musical creators and showing them rehearsing, recording and performing a live rooftop concert.

A United Artists Picture, directed by Michael Lindsay-Hogg. With Paul McCartney, John Lennon, George Harrison, Ringo Starr. Technicolor. 81 mins.

A LETTER TO THREE WIVES (1949)   ★ ★

★ best direction Joseph L. Mankiewicz
★ best screenplay Joseph L. Mankiewicz

Three small-town wives receive a joint message from their best friend telling them that she has run off with one of their husbands—only she doesn't say which one. During the course of the film each wife examines her marriage in flashback, wondering if her husband is the guilty

party. An intriguing aspect of the film is that the lady who sent the letter is never seen, only heard. Her lines were spoken by Celeste Holm.

A 20th Century-Fox Picture, directed by Joseph L. Mankiewicz. With Jeanne Crain, Linda Darnell, Ann Sothern, Kirk Douglas, Paul Douglas, Barbara Lawrence, Jeffrey Lynn, Connie Gilchrist, Florence Bates, Thelma Ritter. 103 mins.

THE LIFE OF EMILE ZOLA (1937)   ★ ★ ★

★ best film Henry Blanke (producer)
★ best supporting actor Joseph Schildkraut
★ best screenplay Norman Reilly Raine, Heinz Herald & Geza Herczeg

Not really a life story, more a reconstruction of the notorious Dreyfus affair, when the famed novelist (Paul Muni) dared all the powers of France—the army, the law and the government—to stop him in his crusade to free the wrongly imprisoned Dreyfus (Joseph Schildkraut), a French captain condemned to Devil's Island because of anti-Semitism in the hierarchy of the French army. The first Warner Bros. picture to be named best of the year since the awards were started 10 years earlier. Previous Warner nominees that missed out: *Disraeli* (1929), *I Am a Fugitive From a Chain Gang (1932)*, *Forty-Second Street (1933)*, *Here Comes the Navy (1934)*, *Captain Blood* (1935), *A Midsummer Night's Dream* (1935), *Anthony Adverse* (1936), and *The Story of Louis Pasteur* (1936).

A Warner Bros. Picture, directed by William Dieterle. With Paul Muni, Gale Sondergaard, Joseph Schildkraut, Gloria Holden, Donald Crisp, Erin O'Brien-Moore, John Litel, Henry O'Neill. 116 mins.

LILI (1953)   ★

★ best music score of a drama or comedy Bronislau Kaper

Lonely little orphan girl Leslie Caron attaches herself to a traveling French carnival and is adored by a crippled puppeteer (Mel Ferrer) who can only bring himself to speak to her through the mouths of his marionettes. The song "Hi Lili, Hi Lo" was not among the five best-song nominees, but composer Bronislau Kaper received consolation for his admirable music score, which won him his only Oscar.

An MGM Picture, directed by Charles Walters. With Leslie Caron, Mel Ferrer, Jean-Pierre Aumont, Zsa Zsa Gabor, Kurt Kasznar. Technicolor. 81 mins.

LILIES OF THE FIELD (1963) ★

★ best actor Sidney Poitier

Twenty-four years after Hattie McDaniel became the first black performer to win a supporting Academy Award, Sidney Poitier won the main acting Oscar for his portrait of the footloose, light-hearted handyman Homer Smith, who, against his better judgment, agrees to help some refugee nuns build a chapel in the middle of the Arizona desert. McDaniel and Poitier remained the only black performers to win Oscars until Louis Gossett, Jr. was named best supporting actor for *An Officer and a Gentleman* in 1982. Since then, Denzel Washington, best supporting actor for *Glory* (1989), and Whoopi Goldberg, best supporting actress for *Ghost* (1990), have also earned awards.

A United Artists Picture, directed by Ralph Nelson. With Sidney Poitier, Lilia Skala, Lisa Mann, Isa Crino. 94 mins.

LIMELIGHT (1952) ★

★ best original dramatic score of 1972 Charles Chaplin, Raymond Rasch & Larry Russell

An aging, once-famous music hall comedian (Charles Chaplin) saves a young dancer (Claire Bloom) from suicide, restores her self-confidence as he nurses her back to health and finally makes a successful ballerina out of her. The film's music award is unique in that it was awarded 20 years after the picture's first release in Europe, the film being shown in the U.S. but not in Los Angeles (where a picture has to

be shown in order to qualify for Oscar consideration) until 1972.

A United Artists Picture, directed by Charles Chaplin. With Charles Chaplin, Claire Bloom, Sydney Chaplin, Nigel Bruce, Norman Lloyd, Buster Keaton, Marjorie Bennett. 143 mins.

THE LION IN WINTER (1968)

★ best actress Katharine Hepburn
★ best screenplay James Goldman
★ best original music score John Barry

Power politics in the 12th century, depicting the ruthless skirmishing among members of England's royal family—Henry II (Peter O'Toole), his wife Eleanor of Aquitaine (Katharine Hepburn) and their three scheming sons—in choosing a successor to the crown. Based on the play by Goldman and boasting the only shared best-actress award in Academy history (Barbra Streisand won the same year for her portrayal of Fanny Brice in *Funny Girl*).

An Avco-Embassy Picture, directed by Anthony Harvey. With Peter O'Toole, Katharine Hepburn, Jane Merrow, John Castle, Anthony Hopkins, Nigel Terry, Timothy Dalton. Panavision/Eastman Color. 134 mins.

THE LITTLE MERMAID (1989)

★ best original score Alan Menken
★ best original song "Under the Sea" (Alan Menken, music; Howard Ashman, lyrics)

Hans Christian Andersen tale about a mermaid princess who falls in love with a handsome young prince and then longs to become human. The first Disney adaptation of an Andersen story and the first animated feature to win musical awards since *Dumbo* in 1941. The award-winning song "Under the Sea" was voiced on the sound track by Jamaican Samuel E. Wright.

A Buena Vista release of a Walt Disney Pictures presentation. Directors: John Musker and Ron Clements. Voices by Rene Auberjonois, Christopher Daniel Barnes, Jodi Benson, Pat

Carroll, Paddi Edwards, Buddy Hackett, Jason Marin. Technicolor. 83 mins.

A LITTLE NIGHT MUSIC (1977)　★

★ best adaptation music score Jonathan Tunick

Elegant period comedy of manners set in Vienna and adapted from the Stephen Sondheim Broadway musical, which, in turn, was inspired by the Ingmar Bergman film *Smiles of a Summer Night* (1955). Elizabeth Taylor as the immoral actress-mother Desiree, Diana Rigg as an officer's wife and Lesley-Ann Down as an enchanting tease are the women who engage in the love charades; Len Cariou, Laurence Guittard and Christopher Guard are the men who accompany the frolics.

A Sascha Wien Film Production/Elliott Kastner New World Pictures Release, directed by Hal Prince. With Elizabeth Taylor, Diana Rigg, Len Cariou, Hermione Gingold, Lesley-Ann Down, Laurence Guittard, Christopher Guard. Eastman Color. 124 mins.

A LITTLE ROMANCE (1979)　★

★ best original score Georges Delerue

Lightweight adventure romance centering on two children—one a working-class French boy, the other the daughter of a rich American—who travel to Venice in order to experience eternal love beneath the famed Bridge of Sighs. Elderly con man Laurence Olivier and the charming music of Georges Delerue help them on their way.

An Orion Pictures Release, directed by George Roy Hill. With Laurence Olivier, Diane Lane, Thelonious Bernard, Arthur Hill, Sally Kellerman, Broderick Crawford, David Dukes. Technicolor. 108 mins.

LITTLE WOMEN (1932/33)　★

★ best writing: adaptation Sarah Y. Mason & Victor Heerman

Louisa May Alcott's gentle classic about four sisters growing to womanhood during the Civil War in the small Massachusetts town of Concord. A notable adaptation by Mason and Heerman won the Academy Award; George Cukor and the picture itself were both among the nominees. Katharine Hepburn starred as Jo, Joan Bennett as Amy, Frances Dee as Meg and Jean Parker as Beth.

An RKO Picture, directed by George Cukor. With Katharine Hepburn, Joan Bennett, Paul Lukas, Edna May Oliver, Jean Parker, Frances Dee, Henry Stephenson, Douglass Montgomery. 107 mins.

LITTLE WOMEN (1949)　★

★ best color art direction Cedric Gibbons & Paul Groesse
　　　　　　　set decoration Edwin B. Willis & Jack D. Moore

The same story as the 1932/33 version, retold less imaginatively but more lushly in color by MGM. This time June Allyson is the tomboyish Jo, Elizabeth Taylor is Amy, Janet Leigh Meg, and Margaret O'Brien the young Beth.

An MGM Picture, directed by Mervyn LeRoy. With June Allyson, Peter Lawford, Margaret O'Brien, Elizabeth Taylor, Janet Leigh, Rossano Brazzi, Mary Astor, Lucile Watson, C. Aubrey Smith. Technicolor. 121 mins.

LIVES OF A BENGAL LANCER (1935)　★

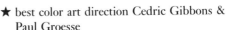

★ best assistant direction Clem Beauchamp & Paul Wing

High adventure on the northwest frontier in India, with Gary Cooper, Franchot Tone and Richard Cromwell as three British officers performing heroic feats of valor against treacherous border tribes on the Khyber Pass. From the novel by Francis Yeats Brown.

A Paramount Picture, directed by Henry Hathaway. With Gary Cooper, Franchot Tone,

Richard Cromwell, Sir Guy Standing, C. Aubrey Smith, Monte Blue. 111 mins.

LOGAN'S RUN (1976) ★

★ best special visual effects* L. B. Abbott, Glen Robinson & Matthew Yuricich

Life in the 23rd century, when human life ends at 30 unless you become a "runner" and escape from the sealed-off existence in a huge domed city where everything is pleasurable until the deadly age of no return. Michael York and Jenny Agutter are featured as the two who try to escape the super-mechanization.

An MGM Picture, directed by Michael Anderson. With Michael York, Richard Jordan, Jenny Agutter, Roscoe Lee Browne, Farrah Fawcett-Majors, Michael Anderson, Jr., Peter Ustinov. Todd-AO 35/Metrocolor. 118 mins.

THE LONGEST DAY (1962) ★★

★ best b/w cinematography Jean Bourgoin & Walter Wottitz

The Longest Day (20th Century-Fox, 1962), Darryl F. Zanuck's retelling of the Allied landings in Normandy on June 6, 1944. The film included 43 international stars in its cast and won awards for cinematography and special effects.

---

* *Note:* The Oscar for best special visual effects was a special achievement award.

★ best special effects Robert MacDonald: visual; Jacques Maumont: audible

The Allied landings in Normandy on June 6, 1944, retold by Darryl F. Zanuck on a grand scale and with an international all-star cast. Financially one of the most successful war movies ever made, it was high up in the Oscar nomination stakes but lost out in the major categories to the year's multi-award winner, *Lawrence of Arabia*.

A 20th Century-Fox Picture, directed by Ken Annakin, Andrew Marton, Bernard Wicki. With John Wayne, Robert Mitchum, Henry Fonda, Robert Ryan, Rod Steiger, Richard Burton, Kenneth More, Peter Lawford, Richard Todd, Curt Jurgens, Robert Wagner, Richard Beymer. CinemaScope. 180 mins.

LOST HORIZON (1937) ★★

★ best art direction Stephen Goosson
★ best editing Gene Milford & Gene Havlick

James Hilton fantasy with Ronald Colman as a young English diplomat who, along with a group of other passengers, survives a plane crash and stumbles across an idyllic Utopian community hidden away in the Himalayas in Tibet. Art director Goosson won his Oscar for his ingenious Shangri La set designs.

A Columbia Picture, directed by Frank Capra. With Ronald Colman, Jane Wyatt, Margo, Joan Howard, Edward Everett Horton, Isabel Jewell, H. B. Warner, Sam Jaffe. 125 mins.

THE LOST WEEKEND (1945) ★★★★

★ best film Charles Brackett (producer)
★ best direction Billy Wilder
★ best actor Ray Milland
★ best screenplay Billy Wilder & Charles Brackett

Three harrowing days in the life of a failed novelist (Ray Milland) driven to the verge of suicide by his addiction to drink. A history-making picture in two ways, both as the first film to treat alcoholism with any seriousness and as the first so-called message picture to win the top award.

A Paramount Picture, directed by Billy Wilder. With Ray Milland, Jane Wyman, Philip Terry, Howard da Silva, Doris Dowling, Frank Faylen. 102 mins.

LOVE IS A MANY SPLENDORED THING (1955)   ★ ★ ★

- ★ best color costume design Charles LeMaire
- ★ best music score of a drama or comedy Alfred Newman
- ★ best song "Love Is a Many Splendored Thing" (Sammy Fain, music; Paul Francis Webster, lyrics)

Tragic love affair between an unhappily married foreign correspondent (William Holden) and a beautiful Eurasian doctor (Jennifer Jones) working in a Hong Kong hospital at the time of the Korean War. Lush backgrounds in CinemaScope and a title love song helped earn the film millions.

A 20th Century-Fox Picture, directed by Henry King. With William Holden, Jennifer Jones, Torin Thatcher, Isobel Elsom, Murray Matheson, Virginia Gregg. CinemaScope. DeLuxe Color. 102 mins.

LOVE ME OR LEAVE ME (1955)   ★

- ★ best motion picture story Daniel Fuchs

Real-life drama of Prohibition days, covering the stormy marriage between 1920s torch singer Ruth Etting (Doris Day) and tough little racketeer Martin Snyder (James Cagney). Vintage numbers from Miss Day and a crackerjack performance from Cagney, who here earned the last of his three Oscar nominations for best actor. Previously he had won for *Yankee Doodle Dandy* (1942) and been nominated for *Angels with Dirty Faces* (1938).

An MGM Picture, directed by Charles Vidor. With Doris Day, James Cagney, Cameron Mitchell, Robert Keith, Tom Tully, Harry Bellaver. CinemaScope/Eastman Color. 122 mins.

LOVERS AND OTHER STRANGERS (1970)   ★

- ★ best song "For All We Know" (Fred Karlin, music; Robb Wilson & Arthur James, lyrics)

Comedy about a young couple who decide to take the plunge and get married after 18 months of living together, and the subsequent repercussions among friends and relatives, who find at the reception that they have plenty of problems of their own to deal with.

A Cinerama Distribution-ABC Picture, directed by Cy Howard. With Gig Young, Bonnie Bedelia, Beatrice Arthur, Michael Brandon, Richard Castellano. Metrocolor. 104 mins.

LOVE STORY (1970)   ★

- ★ best original music score Francis Lai

Simple love story between two college students, Harvard boy Ryan O'Neal and Radcliffe girl Ali MacGraw, which ends in tragedy with the girl's sudden death and which somehow caught the public mood of the early 1970s, earning $50 million at the box office. At Oscar time only Francis Lai's lush music score was recognized.

A Paramount Picture, directed by Arthur Hiller. With Ali MacGraw, Ryan O'Neal, John Marley, Ray Milland, Russell Nype, Katherine Balfour. Movielab Color. 100 mins.

LUST FOR LIFE (1956)   ★

- ★ best supporting actor Anthony Quinn

The turbulent life of tormented artist Vincent Van Gogh (Kirk Douglas), from his early manhood and his endeavors to do religious work to his final anguished years as a painter of genius. Anthony Quinn's Gauguin was recognized by the Academy, but the year's best-actor award went to Yul Brynner for a repeat of his Broadway performance in *The King and I*. Douglas had to be content with a nomination and the award of the New York Film Critics Circle, who recognized the quality of his extraordinary performance.

An MGM Picture, directed by Vincente Minnelli. With Kirk Douglas, Anthony Quinn, James Donald, Pamela Brown, Everett Sloane, Niall MacGinnis, Noel Purcell, Henry Daniell. CinemaScope/Metrocolor. 122 mins.

M

MADAME ROSA (1977)   ★

★ best foreign language film France

The moving relationship between an aging, ailing Jewish woman who cares for the children of prostitutes, and one of her charges, a young Arab boy. Set mainly in the milieu of prostitutes and pimps in the Arab and Jewish working-class section of Paris and starring Simone Signoret as Madame Rosa, herself a former prostitute and concentration camp victim.

A Lira Films Production, directed by Moshe Mizrahi. With Simone Signoret, Claude Dauphin, Samy Ben Youb, Gabriel Jabbour, Michal Bat Adam, Costa Gavras, Stella Anicette. Eastman-Color. 105 mins.

A MAN AND A WOMAN (1966)   ★ ★

★ best foreign language film France
★ best story & screenplay Claude Lelouch, story; Pierre Uytterhoeven & Claude Lelouch, screenplay

Romantic and very lush treatment of a simple love affair between two glamorous people—he a racing driver, she a script girl—who have both lost their partners in death and who first meet while visiting their respective children at a school in Deauville. The famous Francis Lai music score was not even among the year's five nominees.

A Les Films 13 Production, directed by Claude Lelouch. With Anouk Aimee, Jean-Louis Trintignant, Pierre Barouh, Valerie Lagrange, Simone Paris. Eastman Color. 102 mins.

A MAN FOR ALL SEASONS (1966)   ★ ★ ★ ★ ★ ★

★ best film Fred Zinnemann (producer)
★ best direction Fred Zinnemann
★ best actor Paul Scofield
★ best screenplay Robert Bolt
★ best color cinematography Ted Moore
★ best color costume design Elizabeth Haffenden & Joan Bridge

The battle of wills between Sir Thomas More (Paul Scofield), Chancellor of England and one of the most widely respected Catholics in Europe, and the ebullient Henry VIII (Robert Shaw), who in 1528 was seeking a divorce from Catherine of Aragon in order to marry Anne Boleyn. Adapted by Robert Bolt from his own stage play.

A Columbia Picture, directed by Fred Zinnemann. With Paul Scofield, Wendy Hiller, Leo McKern, Robert Shaw, Orson Welles, Susannah York, Nigel Davenport, John Hurt. Technicolor. 120 mins.

MANHATTAN MELODRAMA (1934)   ★

★ best original story Arthur Caesar

Crime melodrama most famous for being the last film Public Enemy Number One, John Dillinger, saw just prior to his death outside a Chicago movie house. William Powell is featured as a D.A. who has to prosecute his boyhood friend, gangster Clark Gable. Myrna Loy is the latter's mistress.

An MGM Picture, directed by W. S. Van Dyke. With Clark Gable, William Powell, Myrna Loy, Leo Carrillo, Nat Pendleton. 93 mins.

THE MAN WHO KNEW TOO MUCH (1956)   ★

★ best song "Que Sera, Sera" (Ray Evans & Jay Livingston, music & lyrics)

Hitchcock's remake of his British classic of 20 years earlier, with James Stewart and Doris Day as two American tourists whose son is kidnapped while they are vacationing in Morocco and who become involved in a plot to assassinate a foreign political leader in London. Despite Hitch's genius, it is for the song "Que Sera, Sera" that the film stands firmly in the Oscar record books.

A Paramount Picture, directed by Alfred Hitchcock. With James Stewart, Doris Day, Daniel Gelin, Bernard Miles, Brenda de Banzie. Technicolor/Vista Vision. 119 mins.

MARIE-LOUISE (1945) ★

★ best original screenplay Richard Schweizer

Simply told story from Switzerland about a group of French children, and one girl in particular, who seek refuge for a few months from the bombs of war-torn France in the peace of neutral Switzerland. The first European movie to win an award in one of the major Oscar categories.

Praesens–Films Ltd, Zurich, directed by Leopold Lindtberg. With Josiane, Heinrich Gretler, Margrit Winter, Anne-Marie Blane, Armin Schweizer. 93 mins.

MAROONED (1969) ★

★ best special visual effects Robbie Robinson

Modern science-fact drama about three American astronauts—Richard Crenna, James Franciscus, Gene Hackman—who are launched into space to link up with an orbiting space laboratory and then find that, through technical malfunctions, the ground crew is unable to bring them back to earth.

A Columbia Picture, directed by John Sturges. With Gregory Peck, Richard Crenna, David Janssen, James Franciscus, Gene Hackman, Lee Grant. Panavision 70/Technicolor. 133 mins.

MARTY (1955)

★ best film Harold Hecht (producer)
★ best direction Delbert Mann
★ best actor Ernest Borgnine
★ best screenplay Paddy Chayefsky

The "sleeper" best-picture winner of the 1950s, an adaptation of Paddy Chayefsky's TV drama about a fat, ugly butcher (Ernest Borgnine) from the Bronx who, after despairing of ever getting married, at last finds romance with a homely schoolteacher (Betsy Blair) who has been stood up at a dance. Also the Grand Prize winner at Cannes, it defeated such heavyweight best-picture contenders as *Picnic*, *The Rose Tattoo* and *Mister Roberts*.

A United Artists Picture, directed by Delbert Mann. With Ernest Borgnine, Betsy Blair, Esther Minciotti, Augusta Ciolli, Joe Mantell, Karen Steele, Jerry Paris. 99 mins.

MARY POPPINS (1964)

★ best actress Julie Andrews
★ best editing Cotton Warburton
★ best visual effects Peter Ellenshaw, Hamilton Luske, Eustace Lycett
★ best original music score Richard M. & Robert B. Sherman
★ best song "Chim Chim Cher-ee" (Richard M. & Robert B. Sherman, music & lyrics)

Julie Andrews "descending" to movie stardom with umbrella and carpetbag as P. L. Travers' no-nonsense nanny and providing two London children with a whole series of magical adventures. The irony of Julie Andrews' award was that in the same year, Warners had turned her down for the part of Eliza Doolittle in *My Fair Lady* (which she had played on stage) and opted instead for Audrey Hepburn, who didn't even figure in 1964's list of nominees. Until *Beauty and the Beast* some 27 years later, *Mary Poppins* remained the only Disney film ever to be nominated for best picture.

A Walt Disney Picture, directed by Robert Stevenson. With Julie Andrews, Dick Van Dyke, David Tomlinson, Glynis Johns, Hermione Baddeley, Karen Dotrice, Matthew Garber, Elsa Lanchester, Ed Wynn, Jane Darwell. Technicolor. 140 mins.

M*A*S*H (1970)   ★

★ best screenplay Ring Lardner, Jr.

Black comedy, set in a mobile hospital unit during the Korean War, which exposes through humor the brutal effects of war itself. Elliott Gould and Donald Sutherland star as the two irreverent soldier surgeons who share a liking for martinis and nurses and who don't give a damn for red tape or authority.

A 20th Century-Fox Picture, directed by Robert Altman. With Donald Sutherland, Elliott Gould, Tom Skerritt, Sally Kellerman, Robert Duvall, Jo Ann Pflug. Panavision/DeLuxe Color. 116 mins.

MASK (1985)   ★

★ best makeup Michael Westmore & Zoltan Elek

The struggles of an intelligent teenage boy suffering from a rare and disfiguring bone disease, and also those of his promiscuous mother, hooked on drugs but continually instilling a sense of confidence in her son. Based on the true story of Rocky Dennis and movingly played by Eric Stoltz, whose features, apart from his eyes, were entirely hidden behind the Oscar-winning makeup. For his work on the film Michael became the first of the famous Westmore family to win an Academy Award. The category was not in existence when Perc, Frank, Wally, Bud and the others were working in Hollywood during the Golden Age.

A Universal Picture, directed by Peter Bogdanovich. With Cher, Sam Elliott, Eric Stoltz, Estelle Getty, Richard Dysart, Laura Dern, Micole Mercurio, Harry Carey, Jr., Dennis Burkley. Technicolor. 120 mins.

MEDITERRANEO (1991)   ★

★ best foreign language film* Italy

Eight Italian soldiers, believed dead when their ship is destroyed and their radio broken, have to adapt to a new and very appealing way of life on a remote, strategically unimportant Greek island during World War II. The third and final installment of Gabriele Salvatores' road picture trilogy begun with *Marrakesh Express* (1989) and *Turné* (1990). Seductive locations, all of them shot on the tucked-away island of Kastellorizo in the Dodecanese.

A Pentafilm and AMA Film Production, directed by Gabriele Salvatores. With Diego Abatantuono, Claudio Bigagli, Giuseppe Cederna, Claudio Bisio, Gigio Alberti, Ugo Conti, Vanna Barba. Telecolor. 105 mins.

MELVIN AND HOWARD (1980)   ★ ★

★ best supporting actress Mary Steenburgen
★ best original screenplay Bo Goldman

Pungent fable of the elusive American dream, with Paul LeMat as perpetual "loser" Melvin Dummar and Jason Robards as the eccentric Howard Hughes, who leaves him $156 million in a Mormon will. Sometimes reminiscent of the Preston Sturges satires of the early 1940s; Mary Steenburgen won her Oscar for her performance as the unlucky Melvin's two-time bride and divorcee.

---

* *Note:* The award for *Mediterraneo* brought Italy's foreign language wins to nine, a record equaled by France a year later when *Indochine* (1992) was named best foreign film of the year. Previous Italian winners of the foreign language film award: *La Strada (1956)*, *The Nights of Cabíria* (1957), *8½ (1963)*, *Yesterday, Today and Tomorrow* (1964), *Investigation of a Citizen Above Suspicion* (1970), *The Garden of the Finzi-Continis* (1971), *Amarcord* (1974), and *Cinema Paradiso* (1989).

Mary Steenburgen, best supporting actress of 1980 for her performance in *Melvin and Howard* (Universal).

A Universal Picture, directed by Jonathan Demme. With Paul LeMat, Jason Robards, Mary Steenburgen, Jack Kehoe, Michael J. Pollard, Pamela Reed. Technicolor. 93 mins.

MEPHISTO (1981)   ★

★ best foreign language film Hungary

Hungarian film tracing the rise of an ambitious German actor who marries the daughter of a pro-Nazi figure, thrives when the Nazis come to power, then subverts classic figures (notably Mephisto in Goethe's *Faust*) to the Nazi outlook. A vivid portrait of moral corruption in a malignant society; named as best foreign film of 1981 over Wajda's *Man of Iron*.

Mafilm (Studio Objektiy), in association with Manfred Durniok Productions. Directed by Istvan Szabo. With Klaus Maria Brandauer, Ildiko Bansagi, Krystyna Janda, Rolf Hoppe, Gyorgy Cserhalmi, Peter Andorai. Eastman Color. 144 mins.

THE MERRY WIDOW (1934)   ★

★ best art direction Cedric Gibbons & Frederic Hope

Lubitsch version of the Lehar operetta, set in romantic Paris, with Chevalier as the roguish Prince Danilo and Jeanette MacDonald as the beautiful rich widow of the title. Also around: George Barbier as the cuckolded King Achmed, Una Merkel as his wife and Edward Everett Horton as the hapless ambassador.

An MGM Picture, directed by Ernst Lubitsch. With Maurice Chevalier. Jeanette MacDonald, Edward Everett Horton, Una Merkel. 110 mins.

MIDNIGHT COWBOY (1969)   ★★★

★ best film Jerome Hellman (producer)
★ best direction John Schlesinger
★ best screenplay Waldo Salt

Two young drifters—Jon Voight as a would-be stud in leather cowboy gear and Dustin Hoffman as a tubercular down-and-outer—come gradually to depend on each other as they struggle to exist in the seamy, unfriendly back streets of New York. The best-film winner of its particular year, although *Butch Cassidy and the Sundance Kid* with four wins against *Cowboy's* three was the year's biggest overall winner in terms of Oscars.

A United Artists Picture, directed by John Schlesinger. With Jon Voight, Dustin Hoffman, Sylvia Miles, Brenda Vaccaro, John McGiver, Barnard Hughes, Ruth White. DeLuxe Color. 113 mins.

MIDNIGHT EXPRESS (1978)   ★★

★ best screenplay Oliver Stone
★ best music score Giorgio Moroder

An indictment of the Turkish judicial system detailing the real-life case of Billy Hayes, who served five years in the notorious Sagamilcar prison after being arrested with two kilos of hashish in his possession. Brad Davis is featured as Hayes; John Hurt earned a supporting actor nomination for his portrait of a dissipated fellow prisoner.

John Hurt and Brad Davis in *Midnight Express* (Columbia), winner of awards for best screenplay and music score in 1978.

A Casablanca Filmworks (UK) Production for Columbia, directed by Alan Parker. With Brad Davis, Randy Quaid, John Hurt, Irene Miracle, Bo Hopkins, Paolo Bonacelli. Eastman Color. 121 mins.

A MIDSUMMER NIGHT'S DREAM (1935)   ★ ★

★ best cinematography Hal Mohr
★ best editing Ralph Dawson

Shakespeare's woodland comedy-fantasy, cut to ribbons text-wise, but retaining as compensations handsome sets and costumes as well as music by Mendelssohn. James Cagney is Bottom, Dick Powell Lysander, Victor Jory a majestic Oberon, the 11-year-old Mickey Rooney a mischievous Puck and Olivia de Havilland, in her first film, a lovely Hermia.

A Warner Bros. Picture, directed by William Dieterle and Max Reinhardt. With James Cagney, Dick Powell, Joe E. Brown, Jean Muir, Hugh Herbert, Ian Hunter, Frank McHugh, Victor Jory, Olivia de Havilland, Mickey Rooney. 132 mins.

MIGHTY JOE YOUNG (1949)   ★

★ best special effects Willis O'Brien

A sort of post-war version of *King Kong* (1933), about a 10-foot giant ape named Joe who is found in Africa and taken to Hollywood to appear in a nightclub act. The special effects award to Willis O'Brien compensated somewhat for his not receiving anything for his brilliant efforts on *King Kong*, the special effects category not having been in existence at the time of that film's release.

An RKO Picture, directed by Ernest B. Schoedsack. With Terry Moore, Ben Johnson, Robert Armstrong, Frank McHugh, Douglas Fowley. 93 mins.

THE MILAGRO BEANFIELD WAR (1988)   ★

★ best original score Dave Grusin

Well-intentioned fable directed by Robert Redford about the clash between New Mexican farmers and the brash outside developers who want to take over their land and turn it into a golf course. Capra-esque in its attitudes, with much charm and whimsy and some stunningly photographed southwestern vistas but most notable for Dave Grusin's lyrical score, which earned him a deserved Academy Award. Grusin's previous nominations: *Heaven Can Wait* (1978), *The Champ* (1979) and *On Golden Pond* (1981). Nominations since: *The Fabulous Baker Boys* (1989) and *Havana* (1990).

A Universal Picture, directed by Robert Redford. With Ruben Blades, Richard Bradford, Sonia Braga, Julie Carmen, James Gammon, Melanie Griffith, John Heard, Carlos Riquelme, Christopher Walken. MGM Color. 118 mins.

MILDRED PIERCE (1945)   ★

★ best actress Joan Crawford

The story of a self-sacrificing mother (Crawford) who determines to give her selfish little monster of a daughter all the opportunities and luxuries she never had herself. Zachary Scott costars as a wealthy playboy, Jack Carson as an unscrupulous real estate agent and Eve Arden as a wisecracking pal. Crawford's edgy, tear-stained performance won her her only Academy Award; Ann Blyth's as the daughter her only nomination.

A Warner Bros. Picture, directed by Michael Curtiz. With Joan Crawford, Jack Carson, Zachary Scott, Eve Arden, Ann Blyth, Bruce Bennett, George Tobias, Lee Patrick, Moroni Olsen. 113 mins.

MIN AND BILL (1930/31) ★

★ best actress Marie Dressler

Sixty-one-year-old Marie Dressler as the hard-boiled proprietress of a waterfront hotel who brings up a young girl deserted by her mother in infancy and is then forced to kill the dissolute mother when, years later, she tries to reclaim the child. The film proved the biggest box-office hit of the year and was the peak of Dressler's career. She died just four years later.

An MGM Picture, directed by George Hill. With Marie Dressler, Wallace Beery, Dorothy Jordan, Marjorie Rambeau, Donald Dillaway, DeWitt Jennings. 69 mins.

MIRACLE ON 34TH STREET (1947) ★★★

★ best supporting actor Edmund Gwenn
★ best screenplay George Seaton
★ best original story Valentine Davies

Gentle department store Santa (Edmund Gwenn), employed by Macy's in New York for the Christmas season, encounters among his young visitors an unbelieving child (Natalie Wood) and finds that he has to prove that he really is Santa Claus. The first of George Seaton's two writing Oscars, the second being earned for his script for *The Country Girl* (1954).

A 20th Century-Fox Picture, directed by George Seaton. With Maureen O'Hara, John Payne, Edmund Gwenn, Gene Lockhart, Natalie Wood, Porter Hall, William Frawley, Jerome Cowan. 96 mins.

A young Natalie Wood tries out Santa's beard in the 1947 comedy *Miracle on 34th Street* (20th Century-Fox). Playing Santa? The year's supporting actor winner, Edmund Gwenn.

THE MIRACLE WORKER (1962) ★★

★ best actress Anne Bancroft
★ best supporting actress Patty Duke

The story of how blind deaf-mute Helen Keller (Patty Duke), who seemed little more than a savage animal as a child, was gradually helped to develop into a young woman of intelligence and intellect by Annie Sullivan (Anne Bancroft), a dedicated young teacher from Boston. A *tour de force* of power acting by both Bancroft and Duke. From the play by William Gibson.

A United Artists Picture, directed by Arthur Penn. With Anne Bancroft, Patty Duke, Victor Jory, Inga Swenson, Andrew Prince, Kathleen Comegys. 106 mins.

MISERY (1990) ★

★ best actress Kathy Bates

A popular novelist (James Caan) finds his life and sanity threatened when he is rescued from a car crash by his self-proclaimed greatest fan–psychotic ex-nurse Kathy Bates—and then held prisoner until he brings back to life the romantic heroine he has just disposed of in his latest novel. To make sure he complies with her wishes, Bates smashes both of his ankles with a hammer. Bette Midler and Warren Beatty were originally slated for the leading roles. Adapted by William Goldman from the novel by Stephen King.

Castle Rock Entertainment, in association with Nelson Entertainment. Directed by Rob Reiner. With James Caan, Kathy Bates, Richard Farnsworth, Frances Sternhagen, Lauren Bacall, Graham Jarvis, Jerry Potter, Tom Brunelle. Color: CFI. 107 mins.

MISSING (1982)   ★

★ best screenplay Costa-Gavras & Donald Stewart

A New York businessman (Jack Lemmon) journeys to Chile to search for his son, a politically active journalist who disappeared in Santiago during the fall of the Allende government in September 1973. A no-holds-barred political thriller based on the true experiences of Ed Horman, who searched in vain for his son in the hospitals, morgues and prison stadiums and discovered that American intelligence may well have been behind the coup that led to the fall of the country's liberal regime. Filmed and co-written by Costa-Gavras, who directed the Award-winning *Z* some 13 years earlier.

A Universal Picture, directed by Costa-Gavras. With Jack Lemmon, Sissy Spacek, Melanie Mayron, John Shea, Charles Cioffi, David Clennon, Richard Venture, Jerry Hardin. Technicolor. 122 mins.

THE MISSION (1986)   ★

★ best cinematography Chris Menges

A priest (Jeremy Irons) and a mercenary-turned-Jesuit (Robert De Niro) defend a thriving 18th-century mission in the jungles of Brazil against avaricious merchants and political factions within the Church itself. Ambitious, thought-provoking David Puttnam epic that earned cameraman

Robert De Niro, mercenary turned priest in *The Mission* (Enigma/Goldcrest/Warner Bros.), winner of the cinematography award in 1986.

Chris Menges his second award for cinematography in three years. He won his first Oscar for his work on another Puttnam film, *The Killing Fields*, in 1984.

A Goldcrest Picture/Warner Bros. Directed by Roland Joffe. With Robert De Niro, Jeremy Irons, Ray McAnally, Aidan Quinn, Cherie Lunghi, Ronald Pickup, Liam Neeson. Scope/Eastman Color. 125 mins.

MISSISSIPPI BURNING (1988)   ★

★ best cinematography Peter Biziou

True and terrifying tale of two FBI agents (Gene Hackman and William Dafoe) sent down south by Washington to investigate the murder of three civil rights workers—two white and one black—in Mississippi in 1964. Powerful direction from Alan Parker, who vividly creates the racism and terrorism of the Ku Klux Klan;

Gene Hackman and Willem Dafoe in Alan Parker's *Mississippi Burning* (Orion, 1988). Cinematographer Peter Biziou was named best of the year for his work on the picture.

a notable performance by Gene Hackman as the world-weary agent who is only too well aware that desperate poverty can lead to racial hatred.

An Orion Picture, directed by Alan Parker. With Gene Hackman, Willem Dafoe, Frances McDormand, Brad Dourif, R. Lee Ermey, Gailard Sartain, Stephen Tobolowsky, Michael Rooker, Pruitt Taylor Vince. Color: DuArt; prints by DeLuxe. 127 mins.

MISTER ROBERTS (1955)   ★

★ best supporting actor Jack Lemmon

Henry Fonda repeating his famous stage role as the restless Lieutenant Roberts, who finds himself stuck aboard a "cargo bucket" during World War II and longs to be transferred to the fighting zone. James Cagney stars as his eccentric captain, William Powell as the philosophical ship's doctor, and the young Oscar-winning Jack Lemmon as the opportunistic Ensign Pulver.

A Warner Bros. Picture, directed by John Ford and Mervyn LeRoy. With Henry Fonda, James Cagney, William Powell, Jack Lemmon, Betsy Palmer, Ward Bond, Phil Carey, Martin Milner. CinemaScope/Warner Color. 123 mins.

MON ONCLE (1958)

★ best foreign language film France/Italy

The second of Jacques Tati's Monsieur Hulot films, with the accident-prone humanitarian constantly at odds with the mechanized society of today, particularly with his sister's ultramodern house with all its gadgets, its electronic garage and its fully mechanized kitchen.

A Specta Films/Gray Film/Alter Film (Paris) and Film del Centauro (Rome) Production, directed by Jacques Tati. With Jacques Tati, Jean-Pierre Zola, Alain Becourt, Lucien Fregis, Dominique Marie. Eastman Color. 116 mins.

MOONSTRUCK (1987)

★ best actress Cher
★ best supporting actress Olympia Dukakis
★ best original screenplay John Patrick Shanley

Attractive Brooklyn widow Cher opts for second best when she agrees to marry an older man for security, but quickly has other ideas when she meets—and is passionately drawn to—his misfit younger brother. A warm-hearted portrait of the trials and tribulations of Italian-American family life, with any number of exquisite performances (notably from Vincent Gardenia as Cher's philandering father and

A proposal, but from the wrong man. Cher and Danny Aiello in Norman Jewison's romantic comedy *Moonstruck* (MGM, 1987). Cher was named best actress of the year for her role as attractive widow Loretta Castorini.

Olympia Dukakis as her long-suffering mother) and a bonus on the sound track with Dean Martin singing "That's Amore!"

An MGM Picture, directed by Norman Jewison. With Cher, Nicolas Cage, Vincent Gardenia, Olympia Dukakis, Danny Aiello, Julie Bovasso, John Mahoney, Louis Guss, Feodor Chaliapin, Anita Gillette. Technicolor & Medallion. 102 mins.

THE MORE THE MERRIER (1943)   ★

★ best supporting actor Charles Coburn

George Stevens' comedy about the housing shortage in wartime Washington, with Jean Arthur as a government employee subletting half of her flat to elderly industrialist Charles Coburn, who, in turn, sublets half of his half to homeless aircraft technician Joel McCrea.

A Columbia Picture, directed by George Stevens. With Jean Arthur, Joel McCrea, Charles Coburn, Richard Gaines, Bruce Bennett, Clyde Fillmore. 104 mins.

MORNING GLORY (1932/33)   ★

★ best actress Katharine Hepburn

Adaptation of Zoe Akin's play about a stage-struck girl (Hepburn) from Vermont who struggles to become a great Broadway actress and finally gets her chance when temperamental star Mary Duncan walks out on opening night. Douglas Fairbanks, Jr. as a young playwright, Adolphe Menjou as a theatrical manager, and C. Aubrey Smith as a veteran actor, co-star. This was the first of Katharine Hepburn's four Oscar wins. She was 26 when she won the award. Her subsequent Oscars were won more than 30 years later for *Guess Who's Coming To Dinner* (1967), *The Lion in Winter* (1968) and *On Golden Pond* (1981).

An RKO Picture, directed by Lowell Sherman. With Katharine Hepburn, Douglas Fairbanks, Jr., Adolphe Menjou, Mary Duncan, C. Aubrey Smith, Don Alvarado. 74 mins.

MOSCOW DOES NOT BELIEVE IN TEARS (1980)   ★

★ best foreign language film USSR

A surprise winner of the foreign language award, recounting the experiences of three Russian country girls when they arrive in Moscow and seek out challenging new lives. An engaging and often forthright Russian comedy spanning a period of 20 years, that won out over such favored contenders as Truffaut's *The Last Metro* and Kurosawa's *Kagemusha*.

A Mosfilm Production, directed by Vladimir Menshov. With Vera Alentova, Alexei Batalov, Irina Murawjova, Raissa Rjasanova, Juri Wassiliev. Sovcolor. 145 mins.

MOTHER WORE TIGHTS (1947)   ★

★ best scoring of a musical Alfred Newman

Archetypal Fox movie of the late 1940s with vaudeville couple Betty Grable and Dan Dailey suddenly running into family trouble when the eldest of their two daughters (Mona Freeman) realizes she lacks social standing at finishing school.

A 20th Century-Fox Picture, directed by Walter Lang. With Betty Grable, Dan Dailey, Mona Freeman, Connie Marshall, Vanessa Brown, Robert Arthur, Sara Allgood, William Frawley. Technicolor. 107 mins.

MOULIN ROUGE (1952)   ★ ★

★ best color art direction Paul Sheriff
set decoration Marcel Vertes
★ best color costume design Marcel Vertes

Biography of the crippled French painter Toulouse-Lautrec (Jose Ferrer), whose stunted growth as a child led to his living a life of despair and loneliness among the whores and entertainers of old Montmartre. The brilliant use of color and design led to two Oscar awards, although cameraman Oswald Morris was undeservedly not among the winning names. Top color cinematographers of 1952 were Winton C. Hoch and Archie Stout for *The Quiet Man*.

A Romulus Films Production, directed by John Huston. With Jose Ferrer, Colette Marchand, Suzanne Flon, Zsa Zsa Gabor, Katherine Kath, Claude Nollier, Muriel Smith. Technicolor. 123 mins.

MR. DEEDS GOES TO TOWN (1936)   ★

★ best direction Frank Capra

Gary Cooper as Longfellow Deeds, a tuba-playing country boy who inherits a million dollars and then gives it all away when he discovers that his big city "associates" are crooks and swindlers. Capra won the direction award for the second time in three years, but the film, although nominated, lost out somewhat surprisingly to *The Great Ziegfeld* as the best of the year.

A Columbia Picture, directed by Frank Capra. With Gary Cooper, Jean Arthur, George Bancroft, Lionel Stander, Douglas Dumbrille, Raymond Walburn, H. B. Warner. 115 mins.

MRS. MINIVER (1942)

★ best film Sidney Franklin (producer)
★ best direction William Wyler
★ best actress Greer Garson
★ best supporting actress Teresa Wright
★ best screenplay Arthur Wimperis, George Froeschel, James Hilton & Claudine West
★ best b/w cinematography Joseph Ruttenberg

Greer Garson and Walter Pidgeon as the mother and father of a supposedly typical English family struggling against the Blitz and surviving through Dunkirk in the darkest days of World War II. Teresa Wright co-starred as the Minivers' daughter-in-law, Dame May Whitty as the lady of the manor. A propaganda piece of its time that took six Oscars, its nearest contender, *Yankee Doodle Dandy*, winning three awards. Other best-picture nominees of that

One of the reasons the Germans lost—Walter Pidgeon and Greer Garson in William Wyler's *Mrs. Miniver* (MGM), best picture of 1942.

year included *The Magnificent Ambersons*, *Wake Island*, *King's Row*, *Random Harvest* and *Talk of the Town*.

An MGM Picture, directed by William Wyler. With Greer Garson, Walter Pidgeon, Teresa Wright, Dame May Whitty, Henry Travers, Reginald Owen, Henry Wilcoxon, Richard Ney. 134 mins.

MR. SMITH GOES TO WASHINGTON (1939)   ★

★ best original story Lewis R. Foster

Not quite the same story as *Mr. Deeds Goes to Town* (1936) but with the same theme—the people against big business and politics—as naive Wisconsin senator James Stewart, determined to do his best for his state, comes face to face with Washington graft and corruption and eventually exposes it in an idealistic speech to the Senate. The film would have been a surefire winner of top awards in most years, but it was unlucky enough to be released the same year as *Gone With the Wind* and had to be content with a solitary best-story Oscar.

A Columbia Picture, directed by Frank Capra. With James Stewart, Jean Arthur, Claude Rains, Edward Arnold, Guy Kibbee, Thomas Mitchell, Eugene Pallette. 126 mins.

MURDER ON THE ORIENT EXPRESS (1974)   ★

★ best supporting actress Ingrid Bergman*

Who killed nasty American millionaire Richard Widmark on the train journey between Istanbul and Paris? English army officer Sean Connery; the dead man's personal assistant, Anthony Perkins; aged countess Wendy Hiller; or any of a dozen other passengers, including timid Swedish spinster Ingrid Bergman? Private detective Hercule Poirot (Albert Finney) duly finds out. From the classic thriller by Agatha Christie.

An EMI Picture, directed by Sidney Lumet. With Albert Finney, Lauren Bacall, Martin Balsam, Ingrid Bergman, Jacqueline Bisset, Jean-Pierre Cassel, Sean Connery, John Gielgud, Wendy Hiller, Anthony Perkins, Vanessa Redgrave, Rachel Roberts, Richard Widmark, Michael York. Technicolor. 131 mins.

THE MUSIC MAN (1962)   ★

★ best score: adaptation or treatment Ray Heindorf

Breezy stage musical, set in the early 1900s, with Robert Preston repeating his Broadway role as the dynamic Professor Harold Hill, a

---

* *Note:* For her role in this film Miss Bergman became the second actress to win both a major acting Oscar (for *Anastasia* in 1956 and *Gaslight* in 1944) and a supporting award. Helen Hayes (for *The Sin of Madelon Claudet* in 1931/32 and *Airport* in 1970) was the first; Maggie Smith (*The Prime of Miss Jean Brodie* in 1969 and *California Suite* in 1978) and Meryl Streep (*Kramer vs. Kramer* in 1979 and *Sophie's Choice* in 1982) have both subsequently achieved the honor.

traveling salesman of musical instruments who tries to organize a boys' band in the small town of River City, Iowa. Preston was not as lucky as Yul Brynner (*The King and I*) and Rex Harrison (*My Fair Lady*), who both won Oscars for repeating their Broadway successes, and was not even among the year's five best-actor nominees. The year's best actor was Gregory Peck for *To Kill a Mockingbird*.

A Warner Bros. Picture, directed by Morton Da Costa. With Robert Preston, Shirley Jones, Paul Ford, Buddy Hackett, Hermione Gingold. Technirama/Technicolor. 151 mins.

MUTINY ON THE BOUNTY (1935)   ★

★ best film Irving Thalberg (producer), with Albert Lewin

The story of the famous mutiny on HMS *Bounty*, which under the command of the ruthless Captain Bligh set sail for Tahiti on a scientific expedition in 1787. The best-picture winner of 1935 and the only film in the history of the Academy to boast three best-actor nominees—Clark Gable (as Fletcher Christian), Charles Laughton (as Bligh) and Franchot Tone—out of the four actors nominated. But none of them won. The award went to the fourth nominee, Victor McLaglen, for *The Informer*.

An MGM Picture, directed by Frank Lloyd. With Charles Laughton, Clark Gable, Franchot Tone, Herbert Mundin, Eddie Quillan, Dudley Digges, Donald Crisp, Henry Stephenson. 131 mins.

MY COUSIN VINNY (1992)   ★

★ best supporting actress Marisa Tomei

Small-scale comedy about a hopelessly inept Brooklyn lawyer (Joe Pesci) who battles to defend his young cousin and his cousin's friend when they are falsely accused of murder in the Deep South. For her performance as "Mona Lisa Vito," Pesci's gum-chewing, streetwise girlfriend, Marisa Tomei caused the major upset of 1992, defeating such strong contenders as

Miranda Richardson (*Damage*), Joan Plowright (*Enchanted April*) and Judy Davis (*Husbands and Wives*) in the supporting actress category.

A 20th Century-Fox Picture, directed by Jonathan Lynn. With Joe Pesci, Ralph Macchio, Marisa Tomei, Mitchell Whitfield, Fred Gwynne, Lane Smith, Austin Pendleton. DeLuxe Color. 119 mins.

MY FAIR LADY (1964) ★★★★★★★★

★ best film Jack L. Warner (producer)
★ best direction George Cukor
★ best actor Rex Harrison
★ best color cinematography Harry Stradling
★ best color art direction Gene Allen & Cecil Beaton
    set decoration George James Hopkins
★ best color costume design Cecil Beaton
★ best sound George R. Groves
★ best music score: adaptation or treatment Andre Previn

Broadway's musical version of Shaw's *Pygmalion*, filmed completely straight and taking eight Oscars with ease, including one to Rex Harrison for his arrogant Professor Higgins and two to Cecil Beaton for his costumes and designs. The only surprise was that Audrey Hepburn as cockney flower girl Eliza Doolittle was not among the best actress nominees.

A Warner Bros. Picture, directed by George Cukor. With Rex Harrison, Audrey Hepburn, Stanley Holloway, Wilfrid Hyde-White, Gladys Cooper, Jeremy Brett, Theodore Bikel. Super Panavision 70/Technicolor. 170 mins.

MY GAL SAL (1942) ★

★ best color art direction Richard Day & Joseph C. Wright
    interior decoration Thomas Little

An 1890s songwriter, Paul Dresser (Victor Mature), falls in love with a beautiful musical queen (Rita Hayworth) and after innumerable ups and downs finally manages to settle down with her to a life of happiness. Formula Fox

musical for the period, richly designed and with songs such as "On the Banks of the Wabash" and "Come Tell Me What's Your Answer."

A 20th Century-Fox Picture, directed by Irving Cummings. With Rita Hayworth, Victor Mature, John Sutton, Carole Landis, James Gleason, Phil Silvers. Technicolor. 103 mins.

MY LEFT FOOT (1989)

★ best actor Daniel Day-Lewis
★ best supporting actress Brenda Fricker

The true story of cerebral palsy victim Christy Brown (Daniel Day-Lewis), who succeeded against all odds and became both an articulate writer and a talented painter by using his left foot, the only part of his body he could move and control. A skillful, physically strenuous performance by Day-Lewis, who spent eight weeks at a clinic studying for his role; a warm, sympathetic one from Brenda Fricker as Brown's supportive mother.

Ferndale Films/Granada Television International, in association with Radio Telefís Eireann. Directed by Jim Sheridan. With Daniel Day-Lewis, Ray McAnally, Brenda Fricker, Ruth McCabe, Fiona Shaw, Eanna MacLiam, Alison Whelan, Declan Croghan, Hugh O'Connor. Technicolor. 103 mins.

Fiona Shaw painstakingly trains Daniel Day-Lewis (as Christy Brown) to control his speech in *My Left Foot* (Granada/Palace, 1989). The film earned Academy Awards for both Day-Lewis and Brenda Fricker as Brown's mother.

N

THE NAKED CITY (1948)

★ best b/w cinematography William Daniels
★ best editing Paul Weatherwax

Realistic crime story of New York—the murder of a beautiful model and the tracking down of her killer—filmed almost entirely on location when the streets and buildings of the great city were sweltering in a heat wave. The last picture of producer Mark Hellinger, it also marked the only time that Garbo's favorite cameraman of the 1930's, William Daniels, was honored by the Academy.

A Universal-International Picture, directed by Jules Dassin. With Barry Fitzgerald, Howard Duff, Dorothy Hart, Don Taylor, Ted De Corsia, Jean Adair. 96 mins.

NASHVILLE (1975)

★ best song "I'm Easy" (Keith Carradine, music & lyrics)

Robert Altman parody of life in Nashville, the country music capital since the 1950s. Almost plotless, the film presents a cross-section of Nashville society during the preparation and performance of a gigantic concert being held in the city to aid the campaign of a leading presidential candidate.

A Paramount Picture, directed by Robert Altman. With David Arkin, Barbara Baxley, Ned Beatty, Karen Black, Ronee Blakley, Timothy Brown, Keith Carradine, Geraldine Chaplin, Robert Doqui, Shelley Duvall, Allen Garfield, Henry Gibson, Scott Glenn, Jeff Goldblum, Barbara Harris, David Hayward, Michael Murphy, Allan Nicholls, Dave Peel, Christina Raines, Bert Remsen, Lily Tomlin,

Gwen Welles, Keenan Wynn. Panavision/Color by MGM Film Laboratories. 161 mins.

NATIONAL VELVET (1945)

★ best supporting actress Anne Revere
★ best editing Robert J. Kern

Enid Bagnold's famous story about a little girl's love for her horse and her subsequent ride to victory (disguised as a boy) in the Grand National. Twelve-year-old Elizabeth Taylor plays the girl, Mickey Rooney the ex-jockey who helps her train her horse, and Oscar winner Anne Revere Liz's quiet, understanding mother.

An MGM Picture, directed by Clarence Brown. With Mickey Rooney, Donald Crisp, Elizabeth Taylor, Anne Revere, Angela Lansbury. Technicolor. 125 mins.

NAUGHTY MARIETTA (1935)   ★

★ best sound recording Douglas Shearer

The first teaming of Jeanette MacDonald and Nelson Eddy, a version of the operetta by Victor Herbert with Jeanette as a French princess who runs away to America and Nelson as her loving Indian scout. Songs include "Tramp, Tramp, Tramp" and "Ah, Sweet Mystery of Life."

An MGM Picture, directed by W. S. Van Dyke. With Jeanette MacDonald, Nelson Eddy, Frank Morgan, Elsa Lanchester, Douglas Dumbrille. 106 mins.

NEPTUNE'S DAUGHTER (1949)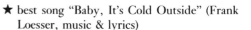

★ best song "Baby, It's Cold Outside" (Frank Loesser, music & lyrics)

Swimming star Esther Williams as a bathing suit designer, Ricardo Montalban as a handsome polo player, Red Skelton as a comic masquerader, South American settings, but best of all the catchy song "Baby, It's Cold Outside," which became a big hit the world over and won 1949's best-song award.

An MGM Picture, directed by Edward Buzzell. With Esther Williams, Red Skelton, Ricardo Montalban, Betty Garrett, Keenan Wynn, Xavier Cugat and His Orchestra, Ted De Corsia, Mike Mazurki. Technicolor. 93 mins.

NETWORK (1976)   ★★★★

★ best actor Peter Finch
★ best actress Faye Dunaway
★ best supporting actress Beatrice Straight
★ best original screenplay Paddy Chayefsky

Savage satire on contemporary TV, with Peter Finch as a deranged news commentator who threatens to kill himself on the air, thus increasing his ratings overnight. Faye Dunaway dominates as the ruthlessly ambitious TV executive determined to climb to the top at any cost and William Holden co-stars as a director of the TV news division. Finch's Oscar made him the first posthumous best-actor winner in the history of the Academy; Beatrice Straight won her supporting award for her one sequence as Holden's neglected wife. Along with *A Streetcar Named Desire* (1951) the only film in which three of the leading performers were named best of the year. No film has yet managed all four acting awards.

Program executive Faye Dunaway playing the ratings game in Sidney Lumet's *Network* (United Artists, 1976) and winning an Oscar as best actress.

An MGM-United Artists Picture, directed by Sidney Lumet. With Faye Dunaway, William Holden, Peter Finch, Robert Duvall, Wesley Addy, Ned Beatty, Beatrice Straight. Panavision/Metrocolor. 121 mins.

NEVER ON SUNDAY (1960)   ★

★ best song "Never on Sunday" (Manos Hadjidakis, music & lyrics)

Jules Dassin shoestring comedy about an American writer (played by Dassin himself) who tries to persuade happy-go-lucky prostitute Melina Mercouri to concentrate on the high-minded ideals of Aristotle instead of parading her ample wares on the waterfront of Piraeus in the Port of Athens. Needless to say, he fails. The happy, infectious theme song became one of the biggest hits of the early 1960s.

A Lopert Pictures-Melina Film (distributed through United Artists), directed by Jules Dassin. With Melina Mercouri, Jules Dassin, George Foundas, Tito Vandis, Mitsos Liguisos, Despo Diamantidou. 91 mins.

NICHOLAS AND ALEXANDRA (1971)   ★★

★ best art direction John Box, Ernest Archer, Jack A. Maxsted & Gil Parrondo
    set decoration Vernon Dixon
★ best costume design Yvonne Blake & Antonio Castillo

The last turbulent years of Tsar Nicholas II (Michael Jayston) and his German-born wife Alexandra (Janet Suzman) before the 1917 revolution caused the upheaval of the Russian social order and led to the deaths of the Russian rulers and their families. As in most films of its type, the settings and costumes dazzled the eye far more than the performances, all Oscar recipients thoroughly deserving their awards for their re-creation of the Russian imperial scene.

A Columbia Picture, directed by Franklin J. Schaffner. With Michael Jayston, Janet Suzman, Roderic Noble, Harry Andrews, Tom Baker, Timothy West, Jack Hawkins, Laurence Olivier. Panavision/Eastman Color. 189 mins.

THE NIGHT OF THE IGUANA (1964) ★

★ best b/w costume design Dorothy Jeakins

Richard Burton as a defrocked priest turned tourist coach driver, set firmly in Tennessee Williams country at a seedy Mexican resort hotel where he becomes involved with proprietress Ava Gardner, rapacious teenager Sue Lyon and anguished spinster Deborah Kerr. Symbolic writing, brilliant black-and-white photography.

An MGM Picture, directed by John Huston. With Richard Burton, Ava Gardner, Deborah Kerr, Sue Lyon, James Ward, Grayson Hall. 125 mins.

THE NIGHTS OF CABIRIA (1957) ★

★ best foreign language film Italy/France

The hopes, fears and sorrows of waifish Italian prostitute Giulietta Masina, always dreaming of a wonderful life just around the corner but always ending up penniless with only another unhappy experience to remember. The second of Fellini's four best-foreign-film awards (the others being *La Strada* in 1956 *8½* in 1963 and *Amarcord* in 1974) and the basis for the subsequent stage and film musical *Sweet Charity* (1966 and 1969, respectively).

Dino De Laurentiis/Films Marceau Production, directed by Federico Fellini. With Giulietta Masina, Francois Perier, Amadeo Nazzari, Franca Marzi, Dorian Gray, Aldo Silvana. 110 mins.

NONE BUT THE LONELY HEART (1944) ★

★ best supporting actress Ethel Barrymore

Version of Richard Llewellyn's novel about a cockney drifter (Cary Grant) who, embittered by the death of his father in the First World War and his mother's subsequent struggle against poverty, tries to find some kind of spiritual fulfillment in the days leading up to World War II. Set in London's prewar slums, it provided Grant with a rare dramatic acting role which earned him a best-actor Academy nomination; Ethel Barrymore's Oscar was for her performance as Grant's mother.

An RKO Picture, directed by Clifford Odets. With Cary Grant, Ethel Barrymore, Barry Fitzgerald, June Duprez, Jane Wyatt, George Coulouris. 113 mins.

NORMA RAE (1979) ★★

★ best actress Sally Field
★ best song "It Goes Like It Goes" (music by David Shire; lyrics by Norman Gimbel)

Sally Field as a small-town Southern girl who fights to establish a union in the textile mill where she works. A distinguished Martin Ritt political movie, scripted by his long-time collaborators Irving Ravetch and Harriet Frank, Jr. (*The Long Hot Summer* in 1958; *Hud* in 1963; and *Hombre* in 1967). *Norma Rae* was nominated for best picture, but Ritt was overlooked in the list of director nominees.

A 20th Century-Fox Picture, directed by Martin Ritt. With Sally Field, Beau Bridges, Ron Leibman, Pat Hingle, Barbara Baxley, Gail Strickland. DeLuxe Color. 114 mins.

NORTHWEST MOUNTED POLICE (1940) ★

★ best editing Anne Bauchens

DeMille's first all-color picture, an adventure of three men (Texas Ranger Gary Cooper, Canadian Mounties Preston Foster and Robert Preston) and two women (frontier nurse Madeleine Carroll and half-breed Paulette Goddard) all caught up in Canada's "Civil War," an abortive frontier rebellion led by Louis Riel in 1885. Anne Bauchens, who won the year's editing award, cut all of DeMille's pictures between *We Can't Have Everything* in 1918 and *The Ten Commandments* in 1956.

A Paramount Picture, directed by Cecil B. DeMille. With Gary Cooper, Madeleine Carroll, Paulette Goddard, Preston Foster, Robert Preston, George Bancroft, Lynne Overman, Akim Tamiroff. Technicolor. 125 mins.

NOW VOYAGER (1942)

★ best music score of a drama or comedy Max Steiner

The story of a plain, neurotic young spinster (Bette Davis) who eventually escapes her mother's petty tyranny through a course in Claude Rains' psychiatry and Paul Henreid's love-making. Chiefly remembered for Max Steiner's famous music score, one of the lushest that celebrated composer ever wrote, and for Henreid's trick of lighting two cigarettes in his mouth at the same time.

A Warner Bros. Picture, directed by Irving Rapper. With Bette Davis, Paul Henreid, Claude Rains, Gladys Cooper, Bonita Granville, John Loder, Ilka Chase, Lee Patrick. 117 mins.

O

AN OFFICER AND A GENTLEMAN (1982)   ★ ★

- ★ best supporting actor Louis Gossett, Jr.
- ★ best song "Up Where We Belong" (music, Jack Nitzsche & Buffy Sainte-Marie; lyrics, Will Jennings)

A kind of *From Here to Eternity* of the 1980s, with Richard Gere enduring 13 weeks of hell to become a naval officer, Debra Winger offering him steamy sex whenever he can get away, and drill sergeant Louis Gossett, Jr. offering him discipline when he can't. An artful mix of key box-office ingredients plus an Oscar-winning song performed by Joe Cocker and Jennifer Warnes. Gossett became the first black performer to win an Oscar since Sidney Poitier was honored for *Lilies of the Field* nearly 20 years before. Denzel Washington, for *Glory* (1989) and Whoopi Goldberg for *Ghost* (1990) complete

Richard Gere and Debra Winger in *An Officer and a Gentleman* (Paramount). The film's hit song "Up Where We Belong" was named the best of 1982 at Oscar time.

the trio of black acting winners in the eight-year period 1982–1990.

A Lorimar/Elfand Picture distributed by Paramount. Directed by Taylor Hackford. With Richard Gere, Debra Winger, David Keith, Robert Loggia, Lisa Blount, Lisa Eilbacher, Louis Gossett, Jr., Tony Plana, Harold Sylvester, David Caruso. Metrocolor. 124 mins.

THE OFFICIAL STORY (1985)   ★

- ★ best foreign language film Argentina

A complacent middle-class woman, sheltered from the political turmoil that surrounds her in Argentina, finds that she may be more involved than she had realized when she discovers that her five-year-old adopted daughter is the offspring of political prisoners. Set in Buenos Aires in 1983 and based on many similar real-life cases that occurred during the Argentinian dictatorship, the film was the first Argentinian production to win the foreign language award. Also nominated that year: the Hungarian *Colonel Redl* and France's *Three Men and a Cradle*.

Historias Cinematograficas/Progress Communications, directed by Luis Puenzo. With Hector Alterio, Norma Aleandro, Chela Ruiz, Chunchuna Villafane, Hugo Arana, Patricio Contreras, Guillermo Battaglia. Eastman Color. 114 mins.

OKLAHOMA! (1955)

- ★ best scoring of a musical Robert Russell Bennett, Jay Blackton & Adolph Deutsch
- ★ best sound recording Fred Hynes

Trendsetting Rodgers and Hammerstein musical about the rivalry between the farmers and the cowmen in Old Oklahoma. Gordon MacRae and Shirley Jones star as the romantic leads, Gloria Grahame is Ado Annie, and Rod Steiger is the psychopathic Jud Fry. Hit songs include "Oh, What a Beautiful Mornin'," "The Surrey with the Fringe on Top" and "People Will Say We're in Love."

A Magna Picture (released by RKO), directed by Fred Zinnemann. With Gordon MacRae, Shirley Jones, Gloria Grahame, Gene Nelson, Rod Steiger, Charlotte Greenwood, Eddie Albert, James Whitmore. Todd-AO/Eastman Color. 145 mins.

THE OLD MAN AND THE SEA (1958) ★

★ best music score of a drama or comedy Dimitri Tiomkin

Hemingway's simple parable of an old Cuban fisherman (Spencer Tracy) who battles to hold on to the giant marlin he has hooked at sea—his first fish in three months—and then has to watch it gradually eaten away by attacking sharks. Felipe Pazes plays the small boy who alone still has faith in the old man.

A Warner Bros. Picture, directed by John Sturges. With Spencer Tracy, Felipe Pazes, Harry Bellaver, Donald Diamond, Don Blackman, Joey Ray, Richard Alameda. Warner Color. 86 mins.

OLIVER! (1968) ★★★★★★

★ best film John Woolf (producer)
★ best direction Carol Reed
★ best art direction John Box & Terence Marsh set decoration Vernon Dixon & Ken Muggleston
★ best sound Shepperton Studios Sound Dept.
★ best music score adaptation John Green
★ best choreography* Onna White

Lionel Bart's musical version of Dickens' *Oliver Twist*, with Mark Lester as the orphan boy who falls into the clutches of a gang of thieves in 19th-century London. Ron Moody is a merry Fagin, Oliver Reed a surly Bill Sikes and Shani Wallis the pathetic street girl Nancy. The first and only Oscar won by Carol Reed—his only

---

* *Note:* Onna White's award for choreography was not a competitive award but a special award bestowed by the Academy.

other nominations coming for *The Fallen Idol* in 1949 and *The Third Man* in 1950—and the only British born and bred musical to win the best film award.

A Columbia Picture, directed by Carol Reed. With Ron Moody, Shani Wallis, Oliver Reed, Harry Secombe, Hugh Griffith, Jack Wild. Panavision 70/Technicolor. 146 mins.

THE OMEN (1976)

★ best original music score Jerry Goldsmith

The commercial "sleeper" of 1976, a horror drama with U.S. ambassador Gregory Peck and wife Lee Remick adopting a baby in a Rome hospital only to find as he grows to boyhood that he is the child of the Devil and destroys everyone he comes in contact with.

A 20th Century-Fox Picture, directed by Richard Donner. With Gregory Peck, Lee Re-

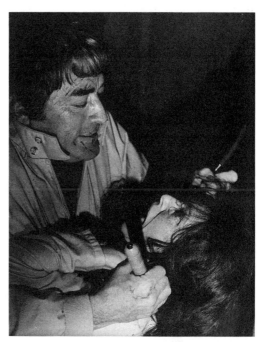

Gregory Peck survives—barely—but it's the end for nanny Billie Whitelaw in Richard Donner's 1976 surprise hit *The Omen* (20th Century-Fox). Jerry Goldsmith won an Academy Award for his music for the film.

mick, David Warner, Billie Whitelaw, Harvey Stephens, Leo McKern, Patrick Troughton. Panavision/DeLuxe Color. 111 mins.

ONE FLEW OVER THE CUCKOO'S NEST (1975)   ★★★★★

- ★ best film Mike Douglas & Saul Zaentz (producers)
- ★ best direction Milos Forman
- ★ best actor Jack Nicholson
- ★ best actress Louise Fletcher
- ★ best screenplay Lawrence Hauben & Bo Goldman

The staff of a state mental hospital—symbolized by stern disciplinarian Louise Fletcher—against the normally apathetic patients, who suddenly find a hero in the character of effervescent Jack Nicholson, a criminal transferred from a penal work farm for clinical observation. The first movie since *It Happened One Night* (1934) to win all five major awards, a feat subsequently repeated for a third time 16 years later by *The Silence of the Lambs*.

A United Artists Picture, directed by Milos Forman. With Jack Nicholson, Louise Fletcher, Brad Dourif, Sydney Lassick, William Redfield, Dean R. Brooks, DeLuxe Color. 134 mins.

ONE HUNDRED MEN AND A GIRL (1937)   ★

- ★ best music score Charles Previn

Golden-voiced Deanna Durbin, daughter of a poor, unemployed violinist, reaches the pinnacle of her dreams by singing at a great concert conducted by the celebrated Leopold Stokowski. Typical, fluffy Durbin vehicle and the only one that ever figured in the Oscar Awards.

A Universal Picture, directed by Henry Koster. With Deanna Durbin, Leopold Stokowski, Adolphe Menjou, Alice Brady, Eugene Pallette, Mischa Auer, Billy Gilbert. 84 mins.

ONE NIGHT OF LOVE (1934)   ★★

- ★ best sound recording Paul Neal
- ★ best music score Louis Silvers

Grace Moore as a young American soprano who studies opera in Italy under demanding teacher Tullio Carminati and finally makes it to the top at the Metropolitan. On the way up she renders six famous operatic arias. Moore was nominated for best actress but lost to Claudette Colbert in *It Happened One Night*. The film was the first to win in the best-music-score category.

A Columbia Picture, directed by Victor Schertzinger. With Grace Moore, Tullio Carminati, Lyle Talbot, Mona Barrie, Nydia Westman, Jessie Ralph, Luis Alberni. 82 mins.

ONE WAY PASSAGE (1932/33)   ★

- ★ best original story Robert Lord

Old-fashioned weepie romance, set on board an ocean liner, between con-man William Powell and fatally ill Kay Francis—doomed to an early death by an incurable heart disease. Also on board and accompanying the action, two other con artists—light-fingered Frank McHugh and fake countess Aline MacMahon.

A Warner Bros. Picture, directed by Tay Garnett. With William Powell, Kay Francis, Frank McHugh, Aline MacMahon, Warren Hymer, Frederick Burton. 69 mins.

ON GOLDEN POND (1981)   ★★★

- ★ best actor Henry Fonda
- ★ best actress Katharine Hepburn
- ★ best screenplay adaptation Ernest Thompson

Crusty 80-year-old former college professor Henry Fonda finds himself caring about life once more through his relationship with a 13-

Katharine Hepburn and estranged daughter Jane Fonda in *On Golden Pond* (Universal, 1981). Both Hepburn and her co-star Henry Fonda were honored for their roles in the film.

year-old boy and the loving care of wife Katharine Hepburn. Set in its entirety in a New England lakeside vacation home, the film at last won Henry Fonda his deserved Academy Award, and established Katharine Hepburn as the only performer in Oscar history to earn four major acting awards—a record that is likely to stand for several years to come. Her other Oscars were for *Morning Glory* (1933), *Guess Who's Coming to Dinner* (1967) and *The Lion in Winter* (1968).

An ITC/IPC Picture, directed by Mark Rydell. With Katharine Hepburn, Henry Fonda, Jane Fonda, Doug McKeon, Dabney Coleman, William Lanteau, Chris Rydell. Color. 109 mins.

ON THE TOWN (1949)　★

★ best scoring of a musical Roger Edens & Lennie Hayton

Three sailors (Kelly, Sinatra, Munshin) dance and sing their way gleefully around New York on a 24-hour shore leave in the big city. Slim beauty Vera-Ellen, wisecracking taxi driver Betty Garrett and hoofer Ann Miller are the girls

they meet on the way. An exhilarating, history-making piece of perpetual motion, adapted from the Leonard Bernstein stage ballet *Fancy Free*.

An MGM Picture, directed by Gene Kelly and Stanley Donen. With Gene Kelly, Frank Sinatra, Betty Garrett, Ann Miller, Jules Munshin, Vera-Ellen. Technicolor. 97 mins.

ON THE WATERFRONT (1954)　★★★★★★★★

★ best film Sam Spiegel (producer)
★ best direction Elia Kazan
★ best actor Marlon Brando
★ best supporting actress Eva Marie Saint
★ best story & screenplay Budd Schulberg
★ best b/w cinematography Boris Kaufman
★ best b/w art direction Richard Day
★ best editing Gene Milford

Angry indictment of the corruption and tyranny existing in a New York longshoremen's union in the early 1950s, with Marlon Brando giving arguably the finest performance of his career as a broken-down ex-boxer in the pay of the racketeers. Eva Marie Saint's Oscar, for her portrayal of a murdered longshoreman's sister, was for her first screen role, while the film itself was the first to have three members of its male cast—Lee J. Cobb as a gang boss, Karl Malden as a tough dockland priest and Rod Steiger as Brando's older brother—nominated in the supporting actor category. The same feat was later achieved by Coppola's two Mafia gangster films, *The Godfather* (1972) and *The Godfather Part II* (1974).

A Columbia Picture, directed by Elia Kazan. With Marlon Brando, Eva Marie Saint, Karl Malden, Lee J. Cobb, Rod Steiger, Pat Henning. 108 mins.

ORDINARY PEOPLE (1980)　★★★★

★ best film Ronald L. Schwary (producer)
★ best direction Robert Redford

★ best supporting actor Timothy Hutton
★ best screenplay Alvin Sargent

Notable directorial debut by Robert Redford, hinging on a disturbed youth (Timothy Hutton) whose precarious tightrope walk through his teens is threatened by a selfish, superficial mother (Mary Tyler Moore) but ultimately saved by the love of an understanding father (Donald Sutherland). A somber and very honest look at American suburban life, based on the novel by Judith Guest; the top Oscar-winner of 1980.

A Wildwood Enterprises Production for Paramount, directed by Robert Redford. With Donald Sutherland, Mary Tyler Moore, Judd Hirsch, Timothy Hutton, M. Emmet Walsh, Elizabeth McGovern, Dinah Manoff. Technicolor. 124 mins.

OUT OF AFRICA (1985)  ★★★★★★★

★ best film Sydney Pollack (producer)
★ best direction Sydney Pollack
★ best screenplay Kurt Luedtke
★ best cinematography David Watkin
★ best art direction Stephen Grimes
      set decoration Josie MacAvin
★ best sound Chris Jenkins, Gary Alexander, Larry Stensvold, Peter Handford
★ best music score John Barry

The film with one of the most quoted opening lines in contemporary cinema: "I had a f-a-r-m in Africa," spoken by Meryl Streep as the Danish expatriate Isak Dinesen, who married for convenience, moved from Denmark to Nairobi

Streep and Redford—a potent mix in Sydney Pollack's *Out of Africa* (Universal, 1985). No Oscars for any of the cast but seven for the picture, including best film.

to set up a coffee plantation but eventually found more satisfaction in her romance with great white hunter Denys Finch Hatton (Robert Redford). An old-fashioned entertainment that emerged as the biggest Oscar winner of 1985, the year when Steven Spielberg's much-admired *The Color Purple* was nominated for 11 Oscars and ended up empty-handed. Spielberg, who was the choice of the Director's Guild, failed to garner even a nomination as best director.

A Universal-Mirage Production, directed by Sydney Pollack. With Meryl Streep, Robert Redford, Klaus Maria Brandauer, Michael Kitchen, Malick Bowens, Joseph Thiaka, Stephen Kinyanjui, Michael Gough, Suzanna Hamilton, Rachel Kempson. 70 mm. Technovision/Technicolor. 162 mins.

P

THE PALEFACE (1948)   ★

★ best song "Buttons and Bows" (Jay
Livingston & Ray Evans, music & lyrics)

Bob Hope as traveling dentist "Painless" Peter
Potter involved with Jane Russell's Calamity
Jane in the Wild West of the 1870s. More satire
than usual in a Hope comedy and also the
winning song "Buttons and Bows."

A Paramount Picture, directed by Norman
Z. McLeod. With Bob Hope, Jane Russell,
Robert Armstrong, Iris Adrian, Robert Wat-
son, Jack Searle. Technicolor. 91 mins.

PANIC IN THE STREETS (1950)   ★

★ best motion picture story Edna & Edward
Anhalt

Best original story of 1950. Richard Widmark and Paul
Douglas in *Panic in the Streets*, Elia Kazan's thriller about
a plague carrier loose in New Orleans (20th Century-
Fox).

Documentary-style thriller by Elia Kazan, with
medical health officer Richard Widmark and
weary cop Paul Douglas tracking down Jack
Palance, an on-the-lam criminal carrying a deadly
plague germ through the city streets. The film
won for its story, although Joe MacDonald's
lensing of the back alleys, low bars and wharves
of New Orleans deserved, but did not receive,
mention.

A 20th Century-Fox Picture, directed by Elia
Kazan. With Richard Widmark, Paul Douglas,
Barbara Bel Geddes, Walter [Jack] Palance, Zero
Mostel. 96 mins.

PAPA'S DELICATE CONDITION (1963)   ★

★ best song "Call Me Irresponsible" (James
Van Heusen, music; Sammy Cahn, lyrics)

Another movie remembered more for its hit
song—"Call Me Irresponsible"—than for its story
about the family life of silent film actress Corinne Griffith when she was a child back in the
1900s. Jackie Gleason is featured as Griffith's
semi-drunk railroad inspector father, Glynis
Johns as his elegant wife—but the song still
comes out tops.

A Paramount Picture, directed by George
Marshall. With Jackie Gleason, Glynis Johns,
Linda Bruhl, Charles Ruggles, Laurel Good-
win, Ned Glass. Technicolor. 98 mins.

THE PAPER CHASE (1973)   ★

★ best supporting actor John Houseman

The pressures on a young college graduate
(Timothy Bottoms) when he arrives at Harvard
Law School determined to do his best in ob-
taining good grades, but finding his best is more
appreciated elsewhere by the daughter (Lindsay
Wagner) of his tyrannical professor (John Houseman). For this last-named role the then-71-
year-old Houseman won a supporting Oscar
after a lifetime of quality work as a producer,
both on stage and in films.

A 20th Century-Fox Picture, directed by James Bridges. With Timothy Bottoms, Lindsay Wagner, John Houseman, Graham Beckel, James Naughton, Edward Herrmann. Panavision/DeLuxe Color. 111 mins.

PAPER MOON (1973)   ★

★ best supporting actress Tatum O'Neal

Con man Ryan O'Neal, pressured into delivering the nine-year-old daughter (Tatum O'Neal) of an old flame to an aunt in Missouri, finds that instead of becoming a burden, his artful little companion becomes a valuable asset in the con game. Tatum O'Neal remains the youngest-ever supporting actress winner; Madeline

Kahn was also nominated in the supporting category for her fading floozie Trixie Delight.

A Paramount Picture, directed by Peter Bogdanovich. With Ryan O'Neal, Tatum O'Neal, Madeline Kahn, John Hillerman, P. J. Johnson, Jessie Lee Fulton. 103 mins.

A PASSAGE TO INDIA (1984)

★ best supporting actress Peggy Ashcroft
★ best original score Maurice Jarre

David Lean's comeback film: a visual feast focusing on a young Englishwoman (Judy Davis) whose visit with an Indian doctor to the eerie Marabar caves leads to an accusation of rape

Entering the sinister Marabar caves. Peggy Ashcroft as Mrs. Moore in David Lean's 1984 version of E. M. Forster's *A Passage to India* (GW Films). Ashcroft was named best supporting actress of the year for her performance.

and an ensuing court trial. Set in India in the 1920s and based on the novel by E. M. Forster, the film earned an Oscar for Peggy Ashcroft (who made just 16 films between 1933 and 1989) as Davis' elderly traveling companion, Mrs. Moore. Maurice Jarre won his third Oscar for a David Lean film following those he received in the 1960s for *Lawrence of Arabia* (1962) and *Doctor Zhivago* (1965).

A GW Film, in association with John Heyman, Edward Sands & Home Box Office. Directed by David Lean. With Judy Davis, Victor Banerjee, Peggy Ashcroft, James Fox, Alec Guinness, Nigel Havers, Richard Wilson, Antonia Pemberton, Michael Culver. Technicolor; prints by Metrocolor. 163 mins.

A PATCH OF BLUE (1965) ★

★ best supporting actress Shelley Winters

Blind white girl Elizabeth Hartman falls in love with Sidney Poitier, not realizing during their affair that her compassionate friend is black. For her portrayal of the blowsy, overbearing mother of the blind Hartman, Shelley Winters won her second supporting actress Oscar, having received her first six years earlier for her portrayal of another mother—Mrs. Van Daan in *The Diary of Anne Frank* (1959).

An MGM Picture, directed by Guy Green. With Sidney Poitier, Shelley Winters, Elizabeth Hartman, Wallace Ford, Ivan Dixon, Elisabeth Fraser, John Qualen. 105 mins.

THE PATRIOT (1928/29) ★

★ best writing achievement Hans Kraly

Emil Jannings as Tsar Paul the First of 18th-century Russia, who finally meets his death after being surrounded on all sides by murderous plots to remove him from the throne.

A Paramount Picture, directed by Ernst Lubitsch. With Emil Jannings, Florence Vidor, Lewis Stone, Vera Voronina, Neil Hamilton, Harry Cording. 12 reels.

PATTON (1970) ★★★★★★★

★ best film Frank McCarthy (producer)
★ best direction Franklin J. Schaffner
★ best actor George C. Scott
★ best story & screenplay Francis Ford Coppola & Edmund H. North
★ best art direction Urie McCleary & Gil Parrondo
      set decoration Antonio Mateos & Pierre-Louis Thevenet
★ best editing Hugh S. Fowler
★ best sound Douglas Williams & Don Bassman

The wartime career of one of the most controversial American commanders of World War II, "Blood and Guts" Patton (George C. Scott), who forfeited command of the 7th Army in Sicily after striking a soldier suffering from battle fatigue. Scott made history by becoming the first actor to refuse his Oscar, contending that he wasn't in a race for awards.* "Life isn't a race," he said. "And because it is not a race I don't consider myself in competition with my fellow actors for awards or recognition. That is why I have rejected the nomination and Oscar for playing Patton."

A 20th Century-Fox Picture, directed by Franklin J. Schaffner. With George C. Scott, Karl Malden, Michael Bates, Stephen Young, Michael Strong, Cary Loftin. Dimension 150/DeLuxe Color. 173 mins.

PELLE THE CONQUEROR (1988) ★

★ best foreign language film Denmark

An immigrant widower and his young son Pelle try to make a new life for themselves as farm laborers as they struggle against the elements,

---

* *Note:* Marlon Brando subsequently refused his Oscar for *The Godfather* (1972), his main reason being his objections to the industry's treatment of Native Americans in films and on TV.

Max Von Sydow and Pelle Hvengegaard in *Pelle the Conqueror* (Denmark), best foreign language film of 1988.

prejudice and poverty in early 20th-century Denmark. Poignant movie based on the four-volume novel of Martin Andersen Nexo, and the second Danish film (following *Babette's Feast*, the winner a year earlier) to win the foreign language award. Max Von Sydow earned a best-actor nomination for his portrait of the widower.

A Per Holst/Kaerne Films Production, directed by Bille August. With Max Von Sydow, Pelle Hvenegaard, Erik Paaske, Kristina Tornqvist, Morten Jorgensen, Axel Strobye, Astrid Villaume, Bjorn Granath. Color. 150 mins.

THE PHANTOM OF THE OPERA (1943)

★ best color cinematography Hal Mohr & W. Howard Greene
★ best color art direction Alexander Golitzen & John B. Goodman
          interior decoration R. A. Gausman & Ira Webb

Gaston LeRoux's tale of a demented violinist whose face has been hideously disfigured by acid and who is forced to haunt the innermost depths of the Paris Opera House. Claude Rains stars as the masked phantom, but the Oscar-winning color and sets, dominated by the huge

chandelier hanging high above the opera audience, impress the most.

A Universal Picture, directed by Arthur Lubin. With Nelson Eddy, Susanna Foster, Claude Rains, Edgar Barrier, Leo Carrillo, Jane Farrar, J. Edward Bromberg. Technicolor. 92 mins.

THE PHILADELPHIA STORY (1940)

★ best actor James Stewart
★ best screenplay Donald Ogden Stewart

Philip Barry's play about a spoiled society girl (Katharine Hepburn) whose impending second marriage is disrupted suddenly by the appearance of ex-husband Cary Grant and two gossip columnists (James Stewart and Ruth Hussey) covering the marriage for their magazine. The film earned James Stewart his only Academy Award, although he subsequently received a special Oscar in 1984. His other nominations: *Mr. Smith Goes to Washington* (1939), *It's a Wonderful Life* (1946), *Harvey* (1950) and *Anatomy of a Murder* (1959).

An MGM Picture, directed by George Cukor. With Cary Grant, Katharine Hepburn, James Stewart, Ruth Hussey, John Howard, Roland Young, John Halliday. 112 mins.

PICNIC (1955)   ★★

★ best color art direction William Flannery & Jo Mielziner
          set decoration Robert Priestley
★ best editing Charles Nelson & William A. Lyon

William Holden as a wandering young hobo who arrives in a small Kansas town on Labor Day and during his brief stay there changes the lives of a number of its inhabitants. Rosalind Russell as a frustrated schoolmistress on the brink of spinsterhood, Arthur O'Connell as a lonely bachelor and Kim Novak as a small-town beauty co-star.

A Columbia Picture, directed by Joshua Logan. With William Holden, Rosalind Russell,

Kim Novak, Betty Field, Susan Strasberg, Cliff Robertson, Arthur O'Connell. CinemaScope/Technicolor. 113 mins.

THE PICTURE OF DORIAN GRAY (1945) ★

★ best b/w cinematography Harry Stradling

Oscar Wilde's frightening fantasy of a handsome young man (Hurd Hatfield) who attains the gift of eternal youth from the gods and remains young while his portrait—the only part of the film to be photographed in Technicolor—shows the horrific marks of age, vice and corruption. Set in gaslit London and starring George Sanders as Wilde's evil genius Lord Henry Wotton, who appropriately delivers the author's witty dialogue and epigrams.

An MGM Picture, directed by Albert Lewin. With George Sanders, Hurd Hatfield, Donna Reed, Angela Lansbury, Peter Lawford, Lowell Gilmore. 110 mins.

PILLOW TALK (1959) ★

★ best story & screenplay Russell Rouse, Clarence Greene, story; Stanley Shapiro, Maurice Richlin, screenplay

Pert interior decorator Doris Day and songwriting wolf Rock Hudson get together—after many squabbles—via the good old-fashioned device of a telephone party line. Thelma Ritter as Day's inebriated maid won the fifth of her six supporting Oscar nominations, a record that still stands in that category. For all her nominations she never came out a winner.

A Universal-International Picture, directed by Michael Gordon. With Rock Hudson, Doris Day, Tony Randall, Thelma Ritter. CinemaScope/Eastman Color. 110 mins.

PINOCCHIO (1940) ★★

★ best original music score Leigh Harline, Paul J. Smith & Ned Washington
★ best song "When You Wish Upon a Star"

(Leigh Harline, music; Ned Washington, lyrics)

Disney's second full-length feature cartoon, based on the Carlo Collodi fairy tale of a wooden puppet who is turned into a real boy. Contains some of the early Disney's most memorable creations—i.e., Pinocchio's "conscience" Jiminy Cricket, puppet master Stromboli, and the roguish fox J. Worthington Foulfellow, as well as some of his best songs—the Oscar-winning "When You Wish Upon a Star," "Hi-Diddle-Dee-Dee" and "Give a Little Whistle." The first Disney full-length feature to be honored by the Academy.

A Walt Disney Picture, released by RKO. Supervising directors—Ben Sharpsteen and Hamilton Luske. With the voices of Dickie Jones, Christian Rub, Cliff Edwards, Evelyn Venable, Walter Catlett, Frankie Darro, Charles Judels. Technicolor. 88 mins.

A PLACE IN THE SUN (1951)

★ best direction George Stevens
★ best screenplay Michael Wilson & Harry Brown
★ best b/w cinematography William C. Mellor
★ best b/w costume design Edith Head
★ best editing William Hornbeck
★ best music score of a drama or comedy Franz Waxman

The tragic story of a poor factory worker (Montgomery Clift) who becomes hopelessly involved with two women in different strata of society—one a plain working girl (Shelley Winters), the other an alluring society beauty (Elizabeth Taylor)—and finds that murder is the only way out of his dilemma. A strong candidate, like *A Streetcar Named Desire*, for the best-film award of 1951, it lost, surprisingly, to the musical *An American in Paris*, Both Clift and Winters earned nominations in the major acting categories but lost—to Humphrey Bogart (*The African Queen*) and Vivien Leigh (*A Streetcar Named Desire*), respectively.

A Place in the Sun (Paramount, 1951), George Stevens' version of Theodore Dreiser's novel *An American Tragedy*. Starring as the doomed lovers: Montgomery Clift and Elizabeth Taylor.

A Paramount Picture, directed by George Stevens. With Montgomery Clift, Elizabeth Taylor, Shelley Winters, Anne Revere, Raymond Burr, Herbert Heyes, Keefe Brasselle, Shepperd Strudwick. 122 mins.

PLACES IN THE HEART (1984)　★★

★ best actress Sally Field
★ best original screenplay Robert Benton

Strong-willed young widow Sally Field raises a family and survives as a cotton farmer in a small Texas town during the Depression. A lynching, threats from the Ku Klux Klan, a tornado and all manner of small-town gossip punctuate the action of the film, which is based on writer-director Robert Benton's early life in the town of Waxahachie. Field's Oscar was her second (she won her first in 1979 for *Norma Rae*); Benton received his third, following the

two he won for his work on *Kramer vs. Kramer* (1979).

A TriStar-Delphi Picture, directed by Robert Benton. With Sally Field, Lindsay Crouse, Ed Harris, Amy Madigan, John Malkovich, Danny Glover, Yankton Hatten, Gennie James, Lane Smith. Technicolor; prints by Metrocolor. 111 mins.

PLATOON (1986)　

★ best film Arnold Kopelson (producer)
★ best direction Oliver Stone
★ best editing Claire Simpson
★ best sound John K. Wilkinson, Richard Rogers, Charles "Bud" Grenzbach & Simon Kaye

The horrific baptism by fire of a young recruit (Charlie Sheen) in Vietnam in the late 1960s, opening with his arrival on a landing strip and the sight of body bags being loaded into a trailer, and closing with his departure as he is lifted out of the country by helicopter. Based very closely on Oliver Stone's own experiences in Vietnam and one of the few films to deal exclusively with the "grunts"—the soldiers in the combat zone who were directly in the line of fire. The second Vietnam picture (*The Deer Hunter* having been the first, some eight years

Sergeant Tom Berenger threatens a terrified Vietnamese girl in Oliver Stone's Oscar-winning best picture of 1986, *Platoon* (Hemdale).

earlier) to be named best of the year. Filmed on location in the Philippines.

Hemdale Film Corporation. Directed by Oliver Stone. With Tom Berenger, Willem Dafoe, Charlie Sheen, Forest Whitaker, Francesco Quinn, John C. McGinley, Richard Edson, Kevin Dillon, Reggie Johnson. Color: CFI. 120 mins.

PLYMOUTH ADVENTURE (1952) ★

★ best special effects A. Arnold Gillespie

A retelling of the voyage of the *Mayflower* to the New World in the 17th century, with Spencer Tracy as the down-to-earth ship's captain and Gene Tierney—wife of staunch Pilgrim leader Leo Genn—as the woman he yearns for.

An MGM Picture, directed by Clarence Brown. With Spencer Tracy, Gene Tierney, Van Johnson, Leo Genn, Lloyd Bridges, Dawn Addams, Barry Jones. Technicolor. 105 mins.

PORGY AND BESS (1959) ★

★ best scoring of a musical Andre Previn & Ken Darby

George Gershwin's classic folk opera about life in the South Carolina slums of Catfish Row. Sidney Poitier is the crippled beggar Porgy, Dorothy Dandridge the beautiful, reckless girl who loves and eventually leaves him, and Sammy Davis, Jr. is "Sportin' Life."

A Samuel Goldwyn Production (released through Columbia) directed by Otto Preminger. With Sidney Poitier, Dorothy Dandridge, Sammy Davis, Jr., Pearl Bailey, Brock Peters, Leslie Scott, Diahann Carroll. Todd-AO/Technicolor. 138 mins.

PORTRAIT OF JENNIE (1948) ★

★ best special effects Paul Eagler, J. McMillan Johnson, Russell Shearman, Clarence Slifer: visual; Charles Freeman, James G. Stewart: audible

Fantasy about a struggling artist (Joseph Cotten) who becomes infatuated with a young woman (Jennifer Jones) he meets in Central Park, then finds that she is no more than the spirit of a girl who died several years before. An imaginative use of color (in an otherwise black-and-white film) in the climactic storm sequence helped earn the special effects men their Oscar.

A David O. Selznick Production (released through the Selznick Releasing Organization) directed by William Dieterle. With Joseph Cotten, Jennifer Jones, Ethel Barrymore, Lillian Gish, Cecil Kellaway, David Wayne, Albert Sharpe, Henry Hull. 86 mins.

THE POSEIDON ADVENTURE (1972) ★★

★ best song "The Morning After" (Al Kasha & Joel Hirschhorn, music & lyrics)
★ best visual effects* L. B. Abbot & A. D. Flowers

Two hours of "will they, won't they make it" suspense as a small band of passengers struggle to the top (i.e., the bottom) of a luxury ocean liner when it capsizes after being struck by a tidal wave in the Mediterranean. Gene Hackman, Ernest Borgnine, Shelley Winters, Jack Albertson and Carol Lynley are among those fighting for survival.

A 20th Century-Fox Picture, directed by Ronald Neame. With Gene Hackman, Ernest Borgnine, Red Buttons, Carol Lynley, Roddy McDowall, Stella Stevens, Shelley Winters, Jack Albertson. Panavision/DeLuxe Color. 117 mins.

PRIDE AND PREJUDICE (1940) ★

★ best b/w art direction Cedric Gibbons & Paul Groesse

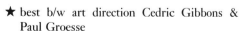

* *Note:* The Oscar for visual effects was a special achievement award.

Adaptation of Helen Jerome's play (based on Jane Austen's classic novel) about the mode of life, manners and customs in a 19th-century English village, when family pride and position were considered to be all that mattered in life. Laurence Olivier stars as the dashing Mr. Darcy seeking the hand of Greer Garson. Edmund Gwenn features as the harassed father with five unwed daughters on his hands.

An MGM Picture, directed by Robert Z. Leonard. With Laurence Olivier, Greer Garson, Mary Boland, Edna May Oliver, Maureen O'Sullivan, Ann Rutherford, Frieda Inescort, Edmund Gwenn. 118 mins.

PRIDE OF THE YANKEES (1942)   ★

★ best editing Daniel Mandell

Biography of the famous American baseball star Lou Gehrig (Gary Cooper), the Yankee first baseman who played 2,130 consecutive games for the Yankees before falling victim to the rare neurological disease amyotrophic lateral sclerosis (ALS)—a disease that resulted in his early death at the age of 37 in June of 1941.

A Sam Goldwyn Production (released through RKO), directed by Sam Wood. With Gary Cooper, Teresa Wright, Walter Brennan, Dan Duryea, Babe Ruth, Elsa Janssen, Ludwig Stossel, Virginia Gilmore. 128 mins.

THE PRIME OF MISS JEAN BRODIE (1969)   ★

★ best actress Maggie Smith

Maggie Smith as novelist Muriel Spark's eccentric Scottish schoolmistress, who ignores the prescribed school curriculum and teaches her own individual concepts of life—which include supporting fascism—to the children in her care. Pamela Franklin is the pupil who rebels against her insidious influence and destroys her; Celia Johnson is the headmistress. Set in Edinburgh in the 1930s.

A 20th Century-Fox Picture, directed by Ronald Neame. With Maggie Smith, Robert Stephens, Pamela Franklin, Gordon Jackson, Celia Johnson. DeLuxe Color. 116 mins.

PRINCESS O'ROURKE (1943)   ★

★ best original screenplay Norman Krasna

Norman Krasna's comedy-romance about an all-American pilot (Robert Cummings), who finds that his fiancee (Olivia de Havilland) is a bonafide exiled princess. Directed by Krasna—one of the few occasions he directed from one of his own screenplays.

A Warner Bros. Picture, directed by Norman Krasna. With Olivia de Havilland, Robert Cummings, Charles Coburn, Jack Carson, Jane Wyman, Harry Davenport, Gladys Cooper. 94 mins.

THE PRIVATE LIFE OF HENRY VIII (1932/33)   ★

★ best actor Charles Laughton

The matrimonial misadventures of one of Britain's most tyrannical kings, with Charles Laughton giving a virtuoso performance as the restless Henry and becoming the first Englishman to win an Oscar in a British-made film. Elsa Lanchester costars as Anne of Cleves, Binnie Barnes as Katherine Howard, Wendy Barrie as Jane Seymour, Merle Oberon as Anne Boleyn and Everley Gregg as Catherine Parr.

A London Films Picture, directed by Alexander Korda. With Charles Laughton, Robert Donat, Merle Oberon, Binnie Barnes, Lady Tree, Elsa Lanchester, Franklin Dyall, Miles Mander. 97 mins.

PRIZZI'S HONOR (1985)   ★

★ best supporting actress Anjelica Huston

None-too-bright hit man Jack Nicholson falls for cool beauty Kathleen Turner and then finds,

Anjelica Huston, best supporting actress of 1985 for her portrayal of a Mafia daughter in *Prizzi's Honor* (ABC/20th Century-Fox).

The Producers (Avco Embassy)—the only Mel Brooks movie to earn an Oscar—winner for best story and screenplay in 1968. Watching their hit show taking shape are Zero Mostel (left) and Gene Wilder (center).

to his dismay, that he has to bump her off before she does it to him. Plenty of Brando-type mumbling from Nicholson, sultry sex from Turner, and heart searching from Anjelica Huston as the black sheep of a Mafia dynasty. Anjelica became the third member of the Huston family to win an Academy Award, following father John and grandfather Walter, both of whom won for *The Treasure of the Sierra Madre* in 1948.

ABC Motion Pictures/20th Century Fox, directed by John Huston. With Jack Nicholson, Kathleen Turner, Robert Loggia, John Randolph, William Hickey, Lee Richardson, Michael Lombard, Anjelica Huston, George Santopietro, Lawrence Tierney. DeLuxe Color. 129 mins.

THE PRODUCERS (1968) ★

★ best story & screenplay Mel Brooks

Brash Mel Brooks comedy with Zero Mostel as a down-and-out ham producer conning meek accountant Gene Wilder into a fraudulent scheme to get rich quick by producing a flop Broadway show called *Springtime for Hitler*. Their plot backfires, however, when the show turns out to be a hit.

An Avco-Embassy Picture, directed by Mel Brooks. With Zero Mostel, Gene Wilder, Dick Shawn, Kenneth Mars, Estelle Winwood. Pathe Color. 88 mins.

PURPLE RAIN (1984) ★

★ best original song score Prince

Flashy and familiar rags-to-riches tale, this time of an American pop star who struggles to rise from the ashes of his past and escape from his alcoholic father. The first movie of the then-24-year-old Prince, and packed wall-to-wall with original songs written by the star.

A Purple Films Company/Warner Bros. Picture, directed by Albert Magnoli. With Prince, Apollonia Kotero, Morris Day, Olga Karlatos,

Clarence Williams III, Jerome Benton, Billy Sparks, Jill Jones. Technicolor. 111 mins.

PYGMALION (1938)

★ best writing adaptation W. P. Lipscomb, Cecil Lewis & Ian Dalrymple
★ best screenplay George Bernard Shaw

The screen version of George Bernard Shaw's stage play on which the musical *My Fair Lady* was based, with Leslie Howard as Professor Higgins and Wendy Hiller as the cockney guttersnipe he turns into a lady. Not the multiple Oscar winner the musical later turned out to be, but the first British movie to win writing awards, one of the four recipients being Shaw himself.

A Gabriel Pascal Production (released through GFD), directed by Anthony Asquith and Leslie Howard. With Leslie Howard, Wendy Hiller, Wilfrid Lawson, Marie Lohr, Scott Sunderland, Jean Cadell, David Tree. 96 mins.

Q

QUEST FOR FIRE (1982)　★

★ best makeup Sarah Monzani & Michele Burke

How the warring tribes of prehistoric times (80,000 B.C.) overcame attacks from apes, wolves, saber-toothed tigers and each other and managed to survive by using the life-giving source of fire. No dialogue, but a great deal of body language (created by Desmond Morris) and a wealth of sense sounds provided by Anthony Burgess. Filmed on location in Kenya, Scotland, Iceland and Canada and based loosely on a French children's fantasy written in 1911.

ICC-Cine-Trail (Montreal)/Belstar Productions/Stephan Films (Paris)/distributed by 20th Century-Fox. Directed by Jean-Jacques Annaud. With Everett McGill, Ron Perlman, Nameer El-Kadi, Rae Dawn Chong, Gary Schwartz, Frank Olivier Bonnet, Jean-Michel Kindt. Panavision/70mm/Color: Bellevue-Pathe. 100 mins.

THE QUIET MAN (1952)　★★

★ best direction John Ford
★ best color cinematography Winton C. Hoch
　& Archie Stout

The film for which John Ford won his fourth directorial Oscar (a record) and cameraman Winton Hoch his third in four years—a whimsical tale set in an idyllic Ireland, with ex-boxer John Wayne returning to his native Galway to court fiery Irish colleen Maureen O'Hara.

A Republic Picture, directed by John Ford. With John Wayne, Maureen O'Hara, Barry Fitzgerald, Ward Bond, Victor McLaglen, Mildred Natwick, Francis Ford. Technicolor. 129 mins.

R

RAGING BULL (1980)   ★ ★

★ best actor Robert De Niro
★ best editing Thelma Schoonmaker

Martin Scorsese at his most unrelenting; a searing portrait of the boxer Jake La Motta, who rose to become middleweight champion of the world and then slid into a life of near obscurity as an entertainer on the sleazy nightclub circuit. Only 12 minutes of boxing sequences, but they remain the most ferocious ever filmed; Robert De Niro's Oscar made him the second actor in the history of the Academy to win both a supporting award (*The Godfather Part II*) and a best-actor honor. Jack Lemmon was the first to achieve the double, with *Mister Roberts* (1955) and *Save the Tiger* (1973). Jack Nicholson and Gene Hackman have accomplished it since: Nicholson for *One Flew Over the Cuckoo's Nest* (1975) and *Terms of Endearment* (1983); Hackman for *The French Connection* (1971) and *Unforgiven* (1992).

A United Artists Picture, directed by Martin Scorsese. With Robert De Niro, Cathy Moriarty, Joe Pesci, Frank Vincent, Nicholas Co-

Robert De Niro as Jake La Motta winning the fight—and an Oscar—for his performance in Martin Scorsese's *Raging Bull*. (United Artists, 1980).

Indiana Jones begins his screen adventures. Harrison Ford in Spielberg's 1981 blockbuster *Raiders of the Lost Ark* (Paramount).

lasanto, Theresa Saldana, Mario Gallo. B/w, and partly Technicolor. 129 mins.

RAIDERS OF THE LOST ARK (1981)   ★ ★ ★ ★ ★

★ best editing Michael Kahn
★ best art direction Norman Reynolds & Leslie Dilley
        set decoration Michael Ford
★ best sound Bill Varney, Steve Maslow, Gregg Landaker & Roy Charman
★ best visual effects Richard Edlund, Kit West, Bruce Nicholson & Joe Johnston
★ best sound effects editing* Ben Burtt & Richard L. Anderson

Fast-moving 1930s-style adventure tale brought up to date with all the technical advantages of modern-day cinema. Harrison Ford stars as American archaeologist Indiana Jones in search of the Ark containing the tablets of God's Law. Also searching: Nazi treasure hunters led by rival archaeologist Paul Freeman. Set in South America and Egypt and, together with *Chariots of Fire*, the major Oscar winner of 1981.

A Lucasfilm for Paramount, directed by Steven Spielberg. With Harrison Ford, Karen Allen, Paul Freeman, Ronald Lacey, John

---

* *Note:* The movie's Oscar for sound effects editing was a special achievement award.

Rhys-Davies, Denholm Elliott, Alfred Molina. Metrocolor. 115 mins.

RAIN MAN (1988) ★★★★

- ★ best film Mark Johnson (producer)
- ★ best direction Barry Levinson
- ★ best actor Dustin Hoffman
- ★ best original screenplay Ronald Base & Barry Morrow; story by Morrow

Two brothers, one an autistic savant (Dustin Hoffman), the other a brash young hustler (Tom Cruise), journey across America together to try to get Cruise cut in on their late father's will. A glossy showcase for Hoffman's ability to create a character in depth; more important, the most revealing and intelligent examination of autism yet put on screen. The film enabled Hoffman to join the select band of actors who

Dustin Hoffman's second best-actor Academy Award, earned for his portrayal of autistic savant Raymond Babbitt in Barry Levinson's *Rain Man* (United Artists, 1988).

have won two best-actor Academy Awards. The other previous double winners: Fredric March *(Dr. Jekyll And Mr. Hyde, The Best Years of Our Lives)*; Spencer Tracy *(Captains Courageous, Boys' Town)*; Gary Cooper *(Sergeant York, High Noon)*; and Marlon Brando *(On the Waterfront, The Godfather)*.

A United Artists Picture (A Guber-Peters Company Production), directed by Barry Levinson. With Dustin Hoffman, Tom Cruise, Valeria Golino, Jerry Molen, Jack Murdock, Michael D. Roberts, Ralph Seymour, Lucinda Jenney. Color; prints by DeLuxe. 133 mins.

THE RAINS CAME (1939) ★

- ★ best special effects E. H. Hansen & Fred Sersen

The first film to win a special effects award, an adaptation of Louis Bromfield's novel about the love affair between an English socialite wife (Myrna Loy) and a handsome young Indian doctor (Tyrone Power). Full of brilliantly staged monsoon floods, earthquakes, toppling temples, etc.

A 20th Century-Fox Picture, directed by Clarence Brown. With Myrna Loy, Tyrone Power, George Brent, Brenda Joyce, Nigel Bruce, Maria Ouspenskaya, Joseph Schildkraut, Mary Nash, Jane Darwell. 103 mins.

RAN (1985) ★

- ★ best costume design Emi Wada

Akira Kurosawa transfers Shakespeare's *King Lear* to 16th-century Japan and weaves it together with a Japanese folk legend. The result: madness, power struggles, warring tribes and bloodshed as a senile 70-year-old warrior divides up his kingdom among his three sons. Kurosawa earned his first Academy Award nomination for his direction of the film, although he subsequently received a special award from the Academy in the spring of 1990. Two previous Kurosawa films won foreign language Oscars—*Rashomon* (a special award in 1951) and

Dersu Uzala in 1975. *Ran* was not among the five nominated foreign language pictures of 1985.

Greenwich Film Productions (Paris)/Herald Ace/Nippon Herald Films (Tokyo). Directed by Akira Kurosawa. With Tatsuya Nakadai, Akira Terao, Jinpachi Nezu, Daisuke Ryu, Mieko Harada, Yoshiko Miyazaki, Kazuo Kato. Color. 160 mins.

THE RAZOR'S EDGE (1946)   ★

★ best supporting actress Anne Baxter

Somerset Maugham's philosophical novel about an idealistic young man (Tyrone Power) who sheds his rich background to search for faith and spiritual fulfillment in his life. Gene Tierney co-stars as a deceitful old flame, Clifton Webb as an aristocratic snob and Anne Baxter (the film's only Oscar winner) as a tragic young woman who becomes an alcoholic after the death of her husband and child in a car crash.

A 20th Century-Fox Picture, directed by Edmund Goulding. With Tyrone Power, Gene Tierney, John Payne, Anne Baxter, Clifton Webb, Herbert Marshall, Lucile Watson, Frank Latimore, Elsa Lanchester. 146 mins.

REAP THE WILD WIND (1942)   ★

★ best special effects Gordon Jennings, Farciot Edouart & William L. Pereira (photo); Louis Mesenkop (sound)

DeMille spectacular—set in the 1840s—about America's fight to crush the pirate wreckers who ransacked ships that went to pieces on the treacherous Florida reefs. John Wayne, Paulette Goddard and Ray Milland provide a three-way romance; the special effects men created a giant squid which, in a thrilling fight to the death, conveniently gets rid of one of the lovers so that Miss Goddard is left free to marry the other.

A Paramount Picture, directed by Cecil B. DeMille. With Ray Milland, John Wayne, Paulette Goddard, Raymond Massey, Robert Preston, Lynne Overman, Susan Hayward, Charles Bickford. Technicolor. 124 mins.

REBECCA (1940)

★ best film David O. Selznick (producer)
★ best b/w cinematography George Barnes

Daphne du Maurier's romantic novel about a timid young newlywed (Joan Fontaine) who finds that her aristocratic husband (Laurence Olivier) is still dominated by the memory of his mysteriously deceased first wife. Set for the most part in the somber Cornish mansion of Manderley, the film was Hitchcock's first in the U.S. and proved an Oscar winner first time out, although Hitch himself—nominated for this one and for four other films—never won. Hitchcock's other nominations were for *Lifeboat* (1944), *Spellbound* (1945), *Rear Window* (1954) and *Psycho* (1960).

A Selznick International Picture (released through United Artists), directed by Alfred Hitchcock. With Laurence Olivier, Joan Fontaine, George Sanders, Judith Anderson, Nigel Bruce, C. Aubrey Smith, Reginald Denny, Gladys Cooper. 130 mins.

THE RED BALLOON (1956)   ★

★ best original screenplay Albert Lamorisse

Half-hour fantasy about the adventures of a little boy and a big red balloon he rescues from a Paris lamppost. Photographed entirely in the picturesque backstreets and alleys of Old Montmartre and starring the director's own six-year-old son, Pascal.

A Films Montsouris Production, directed by Albert Lamorisse. With Pascal Lamorisse, the children of Menilmontant and all the balloons of Paris. Technicolor. 35 mins.

THE RED SHOES (1948)   ★ ★

★ best color art direction Hein Heckroth
        set decoration Arthur Lawson
★ best scoring of a drama or comedy Brian Easdale

One of only a few successful box-office ballet films, hampered by its trite story—young ballerina torn between her love for her composer husband and her love for dancing—but almost completely redeemed by Brian Easdale's exciting music and the brilliant color of cameraman Jack Cardiff. The central 20-minute ballet is based on the Hans Christian Andersen story about the magic red shoes that dance a little girl to death.

An Archers Film, directed by Michael Powell and Emeric Pressburger. With Moira Shearer, Leonide Massine, Robert Helpmann, Anton Walbrook, Marius Goring. Technicolor. 133 mins.

REDS (1981)   ★ ★ ★

★ best direction Warren Beatty
★ best supporting actress Maureen Stapleton
★ best cinematography Vittorio Storaro

This 196-minute epic deals with the life of American communist journalist John Reed, who witnessed the Russian Revolution of 1917 and recorded the events in his book *Ten Days That Shook the World*. The film follows Reed's life from 1915 to his death in Russia and was nom-

Warren Beatty as American journalist John Reed in *Reds* (Paramount, 1981). Beatty was nominated for his performance—and also for his writing and production—but was named by the Academy for his direction. The film also won in the supporting actress and cinematography categories.

inated for 12 Academy Awards. Warren Beatty (like Orson Welles before him for *Citizen Kane*) was nominated in four categories—producer, director, writer and actor—but won only as best director. Maureen Stapleton earned her Oscar for her portrait of disillusioned anarchist Emma Goldman.

A Paramount Picture, directed by Warren Beatty. With Warren Beatty, Diane Keaton, Edward Herrmann, Jerzy Kosinski, Jack Nicholson, Paul Sorvino, Maureen Stapleton, Nicolas Coster. Technicolor. 196 mins.

RETURN OF THE JEDI (1983)   ★

★ best visual effects* Richard Edlund, Dennis Muren, Ken Ralston & Phil Tippett

The last of the *Star Wars* trilogy, with Luke Skywalker discovering that the villainous Darth Vader is really his father and Princess Leia his sister. New additions to the creature and monster gallery: the ingenious little Ewoks and the huge, splendidly repulsive Jabba the Hutt, whose lust for Princess Leia leads to his early demise.

A Lucasfilm for 20th Century-Fox, directed by Richard Marquand. With Mark Hamill, Harrison Ford, Carrie Fisher, Billy Dee Williams, Anthony Daniels, Peter Mayhew, Sebastian Shaw, Ian McDiarmid, Frank Oz, David Prowse, James Earl Jones. Color: Rank, prints by Deluxe. 132 mins.

REVERSAL OF FORTUNE (1990)   ★

★ best actor Jeremy Irons

Did European aristocrat Claus Von Bulow (Jeremy Irons) try to murder his rich wife Sunny (Glenn Close) with an injection of insulin and bungle the job by putting her in a coma instead? The jury says "yes" and sentences him to 30 years. A retrial, led by defense lawyer Alan Dershowitz, says "no" and allows Von Bulow to remain a free man. Oscar-winner Jeremy

---

* *Note:* The film's solitary Oscar was a special achievement award.

Jeremy Irons (best actor, 1990) as Claus Von Bulow in *Reversal of Fortune* (Sovereign Pictures).

Irons supposedly based his enigmatic ice-cold performance on the many screen characterizations of George Sanders.

Sovereign Pictures (in association with Shochiku Fuji Co.), directed by Barbet Schroeder. With Glenn Close, Jeremy Irons, Ron Silver, Annabella Sciorra, Uta Hagen, Fisher Stevens, Jack Gilpin, Christine Baranski. Technicolor. 111 mins.

THE RIGHT STUFF (1983) ★★★★

★ best sound Mark Berger, Tom Scott, Randy Thom & David MacMillan
★ best editing Glenn Farr, Lisa Fruchtman, Stephen A. Rotter, Douglas Stewart & Tom Rolf
★ best sound effects editing Jay Boekelheide
★ best original score Bill Conti

The exhilarating saga of the birth of America's space program, concentrating on each of the seven astronauts who pioneered the first space flights. Based on the novel by Tom Wolfe, who linked the astronauts' heroic story with that of

Chuck Yeager, the test pilot who first broke the sound barrier back in 1947. Three hours of stunning effects and satirical observation, all of it enhanced by the majestic score of Bill Conti.

A Ladd Company Production for Warner Bros., directed by Philip Kaufman. With Sam Shepard, Scott Glenn, Ed Harris, Dennis Quaid, Fred Ward, Barbara Hershey, Kim Stanley, Veronica Cartwright, Pamela Reed, Scott Paulin. 70 mm/Technicolor. 193 mins.

THE RIVER (1984) ★

★ best sound effects editing* Kay Rose

Stolid drama about a Tennessee family struggling to make good on their farm and constantly battling a local tycoon, who wants to claim the river that runs alongside their home and flood their existing farmland. Spectacular storm scenes and beautiful camerawork from Oscar-nominated Vilmos Zsigmond.

A Universal Picture, directed by Mark Rydell. With Mel Gibson, Sissy Spacek, Shane Bailey, Becky Jo Lynch, Scott Glenn, Don Hood, Billy Green Bush, James Tolkan. Technicolor. 124 mins.

A RIVER RUNS THROUGH IT (1992) ★

★ best cinematography Philippe Rousselot

Robert Redford's adaptation of Norman Maclean's autobiographical novella, set against the elegiac backdrop of fly-fishing and tracing the author's relationship with his wilder younger brother in a small Montana community. A loving, affectionate portrait of a virtually vanished American West, handsomely photographed by Philippe Rousselot, who earned his first Oscar for his photography of the mountains and rivers of Montana. Rousselot had previously been nominated for John Boorman's *Hope and Glory* (1987) and for Philip Kaufman's *Henry and June* (1990).

---

* *Note:* The film's solitary Oscar was a special achievement award.

A Columbia Picture, directed by Robert Redford. With Craig Sheffer, Brad Pitt, Tom Skerritt, Brenda Blethyn, Emily Lloyd, Edie McClurg, Stephen Shellen. Technicolor. 123 mins.

THE ROBE (1953) ★★

★ best color art direction Lyle Wheeler & George W. Davis
                set decoration Walter M. Scott & Paul S. Fox
★ best color costume design Charles LeMaire & Emile Santiago

Lloyd C. Douglas' story of the conversion to Christianity of the Roman tribune (Richard Burton) in charge of Christ's crucifixion on Calvary. Jean Simmons is featured as the innocent maid, Jay Robinson as the screaming Emperor Caligula, but, not surprisingly, it was CinemaScope that received the biggest accolades, this being the first film to be shot in the then-revolutionary process.

A 20th Century-Fox Picture, directed by Henry Koster. With Richard Burton, Jean Simmons, Victor Mature, Michael Rennie, Jay Robinson, Dean Jagger. CinemaScope/Technicolor. 135 mins.

ROBOCOP (1987) ★

★ best sound effects* Stephen Flick & John Pospisil

A dead cop, still blessed with a brain and a memory, is transformed into an ultrasophisticated cyborg and stalks the streets of a decaying and futuristic Detroit seeking revenge on the frenzied psychos who shot him to bits. Plenty of noise, carnage and graphic violence, plus— of course—corruption from "the corporation," which sees Robo as the perfect policeman of the future.

An Orion Picture, directed by Paul Verhoeven. With Peter Weller, Nancy Allen, Dan-

_____

* _Note:_ The film's Oscar was a special achievement award bestowed by the Academy.

iel O'Herlihy, Ronny Cox, Kurtwood Smith, Miguel Ferrer, Robert DoQui, Ray Wise. DeLuxe Color. 102 mins.

ROCKY (1976) ★★★

★ best film Irwin Winkler & Robert Chartoff (producers)
★ best direction John G. Avildsen
★ best editing Richard Halsey & Scott Conrad

Cinderella story of an unknown boxer (Sylvester Stallone) who, by a twist of fate, gets his chance to have a crack at the heavyweight title, and in doing so wins for himself the self-respect he has been missing all his life. Co-starring Talia Shire as his shy young girlfriend, the film is the only sports movie ever to be named best picture of the year.

A United Artists Picture, directed by John G. Avildsen. With Sylvester Stallone, Talia Shire, Burt Young, Carl Weathers, Burgess Meredith, Thayer David. DeLuxe Color. 119 mins.

ROMAN HOLIDAY (1953) ★★★

★ best actress Audrey Hepburn
★ best motion picture story* Ian McLellan Hunter
★ best b/w costume design Edith Head

_____

* _Note:_ Ian McLellan Hunter co-scripted _Roman Holiday_ with John Dighton, but the "story" for the film was conceived by the blacklisted writer Dalton Trumbo. Hunter agreed to "front" for Trumbo, selling the story for $40,000. At Oscar time he found himself nominated for his own work (the screenplay) and that of Trumbo (story). Embarrassingly, he lost to Daniel Taradash _(From Here to Eternity)_ in the screenplay category, but won for a story that wasn't his. Nearly 40 years later, Trumbo received belated credit for his work. The Writers' Guild of America determined that Trumbo was responsible for the screen story and that his longtime friend had "fronted" for him in 1953. Ironically, Hunter himself was subsequently blacklisted.

Romantic comedy that made Audrey Hepburn a star and earned her an Oscar in her first major role—that of a young princess who escapes from the pomp and ceremony of her surroundings for 24 hours and enjoys a brief romance with American journalist Gregory Peck. Shot entirely in Rome.

A Paramount Picture, directed by William Wyler. With Gregory Peck, Audrey Hepburn, Eddie Albert, Hartley Power, Laura Solari, Harcourt Williams, Margaret Rawlings. 119 mins.

ROMEO AND JULIET (1968)   ★ ★

- ★ best cinematography Pasqualino De Santis
- ★ best costume design Danilo Donati

Shakespeare's immortal tragedy of two young lovers whose families—the Montagues and the Capulets—try to keep them apart but succeed only in being responsible for their suicides. Leonard Whiting and Olivia Hussey are featured as the star-crossed lovers, Michael York as Tybalt, John McEnery as Mercutio.

A Paramount Release, directed by Franco Zeffirelli. With Leonard Whiting, Olivia Hussey, Milo O'Shea, Michael York, John McEnery. Technicolor. 152 mins.

ROOM AT THE TOP (1959)   ★ ★

- ★ best actress Simone Signoret
- ★ best screenplay Neil Paterson

One of the very few British movies to deal openly with the subject of class; the tale of a young working-class accountant (Laurence Harvey) who ruthlessly makes it to the top in one bounce by the simple expedient of making the daughter of a rich industrialist pregnant. Based on the novel by John Braine. The top performance in the movie came from Simone Signoret, who, as Harvey's tragic fading mistress, became the first French actress to win the best actress award.

A Remus Picture, directed by Jack Clayton. With Simone Signoret, Laurence Harvey,

Heather Sears, Donald Wolfit, Donald Houston, Hermione Baddeley. 117 mins.

A ROOM WITH A VIEW (1986)   ★ ★ ★

- ★ best screenplay Ruth Prawer Jhabvala
- ★ best art direction Gianni Quaranta & Brian Ackland-Snow
         set decoration Brian Savegar & Elio Altramura
- ★ best costume design Jenny Beavan & John Bright

E. M. Forster's classic satire of the English abroad and the hypocrisy of Edwardian society at the turn of the century. Helena Bonham Carter and Julian Sands star as the young couple who begin a passionate affair in Florence and then continue it in England, defying convention by overcoming the sterility and snobbery of those around them. Ravishing Florence locations, elegant performances, and Puccini on the sound track courtesy of Kiri Te Kanawa.

Merchant Ivory/Cinecom, directed by James Ivory. With Maggie Smith, Helena Bonham Carter, Denholm Elliott, Julian Sands, Daniel Day-Lewis, Simon Callow, Judi Dench, Rose-

Romance in Florence—Julian Sands and Helena Bonham Carter in the Merchant Ivory production of *A Room with a View* (Merchant Ivory/Cinecom, 1986). The film won awards for screenplay, art direction and costume design.

mary Leach, Rupert Graves. Technicolor. 117 mins.

ROSEMARY'S BABY (1968) ★

★ best supporting actress Ruth Gordon

Thriller about witchcraft and satanism in contemporary New York, with Mia Farrow as the luckless girl chosen to bear the child (unseen) of the Devil. Co-starring John Cassavetes as her husband, Sidney Blackmer as the leader of the coven and Ruth Gordon as the flamboyant witch, Minnie Castevet, who "looks after" Miss Farrow during her pregnancy.

A Paramount Picture, directed by Roman Polanski. With Mia Farrow, John Cassavetes, Ruth Gordon, Sidney Blackmer, Maurice Evans, Ralph Bellamy, Angela Dorian, Patsy Kelly. Technicolor. 136 mins.

THE ROSE TATTOO (1955) ★★★

★ best actress Anna Magnani
★ best b/w cinematography James Wong Howe
★ best b/w art direction Hal Pereira & Tambi Larsen

 set decoration Sam Comer & Arthur Krams

Anna Magnani as Tennessee Williams' tempestuous, Sicilian-born peasant Serafina, who mourns deeply for her dead truckdriver husband and settles in the end for a great sweating oaf of a man (Burt Lancaster) whose body alone reminds her of her former partner. Set in the Italian quarter of a steamy town on the Gulf Coast.

A Paramount Picture, directed by Daniel Mann. With Anna Magnani, Burt Lancaster, Marisa Pavan, Ben Cooper, Jo Van Fleet. Vista Vision. 117 mins.

ROUND MIDNIGHT (1986) ★

★ best original score Herbie Hancock

A veteran, burned-out jazz saxophonist (Dexter Gordon) is persuaded by a devoted French fan to forsake the booze and drugs and opt for a comeback in New York, all of which works for a while, until he eventually resumes his journey to self-destruction. A Bertrand Tavernier film, bittersweet in mood, and one of the few films about jazz (another being *Bird*, 1988) to figure among Academy Award winners. Based in part on the careers of Bud Powell and Lester Young.

A Warner Bros. (Los Angeles)/PECF/Little Bear (Paris) Picture, directed by Bertrand Tavernier. With Dexter Gordon, Francois Cluzet, Gabrielle Haker, Sandra Reaves-Phillips, Lonette McKee, Christine Pascal, Herbie Hancock. Panavision/Eastman Color. 131 mins.

RYAN'S DAUGHTER (1970) ★★

★ best supporting actor John Mills
★ best cinematography Freddie Young

David Lean's simple love story of Ireland in 1916 centering around a romantic and excitable young Irish girl (Sarah Miles) who marries the simple, plodding schoolteacher (Robert Mitchum) of the village—a man twice her age—and has an affair with a shell-shocked young British officer (Christopher Jones) stationed in a nearby garrison. Mills' Oscar was for his portrayal of the misshapen village idiot, Michael; Freddie Young's was his third for his work in a Lean film (the others being for *Lawrence of Arabia* in 1962 and *Doctor Zhivago* in 1965).

An MGM Picture, directed by David Lean. With Sarah Miles, Robert Mitchum, Trevor Howard, Christopher Jones, John Mills, Leo McKern, Barry Foster. Super Panavision 70/Metrocolor. 206 mins.

S

SABRINA (1954) ★

★ best b/w costume design Edith Head

Lubitsch-type sophisticated comedy with chauffeur's daughter Audrey Hepburn being romanced by the two sons of a wealthy Long Island family—aging business tycoon Humphrey Bogart and his playboy brother William Holden. From the Broadway play by Samuel Taylor.

A Paramount Picture, directed by Billy Wilder. With Humphrey Bogart, Audrey Hepburn, William Holden, Walter Hampden, John Williams, Martha Hyer. 113 mins.

SAMSON AND DELILAH (1950) ★★

★ best color art direction Hans Dreier & Walter Tyler
         set decoration Sam Comer & Ray Moyer
★ best color costume design Edith Head, Dorothy Jeakins, Eloise Jenssen, Gile Steele & Gwen Wakeling

DeMille's first postwar Biblical spectacular, the story of mighty Danite strongman Samson (Victor Mature), who destroys an entire army with the jawbone of an ass but falls victim to the wiles of Philistine temptress Hedy Lamarr. Hokum, although the final destruction of the temple of Gaza is impressive.

A Paramount Picture, directed by Cecil B. DeMille. With Hedy Lamarr, Victor Mature, George Sanders, Angela Lansbury, Henry Wilcoxon. Technicolor. 128 mins.

THE SANDPIPER (1965)

★ best song "The Shadow of Your Smile" (John Mandel, music; Paul Francis Webster, lyrics)

An adulterous love affair between free-thinking beatnik mother Elizabeth Taylor and Episcopal clergyman Richard Burton. Big-star soap opera, photographed on California's Big Sur coast and scored to romantic perfection by John Mandel, whose song "The Shadow of Your Smile" came out easily as the year's best.

An MGM Picture, directed by Vincente Minnelli. With Elizabeth Taylor, Richard Burton, Eva Marie Saint, Charles Bronson, Robert Webber, James Edwards, Torin Thatcher. Panavision/Metrocolor. 116 mins.

SAN FRANCISCO (1936) ★

★ best sound recording Douglas Shearer

Robust melodrama of love and adventure on the notorious Barbary Coast, following the intertwined lives of saloon owner/gambler Clark Gable, opera singer Jeanette MacDonald and two-fisted priest Spencer Tracy. Climaxed, of course, by the historic earthquake of 1906.

An MGM Picture, directed by W. S. Van Dyke. With Clark Gable, Jeanette MacDonald, Spencer Tracy, Jack Holt, Jessie Ralph. 115 mins.

SAVE THE TIGER (1973)

★ best actor Jack Lemmon

A day in the life of American businessman Jack Lemmon, who is forced by his partner to consider arson as a way out of financial trouble. For his portrayal of Harry Stoner, Lemmon became the first actor to win both a supporting Oscar (for *Mister Roberts* 18 years earlier) and a major acting Oscar in his career.

A Paramount Picture, directed by John G. Avildsen. With Jack Lemmon, Jack Gilford, Laurie Heineman, Norman Burton, Patricia Smith, Thayer David. Movielab Color. 100 mins.

SAYONARA (1957) ★★★★

★ best supporting actor Red Buttons
★ best supporting actress Miyoshi Umeki
★ best art direction Ted Haworth
        set decoration Robert Priestley
★ best sound recording George R. Groves

U.S. Korean war ace Marlon Brando, sent to Japan for rest and rehabilitation, falls in love with Japanese actress Miiko Taka and finds himself coming up against the brutal racial policies practiced by the American military authorities. The movie's main Oscars went to Red Buttons as an American flier and Miyoshi Umeki as a Japanese girl, who play out a delicate, ultimately doomed love affair.

A Warner Bros. Picture, directed by Joshua Logan. With Marlon Brando, Patricia Owen, James Garner, Martha Scott, Miyoshi Umeki, Miiko Taka, Red Buttons. Technirama/Technicolor. 147 mins.

SCENT OF A WOMAN (1992) ★

★ best actor Al Pacino

Blind, embittered retired lieutenant colonel Al Pacino determines to enjoy the best and last weekend of his life during a riotous couple of days in New York City. Accompanying him on his escapades is troubled teenager and "minder" Chris O'Donnell, whose weekend turns out to be somewhat more eventful than he'd imagined. Pacino won his best-actor award after receiving previous nominations for *The Godfather* (supporting actor, 1972), *Serpico* (1973), *The Godfather Part II* (1974), *Dog Day Afternoon* (1975), *And Justice for All* (1979) and *Dick Tracy* (supporting actor, 1990). In 1992 he was also nominated in the supporting category, for his hotshot real estate salesman in *Glengarry Glen Ross*.

A Universal Picture, directed by Martin Brest. With Al Pacino, Chris O'Donnell, James Rebhorn, Gabrielle Anwar, Philip S. Hoffman, Richard Venture, Bradley Whitford, Rochelle Oliver, Margaret Eginton. DeLuxe Color. 156 mins.

THE SCOUNDREL (1935) ★

★ best original story Ben Hecht & Charles MacArthur

A ruthless and hated New York publisher (Noel Coward), killed suddenly in a plane crash, finds his path into eternity blocked by a divine voice that gives him exactly one month in which to return to life and find someone who will mourn for him. A modern miracle play, wittily scripted by Hecht and MacArthur.

A Paramount Picture, directed by Ben Hecht and Charles MacArthur. With Noel Coward, Julie Haydon, Stanley Ridges, Martha Sleeper, Ernest Cossart, Alexander Woollcott. 68 mins.

THE SEARCH (1948) ★

★ best motion picture story Richard Schweizer & David Wechsler

Deeply moving account of a Czech mother who wanders aimlessly through postwar Germany searching for the child who was taken from her in a German concentration camp. Jarmila Novotna plays the mother, Ivan Jandl the boy and Montgomery Clift the sympathetic American soldier who befriends him. Made by Zinnemann in Switzerland and the American Zone of Germany.

An MGM Picture, directed by Fred Zinnemann. With Montgomery Clift, Aline MacMahon, Jarmila Novotna, Wendell Corey, Ivan Jandl. 105 mins.

SEPARATE TABLES (1958) ★★

★ best actor David Niven
★ best supporting actress Wendy Hiller

Terence Rattigan's two one-act plays about the individual personal dramas of a group of guests at a British seaside resort hotel. Niven won his Oscar for his ex-colonel who is really a fraud, Hiller won hers for portraying the proprietress of the establishment.

A United Artists Picture, directed by Delbert Mann. With Rita Hayworth, Deborah Kerr,

David Niven, Wendy Hiller, Burt Lancaster, Gladys Cooper, Cathleen Nesbitt, Felix Aylmer, Rod Taylor, Audrey Dalton. 98 mins.

SERGEANT YORK (1941)   ★★

★ best actor Gary Cooper
★ best editing William Holmes

Gary Cooper's first Oscar (he won again for *High Noon* in 1952)—as Sergeant Alvin York, a Tennessee hillbilly with pacifist convictions, who is drafted during World War I and becomes America's greatest hero of the conflict, capturing an entire German battalion single-handed.

A Warner Bros. Picture, directed by Howard Hawks. With Gary Cooper, Walter Brennan, Joan Leslie, George Tobias, Stanley Ridges, Margaret Wycherly. 134 mins.

SEVEN BRIDES FOR SEVEN BROTHERS (1954)   ★

★ best scoring of a musical Adolph Deutsch & Saul Chaplin

The last of the great original musicals from MGM, a story of seven Oregon backwoods boys who, influenced by the story of the Rape of the Sabine Women, kidnap several girls from the local township and make them their brides. The extraordinary acrobatic dancing of Messrs. Tamblyn, Rall and Co. helped earn the picture a nomination as best picture of the year.

An MGM Picture, directed by Stanley Donen. With Jane Powell, Howard Keel, Jeff Richards, Russ Tamblyn, Tommy Rall, Howard Petrie, Virginia Gibson. CinemaScope/Ansco Color. 102 mins.

SEVEN DAYS TO NOON (1951)   ★

★ best motion picture story Paul Dehn & James Bernard

Inventive, and for its period, topical tale of an atomic scientist (Barry Jones) who has a nervous breakdown and makes off with an atom bomb, threatening to destroy London unless the British government agrees to make a public announcement that it will cease production of all nuclear weapons.

A London Films Production, directed by Roy Boulting. With Barry Jones, Andre Morell, Olive Sloane, Sheila Manahan, Hugh Cross, Joan Hickson. 94 mins.

SEVENTH HEAVEN (1927/28)   ★★★

★ best direction Frank Borzage
★ best actress Janet Gaynor
★ best writing adaptation Benjamin Glazer

Among the most famous screen romances of all time, set prior to and during World War I, with Janet Gaynor in the role that won her the first best-actress Oscar (her others were for *Street Angel* and *Sunrise*). As Diane, a mistreated Parisian waif, she is victimized by her unscrupulous lover, but redeemed by the love of honest sewer worker Chico. Gaynor's competitors in the first best-actress race were Gloria Swanson in *Sadie Thompson* and Louise Dresser in *A Ship Comes In*. Borzage's direction award was also the first in the history of the Academy, although in the same year Lewis Milestone was voted best comedy director for his *Two Arabian Knights*, an award that was not continued in subsequent years.

A Fox Picture, directed by Frank Borzage. With Janet Gaynor, Charles Farrell, Ben Bard, David Butler, Marie Mosquini, Albert Gran. 12 reels.

THE SEVENTH VEIL (1946)   ★

★ best original screenplay Muriel & Sydney Box

Famous British tearjerker about a young woman (Ann Todd) who runs away from home to become a concert pianist, achieves her goal, but finds that her personal life with several different men is distinctly less successful. James Mason, in one of his most famous roles, co-stars as Todd's brutal guardian.

A Theatrecraft/Sydney Box/Ortus Production, directed by Compton Bennett. With James Mason, Ann Todd, Herbert Lom, Hugh McDermott, Albert Lieven. 94 mins.

SHAFT (1971) ★

★ best song "Theme from Shaft" (Isaac Hayes, music & lyrics)

Black private eye John Shaft (Richard Roundtree) is hired to find the kidnapped daughter of a wealthy Harlem racketeer. Workmanlike all-black action film, which won the year's best-song award, defeating, among other competitors, the Sherman Brothers' song "The Age of Not Believing" from *Bedknobs and Broomsticks*.

An MGM Picture, directed by Gordon Parks. With Richard Roundtree, Moses Gunn, Charles Cioffi, Christopher St. John, Gwenn Mitchell, Lawrence Pressman. Metrocolor. 100 mins.

SHAMPOO (1975) ★

★ best supporting actress Lee Grant

The complex and amorous adventures of a young hairdresser (Warren Beatty) in Beverly Hills at the time of the 1968 presidential elections. A brilliantly written social comedy that, through the exploits of its main character, looks at the moral and political atmosphere of America in the late 1960s. Lee Grant's Oscar was for her portrayal of the frustrated wife of businessman Jack Warden.

A Columbia Picture, directed by Hal Ashby. With Warren Beatty, Julie Christie, Goldie Hawn, Lee Grant, Jack Warden, Tony Bill, Carrie Fisher, Jay Robinson. Technicolor. 110 mins.

SHANE (1953) ★

★ best color cinematography Loyal Griggs

Classic Western about a mysterious gunfighter (Alan Ladd) who rides into a Wyoming valley and helps the homesteaders in their fight against the cattlemen. Van Heflin and Jean Arthur co-star as the farming Starrett family; Jack Palance is a hired killer. A surefire best-picture winner in any normal year (it garnered six nominations), it won only in the color photography category, being up against *From Here to Eternity*, which swept the 1953 awards.

A Paramount Picture, directed by George Stevens. With Alan Ladd, Jean Arthur, Van Heflin, Brandon De Wilde, Jack Palance, Ben Johnson, Edgar Buchanan, Emile Meyer, Elisha Cook, Jr. Technicolor. 118 mins.

SHANGHAI EXPRESS (1931/32) ★

★ best cinematography Lee Garmes

Sternberg and Dietrich's greatest commercial success ($3 million gross), an Oriental extravaganza set on board a train traveling from Peking to Shanghai, with Dietrich as the notorious prostitute Shanghai Lily saving the life of former lover Clive Brook when he is held hostage by revolutionaries.

A Paramount Picture, directed by Josef von Sternberg. With Marlene Dietrich, Clive Brook, Anna May Wong, Warner Oland, Eugene Pallette, Lawrence Grant. 80 mins.

SHE WORE A YELLOW RIBBON (1949) ★

★ best color cinematography Winton C. Hoch

Retiring captain Nathan Brittles (John Wayne) and the U.S. Cavalry successfully put down a large-scale Indian uprising just after the Civil War. John Ford's first Western in color and a deserved winner in the color photography category, full of glowing sunsets, red mountain peaks and men riding silhouetted against the skyline.

An RKO Picture, directed by John Ford. With John Wayne, Joanne Dru, John Agar, Ben Johnson, Harry Carey, Jr., Victor Mc-

Laglen, Mildred Natwick. Technicolor. 103 mins.

SHIP OF FOOLS (1965)   ★ ★

★ best b/w cinematography Ernest Laszlo
★ best b/w art direction Robert Clatworthy
        set decoration Joseph Kish

Katherine Anne Porter's symbolic, floating *Grand Hotel* about a shipful of assorted passengers going back to Germany from South America in the early Nazi days of 1933. Vivien Leigh as a disillusioned divorcee, Oskar Werner and Simone Signoret as two doomed illicit lovers and Lee Marvin as a punchy baseball player head an all-star cast.

A Columbia Picture, directed by Stanley Kramer. With Vivien Leigh, Simone Signoret, Jose Ferrer, Lee Marvin, Oskar Werner, Elizabeth Ashley, George Segal, Jose Greco, Michael Dunn, Charles Korvin. 149 mins.

THE SHOP ON MAIN STREET (1965)   ★

★ best foreign language film Czechoslovakia

World War II story, set in a small provincial town in occupied Czechoslovakia, about a henpecked carpenter who becomes the Aryan controller of a button shop, kept going by the Jewish community so that its widow proprietress will think she is earning her own living from the proceeds.

A Czechoslovakian Picture, directed by Jan Kadar and Elmar Klos. With Josef Kroner, Ida Kaminska, Hans Slivkova, Frantisek Zvarik, Helen Zvarikova, Martin Holly. 128 mins.

THE SILENCE OF THE LAMBS (1991)   ★ ★ ★ ★ ★

★ best film Edward Saxon, Kenneth Utt & Ron Bozman (producers)
★ best direction Jonathan Demme
★ best actor Anthony Hopkins
★ best actress Jodie Foster
★ best screenplay Ted Tally

Man or monster? Anthony Hopkins, best actor in 1991, for his portrayal of Dr. Hannibal Lecter in *The Silence of the Lambs* (Orion).

FBI trainee Jodie Foster is assigned to track down a serial killer, and finds that the only way she can get close to her quarry is by seeking help from Dr. Hannibal Lecter (Anthony Hopkins), a brilliant psychiatrist who has come unglued and started murdering people and then eating them for lunch. The most recent of the three pictures to win all four major awards on Oscar night (the others being *It Happened One Night* in 1934 and *One Flew Over the Cuckoo's Nest* in 1975) and the only film of its kind (schlock-thriller) to win as best picture. Foster's Oscar was her second in three years, following her award for *The Accused* in 1988.

A Strongheart/Demme production, Orion Pictures. Directed by Jonathan Demme. With Jodie Foster, Anthony Hopkins, Scott Glenn, Ted Levine, Anthony Heald, Lawrence A. Bonney, Kasi Lemmons, Lawrence T. Wrentz,

Frankie Faison. Panavision/Technicolor. 118 mins.

SINCE YOU WENT AWAY (1944) ★

★ best scoring of a drama or comedy Max Steiner

Selznick's companion piece to MGM's *Mrs. Miniver* (1942), a supreme tearjerker about a middle-class American family—its hopes, sacrifices, tragedies—as it goes about its normal everyday life while its menfolk are overseas fighting the war. Set throughout the year 1943, it featured Claudette Colbert as the mother of the family, Shirley Temple and Jennifer Jones as her two daughters and Hattie McDaniel as their maid. Composer Max Steiner won his third and final Oscar for his music score, having won earlier for *The Informer* (1935) and *Now Voyager* (1942).

A David O. Selznick Production (released through United Artists), directed by John Cromwell. With Claudette Colbert, Jennifer Jones, Joseph Cotten, Shirley Temple, Monty Woolley, Lionel Barrymore, Robert Walker, Hattie McDaniel, Agnes Moorehead. 172 mins.

THE SIN OF MADELON CLAUDET (1931/32) ★

★ best actress Helen Hayes

Helen Hayes' first Oscar-winning role, as a tragic mother who makes all manner of sacrifices so that her illegitimate son can be educated and become a physician. Almost a remake of *Madame X* (1929), and Hayes' first try at the talkies. She won a supporting Oscar nearly 40 years later for *Airport* (1970).

An MGM Picture, directed by Edgar Selwyn. With Helen Hayes, Lewis Stone, Neil Hamilton, Robert Young, Cliff Edwards, Jean Hersholt, Marie Prevost. 74 mins.

SKIPPY (1930/31) ★

★ best direction Norman Taurog

Film version of the adventures of Percy Crosby's comic-strip boy character Skippy Skinner and his child friends—Eloise, the tell-tale Sidney, and Sooky of Shanty Town. For his direction of the almost all-child cast, Norman Taurog (perhaps the most forgotten best-director winner in Oscar history) defeated such star names as Josef von Sternberg *(Morocco)* and Lewis Milestone *(The Front Page)*.

A Paramount Picture, directed by Norman Taurog. With Jackie Cooper, Robert Coogan, Mitzi Green, Jackie Searl, Willard Robertson, Enid Bennett. 88 mins.

THE SNAKE PIT (1948)

★ best sound recording Thomas Moulton

Grippingly effective film about the horrors of overcrowding in an understaffed American mental hospital. Olivia de Havilland challenged Jane Wyman (the year's best-actress winner for *Johnny Belinda*) with her portrait of a young woman writer who has a mental breakdown and undergoes treatment in a squalid mental institution.

A 20th Century-Fox Picture, directed by Anatole Litvak. With Olivia de Havilland, Mark Stevens, Leo Genn, Celeste Holm, Glenn Langan, Helen Craig, Leif Erickson, Beulah Bondi, Lee Patrick. 108 mins.

THE SOLID GOLD CADILLAC (1956)

★ best b/w costume design Jean Louis

Judy Holliday in one of her most delightful roles, as an unemployed actress who owns just ten shares in a vast business corporation and sets about proving that the board of directors is riddled with corruption. A Wall Street fairy tale, helped along considerably by actors of the quality of Fred Clark and John Williams.

A Columbia Picture, directed by Richard Quine. With Judy Holliday, Paul Douglas, Fred Clark, John Williams, Hiram Sherman, Neva Patterson, Ralph Dumke, Ray Collins, Arthur O'Connell. 99 mins.

SOMEBODY UP THERE LIKES ME (1956)   ★ ★

★ best b/w cinematography Joseph Ruttenberg
★ best b/w art direction Cedric Gibbons &
  Malcolm F. Brown
              set decoration Edwin B. Willis &
              F. Keogh Gleason

Screen biography of rebellious East Side delinquent Rocky Graziano (Paul Newman), who rises above reform school, jail and army detention barracks to become middleweight boxing champion of the world. Newman starred in the role originally intended for James Dean, and cameraman Joseph Ruttenberg earned the third of his four Academy Awards. The others: *The Great Waltz* (1938), *Mrs. Miniver* (1942) and *Gigi* (1958).

An MGM Picture, directed by Robert Wise. With Paul Newman, Pier Angeli, Everett Sloane, Eileen Heckart, Sal Mineo, Harold J. Stone. 112 mins.

SOME LIKE IT HOT (1959)   ★

★ best b/w costume design Orry-Kelly

One of the funniest American comedies of all time, with jazz musicians Jack Lemmon and Tony Curtis fleeing gangsters after witnessing a gangland massacre in Chicago and disguising themselves as members of an all-girl dance band traveling by train to Florida. Like other top films of 1959, the picture was trampled on by *Ben-Hur* and ended up with only a solitary costume award.

A United Artists Picture, directed by Billy Wilder. With Marilyn Monroe, Tony Curtis, Jack Lemmon, George Raft, Pat O'Brien, Joe E. Brown, Nehemiah Persoff, Joan Shawlee. 120 mins.

THE SONG OF BERNADETTE (1943)   ★ ★ ★ ★

★ best actress Jennifer Jones
★ best b/w cinematography Arthur Miller

★ best b/w art direction James Basevi &
  William Darling
              int. decoration Thomas Little
★ best score of a drama or comedy Alfred
  Newman

Jennifer Jones as Bernadette Soubirous, the French peasant girl who, in 1858, saw visions of the Virgin Mary and discovered a miraculous healing spring at Lourdes. The most prestigious American film of 1943 and the biggest winner of its year, although *Casablanca*, the surprise hit of the period, took the best-picture award.

A 20th Century-Fox Picture, directed by Henry King. With Jennifer Jones, William Eythe, Charles Bickford, Vincent Price, Lee J. Cobb, Gladys Cooper. 156 mins.

SONG OF THE SOUTH (1947)   ★

★ best song "Zip-a-Dee-Doo-Dah" (Allie
  Wrubel, music; Ray Gilbert, lyrics)

Disney version of the Tales of Uncle Remus by Joel Chandler Harris. The Oscar-winning song "Zip-a-Dee-Doo-Dah" was sung by James Baskett against a cartoon background with animated birds perched on his shoulder—one of the earliest uses of the combined live-action/animation process.

A Walt Disney Picture (released through RKO), directed by Harve Foster; cartoons directed by Wilfred Jackson. With Ruth Warrick, James Baskett, Bobby Driscoll, Luanna Patten, Lucile Watson, Hattie McDaniel. Technicolor. 94 mins.

SONG WITHOUT END (1960)   ★

★ best scoring of a musical Morris Stoloff &
  Harry Sukman

Hollywood version of the life of Franz Liszt (Dirk Bogarde), and in particular of his romantic interlude with Princess Carolyne of Russia (Capucine).

A Columbia Picture, directed by Charles Vidor and George Cukor. With Dirk Bogarde, Capucine, Genevieve Page, Patricia Morison,

Ivan Desny, Martita Hunt, Lou Jacobi. CinemaScope/Technicolor. 130 mins.

SONS AND LOVERS (1960) ★

★ best b/w cinematography Freddie Francis

The story of a young boy's growth to manhood in pre-World War I England, with Dean Stockwell as D. H. Lawrence's sensitive Nottingham youth torn between his love for two women (Mary Ure and Heather Sears) and his desire to break away from the drab coal town in which he lives. Trevor Howard as the boy's drunken miner father was nominated for a best-actor Academy Award.

A 20th Century-Fox Picture, directed by Jack Cardiff. With Trevor Howard, Dean Stockwell, Wendy Hiller, Mary Ure, Heather Sears, William Lucas. CinemaScope. 100 mins.

SOPHIE'S CHOICE (1982) ★

★ best actress Meryl Streep

A young Polish woman (Meryl Streep) attempts to justify her existence in postwar America after surviving a living hell in Auschwitz. The terrible choice of the title? To decide which of her two children can survive when the Nazis say that one of them has to go to the gas chamber.

Meryl Streep, winner of the best-actress Oscar, with Peter MacNicol in *Sophie's Choice* (ITC Entertainment, 1982). She won a supporting award three years earlier for her performance in *Kramer vs. Kramer*.

Based on the novel by William Styron and told in flashback from Sophie's new life in Brooklyn, the film earned Streep her best-actress award and was part of a remarkable body of work for which she was nominated in the 1980s: *The French Lieutenant's Woman* (1981), *Silkwood* (1983), *Out of Africa* (1985), *Ironweed* (1987), *A Cry in the Dark* (1988) and *Postcards from the Edge* (1990). *Sophie's Choice* marked Streep's second Academy Award. In 1979 she was named best supporting actress for *Kramer vs. Kramer*.

ITC Entertainment/A Keith Barish Production, directed by Alan J. Pakula. With Meryl Streep, Kevin Kline, Peter MacNicol, Rita Karin, Stephen D. Newman, Greta Turken, Josh Mostel, Marc Rosenblatt. Technicolor. 158 mins.

THE SOUND OF MUSIC (1965) ★★★★★

★ best film Robert Wise (producer)
★ best direction Robert Wise
★ best editing William Reynolds
★ best sound James P. Corcoran & Fred Hynes
★ best music score: adaptation Irwin Kostal

Just a year after winning her Oscar for *Mary Poppins*, Julie Andrews was again up for the award for her performance in this picture—as the singing governess of the Von Trapp family in prewar Austria. This time, however, she failed to win, losing to Julie Christie's much more down-to-earth 1960s gal in John Schlesinger's *Darling*. The Oscar Hammerstein-Richard Rodgers musical did, on the other hand, capture the best-picture award, plus four others.

A 20th Century-Fox Picture, directed by Robert Wise. With Julie Andrews, Christopher Plummer, Eleanor Parker, Richard Haydn, Peggy Wood. Todd-AO/DeLuxe Color. 171 mins.

SOUTH PACIFIC (1958) ★

★ best sound recording Fred Hynes

Another famous Rodgers and Hammerstein musical, not by any means the big winner *The Sound of Music* (1965) would turn out to be, but in its day very nearly as big a financial success. Rossano Brazzi, Mitzi Gaynor, John Kerr and France Nuyen are among those involved in romantic and racial intrigues on a Pacific Island in World War II. Adapted from stories by James A. Michener.

A Magna Theatre Corp Picture (released by 20th Century-Fox), directed by Joshua Logan. With Rossano Brazzi, Mitzi Gaynor, John Kerr, Ray Walston, Juanita Hall, France Nuyen. Todd-AO/Technicolor. 171 mins.

SPARTACUS (1960)

- ★ best supporting actor Peter Ustinov
- ★ best color cinematography Russell Metty
- ★ best color art direction Alexander Golitzen & Eric Orbom
        set decoration Russell A.
            Gausman & Julia Heron
- ★ best color costume design Valles & Bill Thomas

Howard Fast's epic tale of the slaves' revolt (under the leadership of Spartacus) against their Roman masters in 73 B.C. One of the most unusual of Hollywood epics in that it did not feature the coming of Christianity as its major theme. Peter Ustinov won his supporting Oscar for his master of a school of gladiators; Russell Metty, Universal's top cameraman for many years, won his for his magnificent color photography.

A Universal Picture, directed by Stanley Kubrick. With Kirk Douglas, Laurence Olivier, Tony Curtis, Jean Simmons, Charles Laughton, Peter Ustinov, John Gavin, Nina Foch. Super Technirama 70/Technicolor. 196 mins.

SPELLBOUND (1945)   ★

- ★ best scoring of a drama or comedy Miklos Rozsa

The first picture about psychoanalysis—an engaging Hitchcock thriller revolving around an amnesiac doctor (Gregory Peck) who subconsciously believes himself to be a murderer, and the woman psychiatrist (Ingrid Bergman) who tries to prove his innocence. Full of trick effects, including a Salvador Dali dream sequence, and a lush romantic Rozsa score which even today is world-famous and instantly recognizable.

A David O. Selznick Production (released through United Artists), directed by Alfred Hitchcock. With Ingrid Bergman, Gregory Peck, Jean Acker, Donald Curtis, Rhonda Fleming, John Emery, Leo G. Carroll. 111 mins.

SPLENDOR IN THE GRASS (1961)   ★

- ★ best story & screenplay William Inge

A William Inge original about adolescent love and frustration in a puritanical Kansas town in the 1920s just prior to the Wall Street crash. Warren Beatty (making his debut) and Natalie Wood star as the tormented couple.

A Warner Bros. Picture, directed by Elia Kazan. With Natalie Wood, Warren Beatty, Pat Hingle, Audrey Christie, Barbara Loden. Technicolor. 124 mins.

STAGECOACH (1939)   ★★

- ★ best supporting actor Thomas Mitchell
- ★ best music score Richard Hageman, Franke Harling, John Leipold & Leo Shuken

John Ford's famous Western about a stagecoach journey across the plains of Arizona in the 1870s. John Wayne, in the Ringo Kid role that made him famous, remains the best-remembered of the passengers, although it was Thomas Mitchell as the drunken Doc Boone, who has to be forcibly sobered up *en route* to deliver a baby, who deservedly won the acting honors.

A United Artists Picture, directed by John Ford. With John Wayne, Claire Trevor, Thomas Mitchell, George Bancroft, Andy Devine, John Carradine, Louise Platt, Donald Meek, Berton Churchill, Tim Holt. 96 mins.

The many faces of William Holden: winner of the best-actor Oscar for *Stalag 17* (Paramount) in 1953 (top right), he was also nominated for his roles in *Sunset Boulevard* (bottom right) and *Network* (center).

STALAG 17 (1953) ★

★ best actor William Holden

Comedy-drama by Billy Wilder about the life of American airmen in a bleak German POW camp in World War II. A film of many moods—humorous, suspenseful, disturbing—dominated by an Oscar-winning performance by William Holden as the scrounging camp opportunist, a cynical heel who, among other things, arranges horse races using mice, builds a gin distillery and rigs a telescope for peeping into the Russian women's barracks.

A Paramount Picture, directed by Billy Wilder. With William Holden, Don Taylor, Otto Preminger, Robert Strauss, Harvey Lembeck, Richard Erdman, Peter Graves, Neville Brand, Sig Ruman. 120 mins.

A STAR IS BORN (1937) ★★

★ best original story Robert Carson & William A. Wellman
★ color photography* W. Howard Greene

Fredric March, as a famous film actor on the way down because of drink, discovers talented farmgirl Janet Gaynor in Hollywood and turns her into a star. Director Wellman's Oscar for his story of this famous film was the only Academy Award he ever won, even though he was also nominated for his direction of such subsequent films as *Battleground* (1949) and *The High and the Mighty* (1954).

A Selznick International Picture (released through United Artists), directed by William A. Wellman. With Janet Gaynor, Fredric March, Adolphe Menjou, Andy Devine, May Robson, Lionel Stander. Technicolor. 111 mins.

A STAR IS BORN (1976)

★ best song "Evergreen" (Barbra Streisand, music; Paul Williams, lyrics)

Third time out for this famous story of a star on the skids helping a young one on the rise, transferred this time to the rock scene, with Kris Kristofferson as the rock star on the downward path and Barbra Streisand as the young hopeful. Streisand's second Oscar, her first coming nine years earlier as best actress in *Funny Girl*. The Judy Garland version (1954) failed to win an Oscar, despite six nominations, including best actress (Garland), best actor (James Mason) and best song—"The Man That Got Away."

---

* *Note:* The color photography award was a special Oscar (a plaque, not a statuette) recommended by a committee of leading cinematographers after viewing all the color films made during the year.

A Star Is Born (Warner Bros., 1976). Barbra Streisand, seen here with Kris Kristofferson, won her second Oscar for this film, as the composer of the award-winning song "Evergreen." She won earlier as best actress for *Funny Girl.*

A Warner Bros. Picture, directed by Frank Pierson. With Barbra Streisand, Kris Kristofferson, Paul Mazursky, Gary Busey, Oliver Clark. Metrocolor. 140 mins.

STAR WARS (1977)

★ best art direction John Barry, Norman Reynolds & Leslie Dilley
        set decoration Roger Christian
★ best costume design John Mollo
★ best sound Don MacDougall, Ray West, Bob Minkler & Derek Ball
★ best editing Paul Hirsch, Marcia Lucas & Richard Chew
★ best music score John Williams
★ best visual effects John Stears, John Dykstra, Richard Edlund, Grant McCune & Robert Blalack
★ best sound effects creations* Benjamin Burtt, Jr.

---

*   *Note:* Benjamin Burtt's Oscar for creating the alien, creature and robot voices was a special achievement award.

A Darth Vader minion in action in George Lucas' *Star Wars* (20th Century-Fox), winner of seven Academy Awards in 1977.

Vigorous space spectacular out of *Flash Gordon* (1936), but with all the advantages of modern special effects and sound techniques. Peter Cushing is an advanced megalomaniac with plans not just to rule the world but the universe; young adventurers Mark Hamill, Harrison Ford and princess Carrie Fisher are out to stop him. Also on the side of right: Alec Guinness, who provides the spiritual guidance, and robots See-Threepio and Artoo-Detoo, who provide mechanical chatter and mini-beeps. The biggest Oscar winner of its year.

A 20th Century-Fox Picture, directed by George Lucas. With Mark Hamill, Harrison Ford, Carrie Fisher, Peter Cushing, Alec Guinness, Anthony Daniels, Kenny Baker, Peter Mayhew, David Prowse. Panavision/Technicolor; prints by DeLuxe. 121 mins.

STATE FAIR (1945)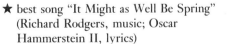

★ best song "It Might as Well Be Spring" (Richard Rodgers, music; Oscar Hammerstein II, lyrics)

The second of the three versions of Philip Stong's perennial tale about a country farm family and their disappointments, romances and minor triumphs during their annual visit to the Iowa

State Fair. The Oscar-winning "It Might as Well Be Spring" was sung by Louanne Hogan, who dubbed for Jeanne Crain.

A 20th Century-Fox Picture, directed by Walter Lang. With Jeanne Crain, Dana Andrews, Dick Haymes, Vivian Blaine, Charles Winninger, Fay Bainter, Donald Meek. Technicolor. 101 mins.

THE STING (1973)

* best film Tony Bill, Michael & Julia Phillips (producers)
* best direction George Roy Hill
* best story & screenplay David S. Ward
* best art direction Henry Bumstead
      set decoration James Payne
* best costume design Edith Head
* best editing William Reynolds
* best music score: adaptation Marvin Hamlisch

Two confidence men, Paul Newman and Robert Redord, set out to "take" big-time racketeer Robert Shaw for a vast sum of money after he has been responsible for the murder of Redford's elderly black partner. Set in Chicago in the 1930s, the film cleaned up at the 1973 awards, pushing the other hot contender, *The Exorcist*, right out of contention for the major honors. Not the least of its merits was its unique use of piano rags by Scott Joplin for its major music themes.

A Universal Picture, directed by George Roy Hill. With Paul Newman, Robert Redford, Robert Shaw, Charles Durning, Ray Walston, Eileen Brennan, Harold Gould. Technicolor. 129 mins.

THE STORY OF LOUIS PASTEUR (1936) ★★★

* best actor Paul Muni
* best written screenplay Pierre Collings & Sheridan Gibney
* best original story Pierre Collings & Sheridan Gibney

The career of French chemist Louis Pasteur (Muni), who almost single-handedly battled with and defeated the diseases of anthrax and chicken cholera in 19th century France. The first of William Dieterle's distinguished Warner biographies of the 1930s. Later additions included *The Life of Emile Zola* (1937), *Juarez* (1939) and *Dr. Ehrlich's Magic Bullet* (1940).

A Warner Bros. Picture, directed by William Dieterle. With Paul Muni, Josephine Hutchinson, Anita Louise, Donald Woods, Fritz Leiber, Henry O'Neill. 85 mins.

LA STRADA (1956)

★ best foreign language film Italy

Fellini's first great film and the first *official* foreign language winner, all the previous awards to overseas movies being in the "special award" category. The film concentrates on the tragic relationship between a brutish strongman (Anthony Quinn) and his simple-minded waiflike assistant (Giulietta Masina) as they travel around Italy entertaining in bleak, desolate towns. The hit song "Stars Shine in Your Eyes" was not among the five best-song nominees (it was played orchestrally; lyrics were added later) even though it later swept to success all around the world.

A Ponti-De Laurentiis Production, directed by Federico Fellini. With Giulietta Masina, Anthony Quinn, Richard Basehart, Aldo Silvana, Marcella Rovena, Lidia Venturini. 115 mins.

THE STRATTON STORY (1949)

★ best motion picture story Douglas Morrow

Biography of baseball pitcher Monty Stratton (James Stewart), who lost his leg in a hunting accident but still managed to make a comeback to the professional game with an artificial limb.

An MGM Picture, directed by Sam Wood. With James Stewart, June Allyson, Frank Morgan, Agnes Moorehead, Bill Williams, Bruce Cowling. 106 mins.

STREET ANGEL (1927/28)

★ best actress Janet Gaynor

Janet Gaynor suffering for the third time in the first Oscar year (she was recognized also for *Seventh Heaven* and *Sunrise*) as a poor Neapolitan girl who falls in love with an itinerant artist but is arrested and separated from him on the eve of their marriage. It was said later that actresses had to suffer to win Oscars. Gaynor proved it the first time out!

A Fox Film, directed by Frank Borzage. With Janet Gaynor, Charles Farrell, Alberto Rabagliati, Gino Conti, Guido Trento, Henry Armetta. 10 reels.

A STREETCAR NAMED DESIRE (1951)   ★ ★ ★ ★

★ best actress Vivien Leigh
★ best supporting actor Karl Malden
★ best supporting actress Kim Hunter
★ best b/w art direction Richard Day
        set decoration George James
        Hopkins

High-voltage Tennessee Williams drama about the sordid fate of faded Southern belle Blanche du Bois (Leigh), who brings her ladylike manners and sad tale of a marriage that went wrong to the sleazy slum apartment of her sister (Hunter) in New Orleans. A feast of method acting, with Leigh, Hunter and Karl Malden (as Blanche's middle-aged beau) all winning awards. Only Marlon Brando as Stanley Kowalski, Hunter's brutal Polish-American husband, a brilliant performance in every way, missed out. Bogart in *The African Queen* was the year's best-actor winner.

A Warner Bros. Picture, directed by Elia Kazan. With Vivien Leigh, Marlon Brando, Kim Hunter, Karl Malden, Rudy Bond, Nick Dennis. 125 mins.

STRIKE UP THE BAND (1940)   ★

★ best sound recording Douglas Shearer

Judy Garland–Mickey Rooney musical about a group of high school youngsters who form their own juvenile band and rise to national fame on Paul Whiteman's nationwide radio show.

An MGM Picture, directed by Busby Berkeley. With Mickey Rooney, Judy Garland, Paul Whiteman, June Preisser, William Tracy, Larry Nunn. 120 mins.

THE SUBJECT WAS ROSES (1968)   ★

★ best supporting actor Jack Albertson

Adaptation of Frank Gilroy's prize-winning play about a young army veteran's return to his Bronx home and his increasingly strained relationship with his parents (Patricia Neal and Jack Albertson), who gradually poison him with their own bitterness. Martin Sheen appears in an early role as the young man.

An MGM Picture, directed by Ulu Grosbard. With Patricia Neal, Jack Albertson, Martin Sheen, Don Saxon, Elaine Williams, Grant Gordon. Metrocolor. 107 mins.

SUMMER OF '42 (1971)   ★

★ best original dramatic score Michel Legrand

Nostalgic, sentimental account of a young teenager's obsession with an attractive war bride (Jennifer O'Neill) during one lazy, idyllic summer on an island off the New England coast. Legrand's lushest of melancholy themes—one of the most romantic in years—won him the Academy Award for best score of the year.

A Warner Bros. Picture, directed by Robert Mulligan. With Jennifer O'Neill, Gary Grimes, Jerry Houser, Oliver Conant, Katherine Allentuck. Technicolor. 104 mins.

SUNDAYS AND CYBELE (1962)

★ best foreign language film France

Delicate story of the strange, ultimately tragic friendship that develops between an ex-war-plane pilot (Hardy Kruger) suffering from a guilt complex and loss of memory and the small girl in a convent school (Patricia Gozzi) whom he takes out with him on Sundays.

A Terra Film-Fides-Orsay Film/Les Films Trocadero, directed by Serge Bourguignon. With Hardy Kruger, Nicole Courcel, Patricia Gozzi, Daniel Ivernel, Michel de Re, Andre Oumansky. Transcope. 110 mins.

SUNRISE (1927/28)

★ best actress Janet Gaynor
★ best cinematography Charles Rosher & Karl Struss
★ best artistic quality of production Fox Studio

F. W. Murnau's drama of a young farmer, happily married with a wife and child, who suddenly becomes infatuated by a temptress from the city and is almost enticed to murder. Tremendously stylish film, marvelously acted by Gaynor (as the wife), George O'Brien as the husband and Margaret Livingston as the other woman. The Oscars for Struss and Rosher were the first to be awarded for cinematography; Gaynor's portrayal was the third for which she was named best actress in the same year (the others being for *Street Angel* and *Seventh Heaven*).

A Fox Picture, directed by F. W. Murnau. With George O'Brien, Janet Gaynor, Bodil Rossing, Margaret Livingston, J. Farrell MacDonald, Ralph Sipperly. 10–11 reels.

SUNSET BOULEVARD (1950) ★★★

★ best story & screenplay Charles Brackett, Billy Wilder & D. M. Marshman, Jr.
★ best art direction Hans Dreier & John Meehan
      set decoration Sam Comer & Ray Moyer
★ best music score of a drama or comedy Franz Waxman

Billy Wilder's ruthless story of a down-and-out screenwriter (William Holden) who is persuaded by a faded silent movie queen (Gloria

"I'm ready for my closeup, Mr. De Mille"—Gloria Swanson at the climax of Billy Wilder's Hollywood classic *Sunset Boulevard* (Paramount, 1950). The film won awards for screenplay, art direction and music.

Swanson) to be her gigolo and write the screenplay for her "comeback" film. Another case of "if only it had been released another year." As it was, it clashed with *All About Eve*, a six-Oscar winner, and had to be content with the runner-up position on presentations night. It remains, however, one of the finest movies about Hollywood and one of the best never to win a best-picture Oscar.

A Paramount Picture, directed by Billy Wilder. With William Holden, Gloria Swanson, Erich von Stroheim, Nancy Olson, Fred Clark, Jack Webb. 110 mins.

THE SUNSHINE BOYS (1975)

★ best supporting actor George Burns

The trials and tribulations of a harassed young theatrical agent (Richard Benjamin) when he tries to bring together two veteran vaudeville comics (Walter Matthau and George Burns) who haven't spoken to each other personally or professionally for 11 years. Until Jessica Tandy's 1989 win for her performance in *Driving Miss Daisy*, George Burns was the oldest winner for acting in the Academy's history.

An MGM Picture, directed by Herbert Ross. With Walter Matthau, George Burns, Richard Benjamin, Lee Meredith, Carol Arthur, Rosetta Le Noire. Metrocolor. 111 mins.

SUPERMAN (1978) ★

★ best visual effects* Les Bowie, Colin
   Chilvers, Denys Coop, Roy Field, Derek
   Meddings and Zoran Perisic

The former comic book hero lives again in a
large-scale production that pits the flying man
of steel against arch villain Lex Luthor. Christopher Reeve stars as the All-American super-
hero, Gene Hackman is the super villain and
Marlon Brando appears as superdad in the pro-
logue on the doomed planet of Krypton.

A Dovemead Production/Warner Bros. Directed by Richard Donner. With Christopher
Reeve, Marlon Brando, Gene Hackman, Margot Kidder, Jackie Cooper, Glenn Ford, Phyllis
Thaxter, Trevor Howard, Ned Beatty, Susannah York, Valerie Perrine. Panavision/Techni-
color. 143 mins.

SUSPICION (1941) ★

★ best actress Joan Fontaine

Stylish Hitchcock thriller with wealthy young
wife Joan Fontaine believing that her irresponsible playboy husband (Cary Grant) is trying
to murder her. Very reminiscent of Hitch's
British thrillers of the 1930s and containing the
only performance in a Hitchcock film ever to
be awarded an Oscar. Actors nominated for
their performances in Hitchcock films: Laurence Olivier, Joan Fontaine and Judith Anderson in *Rebecca* (1940); Albert Basserman in
Foreign Correspondent (1940); Michael Chekhov
in *Spellbound* (1945); Claude Rains in *Notorious*

---

* *Note:* The award for visual effects was a
special achievement award.

(1946); Ethel Barrymore in *The Paradine Case*
(1947); and Janet Leigh in *Psycho* (1960).

An RKO Picture, directed by Alfred Hitch-
cock. With Cary Grant, Joan Fontaine, Cedric
Hardwicke, Nigel Bruce, Dame May Whitty,
Isabel Jeans, Heather Angel. 99 mins.

SWEET BIRD OF YOUTH (1962) ★

★ best supporting actor Ed Begley

Tennessee Williams drama about a tarnished
Southern Apollo (Paul Newman) who brings a
load of trouble with him when he returns to his
hometown in the company of dissipated, drunken
movie queen Geraldine Page. In a film full of
fine performances, Ed Begley's corrupt town
boss who goes after Newman to "fix him for
ruining his daughter" stands out.

An MGM Picture, directed by Richard
Brooks. With Paul Newman, Geraldine Page,
Shirley Knight, Ed Begley, Rip Torn, Mildred
Dunnock, Madeleine Sherwood. CinemaScope/
Metrocolor. 120 mins.

SWING TIME (1936) ★

★ best song "The Way You Look Tonight"
   (Jerome Kern, music; Dorothy Fields, lyrics)

Astaire and Rogers' sixth film together, containing the usual boy and girl romance, one of
Astaire's all-time top dancing routines—"Bojangles of Harlem"—and the Academy Award-
winning song "The Way You Look Tonight."

An RKO Picture, directed by George Stevens. With Fred Astaire, Ginger Rogers, Victor
Moore, Helen Broderick, Eric Blore, Betty Furness. 103 mins.

T

TABU (1930/31) ★

★ best cinematography Floyd Crosby

A simple tale of two young Polynesian lovers who defy the ancient taboos of their tribe. Filmed by Murnau and Flaherty in Tahiti and Bora Bora with a locally recruited nonprofessional cast.

A Paramount Picture, directed by F. W. Murnau and Robert Flaherty. With Reri, Matahi, Hitu, Jean, Jules, Kong Ah. 81 mins.

TELLING THE WORLD (1927/28) ★

★ best title writing Joseph Farnham

William Haines comedy-drama about an eager young newspaper reporter (Haines) who finds romance with chorus girl Anita Page, plus adventure in the remote corners of China. One of three films (the others being *The Fair Co-Ed* and *Laugh, Clown, Laugh*) for which Farnham won his title-writing Oscar.

An MGM Picture, directed by Sam Wood. With William Haines, Anita Page, Eileen Percy, Frank Currier, Polly Moran, Bert Roach. 8 reels.

THE TEMPEST (1927/28) ★

★ best art direction William Cameron Menzies

John Barrymore as a Russian peasant who, during the Revolution of 1917, becomes an officer in the Russian Army and finds himself controlling the fate of the beautiful princess (Camilla Horn) who had earlier spurned him. Cameron

Menzies was also named for his work on *The Dove* in his Oscar award.

A United Artists Picture, directed by Sam Taylor. With John Barrymore, Camilla Horn, Louis Wolheim, Boris De Fas, George Fawcett. 10 reels.

THE TEN COMMANDMENTS (1956)

★ best special effects John Fulton

DeMille's massive biblical epic about the life of Moses from his birth and abandonment as a baby to the eventual time he led the Israelites out of Egypt. Charlton Heston stars as Moses, Yul Brynner as Rameses II and Anne Baxter as Nefretiri. The parting of the Red Sea sequence earned the film its special effects award.

A Paramount Picture, directed by Cecil B. DeMille. With Charlton Heston, Yul Brynner, Anne Baxter, Edward G. Robinson, Yvonne De Carlo, Debra Paget, John Derek, Cedric Hardwicke, Nina Foch, Martha Scott, Judith Anderson, Vincent Price. Vista Vision. Technicolor. 219 mins.

TENDER MERCIES (1983) ★ ★

★ best actor Robert Duvall
★ best original screenplay Horton Foote

Australian director Bruce Beresford's first American film, a low-key tale built around a destitute country-and-western singer (Robert Duvall) who finds a new life with an attractive Vietnam war widow (Tess Harper) who runs a small hotel in a remote part of Texas. Robert Duvall wrote and performed his own songs and at Oscar time defeated four British actors for best actor—Michael Caine (*Educating Rita*), Tom Conti (*Reuben, Reuben*) and Albert Finney and Tom Courtenay (*The Dresser*).

EMI/Universal/AFD. Directed by Bruce Beresford. With Robert Duvall, Tess Harper, Betty Buckley, Wilford Brimley, Ellen Barkin, Allan Hubbard, Lenny Von Dohlen, Paul

Gleason. Color: Movielab, prints by Techni-color. 92 mins.

TERMINATOR 2: JUDGMENT DAY (1991) ★★★★

★ best makeup Stan Winston & Jeff Dawn
★ best sound Tom Johnson, Gary Rydstrom, Gary Summers & Lee Orloff
★ best sound effects editing Gary Rydstrom & Gloria S. Borders
★ best visual effects Dennis Muren, Stan Winston, Gene Warren, Jr. & Robert Skotak

Cyborg Arnold Schwarzenegger turns hero as he battles it out with a lethal enemy, a T-1000 model made up largely of liquid metal but ingeniously capable of taking on human and mechanical forms. The reason for the confrontation? A young boy is destined to become leader of the human resistance against machines and must be saved at all costs. Ample effects, noise, carnage, etc.

A Mario Kassar presentation of a Pacific Western production in association with Light-storm Entertainment. TriStar (from Carolco). Directed by James Cameron. With Arnold Schwarzenegger, Linda Hamilton, Edward Furlong, Robert Patrick, Earl Boen, Joe Morton, S. Epatha Merkerson. 70 mm/Color: CFI, prints by Technicolor. 135 mins.

Terminator 2: Judgment Day (Carolco), winner of four technical Academy Awards in 1991.

Best actress and best supporting actor, Shirley MacLaine and Jack Nicholson, in *Terms of Endearment* (Paramount), directed by James L. Brooks in 1983.

TERMS OF ENDEARMENT (1983) ★★★★★

★ best film James L. Brooks (producer)
★ best direction James L. Brooks
★ best actress Shirley MacLaine
★ best supporting actor Jack Nicholson
★ best screenplay James L. Brooks

The film that at last earned Shirley MacLaine her Academy Award for her performance as the flamboyant Texas widow Aurora Green-way, who enjoys—and endures—a stormy 30-year relationship with daughter Debra Winger. Spicing things up still further: next-door neighbor Jack Nicholson, a former astronaut who indulges his taste for booze and women while dreaming of the old glory days. MacLaine's earlier nominations as an actress: *Some Came Running* (1958), *The Apartment* (1960), *Irma La Douce* (1963), *The Turning Point* (1977). As a documentary producer: *The Other Half of the Sky: A China Memoir* (1975).

A Paramount Picture, directed by James L. Brooks. With Shirley MacLaine, Debra Winger, Jack Nicholson, Danny DeVito, Jeff Daniels, John Lithgow, Lisa Hart Carroll, Betty R. King. Metrocolor. 132 mins.

TESS (1980) ★ ★ ★

- ★ best cinematography Geoffrey Unsworth & Ghislain Cloquet
- ★ best art direction Pierre Guffroy & Jack Stevens
- ★ best costume design Anthony Powell

Thomas Hardy's novel of a beautiful peasant girl's tragic experiences in 19th-century English society, impeccably transferred to the screen by Roman Polanski. The stunning camerawork of Geoffrey Unsworth and Ghislain Cloquet (the film was shot entirely in France) and the production design of Pierre Guffroy help recreate the splendors of Hardy country; Nastassia Kinski brings the tragic Tess to screen life.

A Renn Productions (Paris)/Burrill Productions (London) co-production released by Columbia. Directed by Roman Polanski. With

Nastassia Kinski in Roman Polanski's version of Thomas Hardy's *Tess* (Columbia), winner of Oscars for cinematography, art direction and costume design in 1980.

Nastassia Kinski, Leigh Lawson, Peter Firth, John Collin, David Markham, Rosemary Martin, Richard Pearson, Panavision/Color. 180 mins.

THANK GOD IT'S FRIDAY (1978)

- ★ best song "Last Dance" (Paul Jabara, music & lyrics)

A few hours in the lives of an assorted group of kids, disc jockeys, musicians, singers, and dance fanatics during a Friday night out at a Hollywood disco club. A modest little movie with a Donna Summer song that won out over such contenders as "Hopelessly Devoted to You" from *Grease* and Marvin Hamlisch's "The Last Time I Felt Like This" from *Same Time, Next Year*.

A Casablanca-Motown Production for Columbia, directed by Robert Klane. With Valerie Landsburg, Terri Nunn, Chick Vennera, Donna Summer, Ray Vitte, Mark Lonow, Andrea Howard, Jeff Goldblum, Robert Menken. Metrocolor. 89 mins.

THAT HAMILTON WOMAN (1941)

(Original U.K. title: *Lady Hamilton*)

- ★ best sound recording Jack Whitney

Romanticized version of the life of humbly-born blacksmith's daughter Emma Hart (Vivien Leigh)—her marriage to Sir William Hamilton, ambassador at the British embassy in Naples; her notorious love affair with England's naval hero Horatio Nelson (Laurence Olivier); and her poverty-stricken old age as a wrinkled old thief scrounging a living in the quayside cafes of Calais.

A United Artists Picture, directed by Alexander Korda. With Vivien Leigh, Laurence Olivier, Alan Mowbray, Sara Allgood, Gladys Cooper, Henry Wilcoxon. 128 mins.

Thelma and Louise (MGM), directed by Ridley Scott and co-starring Susan Sarandon and Geena Davis, winner for best original screenplay in 1991.

THELMA AND LOUISE (1991) ★

★ best original screenplay Callie Khouri

A *Bonnie and Clyde* of the 1990s, with bored housewife Geena Davis and frustrated waitress Susan Sarandon setting off by car on a weekend spree only to find that the trip turns into a nightmare of attempted rape, murder, and police pursuit and eventually to their own deaths as they sail off a precipice to their doom. Both Davis and Sarandon were nominated for best actress but, as so often happens when two performers are named for the same film, neither emerged the winner.

A Pathe Entertainment Production, MGM. Directed by Ridley Scott. With Susan Sarandon, Geena Davis, Harvey Keitel, Michael Madsen, Christopher McDonald, Stephen Tobolowsky, Brad Pitt, Timothy Carhart, Lucinda Jenney. Panavision/Color: DeLuxe. 129 mins.

THEY SHOOT HORSES, DON'T THEY? (1969) ★

★ best supporting actor Gig Young

The hopes, fears and disillusionments of some of the entrants in one of Hollywood's dance marathons of the Depression 1930s. Gig Young won his Oscar for playing the oily MC of the grueling contest, having been nominated in the supporting category twice earlier in his career— in Cagney's *Come Fill the Cup* (1951) and in Gable's *Teacher's Pet* (1958).

A Palomar-Cinerama Picture, directed by Sydney Pollack. With Jane Fonda, Michael Sarrazin, Susannah York, Gig Young, Red Buttons, Bonnie Bedelia, Michael Conrad, Bruce Dern. Panavision/DeLuxe Color. 129 mins.

THE THIEF OF BAGHDAD (1940) ★★★

★ best color cinematography Georges Perinal
★ best color art direction Vincent Korda
★ best special effects Lawrence Butler, photographic; Jack Whitney, sound

Conrad Veidt and June Duprez in *The Thief of Baghdad* (London Films, 1940), directed by Michael Powell, Ludwig Berger and Tim Whelan and winner of Academy Awards for cinematography, art direction and special effects.

Arabian Nights fantasy with Sabu as the wily native boy who outwits the wicked Grand Vizier of Baghdad. Superior Technicolor special effects, including a deadly combat with a giant spider.

A London Films Production, directed by Michael Powell, Ludwig Berger and Tim Whelan. With Conrad Veidt, Sabu, June Duprez, John Justin, Rex Ingram, Miles Malleson. Technicolor. 106 mins.

THE THIRD MAN (1950)   ★

★ best b/w cinematography Robert Krasker

Black marketeering in postwar Vienna, with Orson Welles in one of his most famous roles as Harry Lime, infamous dealer in watered-down penicillin. Robert Krasker's somber images of a ruined city earned him his sole Oscar for cinematography, but neither Graham Greene (for his screenplay) nor Anton Karas (for his famous zither score) figured among the nominees.

A London Films Production, directed by Carol Reed. With Joseph Cotten, Alida Valli, Orson Welles, Trevor Howard, Paul Hoerbiger, Ernst Deutsch, Bernard Lee, Wilfrid Hyde-White. 104 mins.

THIRTY SECONDS OVER TOKYO (1944)   ★

★ best special effects A. Arnold Gillespie, Donald Jahraus & Warren Newcombe: photographic; Douglas Shearer: sound

Semidocumentary account of the first American bomber attack on Japan in World War II. The movie covered the preparations for the raid, the takeoff from the aircraft carriers, the raid itself and the return to ship. Spencer Tracy appeared as Colonel Doolittle, commander-in-chief of the attack.

An MGM Picture, directed by Mervyn LeRoy. With Spencer Tracy, Van Johnson, Robert Walker, Phyllis Thaxter, Tim Mur-

dock, Scott McKay, Gordon MacDonald, Don DeFore, Robert Mitchum. 138 mins.

THIS ABOVE ALL (1942)   ★

★ best b/w art direction Richard Day & Joseph Wright
                          interior decoration Thomas Little

British wartime deserter Tyrone Power, disillusioned and bitter about the war, regains his courage through the love of gentle W.A.A.F. girl Joan Fontaine in this 1940s propaganda movie, taken from the novel by Eric Knight.

A 20th Century-Fox Picture, directed by Anatole Litvak. With Tyrone Power, Joan Fontaine, Thomas Mitchell, Henry Stephenson, Nigel Bruce, Gladys Cooper. 110 mins.

THIS IS THE ARMY (1943)   ★

★ best scoring of a musical Ray Heindorf

Technicolor film version of the Irving Berlin stage hit that boasted 350 World War II soldiers in its chorus, a morale booster in its message for millions of American fighting men, and hit numbers such as "Oh, How I Hate to Get Up in the Morning" and "I Left My Heart at the Stage Door Canteen."

A Warner Bros. Picture, directed by Michael Curtiz. With Irving Berlin as himself, George Murphy, Joan Leslie, George Tobias, Alan Hale, Charles Butterworth, Rosemary De Camp, Dolores Costello, Una Merkel. Technicolor. 121 mins.

THIS LAND IS MINE (1943)   ★

★ best sound recording Stephen Dunn

Meek French schoolteacher Charles Laughton suddenly emerges as a figure of stature when his country is overrun by the Nazis in World War II. One of the five films made by Renoir in America during the war period.

An RKO Picture, directed by Jean Renoir. With Charles Laughton, Maureen O'Hara,

George Sanders, Walter Slezak, Kent Smith, Una O'Connor. 103 mins.

THE THOMAS CROWN AFFAIR (1968) ★

★ best song "The Windmills of Your Mind" (Michel Legrand, music; Alan & Marilyn Bergman, lyrics)

The romantic, intellectual duel between a Boston business tycoon (Steve McQueen) who has successfully organized a spectacular bank raid without revealing his identity, and the attractive insurance investigator (Faye Dunaway) sent to look into the case. An already lush and romantic film is made even lusher by the Academy Award-winning song "The Windmills of Your Mind" sung by Noel Harrison.

A United Artists Picture, directed by Norman Jewison. With Steve McQueen, Faye Dunaway, Paul Burke, Jack Weston, Biff McGuire, Yaphet Kotto. Panavision/DeLuxe Color. 102 mins.

THOROUGHLY MODERN MILLIE (1967) ★

★ best music score Elmer Bernstein

Spoof musical of the 1920s with Julie Andrews and Mary Tyler Moore as a couple of innocent flapper girls neatly avoiding the clutches of homicidal Chinese white slave trader Beatrice Lillie. Elmer Bernstein's Oscar for his musical work on the film remains his only one to date, something of a surprise when one considers he composed scores of the caliber of *The Ten Commandments* (1956), *The Magnificent Seven* (1960), *To Kill A Mockingbird* (1962) and *A Walk on the Wild Side* (1962).

A Universal Picture, directed by George Roy Hill. With Julie Andrews, Mary Tyler Moore, Carol Channing, James Fox, John Gavin, Beatrice Lillie. Technicolor. 138 mins.

Julie Andrews tries out the flapper style in *Thoroughly Modern Millie* (Universal, 1967), a musical of the 1920s that earned Elmer Bernstein an Academy Award for best music score.

A THOUSAND CLOWNS (1965) ★

★ best supporting actor Martin Balsam

Screen adaptation of Herb Gardner's play about a hack TV gag writer (Jason Robards) who, fed up with writing scripts for the terrible comedian on his show, determines that his young nephew will not finish up the same way and go to work like a thousand clowns. Martin Balsam's Oscar was for his portrayal of Robards' go-getting agent brother.

A United Artists Picture, directed by Fred Coe. With Jason Robards, Barbara Harris, Martin Balsam, Barry Gordon, Gene Saks, William Daniels. 118 mins.

THREE COINS IN THE FOUNTAIN (1954) ★★

★ best color cinematography Milton Krasner
★ best song "Three Coins in the Fountain" (Jule Styne, music; Sammy Cahn, lyrics)

Early CinemaScope production about three American secretaries (McGuire, Peters, McNamara) who journey to Rome primarily to find themselves attractive husbands. Clifton Webb, Louis Jourdan and Rossano Brazzi prove themselves the most likely candidates. Milton Krasner's staggeringly beautiful shots of the Eternal City earned him his only Oscar award.

A 20th Century-Fox Picture, directed by Jean Negulesco. With Clifton Webb, Dorothy McGuire, Jean Peters, Louis Jourdan, Maggie McNamara, Rossano Brazzi. CinemaScope/DeLuxe Color. 102 mins.

THE THREE FACES OF EVE (1957) ★

★ best actress Joanne Woodward

Supposedly true story of a young American housewife who finds she is a schizophrenic with three contrasting personalities. A *tour de force* performance by the then-unknown Joanne Woodward in the leading role put her in the front rank of leading actresses. Lee J. Cobb is featured as the psychiatrist whose patience and probing eventually help the woman to lead a normal life.

A 20th Century-Fox Picture, directed by Nunnally Johnson. With Joanne Woodward, David Wayne, Lee J. Cobb, Nancy Kulp, Vince Edwards. CinemaScope. 91 mins.

THROUGH A GLASS DARKLY (1961) ★

★ best foreign language film Sweden

Ingmar Bergman raises questions about the significance of God and the meaning of life as he traces a few days in the lives of four people—a just-released mental patient, her husband, her dissatisfied novelist-father and her younger brother—when they spend a summer together on a bleak island in the Baltic.

Svensk Filmindustri Production, directed by Ingmar Bergman. With Harriet Andersson, Max Von Sydow, Gunnar Bjornstrand, Lars Passgard. 91 mins.

THUNDERBALL (1965) ★

★ best special visual effects John Stears

Fourth James Bond adventure, with 007 attempting to find out who is holding the world hostage with two hijacked nuclear bombs. One-eyed Adolfo Celi is the man behind it all. Long underwater sequences at the film's climax earned it its special effects award.

A United Artists Picture, directed by Terence Young. With Sean Connery, Claudine Auger, Adolfo Celi, Luciana Paluzzi, Rik Van Nutter, Bernard Lee. Panavision/Technicolor. 132 mins.

THE TIME MACHINE (1960) ★

★ best special effects Gene Warren, Tim Baar: visual effects

Adaptation of H. G. Wells' novel about a young Victorian (Rod Taylor) who invents a scientific machine that will take him into the distant future—through two world wars and into a time when strange beings inhabit the earth. The fifth George Pal production to win in the special effects category. The others: *Destination Moon* (1950), *When Worlds Collide* (1951), *The War of the Worlds* (1953) and *Tom Thumb* (1958).

An MGM Picture, directed by George Pal. With Rod Taylor, Alan Young, Yvette Mimieux, Sebastian Cabot, Tom Helmore, Whit Bissell. Metroscope/Metrocolor. 103 mins.

David and Heinz Bennent in *The Tin Drum* (West Germany/France), best foreign language film of 1979.

THE TIN DRUM (1979)   ★

★ best foreign language film West Germany
/France

The rise of Nazism in the divided city of Danzig and the subsequent horrors of World War II as seen through the eyes of a small boy who resolves to stop growing at the age of three and accompany the terrifying events on his toy drum. Based on the contemporary classic novel by Gunter Grass. David Bennent, a 12-year-old boy hindered in his own growth, plays the precocious drummer.

Franz Seitz Film/Bioskop-Film/GGB 14 KG/Hallelujah-Film (Munich)/Artemis Film (Berlin)/Argos Films (Paris). In association with Jadran Film (Zagreb), Film Polski (Warsaw). Directed by Volker Schlondorff. With David Bennent, Mario Adorf, Angela Winkler, Daniel Olbrychski, Katharina Thalbach, Heinz Bennent, Charles Aznavour. Eastman Color. 142 mins.

TIN PAN ALLEY (1940)   ★

★ best music score Alfred Newman

Formula Fox musical of the early 1940s following the adventures of two songwriters (John Payne, Jack Oakie) and their girlfriends (Alice Faye and Betty Grable) in the years immediately preceding and during World War I.

A 20th Century-Fox Picture, directed by Walter Lang. With Alice Faye, Betty Grable, Jack Oakie, John Payne, Allen Jenkins, Esther Ralston. 94 mins.

TITANIC (1953)   ★

★ best story & screenplay Charles Brackett,
Walter Reisch & Richard Breen

Story of the doomed maiden voyage of the *Titanic*, concentrating for most of its length on the private lives and fears of selected passengers—captain Brian Aherne, estranged American couple Clifton Webb and Barbara Stanwyck, young lovers Robert Wagner and Audrey Dalton, wisecracking wealthy widow Thelma Ritter and drunken defrocked priest Richard Basehart.

A 20th Century-Fox Picture, directed by Jean Negulesco. With Clifton Webb, Barbara Stanwyck, Robert Wagner, Audrey Dalton, Thelma Ritter, Brian Aherne, Richard Basehart, Allyn Joslyn. 98 mins.

TO BEGIN AGAIN (1982)   ★

(Spanish title: *Volver A Empezar*)

★ best foreign language film Spain

A Nobel Prize-winner for literature revisits the Spain he knew before the Spanish Civil War (when he fought on the side of the Loyalists) and meets some of those he knew in his youth, including the woman he loved and lost when they were torn apart by the conflict. A sentimental, poetic, often moving piece of cinema, the first Spanish film to be honored with the foreign language award.

A Nickel Odeón Picture, directed by José Luis Garci. With Antonio Ferrándis, Encarna Paso, José Bódalo, Agustin González, Pablo Hoyos, Marta Fernandez Muro, Pablo del Hoyo. Eastman Color. 92 mins.

TO CATCH A THIEF (1955)   ★

★ best color cinematography Robert Burks

Hitchcock on the French Riviera, with debonair Cary Grant as a former cat burglar forced out of retirement to catch a new thief who is copying his methods. Grace Kelly (her last picture for Hitch) adds cool blonde beauty and slick repartee. Cameraman Robert Burks made 12 films for Hitchcock, starting with *Strangers on a Train* in 1951 and ending with *Marnie* in 1964. This was the only time he figured among the Oscar winners.

A Paramount Picture, directed by Alfred Hitchcock. With Cary Grant, Grace Kelly, Jessie Royce Landis, John Williams, Charles Vanel, Brigitte Auber. Vista Vision/Technicolor. 97 mins.

TO EACH HIS OWN (1946)   ★

★ best actress Olivia de Havilland

Movie with a weepie theme used by Hollywood since the silent days—that of an unwed mother (Olivia de Havilland) who gives up her baby for fear of scandal and then watches him grow to manhood, pretending to be his aunt in order to be near him. The first of de Havilland's two Oscars (the other being for *The Heiress* in 1949); John Lund appears in a dual role, those of de Havilland's lover and son, both of whom become air aces—the first in World War I, the second in World War II.

A Paramount Picture, directed by Mitchell Leisen. With Olivia de Havilland, John Lund, Mary Anderson, Roland Culver, Philip Terry, Bill Goodwin. 100 mins.

Gregory Peck's Oscar-winning performance as Atticus Finch in *To Kill a Mockingbird* (Universal), directed by Robert Mulligan in 1962. Sharing things with him in this scene: Mary Badham.

TO KILL A MOCKINGBIRD (1962)   ★★★

★ best actor Gregory Peck
★ best screenplay Horton Foote
★ best b/w art direction Alexander Golitzen & Henry Bumstead
        set decoration Oliver Emert

Harper Lee's prizewinning tale of two motherless children growing up with their widowed lawyer father (Gregory Peck) amid racial prejudice in a small Southern town during the Depression. One of the most effective of Hollywood's films about race relations, and one that finally earned Peck his Academy Award after many years of nominations—*The Keys of the Kingdom* (1945), *The Yearling* (1946), *Gentle-*

man's Agreement (1947) and *Twelve O'Clock High* (1949).

A Universal Picture, directed by Robert Mulligan. With Gregory Peck, Mary Badham, Philip Alford, John Megna, Frank Overton, Rosemary Murphy, Ruth White, Brock Peters. 129 mins.

TOM JONES (1963)　★★★★

★ best film Tony Richardson (producer)
★ best direction Tony Richardson
★ best screenplay John Osborne
★ best music score John Addison

Henry Fielding's tale of life in bawdy 18th-century England, with Albert Finney as the illegitimate son of a servant girl who is fostered by a kindly country squire and then pursued lasciviously by every beautiful woman he meets on his way to manhood. The first entirely British-made best-picture winner since *Hamlet* (1948) and the only film in the history of the Academy to boast three supporting actress nominees in its cast—Diane Cilento as a wild gamekeeper's daughter, Edith Evans as Miss Western and Joyce Redman as a lady of easy virtue who seduces Tom over a large tavern meal. None of them won, Margaret Rutherford taking the award for her performance in *The V.I.P.s.* Finney and Hugh Griffith, as Squire Western, also won nominations.

A Woodfall Production (released through United Artists), directed by Tony Richardson. With Albert Finney, Susannah York, Hugh Griffith, Edith Evans, Joan Greenwood, Diane Cilento, Joyce Redman. Eastman Color. 128 mins.

TOM THUMB (1958)　★

★ best special effects Tom Howard

Tiny boy Russ Tamblyn becomes the adopted son of childless woodland couple Bernard Miles and Jessie Matthews but is exploited by villainous robbers Terry-Thomas and Peter Sellers.

Minor children's fantasy that earned an Academy Award for its mixture of live and animated special effects.

An MGM Picture, directed by George Pal. With Russ Tamblyn, Alan Young, Terry-Thomas, Peter Sellers, June Thorburn, Jessie Matthews, Bernard Miles. Eastman Color. 92 mins.

TOOTSIE (1982)　★

★ best supporting actress Jessica Lange

Out-of-work actor Dustin Hoffman disguises himself as a woman in order to win a key role in a TV soap opera and suddenly finds himself a national institution. Complications arise when he falls for one of the show's young stars, Jessica Lange. A previous drag movie, *Some Like It Hot* (1959), ended up as something of an also-ran at Oscar time; the same fate befell *Tootsie*, which won only one award out of ten nominations. It was a tough year, however, with *E.T.* and *Gandhi* carving up 12 awards between them.

A Columbia Picture (Delphi Productions), directed by Sydney Pollack. With Dustin Hoffman, Jessica Lange, Teri Garr, Dabney Coleman, Charles Durning, Bill Murray, George Gaynes, Geena Davis. Technicolor. 116 mins.

Dustin Hoffman and Jessica Lange (best supporting actress) in Sydney Pollack's 1982 drag comedy *Tootsie* (Columbia).

TOP GUN (1986) ★

★ best song "Take My Breath Away" (Giorgio Moroder, music; Tom Whitlock, lyrics)

Brash young fighter pilot Tom Cruise, crippled with guilt because of the death of his partner in maneuvers, tries to get things out of his system by shooting down MiG fighters and making love to Kelly McGillis. A do-it-by-numbers plot interspersed with gung-ho politics and some quite stunning visuals of aerial combat. The Oscar-winning and chart-topping song was performed on the sound track by Berlin.

A Paramount Picture, directed by Tony Scott. With Tom Cruise, Kelly McGillis, Val Kilmer, Anthony Edwards, Tom Skerritt, Michael Ironside, John Stockwell. 70 mm/Metrocolor. 110 mins.

TOPKAPI (1964) ★

★ best supporting actor Peter Ustinov

Jules Dassin sends a raffish group of criminals to Istanbul to steal the emerald-studded dagger from the famous Topkapi museum. Schell, Mercouri and Morley all participate, although it is Peter Ustinov, employed by the gang for his strength rather than for his brains, who comes out ahead from an acting point of view. Based on the novel *The Light of Day* by Eric Ambler.

A United Artists Picture, directed by Jules Dassin. With Melina Mercouri, Peter Ustinov, Maximilian Schell, Robert Morley, Akim Tamiroff. Technicolor. 120 mins.

TORA! TORA! TORA! (1970) ★

★ best special visual effects A. D. Flowers & L. B. Abbott

The full story of the Japanese attack on Pearl Harbor on December 7, 1941, told from both points of view, with scenes of American intelligence officers code-breaking in Washington intercut with those of Japanese strategists preparing their offensive. The title, when translated, means "Tiger, Tiger, Tiger—Attack Launched."

A 20th Century-Fox Picture, directed by Richard Fleischer. With Martin Balsam, Soh Yamamura, Jason Robards, Joseph Cotten, Tatsuya Mihashi, E. G. Marshall, Takahiro Tamura, James Whitmore. Panavision/DeLuxe Color. 144 mins.

TOTAL RECALL (1990)

★ best visual effects* Eric Brevig, Rob Bottin, Tim McGovern, Alex Funke

A nonstop parade of action, destruction, dazzling effects, stuntwork and violence, with Arnold Schwarzenegger suffering a recurring nightmare about living another life on Mars and eventually making a visit to the red planet to find out who he is and just what is going on. Set in the 21st century and adapted from Phillip K. Dick's short story "We Can Remember It for You Wholesale."

A Carolco Picture, directed by Paul Verhoeven. With Arnold Schwarzenegger, Rachel Ticotin, Sharon Stone, Ronny Cox, Michael Ironside, Marshall Bell, Mel Johnson, Jr., Michael Champion, Roy Brocksmith. Technicolor. 113 mins.

A TOUCH OF CLASS (1973) ★

★ best actress Glenda Jackson

Mel Frank comedy about a well-heeled married insurance agent (George Segal) who drifts into a lighthearted affair with a smart rag-trade pirate (Glenda Jackson), then finds himself becoming too involved. Glenda Jackson's second Oscar (the first having been in 1970 for *Women in Love*).

---

* *Note:* The Oscar for visual effects was a special achievement award.

An Avco Embassy Picture, directed by Melvin Frank. With George Segal, Glenda Jackson, Paul Sorvino, Hildegard Neil, Cec Linder. Panavision/ Technicolor. 106 mins.

THE TOWERING INFERNO (1974)   ★★★

★ best cinematography Fred Koenekamp & Joseph Biroc
★ best editing Harold F. Kress & Carl Kress
★ best song "We May Never Love Like This Again" (music & lyrics by Al Kasha & Joel Hirschhorn)

Massive disaster movie about the fight to save hundreds of people trapped by fire on the top floor of the world's tallest building—a 138-story tower block—on the day of its inauguration ceremony in San Francisco. Fire chief Steve McQueen and designer-architect Paul Newman are the superheroes who help many of the trapped guests escape.

A 20th Century-Fox–Warner Bros. Picture, directed by John Guillermin and Irwin Allen. With Steve McQueen, Paul Newman, William Holden, Faye Dunaway, Fred Astaire, Susan Blakely, Richard Chamberlain, Jennifer Jones, O. J. Simpson, Robert Vaughn, Robert Wagner. Panavision/DeLuxe Color. 165 mins.

TRANSATLANTIC (1931/32)   ★

★ best art direction Gordon Wiles

Conventional Hollywood melodrama set on board an Atlantic liner and centering on a master-gambler (Edmund Lowe) who comes up against a gang of crooks trying to engineer a robbery on board ship. Lois Moran adds female decoration; Gordon Wiles' excellent Oscar-winning art direction takes in nearly every aspect of the liner from deck to boiler room.

A Fox Picture, directed by William K. Howard. With Edmund Lowe, Lois Moran, John Halliday, Greta Nissen, Jean Hersholt, Myrna Loy, Earle Fox. 74 mins.

TRAVELS WITH MY AUNT (1972)   ★

★ best costume design Anthony Powell

Strait-laced bank manager (Alec McCowen) is swept into the crazy world of his eccentric Aunt Augusta (Maggie Smith), who takes him all over Europe and involves him in a shady scheme to smuggle illegal currency into Turkey—a ransom payment for the only real love in her life, Robert Stephens. From the novel by Graham Greene.

An MGM Picture, directed by George Cukor, With Maggie Smith, Alec McCowen, Lou Gossett, Jr., Robert Stephens, Cindy Williams, Jose Luis Lopez Vasquez. Panavision/Metrocolor. 109 mins.

THE TREASURE OF THE SIERRA MADRE (1948)   ★★★

★ best direction John Huston
★ best supporting actor Walter Huston
★ best screenplay John Huston

The effects of greed on three penniless prospectors (Bogart, Huston, Holt) when they strike it rich in the bandit-infested mountains of the Sierra Madre. Set in Mexico in the 1920s, the film was John Huston's first since the end of World War II and marked the first time in Academy history that father and son both won major Oscars in the same year for the same film. In 1974 Francis Ford Coppola (best director) and his father Carmine Coppola (best music) won awards in the same year for *The Godfather Part II*.

A Warner Bros. Picture, directed by John Huston. With Humphrey Bogart, Walter Huston, Tim Holt, Bruce Bennett, Barton MacLane, Alfonso Bedoya. 126 mins.

A TREE GROWS IN BROOKLYN (1945)   ★

★ best supporting actor James Dunn

The childhood of a young girl (Peggy Ann Garner) and her relationships with her friends, neighbors and Irish parents as she grows up in a Brooklyn tenement in the 1900s. Dorothy McGuire is the mother constantly struggling to make ends meet, Oscar-winner James Dunn the weak drunkard father. Director Elia Kazan's first film, adapted from the best-seller by Betty Smith.

A 20th Century-Fox Picture, directed by Elia Kazan. With Dorothy McGuire, Joan Blondell, James Dunn, Lloyd Nolan, Peggy Ann Garner, Ted Donaldson, James Gleason, Ruth Nelson. 128 mins.

THE TRIP TO BOUNTIFUL (1985) ★

★ best actress Geraldine Page

The film for which Geraldine Page gained a belated Oscar for her role as a feisty old widow who is resented by her son and his wife and who determines to pay one last visit to the Texas town in which she spent her youth. Adapted by Horton Foote from his 1953 TV drama and later Broadway play of the same name. Page's previous Oscar nominations: *Hondo* (supporting actress, 1953), *Summer and Smoke* (actress, 1961), *Sweet Bird of Youth* (actress, 1962) *You're a Big Boy Now* (supporting actress, 1966), *Pete 'n' Tillie* (supporting actress, 1972), *Interiors* (actress, 1978) and *The Pope of Greenwich Village* (supporting actress, 1984).

A Bountiful Production/Island Pictures. Directed by Peter Masterson. With Geraldine Page, John Heard, Carlin Glynn, Richard Bradford, Rebecca De Mornay, Kevin Cooney, Norman Bennett. Color. 107 mins.

TRUE GRIT (1969) ★

★ best actor John Wayne

John Wayne's Oscar performance (he had been nominated once before for the war movie *Sands of Iwo Jima* in 1949) as the one-eyed, over-the-hill marshal Rooster Cogburn, who is hired by a teenage girl (Kim Darby) to hunt down the outlaws responsible for the death of her father. From the novel by Charles Portis.

A Paramount Picture, directed by Henry Hathaway. With John Wayne, Glen Campbell, Kim Darby, Jeremy Slate, Robert Duvall, Dennis Hopper, Alfred Ryder, Strother Martin. Technicolor. 128 mins.

TWELVE O'CLOCK HIGH (1949) ★ ★

★ best supporting actor Dean Jagger
★ best sound recording Thomas T. Moulton

Gregory Peck as a ruthless American commanding officer sent from headquarters in World War II to rebuild a heavy-bomber group whose morale has cracked under heavy losses. Set in England during the early days of daylight precision bombing over Germany, the film co-starred Gary Merrill, Millard Mitchell and Dean Jagger as a middle-aged adjutant who remembers the events in flashback from a deserted airfield after the war.

A 20th Century-Fox Picture, directed by Henry King. With Gregory Peck, Hugh Marlowe, Gary Merrill, Millard Mitchell, Dean Jagger, Robert Arthur, Paul Stewart. 132 mins.

20,000 LEAGUES UNDER THE SEA (1954) ★ ★

★ best color art direction John Meehan
　　　　set decoration Emile Kuri
★ best special effects Disney Studios

Jules Verne's 19th-century science-fiction adventure about the mysterious, society-hating Captain Nemo (James Mason) and his underwater submarine Nautilus, which is propelled by "the dynamic force of the universe." The special effects award was primarily for the brilliantly filmed underwater fight between the sub and a giant squid.

A Walt Disney Picture, directed by Richard Fleischer. With Kirk Douglas, James Mason, Paul Lukas, Peter Lorre, Robert J. Wilke,

Carleton Young, Ted de Corsia. CinemaScope/Technicolor. 126 mins.

TWO ARABIAN KNIGHTS (1927/28)

★ best comedy direction Lewis Milestone

William Boyd and Louis Wolheim as two brawling U.S. soldiers who escape from German captivity in World War I by posing as Arabs and head for Jaffa, where they become rivals for the hand of Arab girl Mary Astor. Milestone's award for comedy direction for his work on this film was the only time an Oscar of this kind was presented.

A United Artists Picture, directed by Lewis Milestone. With William Boyd, Mary Astor, Louis Wolheim, Michael Vavitch, Ian Keith, DeWitt Jennings. 9 reels.

2001: A SPACE ODYSSEY (1968)

★ best special visual effects Stanley Kubrick

Spectacular movie prediction of the future revolving around the discovery of a centuries-old monolith on the moon and the subsequent journey by a group of astronauts to Jupiter in search of extraterrestrial life. Breathtaking special effects by Kubrick and his team earned the film an Academy Award in that department, although for many it deserved to win many of the major awards as well. For the record, the film was nominated in the following categories: best direction, art direction, story and screenplay, and special effects.

An MGM Picture, directed by Stanley Kubrick. With Keir Dullea, Gary Lockwood, William Sylvester, Daniel Richter, Douglas Rain, Leonard Rossiter. Cinerama/Metrocolor. 141 mins.

TWO WOMEN (1961)

★ best actress Sophia Loren

Sophia Loren as a young widowed mother who, along with her 13-year-old daughter, is raped by a mob of Moroccan troops during the dark days of battle in Italy in 1943. Harrowing drama, taken from the novel by Alberto Moravia. Loren's portrayal was the first foreign language performance to earn an Academy Award.

A Gala Films-Champion (Rome)/Les Films Marceau-Cocinor/S.G.C. (Paris) co-production, directed by Vittorio De Sica. With Sophia Loren, Eleanora Brown, Raf Vallone, Jean-Paul Belmondo, Renato Salvatori. CinemaScope. 110 mins.

U

UNDERWORLD (1927/28) ★

★ best original story Ben Hecht

Revenge story starring George Bancroft as a big-time underworld hoodlum, Evelyn Brent as his moll "Feathers" and Clive Brook as an alcoholic lawyer. One of the first major gangster films; Ben Hecht's original-story Oscar was the first of its kind awarded by the Academy.

A Paramount Picture, directed by Josef von Sternberg. With George Bancroft, Clive Brook, Evelyn Brent, Larry Semon, Fred Kohler, Helen Lynch. 8 reels.

Clint Eastwood, Hollywood icon, takes aim as bounty hunter William Munny in the allegorical Western *Unforgiven*, the 1992 winner for best picture and best director. It was Eastwood's first nominated film in a career spanning 38 years.

UNFORGIVEN (1992) ★★★★

★ best film Clint Eastwood (producer)
★ best direction Clint Eastwood
★ best supporting actor Gene Hackman
★ best editing Joel Cox

One of only three Westerns (following *Cimarron* [1930/31] and *Dances with Wolves* [1990]) to win best picture, focusing on a former gunfighter (Clint Eastwood) who is lured out of retirement by the offer of a $1,000 reward to track down the two men responsible for slashing a prostitute in the town of Big Whiskey. Joining in the quest: young bounty hunter Jaimz Woolvett and former partner Morgan Freeman. Barring their way is megalomaniac sheriff Gene Hack-

Sean Connery as the Irish beat cop who joins the fight against Al Capone in *The Untouchables* (Paramount). Connery was named best supporting actor of 1987 by the Academy.

man. Eastwood's two awards were earned after a lifetime in films without a single nomination; Hackman's Oscar was his second, having won his first in 1971 for his portrayal of a different kind of lawman—Popeye Doyle in *The French Connection*.

A Warner Bros. Picture, directed by Clint Eastwood. With Clint Eastwood, Gene Hackman, Morgan Freeman, Richard Harris, Jaimz Woolvett, Saul Rubinek, Frances Fisher, Anna Thomson. Technicolor. 131 mins.

THE UNTOUCHABLES (1987)   ★

★ best supporting actor Sean Connery

Or, more appropriately, "The Magnificent Four" (young lawman Kevin Costner, seasoned cop Sean Connery, rookie Andy Garcia and accountant John Martin Smith) as they take on and defeat bootlegger king Al Capone in 1930s Chicago. Previously a TV series starring Robert Stack, but given a new lease on life by the no-holds-barred direction of Brian DePalma. For his Irish beat cop, Sean Connery earned his first nomination at the age of 58 and walked off with the award first time out.

A Paramount Picture, directed by Brian DePalma. With Kevin Costner, Sean Connery, Charles Martin Smith, Andy Garcia, Robert De Niro, Richard Bradford, Jack Kehoe, Brad Sullivan, Billy Drago. Panavision/Technicolor. 120 mins.

V

VACATION FROM MARRIAGE (1946)

(Original U.K. title: *Perfect Strangers*)

★ best original story Clemence Dane

Mild young English couple, Robert Donat and Deborah Kerr, jolted out of their rut by World War II—he joins the Navy, she also joins the service—find they are each rejuvenated by wartime romance and then have to adjust once more to marriage at the war's close.

A London Films-MGM Picture, directed by Alexander Korda. With Robert Donat, Deborah Kerr, Glynis Johns, Ann Todd, Roland Culver. 102 mins.

VICTOR/VICTORIA (1982)

★ best original song score Henry Mancini & Leslie Bricusse

Down-and-out 1930s cabaret singer Julie Andrews masquerades as a man and becomes the toast of Paris, much to the delight of her gay mentor Robert Preston and the bewilderment of her would-be suitor, macho gangster James Garner. Sophisticated American cinema in the style of Lubitsch and Leisen, based on the 1933 German film *Viktor und Victoria*, which was first remade in Britain in 1936 as the Jessie Matthews vehicle *First a Girl*.

A Ladbroke Entertainment Feature from Blake Edwards Entertainment/MGM-UA. Directed by Blake Edwards. With Julie Andrews, James Garner, Robert Preston, Lesley Ann Warren, Alex Karras, John Rhys-Davies, Graham Stark, Peter Arne. Panavision/Technicolor: Prints by Metrocolor. 134 mins.

THE V.I.P.S (1963)

★ best supporting actress Margaret Rutherford

Grand Hotel at London Airport with a set of high-class passengers stranded for hours at the terminal because their flight has been delayed by fog. Elizabeth Taylor, Richard Burton, Louis Jourdan, and Orson Welles head the big guns but they're spiked by Oscar-winner Margaret Rutherford as an eccentric duchess on her first flight. From an original script by Terence Rattigan.

An MGM Picture, directed by Anthony Asquith. With Elizabeth Taylor, Richard Burton, Louis Jourdan, Elsa Martinelli, Margaret Rutherford, Maggie Smith, Rod Taylor, Linda Christian, Orson Welles. Panavision/Metrocolor. 119 mins.

THE VIRGIN SPRING (1960) ★

★ best foreign language film Sweden

Ingmar Bergman film set in the 14th century, retelling a dramatic fable about a young virgin who is raped and murdered by three herdsmen while on a holy errand, avenged by her grief-stricken father and then miraculously commemorated by a magical spring that suddenly flows from the spot where she met her death.

Svensk Filmindustri, directed by Ingmar Bergman. With Max Von Sydow, Birgitta Valberg, Gunnel Lindblom, Birgitta Pettersson, Axel Duberg, Tor Isedal. 88 mins.

VIVA VILLA! (1934)

★ best assistant direction John Waters

Part fact, part fiction adventure of the revolutionary bandit Pancho Villa (Wallace Beery), who led the fight for Madero's Mexican republic. Begun by Howard Hawks, the film was completed by and credited to Jack Conway.

An MGM Picture, directed by Jack Conway. With Wallace Beery, Fay Wray, Leo Carrillo,

Donald Cook, Stuart Erwin, George E. Stone, Joseph Schildkraut, Henry B. Walthall. 115 mins.

VIVA ZAPATA! (1952)   ★

★ best supporting actor Anthony Quinn

Biography of Mexican revolutionary Emiliano Zapata (Marlon Brando), who fought for Mad-ero at the same time as Villa and rose to almost legendary stature before being assassinated by soldiers of the Mexican army. Steinbeck wrote the original screenplay; Oscar winner Anthony Quinn plays Zapata's brother Eufemio.

A 20th Century-Fox Picture, directed by Elia Kazan, With Marlon Brando, Jean Peters, Anthony Quinn, Joseph Wiseman, Arnold Moss, Alan Reed, Margo, Lou Gilbert, Harold Gordon, Mildred Dunnock. 113 mins.

WAIKIKI WEDDING (1937)

★ best song "Sweet Leilani" (Harry Owens, music & Lyrics)

Early Crosby comedy musical, with Bing as a press agent promoting Shirley Ross as a pineapple queen in Hawaii. Among Bing's songs: "Blue Hawaii" and the Academy Award-winning "Sweet Leilani."

A Paramount Picture, directed by Frank Tuttle. With Bing Crosby, Bob Burns, Martha Raye, Shirley Ross, George Barbier, Leif Erikson. 89 mins.

WALL STREET (1987) ★

★ best actor Michael Douglas

Oliver Stone casts a jaundiced eye on the dangerous and treacherous world or the New York moneymakers. Chief among the players: Michael Douglas as the corrupt corporate raider Gordon Gekko, and Charlie Sheen as a young hotshot who falls under Gekko's spell when he tries for a quick fortune. The film earned Douglas his second Academy Award; 13 years earlier he had produced, with Saul Zaentz, the Oscar-winning best picture *One Flew Over the Cuckoo's Nest*. His father Kirk, despite being nominated three times—*Champion* (1949), *The Bad and the Beautiful* (1952) and *Lust for Life* (1956)—never won as best actor.

A 20th Century-Fox Picture, directed by Oliver Stone. With Michael Douglas, Charlie Sheen, Daryl Hannah, Martin Sheen, Terence Stamp, Hal Holbrook, Sean Young, Sylvia Miles, Richard Dysart. DeLuxe Color. 126 mins.

WAR AND PEACE (1968) ★

★ best foreign language film U.S.S.R.

Russia's mammoth six-hour-plus version of Tolstoy's classic novel, spanning the years 1805–1812 and following the fortunes of several aristocratic families during the tremendous upheavals during the war with France and Napoleon's attack and retreat from Moscow. Ludmila Savelyeva is the young adolescent Natasha who grows to tragic womanhood, Vyacheslav Tikhonov is Prince Andrei, and Sergei Bondarchuk, who also directed, is the clumsy idealist Pierre.

MosFilm (Russia), directed by Sergei Bondarchuk. With Ludmila Savelyeva, Sergei Bondarchuk, Vyacheslav Tikhonov, Anastasia Vertinskaya, Vasily Lanovoi, Viktor Stanitsin. Sovcolor/70mm. 373 mins.

THE WAR OF THE WORLDS (1953)

★ best special effects Paramount Studios

Producer George Pal transfers H. G. Wells' novel of a deadly Martian invasion from England to the United States, updating the story to the postwar era and even introducing nuclear weapons—used (unsuccessfully) against the invaders. The end result is the same as in the book, however—the death of the Martians from a common cold. Brilliant special effects of the alien spacecraft, their war machines and, in one brief sequence, the Martians themselves.

A Paramount Picture, directed by Byron Haskin. With Gene Barry, Ann Robinson, Les Tremayne, Bob Cornthwaite, Sandra Giglio, Lewis Martin. Technicolor. 85 mins.

WATCH ON THE RHINE (1943) ★

★ best actor Paul Lukas

Version of Lillian Hellman's World War II play about an important member of the anti-Nazi underground movement (Paul Lukas) who escapes with his wife (Bette Davis) to Washington only to find himself being blackmailed and harried by Nazi agents in the States. Lukas' Oscar remains one of the most forgotten in the history of the awards.

A Warner Bros. Picture, directed by Herman Shumlin. With Bette Davis, Paul Lukas, Geraldine Fitzgerald, Lucile Watson, Beulah Bondi, George Coulouris, Donald Woods, Henry Daniell. 114 mins.

THE WAY OF ALL FLESH (1927/28)   ★

★ best actor Emil Jannings

The demoralization and complete downfall of an elderly German-American bank cashier (Emil Jannings) who sinks to vagrancy after being accosted on a train journey by a femme fatale and relieved of the bank bonds he is carrying for his employers. Jannings' first U.S. feature and one of the two films (the other being *The Last Command*) for which he won an Oscar.

A Paramount Picture, directed by Victor Fleming. With Emil Jannings, Belle Bennett, Phyllis Haver, Donald Keith, Fred Kohler, Philippe De Lacey. 9 reels.

THE WAY WE WERE (1973)   ★★

★ best original dramatic score Marvin Hamlisch
★ best song "The Way We Were" (Marvin Hamlisch, music; Alan & Marilyn Bergman, lyrics)

The story of a tempestuous, doomed love affair between two irreconcilable opposites—Barbra Streisand, an outspoken, aggressive Jewish activist who retains her ideals throughout her life, and Robert Redford, the all-American golden-haired college boy who, after becoming a successful novelist, switches to Hollywood to become a screenwriter. Expertly made weepie covering the period from the late 1930s to the early 1950s and containing just the right ingre-

dients in its melancholy score to accompany the tear-soaked events.

A Columbia Picture, directed by Sydney Pollack. With Barbra Streisand, Robert Redford, Bradford Dillman, Lois Chiles, Patrick O'Neal, Viveca Lindfors, Murray Hamilton. Panavision/Eastman color. 118 mins.

THE WESTERNER (1940)   ★

★ best supporting actor Walter Brennan

Goldwyn-Wyler Western about the battle between the cattlemen—the original settlers on the land—and the homesteaders in Texas in the rip-roaring days of the 1880s. Brennan's performance as the real-life character Judge Roy Bean, leader of the cattlemen and "the law west of the Pecos," earned him his third supporting Oscar in five years, a record that stands to this day.

A Sam Goldwyn Production (released through United Artists), directed by William Wyler. With Gary Cooper, Walter Brennan, Doris Davenport, Fred Stone, Paul Hurst, Chill Wills, Charles Halton, Forrest Tucker. 99 mins

WEST SIDE STORY (1961)   ★★★★★★★★★★

★ best film Robert Wise (producer)
★ best direction Robert Wise & Jerome Robbins
★ best supporting actor George Chakiris
★ best supporting actress Rita Moreno
★ best color cinematography Daniel L. Fapp
★ best color art direction Boris Leven
       set decoration Victor A. Gangelin
★ best color costume design Irene Sharaff
★ best sound Fred Hynes & Gordon E. Sawyer
★ best editing Thomas Stanford
★ best scoring of a musical Saul Chaplin, Johnny Green, Sid Ramin & Irwin Kostal

A musical transposition of Shakespeare's *Romeo and Juliet* to the slums of New York, with Richard Beymer and Natalie Wood trying to find peace and love despite the gang wars—between the immigrant Puerto Ricans (the Sharks) and the native New Yorkers (the Jets)—going on around them. Chakiris and Moreno as a pair of young Puerto Rican lovers proved to be the only winners in the acting categories, but the film itself emerged as the biggest musical best-picture winner of all time, and with 10 awards stand second only to the Oscar record-holder *Ben Hur*. Wise and Robbins shared the director's award (the first time in Oscar history) and Robbins was also voted a special award for his outstanding choreography.

A United Artists Picture, directed by Robert Wise and Jerome Robbins. With Natalie Wood, Richard Beymer, Russ Tamblyn, Rita Moreno, George Chakiris. Panavision 70/Technicolor. 155 mins.

WHATEVER HAPPENED TO BABY JANE? (1962)   ★

★ best b/w costume design Norma Koch

Grand Guignol from Robert Aldrich with Bette Davis as a drunken, demented ex-child star getting her kicks by slowly torturing her crippled sister Joan Crawford in the decaying Hollywood mansion in which they live. The first time that the two former Warner stars appeared together, with only Davis receiving an Academy nomination.

A Warner Bros. Picture, directed by Robert Aldrich. With Joan Crawford, Bette Davis, Victor Buono, Marjorie Bennett, Maidie Norman, Anna Lee, Barbara Merrill 132 mins.

WHEN TOMORROW COMES (1939)   ★

★ best sound recording Bernard B. Brown

Lush tearjerker with world-famous concert pianist and married man Charles Boyer falling in love with beautiful waitress Irene Dunne. Based on a story by James M. Cain.

A Universal Picture, directed by John M. Stahl. With Charles Boyer, Irene Dunne, Bar-bara O'Neil, Onslow Stevens, Nydia Westman, Fritz Feld. 90 mins.

WHEN WORLDS COLLIDE (1951)   ★

★ best special effects Paramount Studios

Another of George Pal's science fiction fantasies of the early 1950s with the Planet Earth about to be destroyed by a giant star hurtling towards it. Richard Derr and Barbara Rush lead the group of people racing against time to build a rocket ship that will take them to a new planet and a new life. The Technicolor special effects, as always in Pal's films, were far superior to those in other science fiction films of the period.

A Paramount Picture, directed by Rudoph Mate. With Richard Derr, Barbara Rush, Peter Hanson, Judith Ames, John Hoyt. Technicolor. 81 mins.

WHITE NIGHTS (1985)   ★

★ best song "Say You, Say Me" (Lionel Richie, music & lyrics)

An international thriller, racial romance and classical-and-pop musical all rolled into one, as tap-dancing expatriate Gregory Hines and Russian ballet star Mikhail Baryshnikov escape the KGB and make a dash for freedom and safety to the U.S. embassy in Moscow. A dozen or so songs and musical numbers help rather than hinder the unlikely goings-on, one of them earning an Oscar as best song of its year. A second, "Separate Lives," with music and lyrics by Stephen Bishop, earned a nomination.

A Columbia-Delphi V Production/New Visions Production, directed by Taylor Hackford. With Mikhail Baryshnikov, Gregory Hines, Jerzy Skolimowski, Helen Mirren, Geraldine Page, Isabella Rossellini, John Glover, Stefan Gryff. 70mm/Metrocolor. 134 mins.

WHITE SHADOWS IN THE SOUTH SEAS (1928/29)   ★

★ best cinematography Clyde De Vinna

The first MGM sound film—synchronized sound effects and music were added after the film's completion. The plot deals with a drunken doctor (Monte Blue) who tries to defend a tribe of South Seas natives from the machinations of unscrupulous trader Robert Anderson. Raquel Torres co-stars as a native girl. Photographed entirely on location in the Marquesas Islands.

An MGM Picture, directed by W. S. Van Dyke. With Monte Blue, Raquel Torres, Robert Anderson. 9 reels

WHO FRAMED ROGER RABBIT? (1988)   ★★★

- ★ best editing Arthur Schmidt
- ★ best sound effects editing Charles L. Campbell & Louis L. Edemann
- ★ best visual effects Ken Ralston, Richard Williams, Edward Jones & George Gibbs

The most advanced combination of live action and animation yet put on screen, with Bob Hoskins as a washed-up private eye trying to prove the innocence of a rabbit suspected of murder. Many cameo performances from old cartoon favorites such as Donald Duck, Goofy, Mickey Mouse, Tweetie Pie, etc., plus a voluptuous new character, a slinky nightclub singer named Jessica, voiced by Kathleen Turner. Animator Richard Williams, who had previously

Private-eye Bob Hoskins meets up with Jessica in *Who Framed Roger Rabbit?* (Touchstone Pictures/Amblin). The picture was named for its sound effects editing, editing and visual effects.

won an Academy Award for his 30-minute version of Dickens' *A Christmas Carol*, was also awarded an honorary Oscar for his work in animation.

A Touchstone Pictures/Amblin Entertainment Production, directed by Robert Zemeckis. With Bob Hoskins, Christopher Lloyd, Joanna Cassidy, Charles Fleischer (voice of Roger Rabbit, Benny the Cab, Greasy, Psycho), Stubby Kaye, Alan Tilvern, Richard Le Parmentier. In color. 104 mins.

WHO'S AFRAID OF VIRGINIA WOOLF? (1966)   ★★★★★

- ★ best actress Elizabeth Taylor
- ★ best supporting actress Sandy Dennis
- ★ best b/w cinematography Haskell Wexler
- ★ best b/w art direction Richard Sylbert set decoration George James Hopkins
- ★ best b/w costume design Irene Sharaff

The desperate infighting between a college professor (Richard Burton) and his blowsy, shrewish wife (Elizabeth Taylor) and the innocent young faculty couple (George Segal and Sandy Dennis) they invite to join them for one of their vicious no-holds-barred evenings of marital fun and games. All four of the principal performers earned Oscar nominations, although it was only the women who came out winners on awards night. Based on the play by Edward Albee.*

A Warner Bros. Picture, directed by Mike Nichols. With Elizabeth Taylor, Richard Burton, George Segal, Sandy Dennis. 131 mins.

---

* *Note:* Elizabeth Taylor earned two Oscars in the 1960s, winning her first for *Butterfield 8* in 1960. Burton, despite being nominated on seven occasions, never emerged a winner. His nominations: *My Cousin Rachel* (supporting actor, 1952), *The Robe* (1953), *Becket* (1964), *The Spy Who Came In from the Cold* (1965), *Who's Afraid of Virginia Woolf?* (1966), *Anne of the Thousand Days* (1969) and *Equus* (1977).

WILSON (1944)

★ best original screenplay Lamar Trotti
★ best color cinematography Leon Shamroy
★ best color art direction Wiard Ihnen
       int. decoration Thomas Little
★ best sound recording E. H. Hansen
★ best film editing Barbara McLean

The prestige production of 1944—a painstaking biography of America's 28th president, Woodrow Wilson, covering his period as a schoolteacher at Princeton and as governor of New Jersey, his election to the presidency, his postwar fight for the League of Nations and his final illness and defeat. For all its production values and important themes, it lost out to a much lighter vehicle, Crosby's *Going My Way*, as best picture of the year.

A 20th Century-Fox Picture, directed by Henry King. With Alexander Knox, Charles Coburn, Geraldine Fitzgerald, Thomas Mitchell, Cedric Hardwicke, Ruth Nelson, Vincent Price. Technicolor. 154 mins.

WINGS (1927/28)

★ best film Lucien Hubbard (producer)
★ best engineering effects Roy Pomeroy

The first best-picture winner, a routine World War I aviation story of two American pilots (Charles "Buddy" Rogers and Richard Arlen) who find themselves rivals for the affections of small-town girl Clara Bow. Turned into something special, however, by William Wellman's expertly staged action sequences—both in the air and on the ground. Besides being the first Oscar winner, the picture was also the only non-speaking film to win the award, its only sound being synchronized music and sound effects. The following year's winner, *The Broadway Melody*, was a talkie. Other best-picture nominees in that historic first year: *The Last Command*, *The Racket*, *The Way of All Flesh* (all Paramount) and *Seventh Heaven* (Fox).

A Paramount Picture, directed by William A. Wellman. With Clara Bow, Charles "Buddy"

Rogers, Richard Arlen, Jobyna Ralston, Gary Cooper, Arlette Marchal. 13 reels.

WITH A SONG IN MY HEART (1952) ★

★ best scoring of a musical Alfred Newman

The dramatic life of singer Jane Froman (Susan Hayward), who fought her way back to stardom after being badly crippled in an airplane crash. Susan Hayward's third best-actress nomination.

A 20th Century-Fox Picture, directed by Walter Lang. With Susan Hayward, Rory Calhoun, David Wayne, Thelma Ritter, Robert Wagner, Helen Westcott, Una Merkel. Technicolor. 117 mins.

WITH BYRD AT THE SOUTH POLE (1929/30)

★ best cinematography Willard Van Der Veer
  & Joseph T. Rucker

Documentary account of an incident-packed expedition by Rear Admiral Richard E. Byrd and his men to the South Pole. Blizzards, storms at sea, battles with Antarctic icepacks, all handsomely photographed by the two Oscar-winning cameramen.

A Paramount Picture, synchronized narration by Floyd Gibbons. 8 reels.

WITNESS (1985)

★ best original screenplay William Kelley,
  Pamela Wallace & Earl W. Wallace
★ best editing Thom Noble

Philadelphia cop Harrison Ford discovers his bosses are corrupt and goes into hiding with peace-loving Amish farmers who care for him when he is wounded. A beguiling performance from Lukas Haas as the young boy who starts the events in motion when he witnesses a killing, and a tender one from Kelly McGillis as an Amish widow who falls for Ford. Arguably Australian director Peter Weir's best American

Harrison Ford's only Oscar nomination, as the police captain hiding out with the peace-loving Amish community in *Witness* (Paramount, 1985). The film won awards for screenplay and editing.

film, although he failed to win the directing award (Sydney Pollack won that year for *Out of Africa*), and to date Ford's only Academy Award nomination.

A Paramount Picture, directed by Peter Weir, With Harrison Ford, Kelly McGillis, Josef Sommer, Lukas Haas, Jan Rubes, Alexander Godunov, Danny Glover, Brent Jennings, Patti LuPone. Technicolor. 112 mins.

THE WIZARD OF OZ (1939) ★★

- ★ best original score Herbert Stothart
- ★ best song "Over the Rainbow" (Harold Arlen, music; E. Y. Harburg, lyrics)

Aside from the Disney films, the most famous children's classic of the screen—a part-Technicolor, part-monochrome recreation of Frank Baum's magical land of Oz, with Judy Garland as the lost little Kansas girl making her way to the Emerald City in the company of scarecrow Ray Bolger, tin man Jack Haley and cowardly lion Bert Lahr.

An MGM Picture, directed by Victor Fleming. With Judy Garland, Frank Morgan, Ray Bolger, Bert Lahr, Jack Haley, Billie Burke, Margaret Hamilton, Charley Grapewin. Technicolor. 101 mins.

THE WOMAN IN RED (1984)   ★

- ★ best song "I Just Called to Say I Love You" (Stevie Wonder, music & lyrics)

Happily married public relations man Gene Wilder finds himself aroused by a model in a red dress and frantically pursues her. Based on *Pardon Mon Affaire*, a French success of the mid-1970s, and more famous for its Oscar-winning song than for anything else. Attractive Kelly Le Brock is featured as the girl who inadvertently starts all the trouble.

An Orion Picture, directed by Gene Wilder. With Gene Wilder, Charles Grodin, Joseph Bologna, Judith Ivey, Michael Huddleston, Kelly Le Brock, Gilda Radner, Kyle T. Heffner, DeLuxe Color. 86 mins.

WOMAN OF THE YEAR (1942)   ★

- ★ best original screenplay Ring Lardner Jr. & Michael Kanin

The first teaming of Tracy and Hepburn, he a down-to-earth baseball writer, she a world-famous international affairs journalist. Their resulting marriage produced a script on the husband-versus-career theme that has rarely, if ever, been bettered.

An MGM Picture, directed by George Stevens. With Spencer Tracy, Katharine Hepburn, Fay Bainter, Reginald Owen, Minor Watson, William Bendix. 112 mins.

WOMEN IN LOVE (1970)   ★

- ★ best actress Glenda Jackson

D. H. Lawrence's powerful novel of two less-than-peaceful love affairs in a small English coal-mining town in the early 1920s. Glenda Jackson and Jennie Linden star as the two emancipated Brangwen sisters, Oliver Reed as

Gerald Crich, the vigorous son of a local mine owner, and Alan Bates as the less exuberant but equally passionate school inspector Rupert Birkin.

A United Artists Picture, directed by Ken Russell. With Alan Bates, Oliver Reed, Glenda Jackson, Jennie Linden, Eleanor Bron, Michael Gough. DeLuxe Color. 130 mins.

THE WONDERFUL WORLD OF THE BROTHERS GRIMM (1962) ★

★ best color costume design Mary Wills

A combination of historical fact and fantasy, retelling the lives of the famous children's writers as well as some of the stories that made them famous. The first Cinerama movie to tell a story; George Pal directed the fantasy sequences, Henry Levin the main story line.

An MGM Picture, directed by Henry Levin. With Laurence Harvey, Karl Boehm, Claire Bloom, Walter Slezak, Barbara Eden, Oscar Homolka. Cinerama/Technicolor. 135 mins.

WONDER MAN (1945) ★

★ best special effects John Fulton, photo graphic; Arthur W. Johns, sound

Danny Kaye's second movie, a special effects bonanza with Kaye as a quiet, bespectacled bookworm taking the place of his nightclub entertainer twin brother when the latter is bumped off by gangsters. The trick photography occurs when the bookworm is constantly bothered by his brother's frolicsome ghost.

A Sam Goldwyn Production (released through RKO), directed by Bruce Humberstone. With Danny Kaye, Virginia Mayo, Vera-Ellen, Allen Jenkins, Edward S. Brophy, S. Z. Sakall, Steve Cochran. Technicolor. 98 mins.

WORKING GIRL (1988) ★

★ best song "Let the River Run" (Carly Simon, music & lyrics)

Secretary Melanie Griffith makes the most of the absence of high-flying boss Sigourney Weaver by stepping into her shoes when she's injured in a skiing accident, and snaring not only her best clients but also her boyfriend, struggling broker Harrison Ford. A classic role-swapping comedy from Mike Nichols, set in the wheeling-dealing world of Manhattan and directed with more than one backward glance to the 1940s.

A 20th Century-Fox Picture, directed by Mike Nichols. With Harrison Ford, Sigourney Weaver, Melanie Griffith, Alec Baldwin, Joan Cusack, Philip Bosco, Nora Dunn, Oliver Platt, James Lally. Color: Du Art; prints by DeLuxe. 113 mins.

WRITTEN ON THE WIND (1956) ★

★ best supporting actress Dorothy Malone

Texas melodrama that gave Dorothy Malone her chance to win an Oscar as the nymphomaniac sister of multimillionaire Robert Stack, a woman who almost manages to destroy both her brother and the man she sets out to get— Rock Hudson. Lauren Bacall as Stack's wife completes the melodramatic quartet.

A Universal International Picture, directed by Douglas Sirk. With Rock Hudson, Lauren Bacall, Robert Stack, Dorothy Malone, Robert Keith, Grant Williams, Robert J. Wilke. Technicolor. 99 mins.

WUTHERING HEIGHTS (1939) ★

★ best b/w cinematography Gregg Toland

Goldwyn's favorite among all his pictures—an atmospheric rendering of Emily Bronte's brooding love story of the Yorkshire moors, with Laurence Olivier as the wild Heathcliff and Merle Oberon as his tragic love, Cathy. Gregg Toland—in the opinion of many the finest

cameraman Hollywood has ever produced—
won his only Academy Award for this film,
although he was also nominated for *Les Miserables* (1935), *Dead End* (1937), *The Long Voyage
Home* (1940) and *Citizen Kane* (1941) before his
untimely death in 1948, at the age of 44.

A Sam Goldwyn Production (released through
United Artists), directed by William Wyler.
With Merle Oberon, Laurence Olivier, David
Niven, Donald Crisp, Flora Robson, Hugh
Williams, Geraldine Fitzgerald, Cecil Kella-
way, Leo G. Carroll. 103 mins.

Y

YANKEE DOODLE DANDY (1942)

- ★ best actor James Cagney
- ★ best sound recording Nathan Levinson
- ★ best scoring of a musical Ray Heindorf & Heinz Roemheld

James Cagney, sheer dynamite as the immortal George M. Cohan, one of the most popular American composer-entertainers of the early 1900s. Walter Huston co-stars as Cohan, Sr.; songs include "Yankee Doodle Boy," "Give My Regards to Broadway" and "Over There."

A Warner Bros. Picture, directed by Michael Curtiz. With James Cagney, Joan Leslie, Walter Huston, Richard Whorf, George Tobias, Irene Manning, Rosemary De Camp, S. Z. Sakall. 126 mins.

THE YEARLING (1946)

- ★ best color cinematography Charles Rosher, Leonard Smith & Arthur Arling
- ★ best color art direction Cedric Gibbons & Paul Groesse
                    interior decoration Edwin B.
                    Willis

Marjorie Kinnan Rawlings' story of a young boy's love for his pet fawn, an animal that has to be destroyed because it is gradually eating the crops on which the boy's farmer parents depend for their living. Set in the Florida backwoods and handsomely photographed by three of Hollywood's top cameramen.

An MGM Picture, directed by Clarence Brown. With Gregory Peck, Jane Wyman, Claude Jarman, Jr., Chill Wills, Clem Bevans. Technicolor. 134 mins.

THE YEAR OF LIVING DANGEROUSLY (1983)

- ★ best supporting actress Linda Hunt

Australian TV journalist Mel Gibson finds himself on the death list of the Indonesian Communist party when he becomes privy to some vital military information just prior to Sukarno's fall in 1965. Also involved in the dangerous intrigues: Sigourney Weaver as an attaché at the British Embassy, and Linda Hunt, who won an Oscar for her portrayal of a diminutive Chinese-Australian male photographer working for the Australian Broadcasting Service. Hunt's Oscar was the first to be earned by a woman playing a man.

McElroy & McElroy Productions. A Freddie Fields presentation for MGM/UA, directed by Peter Weir. With Mel Gibson, Sigourney Weaver, Linda Hunt, Bembol Roco, Domingo Landicho, Hermino De Guzman, Michael Murphy, Noel Ferrier. Panavision/Metrocolor. 115 mins.

YENTL (1983)

- ★ best original song score Michel Legrand, Alan & Marilyn Bergman

Barbra Streisand starred in, directed, produced and co-wrote this film based on a story by Isaac Bashevis Singer about a young woman in turn-of-the-century Poland who disguises herself as a boy to become a Talmudic scholar. Things work out reasonably well until she falls in love with a fellow student and his fiancée falls in love with her. Streisand's first film as a director.

Ladbroke Entertainments/A Barwood Film for MGM/UA, directed by Barbra Streisand. With Barbra Streisand, Mandy Patinkin, Amy Irving, Nehemiah Persoff, Steven Hill, Allan Corduner, Ruth Goring, David De Keyser. Technicolor. 133 mins.

YESTERDAY, TODAY AND TOMORROW (1964) ★

★ best foreign language film Italy

One of the lightest vehicles ever to win the best foreign film award, an Italian comedy made up of three different stories all featuring Sophia Loren. In the first she appears as a permanently pregnant black marketeer in the slums; in the second as the elegant wife of a rich Milan industrialist; in the third as a call girl having an affair with Bologna playboy Marcello Mastroianni.

A Champion/Concordia Production (Italy), directed by Vittorio De Sica. With Sophia Loren, Marcello Mastroianni, Aldo Giuffre, Armando Trovajoli, Giovanni Ridolfi. Techniscope/Technicolor. 119 mins.

YOU CAN'T TAKE IT WITH YOU (1938) ★ ★

★ best film Frank Capra (producer)
★ best direction Frank Capra

Frank Capra's third Oscar of the 1930s, an adaptation of the Pulitzer Prize–winning Moss Hart–George S. Kaufman play about the zany Vanderhof family, who believe in doing just what they like and to hell with the consequences. Leader of the clan is father Lionel Barrymore, who decided one day that he had earned enough money and would spend the next 30 years having fun. Up against him is Wall Street business tycoon Edward Arnold, who needs to demolish the Vanderhof home as part of his plans to expand his business plant.

A Columbia Picture, directed by Frank Capra. With Jean Arthur, Lionel Barrymore, James Stewart, Edward Arnold, Mischa Auer, Ann Miller, Spring Byington, Samuel S. Hinds, Donald Meek, H. B. Warner. 127 mins.

YOU LIGHT UP MY LIFE (1977) ★

★ best song "You Light Up My Life" (Joseph Brooks, music & lyrics)

Character study of a former child star (DiDi Conn) who tries to leave her past behind her and become a top recording artist in the pop music business. A selfish, second-rate comedian father, a dull fiancée and a faithless sponsor all leave her sadder, wiser and still single.

A Columbia Picture, directed by Joseph Brooks. With DiDi Conn, Joe Silver, Michael Zaslow, Stephen Nathan, Melanie Mayron, Jerry Keller, Lisa Reeves. Technicolor. 91 mins.

Z

Z (1969)

★ best foreign language film Algeria
★ best editing Francoise Bonnot

Chilling political thriller, set in an unidentified Mediterranean country, about a young district magistrate who, when investigating the death of an influential pacifist leader, learns that it has been engineered by officialdom and the country's military authorities. Based on a true incident, the 1963 assassination of a left-wing Greek deputy.

Reggane Film (Paris)-O.N.C.I.C. (Algiers), directed by Costa-Gavras. With Yves Montand, Jean-Louis Trintignant, Jacques Perrin, Francois Perier, Irene Papas, Georges Geret, Charles Denner. Eastman Color. 127 mins.

ZORBA THE GREEK (1964)

★ best supporting actress Lila Kedrova
★ best b/w cinematography Walter Lassally
★ best b/w art direction Vassilis Photopoulos

Anthony Quinn in perhaps his most famous role, as a big-hearted, grizzled old Greek who befriends a quiet young Englishman (Alan Bates) who is attempting to reopen the Cretan mine left him by his father. Quinn, however, had to be content with just a nomination, the acting award in the film being stolen from under his nose by Lila Kedrova as a pathetic aging prostitute living out her last days with only her memories for company.

An International Classics Picture (released by 20th Century-Fox) directed by Michael Cacoyannis. With Anthony Quinn, Alan Bates, Irene Papas, Lila Kedrova, George Foundas. 142 mins.

APPENDIX 1
The Winners Year by Year

A listing by year of the major Oscars presented by the Academy of Motion Picture Arts and Sciences in Hollywood, from 1927 to the present.

1927/28

Production	*Wings* (Paramount)
Actor	Emil Jannings in *The Way of All Flesh* and *The Last Command*.
Actress	Janet Gaynor in *Seventh Heaven*, *Street Angel* and *Sunrise*
Direction	Frank Borzage for *Seventh Heaven*
	Note: Lewis Milestone was voted best comedy director for *Two Arabian Knights*, an award not given after this first year.

1928/29

Production	*The Broadway Melody* (MGM)
Actor	Warner Baxter in *In Old Arizona*
Actress	Mary Pickford in *Coquette*
Direction	Frank Lloyd for *The Divine Lady*

1929/30

Production	*All Quiet on the Western Front* (Universal)
Actor	George Arliss in *Disraeli*
Actress	Norma Shearer in *The Divorcee*
Direction	Lewis Milestone for *All Quiet On the Western Front*

1930/31

Production	*Cimarron* (RKO)
Actor	Lionel Barrymore in *A Free Soul*
Actress	Marie Dressler in *Min and Bill*
Direction	Norman Taurog for *Skippy*

1931/32

Production	*Grand Hotel* (MGM)
Actor	Fredric March in *Dr. Jekyll and Mr. Hyde* and Wallace Beery in *The Champ*
Actress	Helen Hayes in *The Sin of Madelon Claudet*
Direction	Frank Borzage for *Bad Girl*

1932/33

Production	*Cavalcade* (Fox)
Actor	Charles Laughton in *The Private Life of Henry VIII*
Actress	Katharine Hepburn in *Morning Glory*
Direction	Frank Lloyd for *Cavalcade*

1934

Production	*It Happened One Night* (Columbia)
Actor	Clark Gable in *It Happened One Night*
Actress	Claudette Colbert in *It Happened One Night*
Direction	Frank Capra for *It Happened One Night*

1935

Production	*Mutiny on the Bounty* (MGM)
Actor	Victor McLaglen in *The Informer*

Actress   Bette Davis in *Dangerous*
Direction   John Ford for *The Informer*

1936

Production   *The Great Ziegfeld* (MGM)
Actor   Paul Muni in *The Story of Louis Pasteur*
Actress   Luise Rainer in *The Great Ziegfeld*
Supp. Actor   Walter Brennan in *Come and Get It*
Supp. Actress Gale Sondergaard in *Anthony Adverse*
Direction   Frank Capra for *Mr. Deeds Goes to Town*

1937

Production   *The Life of Emile Zola* (Warner Bros.)
Actor   Spencer Tracy in *Captains Courageous*
Actress   Luise Rainer in *The Good Earth*
Supp. Actor   Joseph Schildkraut in *The Life of Emile Zola*
Supp. Actress Alice Brady in *In Old Chicago*
Direction   Leo McCarey for *The Awful Truth*

1938

Production   *You Can't Take It With You* (Columbia)
Actor   Spencer Tracy in *Boys' Town*
Actress   Bette Davis in *Jezebel*
Supp. Actor   Walter Brennan in *Kentucky*
Supp. Actress Fay Bainter in *Jezebel*
Direction   Frank Capra for *You Can't Take It With You*

1939

Production   *Gone With the Wind* (Selznick–MGM)
Actor   Robert Donat in *Goodbye, Mr. Chips*
Actress   Vivien Leigh in *Gone With the Wind*

Supp. Actor   Thomas Mitchell in *Stagecoach*
Supp. Actress Hattie McDaniel in *Gone With the Wind*
Direction   Victor Fleming for *Gone With the Wind*

1940

Production   *Rebecca* (Selznick–United Artists)
Actor   James Stewart in *The Philadelphia Story*
Actress   Ginger Rogers in *Kitty Foyle*
Supp. Actor   Walter Brennan in *The Westerner*
Supp. Actress Jane Darwell in *The Grapes of Wrath*
Direction   John Ford for *The Grapes of Wrath*

1941

Production   *How Green Was My Valley* (20th Century-Fox)
Actor   Gary Cooper in *Sergeant York*
Actress   Joan Fontaine in *Suspicion*
Supp. Actor   Donald Crisp in *How Green Was My Valley*
Supp. Actress Mary Astor in *The Great Lie*
Direction   John Ford for *How Green Was My Valley*

1942

Production   *Mrs. Miniver* (MGM)
Actor   James Cagney in *Yankee Doodle Dandy*
Actress   Greer Garson in *Mrs. Miniver*
Supp. Actor   Van Heflin in *Johnny Eager*
Supp. Actress Teresa Wright in *Mrs. Miniver*
Direction   William Wyler for *Mrs. Miniver*

1943

Production   *Casablanca* (Warner Bros.)
Actor   Paul Lukas in *Watch on the Rhine*

Actress	Jennifer Jones in *The Song of Bernadette*
Supp. Actor	Charles Coburn in *The More the Merrier*
Supp. Actress	Katina Paxinou in *For Whom the Bell Tolls*
Direction	Michael Curtiz for *Casablanca*

1944

Production	*Going My Way* (Paramount)
Actor	Bing Crosby in *Going My Way*
Actress	Ingrid Bergman in *Gaslight*
Supp. Actor	Barry Fitzgerald in *Going My Way*
Supp. Actress	Ethel Barrymore in *None But the Lonely Heart*
Direction	Leo McCarey for *Going My Way*

1945

Production	*The Lost Weekend* (Paramount)
Actor	Ray Milland in *The Lost Weekend*
Actress	Joan Crawford in *Mildred Pierce*
Supp. Actor	James Dunn in *A Tree Grows in Brooklyn*
Supp. Actress	Anne Revere in *National Velvet*
Direction	Billy Wilder for *The Lost Weekend*

1946

Production	*The Best Years of Our Lives* (Goldwyn-RKO)
Actor	Fredric March in *The Best Years of Our Lives*
Actress	Olivia de Havilland in *To Each His Own*
Supp. Actor	Harold Russell in *The Best Years of Our Lives*
Supp. Actress	Anne Baxter in *The Razor's Edge*
Direction	William Wyler for *The Best Years of Our Lives*

1947

Production	*Gentleman's Agreement* (20th Century-Fox)
Actor	Ronald Colman in *A Double Life*
Actress	Loretta Young in *The Farmer's Daughter*
Supp. Actor	Edmund Gwenn in *Miracle on 34th Street*
Supp. Actress	Celeste Holm in *Gentleman's Agreement*
Direction	Elia Kazan for *Gentleman's Agreement*

1948

Production	*Hamlet* (Two-Cities)
Actor	Laurence Olivier in *Hamlet*
Actress	Jane Wyman in *Johnny Belinda*
Supp. Actor	Walter Huston in *The Treasure of the Sierra Madre*
Supp. Actress	Claire Trevor in *Key Largo*
Direction	John Huston for *The Treasure of the Sierra Madre*

1949

Production	*All the King's Men* (Columbia)
Actor	Broderick Crawford in *All the King's Men*
Actress	Olivia de Havilland in *The Heiress*
Supp. Actor	Dean Jagger in *Twelve O'Clock High*
Supp. Actress	Mercedes McCambridge in *All the King's Men*
Direction	Joseph L. Mankiewicz for *A Letter to Three Wives*

1950

Production	*All About Eve* (20th Century-Fox)
Actor	Jose Ferrer in *Cyrano de Bergerac*
Actress	Judy Holliday in *Born Yesterday*
Supp. Actor	George Sanders in *All About Eve*

Supp. Actress	Josephine Hull in *Harvey*
Direction	Joseph L. Mankiewicz for *All About Eve*

1951

Production	*An American in Paris* (MGM)
Actor	Humphrey Bogart in *The African Queen*
Actress	Vivien Leigh in *A Streetcar Named Desire*
Supp. Actor	Karl Malden in *A Streetcar Named Desire*
Supp. Actress	Kim Hunter in *A Streetcar Named Desire*
Direction	George Stevens for *A Place in the Sun*

1952

Production	*The Greatest Show on Earth* (Paramount)
Actor	Gary Cooper in *High Noon*
Actress	Shirley Booth in *Come Back, Little Sheba*
Supp. Actor	Anthony Quinn in *Viva Zapata*
Supp. Actress	Gloria Grahame in *The Bad and the Beautiful*
Direction	John Ford for *The Quiet Man*

1953

Production	*From Here to Eternity* (Columbia)
Actor	William Holden in *Stalag 17*
Actress	Audrey Hepburn in *Roman Holiday*
Supp. Actor	Frank Sinatra in *From Here to Eternity*
Supp. Actress	Donna Reed in *From Here to Eternity*
Direction	Fred Zinnemann for *From Here to Eternity*

1954

Production	*On the Waterfront* (Columbia)
Actor	Marlon Brando in *On the Waterfront*

Actress	Grace Kelly in *The Country Girl*
Supp. Actor	Edmond O'Brien in *The Barefoot Contessa*
Supp. Actress	Eva Marie Saint in *On the Waterfront*
Direction	Elia Kazan for *On the Waterfront*

1955

Production	*Marty* (United Artists)
Actor	Ernest Borgnine in *Marty*
Actress	Anna Magnani in *The Rose Tattoo*
Supp. Actor	Jack Lemmon in *Mister Roberts*
Supp. Actress	Jo Van Fleet in *East of Eden*
Direction	Delbert Mann for *Marty*

1956

Production	*Around the World in 80 Days* (United Artists)
Actor	Yul Brynner in *The King and I*
Actress	Ingrid Bergman in *Anastasia*
Supp. Actor	Anthony Quinn in *Lust for Life*
Supp. Actress	Dorothy Malone in *Written on the Wind*
Direction	George Stevens for *Giant*

1957

Production	*The Bridge on the River Kwai* (Columbia)
Actor	Alec Guinness in *The Bridge on the River Kwai*
Actress	Joanne Woodward in *The Three Faces of Eve*
Supp. Actor	Red Buttons in *Sayonara*
Supp. Actress	Miyoshi Umeki in *Sayonara*
Direction	David Lean for *The Bridge on the River Kwai*

1958

Production	*Gigi* (MGM)
Actor	David Niven in *Separate Tables*

Actress	Susan Hayward in *I Want to Live*
Supp. Actor	Burl Ives in *The Big Country*
Supp. Actress	Wendy Hiller in *Separate Tables*
Direction	Vincente Minnelli for *Gigi*

1959

Production	*Ben-Hur* (MGM)
Actor	Charlton Heston in *Ben-Hur*
Actress	Simone Signoret in *Room at the Top*
Supp. Actor	Hugh Griffith in *Ben-Hur*
Supp. Actress	Shelley Winters in *The Diary of Anne Frank*
Direction	William Wyler for *Ben-Hur*

1960

Production	*The Apartment* (United Artists)
Actor	Burt Lancaster in *Elmer Gantry*
Actress	Elizabeth Taylor in *Butterfield 8*
Supp. Actor	Peter Ustinov in *Spartacus*
Supp. Actress	Shirley Jones in *Elmer Gantry*
Direction	Billy Wilder for *The Apartment*

1961

Production	*West Side Story* (United Artists)
Actor	Maximilian Schell in *Judgment at Nuremberg*
Actress	Sophia Loren in *Two Women*
Supp. Actor	George Chakiris in *West Side Story*
Supp. Actress	Rita Moreno in *West Side Story*
Direction	Robert Wise and Jerome Robbins for *West Side Story*

1962

Production	*Lawrence of Arabia* (Columbia)
Actor	Gregory Peck in *To Kill a Mockingbird*

Actress	Anne Bancroft in *The Miracle Worker*
Supp. Actor	Ed Begley in *Sweet Bird of Youth*
Supp. Actress	Patty Duke in *The Miracle Worker*
Direction	David Lean for *Lawrence of Arabia*

1963

Production	*Tom Jones* (Woodfall-United Artists)
Actor	Sidney Poitier in *Lilies of the Field*
Actress	Patricia Neal in *Hud*
Supp. Actor	Melvyn Douglas in *Hud*
Supp. Actress	Margaret Rutherford in *The V.I.P.s*
Direction	Tony Richardson for *Tom Jones*

1964

Production	*My Fair Lady* (Warner Bros.)
Actor	Rex Harrison in *My Fair Lady*
Actress	Julie Andrews in *Mary Poppins*
Supp. Actor	Peter Ustinov in *Topkapi*
Supp. Actress	Lila Kedrova in *Zorba the Greek*
Direction	George Cukor for *My Fair Lady*

1965

Production	*The Sound of Music* (20th Century-Fox)
Actor	Lee Marvin in *Cat Ballou*
Actress	Julie Christie in *Darling*
Supp. Actor	Martin Balsam in *A Thousand Clowns*
Supp. Actress	Shelley Winters in *A Patch of Blue*
Direction	Robert Wise for *The Sound of Music*

1966

Production	*A Man for All Seasons* (Columbia)

Actor	Paul Scofield in *A Man for All Seasons*
Actress	Elizabeth Taylor in *Who's Afraid of Virginia Woolf?*
Supp. Actor	Walter Matthau in *The Fortune Cookie*
Supp. Actress	Sandy Dennis in *Who's Afraid of Virginia Woolf?*
Direction	Fred Zinnemann for *A Man for All Seasons*

1967

Production	*In the Heat of the Night* (United Artists)
Actor	Rod Steiger in *In the Heat of the Night*
Actress	Katharine Hepburn in *Guess Who's Coming to Dinner*
Supp. Actor	George Kennedy in *Cool Hand Luke*
Supp. Actress	Estelle Parsons in *Bonnie and Clyde*
Direction	Mike Nichols for *The Graduate*

1968

Production	*Oliver!* (Columbia)
Actor	Cliff Robertson in *Charly*
Actress	Katharine Hepburn in *The Lion in Winter* and Barbra Streisand in *Funny Girl*
Supp. Actor	Jack Albertson in *The Subject Was Roses*
Supp. Actress	Ruth Gordon in *Rosemary's Baby*
Direction	Carol Reed for *Oliver!*

1969

Production	*Midnight Cowboy* (United Artists)
Actor	John Wayne in *True Grit*
Actress	Maggie Smith in *The Prime of Miss Jean Brodie*
Supp. Actor	Gig Young in *They Shoot Horses, Don't They?*

Supp. Actress	Goldie Hawn in *Cactus Flower*
Direction	John Schlesinger for *Midnight Cowboy*

1970

Production	*Patton* (20th Century-Fox)
Actor	George C. Scott in *Patton*
Actress	Glenda Jackson in *Women in Love*
Supp. Actor	John Mills in *Ryan's Daughter*
Supp. Actress	Helen Hayes in *Airport*
Direction	Franklin J. Schaffner for *Patton*

1971

Production	*The French Connection* (20th Century-Fox)
Actor	Gene Hackman in *The French Connection*
Actress	Jane Fonda in *Klute*
Supp. Actor	Ben Johnson in *The Last Picture Show*
Supp. Actress	Cloris Leachman in *The Last Picture Show*
Direction	William Friedkin for *The French Connection*

1972

Production	*The Godfather* (Paramount)
Actor	Marlon Brando in *The Godfather*
Actress	Liza Minnelli in *Cabaret*
Supp. Actor	Joel Grey in *Cabaret*
Supp. Actress	Eileen Heckart in *Butterflies Are Free*
Direction	Bob Fosse for *Cabaret*

1973

Production	*The Sting* (Universal)
Actor	Jack Lemmon in *Save the Tiger*
Actress	Glenda Jackson in *A Touch of Class*
Supp. Actor	John Houseman in *The Paper Chase*

Supp. Actress	Tatum O'Neal in *Paper Moon*
Direction	George Roy Hill for *The Sting*

1974

Production	*The Godfather Part II* (Paramount)
Actor	Art Carney in *Harry and Tonto*
Actress	Ellen Burstyn in *Alice Doesn't Live Here Anymore*
Supp. Actor	Robert De Niro in *The Godfather Part II*
Supp. Actress	Ingrid Bergman in *Murder on the Orient Express*
Direction	Francis Ford Coppola for *The Godfather Part II*

1975

Production	*One Flew Over the Cuckoo's Nest* (United Artists)
Actor	Jack Nicholson in *One Flew Over the Cuckoo's Nest*
Actress	Louise Fletcher in *One Flew Over the Cuckoo's Nest*
Supp. Actor	George Burns in *The Sunshine Boys*
Supp. Actress	Lee Grant in *Shampoo*
Direction	Milos Forman for *One Flew Over the Cuckoo's Nest*

1976

Production	*Rocky* (United Artists)
Actor	Peter Finch in *Network*
Actress	Faye Dunaway in *Network*
Supp. Actor	Jason Robards in *All the President's Men*
Supp. Actress	Beatrice Straight in *Network*
Direction	John Avildsen for *Rocky*

1977

Production	*Annie Hall* (United Artists)
Actor	Richard Dreyfuss in *The Goodbye Girl*
Actress	Diane Keaton in *Annie Hall*
Supp. Actor	Jason Robards in *Julia*

Supp. Actress	Vanessa Redgrave in *Julia*
Direction	Woody Allen for *Annie Hall*

1978

Production	*The Deer Hunter* (EMI/ Universal)
Actor	Jon Voight in *Coming Home*
Actress	Jane Fonda in *Coming Home*
Supp. Actor	Christopher Walken in *The Deer Hunter*
Supp. Actress	Maggie Smith in *California Suite*
Direction	Michael Cimino for *The Deer Hunter*

1979

Production	*Kramer vs. Kramer* (Columbia)
Actor	Dustin Hoffman in *Kramer vs. Kramer*
Actress	Sally Field in *Norma Rae*
Supp. Actor	Melvyn Douglas in *Being There*
Supp. Actress	Meryl Streep in *Kramer vs. Kramer*
Direction	Robert Benton for *Kramer vs. Kramer*

1980

Production	*Ordinary People* (Paramount)
Actor	Robert De Niro in *Raging Bull*
Actress	Sissy Spacek in *Coal Miner's Daughter*
Supp. Actor	Timothy Hutton in *Ordinary People*
Supp. Actress	Mary Steenburgen in *Melvin and Howard*
Direction	Robert Redford for *Ordinary People*

1981

Production	*Chariots of Fire* (Ladd Company/Warner Bros.)
Actor	Henry Fonda in *On Golden Pond*

Actress	Katharine Hepburn in *On Golden Pond*
Supp. Actor	John Gielgud in *Arthur*
Supp. Actress	Maureen Stapleton in *Reds*
Direction	Warren Beatty for *Reds*

1982

Production	*Gandhi* (Columbia)
Actor	Ben Kingsley in *Gandhi*
Actress	Meryl Streep in *Sophie's Choice*
Supp. Actor	Louis Gossett, Jr. in *An Officer and a Gentleman*
Supp. Actress	Jessica Lange in *Tootsie*
Direction	Richard Attenborough for *Gandhi*

1983

Production	*Terms of Endearment* (Paramount)
Actor	Robert Duvall in *Tender Mercies*
Actress	Shirley MacLaine in *Terms of Endearment*
Supp. Actor	Jack Nicholson in *Terms of Endearment*
Supp. Actress	Linda Hunt in *The Year of Living Dangerously*
Direction	James L. Brooks for *Terms of Endearment*

1984

Production	*Amadeus* (Zaentz/Orion)
Actor	F. Murray Abraham in *Amadeus*
Actress	Sally Field in *Places in the Heart*
Supp. Actor	Haing S. Ngor in *The Killing Fields*
Supp. Actress	Peggy Ashcroft in *A Passage to India*
Direction	Milos Forman for *Amadeus*

1985

Production	*Out of Africa* (Universal)
Actor	William Hurt in *Kiss of the Spider Woman*
Actress	Geraldine Page in *The Trip to Bountiful*
Supp. Actor	Don Ameche in *Cocoon*
Supp. Actress	Anjelica Huston in *Prizzi's Honor*
Direction	Sydney Pollack for *Out of Africa*

1986

Production	*Platoon* (Hemdale/Orion)
Actor	Paul Newman in *The Color of Money*
Actress	Marlee Matlin in *Children of a Lesser God*
Supp. Actor	Michael Caine in *Hannah and Her Sisters*
Supp. Actress	Dianne Wiest in *Hannah and Her Sisters*
Direction	Oliver Stone for *Platoon*

1987

Production	*The Last Emperor* (Hemdale/Columbia)
Actor	Michael Douglas in *Wall Street*
Actress	Cher in *Moonstruck*
Supp. Actor	Sean Connery in *The Untouchables*
Supp. Actress	Olympia Dukakis in *Moonstruck*
Direction	Bernardo Bertolucci for *The Last Emperor*

1988

Production	*Rain Man* (United Artists)
Actor	Dustin Hoffman in *Rain Man*
Actress	Jodie Foster in *The Accused*
Supp. Actor	Kevin Kline in *A Fish Called Wanda*
Supp. Actress	Geena Davis in *The Accidental Tourist*
Direction	Barry Levinson for *Rain Man*

1989

Production	*Driving Miss Daisy* (Warner Bros.)

Actor   Daniel Day-Lewis in *My Left Foot*
Actress   Jessica Tandy in *Driving Miss Daisy*
Supp. Actor   Denzel Washington in *Glory*
Supp. Actress   Brenda Fricker in *My Left Foot*
Direction   Oliver Stone for *Born on the Fourth of July*

1990

Production   *Dances With Wolves* (Orion)
Actor   Jeremy Irons in *Reversal of Fortune*
Actress   Kathy Bates in *Misery*
Supp. Actor   Joe Pesci in *Goodfellas*
Supp. Actress   Whoopi Goldberg in *Ghost*
Direction   Kevin Costner for *Dances With Wolves*

1991

Production   *The Silence of the Lambs* (Orion)
Actor   Anthony Hopkins in *The Silence of the Lambs*
Actress   Jodie Foster in *The Silence of the Lambs*
Supp. Actor   Jack Palance in *City Slickers*
Supp. Actress   Mercedes Ruehl in *The Fisher King*
Direction   Jonathan Demme for *The Silence of the Lambs*

1992

Production   *Unforgiven* (Warner Bros.)
Actor   Al Pacino in *Scent of a Woman*
Actress   Emma Thompson in *Howards End*
Supp. Actor   Gene Hackman in *Unforgiven*
Supp. Actress   Marisa Tomei in *My Cousin Vinny*
Direction   Clint Eastwood for *Unforgiven*

APPENDIX 2
Nominees Year by Year

A companion listing, by year, of all acting, directing and best-film nominees from 1927 to the present.

1927/28

Production	*The Last Command* (Paramount); *The Racket* (Paramount); *Seventh Heaven* (Fox); *The Way of All Flesh* (Paramount); *Wings* (Paramount)
Actor	Richard Barthelmess in *The Noose*; Richard Barthelmess in *The Patent Leather Kid*; Charles Chaplin in *The Circus*; Emil Jannings in *The Last Command*; Emil Jannings in *The Way of All Flesh*
Actress	Louise Dresser in *A Ship Comes In*; Janet Gaynor in *Seventh Heaven*; Janet Gaynor in *Street Angel*; Janet Gaynor in *Sunrise*; Gloria Swanson in *Sadie Thompson*
Direction	Frank Borzage for *Seventh Heaven*; Herbert Brenon for *Sorrell and Son*; King Vidor for *The Crowd* Comedy Direction (Not given after this year): Charles Chaplin for *The Circus*; Lewis Milestone for *Two Arabian Knights*; Ted Wilde for *Speedy*

1928/29

Production	*Alibi* (United Artists); *The Broadway Melody* (MGM); *Hollywood Revue* (MGM); *In Old Arizona* (Fox); *The Patriot* (Paramount)

Actor	Warner Baxter in *In Old Arizona*; Chester Morris in *Alibi*; Paul Muni in *The Valiant*; George Bancroft in *Thunderbolt*; Lewis Stone in *The Patriot*
Actress	Ruth Chatterton in *Madame X*; Betty Compson in *The Barker*; Jeanne Eagels in *The Letter*; Bessie Love in *The Broadway Melody*; Mary Pickford in *Coquette*
Direction	Lionel Barrymore for *Madame X*; Harry Beaumont for *The Broadway Melody*; Irving Cummings for *In Old Arizona*; Frank Lloyd for *The Divine Lady*; Frank Lloyd for *Weary River*; Frank Lloyd for *Drag*; Ernst Lubitsch for *The Patriot*

1929/30

Production	*All Quiet on the Western Front* (Universal); *The Big House* (MGM); *Disraeli* (Warner Bros.); *The Divorcee* (MGM); *The Love Parade* (Paramount)
Actor	George Arliss in *Disraeli*; George Arliss in *The Green Goddess*; Wallace Beery in *The Big House*; Maurice Chevalier in *The Love Parade*; Maurice Chevalier in *The Big Pond*; Ronald Colman in *Bulldog Drummond*; Ronald Colman in *Condemned*; Lawrence Tibbett in *The Rogue Song*
Actress	Nancy Carroll in *The Devil's Holiday*; Ruth Chatterton in

Sarah and Son; Greta Garbo in *Anna Christie;* Greta Garbo in *Romance;* Norma Shearer in *The Divorcee;* Norma Shearer in *Their Own Desire;* Gloria Swanson in *The Trespasser*

Direction　Clarence Brown for *Anna Christie;* Clarence Brown for *Romance;* Robert Z. Leonard for *The Divorcee;* Ernst Lubitsch for *The Love Parade;* Lewis Milestone for *All Quiet on the Western Front;* King Vidor for *Hallelujah*

1930/31

Production　*Cimarron* (RKO Radio); *East Lynne* (Fox); *The Front Page* (United Artists); *Skippy* (Paramount); *Trader Horn* (MGM)

Actor　Lionel Barrymore in *A Free Soul;* Jackie Cooper in *Skippy;* Richard Dix in *Cimarron;* Fredric March in *The Royal Family of Broadway;* Adolphe Menjou in *The Front Page*

Actress　Marlene Dietrich in *Morocco;* Marie Dressler in *Min and Bill;* Irene Dunne in *Cimarron;* Ann Harding in *Holiday;* Norma Shearer in *A Free Soul*

Direction　Clarence Brown for *A Free Soul;* Lewis Milestone for *The Front Page;* Wesley Ruggles for *Cimarron;* Josef von Sternberg for *Morocco;* Norman Taurog for *Skippy*

1931/32

Production　*Arrowsmith* (United Artists); *Bad Girl* (Fox); *The Champ* (MGM); *Five Star Final* (First National); *Grand Hotel* (MGM); *One Hour with You*

(Paramount); *Shanghai Express* (Paramount); *The Smiling Lieutenant* (Paramount)

Actor　Wallace Beery in *The Champ;* Alfred Lunt in *The Guardsman;* Fredric March in *Dr. Jekyll and Mr. Hyde*

Actress　Marie Dressler in *Emma;* Lynne Fontanne in *The Guardsman;* Helen Hayes in *The Sin of Madelon Claudet*

Direction　Frank Borzage for *Bad Girl;* King Vidor for *The Champ;* Josef von Sternberg for *Shanghai Express*

1932/33

Production　*Cavalcade* (Fox); *A Farewell to Arms* (Paramount); *Forty-Second Street* (Warner Bros.); *I Am a Fugitive from a Chain Gang* (Warner Bros.); *Lady for a Day* (Columbia); *Little Women* (RKO Radio); *The Private Life of Henry VIII* (London Films); *She Done Him Wrong* (Paramount); *Smilin' Through* (MGM); *State Fair* (Fox)

Actor　Leslie Howard in *Berkeley Square;* Charles Laughton in *The Private Life of Henry VIII;* Paul Muni in *I Am a Fugitive From a Chain Gang*

Actress　Katharine Hepburn in *Morning Glory;* May Robson in *Lady for a Day;* Diana Wynyard in *Cavalcade*

Direction　Frank Capra for *Lady for a Day;* George Cukor for *Little Women;* Frank Lloyd for *Cavalcade*

1934

Production　*The Barretts of Wimpole Street* (MGM); *Cleopatra* (Paramount); *Flirtation Walk* (First National); *The Gay*

Divorcee (RKO Radio); *Here Comes the Navy* (Warner Bros.); *The House of Rothschild* (Twentieth Century); *Imitation of Life* (Universal); *It Happened One Night* (Columbia); *One Night of Love* (Columbia); *The Thin Man* (MGM); *Viva Villa* (MGM); *The White Parade* (Fox)

Actor — Clark Gable in *It Happened One Night*; Frank Morgan in *Affairs of Cellini*; William Powell in *The Thin Man*

Actress — Claudette Colbert in *It Happened One Night*; Grace Moore in *One Night of Love*; Norma Shearer in *The Barretts of Wimpole Street*

Direction — Frank Capra for *It Happened One Night*; Victor Schertzinger for *One Night of Love*; W. S. Van Dyke for *The Thin Man*

1935

Production — *Alice Adams* (RKO Radio); *The Broadway Melody of 1936* (MGM); *Captain Blood* (Warner Bros.); *David Copperfield* (MGM); *The Informer* (RKO Radio); *Les Misérables* (Twentieth Century); *Lives of a Bengal Lancer* (Paramount); *A Midsummer Night's Dream* (Warner Bros.); *Mutiny on the Bounty* (MGM); *Naughty Marietta* (MGM); *Ruggles of Red Gap* (Paramount); *Top Hat* (RKO Radio)

Actor — Clark Gable in *Mutiny on the Bounty*; Charles Laughton in *Mutiny on the Bounty*; Victor McLaglen in *The Informer*; Franchot Tone in *Mutiny on the Bounty*

Actress — Elisabeth Bergner in *Escape Me Never*; Claudette Colbert in *Private Worlds*; Bette Davis in *Dangerous*; Katharine Hepburn in *Alice Adams*; Miriam Hopkins in *Becky Sharp*; Merle Oberon in *The Dark Angel*

Direction — John Ford for *The Informer*; Henry Hathaway for *Lives of a Bengal Lancer*; Frank Lloyd for *Mutiny on the Bounty*

1936

Production — *Anthony Adverse* (Warner Bros.); *Dodsworth* (Goldwyn UA); *The Great Ziegfeld* (MGM); *Libeled Lady* (MGM); *Mr. Deeds Goes to Town* (Columbia); *Romeo and Juliet* (MGM); *San Francisco* (MGM); *The Story of Louis Pasteur* (Warner Bros.); *A Tale of Two Cities* (MGM); *Three Smart Girls* (Universal)

Actor — Gary Cooper in *Mr. Deeds Goes to Town*; Walter Huston in *Dodsworth*; Paul Muni in *The Story of Louis Pasteur*; William Powell in *My Man Godfrey*; Spencer Tracy in *San Francisco*

Actress — Irene Dunne in *Theodora Goes Wild*; Gladys George in *Valiant Is the Word for Carrie*; Carole Lombard in *My Man Godfrey*; Luise Rainer in *The Great Ziegfeld*; Norma Shearer in *Romeo and Juliet*

Supp. Actor — Mischa Auer in *My Man Godfrey*; Walter Brennan in *Come and Get It*; Stuart Erwin in *Pigskin Parade*; Basil Rathbone in *Romeo and Juliet*; Akim Tamiroff in *The General Died at Dawn*

Supp. Actress — Beulah Bondi in *The Gorgeous*

Hussy; Alice Brady in *My Man Godfrey;* Bonita Granville in *These Three;* Maria Ouspenskaya in *Dodsworth;* Gale Sondergaard in *Anthony Adverse*

Direction   Frank Capra for *Mr. Deeds Goes to Town;* Gregory LaCava for *My Man Godfrey;* Robert Z. Leonard for *The Great Ziegfeld;* W. S. Van Dyke for *San Francisco;* William Wyler for *Dodsworth*

1937

Production   *The Awful Truth* (Columbia); *Captains Courageous* (MGM); *Dead End* (Goldwyn, UA); *The Good Earth* (MGM); *In Old Chicago* (20th Century-Fox); *The Life of Emile Zola* (Warner Bros.); *Lost Horizon* (Columbia); *One Hundred Men and a Girl* (Universal); *Stage Door* (RKO Radio); *A Star Is Born* (Selznick International, UA)

Actor   Charles Boyer in *Conquest;* Fredric March in *A Star Is Born;* Robert Montgomery in *Night Must Fall;* Paul Muni in *The Life of Emile Zola;* Spencer Tracy in *Captains Courageous*

Actress   Irene Dunne in *The Awful Truth;* Greta Garbo in *Camille;* Janet Gaynor in *A Star Is Born;* Luise Rainer in *The Good Earth;* Barbara Stanwyck in *Stella Dallas*

Supp. Actor   Ralph Bellamy in *The Awful Truth;* Thomas Mitchell in *The Hurricane;* Joseph Schildkraut in *The Life of Emile Zola;* H. B. Warner in *Lost Horizon;* Roland Young in *Topper*

Supp. Actress   Alice Brady in *In Old Chicago;*

Andrea Leeds in *Stage Door;* Anne Shirley in *Stella Dallas;* Claire Trevor in *Dead End;* Dame May Whitty in *Night Must Fall*

Direction   William Dieterle for *The Life of Emile Zola;* Sidney Franklin for *The Good Earth;* Gregory LaCava for *Stage Door;* Leo McCarey for *The Awful Truth;* William Wellman for *A Star Is Born*

1938

Production   *The Adventures of Robin Hood* (Warner Bros.); *Alexander's Ragtime Band* (20th Century-Fox); *Boys' Town* (MGM); *The Citadel* (MGM); *Four Daughters* (Warner Bros.); *La Grande Illusion* (France); *Jezebel* (Warner Bros.); *Pygmalion* (MGM); *Test Pilot* (MGM); *You Can't Take It With You* (Columbia)

Actor   Charles Boyer in *Algiers;* James Cagney in *Angels with Dirty Faces;* Robert Donat in *The Citadel;* Leslie Howard in *Pygmalion;* Spencer Tracy in *Boys' Town*

Actress   Fay Bainter in *White Banners;* Bette Davis in *Jezebel;* Wendy Hiller in *Pygmalion;* Norma Shearer in *Marie Antoinette;* Margaret Sullavan in *Three Comrades*

Supp. Actor   Walter Brennan in *Kentucky;* John Garfield in *Four Daughters;* Gene Lockhart in *Algiers;* Robert Morley in *Marie Antoinette;* Basil Rathbone in *If I Were King*

Supp. Actress   Fay Bainter in *Jezebel;* Beulah Bondi in *Of Human Hearts;* Spring Byington in *You Can't Take It With You;* Billie Burke

Direction — in *Merrily We Live*; Miliza Korjus in *The Great Waltz* Frank Capra for *You Can't Take It With You*; Michael Curtiz for *Angels with Dirty Faces*; Michael Curtiz for *Four Daughters*; Norman Taurog for *Boys' Town*; King Vidor for *The Citadel*

1939

Production — *Dark Victory* (Warner Bros.); *Gone With the Wind* (Selznick/MGM); *Goodbye, Mr. Chips* (MGM); *Love Affair* (RKO Radio); *Mr. Smith Goes to Washington* (Columbia); *Ninotchka* (MGM); *Of Mice and Men* (United Artists); *Stagecoach* (United Artists); *The Wizard of Oz* (MGM); *Wuthering Heights* (Goldwyn, UA)

Actor — Robert Donat in *Goodbye, Mr. Chips*; Clark Gable in *Gone With the Wind*; Laurence Olivier in *Wuthering Heights*; Mickey Rooney in *Babes in Arms*; James Stewart in *Mr. Smith Goes to Washington*

Actress — Bette Davis in *Dark Victory*; Irene Dunne in *Love Affair*; Greta Garbo in *Ninotchka*; Greer Garson in *Goodbye, Mr. Chips*; Vivien Leigh in *Gone With the Wind*

Supp. Actor — Brian Aherne in *Juarez*; Harry Carey in *Mr. Smith Goes to Washington*; Brian Donlevy in *Beau Geste*; Thomas Mitchell in *Stagecoach*; Claude Rains in *Mr. Smith Goes to Washington*

Supp. Actress — Olivia de Havilland in *Gone With The Wind*; Geraldine Fitzgerald in *Wuthering Heights*; Hattie McDaniel in

Direction — *Gone With The Wind*; Edna May Oliver in *Drums Along the Mohawk*; Maria Ouspenskaya in *Love Affair* Frank Capra for *Mr. Smith Goes to Washington*; Victor Fleming for *Gone With the Wind*; John Ford for *Stagecoach*; Sam Wood for *Goodbye, Mr. Chips*; William Wyler for *Wuthering Heights*

1940

Production — *All This and Heaven Too* (Warner Bros.); *Foreign Correspondent* (United Artists); *The Grapes of Wrath* (20th Century-Fox); *The Great Dictator* (United Artists); *Kitty Foyle* (RKO Radio); *The Letter* (Warner Bros.); *The Long Voyage Home* (United Artists); *Our Town* (United Artists); *The Philadelphia Story* (MGM); *Rebecca* (Selznick, United Artists)

Actor — Charles Chaplin in *The Great Dictator*; Henry Fonda in *The Grapes of Wrath*; Raymond Massey in *Abe Lincoln in Illinois*; Laurence Olivier in *Rebecca*; James Stewart in *The Philadelphia Story*

Actress — Bette Davis in *The Letter*; Joan Fontaine in *Rebecca*; Katharine Hepburn in *The Philadelphia Story*; Ginger Rogers in *Kitty Foyle*; Martha Scott in *Our Town*

Supp. Actor — Albert Basserman in *Foreign Correspondent*; Walter Brennan in *The Westerner*; William Gargan in *They Knew What They Wanted*; Jack Oakie in *The Great Dictator*; James Stephenson in *The Letter*

Supp. Actress	Judith Anderson in *Rebecca;* Jane Darwell in *The Grapes of Wrath;* Ruth Hussey in *The Philadelphia Story;* Barbara O'Neil in *All This and Heaven Too;* Marjorie Rambeau in *Primrose Path*
Direction	George Cukor for *The Philadelphia Story;* John Ford for *The Grapes of Wrath;* Alfred Hitchcock for *Rebecca;* Sam Wood for *Kitty Foyle;* William Wyler for *The Letter*

1941

Production	*Blossoms in the Dust* (MGM); *Citizen Kane* (RKO Radio); *Here Comes Mr. Jordan* (Columbia); *Hold Back the Dawn* (Paramount); *How Green Was My Valley* (20th Century-Fox); *The Little Foxes* (Goldwyn, RKO Radio); *The Maltese Falcon* (Warner Bros.); *One Foot in Heaven* (Warner Bros.); *Sergeant York* (Warner Bros.); *Suspicion* (RKO Radio)
Actor	Gary Cooper in *Sergeant York;* Cary Grant in *Penny Serenade;* Walter Huston in *All That Money Can Buy;* Robert Montgomery in *Here Comes Mr. Jordan;* Orson Welles in *Citizen Kane*
Actress	Bette Davis in *The Little Foxes;* Joan Fontaine in *Suspicion;* Greer Garson in *Blossoms in the Dust;* Olivia de Havilland in *Hold Back the Dawn;* Barbara Stanwyck in *Ball of Fire*
Supp. Actor	Walter Brennan in *Sergeant York;* Charles Coburn in *The Devil and Miss Jones;* Donald Crisp in *How Green Was My Valley;* James Gleason in *Here Comes Mr. Jordan;* Sydney

	Greenstreet in *The Maltese Falcon*
Supp. Actress	Sara Allgood in *How Green Was My Valley;* Mary Astor in *The Great Lie;* Patricia Collinge in *The Little Foxes;* Teresa Wright in *The Little Foxes;* Margaret Wycherly in *Sergeant York*
Direction	John Ford for *How Green Was My Valley;* Alexander Hall for *Here Comes Mr. Jordan;* Howard Hawks for *Sergeant York;* Orson Welles for *Citizen Kane;* William Wyler for *The Little Foxes*

1942

Production	*The Invaders* (British–UK *The 49th Parallel*); *Kings Row* (Warner Bros.); *The Magnificent Ambersons* (RKO Radio); *Mrs. Miniver* (MGM); *The Pied Piper* (20th Century-Fox); *The Pride of the Yankees* (Goldwyn, RKO); *Random Harvest* (MGM); *The Talk of the Town* (Columbia); *Wake Island* (Paramount); *Yankee Doodle Dandy* (Warner Bros.)
Actor	James Cagney in *Yankee Doodle Dandy;* Ronald Colman in *Random Harvest;* Gary Cooper in *The Pride of the Yankees;* Walter Pidgeon in *Mrs. Miniver;* Monty Woolley in *The Pied Piper*
Actress	Bette Davis in *Now Voyager;* Greer Garson in *Mrs. Miniver;* Katharine Hepburn in *Woman of the Year;* Rosalind Russell in *My Sister Eileen;* Teresa Wright in *The Pride of the Yankees*
Supp. Actor	William Bendix in *Wake Island;* Van Heflin in *Johnny Eager;* Walter Huston in

Yankee Doodle Dandy; Frank Morgan in *Tortilla Flat;* Henry Travers in *Mrs. Miniver*

Supp. Actress — Gladys Cooper in *Now Voyager;* Agnes Moorehead in *The Magnificent Ambersons;* Susan Peters in *Random Harvest;* Dame May Whitty in *Mrs. Miniver;* Teresa Wright in *Mrs. Miniver*

Direction — Michael Curtiz for *Yankee Doodle Dandy;* John Farrow for *Wake Island;* Mervyn LeRoy for *Random Harvest;* Sam Wood for *Kings Row;* William Wyler for *Mrs. Miniver*

1943

Production — *Casablanca* (Warner Bros.); *For Whom the Bell Tolls* (Paramount); *Heaven Can Wait* (20th Century-Fox); *The Human Comedy* (MGM); *In Which We Serve* (British); *Madame Curie* (MGM); *The More the Merrier* (Columbia); *The Ox-Bow Incident* (20th Century-Fox); *The Song of Bernadette* (20th Century-Fox); *Watch on the Rhine* (Warner Bros.)

Actor — Humphrey Bogart in *Casablanca;* Gary Cooper in *For Whom the Bell Tolls;* Paul Lukas in *Watch on the Rhine;* Walter Pidgeon in *Madame Curie;* Mickey Rooney in *The Human Comedy*

Actress — Jean Arthur in *The More the Merrier;* Ingrid Bergman in *For Whom the Bell Tolls;* Joan Fontaine in *The Constant Nymph;* Greer Garson in *Madame Curie;* Jennifer Jones in *The Song of Bernadette*

Supp. Actor — Charles Bickford in *The Song of Bernadette;* Charles Coburn in *The More the Merrier;* J. Carrol Naish in *Sahara;* Claude Rains in *Casablanca;* Akim Tamiroff in *For Whom the Bell Tolls*

Supp. Actress — Gladys Cooper in *The Song of Bernadette;* Paulette Goddard in *So Proudly We Hail;* Katina Paxinou in *For Whom the Bell Tolls;* Anne Revere in *The Song of Bernadette;* Lucile Watson in *Watch on the Rhine*

Direction — Clarence Brown for *The Human Comedy;* Michael Curtiz for *Casablanca;* Henry King for *The Song of Bernadette;* Ernst Lubitsch for *Heaven Can Wait;* George Stevens for *The More the Merrier*

1944

Production — *Double Indemnity* (Paramount); *Gaslight* (MGM); *Going My Way* (Paramount); *Since You Went Away* (Selznick International, UA); *Wilson* (20th Century-Fox)

Actor — Charles Boyer in *Gaslight;* Bing Crosby in *Going My Way;* Barry Fitzgerald in *Going My Way;* Cary Grant in *None But the Lonely Heart;* Alexander Knox in *Wilson*

Actress — Ingrid Bergman in *Gaslight;* Claudette Colbert in *Since You Went Away;* Bette Davis in *Mr. Skeffington;* Greer Garson in *Mrs. Parkington;* Barbara Stanwyck in *Double Indemnity*

Supp. Actor — Hume Cronyn in *The Seventh Cross;* Barry Fitzgerald in *Going My Way;* Claude Rains in *Mr. Skeffington;* Clifton Webb in *Laura;* Monty

Woolley in *Since You Went Away*

Supp. Actress   Ethel Barrymore in *None But the Lonely Heart*; Jennifer Jones in *Since You Went Away*; Angela Lansbury in *Gaslight*; Aline MacMahon in *Dragon Seed*; Agnes Moorehead in *Mrs. Parkington*

Direction   Alfred Hitchcock for *Lifeboat*; Henry King for *Wilson*; Leo McCarey for *Going My Way*; Otto Preminger for *Laura*; Billy Wilder for *Double Indemnity*

1945

Production   *Anchors Aweigh* (MGM); *The Bells of St. Mary's* (RKO Radio); *The Lost Weekend* (Paramount); *Mildred Pierce* (Warner Bros.); *Spellbound* (Selznick International, UA)

Actor   Bing Crosby in *The Bells of St. Mary's*; Gene Kelly in *Anchors Aweigh*; Ray Milland in *The Lost Weekend*; Gregory Peck in *The Keys of the Kingdom*; Cornel Wilde in *A Song to Remember*

Actress   Ingrid Bergman in *The Bells of St. Mary's*; Joan Crawford in *Mildred Pierce*; Greer Garson in *The Valley of Decision*; Jennifer Jones in *Love Letters*; Gene Tierney in *Leave Her to Heaven*

Supp. Actor   Michael Chekhov in *Spellbound*; John Dall in *The Corn Is Green*; James Dunn in *A Tree Grows in Brooklyn*; Robert Mitchum in *The Story of G.I. Joe*; J. Carrol Naish in *A Medal for Benny*

Supp. Actress   Eve Arden in *Mildred Pierce*; Ann Blyth in *Mildred Pierce*; Angela Lansbury in *The*

Picture of Dorian Gray; Joan Lorring in *The Corn Is Green*; Anne Revere in *National Velvet*

Direction   Clarence Brown for *National Velvet*; Alfred Hitchcock for *Spellbound*; Leo McCarey for *The Bells of St. Mary's*; Jean Renoir for *The Southerner*; Billy Wilder for *The Lost Weekend*

1946

Production   *The Best Years of Our Lives* (Goldwyn, RKO); *Henry V* (Rank/Two Cities/British); *It's a Wonderful Life* (RKO Radio); *The Razor's Edge* (20th Century-Fox); *The Yearling* (MGM)

Actor   Fredric March in *The Best Years of Our Lives*; Laurence Olivier in *Henry V*; Larry Parks in *The Jolson Story*; Gregory Peck in *The Yearling*; James Stewart in *It's a Wonderful Life*

Actress   Olivia de Havilland in *To Each His Own*; Celia Johnson in *Brief Encounter*; Jennifer Jones in *Duel in the Sun*; Rosalind Russell in *Sister Kenny*; Jane Wyman in *The Yearling*

Supp. Actor   Charles Coburn in *The Green Years*; William Demarest in *The Jolson Story*; Claude Rains in *Notorious*; Harold Russell in *The Best Years of Our Lives*; Clifton Webb in *The Razor's Edge*

Supp. Actress   Ethel Barrymore in *The Spiral Staircase*; Anne Baxter in *The Razor's Edge*; Lillian Gish in *Duel in the Sun*; Flora Robson in *Saratoga Trunk*; Gale

	Sondergaard in *Anna and the King of Siam*	Direction	*The Egg and I*; Anne Revere in *Gentleman's Agreement*
Direction	Clarence Brown for *The Yearling*; Frank Capra for *It's a Wonderful Life*; David Lean for *Brief Encounter*; Robert Siodmak for *The Killers*; William Wyler for *The Best Years of our Lives*		George Cukor for *A Double Life*; Edward Dmytryk for *Crossfire*; Elia Kazan for *Gentleman's Agreement*; Henry Koster for *The Bishop's Wife*; David Lean for *Great Expectations*

1947

Production	*The Bishop's Wife* (Goldwyn, RKO); *Crossfire* (RKO Radio); *Gentleman's Agreement* (20th Century-Fox); *Great Expectations* (Rank-Cineguild/British); *Miracle on 34th Street* (20th Century-Fox)
Actor	Ronald Colman in *A Double Life*; John Garfield in *Body and Soul*; Gregory Peck in *Gentleman's Agreement*; William Powell in *Life with Father*; Michael Redgrave in *Mourning Becomes Electra*
Actress	Joan Crawford in *Possessed*; Susan Hayward in *Smash-Up—The Story of a Woman*; Dorothy McGuire in *Gentleman's Agreement*; Rosalind Russell in *Mourning Becomes Electra*; Loretta Young in *The Farmer's Daughter*
Supp. Actor	Charles Bickford in *The Farmer's Daughter*; Thomas Gomez in *Ride the Pink Horse*; Edmund Gwenn in *Miracle on 34th Street*; Robert Ryan in *Crossfire*; Richard Widmark in *Kiss of Death*
Supp. Actress	Ethel Barrymore in *The Paradine Case*; Gloria Grahame in *Crossfire*; Celeste Holm in *Gentleman's Agreement*; Marjorie Main in

1948

Production	*Hamlet* (Rank-Two Cities/British); *Johnny Belinda* (Warner Bros.); *The Red Shoes* (Rank-Archers/British); *The Snake Pit* (20th Century-Fox); *The Treasure of the Sierra Madre* (Warner Bros.)
Actor	Lew Ayres in *Johnny Belinda*; Montgomery Clift in *The Search*; Dan Dailey in *When My Baby Smiles at Me*; Laurence Olivier in *Hamlet*; Clifton Webb in *Sitting Pretty*
Actress	Ingrid Bergman in *Joan of Arc*; Olivia de Havilland in *The Snake Pit*; Irene Dunne in *I Remember Mama*; Barbara Stanwyck in *Sorry, Wrong Number*; Jane Wyman in *Johnny Belinda*
Supp. Actor	Charles Bickford in *Johnny Belinda*; Jose Ferrer in *Joan of Arc*; Oscar Homolka in *I Remember Mama*; Walter Huston in *The Treasure of the Sierra Madre*; Cecil Kellaway in *The Luck of the Irish*
Supp. Actress	Barbara Bel Geddes in *I Remember Mama*; Ellen Corby in *I Remember Mama*; Agnes Moorehead in *Johnny Belinda*; Jean Simmons in *Hamlet*; Claire Trevor in *Key Largo*
Direction	John Huston for *The Treasure of the Sierra Madre*; Anatole

Litvak for *The Snake Pit*; Jean
Negulesco for *Johnny Belinda*;
Laurence Olivier for *Hamlet*;
Fred Zinnemann for *The
Search*

1949

Production   *All the King's Men* (Columbia);
                  Battleground (MGM); *The
                  Heiress* (Paramount); *A Letter
                  to Three Wives* (20th Century-
                  Fox); *Twelve O'Clock High*
                  (20th Century-Fox)

Actor   Broderick Crawford in *All the
                  King's Men*; Kirk Douglas in
                  Champion; Gregory Peck in
                  Twelve O'Clock High; Richard
                  Todd in *The Hasty Heart*;
                  John Wayne in *Sands of Iwo
                  Jima*

Actress   Jeanne Crain in *Pinky*; Olivia
                  de Havilland in *The Heiress*;
                  Susan Hayward in *My Foolish
                  Heart*; Deborah Kerr in
                  Edward, My Son; Loretta
                  Young in *Come to the Stable*

Supp. Actor   John Ireland in *All the King's
                  Men*; Dean Jagger in *Twelve
                  O'Clock High*; Arthur
                  Kennedy in *Champion*; Ralph
                  Richardson in *The Heiress*;
                  James Whitmore in
                  Battleground

Supp. Actress   Ethel Barrymore in *Pinky*;
                  Celeste Holm in *Come to the
                  Stable*; Elsa Lanchester in
                  Come to the Stable; Mercedes
                  McCambridge in *All the
                  King's Men*; Ethel Waters in
                  Pinky

Direction   Joseph L. Mankiewicz for *A
                  Letter to Three Wives*; Carol
                  Reed for *The Fallen Idol*;
                  Robert Rossen for *All the
                  King's Men*; William A.
                  Wellman for *Battleground*;
                  William Wyler for *The Heiress*

1950

Production   *All About Eve* (20th Century-
                  Fox); *Born Yesterday*
                  (Columbia); *Father of the Bride*
                  (MGM); *King Solomon's Mines*
                  (MGM); *Sunset Boulevard*
                  (Paramount)

Actor   Louis Calhern in *The
                  Magnificent Yankee*; Jose Ferrer
                  in *Cyrano de Bergerac*; William
                  Holden in *Sunset Boulevard*;
                  James Stewart in *Harvey*;
                  Spencer Tracy in *Father of the
                  Bride*

Actress   Anne Baxter in *All About
                  Eve*; Bette Davis in *All About
                  Eve*; Judy Holliday in *Born
                  Yesterday*; Eleanor Parker in
                  Caged; Gloria Swanson in
                  Sunset Boulevard

Supp. Actor   Jeff Chandler in *Broken
                  Arrow*; Edmund Gwenn in
                  Mister 880; Sam Jaffe in *The
                  Asphalt Jungle*; George
                  Sanders in *All About Eve*;
                  Erich Von Stroheim in *Sunset
                  Boulevard*

Supp. Actress   Hope Emerson in *Caged*;
                  Celeste Holm in *All About
                  Eve*; Josephine Hull in
                  Harvey; Nancy Olson in
                  Sunset Boulevard; Thelma
                  Ritter in *All About Eve*

Direction   George Cukor for *Born
                  Yesterday*; John Huston for
                  The Asphalt Jungle; Joseph L.
                  Mankiewicz for *All About
                  Eve*; Carol Reed for *The Third
                  Man*; Billy Wilder for *Sunset
                  Boulevard*

1951

Production   *An American in Paris* (MGM);
                  Decision Before Dawn (20th
                  Century-Fox); *A Place in the
                  Sun* (Paramount); *Quo Vadis*

Actor
(MGM); *A Streetcar Named Desire* (Warner Bros.)

Actor
Humphrey Bogart in *The African Queen*; Marlon Brando in *A Streetcar Named Desire*; Montgomery Clift in *A Place in the Sun*; Arthur Kennedy in *Bright Victory*; Fredric March in *Death of a Salesman*

Actress
Katharine Hepburn in *The African Queen*; Vivien Leigh in *A Streetcar Named Desire*; Eleanor Parker in *Detective Story*; Shelley Winters in *A Place in the Sun*; Jane Wyman in *The Blue Veil*

Supp. Actor
Leo Genn in *Quo Vadis*; Karl Malden in *A Streetcar Named Desire*; Kevin McCarthy in *Death of a Salesman*; Peter Ustinov in *Quo Vadis*; Gig Young in *Come Fill the Cup*

Supp. Actress
Joan Blondell in *The Blue Veil*; Mildred Dunnock in *Death of a Salesman*; Lee Grant in *Detective Story*; Kim Hunter in *A Streetcar Named Desire*; Thelma Ritter in *The Mating Season*

Direction
John Huston for *The African Queen*; Vincente Minnelli for *An American in Paris*; William Wyler for *Detective Story*; George Stevens for *A Place in the Sun*; Elia Kazan for *A Streetcar Named Desire*

1952

Production
The Greatest Show on Earth (Paramount); *High Noon* (United Artists); *Ivanhoe* (MGM); *Moulin Rouge* (United Artists); *The Quiet Man* (Republic)

Actor
Marlon Brando in *Viva Zapata*; Gary Cooper in *High Noon*; Kirk Douglas in *The Bad and the Beautiful*; Jose Ferrer in *Moulin Rouge*; Alec Guinness in *The Lavender Hill Mob*

Actress
Shirley Booth in *Come Back Little Sheba*; Joan Crawford in *Sudden Fear*; Bette Davis in *The Star*; Julie Harris in *The Member of the Wedding*; Susan Hayward in *With a Song in My Heart*

Supp. Actor
Richard Burton in *My Cousin Rachel*; Arthur Hunnicutt in *The Big Sky*; Victor McLaglen in *The Quiet Man*; Jack Palance in *Sudden Fear*; Anthony Quinn in *Viva Zapata*

Supp. Actress
Gloria Grahame in *The Bad and the Beautiful*; Jean Hagen in *Singin' in the Rain*; Colette Marchand in *Moulin Rouge*; Terry Moore in *Come Back Little Sheba*; Thelma Ritter in *With a Song in My Heart*

Direction
Cecil B. DeMille for *The Greatest Show on Earth*; John Ford for *The Quiet Man*; John Huston for *Moulin Rouge*; Joseph L. Mankiewicz for *Five Fingers*; Fred Zinnemann for *High Noon*

1953

Production
From Here to Eternity (Columbia); *Julius Caesar* (MGM); *The Robe* (20th Century-Fox); *Roman Holiday* (Paramount); *Shane* (Paramount)

Actor
Marlon Brando in *Julius Caesar*; Richard Burton in *The Robe*; Montgomery Clift in *From Here to Eternity*; William Holden in *Stalag 17*; Burt Lancaster in *From Here to Eternity*

Actress	Leslie Caron in *Lili*; Ava Gardner in *Mogambo*; Audrey Hepburn in *Roman Holiday*; Deborah Kerr in *From Here to Eternity*; Maggie McNamara in *The Moon Is Blue*
Supp. Actor	Eddie Albert in *Roman Holiday*; Brandon De Wilde in *Shane*; Jack Palance in *Shane*; Frank Sinatra in *From Here to Eternity*; Robert Strauss in *Stalag 17*
Supp. Actress	Grace Kelly in *Mogambo*; Geraldine Page in *Hondo*; Marjorie Rambeau in *Torch Song*; Donna Reed in *From Here to Eternity*; Thelma Ritter in *Pickup on South Street*
Direction	George Stevens for *Shane*; Charles Walters for *Lili*; Billy Wilder for *Stalag 17*; William Wyler for *Roman Holiday*; Fred Zinnemann for *From Here to Eternity*

1954

Production	*The Caine Mutiny* (Columbia); *The Country Girl*; (Paramount); *On the Waterfront* (Columbia); *Seven Brides for Seven Brothers* (MGM); *Three Coins in the Fountain* (20th Century-Fox)
Actor	Humphrey Bogart in *The Caine Mutiny*; Marlon Brando in *On the Waterfront*; Bing Crosby in *The Country Girl*; James Mason in *A Star Is Born*; Dan O'Herlihy in *The Adventures of Robinson Crusoe*
Actress	Dorothy Dandridge in *Carmen Jones*; Judy Garland in *A Star Is Born*; Audrey Hepburn in *Sabrina*; Grace Kelly in *The Country Girl*; Jane Wyman in *Magnificent Obsession*

Supp. Actor	Lee J. Cobb in *On the Waterfront*; Karl Malden in *On the Waterfront*; Edmond O'Brien in *The Barefoot Contessa*; Rod Steiger in *On the Waterfront*; Tom Tully in *The Caine Mutiny*
Supp. Actress	Nina Foch in *Executive Suite*; Katy Jurado in *Broken Lance*; Eva Marie Saint in *On the Waterfront*; Jan Sterling in *The High and the Mighty*; Claire Trevor in *The High and the Mighty*
Direction	Alfred Hitchcock for *Rear Window*; Elia Kazan for *On the Waterfront*; George Seaton for *The Country Girl*; William A. Wellman for *The High and the Mighty*; Billy Wilder for *Sabrina*

1955

Production	*Love Is a Many-Splendored Thing* (20th Century-Fox); *Marty* (United Artists); *Mister Roberts* (Warner Bros.); *Picnic* (Columbia); *The Rose Tattoo* (Paramount)
Actor	Ernest Borgnine in *Marty*; James Cagney in *Love Me or Leave Me*; James Dean in *East of Eden*; Frank Sinatra in *The Man with the Golden Arm*; Spencer Tracy in *Bad Day at Black Rock*
Actress	Susan Hayward in *I'll Cry Tomorrow*; Katharine Hepburn in *Summertime*; Jennifer Jones in *Love Is a Many-Splendored Thing*; Anna Magnani in *The Rose Tattoo*; Eleanor Parker in *Interrupted Melody*
Supp. Actor	Arthur Kennedy in *Trial*; Jack Lemmon in *Mister Roberts*; Joe Mantell in *Marty*;

Sal Mineo in *Rebel Without a Cause*; Arthur O'Connell in *Picnic*

Supp. Actress   Betsy Blair in *Marty*; Peggy Lee in *Pete Kelly's Blues*; Marisa Pavan in *The Rose Tattoo*; Jo Van Fleet in *East of Eden*; Natalie Wood in *Rebel Without a Cause*

Direction   Elia Kazan for *East of Eden*; David Lean for *Summertime*; Joshua Logan for *Picnic*; Delbert Mann for *Marty*; John Sturges for *Bad Day at Black Rock*

1956

Production   *Around the World in 80 Days* (United Artists); *Friendly Persuasion* (Allied Artists); *Giant* (Warner Bros.); *The King and I* (20th Century-Fox); *The Ten Commandments* (Paramount)

Actor   Yul Brynner in *The King and I*; James Dean in *Giant*; Kirk Douglas in *Lust For Life*; Rock Hudson in *Giant*; Laurence Olivier in *Richard III*

Actress   Carroll Baker in *Baby Doll*; Ingrid Bergman in *Anastasia*; Katharine Hepburn in *The Rainmaker*; Nancy Kelly in *The Bad Seed*; Deborah Kerr in *The King and I*

Supp. Actor   Don Murray in *Bus Stop*; Anthony Perkins in *Friendly Persuasion*; Anthony Quinn in *Lust for Life*; Mickey Rooney in *The Bold and the Brave*; Robert Stack in *Written on the Wind*

Supp. Actress   Mildred Dunnock in *Baby Doll*; Eileen Heckart in *The Bad Seed*; Mercedes

McCambridge in *Giant*; Patty McCormack in *The Bad Seed*; Dorothy Malone in *Written on the Wind*

Direction   Michael Anderson for *Around the World in 80 Days*; William Wyler for *Friendly Persuasion*; George Stevens for *Giant*; Walter Lang for *The King and I*; King Vidor for *War and Peace*

1957

Production   *The Bridge on the River Kwai* (Columbia); *Peyton Place* (20th Century-Fox); *Sayonara* (Warner Bros.); *Twelve Angry Men* (United Artists); *Witness for the Prosecution* (United Artists)

Actor   Marlon Brando in *Sayonara*; Anthony Franciosa in *A Hatful of Rain*; Alec Guinness in *The Bridge on the River Kwai*; Charles Laughton in *Witness for the Prosecution*; Anthony Quinn in *Wild Is the Wind*

Actress   Deborah Kerr in *Heaven Knows, Mr. Allison*; Anna Magnani in *Wild Is the Wind*; Elizabeth Taylor in *Raintree County*; Lana Turner in *Peyton Place*; Joanne Woodward in *The Three Faces of Eve*

Supp. Actor   Red Buttons in *Sayonara*; Vittorio De Sica in *A Farewell to Arms*; Sessue Hayakawa in *The Bridge on the River Kwai*; Arthur Kennedy in *Peyton Place*; Russ Tamblyn in *Peyton Place*

Supp. Actress   Carolyn Jones in *The Bachelor Party*; Elsa Lanchester in *Witness for the Prosecution*;

Hope Lange in *Peyton Place*; Miyoshi Umeki in *Sayonara*; Diane Varsi in *Peyton Place*

Direction   David Lean for *The Bridge on the River Kwai*; Mark Robson for *Peyton Place*; Joshua Logan for *Sayonara*; Sidney Lumet for *Twelve Angry Men*; Billy Wilder for *Witness for the Prosecution*

1958

Production   *Auntie Mame* (Warner Bros.); *Cat on a Hot Tin Roof* (MGM); *The Defiant Ones* (United Artists); *Gigi* (MGM); *Separate Tables* (United Artists)

Actor   Tony Curtis in *The Defiant Ones*; Paul Newman in *Cat on a Hot Tin Roof*; David Niven in *Separate Tables*; Sidney Poitier in *The Defiant Ones*; Spencer Tracy in *The Old Man and the Sea*

Actress   Susan Hayward in *I Want to Live*; Deborah Kerr in *Separate Tables*; Shirley MacLaine in *Some Came Running*; Rosalind Russell in *Auntie Mame*; Elizabeth Taylor in *Cat on a Hot Tin Roof*

Supp. Actor   Theodore Bikel in *The Defiant Ones*; Lee J. Cobb in *The Brothers Karamazov*; Burl Ives in *The Big Country*; Arthur Kennedy in *Some Came Running*; Gig Young in *Teacher's Pet*

Supp. Actress   Peggy Cass in *Auntie Mame*; Wendy Hiller in *Separate Tables*; Martha Hyer in *Some Came Running*; Maureen Stapleton in *Lonelyhearts*; Cara Williams in *The Defiant Ones*

Direction   Richard Brooks for *Cat on a Hot Tin Roof*; Stanley Kramer for *The Defiant Ones*; Vincente Minnelli for *Gigi*; Robert Wise for *I Want to Live*; Mark Robson for *The Inn of The Sixth Happiness*

1959

Production   *Anatomy of a Murder* (Columbia); *Ben-Hur* (MGM); *The Diary of Anne Frank* (20th Century-Fox); *The Nun's Story* (Warner Bros.); *Room at the Top* (Romulus Films/British)

Actor   Laurence Harvey in *Room at the Top*; Charlton Heston in *Ben-Hur*; Jack Lemmon in *Some Like It Hot*; Paul Muni in *The Last Angry Man*; James Stewart in *Anatomy of a Murder*

Actress   Doris Day in *Pillow Talk*; Audrey Hepburn in *The Nun's Story*; Katharine Hepburn in *Suddenly, Last Summer*; Simone Signoret in *Room at the Top*; Elizabeth Taylor in *Suddenly, Last Summer*

Supp. Actor   Hugh Griffith in *Ben-Hur*; Arthur O'Connell in *Anatomy of a Murder*; George C. Scott in *Anatomy of a Murder*; Robert Vaughn in *The Young Philadelphians*; Ed Wynn in *The Diary of Anne Frank*

Supp. Actress   Hermione Baddeley in *Room at the Top*; Susan Kohner in *Imitation of Life*; Juanita Moore in *Imitation of Life*; Thelma Ritter in *Pillow Talk*; Shelley Winters in *The Diary of Anne Frank*

Direction   William Wyler for *Ben-Hur*; George Stevens for *The Diary of Anne Frank*; Fred

Zinnemann for *The Nun's Story;* Jack Clayton for *Room at the Top;* Billy Wilder for *Some Like It Hot*

1960

Production | *The Alamo* (United Artists); *The Apartment* (United Artists); *Elmer Gantry* (United Artists); *Sons and Lovers* (20th Century-Fox); *The Sundowners* (Warner Bros.)

Actor | Trevor Howard in *Sons and Lovers;* Burt Lancaster in *Elmer Gantry;* Jack Lemmon in *The Apartment;* Laurence Olivier in *The Entertainer;* Spencer Tracy in *Inherit the Wind*

Actress | Greer Garson in *Sunrise at Campobello;* Deborah Kerr in *The Sundowners;* Shirley MacLaine in *The Apartment;* Melina Mercouri in *Never on Sunday;* Elizabeth Taylor in *Butterfield 8*

Supp. Actor | Peter Falk in *Murder Inc.;* Jack Kruschen in *The Apartment;* Sal Mineo in *Exodus;* Peter Ustinov in *Spartacus;* Chill Wills in *The Alamo*

Supp. Actress | Glynis Johns in *The Sundowners;* Shirley Jones in *Elmer Gantry;* Shirley Knight in *The Dark at the Top of the Stairs;* Janet Leigh in *Psycho;* Mary Ure in *Sons and Lovers*

Direction | Jack Cardiff for *Sons and Lovers;* Jules Dassin for *Never on Sunday;* Alfred Hitchcock for *Psycho;* Billy Wilder for *The Apartment;* Fred Zinnemann for *The Sundowners*

1961

Production | *Fanny* (Warner Bros.); *The Guns of Navarone* (Columbia); *The Hustler* (20th Century-Fox); *Judgment at Nuremberg* (United Artists); *West Side Story* (United Artists)

Actor | Charles Boyer in *Fanny;* Paul Newman in *The Hustler;* Maximilian Schell in *Judgment at Nuremberg;* Spencer Tracy in *Judgment at Nuremberg;* Stuart Whitman in *The Mark*

Actress | Audrey Hepburn in *Breakfast at Tiffany's;* Piper Laurie in *The Hustler;* Sophia Loren in *Two Women;* Geraldine Page in *Summer and Smoke;* Natalie Wood in *Splendor in the Grass*

Supp. Actor | George Chakiris in *West Side Story;* Montgomery Clift in *Judgment at Nuremberg;* Peter Falk in *Pocketful of Miracles;* Jackie Gleason in *The Hustler;* George C. Scott in *The Hustler*

Supp. Actress | Fay Bainter in *The Children's Hour;* Judy Garland in *Judgment at Nuremberg;* Lotte Lenya in *The Roman Spring of Mrs. Stone;* Una Merkel in *Summer and Smoke;* Rita Moreno in *West Side Story*

Direction | J. Lee Thompson for *The Guns of Navarone;* Robert Rossen for *The Hustler;* Stanley Kramer for *Judgment at Nuremberg;* Federico Fellini for *La Dolce Vita;* Robert Wise and Jerome Robbins for *West Side Story*

1962

Production | *Lawrence of Arabia* (Columbia); *The Longest Day*

(20th Century-Fox); *The Music Man* (Warner Bros.); *Mutiny on the Bounty* (MGM); *To Kill a Mockingbird* (Universal-International)

Actor — Burt Lancaster in *Birdman of Alcatraz*; Jack Lemmon in *Days of Wine and Roses*; Marcello Mastroianni in *Divorce Italian Style*; Peter O'Toole in *Lawrence of Arabia*; Gregory Peck in *To Kill a Mockingbird*

Actress — Anne Bancroft in *The Miracle Worker*; Bette Davis in *What Ever Happened to Baby Jane?*; Katharine Hepburn in *Long Day's Journey Into Night*; Geraldine Page in *Sweet Bird of Youth*; Lee Remick in *Days of Wine and Roses*

Supp. Actor — Ed Begley in *Sweet Bird of Youth*; Victor Buono in *What Ever Happened to Baby Jane?*; Telly Savalas in *Birdman of Alcatraz*; Omar Sharif in *Lawrence of Arabia*; Terence Stamp in *Billy Budd*

Supp. Actress — Mary Badham in *To Kill a Mockingbird*; Patty Duke in *The Miracle Worker*; Shirley Knight in *Sweet Bird of Youth*; Angela Lansbury in *The Manchurian Candidate*; Thelma Ritter in *Birdman of Alcatraz*

Direction — Frank Perry for *David and Lisa*; Pietro Germi for *Divorce Italian Style*; David Lean for *Lawrence of Arabia*; Arthur Penn for *The Miracle Worker*; Robert Mulligan for *To Kill a Mockingbird*

1963

Production — *Tom Jones* (United Artists); *America, America* (Warner Bros.); *Cleopatra* (20th Century-Fox); *How the West Was Won* (MGM); *Lilies of the Field* (United Artists)

Actor — Albert Finney in *Tom Jones*; Richard Harris in *This Sporting Life*; Rex Harrison in *Cleopatra*; Paul Newman in *Hud*; Sidney Poitier in *Lilies of the Field*

Actress — Leslie Caron in *The L-Shaped Room*; Shirley MacLaine in *Irma La Douce*; Patricia Neal in *Hud*; Rachel Roberts in *This Sporting Life*; Natalie Wood in *Love with the Proper Stranger*

Supp. Actor — Nick Adams in *Twilight of Honor*; Bobby Darin in *Captain Newman, M.D.*; Melvyn Douglas in *Hud*; Hugh Griffith in *Tom Jones*; John Huston in *The Cardinal*

Supp. Actress — Diane Cilento in *Tom Jones*; Edith Evans in *Tom Jones*; Joyce Redman in *Tom Jones*; Margaret Rutherford in *The V.I.P.s*; Lilia Skala in *Lilies of the Field*

Direction — Tony Richardson for *Tom Jones*; Elia Kazan for *America, America*; Otto Preminger for *The Cardinal*; Federico Fellini for *8½*; Martin Ritt for *Hud*

1964

Production — *Becket* (Paramount); *Dr. Strangelove* (Columbia); *Mary Poppins* (Walt Disney); *My Fair Lady* (Warner Bros.); *Zorba the Greek* (20th Century-Fox)

Actor — Rex Harrison in *My Fair Lady*; Peter O'Toole in *Becket*; Anthony Quinn in *Zorba the Greek*; Peter Sellers in *Dr.*

	Strangelove; Richard Burton in *Becket*
Actress	Julie Andrews in *Mary Poppins*; Anne Bancroft in *The Pumpkin Eater*; Sophia Loren in *Marriage Italian-Style*; Debbie Reynolds in *The Unsinkable Molly Brown*; Kim Stanley in *Seance on a Wet Afternoon*
Supp. Actor	John Gielgud in *Becket*; Stanley Holloway in *My Fair Lady*; Edmond O'Brien in *Seven Days in May*; Lee Tracy in *The Best Man*; Peter Ustinov in *Topkapi*
Supp. Actress	Gladys Cooper in *My Fair Lady*; Edith Evans in *The Chalk Garden*; Grayson Hall in *Night of the Iguana*; Lila Kedrova in *Zorba the Greek*; Agnes Moorehead in *Hush . . . Hush, Sweet Charlotte*
Direction	Peter Glenville for *Becket*; Stanley Kubrick for *Dr. Strangelove*; Robert Stevenson for *Mary Poppins*; George Cukor for *My Fair Lady*; Michael Cacoyannis for *Zorba the Greek*

1965

Production	*Darling* (Embassy/British); *Dr. Zhivago* (MGM); *Ship of Fools* (Columbia); *The Sound of Music* (20th Century-Fox); *A Thousand Clowns* (United Artists)
Actor	Richard Burton in *The Spy Who Came In from the Cold*; Lee Marvin in *Cat Ballou*; Laurence Olivier in *Othello*; Rod Steiger in *The Pawnbroker*; Oskar Werner in *Ship of Fools*
Actress	Julie Andrews in *The Sound of Music*; Julie Christie in

	Darling; Samantha Eggar in *The Collector*; Elizabeth Hartman in *A Patch of Blue*; Simone Signoret in *Ship of Fools*
Supp. Actor	Martin Balsam in *A Thousand Clowns*; Ian Bannen in *Flight of the Phoenix*; Tom Courtenay in *Dr. Zhivago*; Michael Dunn in *Ship of Fools*; Frank Finlay in *Othello*
Supp. Actress	Ruth Gordon in *Inside Daisy Clover*; Joyce Redman in *Othello*; Maggie Smith in *Othello*; Shelley Winters in *A Patch of Blue*; Peggy Wood in *The Sound of Music*
Direction	William Wyler for *The Collector*; John Schlesinger for *Darling*; David Lean for *Dr. Zhivago*; Robert Wise for *The Sound of Music*; Hiroshi Teshigahara for *Woman of the Dunes*

1966

Production	*Alfie* (Paramount/British); *A Man for All Seasons* (Columbia); *The Russians Are Coming, The Russians Are Coming* (United Artists); *The Sand Pebbles* (20th Century-Fox); *Who's Afraid of Virginia Woolf?* (Warner Bros.)
Actor	Alan Arkin in *The Russians Are Coming, The Russians Are Coming*; Richard Burton in *Who's Afraid of Virginia Woolf?*; Michael Caine in *Alfie*; Steve McQueen in *The Sand Pebbles*; Paul Scofield in *A Man for All Seasons*
Actress	Anouk Aimee in *A Man and a Woman*; Ida Kaminska in *The Shop on Main Street*; Lynn Redgrave in *Georgy Girl*; Vanessa Redgrave in *Morgan:*

Supp. Actor | *A Suitable Case for Treatment;* Elizabeth Taylor in *Who's Afraid of Virginia Woolf?* Mako in *The Sand Pebbles;* James Mason in *Georgy Girl;* Walter Matthau in *The Fortune Cookie;* George Segal in *Who's Afraid of Virginia Woolf?;* Robert Shaw in *A Man for All Seasons*

Supp. Actress | Sandy Dennis in *Who's Afraid of Virginia Woolf?;* Wendy Hiller in *A Man for All Seasons;* Jocelyn LaGarde in *Hawaii;* Vivien Merchant in *Alfie;* Geraldine Page in *You're a Big Boy Now*

Direction | Michelangelo Antonioni for *Blowup;* Claude Lelouch for *A Man and a Woman;* Fred Zinnemann for *A Man for All Seasons;* Richard Brooks for *The Professionals;* Mike Nichols for *Who's Afraid of Virginia Woolf?*

1967

Production | *Bonnie and Clyde* (Warner Bros.); *Doctor Dolittle* (20th Century-Fox); *The Graduate* (United Artists); *Guess Who's Coming to Dinner* (Columbia); *In the Heat of the Night* (United Artists)

Actor | Warren Beatty in *Bonnie and Clyde;* Dustin Hoffman in *The Graduate;* Paul Newman in *Cool Hand Luke;* Rod Steiger in *In the Heat of the Night;* Spencer Tracy in *Guess Who's Coming to Dinner*

Actress | Anne Bancroft in *The Graduate;* Faye Dunaway in *Bonnie and Clyde;* Edith Evans in *The Whisperers;* Audrey Hepburn in *Wait Until Dark;*

Katharine Hepburn in *Guess Who's Coming to Dinner*

Supp. Actor | John Cassavetes in *The Dirty Dozen;* Gene Hackman in *Bonnie and Clyde;* Cecil Kellaway in *Guess Who's Coming to Dinner;* George Kennedy in *Cool Hand Luke;* Michael J. Pollard in *Bonnie and Clyde*

Supp. Actress | Carol Channing in *Thoroughly Modern Millie;* Mildred Natwick in *Barefoot in the Park;* Estelle Parsons in *Bonnie and Clyde;* Beah Richards in *Guess Who's Coming to Dinner;* Katharine Ross in *The Graduate*

Direction | Arthur Penn for *Bonnie and Clyde;* Mike Nichols for *The Graduate;* Stanley Kramer for *Guess Who's Coming to Dinner;* Richard Brooks for *In Cold Blood;* Norman Jewison for *In the Heat of the Night*

1968

Production | *Funny Girl* (Columbia); *The Lion in Winter* (Avco Embassy); *Oliver!* (Columbia); *Rachel, Rachel* (Warner Bros.); *Romeo and Juliet* (Paramount)

Actor | Alan Arkin in *The Heart Is a Lonely Hunter;* Alan Bates in *The Fixer;* Ron Moody in *Oliver!;* Peter O'Toole in *The Lion in Winter;* Cliff Robertson in *Charly*

Actress | Katharine Hepburn in *The Lion in Winter;* Patricia Neal in *The Subject Was Roses;* Vanessa Redgrave in *Isadora;* Barbra Streisand in *Funny Girl;* Joanne Woodward in *Rachel, Rachel*

Supp. Actor | Jack Albertson in *The Subject Was Roses;* Seymour Cassel in

	Faces; Daniel Massey in *Star!*; Jack Wild in *Oliver!*; Gene Wilder in *The Producers*		in *They Shoot Horses, Don't They?*
Supp. Actress	Lynn Carlin in *Faces*; Ruth Gordon in *Rosemary's Baby*; Sondra Locke in *The Heart Is A Lonely Hunter*; Kay Medford in *Funny Girl*; Estelle Parsons in *Rachel, Rachel*	Supp. Actress	Cathy Burns in *Last Summer*; Dyan Cannon in *Bob and Carol and Ted and Alice*; Goldie Hawn in *Cactus Flower*; Sylvia Miles in *Midnight Cowboy*; Susannah York in *They Shoot Horses, Don't They?*
Direction	Gillo Pontecorvo for *The Battle of Algiers*; Franco Zeffirelli for *Romeo and Juliet*; Anthony Harvey for *The Lion in Winter*; Carol Reed for *Oliver!*; Stanley Kubrick for *2001: A Space Odyssey*	Direction	Arthur Penn for *Alice's Restaurant*; George Roy Hill for *Butch Cassidy and the Sundance Kid*; John Schlesinger for *Midnight Cowboy*; Sydney Pollack for *They Shoot Horses, Don't They?*; Costa-Gavras for *Z*

1969

Production	*Anne of the Thousand Days* (Universal); *Butch Cassidy and the Sundance Kid* (20th Century-Fox); *Hello, Dolly!* (20th Century-Fox); *Midnight Cowboy* (United Artists); *Z* (Algeria/France)		

1970

		Production	*Airport* (Universal); *Five Easy Pieces* (Columbia); *Love Story* (Paramount); *M*A*S*H* (20th Century-Fox); *Patton* (20th Century-Fox)
Actor	Richard Burton in *Anne of the Thousand Days*; Dustin Hoffman in *Midnight Cowboy*; Peter O'Toole in *Goodbye, Mr. Chips*; Jon Voight in *Midnight Cowboy*; John Wayne in *True Grit*	Actor	Melvyn Douglas in *I Never Sang for My Father*; James Earl Jones in *The Great White Hope*; Jack Nicholson in *Five Easy Pieces*; Ryan O'Neal in *Love Story*; George C. Scott in *Patton*
Actress	Genevieve Bujold in *Anne of the Thousand Days*; Jane Fonda in *They Shoot Horses, Don't They?*; Liza Minnelli in *The Sterile Cuckoo*; Jean Simmons in *The Happy Ending*; Maggie Smith in *The Prime of Miss Jean Brodie*	Actress	Jane Alexander in *The Great White Hope*; Glenda Jackson in *Women in Love*; Ali MacGraw in *Love Story*; Sarah Miles in *Ryan's Daughter*; Carrie Snodgress in *Diary of a Mad Housewife*
Supp. Actor	Rupert Crosse in *The Reivers*; Elliott Gould in *Bob and Carol and Ted and Alice*; Jack Nicholson in *Easy Rider*; Anthony Quayle in *Anne of the Thousand Days*; Gig Young	Supp. Actor	Richard Castellano in *Lovers and Other Strangers*; Chief Dan George in *Little Big Man*; Gene Hackman in *I Never Sang for My Father*; John Mills in *Ryan's Daughter*; John Marley in *Love Story*
		Supp. Actress	Karen Black in *Five Easy*

Pieces; Lee Grant in *The Landlord;* Helen Hayes in *Airport;* Sally Kellerman in *M*A*S*H;* Maureen Stapleton in *Airport*

Direction   Federico Fellini for *Satyricon;* Arthur Hiller for *Love Story;* Robert Altman for *M*A*S*H;* Franklin J. Schaffner for *Patton;* Ken Russell for *Women in Love*

1971

Production   *A Clockwork Orange* (Warner Bros.); *Fiddler on the Roof* (United Artists); *The French Connection* (20th Century-Fox); *The Last Picture Show* (Columbia); *Nicholas and Alexandra* (Columbia)

Actor   Peter Finch in *Sunday Bloody Sunday;* Gene Hackman in *The French Connection;* Walter Matthau in *Kotch;* George C. Scott in *The Hospital;* Topol in *Fiddler on the Roof*

Actress   Jane Fonda in *Klute;* Julie Christie in *McCabe and Mrs. Miller;* Glenda Jackson in *Sunday Bloody Sunday;* Vanessa Redgrave in *Mary, Queen of Scots;* Janet Suzman in *Nicholas and Alexandra*

Supp. Actor   Jeff Bridges in *The Last Picture Show;* Leonard Frey in *Fiddler on the Roof;* Richard Jaeckel in *Sometimes a Great Notion;* Ben Johnson in *The Last Picture Show;* Roy Scheider in *The French Connection*

Supp. Actress   Ellen Burstyn in *The Last Picture Show;* Barbara Harris in *Who Is Harry Kellerman?;* Cloris Leachman in *The Last Picture Show;* Margaret Leighton in *The Go-Between;*

Ann-Margret in *Carnal Knowledge*

Direction   Stanley Kubrick for *A Clockwork Orange;* Norman Jewison for *Fiddler on the Roof;* William Friedkin for *The French Connection;* Peter Bogdanovich for *The Last Picture Show;* John Schlesinger for *Sunday Bloody Sunday*

1972

Production   *Cabaret* (Allied Artists); *Deliverance* (Warner Bros.); *The Emigrants* (Sweden); *The Godfather* (Paramount); *Sounder* (20th Century-Fox)

Actor   Marlon Brando in *The Godfather;* Michael Caine in *Sleuth;* Laurence Olivier in *Sleuth;* Peter O'Toole in *The Ruling Class;* Paul Winfield in *Sounder*

Actress   Liza Minnelli in *Cabaret;* Diana Ross in *Lady Sings the Blues;* Maggie Smith in *Travels with My Aunt;* Cicely Tyson in *Sounder;* Liv Ullmann in *The Emigrants*

Supp. Actor   Eddie Albert in *The Heartbreak Kid;* James Caan in *The Godfather;* Robert Duvall in *The Godfather;* Al Pacino in *The Godfather;* Joel Grey in *Cabaret*

Supp. Actress   Eileen Heckart in *Butterflies Are Free;* Geraldine Page in *Pete 'n' Tillie;* Susan Tyrrell in *Fat City;* Shelley Winters in *The Poseidon Adventure;* Jeannie Berlin in *The Heartbreak Kid*

Direction   Bob Fosse for *Cabaret;* John Boorman for *Deliverance;* Jan Troell for *The Emigrants;* Francis Ford Coppola for *The*

Godfather; Joseph L. Mankiewicz for *Sleuth*

1973

Production	*American Graffiti* (Universal); *Cries and Whispers* (Sweden); *The Exorcist* (Warner Bros.); *The Sting* (Universal); *A Touch of Class* (Avco Embassy)
Actor	Marlon Brando in *Last Tango in Paris;* Jack Lemmon in *Save the Tiger;* Jack Nicholson in *The Last Detail;* Al Pacino in *Serpico;* Robert Redford in *The Sting*
Actress	Ellen Burstyn in *The Exorcist;* Glenda Jackson in *A Touch of Class;* Marsha Mason in *Cinderella Liberty;* Barbra Streisand in *The Way We Were;* Joanne Woodward in *Summer Wishes, Winter Dreams*
Supp. Actor	Vincent Gardenia in *Bang the Drum Slowly;* Jack Gilford in *Save the Tiger;* John Houseman in *The Paper Chase;* Jason Miller in *The Exorcist;* Randy Quaid in *The Last Detail*
Supp. Actress	Linda Blair in *The Exorcist;* Candy Clark in *American Graffiti;* Madeline Kahn in *Paper Moon;* Tatum O'Neal in *Paper Moon;* Sylvia Sidney in *Summer Wishes, Winter Dreams*
Direction	George Lucas for *American Graffiti;* Ingmar Bergman for *Cries and Whispers;* William Friedkin for *The Exorcist;* George Roy Hill for *The Sting;* Bernardo Bertolucci for *Last Tango in Paris*

1974

Production	*Chinatown* (Paramount); *The Conversation* (Paramount); *The Godfather Part II* (Paramount); *Lenny* (United Artists); *The Towering Inferno* (20th Century-Fox/Warner Bros.)
Actor	Art Carney in *Harry and Tonto;* Albert Finney in *Murder on the Orient Express;* Dustin Hoffman in *Lenny;* Jack Nicholson in *Chinatown;* Al Pacino in *The Godfather Part II*
Actress	Ellen Burstyn in *Alice Doesn't Live Here Anymore;* Diahann Carroll in *Claudine;* Faye Dunaway in *Chinatown;* Valerie Perrine in *Lenny;* Gena Rowlands in *A Woman Under the Influence*
Supp. Actor	Fred Astaire in *The Towering Inferno;* Jeff Bridges in *Thunderbolt and Lightfoot;* Robert De Niro in *The Godfather Part II;* Michael V. Gazzo in *The Godfather Part II;* Lee Strasberg in *The Godfather Part II*
Supp. Actress	Ingrid Bergman in *Murder on the Orient Express;* Valentina Cortese in *Day for Night;* Madeline Kahn in *Blazing Saddles;* Diane Ladd in *Alice Doesn't Live Here Anymore;* Talia Shire in *The Godfather Part II*
Direction	Roman Polanski for *Chinatown;* Francois Truffaut for *Day for Night;* Francis Ford Coppola for *The Godfather Part II;* Bob Fosse for *Lenny;* John Cassavetes for *A Woman Under the Influence*

1975

Production	*Barry Lyndon* (Warner Bros.); *Dog Day Afternoon* (Warner Bros.); *Jaws* (Universal); *Nashville* (Paramount); *One*

Flew Over the Cuckoo's Nest (United Artists)

Actor — Walter Matthau in *The Sunshine Boys;* Jack Nicholson in *One Flew Over the Cuckoo's Nest;* Al Pacino in *Dog Day Afternoon;* Maximilian Schell in *The Man in the Glass Booth;* James Whitmore in *"Give 'Em Hell, Harry"*

Actress — Isabelle Adjani in *The Story of Adele H.;* Ann-Margret in *Tommy;* Louise Fletcher in *One Flew Over the Cuckoo's Nest;* Glenda Jackson in *Hedda;* Carol Kane in *Hester Street*

Supp. Actor — George Burns in *The Sunshine Boys;* Brad Dourif in *One Flew Over the Cuckoo's Nest;* Burgess Meredith in *The Day of the Locust;* Chris Sarandon in *Dog Day Afternoon;* Jack Warden in *Shampoo*

Supp. Actress — Ronee Blakley in *Nashville;* Lee Grant in *Shampoo;* Sylvia Miles in *Farewell My Lovely;* Lily Tomlin in *Nashville;* Brenda Vaccaro in *Once Is Not Enough*

Direction — Federico Fellini for *Amarcord;* Stanley Kubrick for *Barry Lyndon;* Sidney Lumet for *Dog Day Afternoon;* Robert Altman for *Nashville;* Milos Forman for *One Flew Over the Cuckoo's Nest*

1976

Production — *All the President's Men* (Warner Bros.); *Bound for Glory* (United Artists); *Network* (United Artists); *Rocky* (United Artists); *Taxi Driver* (Columbia)

Actor — Robert De Niro in *Taxi Driver;* Peter Finch in *Network;* Giancarlo Giannini in *Seven Beauties;* William Holden in *Network;* Sylvester Stallone in *Rocky*

Actress — Marie-Christine Barrault in *Cousin, Cousine;* Faye Dunaway in *Network;* Talia Shire in *Rocky;* Sissy Spacek in *Carrie;* Liv Ullmann in *Face to Face*

Supp. Actor — Ned Beatty in *Network;* Burgess Meredith in *Rocky;* Laurence Olivier in *Marathon Man;* Jason Robards in *All the President's Men;* Burt Young in *Rocky*

Supp. Actress — Jane Alexander in *All the President's Men;* Jodie Foster in *Taxi Driver;* Lee Grant in *Voyage of the Damned;* Piper Laurie in *Carrie;* Beatrice Straight in *Network*

Direction — Alan J. Pakula for *All the President's Men;* Ingmar Bergman for *Face to Face;* Sidney Lumet for *Network;* John G. Avildsen for *Rocky;* Lina Wertmuller for *Seven Beauties*

1977

Production — *Annie Hall* (United Artists); *The Goodbye Girl* (MGM-Warner Bros.); *Julia* (20th Century-Fox); *Star Wars* (20th Century-Fox); *The Turning Point* (20th Century-Fox)

Actor — Woody Allen in *Annie Hall;* Richard Burton in *Equus;* Richard Dreyfuss in *The Goodbye Girl;* Marcello

	Mastroianni in *A Special Day*; John Travolta in *Saturday Night Fever*
Actress	Anne Bancroft in *The Turning Point*; Jane Fonda in *Julia*; Diane Keaton in *Annie Hall*; Shirley MacLaine in *The Turning Point*; Marsha Mason in *The Goodbye Girl*
Supp. Actor	Mikhail Baryshnikov in *The Turning Point*; Peter Firth in *Equus*; Alec Guinness in *Star Wars*; Jason Robards in *Julia*; Maximilian Schell in *Julia*
Supp. Actress	Leslie Browne in *The Turning Point*; Quinn Cummings in *The Goodbye Girl*; Melinda Dillon in *Close Encounters of the Third Kind*; Vanessa Redgrave in *Julia*; Tuesday Weld in *Looking for Mr. Goodbar*
Direction	Woody Allen for *Annie Hall*; Steven Spielberg for *Close Encounters of the Third Kind*; Fred Zinnemann for *Julia*; George Lucas for *Star Wars*; Herbert Ross for *The Turning Point*

1978

Production	*Coming Home* (United Artists); *The Deer Hunter* (EMI/Universal); *Heaven Can Wait* (Paramount); *Midnight Express* (Columbia); *An Unmarried Woman* (20th Century-Fox)
Actor	Warren Beatty in *Heaven Can Wait*; Gary Busey in *The Buddy Holly Story*; Robert De Niro in *The Deer Hunter*; Laurence Olivier in *The Boys from Brazil*; Jon Voight in *Coming Home*
Actress	Ingrid Bergman in *Autumn Sonata*; Ellen Burstyn in *Same Time, Next Year*; Jill

	Clayburgh in *An Unmarried Woman*; Jane Fonda in *Coming Home*; Geraldine Page in *Interiors*
Supp. Actor	Bruce Dern in *Coming Home*; Richard Farnsworth in *Comes a Horseman*; John Hurt in *Midnight Express*; Christopher Walken in *The Deer Hunter*; Jack Warden in *Heaven Can Wait*
Supp. Actress	Dyan Cannon in *Heaven Can Wait*; Penelope Milford in *Coming Home*; Maggie Smith in *California Suite*; Maureen Stapleton in *Interiors*; Meryl Streep in *The Deer Hunter*
Best Direction	Hal Ashby for *Coming Home*; Michael Cimino for *The Deer Hunter*; Warren Beatty and Buck Henry for *Heaven Can Wait*; Woody Allen for *Interiors*; Alan Parker for *Midnight Express*

1979

Production	*All That Jazz* (Columbia/20th Century-Fox); *Apocalypse Now* (United Artists); *Breaking Away* (20th Century-Fox); *Kramer vs. Kramer* (Columbia); *Norma Rae* (20th Century-Fox)
Actor	Dustin Hoffman in *Kramer vs. Kramer*; Jack Lemmon in *The China Syndrome*; Al Pacino in *And Justice for All*; Roy Scheider in *All That Jazz*; Peter Sellers in *Being There*
Actress	Jill Clayburgh in *Starting Over*; Sally Field in *Norma Rae*; Jane Fonda in *The China Syndrome*; Marsha Mason in *Chapter Two*; Bette Midler in *The Rose*
Supp. Actor	Melvyn Douglas in *Being*

There; Robert Duvall in
Apocalypse Now; Frederic
Forrest in *The Rose;* Justin
Henry in *Kramer vs. Kramer;*
Mickey Rooney in *The Black
Stallion*

Supp. Actress   Jane Alexander in *Kramer vs.
Kramer;* Barbara Barrie in
Breaking Away; Candice
Bergen in *Starting Over;*
Mariel Hemingway in
Manhattan; Meryl Streep in
Kramer vs. Kramer

Direction   Bob Fosse for *All That Jazz;*
Francis Ford Coppola for
Apocalypse Now; Peter Yates
for *Breaking Away;* Robert
Benton for *Kramer vs. Kramer;*
Edouard Molinaro for *La
Cage Aux Folles*

1980

Production   *Coal Miner's Daughter*
(Universal); *The Elephant Man*
(Paramount); *Ordinary People*
(Paramount); *Raging Bull*
(United Artists); *Tess*
(Columbia)

Actor   Robert De Niro in *Raging
Bull;* Robert Duvall in *The
Great Santini;* John Hurt in
The Elephant Man; Jack
Lemmon in *Tribute;* Peter
O'Toole in *The Stunt Man*

Actress   Ellen Burstyn in *Resurrection;*
Goldie Hawn in *Private
Benjamin;* Mary Tyler Moore
in *Ordinary People;* Gena
Rowlands in *Gloria;* Sissy
Spacek in *Coal Miner's
Daughter*

Supp. Actor   Judd Hirsch in *Ordinary
People;* Timothy Hutton in
Ordinary People; Michael
O'Keefe in *The Great Santini;*
Joe Pesci in *Raging Bull;*

Jason Robards in *Melvin and
Howard*

Supp. Actress   Eileen Brennan in *Private
Benjamin;* Eva Le Gallienne
in *Resurrection;* Cathy
Moriarty in *Raging Bull;*
Diana Scarwid in *Inside
Moves;* Mary Steenburgen in
Melvin and Howard

Direction   David Lynch for *The Elephant
Man;* Robert Redford for
Ordinary People; Martin
Scorsese for *Raging Bull;*
Richard Rush for *The Stunt
Man;* Roman Polanski for *Tess*

1981

Production   *Atlantic City* (Paramount);
Chariots of Fire (The Ladd
Company/Warner Bros); *On
Golden Pond* (ITC/Universal);
Raiders of the Lost Ark
(Paramount); *Reds*
(Paramount)

Actor   Warren Beatty in *Reds;*
Henry Fonda in *On Golden
Pond;* Burt Lancaster in
Atlantic City; Dudley Moore
in *Arthur;* Paul Newman in
Absence of Malice

Actress   Katharine Hepburn in *On
Golden Pond;* Diane Keaton in
Reds; Marsha Mason in *Only
When I Laugh;* Susan
Sarandon in *Atlantic City;*
Meryl Streep in *The French
Lieutenant's Woman*

Supp. Actor   James Coco in *Only When I
Laugh;* John Gielgud in
Arthur; Ian Holm in *Chariots
of Fire;* Jack Nicholson in
Reds; Howard E. Rollins, Jr.
in *Ragtime*

Supp. Actress   Melinda Dillon in *Absence of
Malice;* Jane Fonda in *On
Golden Pond;* Joan Hackett in
Only When I Laugh; Elizabeth

Direction	McGovern in *Ragtime*; Maureen Stapleton in *Reds* Louis Malle for *Atlantic City*; Hugh Hudson for *Chariots of Fire*; Mark Rydell for *On Golden Pond*; Steven Spielberg for *Raiders of the Lost Ark*; Warren Beatty for *Reds*

1982

Production	*E.T. The Extra-Terrestrial* (Universal); *Gandhi* (Columbia); *Missing* (Universal); *Tootsie* (Columbia); *The Verdict* (20th Century-Fox)
Actor	Dustin Hoffman in *Tootsie*; Ben Kingsley in *Gandhi*; Jack Lemmon in *Missing*; Paul Newman in *The Verdict*; Peter O'Toole in *My Favorite Year*
Actress	Julie Andrews in *Victor/Victoria*; Jessica Lange in *Frances*; Sissy Spacek in *Missing*; Meryl Streep in *Sophie's Choice*; Debra Winger in *An Officer and a Gentleman*
Supp. Actor	Charles Durning in *The Best Little Whorehouse in Texas*; Louis Gossett, Jr. in *An Officer and a Gentleman*; John Lithgow in *The World According to Garp*; James Mason in *The Verdict*; Robert Preston in *Victor/Victoria*
Supp. Actress	Glenn Close in *The World According to Garp*; Teri Garr in *Tootsie*; Jessica Lange in *Tootsie*; Kim Stanley in *Frances*; Lesley Ann Warren in *Victor/Victoria*
Direction	Wolfgang Peterson for *Das Boot*; Steven Spielberg for *E.T. The Extra-Terrestrial*; Richard Attenborough for *Gandhi*; Sydney Pollack for *Tootsie*; Sidney Lumet for *The Verdict*

1983

Production	*The Big Chill* (Columbia); *The Dresser* (Goldcrest/Columbia); *The Right Stuff* (The Ladd Co./Warner Bros.); *Tender Mercies* (EMI/Universal); *Terms of Endearment* (Paramount)
Actor	Michael Caine in *Educating Rita*; Tom Conti in *Reuben, Reuben*; Tom Courtenay in *The Dresser*; Robert Duvall in *Tender Mercies*; Albert Finney in *The Dresser*
Actress	Jane Alexander in *Testament*; Shirley MacLaine in *Terms of Endearment*; Meryl Streep in *Silkwood*; Julie Walters in *Educating Rita*; Debra Winger in *Terms of Endearment*
Supp. Actor	Charles Durning in *To Be or Not To Be*; John Lithgow in *Terms of Endearment*; Jack Nicholson in *Terms of Endearment*; Sam Shepard in *The Right Stuff*; Rip Torn in *Cross Creek*
Supp. Actress	Cher in *Silkwood*; Glenn Close in *The Big Chill*; Linda Hunt in *The Year of Living Dangerously*; Amy Irving in *Yentl*; Alfre Woodard in *Cross Creek*
Direction	Peter Yates for *The Dresser*; Ingmar Bergman for *Fanny and Alexander*; Mike Nichols for *Silkwood*; Bruce Beresford for *Tender Mercies*; James L. Brooks for *Terms of Endearment*

1984

Production	*Amadeus* (Zaentz/Orion); *The Killing Fields* (Enigma/Warner Bros.); *A Passage to India* (G.W. Films/Columbia); *Places in the Heart* (Tri-Star); *A Soldier's Story* (Columbia)

Actor | F. Murray Abraham in *Amadeus;* Jeff Bridges in *Starman;* Albert Finney in *Under the Volcano;* Tom Hulce in *Amadeus;* Sam Waterston in *The Killing Fields*

Actress | Judy Davis in *A Passage to India;* Sally Field in *Places in the Heart;* Jessica Lange in *Country;* Vanessa Redgrave in *The Bostonians;* Sissy Spacek in *The River*

Supp. Actor | Adolph Caesar in *A Soldier's Story;* John Malkovich in *Places in the Heart;* Noriyuki "Pat" Morita in *The Karate Kid;* Haing S. Ngor in *The Killing Fields;* Ralph Richardson in *Greystoke: The Legend of Tarzan, Lord of the Apes*

Supp. Actress | Peggy Ashcroft in *A Passage to India;* Glenn Close in *The Natural;* Lindsay Crouse in *Places in the Heart;* Christine Lahti in *Swing Shift;* Geraldine Page in *The Pope of Greenwich Village*

Direction | Milos Forman for *Amadeus;* Woody Allen for *Broadway Danny Rose;* Roland Joffe for *The Killing Fields;* David Lean for *A Passage to India;* Robert Benton for *Places in the Heart*

1985

Production | *The Color Purple* (Warner Bros.); *Kiss of the Spider Woman* (Island Alive); *Out of Africa* (Universal); *Prizzi's Honor* (ABC/20th Century-Fox); *Witness* (Paramount)

Actor | Harrison Ford in *Witness;* James Garner in *Murphy's Romance;* William Hurt in *Kiss of the Spider Woman;* Jack Nicholson in *Prizzi's Honor;* Jon Voight in *Runaway Train*

Actress | Anne Bancroft in *Agnes of God;* Whoopi Goldberg in *The Color Purple;* Jessica Lange in *Sweet Dreams;* Geraldine Page in *The Trip to Bountiful;* Meryl Streep in *Out of Africa*

Supp. Actor | Don Ameche in *Cocoon;* Klaus Maria Brandauer in *Out of Africa;* William Hickey in *Prizzi's Honor;* Robert Loggia in *Jagged Edge;* Eric Roberts in *Runaway Train*

Supp. Actress | Margaret Avery in *The Color Purple;* Anjelica Huston in *Prizzi's Honor;* Amy Madigan in *Twice in a Lifetime;* Meg Tilly in *Agnes of God;* Oprah Winfrey in *The Color Purple*

Direction | Hector Babenco for *Kiss of the Spider Woman;* Sydney Pollack for *Out of Africa;* John Huston for *Prizzi's Honor;* Akira Kurosawa for *Ran;* Peter Weir for *Witness*

1986

Production | *Children of a Lesser God* (Paramount); *Hannah and Her Sisters* (Orion); *The Mission* (Warner Bros.); *Platoon* (Hemdale/Orion); *A Room with a View* (Merchant Ivory/Cinecom)

Actor | Dexter Gordon in *'Round Midnight;* Bob Hoskins in *Mona Lisa;* William Hurt in *Children of a Lesser God;* Paul Newman in *The Color of Money;* James Woods in *Salvador*

Actress | Jane Fonda in *The Morning After;* Marlee Matlin in *Children of a Lesser God;* Sissy Spacek in *Crimes of the Heart;* Kathleen Turner in *Peggy Sue Got Married;* Sigourney Weaver in *Aliens*

Supp. Actor | Tom Berenger in *Platoon;*

Michael Caine in *Hannah and Her Sisters*; Willem Dafoe in *Platoon*; Denholm Elliott in *A Room with a View*; Dennis Hopper in *Hoosiers*

Supp. Actress
Tess Harper in *Crimes of the Heart*; Piper Laurie in *Children of a Lesser God*; Mary Elizabeth Mastrantonio in *The Color of Money*; Maggie Smith in *A Room with a View*; Dianne Wiest in *Hannah and Her Sisters*

Direction
David Lynch for *Blue Velvet*; Woody Allen for *Hannah and Her Sisters*; Roland Joffe for *The Mission*; Oliver Stone for *Platoon*; James Ivory for *A Room with a View*

1987

Production
Broadcast News (20th Century-Fox); *Fatal Attraction* (Paramount); *Hope and Glory* (Davros/Columbia); *The Last Emperor* (Hemdale/Columbia); *Moonstruck* (MGM)

Actor
William Hurt in *Broadcast News*; Michael Douglas in *Wall Street*; Robin Williams in *Good Morning, Vietnam*; Marcello Mastroianni in *Dark Eyes*; Jack Nicholson in *Ironweed*

Actress
Cher in *Moonstruck*; Meryl Streep in *Ironweed*; Sally Kirkland in *Anna*; Glenn Close in *Fatal Attraction*; Holly Hunter in *Broadcast News*

Supp. Actor
Albert Brooks in *Broadcast News*; Morgan Freeman in *Street Smart*; Sean Connery in *The Untouchables*; Denzel Washington in *Cry Freedom*; Vincent Gardenia in *Moonstruck*

Supp. Actress
Norma Aleandro in *Gaby—A True Story*; Ann Sothern in *The Whales of August*; Olympia Dukakis in *Moonstruck*; Anne Archer in *Fatal Attraction*; Anne Ramsey in *Throw Momma from the Train*

Direction
Bernardo Bertolucci for *The Last Emperor*; John Boorman for *Hope and Glory*; Lasse Hallstrom for *My Life as a Dog*; Norman Jewison for *Moonstruck*; Adrian Lyne for *Fatal Attraction*

1988

Production
The Accidental Tourist (Warner Bros.); *Dangerous Liaisons* (Lorimar/Warner Bros.); *Mississippi Burning* (Orion); *Rain Man* (United Artists); *Working Girl* (20th Century-Fox)

Actor
Gene Hackman in *Mississippi Burning*; Tom Hanks in *Big*; Dustin Hoffman in *Rain Man*; Edward James Olmos in *Stand and Deliver*; Max Von Sydow in *Pelle the Conqueror*

Actress
Glenn Close in *Dangerous Liaisons*; Jodie Foster in *The Accused*; Melanie Griffith in *Working Girl*; Meryl Streep in *A Cry in the Dark*; Sigourney Weaver in *Gorillas in the Mist*

Supp. Actor
Alec Guinness in *Little Dorrit*; Kevin Kline in *A Fish Called Wanda*; Martin Landau in *Tucker: The Man and His Dream*; River Phoenix in *Running on Empty*; Dean Stockwell in *Married to the Mob*

Supp. Actress
Joan Cusack in *Working Girl*; Geena Davis in *The Accidental*

Direction

Tourist; Frances McDormand in *Mississippi Burning*; Michelle Pfeiffer in *Dangerous Liaisons*; Sigourney Weaver in *Working Girl*

Charles Crichton for *A Fish Called Wanda*; Barry Levinson for *Rain Man*; Mike Nichols for *Working Girl*; Alan Parker for *Mississippi Burning*; Martin Scorsese for *The Last Temptation of Christ*

1989

Production

Born on the Fourth of July (Universal); *Dead Poets Society* (Buena Vista/Touchstone); *Driving Miss Daisy* (Warner Bros.); *Field of Dreams* (Universal); *My Left Foot* (Miramax/Ferndale Films)

Actor

Kenneth Branagh in *Henry V*; Tom Cruise in *Born on the Fourth Of July*; Morgan Freeman in *Driving Miss Daisy*; Daniel Day-Lewis in *My Left Foot*; Robin Williams in *Dead Poets Society*

Actress

Isabelle Adjani in *Camille Claudel*; Pauline Collins in *Shirley Valentine*; Jessica Lange in *Music Box*; Michelle Pfeiffer in *The Fabulous Baker Boys*; Jessica Tandy in *Driving Miss Daisy*

Supp. Actor

Danny Aiello in *Do the Right Thing*; Dan Aykroyd in *Driving Miss Daisy*; Marlon Brando in *A Dry White Season*; Martin Landau in *Crimes and Misdemeanors*; Denzel Washington in *Glory*

Supp. Actress

Brenda Fricker in *My Left Foot*; Anjelica Huston in *Enemies: A Love Story*; Lena Olin in *Enemies: A Love Story*; Julia Roberts in *Steel*

Direction

Magnolias; Dianne Wiest in *Parenthood*

Oliver Stone for *Born on the Fourth of July*; Woody Allen for *Crimes and Misdemeanors*; Peter Weir for *Dead Poets Society*; Kenneth Branagh for *Henry V*; Jim Sheridan for *My Left Foot*

1990

Production

Awakenings (Columbia); *Dances with Wolves* (Orion/Tig); *Ghost* (Paramount); *The Godfather Part III* (Paramount); *Goodfellas* (Warner Bros.)

Actor

Kevin Costner in *Dances With Wolves*; Robert De Niro in *Awakenings*; Gerard Depardieu in *Cyrano de Bergerac*; Richard Harris in *The Field*; Jeremy Irons in *Reversal of Fortune*

Actress

Kathy Bates in *Misery*; Anjelica Huston in *The Grifters*; Julia Roberts in *Pretty Woman*; Meryl Streep in *Postcards from the Edge*; Joanne Woodward in *Mr. and Mrs. Bridge*

Supp. Actor

Bruce Davison in *Longtime Companion*; Andy Garcia in *The Godfather Part III*; Graham Greene in *Dances With Wolves*; Al Pacino in *Dick Tracy*; Joe Pesci in *Goodfellas*

Supp. Actress

Annette Bening in *The Grifters*; Lorraine Bracco in *Goodfellas*; Whoopi Goldberg in *Ghost*; Diane Ladd in *Wild at Heart*; Mary McDonnell in *Dances With Wolves*

Direction

Kevin Costner for *Dances With Wolves*; Francis Ford Coppola for *The Godfather Part III*; Martin Scorsese for

Goodfellas; Stephen Frears for *The Grifters*; Barbet Schroeder for *Reversal of Fortune*

Silence of the Lambs; Ridley Scott for *Thelma and Louise*

1991

Production	*Beauty and the Beast* (Buena Vista, Walt Disney Pictures); *Bugsy* (Tristar); *JFK* (Warner Bros.); *The Prince of Tides* (Columbia); *The Silence of the Lambs* (Orion)
Actor	Warren Beatty in *Bugsy*; Robert De Niro in *Cape Fear*; Anthony Hopkins in *The Silence of the Lambs*; Nick Nolte in *The Prince of Tides*; Robin Williams in *The Fisher King*
Actress	Geena Davis in *Thelma and Louise*; Laura Dern in *Rambling Rose*; Jodie Foster in *The Silence of the Lambs*; Bette Midler in *For the Boys*; Susan Sarandon in *Thelma and Louise*
Supp. Actor	Tommy Lee Jones in *JFK*; Harvey Keitel in *Bugsy*; Ben Kingsley in *Bugsy*; Michael Lerner in *Barton Fink*; Jack Palance in *City Slickers*
Supp. Actress	Diane Ladd in *Rambling Rose*; Juliette Lewis in *Cape Fear*; Kate Nelligan in *The Prince of Tides*; Mercedes Ruehl in *The Fisher King*; Jessica Tandy in *Fried Green Tomatoes at the Whistle Stop Cafe*
Direction	John Singleton for *Boyz N The Hood*; Barry Levinson for *Bugsy*; Oliver Stone for *JFK*; Jonathan Demme for *The*

1992

Production	*The Crying Game* (Palace Pictures); *A Few Good Men* (Columbia); *Howards End* (Merchant Ivory/Sony Pictures Classics); *Scent of a Woman* (Universal); *Unforgiven* (Warner Bros.)
Actor	Robert Downey, Jr. in *Chaplin*; Clint Eastwood in *Unforgiven*; Al Pacino in *Scent of a Woman*; Stephen Rea in *The Crying Game*; Denzel Washington in *Malcolm X*
Actress	Catherine Deneuve in *Indochine*; Mary McDonnell in *Passion Fish*; Michelle Pfeiffer in *Love Field*; Susan Sarandon in *Lorenzo's Oil*; Emma Thompson in *Howards End*
Supp. Actor	Jaye Davidson in *The Crying Game*; Gene Hackman in *Unforgiven*; Jack Nicholson in *A Few Good Men*; Al Pacino in *Glengarry Glen Ross*; David Paymer in *Mr. Saturday Night*
Supp. Actress	Judy Davis in *Husbands and Wives*; Joan Plowright in *Enchanted April*; Vanessa Redgrave in *Howards End*; Miranda Richardson in *Damage*; Marisa Tomei in *My Cousin Vinny*
Direction	Neil Jordan for *The Crying Game*; James Ivory for *Howards End*; Robert Altman for *The Player*; Martin Brest for *Scent of a Woman*; Clint Eastwood for *Unforgiven*

Oscar Record-Holders

Who has won the most Oscars in the 65 years of the Academy Awards? This section provides the answers, and a quick check on the performers, directors, writers and craftspeople who have been most honored in each category since the awards were first presented in May, 1929.

FILM

Ben-Hur holds the record for the film with the most Academy Awards, earning 11 Oscars in 1959. It was nominated for 12 but missed out on the best-screenplay award.

Two years later, in 1961, *West Side Story* won 10 awards, putting it one ahead of the three films that have earned nine—*Gone With the Wind* in 1939 (its total included a special achievement award), *Gigi* in 1958 and *The Last Emperor* in 1987.

Six films have, to date, each won eight Academy Awards: *From Here to Eternity* (1953), *On the Waterfront* (1954), *My Fair Lady* (1964), *Cabaret* (1972), *Gandhi* (1982) and *Amadeus* (1984).

PRODUCTION

Darryl F. Zanuck and Sam Spiegel are the only producers to have won the best-picture award on three occasions. Zanuck won for *How Green Was My Valley* (1941), *Gentleman's Agreement* (1947) and *All About Eve* (1951); Spiegel for *On the Waterfront* (1954), *The Bridge on the River Kwai* (1957) and *Lawrence of Arabia* (1962).

DIRECTION

John Ford was named best director on four occasions during his career—for *The Informer*

(1935), *The Grapes of Wrath* (1940), *How Green Was My Valley* (1941) and *The Quiet Man* (1952).

Runners-up: Frank Capra (3) for *It Happened One Night* (1934), *Mr. Deeds Goes to Town* (1936) and *You Can't Take It With You* (1938); and William Wyler (3) for *Mrs. Miniver* (1942), *The Best Years of Our Lives* (1946) and *Ben-Hur* (1959).

ACTING

Katharine Hepburn is the only actress to have won four best-actress awards—for *Morning Glory* (1932/33), *Guess Who's Coming to Dinner* (1967), *The Lion in Winter* (1968) and *On Golden Pond* (1981).

Ingrid Bergman was a triple winner, having won best-actress awards for *Gaslight* (1944) and *Anastasia* (1956) and a supporting Oscar for *Murder on the Orient Express* (1974).

Eleven actresses have earned two awards for acting:

Bette Davis: best actress—*Dangerous* (1935) and *Jezebel* (1938); Olivia de Havilland: best actress—*To Each His Own* (1946) and *The Heiress* (1949); Sally Field: best actress—*Norma Rae* (1979) and *Places in the Heart* (1984); Jane Fonda: best actress—*Klute* (1971) and *Coming Home* (1978); Jodie Foster: best actress—*The Accused* (1988) and *The Silence of the Lambs* (1991); Helen Hayes: best actress—*The Sin of Madelon Claudet* (1931/32) and best supporting actress, *Airport* (1970); Glenda Jackson: best actress—*Women in Love* (1970) and *A Touch of Class* (1973); Vivien Leigh: best actress—*Gone With the Wind* (1939) and *A Streetcar Named Desire* (1951); Luise Rainer: best actress—*The Great Ziegfeld* (1936) and *The Good*

Earth (1937); Maggie Smith: best actress—*The Prime of Miss Jean Brodie* (1969) and best supporting actress, *California Suite* (1978); Meryl Streep: best supporting actress—*Kramer vs. Kramer* (1979) and best actress, *Sophie's Choice* (1982).

No performer has yet won three Oscars in the best-actor category, although five players rank as double winners—Spencer Tracy for *Captains Courageous* (1937) and *Boys' Town* (1938); Fredric March for *Dr. Jekyll and Mr. Hyde* (1931/32) and *The Best Years of Our Lives* (1946); Gary Cooper for *Sergeant York* (1941) and *High Noon* (1952); Marlon Brando for *On the Waterfront* (1954) and *The Godfather* (1972); and Dustin Hoffman for *Kramer vs. Kramer* (1979) and *Rain Man* (1988).

The following actors have also won two Oscars, although their achievement is divided between the major and supporting categories:

Robert De Niro for *The Godfather Part II* (supporting actor, 1974) and *Raging Bull* (actor, 1980); Melvyn Douglas for *Hud* (supporting actor, 1963) and *Being There* (supporting actor, 1979); Gene Hackman for *The French Connection* (actor, 1971) and *Unforgiven* (supporting actor, 1992); Jack Lemmon for *Mister Roberts* (supporting actor, 1955) and *Save the Tiger* (actor, 1973); Jack Nicholson for *One Flew Over the Cuckoo's Nest* (actor, 1975) and *Terms of Endearment* (supporting actor, 1983); Anthony Quinn for *Viva Zapata* (supporting actor, 1952) and *Lust for Life* (supporting actor, 1956); Jason Robards for *All The President's Men* (supporting actor, 1976) and *Julia* (supporting actor, 1977).

In the supporting actor category, Walter Brennan is the only three-time winner. He won in 1936 for *Come and Get It*, in 1938 for *Kentucky* and in 1940 for *The Westerner*.

Shelley Winters—*The Diary of Anne Frank* (1959) and *A Patch of Blue* (1965)—is the only actress to have won more than once as best supporting actress.

SCREENWRITING

Four writers have been triple winners in the screenwriting categories (although Paddy Chayefsky is the only writer to have won for solo screenplays).

Paddy Chayefsky (3)   *Marty* (1955); *The Hospital* (1971); and *Network* (1976).

Billy Wilder (3)   *The Lost Weekend* (1945) with Charles Brackett; *Sunset Boulevard* (1950) with Charles Brackett & D. M. Marshman, Jr.; and *The Apartment* (1960) with I. A. L. Diamond.

Charles Brackett (3)   *The Lost Weekend* (1945) with Billy Wilder; *Sunset Boulevard* (1950) with Billy Wilder and D. M. Marshman, Jr.; and *Titanic* (1953) with Walter Reisch and Richard Breen.

Francis Ford Coppola (3)   *Patton* (1970) with Edmund H. North; *The Godfather* (1972) with Mario Puzo; and *The Godfather Part II* (1974) with Mario Puzo.

CINEMATOGRAPHY

Joseph Ruttenberg and Leon Shamroy both earned four Academy Awards for camerawork during their respective careers at MGM and 20th Century-Fox.

Ruttenberg won for his black and white camerawork on *The Great Waltz* (1938), *Mrs. Miniver* (1942) and *Somebody Up There Likes Me* (1956) and for his color photography of *Gigi* (1958). Shamroy earned all his awards for color photography: *The Black Swan* (1942), *Wilson* (1944), *Leave Her To Heaven* (1945) and *Cleopatra* (1963).

Five cameramen have won three Oscars for photography:

Arthur Miller (3)   *How Green Was My Valley* (1941); *The Song of Bernadette* (1943); and *Anna and the King Of Siam* (1946).

Winton C. Hoch (3) *Joan of Arc* (1948) with Joseph Valentine and William V. Skall; *She Wore a Yellow Ribbon* (1949); and *The Quiet Man* (1952) with Archie Stout.

Robert L. Surtees (3) *King Solomon's Mines* (1950); *The Bad and the Beautiful* (1952); and *Ben-Hur* (1959).

Freddie Young (3) *Lawrence of Arabia* (1962), *Doctor Zhivago* (1965); and *Ryan's Daughter* (1970).

Vittorio Storaro (3) *Apocalypse Now* (1979); *Reds* (1981); and *The Last Emperor* (1987).

ART DIRECTION

Cedric Gibbons goes down as the art director with the most Academy Awards (11) to his name, although during the 1940s and 1950s he worked purely in a supervisory capacity and most of the design work on his films was done by his associates—men such as William Ferrari, Preston Ames, Malcolm Brown and Edward Carfagno.

Gibbons' Oscar wins (all at MGM) were as follows:

The Bridge of San Luis Rey (1928/29); *The Merry Widow* (1934) with Frederic Hope; *Pride and Prejudice* (1940) with Paul Groesse; *Blossoms in the Dust* (1941) with Urie McCleary; *Gaslight* (1944) with William Ferrari; *The Yearling* (1946) with Paul Groesse; *Little Women* (1949) with Paul Groesse; *An American in Paris* (1951) with Preston Ames; *The Bad and the Beautiful* (1952) with Edward Carfagno; *Julius Caesar* (1953) with Edward Carfagno; and *Somebody Up There Likes Me* (1956) with Malcolm F. Brown.

In view of Gibbons' strong reliance on his collaborators, both Richard Day (with seven wins) and Lyle Wheeler (with five) deserve mention.

Richard Day (7) *The Dark Angel* (1935); *Dodsworth* (1936); *How Green Was My Valley* (1941) with Nathan Juran; *This Above All* (1942) with Joseph Wright; *My Gal Sal* (1942) with Joseph Wright; *A Streetcar Named Desire* (1951); and *On the Waterfront* (1954).

Lyle Wheeler (5) *Gone With the Wind* (1939); *Anna and the King of Siam* (1946) with William Darling; *The Robe* (1953) with George W. Davis; *The King and I* (1956) with John DeCuir; and *The Diary of Anne Frank* (1959) with George W. Davis.

COSTUME DESIGN

Since the inception of this category in 1948 over 50 costume designers have earned Academy Awards. Heading the list is Edith Head, with eight Oscars received over 24 years. Irene Sharaff is runner-up with five. Their wins were as follows:

Edith Head (8) *The Heiress* (1949) with Gile Steele; *All About Eve* (1950) with Charles LeMaire; *Samson and Delilah* (1950) with Dorothy Jeakins, Eloise Jenssen, Gile Steele and Gwen Wakeling; *A Place in the Sun* (1951); *Roman Holiday* (1953); *Sabrina* (1954); *The Facts of Life* (1960); with Edward Stevenson; and *The Sting* (1973).

Irene Sharaff (5) *An American in Paris* (1951) with Orry-Kelly and Walter Plunkett; *The King and I* (1956); *West Side Story* (1961); *Cleopatra* (1963) with Vittorio Nino Novarese and Renie; and *Who's Afraid of Virginia Woolf?* (1966).

EDITING

Two editors have each won three Oscars—Ralph Dawson, who earned his three awards at Warner Bros. during the 1930s, and Daniel Mandell, who worked for Goldwyn for many years and also for director Billy Wilder. Their wins:

Ralph Dawson (3)   _A Midsummer Night's Dream_ (1935); _Anthony Adverse_ (1936); and _The Adventures of Robin Hood_ (1938).

Daniel Mandell (3)   _The Pride of the Yankees_ (1942); _The Best Years of Our Lives_ (1946); and _The Apartment_ (1960).

SOUND RECORDING

Top winners are Douglas Shearer for his work on five movies at MGM, and Fred Hynes, who contributed to the sound tracks of several large-scale Hollywood musicals of the late 1950s and early 1960s. Their wins:

Douglas Shearer (5)   _The Big House_ (1929/30); _Naughty Marietta_ (1935); _San Francisco_ (1936); _Strike Up the Band_ (1940); and _The Great Caruso_ (1951).

Fred Hynes (5)   _Oklahoma_ (1955); _South Pacific_ (1958); _The Alamo_ (1960) with Gordon Sawyer; _West Side Story_ (1961) with Gordon Sawyer; and _The Sound of Music_ (1965) with James P. Corcoran.

MUSIC SCORE

John Barry is the only composer to have won four Oscars in the best-original-score category; six composers have each won three awards for original music:*

John Barry (4)   _Born Free_ (1966); _The Lion in Winter_ (1967); _Out of Africa_ (1985); and _Dances With Wolves_ (1990).

---

* _Note:_ Alan Menken has won three additional Oscars for best song ("Under the Sea" in 1989, "Beauty and the Beast" in 1991, and "Whole New World" in 1992); John Barry earned an additional Oscar for the song "Born Free" in 1966; and John Williams won a fourth Academy Award for best scoring adaptation for his work on _Fiddler on the Roof_ (1971).

Max Steiner (3)   _The Informer_ (1935); _Now Voyager_ (1942); and _Since You Went Away_ (1944).

Dimitri Tiomkin (3)   _High Noon_ (1952); _The High and the Mighty_ (1954); and _The Old Man and the Sea_ (1958).

Miklos Rozsa (3)   _Spellbound_ (1945); _A Double Life_ (1947); and _Ben-Hur_ (1959).

John Williams (3)   _Jaws_ (1975); _Star Wars_ (1977); and _E.T. The Extra-Terrestrial_ (1982).

Maurice Jarre (3)   _Lawrence of Arabia_ (1962); _Doctor Zhivago_ (1965); and _A Passage to India_ (1984).

Alan Menken (3)   _The Little Mermaid_ (1989); _Beauty and the Beast_ (1991); _Aladdin_ (1992).

MUSIC ARRANGING, SCORING, ETC.

This is a category that has been referred to under several titles since its inception—best scoring of a musical, best scoring, best adaptation score—but one that has always been reserved for arrangers and composers who have adapted film music not composed by themselves.

The late Alfred Newman of 20th Century-Fox won seven times in this category; Johnny Green and Andre Previn both earned four Oscars for arranging. Their wins are:

Alfred Newman (7)   _Alexander's Ragtime Band_ (1938); _Tin Pan Alley_ (1940); _Mother Wore Tights_ (1947); _With a Song in My Heart_ (1952); _Call Me Madam_ (1953); _The King and I_ (1956) with Ken Darby; and _Camelot_ (1967) with Ken Darby.

Johnny Green (4)   _Easter Parade_ (1948) with Roger Edens; _An American in Paris_ (1951) with Saul Chaplin; _West Side Story_ (1961) with Saul Chaplin, Sid Ramin and Irwin Kostal; and _Oliver!_ (1968).

**Andre Previn (4)** _Gigi_ (1958); _Porgy and Bess_ (1959) with Ken Darby; _Irma La Douce_ (1963); and _My Fair Lady_ (1964).

SONGWRITING

The top composers of Oscar-winning songs? Not Irving Berlin, Cole Porter or Jerome Kern, but Jimmy Van Heusen and Harry Warren—and, more recently, Alan Menken: *

**James Van Heusen (4)** "Swinging on a Star" from _Going My Way_ (1944), lyrics by Johnny Burke; "All The Way" from _The Joker Is Wild_ (1957), lyrics by Sammy Cahn; "High Hopes" from _A Hole in the Head_ (1959), lyrics by Sammy Cahn; and "Call Me Irresponsible" from _Papa's Delicate Condition_ (1963), lyrics by Sammy Cahn.

**Harry Warren (3)** "Lullaby of Broadway" from _Gold Diggers of 1935_ (1935), lyrics by Al Dubin; "You'll Never Know" from _Hello Frisco, Hello_ (1943), lyrics by Mack Gordon; and "On the Atchison, Topeka and Santa Fe" from _The Harvey Girls_ (1946), lyrics by Johnny Mercer.

**Alan Menken (3)** "Under the Sea" from _The Little Mermaid_ (1989), lyrics by Howard Ash-

---

* _Note:_ Jay Livingston and Ray Evans, who wrote both music and lyrics for their songs, received three Oscars during their careers—for "Buttons and Bows" from _The Paleface_ (1948); "Mona Lisa" from _Captain Carey, U.S.A._ (1950); and "Que Sera Sera" from _The Man Who Knew Too Much_ (1956).

man; "Beauty and the Beast" from _Beauty and the Beast_ (1991), lyrics by Howard Ashman; and "Whole New World" from _Aladdin_ (1992), lyrics by Tim Rice.

The top lyricists? No surprise here—Sammy Cahn, Johnny Mercer and Paul Francis Webster:

**Sammy Cahn (4)** "Three Coins in the Fountain" from _Three Coins in the Fountain_ (1954), music by Jule Styne; "All The Way" from _The Joker Is Wild_ (1957), music by James Van Heusen; "High Hopes" from _A Hole in The Head_ (1959), music by James Van Heusen; and "Call Me Irresponsible" from _Papa's Delicate Condition_ (1963) music by James Van Heusen.

**Johnny Mercer (4)** "On the Atchison, Topeka and Santa Fe" from _The Harvey Girls_ (1946), music by Harry Warren; "In the Cool, Cool, Cool of the Evening" from _Here Comes the Groom_ (1951), music by Hoagy Carmichael; "Moon River" from _Breakfast at Tiffanys_ (1961), music by Henry Mancini; and "Days of Wine and Roses" from _Days of Wine and Roses_ (1962), music by Henry Mancini.

**Paul Francis Webster (3)** "Secret Love" from _Calamity Jane_ (1953), music by Sammy Fain; "Love Is a Many Splendored Thing" from _Love Is a Many Splendored Thing_ (1955), music by Sammy Fain; and "The Shadow of Your Smile" from _The Sandpiper_ (1965), music by Johnny Mandel.

APPENDIX 4
Documentary and Short Subjects

The following pages detail all the documentary and short subjects that have won Academy Awards since short films were first honored in 1931/2.

The films are listed in order by year and include a number of minor classics in the short and documentary categories, among them Laurel and Hardy's *The Music Box* (1931/32), the pair's only Oscar success and the film in which they continually haul a piano up and down a long flight of stairs; John Ford's wartime documentaries *Battle of Midway* (1942) and *December 7th* (1943); Disney's true-life adventures *The Living Desert* (1953) and *The Vanishing Prairie* (1954); the Sanders brothers' *A Time Out of War* (1954), a vignette about an interlude in the Civil War; and Richard Williams' 30-minute animated version of Dickens' *A Christmas Carol* (1972).

All of these films are included in the following list, along with Walt Disney's award-winning cartoons of the 1930s, the Tom and Jerry classics of the 1940s and 1950s, and the Oscar-winning cartoons of Bugs Bunny and Mister Magoo.

1931/32

Best Cartoon	*Flowers and Trees* (Disney, UA)
Best Comedy	*The Music Box* (Roach, MGM—Laurel and Hardy)
Best Novelty	*Wrestling Swordfish* (Mack Sennett—Educational)

1932/33

Best Cartoon	*The Three Little Pigs* (Disney, UA)
Best Comedy	*So This Is Harris* (RKO Radio)
Best Novelty	*Krakatoa* (Educational, Three Reel special)

1934

Best Cartoon	*The Tortoise and the Hare* (Disney, UA)
Best Comedy	*La Cucaracha* (RKO Radio Special)
Best Novelty	*City of Wax* (Educational, Battle For Life)

1935

Best Cartoon	*Three Orphan Kittens* (Disney, UA)
Best Comedy	*How to Sleep* (MGM)
Best Novelty	*Wings Over Mt. Everest* (Gaumont British, Educational)

1936

Best Cartoon	*Country Cousin* (Disney, UA)
Best One-Reel Short Subject	*Bored of Education* (Roach, MGM—Our Gang)
Best Two-Reel Short Subject	*The Public Pays* (MGM—Crime Doesn't Pay)
Best Color Short Subject	*Give Me Liberty* (Warner Bros.—Broadway Brevities)

1937

Best Cartoon	*The Old Mill* (Disney, RKO Radio)
Best One-Reel Short Subject	*Private Life of the Gannets* (Educational)

Best Two-Reel
Short Subject

Torture Money (MGM—
Crime Doesn't Pay)

Best Color Short
Subject

Penny Wisdom (MGM—
Pete Smith Specialties)

1938

Best Cartoon

Ferdinand the Bull (Disney,
RKO Radio)

Best One-Reel
Short Subject

That Mothers Might Live
(MGM—Miniature)

Best Two-Reel
Short Subject

Declaration of Independence
(Warner Bros. Historical
Featurette)

1939

Best Cartoon

The Ugly Duckling (Disney,
RKO Radio)

Best One-Reel
Short Subject

Busy Little Bears
(Paramount—Paragraphics)

Best Two-Reel
Short Subject

Sons of Liberty (Warner
Bros. Historical
Featurette)

1940

Best Cartoon

The Milky Way (MGM—
Rudolph Ising Series)

Best One-Reel
Short Subject

Quicker 'N a Wink
(MGM—Pete Smith)

Best Two-Reel
Short Subject

Teddy, The Rough Rider
(Warner Bros. Historical
Featurette)

1941

Best Cartoon

Lend a Paw (Disney, RKO
Radio)

Best One-Reel
Short Subject

Of Pups and Puzzles
(MGM—Passing Parade
Series)

Best Two-Reel
Short Subject

Main Street on the March
(MGM Special)

Best
Documentary

Churchill's Island (Canadian
Film Board, UA)

1942

Best Cartoon

Der Fuehrer's Face (Disney,
RKO Radio)

Best One-Reel
Short Subject

*Speaking of Animals and
Their Families* (Paramount)

Best Two-Reel
Short Subject

Beyond the Line of Duty
(Warner Bros.—Broadway
Brevities)

Best
Documentary

Battle of Midway (U.S.
Navy, 20th Century-Fox)
Kokoda Front Line
(Australian News
Information Bureau)
Moscow Strikes Back
(Artkino—Russian)
Prelude to War (U.S. Army
Special Services)

1943

Best Cartoon

Yankee Doodle Mouse
(MGM, Fred Quimby,
producer)

Best One-Reel
Short Subject

Amphibious Fighters
(Paramount, Grantland
Rice, producer)

Best Two-Reel
Short Subject

Heavenly Music (MGM,
Jerry Bresler and Sam
Coslow, producers)

Best
Documentary
Short Subject

December 7th (U.S. Navy,
Field Photographic
Branch, Office of Strategic
Services)

Best
Documentary
Feature

Desert Victory (British
Ministry of Information)

1944

Best Cartoon

Mouse Trouble (MGM,
Fred Quimby, producer)

Best One-Reel
Short Subject

Who's Who in Animal Land
(Paramount, Jerry
Fairbanks, producer)

Best Two-Reel
Short Subject

I Won't Play (Warner Bros.
Featurette—Gordon
Hollingshead, producer)

Best
Documentary
Short Subject

With the Marines at Tarawa
(U.S. Marine Corps)

Best
Documentary
Feature

The Fighting Lady (20th
Century-Fox and U.S.
Navy)

1945

Best Cartoon — *Quiet Please* (MGM, Fred Quimby, producer)

Best One-Reel Short Subject — *Stairway to Light* (MGM—John Nesbitt Passing Parade, Herbert Moulton, producer)

Best Two-Reel Short Subject — *Star in the Night* (Warner Bros.—Broadway Brevities, Gordon Hollingshead, producer)

Best Documentary Short Subject — *Hitler Lives?* (Warner Bros.)

Best Documentary Feature — *The True Glory* (Governments of Great Britain and U.S.A.)

1946

Best Cartoon — *The Cat Concerto* (MGM, Fred Quimby, producer)

Best One-Reel Short Subject — *Facing Your Danger* (Warner Bros.—Sports Parade, Gordon Hollingshead, producer)

Best Two-Reel Short Subject — *A Boy and His Dog* (Warner Bros. Featurette, Gordon Hollingshead, producer)

Best Documentary Short Subject — *Seeds of Destiny* (U.S. War Department)

Best Documentary Feature — None nominated this year

1947

Best Cartoon — *Tweetie Pie* (Warner Bros., Edward Selzer, producer)

Best One-Reel Short Subject — *Goodbye Miss Turlock* (MGM—John Nesbitt Passing Parade, Herbert Moulton, producer)

Best Two-Reel Short Subject — *Climbing the Matterhorn* (Monogram, Irving Allen, producer)

Best Documentary Short Subject — *First Steps* (United Nations Division of Films and Visual Education)

Best Documentary Feature — *Design for Death* (RKO Radio, Sid Rogell, executive producer; Theron Warth and Richard Fleischer, producers)

1948

Best Cartoon — *The Little Orphan* (MGM, Fred Quimby, producer)

Best One-Reel Short Subject — *Symphony of a City* (20th Century-Fox, Movietone Specialty, Edmund Reek, producer)

Best Two-Reel Short Subject — *Seal Island* (Disney, RKO Radio—True Life Adventure, Walt Disney, producer)

Best Documentary Short Subject — *Toward Independence* (U.S. Army)

Best Documentary Feature — *The Secret Land* (U.S. Navy, MGM, O. O. Dull, producer)

1949

Best Cartoon — *For Scent-imental Reasons* (Warner Bros., Edward Selzer, producer)

Best One-Reel Short Subject — *Aquatic House-Party* (Paramount, Grantland Rice Sportlights, Jack Eaton, producer)

Best Two-Reel Short Subject — *Van Gogh* (Canton-Weiner, Gaston Diehl and Robert Haessens, producers)

Best Documentary Short Subjects — *A Chance to Live* (March of Time, 20th Century-Fox, Richard de Rochemont, producer) *So Much for So Little* (Warner Bros., Edward Selzer, producer)

Best Documentary Feature	*Daybreak in Udi* (British Information Services, Crown Film Unit)

1950

Best Cartoon	*Gerald McBoing-Boing* (UPA, Columbia, Stephen Bosustow, executive producer)
Best One-Reel Short Subject	*Granddad of Races* (Warner Bros.—Sports Parade, Gordon Hollingshead, producer).
Best Two-Reel Short Subject	*Beaver Valley* (Disney, RKO Radio—True Life Adventure, Walt Disney, producer)
Best Documentary Short Subject	*Why Korea?* (20th Century-Fox Movietone, Edmund Reek, producer)
Best Documentary Feature	*The Titan: Story of Michelangelo* (Michelangelo Co., Classics Pictures Inc., Robert Snyder, producer)

1951

Best Cartoon	*Two Mouseketeers* (MGM, Fred Quimby, producer)
Best One-Reel Short Subject	*World of Kids* (Warner Bros.—Vitaphone Novelties, Robert Youngson, producer)
Best Two-Reel Short Subject	*Nature's Half Acre* (Disney, RKO Radio—True Life Adventure, Walt Disney, producer)
Best Documentary Short Subject	*Benjy* (made by Fred Zinnemann with the cooperation of Paramount Pictures Corp. for the Los Angeles Orthopedic Hospital)
Best Documentary Feature	*Kon-Tiki* (Artfilm Prod., RKO Radio—Norwegian—Olle Nordemar, producer)

1952

Best Cartoon	*Johann Mouse* (MGM, Fred Quimby, producer)
Best One-Reel Short Subject	*Light in the Window* (Art Film Prods., 20th Century-Fox, Art Series, Boris Vermont, producer)
Best Two-Reel Short Subject	*Water Birds* (Disney, RKO Radio—True Life Adventure, Walt Disney, producer)
Best Documentary Short Subject	*Neighbors* (National Film Board of Canada, Mayer-Kingsley, Inc. [Canadian], Norman McLaren, producer)
Best Documentary Feature	*The Sea Around Us* (RKO-Radio, Irwin Allen, producer)

1953

Best Cartoon	*Toot, Whistle, Plunk and Boom* (Disney, Buena Vista—Special Music Series, Walt Disney, producer)
Best One-Reel Short Subject	*The Merry Wives of Windsor Overture* (MGM—Overture Series, Johnny Green, producer)
Best Two-Reel Short Subject	*Bear Country* (Disney, RKO Radio—True Life Adventure—Walt Disney, producer)
Best Documentary Short Subject	*The Alaskan Eskimo* (Disney, RKO-Radio, Walt Disney, producer)
Best Documentary Feature	*The Living Desert* (Disney, Buena Vista, Walt Disney, producer)

1954

Best Cartoon	*When Magoo Flew* (UPA, Columbia. Stephen Bosustow, producer)

Best One-Reel Short Subject	*This Mechanical Age* (Warner Bros., Robert Youngson, producer)
Best Two-Reel Short Subject	*A Time Out of War* (Carnival Prods., Denis and Terry Sanders, producers)
Best Documentary Short Subject	*Thursday's Children* (British Information Services—British—World Wide Pictures and Morse Films, producers)
Best Documentary Feature	*The Vanishing Prairie* (Disney, Buena Vista, Walt Disney, producer)

1955

Best Cartoon	*Speedy Gonzales* (Warner Bros., Edward Selzer, producer)
Best One-Reel Short Subject	*Survival City* (20th Century-Fox, Edmund Reek, producer)
Best Two-Reel Short Subject	*The Face of Lincoln* (University of Southern California, Cavalcade Pictures, Wilbur T. Blume, producer)
Best Documenatry Short Subject	*Men Against the Arctic* (Disney, Buena Vista, Walt Disney, producer)
Best Documentary Feature	*Helen Keller in Her Story* (Nancy Hamilton Presentation, Nancy Hamilton, producer)

1956

Best Cartoon	*Mister Magoo's Puddle Jumper* (UPA, Columbia, Stephen Bosustow, producer)
Best One-Reel Short Subject	*Crashing the Water Babies* (Warner Bros., Konstantin Kalser, producer)
Best Two-Reel Short Subject	*The Bespoke Overcoat* (Romulus Films, George K. Arthur, producer)

Best Documentary Short Subject	*The True Story of the Civil War* (Camera Eye Pictures, Louis Clyde Stoumen, producer)
Best Documentary Feature	*The Silent World* (Filmad-F.S.J.Y.C. Columbia-French—Jacques-Yves Cousteau, producer)

1957

Best Cartoon	*Birds Anonymous* (Warner Bros., Edward Selzer, producer)
Best Live Action Short Subject	*The Wetback Hound* (Disney, Buena Vista, Larry Lansburgh, producer)
Best Documentary Short Subject	No nominations or award this year
Best Documentary Feature	*Albert Schweitzer* (Hill and Anderson Prod., Louis de Rochemont Associates, Jerome Hill, producer)

1958

Best Cartoon	*Knighty Knight Bugs* (Warner Bros., John W. Burton, producer)
Best Live Action Short Subject	*Grand Canyon* (Walt Disney Prods., Buena Vista, Walt Disney, producer)
Best Documentary Short Subject	*Ama Girls* (Disney Prods., Buena Vista, Ben Sharpsteen, producer)
Best Documentary Feature	*White Wilderness* (Disney Prods., Buena Vista, Ben Sharpsteen, producer)

1959

Best Cartoon	*Moonbird* (Storyboard-Harrison, John Hubley, producer)
Best Live Action Short Subject	*The Golden Fish* (Les Requins Associés,

Columbia [French],
Jacques-Yves Cousteau,
producer)

Best
Documentary
Short Subject

Glass (Netherlands
Government, George K.
Arthur—Go Pictures—
The Netherlands—Bert
Haanstra, producer)

Best
Documentary
Feature

Serengeti Shall Not Die
(Okapia Film Prods.,
Transocean Film—
German—Bernhard
Grzimek, producer)

1960

Best Cartoon
Munro (Rembrandt Films,
Film Representations,
William L. Snyder,
producer)

Best Live Action
Short Subject
Day of the Painter (Little
Movies, Kingsley-Union
Films, Ezra R. Baker,
producer)

Best
Documentary
Short Subject
Giuseppina (Schoenfeld
Films—British—James
Hill, producer)

Best
Documentary
Feature
*The Horse with the Flying
Tail* (Disney, Buena Vista,
Larry Lansburgh,
producer)

1961

Best Cartoon
Ersatz (The Substitute)
(Zagreb Film, Herts-Lion
International Corp.)

Best Live Action
Short Subject
Seawards the Great Ships
(Templar Film Studios,
Schoenfeld Films)

Best
Documentary
Short Subject
Project Hope (Klaeger
Films, Frank P. Bibas,
producer)

Best
Documentary
Feature
*The Sky Above and Mud
Below* (Rank Films
[French], Arthur Cohn
and Rene Lafuite,
producers)

1962

Best Cartoon
The Hole (Storyboard Inc.,
Brandon Films, John and
Faith Hubley, producers)

Best Live Action
Short Subject
Happy Anniversary
(Atlantic Pictures
[French], Pierre Etaix and
J. C. Carriere, producers)

Best
Documentary
Short Subject
Dylan Thomas (TWW Ltd.,
Janus Films—Welsh—Jack
Howells, producer)

Best
Documentary
Feature
Black Fox (Image Prods.,
Heritage Films, Louis
Clyde Stoumen, producer)

1963

Best Cartoon
The Critic (Pintoff-
Crossbow Prods.,
Columbia, Ernest Pintoff,
producer)

Best Live Action
Short Subject
*An Occurrence at Owl Creek
Bridge* (Janus Films, Paul
de Roubaix and Marcel
Ichac, producers)

Best
Documentary
Short Subject
Chagall (Auerbach-Flag
Films, Simon Schiffrin,
producer)

Best
Documentary
Feature
*Robert Frost: A Lover's
Quarrel with the World*
(WGBH Educational
Foundation, Robert
Hughes, producer)

1964

Best Cartoon
The Pink Phink (Mirisch-
Geoffrey, UA, David H.
DePatie and Friz Freleng,
producers)

Best Live Action
Short Subject
Casals Conducts: 1964
(Thalia Films, Beckman
Film Corp., Edward
Schreiber, producer)

Best
Documentary
Short Subject
Nine from Little Rock (U.S.
Information Agency,
Guggenheim Productions)

Best
Documentary
Feature

World Without Sun
(Columbia, Jacques-Yves
Cousteau, producer)

1965

Best Cartoon

The Dot and the Line
(MGM; Chuck Jones and
Les Goldman, producers)

Best Live Action
Short Subject

The Chicken (Pathe
Contemporary Films—
French—Claude Berri,
producer)

Best
Documentary
Short Subject

To Be Alive! (Johnson
Wax, Francis Thompson,
Inc., producer)

Best
Documentary
Feature

The Eleanor Roosevelt Story
(American International,
Sidney Glazier, producer)

1966

Best Cartoon

*Herb Alpert and The
Tijuana Brass Double
Feature* (Paramount, John
and Faith Hubley,
producers)

Best Live Action
Short Subject

Wild Wings (British
Transport Films, Manson
Distributing, Edgar
Anstey, producer)

Best
Documentary
Short Subject

A Year Toward Tomorrow
(Sun Dial Films for Office
of Economic Opportunity,
Edmond A. Levy,
producer)

Best
Documentary
Feature

The War Game (BBC Prod.
for the British Film
Institute, Pathe
Contemporary Films,
Peter Watkins, producer)

1967

Best Cartoon

The Box (Brandon Films,
Fred Wolf, producer)

Best Live Action
Short Subject

A Place to Stand (T.D.F.
Prod. for Ontario Dept. of
Economics and

Development, Columbia,
Christopher Chapman,
producer)

Best
Documentary
Short Subject

The Redwoods (King Screen
Prods., Mark Harris and
Trevor Greenwood,
producers)

Best
Documentary
Feature

The Anderson Platoon
(French Broadcasting
System, Pierre
Schoendoerffer, producer)

1968

Best Cartoon

*Winnie the Pooh and the
Blustery Day* (Disney,
Buena Vista, Walt
Disney, producer)

Best Live Action
Short Subject

Robert Kennedy Remembered
(Guggenheim Prods.,
National General, Charles
Guggenheim, producer)

Best
Documentary
Short Subject

Why Man Creates (Saul
Bass and Associates, Saul
Bass, producer)

Best
Documentary
Feature

Journey Into Self (Western
Behavioral Sciences
Institute, Bill McGraw,
producer)

1969

Best Cartoon

It's Tough to Be a Bird
(Disney, Buena Vista,
Ward Kimball, producer)

Best Live Action
Short Subject

The Magic Machines (Fly-
By-Night Prods., Manson
Distributing, Joan Keller
Stern, producer)

Best
Documentary
Short Subject

Czechoslovakia 1968
(Sanders-Fresco Film
Makers for U.S.
Information Agency,
Denis Sanders and Robert
M. Fresco, producers)

Best
Documentary
Feature

*Arthur Rubinstein—The
Love of Life* (Midem, Prod.
Bernard Chevry,
producer)

1970

Best Cartoon   *Is It Always Right to Be Right?* (Stephen Bosustow Prods., Schoenfeld Films, Nick Bosustow, producer)

Best Live Action Short Subject   *The Resurrection of Broncho Billy* (University Of Southern California, Dept. Of Cinema, Universal, John Longenecker, producer)

Best Documentary Short Subject   *Interviews with My Lai Veterans* (Laser Film Corp., Joseph Strick, producer)

Best Documentary Feature   *Woodstock* (Wadleigh-Maurice Warner Bros., Bob Maurice, producer)

1971

Best Animated Short Subject   *The Crunch Bird* (Maxwell-Petok-Petrovich Prods., Regency Films, Ted Perok, producer)

Best Live Action Short Subject   *Sentinels of Silence* (Producciones Concord, Paramount, Manuel Arango and Robert Amram, producers)

Best Documentary Short Subject   *Sentinels of Silence* (Producciones Concord, Paramount, Manuel Arango and Robert Amram, producers)

Best Documentary Feature   *The Hellstrom Chronicle* (David L. Wolper, Cinema V, Walon Green, producer)

1972

Best Animated Short Subject   *A Christmas Carol* (American Broadcasting Company Film Services, Richard Williams, producer)

Best Live Action   *Norman Rockwell's World*

Short Subject   *. . . An American Dream* (Concepts Unlimited, Columbia, Richard Barclay, producer)

Best Documentary Short Subject   *This Tiny World* (A Charles Huguenot van der Linden Production, Charles and Martina Huguenot van der Linden, producers)

Best Documentary Feature   *Marjoe* (Cinema X, Cinema 5, Ltd., Howard Smith and Sarah Kernochan, producers)

1973

Best Animated Short Subject   *Frank Film* (Frank Mouris Production, Frank Mouris, producer)

Best Live Action Short Subject   *The Bolero* (Allan Miller Production, Allan Miller and William Fertik, producers)

Best Documentary Short Subject   *Princeton: A Search for Answers* (Krainin-Sage Prods., Julian Krainin and DeWitt L. Sage, Jr., producers)

Best Documentary Feature   *The Great American Cowboy* (Merrill-Rodeo Film Prods., Kieth Merrill, producer)

1974

Best Animated Short Film   *Closed Mondays* (Lighthouse Productions, Will Vinton and Bob Gardiner, producers)

Best Live Action Short Film   *One-Eyed Men Are Kings* (C.A.P.A.C. Productions [Paris], Paul Claudon and Edmond Sechan, producers)

Best Documentary Short Subject   *Don't* (RA Films, Robin Lehman, producer)

Best
Documentary
Feature
Hearts and Minds
(Touchstone-Audjeff-BBS
Prod., Zuker/Jaglom-
Rainbow Pictures, Peter
Davis and Bert Schneider,
producers)

1975

Best Animated
Short Film
Great (Grantstern, British
Lion Films Ltd., Bob
Godfrey, producer)

Best Live Action
Short Film
Angel and Big Joe (Salzman
Productions, Bert
Salzman, producer)

Best
Documentary
Short Subject
The End of the Game (Opus
Films Ltd., Claire Wilbur
and Robin Lehman,
producers)

Best
Documentary
Feature
*The Man Who Skied Down
Everest* (Crawley Films, F.
R. Crawley, James Hager
and Dale Hartleben,
producers)

1976

Best Animated
Short Film
Leisure (Film Australia,
Suzanne Baker, producer)

Best Live Action
Short Film
In the Region of Ice
(American Film Institute,
Andre Guttfreund and
Peter Werner, producers)

Best
Documentary
Short Subject
Number Our Days
(Community Television of
Southern California,
Lynne Littman, producer)

Best
Documentary
Feature
Harlan County, U.S.A.
(Cabin Creek Films,
Barbara Kopple, producer)

1977

Best Animated
Short Film
Sand Castle (National Film
Board of Canada, Co
Hoedeman, producer)

Best Live Action
Short Film
I'll Find a Way (National
Film Board of Canada,

Beverly Shaffer and Yuki
Yoshida, producers)

Best
Documentary
Short Subject
Gravity Is My Enemy
(Joseph Production, John
Joseph and Jan Stussy,
producers)

Best
Documentary
Feature
*Who Are the Debolts? And
Where Did They Get
Nineteen Kids?* (Korty
Films/Charles M. Schulz,
Sanrio Films, John Korty,
Dan McCann and Warren
L. Lockhart, producers)

1978

Best Animated
Short Film
Special Delivery (National
Film Board of Canada,
Eunice Macaulay and John
Weldon, producers)

Best Live Action
Short Film
Teenage Father (New
Visions Inc. for the
Children's Home Society
of California, Taylor
Hackford, producer)

Best
Documentary
Short Subject
*The Flight of the Gossamer
Condor* (A Shedd
Production, Jacqueline
Phillips Shedd, producer)

Best
Documentary
Feature
Scared Straight (A Golden
West Television
Production, Arnold
Shapiro, producer)

1979

Best Animated
Short Film
Every Child (National Film
Board of Canada, Derek
Lambe, producer)

Best Live Action
Short Film
Board and Care (Ron Ellis
Films, Sarah Pillsburg,
Ron Ellis, producers)

Best
Documentary
Short Subject
*Paul Robeson: Tribute to an
Artist* (Janus Films Inc.)

Best
Documentary
Feature
Best Boy (Only Child
Motion Picture Inc., Ira
Wohl, producer,
Entertainment Marketing)

1980

Best Animated
Short Film
The Fly (Pannonia Film, Budapest, Ferenc Rofusz, producer)

Best Live Action
Short Film
The Dollar Bottom (Rocking Horse Films Ltd., Paramount, Lloyd Phillips, producer)

Best
Documentary
Short Subject
Karl Hess: Toward Liberty (Halle/Ladue Inc., Peter W. Ladue and Roland Halle, producers)

Best
Documentary
Feature
From Mao to Mozart: Isaac Stern in China (The Hopewell Foundation, Murray Lerner, producer)

1981

Best Animated
Short Film
Crac (Societe Radio-Canada, Frederic Back, producer)

Best Live Action
Short Film
Close Harmony (Noble Enterprise, Nigel Noble, producer)

Best
Documentary
Short Subject
Violet (The American Film Institute, Paul Kemp and Shelley Levinson, producers)

Best
Documentary
Feature
Genocide (Arnold Schwartzman Productions, Inc., Arnold Schwartzman and Rabbi Marvin Hier, producers)

1982

Best Animated
Short Film
Tango (Film Polski, Zbigniew Rybczynski, producer)

Best Live Action
Short Film
A Shocking Accident (Flamingo Pictures Ltd., Christine Oestreicher, producer)

Best
Documentary
Short Subject
If You Love This Planet (National Film Board of Canada, Edward Le Lorraine and Terri Nash, producers)

Best
Documentary
Feature
Just Another Missing Kid (Canadian Broadcasting Corporation, John Zaritsky, producer)

1983

Best Animated
Short Film
Sundae in New York (A Motionpicker Production, Jimmy Picker, producer)

Best Live Action
Short Film
Boys and Girls (An Atlantis Films Ltd. Production, Janice L. Platt, producer)

Best
Documentary
Short Subject
Flamenco at 5:15 (A National Film Board of Canada Production, Cynthia Scott and Adam Symansky, producers)

Best
Documentary
Feature
He Makes Me Feel Like Dancin' (An Edgar J. Scherick Associates Production, Emile Ardolino, producer)

1984

Best Animated
Short Film
Charade (A Sheridan College Production, Jon Minnis, producer)

Best Live Action
Short Film
Up (Pyramid Films, Mike Hoover, producer)

Best
Documentary
Short Subject
The Stone Carvers (Paul Wagner Productions, Marjorie Hunt and Paul Wagner, producers)

Best
Documentary
Feature
The Times of Harvey Milk (Black Sand Educational Productions, Inc., Robert Epstein and Richard Schmiechen, producers)

1985

Best Animated
Short Film
Anna and Bella (The Netherlands, Cilia Van Dijk, producer)

Best Live Action
Short Film
Molly's Pilgrim (Phoenix Films, Jeff Brown and Chris Pelzer, producers)

Best Documentary Short Subject — *Witness to War: Dr. Charlie Clements* (A Skylight Picture Production, David Goodman, producer)

Best Documentary Feature — *Broken Rainbow* (An Earthworks Film Production, Maria Florio and Victoria Mudd, Producers)

Best Documentary Short Subject — *Young at Heart* (A Sue Marx Films, Inc., Production, Sue Marx and Pamela Conn, producers)

Best Documentary Feature — *The Ten-Year Lunch: The Wit and Legend of the Algonquin Round Table* (An Aviva Films Production, Aviva Slesin, producer)

1986

Best Animated Short Film — *A Greek Tragedy* (CineTe pvba, Linda Van Tulden and Willem Thijssen, producers)

Best Live Action Short Film — *Precious Images* (A Calliope Films, Inc., Chuck Workman, producer)

Best Documentary Short Subject — *Women—For America, For the World* (Educational Film and Video Project, Vivienne Verdon-Roe, producer)

Best Documentary Feature — *Artie Shaw: Time Is All You've Got* (A Bridge Film Production, Brigette Berman, producer)

and

Down And Out In America (A Joseph Feury Production, Joseph Feury and Milton Justice, producers)

1987

Best Animated Short Film — *The Man Who Planted Trees* (Societé Radio—Canada/Canadian Broadcasting Corporation, Frederic Back, producer)

Best Live Action Short Film — *Ray's Male Heterosexual Dance Hall* (Chanticleer Films, Jonathan Sanger and Jana Sue Memel, producers)

1988

Best Animated Short Film — *Tin Toy* (Pixar, John Lasseter, producer)

Best Live Action Short Film — *The Appointments of Dennis Jennings* (Schooner Productions, Inc., Dean Parisot and Steven Wright, producers)

Best Documentary Short Subject — *You Don't Have to Die* (A Tiger Rose Production in association with Filmworks Inc., William Guttentag and Malcolm Clarke, producers)

Best Documentary Feature — *Hotel Terminus: The Life and Times of Klaus Barbie* (The Memory Pictures Co Production, Marcel Ophuls, producer)

1989

Best Animated Short Film — *Balance* (A Lauenstein Production, Christoph and Wolfgang Lauenstein, producers)

Best Live Action Short Film — *Work Experience* (North Inch Production, Ltd., James Hendrie, producer)

Best Documentary Short Subject — *The Johnstown Flood* (Guggenheim Productions, Inc. Production, Charles Guggenheim, producer)

Best Documentary Feature — *Common Threads: Stories from the Quilt* (Telling Pictures and The Couturie

Co Production, Robert Epstein and Bill Couturie, producers)

1990

Best Animated Short Film — *Creature Comforts* (Aardman Animations Ltd. Production, Nick Park, producer)

Best Live Action Short Film — *The Lunch Date* (Adam Davidson Productions, Adam Davidson, producer)

Best Documentary Short Subject — *Days of Waiting* (Mouchette Films Production, Steven Okazaki, producer)

Best Documentary Feature — *American Dream* (A Cabin Creek Production, Barbara Kopple and Arthur Cohn, producers)

1991

Best Animated Short Film — *Manipulation* (Tandem Films Production, Daniel Greaves, producer)

Best Live Action Short Film — *Session Man* (Chanticleer Films Production, Seth Winston and Rob Fried, producers)

Best Documentary Short Subject — *Deadly Deception: General Electric, Nuclear Weapons and Our Environment* (Women's Educational Media Inc. Production, Debra Chasnoff, producer)

Best Documentary Feature — *In the Shadow of the Stars* (Light-Saraf Films Production, Allie Light and Irving Saraf, producers)

1992

Best Animated Short Film — *Mona Lisa Descending a Staircase* (A Joan C. Gratz Production, Joan Gratz, producer)

Best Live Action Short Film — *Omnibus* (Lazennec tout court/Le CRRAV production, Sam Karmann, producer)

Best Documentary Short Subject — *Educating Peter* (State of the Art, Inc., Production, Thomas C. Goodwin and Gerardine Wurzburg, producers)

Best Documentary Feature — *The Panama Deception* (Empowerment Project Production, Barbara Trent and David Kasper, producers)

APPENDIX 5
Oscar Winners at the Box Office

Oscar wins and best-picture nominations have frequently meant extra revenue at the box office. In the 1950s a film winning the best-picture award would earn something like an extra $4 million. Today, that figure is in excess of $20 million and rising. The award is especially advantageous if the best picture has been in release for only three or four months when the Oscars are announced and its main financial life lies ahead of it.

All films that have been up for best picture (and there are nearly 400 of them) appear in the following list in alphabetical order. Directors and years of release are included in parenthesis after the movie's title.

If a picture earned more than $3 million, the amount is shown in the right-hand column. If no figure is shown it means that the film in question did not reach the $3 million mark—the figure quoted by *Variety* as being the starting point for the listings of all-time box-office/rental champions. An asterisk means the film was named best of its respective year.

All figures quoted are from *Variety's* list of all-time rental champs and apply to the U.S. and Canadian markets. To provide a yardstick with which to measure a film's box-office success I have compiled the following table, which may prove a useful indicator. It illustrates the average take of the top 10 films over a five-year period from the 1940s to the present.

Average box-office takes of the top 10 films:

Five-year period	
1940–44	6.8 million
1945–49	6.3 million
1950–54	7.0 million
1955–59	10.3 million
1960–64	13.0 million
1965–69	19.3 million
1970–74	27.9 million
1975–79	36.8 million
1980–84	56.7 million
1985–89	56.0 million
Early 1990s	69.0 million

The Accidental Tourist (Kasdan, 1988)	$15,900,000
The Adventures of Robin Hood (Curtiz/ Keighley, 1938)	
Airport (Seaton, 1970)	45,220,118
The Alamo (Wayne, 1960)	7,918,776
Alexander's Ragtime Band (King, 1938)	
Alfie (Gilbert, 1966)	8,500,000
Alibi (West, 1928/29)	
Alice Adams (Stevens, 1935)	
*All About Eve (Mankiewicz, 1950)	3,100,000
*All Quiet on the Western Front (Milestone, 1929/30)	
All That Jazz (Fosse, 1979)	20,030,000
*All the King's Men (Rossen, 1949)	
All the President's Men (Pakula, 1976)	30,000,000
All This and Heaven Too (Litvak, 1940)	
*Amadeus (Forman, 1984)	23,034,449
America, America (Kazan, 1963)	
American Graffiti (Lucas, 1973)	55,128,175
*An American in Paris (Minnelli, 1951)	4,212,776
Anatomy of a Murder (Preminger, 1959)	5,500,000
Anchors Aweigh (Sidney, 1945)	4,778,679
Anne of the Thousand Days (Jarrott, 1969)	5,876,068
*Annie Hall (Woody Allen, 1977)	19,002,366
Anthony Adverse (LeRoy, 1936)	
*The Apartment (Wilder, 1960)	6,680,036
Apocalypse Now (Coppola, 1979)	37,980,163

*Around the World in 80 Days (Anderson, 1956)	23,120,000	
Arrowsmith (Ford, 1931/32)		
Atlantic City (Malle, 1981)	5,000,000	
Auntie Mame (DaCosta, 1958)	9,300,000	
Awakenings (Marshall, 1990)	23,240,000	
The Awful Truth (McCarey, 1937)		
Bad Girl (Borzage, 1931/32)		
The Barretts of Wimpole Street (Franklin, 1934)		
Barry Lyndon (Kubrick, 1975)	9,200,000	
Battleground (Wellman, 1949)	5,051,143	
Beauty and the Beast (Animated, 1991)	69,415,000	
Becket (Glenville, 1964)	5,000,000	
The Bells of St. Mary's (McCarey, 1945)	8,000,000	
*Ben-Hur (Wyler, 1959)	36,992,088	
*The Best Years of Our Lives (Wyler, 1946)	11,300,000	
The Big Chill (Kasdan, 1983)	24,060,000	
The Big House (Hill, 1929/30)		
The Bishop's Wife (Koster, 1947)	3,000,000	
Blossoms in the Dust (LeRoy, 1941)		
Bonnie and Clyde (Penn, 1967)	22,800,000	
Born on the Fourth of July (Stone, 1989)	36,803,148	
Born Yesterday (Cukor, 1950)	4,115,000	
Bound for Glory (Ashby, 1976)		
Boys' Town (Taurog, 1938)	3,000,000	
Breaking Away (Yates, 1979)	10,300,000	
*The Bridge on the River Kwai (Lean, 1957)	17,195,000	
Broadcast News (James L. Brooks, 1987)	24,900,000	
*The Broadway Melody (Beaumont, 1928/29)	3,000,000	
The Broadway Melody of 1936 (Del Ruth, 1935)		
Bugsy (Levinson, 1991)	21,000,000	
Butch Cassidy and the Sundance Kid (Roy Hill)	45,953,000	
Cabaret (Fosse, 1972)	20,250,000	
The Caine Mutiny (Dmytyk, 1954)	8,700,000	
Captain Blood (Curtiz, 1935)		
Captains Courageous (Fleming, 1937)		
*Casablanca (Curtiz, 1943)	4,750,000	
Cat on a Hot Tin Roof (Brooks, 1958)	8,785,162	
*Cavalcade (Lloyd, 1932/33)		
The Champ (King Vidor, 1931/32)		

*Chariots of Fire (Hudson, 1981)	30,600,000
Children of a Lesser God (Haines, 1986)	12,056,608
Chinatown (Polanski, 1974)	12,400,000
*Cimarron (Ruggles, 1930/31)	
The Citadel (King Vidor, 1938)	
Citizen Kane (Welles, 1941)	
Cleopatra (DeMille, 1934)	
Cleopatra (Mankiewicz, 1963)	26,000,000
A Clockwork Orange (Kubrick, 1971)	17,000,000
Coal Miner's Daughter (Apted, 1980)	35,030,225
The Color Purple (Spielberg, 1985)	49,800,000
Coming Home (Ashby, 78)	13,470,508
The Conversation (Coppola, 1974)	
The Country Girl (Seaton, 1954)	6,500,000
Cries and Whispers (Bergman, 1973)	3,500,000
Crossfire (Dmytryk, 1947)	3,000,000
The Crying Game (Jordan, 1992)	18,500,000
*Dances with Wolves (Costner, 1990)	81,537,971
Dangerous Liaisons (Frears, 1988)	15,500,000
Dark Victory (Goudling, 1939)	
Darling (Schlesinger, 1965)	3,600,000
David Copperfield (Cukor, 1935)	
Dead End (Wyler, 1937)	
Dead Poets Society (Weir, 1989)	48,427,506
Decision Before Dawn (Litvak, 1951)	
*The Deer Hunter (Cimino, 1978)	27,436,325
The Defiant Ones (Kramer, 1958)	
Deliverance (Boorman, 1972)	22,600,000
The Diary of Anne Frank (Stevens, 1959)	
Disraeli (Green, 1929/30)	
The Divorcee (Leonard, 1929/30)	
Doctor Dolittle (Fleischer, 1967)	6,215,000
Doctor Zhivago (Lean, 1965)	47,253,762
Dodsworth (Wyler, 1936)	
Dog Day Afternoon (Lumet, 1975)	22,500,000
Double Indemnity (Wilder, 1944)	
The Dresser (Yates, 1983)	
*Driving Miss Daisy (Beresford, 1989)	50,500,000
Dr. Strangelove (Kubrick, 1964)	5,000,000
East Lynne (Lloyd, 1930/31)	
The Elephant Man (Lynch, 1980)	12,010,000
Elmer Gantry (Brooks, 1960)	4,623,858
The Emigrants (Troell, 1972)	
E.T. The Extra-Terrestrial (Spielberg, 1982)	228,618,939
The Exorcist (Friedkin, 1973)	89,000,000

Fanny (Logan, 1961)	4,500,000
A Farewell to Arms (Borzage, 1932/33)	
Fatal Attraction (Lyne, 1987)	70,000,000
Father of the Bride (Minnelli, 1950)	4,054,405
A Few Good Men (Reiner, 1992)	67,000,000
Fiddler on the Roof (Jewison, 1971)	38,260,954
Field of Dreams (Robinson, 1989)	30,531,165
Five Easy Pieces (Rafelson, 1970)	8,900,000
Five Star Final (LeRoy, 1931/32)	
Flirtation Walk (Borzage, 1934)	
Foreign Correspondent (Hitchcock, 1940)	
Forty-Second Street (Bacon, 1932/33)	
For Whom the Bell Tolls (Wood, 1943)	7,100,000
Four Daughters (Curtiz, 1938)	
*The French Connection (Friedkin, 1971)	26,315,000
Friendly Persuasion (Wyler, 1956)	5,050,000
*From Here to Eternity (Zinnemann, 1953)	12,200,000
The Front Page (Milestone, 1930/31)	
Funny Girl (Wyler, 1968)	26,325,000
*Gandhi (Attenborough, 1982)	24,970,000
Gaslight (Cukor, 1944)	3,000,000
The Gay Divorcee (Sandrich, 1934)	
*Gentleman's Agreement (Kazan, 1947)	3,900,000
Ghost (Zucker, 1990)	98,200,000
Giant (Stevens, 1956)	14,000,000
*Gigi (Minnelli, 1958)	7,321,423
*The Godfather (Coppola, 1972)	86,275,000
*The Godfather Part II (Coppola, 1974)	30,673,000
The Godfather III (Coppola, 1990)	38,000,000
*Going My Way (McCarey, 1944)	6,500,000
*Gone with the Wind (Fleming, 1939)	79,375,077
The Goodbye Girl (Ross, 1977)	41,839,170
The Good Earth (Franklin, 1937)	
Goodfellas (Scorsese, 1990)	20,500,000
The Graduate (Nichols, 1967)	44,090,729
La Grande Illusion (Renoir, 1938)	
*Grand Hotel (Goulding, 1931/32)	
The Grapes of Wrath (Ford, 1940)	
The Great Dictator (Chaplin, 1940)	3,500,000
*The Greatest Show on Earth (DeMille, 1952)	14,000,000
Great Expectations (Lean, 1947)	
*The Great Ziegfeld (Leonard, 1936)	3,000,000
Guess Who's Coming to Dinner (Kramer, 1967)	25,500,000
The Guns of Navarone (Thompson, 1961)	13,000,000

*Hamlet (Olivier, 1948)	3,400,000
Hannah and Her Sisters (Woody Allen, 1986)	18,196,010
Heaven Can Wait (Lubitsch, 1943)	
Heaven Can Wait (Beatty/Henry, 1978)	49,400,000
The Heiress (Wyler, 1949)	
Hello, Dolly! (Kelly, 1969)	15,200,000
Henry V (Olivier, 1946)	
Here Comes Mr. Jordan (Hall, 1941)	
Here Comes the Navy (Bacon, 1934)	
High Noon (Zinnemann, 1952)	3,400,000
Hold Back the Dawn (Leisen, 1941)	
Hollywood Revue (Reisner, 1928/29)	
Hope and Glory (Boorman, 1987)	4,240,000
House of Rothschild (Werker, 1934)	
Howards End (Ivory, 1992)	11,500,000
*How Green Was My Valley (Ford, 1941)	
How the West Was Won (Ford, Hathaway, Marshall, 1963)	20,932,883
The Human Comedy (Brown, 1943)	
The Hustler (Rossen, 1961)	3,100,000
I Am a Fugitive from a Chain Gang (LeRoy, 1932/33)	
Imitation of Life (Stahl, 1934)	
The Informer (Ford, 1935)	
In Old Arizona (Walsh, 1928/29)	
In Old Chicago (Henry King, 1937)	
*In the Heat of the Night (Jewison, 1967)	10,974,028
The Invaders (Powell, 1942)	
In Which We Serve (Coward/Lean, 1943)	
*It Happened One Night (Capra, 1934)	
It's a Wonderful Life (Capra, 1946)	3,300,000
Ivanhoe (Thorpe, 1952)	6,258,000
Jaws (Spielberg, 1975)	129,549,325
Jezebel (Wyler, 1938)	
JFK (Stone, 1991)	34,000,000
Johnny Belinda (Negulesco, 1948)	4,100,000
Judgment at Nuremberg (Kramer, 1961)	3,900,000
Julia (Zinnemann, 1977)	13,055,000
Julius Caesar (Mankiewicz, 1953)	
The Killing Fields (Joffe, 1984)	15,900,000
The King and I (Walter Lang, 1956)	8,500,000
King Solomon's Mines (Bennett/Marton, 1950)	

King's Row (Wood, 1942)		
Kiss of the Spider Woman (Babenco, 1985)	6,376,000	
Kitty Foyle (Wood, 1940)		
*Kramer vs. Kramer (Benton, 1979)	59,986,335	
Lady for a Day (Capra, 1932/33)		
The Last Command (von Sternberg, 1927/28)		
*The Last Emperor (Bertolucci, 1987)	18,800,000	
The Last Picture Show (Bogdanovich, 1971)	13,110,000	
*Lawrence of Arabia (Lean, 1962)	20,310,000	
Lenny (Fosse, 1974)	11,622,371	
Les Miserables (Boleslawski, 1935)		
The Letter (Wyler, 1940)		
A Letter to Three Wives (Mankiewicz, 1949)		
Libeled Lady (Conway, 1936)		
*The Life of Emile Zola (Dieterle, 1937)		
Lilies of the Field (Nelson, 1963)		
The Lion in Winter (Harvey, 1968)	10,005,707	
The Little Foxes (Wyler, 1941)		
Little Women (Cukor, 1932/33)		
Lives of a Bengal Lancer (Hathaway, 1935)		
The Longest Day (Annakin, Marton, Wicki, 1962)	17,600,000	
The Long Voyage Home (Ford, 1940)		
Lost Horizon (Capra, 1937)	3,500,000	
*The Lost Weekend (Wilder, 1945)	4,300,000	
Love Affair (McCarey, 1939)		
Love Is a Many Splendored Thing (Henry King, 1955)	4,000,000	
The Love Parade (Lubitsch, 1929/30)		
Love Story (Hiller, 1970)	48,700,000	
Madame Curie (LeRoy, 1943)	3,500,000	
The Magnificent Ambersons (Welles, 1941)		
The Maltese Falcon (Huston, 1941)		
*A Man for All Seasons (Zinnemann, 1966)	12,750,000	
*Marty (Delbert Mann, 1955)		
Mary Poppins (Stevenson, 1964)	45,000,000	
M*A*S*H (Altman, 1970)	36,720,000	
*Midnight Cowboy (Schlesinger, 1969)	20,499,282	
Midnight Express (Parker, 1978)	15,065,000	
A Midsummer's Night's Dream (Reinhardt/Dieterle, 1935)		

Mildred Pierce (Curtiz, 1945)	3,483,000	
Miracle on 34th Street (Seaton, 1947)	3,100,000	
Missing (Costa-Gavras, 1982)	7,884,069	
The Mission (Joffe, 1986)	8,300,000	
Mississippi Burning (Parker, 1988)	14,716,129	
Mister Roberts (Ford/LeRoy, 1955)	8,500,000	
Moonstruck (Jewison, 1987)	34,393,000	
The More the Merrier (Stevens, 1943)		
Moulin Rouge (Huston, 1952)	4,251,914	
Mr. Deeds Goes to Town (Capra, 1936)		
*Mrs. Miniver (Wyler, 1942)	5,390,009	
Mr. Smith Goes to Washington (Capra, 1939)	3,500,000	
The Music Man (DaCosta, 1962)	8,100,000	
*Mutiny on the Bounty (Lloyd, 1935)		
Mutiny on the Bounty (Milestone, 1962)	7,409,783	
*My Fair Lady (Cukor, 1964)	34,000,000	
My Left Foot (Sheridan, 1989)	7,000,000	
Nashville (Altman, 1975)	8,744,000	
Naughty Marietta (Van Dyke II, 1935)		
Network (Lumet, 1976)	13,921,739	
Nicholas and Alexandra (Schaffner, 1971)	6,990,000	
Ninotchka (Lubitsch, 1939)		
Norma Rae (Ritt, 1979)	10,000,000	
The Nun's Story (Zinnemann, 1959)	5,750,000	
Of Mice and Men (Milestone, 1939)		
*Oliver! (Reed, 1968)	16,800,000	
*One Flew Over the Cuckoo's Nest (Forman, 1975)	59,939,701	
One Foot in Heaven (Rapper, 1941)		
One Hour With You (Lubitsch, 1931/32)		
One Hundred Men and a Girl (Koster, 1937)		
One Night of Love (Schertzinger, 1934)		
On Golden Pond (Rydell, 1981)	61,175,028	
*On the Waterfront (Kazan, 1954)	4,200,000	
*Ordinary People (Redford, 1980)	23,123,000	
Our Town (Wood, 1940)		
*Out of Africa (Pollack, 1985)	43,448,253	
The Ox-Bow Incident (Wellman, 1943)		
A Passage to India (Lean, 1984)	13,690,000	
The Patriot (Lubitsch, 1928/29)		
*Patton (Schaffner, 1970)	28,100,000	
Peyton Place (Robson, 1957)	11,500,000	
The Philadelphia Story (Cukor, 1940)		
Picnic (Logan, 1955)	6,350,000	

The Pied Piper (Pichel, 1942)
A Place in the Sun (Stevens, 1951)
Places in the Heart (Benton, 1984)   16,000,000
*Platoon (Stone, 1986)   69,937,092
Pride of the Yankees (Wood, 1942)   3,671,000
The Prince of Tides (Streisand, 1991)   36,100,000
The Private Life of Henry VIII (Korda,
    1932/33)
Prizzi's Honor (Huston, 1985)   13,000,000
Pygmalion (Asquith/Howard, 1938)

The Quiet Man (Ford, 1952)   3,800,000
Quo Vadis (LeRoy, 1951)   11,901,662

Rachel, Rachel (Newman, 1968)   6,100,000
The Racket (Milestone, 1927/28)
Raging Bull (Scorsese, 1980)   10,111,078
Raiders of the Lost Ark (Spielberg,   115,598,000
    1981)
*Rain Man (Levinson, 1988)   86,813,000
Random Harvest (LeRoy, 1942)   4,665,501
The Razor's Edge (Goulding, 1946)   5,000,000
*Rebecca (Hitchcock, 1940)   3,000,000
The Red Shoes (Powell/Pressburger,   5,000,000
    1948)
Reds (Beatty, 1981)   21,000,000
The Right Stuff (Kaufman, 1983)   10,400,000
The Robe (Koster, 1953)   17,500,000
*Rocky (Avildsen, 1976)   56,524,972
Roman Holiday (Wyler, 1953)   3,000,000
Romeo and Juliet (Cukor, 1936)
Romeo and Juliet (Zeffirelli, 1968)   17,473,000
Room at the Top (Clayton, 1959)
A Room with a View (Ivory, 1986)   12,000,000
The Rose Tattoo (Daniel Mann, 1955)   4,200,000
Ruggles of Red Gap (McCarey, 1935)
The Russians Are Coming, The   9,771,271
    Russians are Coming (Jewison, 1966)

The Sand Pebbles (Wise, 1966)   13,500,000
San Francisco (Van Dyke II, 1936)   3,785,868
Sayonara (Logan, 1957)   10,500,000
Scent of a Woman (Brest, 1992)   26,000,000
Separate Tables (Delbert Mann, 1958)   3,100,000
Sergeant York (Hawks, 1941)   6,135,707
Seven Brides For Seven Brothers   6,298,000
    (Donen, 1954)
Seventh Heaven (Borzage, 1927/28)
Shane (Stevens, 1953)   9,000,000

Shanghai Express (von Sternberg, 1931/
    32)
She Done Him Wrong (Sherman, 1932/
    33)
Ship of Fools (Kramer, 1965)
*The Silence of the Lambs (Demme,   59,882,870
    1991)
Since You Went Away (Cromwell,   4,924,756
    1944)
Skippy (Taurog, 1930/31)
The Smiling Lieutenant (Lubitsch, 1931/
    32)
Smilin' Through (Franklin, 1932/33)
The Snake Pit (Litvak, 1948)   4,100,000
A Soldier's Story (Jewison, 1984)   10,120,000
The Song of Bernadette (Henry King,   4,701,000
    1943)
Sons and Lovers (Cardiff, 1960)
Sounder (Ritt, 1972)   8,726,000
*The Sound of Music (Wise)   79,975,000
Spellbound (Hitchcock, 1945)   4,970,583
Stagecoach (Ford, 1939)
Stage Door (LaCava, 1937)
A Star Is Born (Wellman, 1937)
Star Wars (Lucas, 1977)   193,777,000
State Fair (Henry King, 1932/33)
*The Sting (Roy Hill, 1973)   78,212,000
The Story of Louis Pasteur (Dieterle,
    1936)
A Streetcar Named Desire (Kazan,   4,414,474
    1951)
The Sundowners (Zinnemann, 1960)   3,800,000
Sunset Boulevard (Wilder, 1950)
Suspicion (Hitchcock, 1941)

A Tale of Two Cities (Conway, 1936)
Talk of the Town (Stevens, 1942)
Taxi Driver (Scorsese, 1976)   12,569,000
The Ten Commandments (DeMille,   43,000,000
    1956)
Tender Mercies (Beresford, 1983)   3,289,225
*Terms of Endearment (James L. Brooks,   50,250,000
    1983)
Tess (Polanski, 1980)   9,869,000
Test Pilot (Fleming, 1938)
The Thin Man (Van Dyke II, 1934)
A Thousand Clowns (Coe, 1965)
Three Coins in the Fountain   5,000,000
    (Negulesco, 1954)

Three Smart Girls (Koster, 1936)	
To Kill a Mockingbird (Mulligan, 1962)	7,112,368
*Tom Jones (Richardson, 1963)	17,070,000
Tootsie (Pollack, 1982)	94,910,000
Top Hat (Sandrich, 1935)	
A Touch of Class (Frank, 1973)	8,400,000
The Towering Inferno (Guillermin/ Allen, 1974)	48,838,000
Trader Horn (Van Dyke II, 1930/31)	
Treasure of the Sierra Madre (Huston, 1948)	
The Turning Point (Ross, 1977)	17,060,000
Twelve Angry Men (Lumet, 1957)	
Twelve O'Clock High (Henry King, 1949)	3,300,000
*Unforgiven (Eastwood, 1992)	39,000,000
An Unmarried Woman (Mazursky, 1978)	12,000,000
The Verdict (Lumet, 1982)	26,650,000
Viva Villa! (Conway, 1934)	

Wake Island (Farrow, 1942)	3,500,000
Watch on the Rhine (Shumlin, 1943)	
The Way of All Flesh (Fleming, 1927/ 28)	
*West Side Story (Wise/Robbins, 1961)	19,645,570
The White Parade (Cummings, 1934)	
Who's Afraid of Virginia Woolf? (Nichols, 1966)	14,500,000
Wilson (Henry King, 1944)	
*Wings (Wellman, 1927/28)	3,800,000
Witness (Weir, 1985)	28,500,000
Witness for the Prosecution (Wilder, 1957)	3,800,000
The Wizard of Oz (Fleming, 1939)	4,759,888
Working Girl (Nichols, 1988)	28,600,000
Wuthering Heights (Wyler, 1939)	
Yankee Doodle Dandy (Curtiz, 1942)	4,719,681
The Yearling (Brown, 1946)	5,567,818
*You Can't Take It With You (Capra, 1938)	
Z (Costa-Gavras, 1969)	7,100,000
Zorba the Greek (Cacoyannis, 1964)	4,400,000

APPENDIX 6
Directors Who Worked With Oscar-Winning Actors

Winning Oscars for acting depends largely on a good script, but, even more importantly, on being directed by a filmmaker who can interpret that script and draw from an actor a performance that stands the test of time. William Wyler, for many the best all-around director in the business, guided some 14 Oscar winners in the space of 32 years, more than any other filmmaker. Elia Kazan was also highly successful in the postwar years, averaging almost one Oscar performance a year between 1945 and 1955. Of the leading eight, only George Cukor directed winners that were solely in the best actor and actress categories.

Note: On the following list, *Come and Get It* was co-directed by Wyler with Howard Hawks; *Mister Roberts* was co-directed by Ford with Mervyn LeRoy.

WILLIAM WYLER (14)

Walter Brennan	*Come and Get It*	supp. actor, 1936
Bette Davis	*Jezebel*	actress, 1938
Fay Bainter	*Jezebel*	supp. actress, 1938
Walter Brennan	*The Westerner*	supp. actor, 1940
Greer Garson	*Mrs. Miniver*	actress, 1942
Teresa Wright	*Mrs. Miniver*	supp. actress, 1942
Fredric March	*The Best Years of Our Lives*	actor, 1946
Harold Russell	*The Best Years of Our Lives*	supp. actor, 1946
Olivia de Havilland	*The Heiress*	actress, 1949
Audrey Hepburn	*Roman Holiday*	actress, 1953
Burl Ives	*The Big Country*	supp. actor, 1958
Charlton Heston	*Ben-Hur*	actor, 1959
Hugh Griffith	*Ben-Hur*	supp. actor, 1959
Barbra Streisand	*Funny Girl*	actress, 1968

ELIA KAZAN (9)

James Dunn	*A Tree Grows in Brooklyn*	supp. actor, 1945
Celeste Holm	*Gentleman's Agreement*	supp. actress, 1947
Vivien Leigh	*A Streetcar Named Desire*	actress, 1951
Karl Malden	*A Streetcar Named Desire*	supp. actor, 1951
Kim Hunter	*A Streetcar Named Desire*	supp. actress, 1951
Anthony Quinn	*Viva Zapata!*	supp. actor, 1952
Marlon Brando	*On the Waterfront*	actor, 1954
Eva Marie Saint	*On the Waterfront*	supp. actress, 1954
Jo Van Fleet	*East of Eden*	supp. actress, 1955

FRED ZINNEMANN (6)

Gary Cooper	*High Noon*	actor, 1952
Frank Sinatra	*From Here to Eternity*	supp. actor, 1953
Donna Reed	*From Here to Eternity*	supp. actress, 1953
Paul Scofield	*A Man For All Seasons*	actor, 1966
Jason Robards	*Julia*	supp. actor, 1977
Vanessa Redgrave	*Julia*	supp. actress, 1977

GEORGE CUKOR (5)

James Stewart	*The Philadelphia Story*	actor, 1940
Ingrid Bergman	*Gaslight*	actress, 1944
Ronald Colman	*A Double Life*	actor, 1947
Judy Holliday	*Born Yesterday*	actress, 1950
Rex Harrison	*My Fair Lady*	actor, 1964

JOHN FORD (5)

Victor McLaglen	*The Informer*	actor, 1935
Thomas Mitchell	*Stagecoach*	supp. actor, 1939
Jane Darwell	*The Grapes of Wrath*	supp. actress, 1940
Donald Crisp	*How Green Was My Valley*	supp. actor, 1941
Jack Lemmon	*Mister Roberts*	supp. actor, 1955

JOHN HUSTON (4)

Walter Huston	*The Treasure of the Sierra Madre*	supp. actor, 1948
Claire Trevor	*Key Largo*	supp. actress, 1948
Humphrey Bogart	*The African Queen*	actor, 1951
Anjelica Huston	*Prizzi's Honor*	supp. actress, 1985

SIDNEY LUMET (4)

Ingrid Bergman	*Murder on the Orient Express*	supp. actress, 1974
Peter Finch	*Network*	actor, 1976
Faye Dunaway	*Network*	actress, 1976
Beatrice Straight	*Network*	supp. actress, 1976

MARTIN SCORSESE (4)

Ellen Burstyn	*Alice Doesn't Live Here Anymore*	actress, 1974
Robert De Niro	*Raging Bull*	actor, 1980
Paul Newman	*The Color of Money*	actor, 1986
Joe Pesci	*Goodfellas*	supp. actor, 1990

APPENDIX 7
Nominated Films That Lost

And the losers? What of them—the films you may have been searching for in the main A–Z part of this book but been unable to find. Well, it's more than likely that you will find them in this appendix, and also the next, both of which concentrate on the "unlucky" films, at least as far as the Academy Awards are concerned.

Below are listed those movies that received nominations but failed to win a single award. Spielberg's *The Color Purple* and Herbert Ross' *The Turning Point* (each with 11 mentions) hold the dubious distinction of being the films that had the most nominations but no wins. They are closely followed by William Wyler's *The Little Foxes* (9), Fred Zinnemann's *The Nun's Story* (8), David Lynch's *The Elephant Man* (8) and Mervyn LeRoy's *Quo Vadis* (8).

Over 200 films make up the list; your favorite may well be among them.

Note: Each of the films listed below is followed (in parentheses) by the name of its director and the year of its release. The column on the right shows the number of nominations the film received. An asterisk preceding a title indicates that the film was a best-picture nominee of its year.

The Adventures of Baron Munchausen (Gilliam, 1989)	4
*Alfie (Gilbert, 1966)	5
Alice (Woody Allen, 1990)	1
*Anatomy of a Murder (Preminger, 1959)	7
Anna Christie (Brown, 1929/30)	3
The Asphalt Jungle (Huston, 1950)	4
*Atlantic City (Malle, 1981)	5
Avalon (Levinson, 1990)	4
*Awakenings (Marshall, 1990)	3
Baby Doll (Kazan, 1956)	4
Bad Day at Black Rock (Sturges, 1955)	3
The Band Wagon (Minnelli, 1953)	3
Barton Fink (Coen, 1991)	3
Basic Instinct (Verhoeven, 1992)	2
Batman Returns (Burton, 1992)	2
Big (Marshall, 1988)	2
*The Big Chill (Kasdan, 1983)	3
Blackboard Jungle (Richard Brooks, 1955)	4
Blade Runner (Scott, 1982)	2
Blazing Saddles (Mel Brooks, 1974)	3
Blue Velvet (Lynch, 1986)	1
The Bostonians (Ivory, 1984)	2
Boyz N The Hood (Singleton, 1991)	2
Brazil (Gilliam, 1985)	2
Brief Encounter (Lean, 1946)	3

*Broadcast News (James L. Brooks, 1987)	7
Broadway Danny Rose (Woody Allen, 1984)	2
*The Caine Mutiny (Dmytryk, 1954)	7
Cape Fear (Scorsese, 1991)	2
*Cat on a Hot Tin Roof (Richard Brooks, 1958)	6
Chaplin (Attenborough, 1992)	3
The China Syndrome (Bridges, 1979)	4
*A Clockwork Orange (Kubrick, 1971)	4
*The Color Purple (Spielberg, 1985)	11
The Commitments (Parker, 1991)	1
*The Conversation (Coppola, 1974)	3
The Cotton Club (Coppola, 1984)	2
Crimes and Misdemeanors (Woody Allen, 1989)	3
Cross Creek (Ritt, 1983)	4
*Crossfire (Dmytryk, 1947)	5
Cry Freedom (Attenborough, 1987)	3
A Cry in the Dark (Schepisi, 1988)	1
*Dark Victory (Goulding, 1939)	3
Das Boot (Peterson, 1982)	6
*David Copperfield (Cukor, 1935)	2
The Dead (Huston, 1987)	2
*Dead End (Wyler, 1937)	4
Death of a Salesman (Benedek, 1951)	5
*Deliverance (Boorman, 1972)	3
Detective Story (Wyler, 1951)	4

Diner (Levinson, 1982)	1
Do the Right Thing (Lee, 1989)	2
*Double Indemnity (Wilder, 1944)	7
*The Dresser (Yates, 1983)	5
*Dr. Strangelove (Kubrick, 1964)	4
Easy Rider (Hopper, 1969)	2
Educating Rita (Gilbert, 1983)	3
Edward Scissorhands (Burton, 1990)	1
El Cid (Anthony Mann, 1961)	3
*The Elephant Man (Lynch, 1980)	8
Empire of the Sun (Spielberg, 1987)	6
Enchanted April (Newell, 1992)	3
Enemies: A Love Story (Mazursky, 1989)	3
Executive Suite (Wise, 1954)	4
The Fabulous Baker Boys (Kloves, 1989)	4
The Fallen Idol (Reed, 1949)	2
*Fatal Attraction (Lyne, 1987)	6
*Father of the Bride (Minnelli, 1950)	3
*A Few Good Men (Reiner, 1992)	4
The Field (Sheridan, 1990)	1
*Field of Dreams (Robinson, 1989)	3
*Five Easy Pieces (Rafelson, 1970)	4
*Foreign Correspondent (Hitchcock, 1940)	6
*Forty-Second Street (Bacon, 1932/33)	2
The French Lieutenant's Woman (Reisz, 1981)	5
Fried Green Tomatoes at the Whistle Stop Cafe (Avnet, 1991)	2
*Friendly Persuasion (Wyler, 1956)	6
*The Front Page (Milestone, 1930/31)	3
Full Metal Jacket (Kubrick, 1987)	1
Ghostbusters (Reitman, 1984)	2
*The Godfather, Part III (Coppola, 1990)	7
Good Morning, Vietnam (Levinson, 1987)	1
Gorillas in the Mist (Apted, 1988)	5
Grand Canyon (Kasdan, 1991)	1
*The Great Dictator (Chaplin, 1940)	5
Green Card (Weir, 1990)	1
Greystoke: The Legend of Tarzan, Lord of the Apes (Hudson, 1984)	3
The Grifters (Frears, 1990)	4
Hamlet (Zeffirelli, 1990)	2
A Handful of Dust (Sturridge, 1988)	1
The Heart Is a Lonely Hunter (Miller, 1968)	2
*Henry V (Olivier, 1946)	4
High Society (Walters, 1956)	3

Hoffa (DeVito, 1992)	2
Home Alone (Columbus, 1990)	2
*Hope and Glory (Boorman, 1987)	5
The Hunchback of Notre Dame (Dieterle, 1939)	2
Husbands and Wives (Woody Allen, 1992)	2
*I Am a Fugitive from a Chain Gang (LeRoy, 1932/33)	3
In Cold Blood (Richard Brooks, 1967)	4
Inherit the Wind (Kramer, 1960)	4
Interiors (Woody Allen, 1978)	5
Ironweed (Babenco, 1987)	2
*It's a Wonderful Life (Capra, 1946)	5
The Killers (Siodmak, 1946)	4
*King's Row (Wood, 1942)	3
Kiss of Death (Hathaway, 1947)	2
*Lady for a Day (Capra, 1932/33)	4
Last Tango in Paris (Bertolucci, 1973)	2
The Last Temptation of Christ (Scorsese, 1988)	1
*Lenny (Fosse, 1974)	6
*The Letter (Wyler, 1940)	7
Life with Father (Curtiz, 1947)	4
Little Dorrit (Edzard, 1988)	2
*The Little Foxes (Wyler, 1941)	9
The Little Shop of Horrors (Oz, 1986)	2
*The Long Voyage Home (Ford, 1940)	6
Lorenzo's Oil (Miller, 1992)	2
*Love Affair (McCarey, 1939)	6
*The Love Parade (Lubitsch, 1929/30)	6
*Madame Curie (LeRoy, 1943)	7
*The Magnificent Ambersons (Welles, 1942)	4
Malcolm X (Lee, 1992)	2
*The Maltese Falcon (Huston, 1941)	3
The Manchurian Candidate (Frankenheimer, 1962)	2
Manhattan (Woody Allen, 1979)	2
The Man Who Shot Liberty Valance (Ford, 1962)	1
Meet Me in St. Louis (Minnelli, 1944)	4
Mona Lisa (Jordan, 1986)	1
Morocco (Von Sternberg, 1930/31)	4
Mr. and Mrs. Bridge (Ivory, 1990)	1
Music Box (Costa-Gavras, 1989)	1
*Mutiny on the Bounty (Milestone, 1962)	7
My Man Godfrey (LaCava, 1936)	6
The Natural (Levinson, 1984)	4
*Ninotchka (Lubitsch, 1939)	4

North by Northwest (Hitchcock, 1959)   3
Notorious (Hitchcock, 1946)   2
*The Nun's Story (Zinnemann, 1959)   8

The Odd Couple (Saks, 1968)   2
Odd Man Out (Reed, 1947)   1
*Of Mice and Men (Milestone, 1939)   4

Parenthood (Howard, 1989)   2
The Player (Altman, 1992)   3
Poltergeist (Hooper, 1982)   3
Postcards from the Edge (Nichols, 1990)   2
Pretty Woman (Marshall, 1990)   1
*The Prince of Tides (Streisand, 1991)   7
The Prisoner of Zenda (Cromwell, 1937)   2
The Private Lives of Elizabeth and Essex (Curtiz,   5
   1939)
Psycho (Hitchcock, 1960)   4
The Purple Rose of Cairo (Woody Allen, 1985)   1

*Quo Vadis (LeRoy, 1951)   8

Radio Days (Woody Allen, 1987)   2
Ragtime (Forman, 1981)   8
Rambling Rose (Coolidge, 1991)   2
*Random Harvest (LeRoy, 1942)   7
Rear Window (Hitchcock, 1954)   4
Rebel Without a Cause (Ray, 1955)   3
Red River (Hawks, 1948)   2
Robin Hood: Prince of Thieves (Reynolds, 1991)   1
The Rose (Rydell, 1979)   4
Running on Empty (Lumet, 1988)   2

Salvador (Oliver Stone, 1986)   2
Sands of Iwo Jima (Dwan, 1949)   4
The Sea Hawk (Curtiz, 1940)   4
Sex, Lies and Videotape (Soderbergh, 1989)   1
Shirley Valentine (Gilbert, 1989)   2
Silkwood (Nichols, 1983)   5
Silverado (Kasdan, 1985)   2

Singin' in the Rain (Kelly/Donen, 1952)   2
Sleuth (Mankiewicz, 1972)   3
*A Soldier's Story (Jewison, 1984)   3
The Spiral Staircase (Siodmak, 1946)   1
The Spy Who Came In from the Cold (Ritt, 1965)   2
Stand and Deliver (Menendez, 1988)   1
A Star is Born (Cukor, 1954)   6
*State Fair (King, 1932/33)   2
The Story of G. I. Joe (Wellman, 1945)   4
The Stunt Man (Rush, 1980)   3
Suddenly Last Summer (Mankiewicz, 1959)   3
Summertime (Lean, 1955)   2
Sunday Bloody Sunday (Schlesinger, 1971)   4

*Taxi Driver (Scorsese, 1976)   4
*The Thin Man (Van Dyke, 1934)   4
*Top Hat (Sandrich, 1935)   4
Trading Places (Landis, 1983)   1
Tucker: The Man and His Dream (Coppola, 1988)   3
*The Turning Point (Ross, 1977)   11
*Twelve Angry Men (Lumet, 1957)   3
2010 (Hyams, 1984)   5

The Unbearable Lightness of Being (Kaufman,   2
   1988)
Under the Volcano (Huston, 1984)   2
*An Unmarried Woman (Mazursky, 1978)   3

*The Verdict (Lumet, 1982)   5
Vertigo (Hitchcock, 1958)   2

*Wake Island (Farrow, 1942)   4
Waterloo Bridge (LeRoy, 1940)   2
When Harry Met Sally (Reiner, 1989)   1
White Heat (Walsh, 1949)   1
Wild at Heart (Lynch, 1990)   1
The Wild Bunch (Peckinpah, 1969)   2
*Witness for the Prosecution (Wilder, 1957)   6

Zelig (Woody Allen, 1983)   2

APPENDIX 8
Over 200 Great Films That Weren't Nominated

This appendix complements the previous listing, drawing attention to more than 200 films that were entirely overlooked by the Academy and did not muster a single nomination among them. The list is a personal one and somewhat idiosyncratic, but has been drawn from acclaimed critical and popular successes of the last 60 years, including such distinguished films as Howard Hawks' *The Big Sleep* (1946), Charlie Chaplin's *City Lights* (1931) and *Modern Times* (1936), Don Siegel's *Dirty Harry* (1971), Charles Laughton's *Night of the Hunter* (1955) and so on. The surprises continue below . . .

Accident (Losey)	1967
Advise and Consent (Preminger)	1962
After Hours (Scorsese)	1985
Angel Heart (Parker)	1987
Another Woman (Woody Allen)	1988
Applause (Mamoulian)	1929
Attack (Aldrich)	1956
Bananas (Woody Allen)	1971
Beat The Devil (Huston)	1954
The Big Clock (Farrow)	1948
The Big Heat (Lang)	1953
The Big Sleep (Hawks)	1946
Billy Bathgate (Benton)	1991
Birdy (Parker)	1984
Blood Simple (Coen)	1985
The Blue Angel (von Sternberg)	1930
Bluebeard's Eighth Wife (Lubitsch)	1938
The Blues Brothers (Landis)	1980
Bob Roberts (Robbins)	1992
Bonfire of the Vanities (DePalma)	1990
The Bounty (Donaldson)	1984
The Boy with Green Hair (Losey)	1948
A Bridge Too Far (Attenborough)	1977
Bringing Up Baby (Hawks)	1938
The Browning Version (Asquith)	1951
Brute Force (Dassin)	1947
Call Northside 777 (Hathaway)	1948
Castaway (Roeg)	1987
The Cincinnati Kid (Jewison)	1965

City Lights (Chaplin)	1931
City Streets (Mamoulian)	1931
The Cook, the Thief, His Wife and Her Lover (Greenaway)	1990
The Court Jester (Panama/Frank)	1956
Cul-de-Sac (Polanski)	1966
The Day the Earth Stood Still (Wise)	1951
Dead of Night (Cavalcanti/Dearden/Hamer/ Crichton)	1945
Dead Ringers (Cronenberg)	1988
Dinner at Eight (Cukor)	1933
Dirty Harry (Siegel)	1971
Distant Voices, Still Lives (Davies)	1989
Don't Look Now (Roeg)	1973
The Doors (Stone)	1991
Down and Out in Beverly Hills (Mazursky)	1986
Dracula (Browning)	1931
The Draughtsman's Contract (Greenaway)	1983
Drugstore Cowboy (Van Sant, Jr.)	1989
Eight Men Out (Sayles)	1988
84 Charing Cross Road (Jones)	1987
Eureka (Roeg)	1984
A Face in the Crowd (Kazan)	1957
Fahrenheit 451 (Truffaut)	1966
Farewell My Lovely (Dmytryk)	1944
Fedora (Wilder)	1978
The Four Feathers (Zoltan Korda)	1939
1492: Conquest of Paradise (Scott)	1992

Frankenstein (Whale)	1931
Freaks (Browning)	1933
The Front Page (Wilder)	1975
Gilda, (Charles Vidor)	1946
The Glass Menagerie (Newman)	1987
The Great Waldo Pepper (Hill)	1975
Gregory's Girl (Forsyth)	1982
The Group (Lumet)	1966
Gunga Din (Stevens)	1939
Heat and Dust (Ivory)	1983
Hell in the Pacific (Boorman)	1968
Hero (Frears)	1992
Hidden Agenda (Loach)	1990
High Anxiety (Brooks)	1977
High Sierra (Walsh)	1941
The Hill (Lumet)	1965
His Girl Friday (Hawks)	1940
Hobson's Choice (Lean)	1954
Hombre (Ritt)	1966
Homicide (Mamet)	1991
House of Games (Mamet)	1987
Hue and Cry (Crichton)	1947
Human Desire (Lang)	1954
I Confess (Hitchcock)	1953
In a Lonely Place (Ray)	1950
The Incredible Shrinking Man (Arnold)	1957
The Innocents (Clayton)	1961
Intruder in the Dust (Brown)	1949
Invasion of the Body Snatchers (Siegel)	1956
Invasion of the Body Snatchers (Kaufman)	1978
The Invisible Man (Whale)	1933
Jungle Fever (Lee)	1991
Junior Bonner (Peckinpah)	1972
The Killing (Kubrick)	1956
Kind Hearts and Coronets (Hamer)	1948
King Kong (Cooper/Schoedsack)	1933
The King of Comedy (Scorsese)	1983
Kiss Me Deadly (Aldrich)	1955
The Lady from Shanghai (Welles)	1948
The Lady Vanishes (Hitchcock)	1938
The Last Hurrah (Ford)	1958
Letter from an Unknown Woman (Ophuls)	1948

The Life and Death of Colonel Blimp (Powell/ Pressburger)	1943
Life Is Sweet (Leigh)	1991
Local Hero (Forsyth)	1983
Lonely Are the Brave (Miller)	1962
Love Me Tonight (Mamoulian)	1932
The Lusty Men (Ray)	1952
Magic (Attenborough)	1978
Major Barbara (Pascal)	1941
Major Dundee (Peckinpah)	1965
Marnie (Hitchcock)	1964
The Mask of Dimitrios (Negulesco)	1944
A Matter of Life and Death (Powel/Pressburger)	1946
Memphis Belle (Caton-Jones)	1990
Merry Christmas, Mr. Lawrence (Oshima)	1983
Midnight (Leisen)	1939
Midnight Run (Brest)	1988
Miller's Crossing (Coen)	1990
The Misfits (Huston)	1961
Modern Times (Chaplin)	1936
The Mosquito Coast (Weir)	1986
The Mummy (Freund)	1933
Murder by Death (Moore)	1976
My Darling Clementine (Ford)	1946
My Own Private Idaho (Van Sant, Jr.)	1991
The Naked Gun (David Zucker)	1988
The Naked Lunch (Cronenberg)	1991
The Name of the Rose (Annaud)	1986
Night of the Hunter (Laughton)	1955
Nothing Sacred (Wellman)	1937
Of Mice and Men (Sinise)	1992
Oliver Twist (Lean)	1948
O Lucky Man (Anderson)	1972
Once Upon a Time in America (Leone)	1984
Our Man in Havana (Reed)	1960
Outcast of the Islands (Reed)	1952
Pale Rider (Eastwood)	1985
Palm Beach Story (Sturges)	1942
Paris, Texas (Wenders)	1984
The Passenger (Antonioni)	1975
Paths of Glory (Kubrick)	1957
People Will Talk (Mankiewicz)	1951
Performance (Roeg)	1970
Peter's Friends (Branagh)	1992

The Plainsman (DeMille)	1936
Point Blank (Boorman)	1967
The Postman Always Rings Twice (Garnett)	1946
Prick Up your Ears (Frears)	1987
The Private Life of Sherlock Holmes (Wilder)	1970
The Railway Children (Jeffries)	1970
The Rainbow (Russell)	1989
The Rake's Progress (Launder/Gilliat)	1945
The Red Badge of Courage (Huston)	1951
Reservoir Dogs (Tarantino)	1992
Rio Bravo (Hawks)	1959
Riot in Cell Block 11 (Siegel)	1954
The Roaring Twenties (Walsh)	1939
Roxanne (Schepisi)	1987
Saturday Night and Sunday Morning (Reisz)	1960
Scarface (Hawks)	1932
The Scarlet Empress (von Sternberg)	1934
Scarlet Street (Lang)	1945
The Searchers (Ford)	1956
September (Woody Allen)	1987
The Servant (Losey)	1964
The Set-Up (Wise)	1949
Seven Women (Ford)	1966
Shadows and Fog (Woody Allen)	1992
The Sheltering Sky (Bertolucci)	1990
The Shining (Kubrick)	1980
The Shooting Party (Bridges)	1985
The Shop Around the Corner (Lubitsch)	1940
Showboat (Whale)	1936
Silent Movie (Brooks)	1976
Silk Stockings (Mamoulian)	1957
Slaughterhouse Five (Hill)	1972
The Small Back Room (Powell/Pressburger)	1948
Something Wicked This Way Comes (Clayton)	1983

Something Wild (Demme)	1986
Stardust Memories (Woody Allen)	1980
State of the Union (Capra)	1948
St. Valentine's Day Massacre (Corman)	1967
Sullivan's Travels (Sturges)	1942
The Sun Shines Bright (Ford)	1953
The Sweet Smell of Success (Mackendrick)	1957
Talk Radio (Stone)	1988
They Won't Forget (LeRoy)	1937
The Thing (Nyby)	1951
The Thing (Carpenter)	1982
Things to Come (Cameron Menzies)	1936
The Thirty-Nine Steps (Hitchcock)	1935
This Gun for Hire (Tuttle)	1942
3:10 to Yuma (Daves)	1957
Tin Men (Levinson)	1987
To Have and Have Not (Hawks)	1944
Touch of Evil (Welles)	1958
Trouble in Paradise (Lubitsch)	1932
The Trouble with Harry (Hitchcock)	1956
Wagonmaster (Ford)	1950
A Walk in the Sun (Milestone)	1946
The War of the Roses (DeVito)	1989
White Hunter, Black Heart (Eastwood)	1990
The Wild One (Benedek)	1953
Wild River (Kazan)	1960
Winchester 73 (Mann)	1950
Wish You Were Here (Leland)	1987
The Witches (Roeg)	1990
The Women (Cukor)	1939
A World Apart (Menges)	1988
The Wrong Man (Hitchcock)	1957
You Only Live Once (Lang)	1937

A P P E N D I X 9
Memorial and Honorary Awards

Irving G. Thalberg Memorial Award

The Thalberg Award was established in 1937 and is voted by the Academy's Board of Governors only in those years in which the Board feels there is a deserving recipient. The Award is for "outstanding motion picture production" and remains one of the most coveted of the Academy prizes.

Winners

1937	Darryl F. Zanuck
1938	Hal B. Wallis
1939	David O. Selznick
1941	Walt Disney
1942	Sidney Franklin
1943	Hal B. Wallis
1944	Darryl F. Zanuck
1946	Samuel Goldwyn
1948	Jerry Wald
1950	Darryl F. Zanuck
1951	Arthur Freed
1952	Cecil B. DeMille
1953	George Stevens
1956	Buddy Adler
1958	Jack L. Warner
1961	Stanley Kramer
1963	Sam Spiegel
1965	William Wyler
1966	Robert Wise
1967	Alfred Hitchcock
1970	Ingmar Bergman
1973	Lawrence Weingarten
1975	Mervyn LeRoy
1976	Pandro S. Berman
1977	Walter Mirisch
1979	Ray Stark
1981	Albert R. Broccoli

1986	Steven Spielberg
1987	Billy Wilder
1990	Richard Zanuck and David Brown
1991	George Lucas

Jean Hersholt Humanitarian Award

First presented in 1956, the Hersholt Award is for "reflecting credit on the industry," and like the Thalberg Award is voted by the Board of Governors. Again, it is awarded only in those years in which, in the Board's opinion, there is a deserving recipient.

Winners

1956	Y. Frank Freeman
1957	Samuel Goldwyn
1959	Bob Hope
1960	Sol Lesser
1961	George Seaton
1962	Steve Broidy
1965	Edmond L. DePatie
1966	George Bagnall
1967	Gregory Peck
1968	Martha Raye
1969	George Jessel
1970	Frank Sinatra
1972	Rosalind Russell
1973	Lew Wasserman
1974	Arthur B. Krim
1975	Dr. Jules Stein
1977	Charlton Heston
1978	Leo Jaffe
1979	Robert S. Benjamin
1981	Danny Kaye
1982	Walter Mirisch
1983	M. J. Frankovich

1984	David L. Wolper
1985	Charles (Buddy) Rogers
1989	Howard W. Koch
1992	Elizabeth Taylor, Audrey Hepburn

The Gordon E. Sawyer Award

Established in 1981 to recognize an individual's long-term contributions to the advancement of motion picture science or technology. Not presented every year.

1981	Joseph B. Walker
1982	John O. Aalberg
1983	Dr. John G. Frayne
1984	Lindwood G. Dunn
1987	Fred Hynes
1988	Gordon Henry Cook
1989	Pierre Angenieux
1990	Stefan Kudelski
1991	Ray Harryhausen
1992	Erich Kaestner

Special and Honorary Awards Presented by the Academy since 1927/28

1927/28	Warner Brothers for producing *The Jazz Singer*, the pioneer talking picture which has revolutionized the industry
	Charles Chaplin, for versatility and genius in writing, acting, directing and producing *The Circus*
1931/32	Walt Disney, for the creation of Mickey Mouse
1934	Shirley Temple, presented in grateful recognition of her outstanding contribution to screen entertainment during the year 1934
1935	David Wark Griffith, for his distinguished creative achievements as director and producer and his invaluable initiative and lasting contributions to the progress of the motion picture arts
1936	The March of Time, for its significance to motion pictures and for having revolutionized one of the most important branches of the industry—the newsreel
	W. Howard Greene and Harold Rosson, for the color cinematography of the Selznick International production, *The Garden of Allah*
1937	The Museum of Modern Art Film Library, for making available to the public the means of studying the development of the motion picture as one of the major arts
	Mack Sennett, for his lasting contribution to the comedy technique of the screen
	Edgar Bergen, for his outstanding comedy creation, Charlie McCarthy
	W. Howard Greene, for the color cinematography of *A Star Is Born*
1938	Deanna Durbin and Mickey Rooney, for their significant contribution in bringing to the screen the spirit and personification of youth and as juvenile players setting a high standard of ability and achievement
	Harry M. Warner, in recognition of patriotic service in the production of historical short subjects presenting significant episodes in the early struggle of the American people for liberty
	Walt Disney for *Snow White and the Seven Dwarfs*, recognized as a significant screen innovation which has charmed millions and pioneered a great new entertainment field for the motion picture cartoon
	J. Arthur Ball for outstanding contributions to the advancement of color in motion picture photography
	Oliver Marsh and Allen Davey for the color cinematography of *Sweethearts*
	Special award to Paramount for

outstanding achievement in creating the special photographic and sound effects in *Spawn of the North*

1939 Douglas Fairbanks (Commemorative Award), recognizing the unique and outstanding contribution of Douglas Fairbanks, first President of the Academy, to the international development of the motion picture

The Technicolor Company, for its contributions in successfully bringing three-color feature production to the screen

Motion Picture Relief Fund, acknowledging the outstanding services to the industry during the past year of the Motion Picture Relief Fund and its progressive leadership

Judy Garland, for her outstanding performance as a screen juvenile during the past year

William Cameron Menzies, for outstanding achievement in the use of color for the enhancement of dramatic mood in the production of *Gone With the Wind*

1940 Bob Hope, in recognition of his unselfish services to the Motion Picture Industry

Colonel Nathan Levinson, for his outstanding services to the industry and the Army which made possible the present efficient mobilization of the Motion Picture Industry facilities for the production of Army training films

1941 *Churchill's Island*, Canadian National Film Board, citation for distinctive achievement

Rey Scott, for his extraordinary achievement in producing *Kukan*

The British Ministry of Information, for *Target for Tonight*

Leopold Stokowski and his associates, for their unique achievement

in the creation of a new form of visualized music in *Fantasia*

Walt Disney, William Garity, John N. A. Hawkins and the RCA Manufacturing Company, for their outstanding contribution to the advancement of the use of sound in motion pictures through the production of *Fantasia*

1942 Charles Boyer for his progressive cultural achievement in establishing the French Research Foundation in Los Angeles

Noel Coward for his outstanding production achievement in *In Which We Serve*

Metro-Goldwyn-Mayer Studio, for its achievement in representing the American Way of Life in the production of the *Andy Hardy* series of films

1943 George Pal, for the development of novel methods and techniques in the production of short subjects known as Puppetoons

1944 Margaret O'Brien, outstanding child actress of 1944

Bob Hope, for his many services to the Academy, a Life Membership in the Academy of Motion Picture Arts and Sciences

1945 Walter Wanger, for his six years' service as President of the Academy of Motion Picture Arts and Sciences

Peggy Ann Garner, outstanding child actress of 1945

The House I Live In, tolerance short subject; directed by Mervyn LeRoy and starring Frank Sinatra. Released by RKO Radio

1946 Laurence Olivier, for his outstanding achievement as actor, producer and director in bringing *Henry V* to the screen

Harold Russell, for bringing hope and courage to his fellow veterans through his appearance in *The Best Years of Our Lives*

Ernst Lubitsch, for his distinguished contributions to the art of the motion picture

Claude Jarman, Jr., outstanding child actor of 1946

1947   James Baskett, for his able and heartwarming characterization of Uncle Remus, friend and storyteller to the children of the world

Bill and Coo, in which artistry and patience blended in a novel and entertaining use of the medium of motion pictures

Shoe Shine (Italy) for the high quality of this film

Colonel William N. Selig, Albert E. Smith, Thomas Armat and George K. Spoor, film pioneers

1948   *Monsieur Vincent* (France), voted by the Academy Board of Governors as the most outstanding foreign language film released in the United States during 1948

Ivan Jandl, for the outstanding juvenile performance of 1948 in *The Search*

Sid Grauman, master showman, who raised the standard of exhibition of motion pictures

Adolph Zukor, a man who has been called the father of the feature film in America, for his services to the industry over a period of forty years

Walter Wanger, for distinguished service to the industry in adding to its moral stature in the world community by his production of the picture *Joan of Arc*

1949   *The Bicycle Thief* (Italy), voted by the Academy Board of Governors as the most outstanding foreign language film released in the United States during 1949

Bobby Driscoll, as the outstanding juvenile actor of 1949

Fred Astaire, for his unique artistry and his contributions to the technique of musical pictures

Cecil B. DeMille, distinguished motion picture pioneer, for 37 years of brilliant showmanship

Jean Hersholt, for distinguished service to the motion picture industry

1950   *The Walls of Malapaga* (France–Italy), voted by the Board of Governors as the most outstanding foreign language film released in the United States in 1950

George Murphy, for his services in interpreting the film industry to the country at large

Louis B. Mayer, for distinguished service to the motion picture industry

1951   *Rashomon* (Japan), voted by the Board of Governors as the most outstanding foreign language film released in the United States during 1951

Gene Kelly, in appreciation of his versatility as an actor, singer, director and dancer, and especially for his brilliant achievements in the art of choreography on film

1952   *Forbidden Games* (France), best foreign language film released in the United States during 1952

George Alfred Mitchell, for the design and development of the camera which bears his name and for his continued and dominant presence in the field of cinematography

Joseph M. Schenck for long and distinguished service to the motion picture industry

Merian C. Cooper, for his many innovations and contributions to the art of motion pictures

Harold Lloyd, master comedian and good citizen

Bob Hope, for his contribution to the laughter of the world

1953   Pete Smith, for his witty and pungent observations on the American scene in the series of *Pete Smith Specialties*

The 20th Century-Fox Film Corporation, in recognition of their imagination, showmanship and foresight in introducing the revolutionary process known as CinemaScope

Joseph I. Breen, for his conscientious, open-minded and dignified management of the Motion Picture Production Code

Bell and Howell Company, for their pioneering and basic achievements in the advancement of the motion picture industry

1954   *Gate of Hell* (Japan), best foreign language film of 1954

Bausch and Lomb Optical Company, for their contributions to the advancement of the motion picture industry

Kemp R. Niver, for the development of the Renovare Process

Greta Garbo, for unforgettable performances

Danny Kaye, for his unique talents, his service to the Academy, the motion picture industry, and the American people

Jon Whitely, for his outstanding juvenile performance in *The Little Kidnappers* (U.K. title *The Kidnappers*)

Vincent Winter, for his outstanding juvenile performance in *The Little Kidnappers*

1955   *Samurai* (Japan), best foreign language film of 1955

1956   Eddie Cantor, for distinguished service to the film industry

1957   Charles Brackett, for outstanding service to the Academy

B. B. Kahane, for distinguished service to the motion picture industry

Gilbert M. ("Broncho Billy") Anderson, motion picture pioneer, for his contributions to the development of motion pictures as entertainment

The Society of Motion Picture and Television Engineers for their contributions to the advancement of the motion picture industry

1958   Maurice Chevalier, for his contributions to the world of entertainment for more than half a century

1959   Lee de Forest, for his pioneering inventions which brought sound to motion pictures.

Buster Keaton, for his unique talents which brought immortal comedies to the screen

1960   Gary Cooper, for his many memorable screen performances and the international recognition he, as an individual, has gained for the motion picture industry

Stan Laurel, for his creative pioneering in the field of cinema comedy

Hayley Mills, for *Pollyanna*, the most outstanding juvenile performance during 1960

1961   William L. Hendricks, for his outstanding patriotic service in the conception, writing and production of the Marine Corps film, *A Force in Readiness*, which has brought honor to the Academy and the motion picture industry

Jerome Robbins, for his brilliant achievements in the art of choreography on film in *West Side Story*

Fred L. Metzler, for his dedication and outstanding service to the Academy of Motion Picture Arts and Sciences

1964   William Tuttle for his outstanding

makeup work in the film *7 Faces of Dr. Lao*

1965   Bob Hope for unique and distinguished service to the motion picture industry and the Academy

1966   Y. Frank Freeman, for unusual and outstanding service to the Academy during his thirty years in Hollywood

Yakima Canutt, for creating the profession of stuntman as it exists today and for the development of many safety devices used by stuntmen everywhere

1967   Arthur Freed, MGM producer, for distinguished service to the Motion Picture Academy of Arts and Sciences in the production of six top-rated Awards telecasts

1968   Onna White for her choreography of *Oliver*

John Chambers for his creative makeup design for *Planet of the Apes*

1969   Cary Grant, for his unique mastery of the art of screen acting, with the respect and affection of his colleagues

1970   Lillian Gish and Orson Welles for their superlative and distinguished service in the making of motion pictures

1971   Charles Chaplin, for the incalculable effect he has had in making motion pictures the art form of this century

1972   Edward G. Robinson for his contribution to the acting art

Charles Boren, leader for 38 years of the industry's enlightened labor relations and architect of its policy of nondiscrimination

1973   Groucho Marx, for his brilliant creativity and for the unequaled achievements of the Marx Brothers in the art of motion picture comedy

Henry Langlois, for his untiring devotion to the art of film, for his massive contributions towards preserving its historical past and for his unswerving faith in its future

1974   Howard Hawks, a giant of the American cinema whose pictures taken as a whole represent one of the most consistent, vivid and varied bodies of work in world cinema

Jean Renoir, a filmmaker who has worked with grace, responsibility and enviable competence through silent film, sound film, feature, documentary and television

1975   Mary Pickford, in recognition of her unique contributions to the film industry and the development of film as an artistic medium

1977   Margaret Booth, for 62 years of exceptionally distinguished service to the motion picture industry as a film editor

Janet Gaynor, for her truly immeasurable contribution to the art of motion pictures and for the pleasure and entertainment her unique artistry has brought to millions of film fans around the globe

1978   Laurence Olivier, for the full body of his work, the unique achievements of his entire career and his lifetime of contribution to the art of film

King Vidor, for his incomparable achievements as a cinematic creator and innovator

Walter Lantz, for his unique animated motion pictures and especially his creation of Woody Woodpecker, featured in more than 250 cartoons

The Museum of Modern Art, for its contribution to the public's perception of movies as an art form

1979   Alec Guinness, for advancing the art of screen acting through a host of memorable and distinguished performances including a best actor

Oscar in 1957 for *The Bridge on the River Kwai*

Hal Elias, for his unswerving dedication and distinguished and continued service to the Academy

1980   Henry Fonda, in recognition of his brilliant accomplishments and enduring contribution to the art of motion pictures

1981   Barbara Stanwyck, for superlative creativity and unique contribution to the art of screen acting

1982   Mickey Rooney, in recognition of his 60 years of versatility in a variety of memorable film performances

1983   Hal Roach, in recognition of his unparalleled record of distinguished contributions to the motion picture art form

1984   James Stewart for his fifty years of memorable performances. For his high ideals both on and off the screen. With the respect and affection of his colleagues

The National Endowment for the Arts in recognition of its 20th anniversary and its dedicated commitment to fostering artistic and creative activity and excellence in every area of the arts

1985   Paul Newman in recognition of his many and memorable compelling screen performances and for his personal integrity and dedication to his craft

Alex North in recognition of his brilliant artistry in the creation of memorable music for a host of distinguished motion pictures

John H. Whitney, Sr. for Cinematic Pioneering (Medal of Commendation)

1986   Ralph Bellamy for his unique artistry and his distinguished service to the profession of acting

E. M. (Al) Lewis in appreciation for outstanding service and dedication in upholding the high standards of The Academy of Motion Picture Arts and Sciences

1987   None presented

1988   National Film Board of Canada in recognition of its 50th anniversary and its dedicated commitment to originate artistic, creative and technological activity and excellence in every area of film-making

Richard Williams for his unique accomplishment as director of animation and creator of all the new cartoon characters in *Who Framed Roger Rabbit?* which has received international acclaim

Eastman Kodak in recognition of the company's fundamental contributions to the art of motion pictures during the first century of film history

1989   Akira Kurosawa for his cinematic accomplishments that have inspired, delighted, enriched and entertained worldwide audiences and influenced filmmakers throughout the world

1990   Myrna Loy in recognition of her extraordinary qualities both on screen and off, with appreciation for a lifetime's worth of indelible performances

Sophia Loren, one of the genuine treasures of world cinema who, in a career rich with memorable performances, has added permanent luster to our art form

1991   Satyajit Ray, for his rare mastery of the art of motion pictures and for his profound humanitarian outlook, which has had an indelible influence on filmmakers and audiences throughout the world

1992   Federico Fellini, in recognition of his cinematic accomplishments that have thrilled and entertained worldwide audiences

APPENDIX 10
Oscar Night Hosts

More than 80 presenters have hosted or co-hosted the Academy Awards since Douglas Fairbanks and William C. DeMille presided over the first ceremony in May, 1929. In the late 1960s and throughout the 1970s and 1980s the Academy opted on occasion for a group of presenters rather than a solo MC, but generally the evening has worked best when a single host (preferably a comedian) has been in charge of the proceedings.

Bob Hope easily outstrips all his rivals. Between 1940 and 1978 he appeared as master of ceremonies on 20 occasions, 13 times as a solo presenter. Johnny Carson dominated the 1980s, hosting five shows; Billy Crystal has established himself as the man for the 1990s.

1929	Douglas Fairbanks and William C. DeMille
1930	William C. DeMille
1930	Conrad Nagel
1931	Lawrence Grant
1932	Conrad Nagel
1934	Will Rogers
1935	Irvin S. Cobb
1936	Frank Capra
1937	George Jessel
1938	Bob Burns
1939	Frank Capra
1940	Bob Hope (for the last half only)
1941	Walter Wanger
1942	Bob Hope
1943	Bob Hope
1944	Jack Benny (for overseas broadcast)
1945	John Cromwell (first half) Bob Hope (second half)
1946	Bob Hope and James Stewart
1947	Jack Benny
1948	Dick Powell and Agnes Moorehead
1949	Robert Montgomery
1950	Paul Douglas
1951	Fred Astaire
1952	Danny Kaye
1953	Bob Hope
1954	Donald O'Connor
1955	Bob Hope
1956	Jerry Lewis
1957	Jerry Lewis
1958	Bob Hope, Jack Lemmon, David Niven, Rosalind Russell, James Stewart and (on film) Donald Duck

1959   Bob Hope, Jerry Lewis, David Niven, Sir Laurence Olivier, Tony Randall and Mort Sahl

1960   Bob Hope

1961   Bob Hope

1962   Bob Hope

1963   Frank Sinatra

1964   Jack Lemmon

1965   Bob Hope

1966   Bob Hope

1967   Bob Hope

1968   Bob Hope

1969   The Friends of Oscar—Ingrid Bergman, Diahann Carroll, Tony Curtis, Jane Fonda, Burt Lancaster, Walter Matthau, Sidney Poitier, Rosalind Russell, Frank Sinatra and Natalie Wood

1970   The Friends of Oscar—Claudia Cardinale, Elliott Gould, Myrna Loy, Barbara McNair, Jon Voight, Fred Astaire, Elizabeth Taylor, Ali MacGraw, Cliff Robertson, Katharine Ross, James Earl Jones, Candice Bergen, Raquel Welch, Clint Eastwood, John Wayne and Bob Hope

1971   The Friends of Oscar—Burt Bacharach, Harry Belafonte, Richard Benjamin, Joan Blondell, Jim Brown, Genevieve Bujold, Glen Campbell, Petula Clark, Angie Dickinson, Melvyn Douglas, Lola Falana, Janet Gaynor, Goldie Hawn, Bob Hope, John Huston, James Earl Jones, Shirley Jones, Sally Kellerman, Burt Lancaster, John Marley, Walter Mat-

thau, Steve McQueen, Sarah Miles, Ricardo Montalban, Jeanne Moreau, Merle Oberon, Ryan O'Neal, Gregory Peck, Paula Prentiss, Eva Marie Saint, George Segal, Maggie Smith and Gig Young

1972   Helen Hayes, Alan King, Sammy Davis, Jr., and Jack Lemmon

1973   Carol Burnett, Michael Caine, Charlton Heston and Rock Hudson

1974   John Huston, Diana Ross, Burt Reynolds and David Niven

1975   Sammy Davis, Jr., Bob Hope, Shirley MacLaine and Frank Sinatra

1976   Walter Matthau, Robert Shaw, George Segal, Goldie Hawn and Gene Kelly

1977   Richard Pryor, Jane Fonda, Ellen Burstyn and Warren Beatty

1978   Bob Hope

1979   Johnny Carson

1980   Johnny Carson

1981   Johnny Carson

1982   Johnny Carson

1983   Liza Minnelli, Dudley Moore, Richard Pryor and Walter Matthau

1984   Johnny Carson

1985   Jack Lemmon

1986   Alan Alda, Jane Fonda, and Robin Williams

1987   Chevy Chase, Goldie Hawn and Paul Hogan

1988   Chevy Chase

1989   The Friends of Oscar—Lily Tomlin,
          Tom Selleck, Jane Fonda, Patrick
          Swayze, Anjelica Huston, Barbara
          Hershey, Billy Crystal, Anne Archer
          and Ali MacGraw

1990   Billy Crystal

1991   Billy Crystal

1992   Billy Crystal

1993   Billy Crystal

Selected Bibliography

The following books are devoted in part or in their entirety to the Awards of The Academy of Motion Picture Arts and Sciences. All are useful for reference, behind-the-scenes information and the overall history of the Oscars.

Bergan, Ronald; Fuller, Graham; and Malcolm, David. *Academy Award Winners*. London: Multimedia Books, 1992.

Brown, Peter H. *The Real Oscar: The Story Behind the Academy Awards*. Westport, Conn.: Arlington House, 1981.

Brown, Peter H. and Pinkston, Jim. *Oscar Dearest: Six Decades of Scandal, Politics and Greed Behind Hollywood's Academy Awards*. New York: Harper & Row, 1987.

Holden, Anthony. *The Oscars: The Secret History of Hollywood's Academy Awards*. New York: Little, Brown, 1992.

Libby, Bill. *They Didn't Win Oscars*. Westport, Conn.: Arlington, House, 1980.

Likeness, George. *The Oscar People*. Mendota, Ill.: The Wayside Press, 1965.

Osborne, Robert. *60 Years of the Oscar: The Official History of the Academy Awards*. New York: Abbeyville Press, 1989.

Shale, Richard. *Academy Awards: An Ungar Reference Index*. New York: Frederick Ungar Publishing Company, 1978.

Simonet, Thomas. *Oscar: A Pictorial History of the Academy Awards*. New York: The Associated Press & Norback and Co., Inc., 1983.

Steinberg, Cobbett. *Reel Facts: The Movie Book of Records*, New York: Vintage Books, 1978.

Wiley, Mason, and Bona, Damien. *Inside Oscar: The Unofficial History of the Academy Awards*. New York: Ballantine, 1986.

Index

Oscar citations within the A to Z film synopsis section are marked in **bold** type.
Footnotes are indicated by "*n*" following the page number.

A

Aalberg, John O. 253
Abatantuono, Diego 100
Abbott, L. B. **43, 95, 125, 163**
Abel, Walter 11, 74
Abe Lincoln in Illinois (1940) 196
Abraham, F. Murray **7**, 190, 217
Absence of Malice (1981) 32, 215
Abyss, The (1989) **1**
Accident (1967) 249
Accidental Tourist, The (1988) **1–2**, 190, 218, 219, 238
Accused, The (1988) **2**, 142, 190, 218, 221
Acheson, James **37, 89**
Acker, Jean 146
Ackland, Joss 77
Ackland-Snow, Brian **136**
acting 183–220 *see also* personal names (e.g., Hepburn, Katharine)
Adair, Jean 110
Adam, Ken **14**
Adams, Brooke 38
Adams, Edie 11
Adams, Nick 207
Adamson, Joy 20
Addams, Dawn 125
Addison, John **162**
Addy, Wesley 111
Adjani, Isabelle 213, 219
Adler, Buddy **55**, 252
Adorf, Mario 160
Adrian, Iris 119
Adventures of Baron Munchausen, The (1989) 246
Adventures of Don Juan, The (1949) **2**
Adventures of Robin Hood, The (1938) **2**, 195, 224, 238
Adventures of Robinson Crusoe, The (1954) 203
Advise and Consent (1962) 249
Affairs of Cellini (1934) 194
African Queen, The (1951) **3**, 123, 150, 186, 202, 245
After Hours (1985) 249
After Midnight (1950) 26
Agar, John 141
"Age of Not Believing, The" 141
Agins, Robert 32
Agnese 30
Agnes of God (1985) 217
Agutter, Jenny 8, 95
"Ah, Sweet Mystery of Life" 110
Aherne, Brian 160, 196
Ahlstedt, Borje 51
Aiello, Danny 106, 219
Aimée, Anouk 44, 46, 98, 208
Air Force (1943) **3**
Airport (1970) **3**, 25*n*, 108*n*, 143, 188, 210, 211, 221, 238
Aitken, Maria 53
Akbas, Erdine 84
Akin, Zoe 106

Akins, Claude 40
Aladdin (1992) **3**, 50*n*, 224, 225
Alameda, Richard 115
Alamo, The (1960) **3–4**, 29, 206, 224, 238
Alaskan Eskimo, The (1953) 229
Albee, Edward 174
Alberni, Luis 116
Albert, Eddie 78, 84, 115, 136, 203, 211
Albert, Edward 24
Alberti, Gigio 100
Alberti, Guido 46
Albert Schweitzer (1957) 230
Albertson, Jack 38, 125, **150**, 188, 209
Albright, Lola 27
Alcott, John **14**
Alcott, Louisa May 94
Alda, Alan 25, 26, 260
Aldredge, Theoni V. **67**
Aldrich, Robert 42, 173, 249, 250
Aleandro, Norma 114, 218
Alentova, Vera 106
Alexander, Dick **7, 17**
Alexander, Gary **118**
Alexander, Jane 7, 61, 88, 210, 213, 215, 216
Alexander, John 84
Alexander's Ragtime Band (1938) **4**, 195, 224, 238
Alfie (1966) **70**, 208, 209, 238, 246
Alford, Philip 162
Algiers (1938) 195
Alibi (1928/29) 192, 238
Alice (1990) 246
Alice Adams (1935) 194, 238
Alice Doesn't Live Here Anymore (1974) **4**, 189, 212, 245
Alice's Restaurant (1969) 210
Alien (1979) **4–5**
Aliens (1986) **5**, 217
Aling, Denys **4**
All About Eve (1950) **5**, 151, 185, 186, 201, 221, 223, 238
Allder, Nick **4**
Allen, Gene **109**
Allen, Gracie 36
Allen, Hervey 10
Allen, Irwin 164, 243
Allen, Karen 130
Allen, Lee 56
Allen, Nancy 135
Allen, Penelope 44
Allen, Peter **12**
Allen, Woody: *Alice* 246; *Annie Hall* **9–10**, 10*n*, 189, 213, 214, 238; *Another Woman* 249; *Bananas* 249; *Broadway Danny Rose* 217, 246; *Crimes and Misdemeanors* 219, 246; *Hannah and Her Sisters* 70, 190, 218, 240; *Husbands and Wives* 247; *Interiors* 214, 247; *Manhattan* 247; *Purple Rose of Cairo* 248; *Radio Days*

248; *September* 251; *Shadows and Fog* 251; *Stardust Memories* 251; *Zelig* 248
Allentuck, Katherine 150
Allgood, Sara 76, 106, 155, 197
All Quiet on the Western Front (1929/30) **5–6**, 183, 192, 193, 238
All That Jazz (1929/30) **6**
All That Jazz (1979) 214, 215, 238
All That Money Can Buy (1941) **6**, 197
All the King's Men (1949) **6**, 185, 201, 238
All the President's Men (1976) **7**, 189, 213, 222, 238
"All the Way" **84**, 225
All This and Heaven Too (1940) 196, 197, 238
Allwin, Pernilla 51
Allyson, June 61, 94, 149
Almendros, Nestor **38**
Alterio, Hector 114
Altman, Robert 100, 110, 211, 213, 220, 241, 248
Alton, John **8**
Altramura, Elio **136**
Alvarado, Don 22, 106
Amadeus (1984) **7–8**, 190, 216, 217, 221, 238
Ama Girls (1958) 230
Amarcord (1974) **8**, 100*n*, 112, 213
Ambler, Eric 163
Ameche, Don 4, **31–32**, 71, 79, 190, 217
America, America (1963) **8**, 207, 238
American Dream (1990) 237
American Graffiti (1973) 212, 238
American in Paris, An (1951) **8**, 123, 186, 201, 202, 223, 225, 238
American Werewolf in London, An (1981) **8**, 71
Ames, Judith 173
Ames, Preston **8, 60**, 223
Amidei, Sergio 8*n*
Amphibious Fighters (1943) 227
Amy, George **3**
Anastasia (1956) **9**, 25*n*, 108*n*, 186, 204, 221
Anatomy of a Murder (1959) 122, 205, 238, 246
Anchors Aweigh (1945) **9**, 199, 238
Andersen, Hans Christian 93, 133
Anderson, Gilbert M. ("Broncho Billy") 256
Anderson, John Murray 87
Anderson, Judith 90, 132, 152, 153, 197
Anderson, Lindsay 28, 250
Anderson, Mary 161
Anderson, Michael 12, 95, 204, 239
Anderson Jr., Michael 95
Anderson, Richard L. **130**

Anderson, Robert 174
Anderson, Warner 40
Anderson Platoon, The (1967) 232
Andersson, Bibi 13
Andersson, Harriet 34, 51, 159
And Justice for All (1979) 139, 214
Andorai, Peter 101
Andre, Annette 56
Andrews, Dana 17, 34, 90, 149
Andrews, Edward 47
Andrews, Harry 39, 112
Andrews, Julie **99–100**, 145, 158, 169, 187, 208, 216
Andy Hardy (film series) 254
Angel, Heather 79, 152
Angel and Big Joe (1975) 234
Angel Heart (1987) 249
Angeli, Pier 144
Angels with Dirty Faces (1938) 96, 195, 196
Angelus, Muriel 67
Angenieux, Pierre 253
Anhalt, Edna **119**
Anhalt, Edward **15, 119**
Anicette, Stella 98
animation 226–237
Anna (1987) 218
Anna and Bella (1985) 235
Anna and the King of Siam (1946) 6, **9**, 87, 200, 222, 223
Anna Christie (1929/30) 193, 246
Annakin, Ken 95, 241
Annaud, Jean-Jacques 18, 129, 250
Anne of the Thousand Days (1969) **9**, 174*n*, 210, 238
Annie Get Your Gun (1950) **9**
Annie Hall (1977) **9–10**, 70, 189, 213, 214, 238
Ann-Margret 211, 213
Another Woman (1988) 249
Anouilh, Jean 15
Anthony Adverse (1936) **10**, 92, 184, 194, 195, 224, 238
Antin, Steve 2
Antonio, Lou 33
Antonioni, Michelangelo 209, 250
Anwar, Gabrielle 139
Apartment, The (1960) **10–11**, 154, 187, 206, 222, 224, 238
Apocalypse Now (1979) **11**, 214, 215, 223, 238
Applause (1929) 249
Appointments of Dennis Jennings, The (1988) 236
"April Showers" **84**
Apted, Michael 31, 239, 247
Aquatic House-Party (1949) 228
Arana, Hugo 114
Arbatt, Alexandre 37
Archer, Anne 218, 261
Archer, Ernest **111**
Archer, John 40
Arden, Eve 34, 103, 199
Ardolino, Emile 42

Argenziano, Carmen 2
Arise My Love (1940) **11**
Arkin, Alan 208, 209
Arkin, David 110
Arlen, Harold **176**
Arlen, Richard 175
Arling, Arthur **179**
Arliss, Florence 42
Arliss, George 42, 183, 192
Armat, Thomas 255
Armetta, Henry 150
Armstrong, Louis 61, 72
Armstrong, Robert 19, 102, 119
Arne, Peter 169
Arnold, Edward 6, 9, 32, 84, 108, 180
Arnold, Jack 250
Arnold, Malcolm **22**
Around the World in 80 Days (1956) **11–12**, 186, 204, 239
Arrighi, Luciana 75
Arrowsmith (1931/32) 193, 239
art direction 223 see also personal names (e.g., Gibbons, Cedric)
Arthur (1981) 12, 190, 215
Arthur, Beatrice 96
Arthur, Carol 151
Arthur, Jean 106, 107, 108, 141, 180, 198
Arthur, Robert 106, 165
Arthur Rubinstein—The Love of Life (1969) 232
"Arthur's Theme" **12**
Artie Shaw: Time Is All You've Got (1986) 236
Ashby, Hal 15, 20, 32, 33, **80**, 141, 214, 239
Ashcroft, Peggy **120–121**, 190, 217
Ashley, Elizabeth 142
Ashley, John 76
Ashman, Howard **14–15**, **93**, 225
Asner, Ed 82
Asp, Anna **50**
Aspegren, Chuck 40
Asphalt Jungle, The (1950) 201, 246
Asquith, Anthony 128, 169, 242, 249
Assault, The (1986) **12**
Astaire, Fred 255, 259, 260; *Damsel in Distress* 36; *Easter Parade* 46; *Gay Divorcee* 58; *Holiday Inn* 74; *Swing Time* 152; *Towering Inferno* 164, 212
Asther, Nils 90
"As Time Goes By" 27
Astor, Mary 44, **67**, 77, 94, 166, 184, 197
Ates, Roscoe 27, 29
Athaiya, Ehanu **57**
Atherton, William 74
Atlantic City (1981) 215, 216, 239, 246
Attack (1956) 249
Attaway, Ruth 15
Attenborough, Richard: *Bridge Too Far* 249; *Chaplin* 246; *Cry Freedom* 246; *Doctor Doolittle* 43; *Gandhi* 36, 48, **57–58**, 190, 216, 240; *Magic* 250
Attili, Antonella 30

Atwill, Lionel 68
Auber, Brigitte 161
Auberjonois, René 87, 93
Audran, Stephane 13, 42
Auer, Mischa 32, 116, 180, 194
Auger, Claudine 159
August, Bille 122
Aumont, Jean-Pierre 38, 93
Aumont, Michel 37
Aumont, Tina 52
Auntie Mame (1958) 205, 239
Au Revoir les Enfants (1987) 13
Austen, Jane 126
Autumn Sonata (1978) 214
Avalon (1990) 246
Avalon, Frankie 4
Avedikian, Serge 37
Avery, Margaret 217
Avildsen, John G. **135**, 138, 189, 213, 242
Avnet, Jon 247
Awakenings (1990) 219, 239, 246
Awful Truth, The (1937) 12, 184, 195, 239
Axel, Gabriel 13
Axton, Hoyt 18
Aykroyd, Dan 45, 219
Aylmer, Felix 9, 70, 140
Ayres, Lew 6, 83, 200
Aznavour, Charles 160

B

Baar, Tim **159**
Babenco, Hector 87, 217, 241, 247
Babes in Arms (1939) 196
Babette's Feast (1987) 13, 122
"Baby, It's Cold Outside" **110–111**
Baby Doll (1956) 204, 246
"Baby Mine" 45
Bacall, Lauren 40, 86, 104, 108, 177
Bacharach, Burt 12, 24, 260
Bachelor and the Bobby-Soxer, The (1947) 13
Bachelor Party, The (1957) 204
Back To The Future (1985) **13**
Bacon, Irving 74
Bacon, Lloyd 240, 247
Bad and the Beautiful, The (1952) **13**, 171, 186, 202, 223
Bad Day at Black Rock (1955) 203, 204, 246
Baddeley, Hermione 100, 136, 205
Bad Girl (1931/32) **14**, 183, 193, 239
Badham, Mary 162, 207
Bad Seed, The (1956) 204
Bagnall, George 252
Bagnold, Enid 110
Bailey, Pearl 125
Bailey, Shane 134
Bainter, Fay 77, **82**, 149, 176, 184, 195, 206, 244
Baker, Carroll 17, 60, 76, 204
Baker, Kenny 8, 47, 71, 148
Baker, Rick 8, **70–71**, 87
Baker, Stanley 69
Baker, Tom 112

Balaban, Bob 31
Balance (1989) 236
Baldwin, Alec 15, 77, 177
Balfour, Katherine 96
Ball, Derek **148**
Ball, J. Arthur 253
Ball, Lucille 54
Ballard, Carroll 18
Ball of Fire (1941) 197
Balsam, Martin 7, 21, 108, **158**, 163, 187, 208
Bananas (1971) 249
Bancroft, Anne: *Agnes of God* 217; *Graduate* 65, 209; *Hindenburg* 74; *Miracle Worker* **103**, 187, 207; *Pumpkin Eater* 208; *Turning Point* 214
Bancroft, George 107, 113, 146, 167, 192
Bando, Kotaro 58
Band Wagon, The (1953) 246
Banerjee, Victor 121
Bang the Drum Slowly (1973) 212
Bannen, Ian 208
Bansagi, Ildiko 101
Baranski, Christine 134
Barba, Vanna 100
Barber, Lyn **44**
Barbier, George 101, 171
Bard, Ben 140
Barefoot Contessa, The (1954) **14**, 186, 203
Barefoot in the Park (1967) 209
Bari, Lynn 72
Barker, Lex **44**
Barker, The (1928/29) 192
Barkin, Ellen 153
Barnes, Binnie 126
Barnes, Christopher Daniel 93
Barnes, George **132**
Barnett, S. H. **51**
Barouh, Pierre 98
Barrault, Marie-Christine 213
Barretts of Wimpole Street, The (1934) 193, 194, 239
Barrie, Barbara 21, 215
Barrie, Mona 116
Barrier, Edgar 122
Barrier, Maurice 18
Barris, Harry 87
Barry, Gene 171
Barry, John **20**, **36**, **93**, **118**, **148**, 224
Barry, Philip 122
Barry, Raymond J. 20
Barry Lyndon (1975) **14**, 212, 213, 239
Barrymore, Drew 48
Barrymore, Ethel 51, **112**, 125, 152, 185, 199, 200, 201
Barrymore, John 65, 153
Barrymore, Lionel: *Captains Courageous* 26; *Free Soul* **54**, 183, 193; *Grand Hotel* 65; *Key Largo* 86; *Lady Be Good* 89; *Madame X* 192; *Since You Went Away* 143; *You Can't Take It With You* 180
Bart, Lionel 115
Barthelmess, Richard 38, 89, 192
Bartholomew, Freddie 26
Barton, James 73
Barton Fink (1991) 220, 246

Baryshnikov, Mikhail 173, 214
Base, Ronald **131**
Basehart, Richard 15, 149, 160
Basevi, James 77, **144**
Basic Instinct (1992) 246
Basinger, Kim 14
Baskett, James 144, 255
Bass, Alfie 90, 91
Basserman, Albert 152, 196
Bassman, Don **121**
Bat Adam, Michal 98
Batalov, Alexei 106
Bates, Alan 177, 181, 209
Bates, Florence 92
Bates, Kathy **103–104**, 191, 219
Bates, Michael 121
Batman (1989) **14**
Batman Returns (1992) 246
Battaglia, Guillermo 114
Battleground (1949) **14**, 147, 201, 239
Battle of Algiers, The (1968) 210
Battle of Midway (1942) 226, 227
Bauchens, Anne **112–113**
Baum, Frank 176
Baum, Vicki 65
Bausch and Lomb Optical Company 256
Baxley, Barbara 110, 112
Baxter, Anne 5, 34, **132**, 153, 185, 199, 201
Baxter, Meredith 7
Baxter, Warner **79**, 183, 192
Beals, Jennifer 53
Bean, Roy 172
Bear Country (1953) 229
Beatles, The (musical group) 32, **92**
Beaton, Cecil **61**, **109**
Beat The Devil (1954) 249
Beatty, Ned 7, 110, 111, 152, 213
Beatty, Warren 260; *Bonnie and Clyde* 19–20, 209; *Bugsy* 23, 220; *Dick Tracy* 41; *Heaven Can Wait* 10n, 71, 214, 240; *Misery* 104; *Reds* 10n, 28, 36, **133**, 190, 215, 216, 242; *Shampoo* 141; *Splendor in the Grass* 146
Beauchamp, Clem **94**
Beau Geste (1939) 196
Beaumont, Harry 23, 192, 239
Beaumont, Lucy 54
"Beauty and the Beast" **14–15**, 50n, 225
Beauty and the Beast (1991) **14–15**, 50n, 99, 220, 224, 225, 239
Beavan, Jenny **136**
Beavers, Dick 46
Beavers, Louise 74
Beaver Valley (1950) 229
Beckel, Graham 120
Becket (1964) **15**, 174n, 207, 208, 239
Becky Sharp (1935) 194
Becourt, Alain 105
Bedelia, Bonnie 96, 156
Bedford, Brian 65, 66
Bedknobs and Broomsticks (1971) **15**, 141
Bedoya, Alfonso 164
Beecher, Janet 37
Beery, Noah 44

264

Beery, Wallace: *Big House* 17, 192; *Champ* **27**, 45, 183, 193; *Grand Hotel* 65; *Min and Bill* 103; *Viva Villa!* 169
Beetlejuice (1988) **15**
Beggs, Richard **11**
Begley, Ed **152**, 187, 207
Begley Jr., Ed 2
Being There (1979) **15–16**, 189, 214, 215, 222
Belafonte, Harry 260
Bel Geddes, Barbara 119, 200
Bell, Marshall 163
Bellamy, Ralph 12, 137, 195, 258
Bell and Howell Company 256
Bellaver, Harry 96, 115
"Belle" 50n
Bells of St. Mary's, The (1945) **16**, 199, 239
Belmondo, Jean-Paul 166
Bendix, William 176, 197
Bendova, Jitka 31
Benedek, Laslo 246, 251
Benedict, Paul 64
Ben-Hur (1959) **16**, 61, 89, 144, 173, 187, 205, 221, 223, 224, 239, 244
Bening, Annette 23, 24, 219
Benjamin, Richard 151, 260
Benjamin, Robert S. 252
Benjy (1951) 229
Bennent, David 160
Bennent, Heinz 160
Bennett, Belle 172
Bennett, Bruce 103, 106, 164
Bennett, Compton 87, 141, 240
Bennett, Enid 143
Bennett, Joan 42, 94
Bennett, Joseph 76
Bennett, Marjorie 93, 173
Bennett, Norman 165
Bennett, Robert Russell **114**
Benny, Jack 23, 259
Benson, Jodi 93
Benson, Martin 87
Benson, Robby 15
Benson, Suzanne **5**
Benton, Bill W. **36**
Benton, Jerome 128
Benton, Robert **88**, **124**, 189, 215, 217, 241, 242, 249
Ben Youb, Samy 98
"Be Our Guest" 50n
Berenger, Tom 20, 125, 217
Berenson, Marisa 14, 25
Beresford, Bruce 44, 45, 153, 216, 239, 242
Bergen, Candice 58, 215, 260
Bergen, Edgar 253
Berger, Helmut 58
Berger, Ludwig 157
Berger, Mark **7**, **11**, **134**
Bergerac, Jacques 61, 92
Bergman, Alan and Marilyn **158**, **172**, **179**
Bergman, Ingmar 252; *Cries and Whispers* 34, 212, 239; *Face to Face* 213; *Fanny and Alexander* 50–51, 216; *Smiles of a Summer Night* 94; *Through a Glass Darkly* 159; *Virgin Spring* 169

Bergman, Ingrid 260; *Anastasia* 9, 25n, 108n, 186, 204, 221; *Autumn Sonata* 214; *Bells of St. Mary's* 16, 199; *Casablanca* 27; *Gaslight* 25n, **58**, 108n, 185, 221, 245; *Joan of Arc* 82–83, 200; *Murder on the Orient Express* 25n, 108, 108n, 189, 198, 212, 221, 245; *Spellbound* 146; *For Whom the Bell Tolls* 54, 198
Bergner, Elisabeth 194
Berkeley, Busby 62, 63, 89, 150
Berkeley Square (1932/33) 193
Berkoff, Steven 14
Berkos, Peter **74**
Berle, Milton 81
Berlin, Irving 4, 9, 26, 33, **74**, 157, 225
Berlin, Jeannie 211
Berman, Henry **65**
Berman, Pandro S. 252
Bern, Paul **65**
Bernard, James **140**
Bernard, Thelonious 94
Bernardi, Herschel 81
Bernhardt, Curtis 80
Bernstein, Elmer 48, **158**
Bernstein, Leonard 73, 117
Berridge, Elizabeth 8
Berry, David **31**
Bertin, Roland 35
Bertolucci, Bernardo **89–90**, 190, 212, 218, 241, 247, 251
Bespoke Overcoat, The (1956) 230
Best, Travilla and Marjorie **2**
Best Boy (1979) 234
Best Little Whorehouse in Texas, The (1982) 216
Best Man, The (1964) 208
"Best That You Can Do" **12**
Best Years of Our Lives, The (1946) **17**, 86, 131, 185, 199, 200, 221, 222, 224, 239, 244, 255
Bevans, Clem 179
Beymer, Richard 41, 95, 172, 173
Beyond the Line of Duty (1942) 227
Bickford, Charles 17, 38, 51, 83, 132, 144, 198, 200
Bicycle Thief, The (1949) 255
Biehn, Michael 1, 5
Big (1988) 218, 246
Bigagli, Claudio 100
Big Broadcast of 1938, The (1938) **17**
Big Chill, The (1983) 216, 239, 246
Big Clock, The (1948) 249
Big Country, The (1958) **17**, 187, 205, 244
Big Heat, The (1953) 249
Big House, The (1929/30) **17**, 192, 224, 239
Big Pond, The (1929/30) 192
Big Sky, The (1952) 202
Big Sleep, The (1946) 249
Bikel, Theodore 3, 40, 47, 81, 109, 205
Bill, Tony 141, **149**
Bill and Coo 255
Billy Bathgate (1991) 249
Billy Budd (1962) 207
Bing, Herman 45, 68
Bird (1988) **17**, 137

Birdman of Alcatraz (1962) 207
Birds Anonymous (1957) 230
Birdy (1984) 249
Birkin, Jane 39
Biroc, Joseph **164**
Bishop, Kelly 42
Bishop, Stephen 173
Bishop's Wife, The (1947) **18**, 200, 239
Bisio, Claudio 100
Bissell, Whit 76, 159
Bisset, Jacqueline 3, 24, 38, 108
Biziou, Peter **104**
Bjornstrand, Gunnar 51, 159
Black, Don **20**
Black, Karen 67, 110
Black and White in Color (1976) **18**
Blackboard Jungle (1955) 246
Black Fox (1962) 231
"Black Hills of Dakota, The" 25
Blackman, Don 115
Blackman, Honor 63
Blackmer, Sidney 73, 137
Black Narcissus (1947) **18**, 67
Black Orpheus (1959) **18**, 78n
Black Stallion, The (1979) **18**, 215
Black Swan, The (1942) **18–19**, 222
Blackton, Jay **114**
Blade Runner (1982) 246
Blades, Ruben 102
Blaine, Vivian 149
Blair, Betsy 99, 204
Blair, Linda 49, 212
Blake, Michael **36**
Blake, Yvonne **111**
Blakely, Susan 164
Blakley, Ronee 110, 213
Blalack, Robert **148**
Blanc, Dominique 79
Blane, Anne-Marie 99
Blanke, Henry **92**
Blatty, William Peter **49**
Blazing Saddles (1974) 212, 246
Blessed, Brian 72
Blethyn, Brenda 135
Blier, Bertrand 59
Blithe Spirit (1946) **19**
Blondell, Joan 165, 202, 260
Blood and Sand (1941) **19**
Blood on the Sun (1945) **19**
Blood Simple (1985) 249
Bloom, Claire 28, 93, 177
Bloom, John **57**
Blore, Eric 54, 58, 152
Blossoms in the Dust (1941) **19**, 197, 223, 239
Blount, Lisa 114
Blowup (1966) 209
Blue, Ben 17
Blue, Monte 95, 174
Blue Angel, The (1930) 249
Bluebeard's Eighth Wife (1938) 249
"Blue Hawaii" 171
Blues Brothers, The (1980) 249
"Blue Skies" 4
Blue Skies (1946) 74
Blue Veil, The (1951) 202
Blue Velvet (1986) 218, 246
Blumenthal, Herman **30**, **72**
Blyth, Ann 66, 103, 199
Board and Care (1979) 234

Bob and Carol and Ted and Alice (1969) 210
Bob Roberts (1992) 249
Bochner, Hart 21
Bock, Jerry 52
Bódalo, José 161
Body and Soul (1947) **19**, 200
Bodyguard, The (1992) 50n
Boehm, Karl 177
Boekelheide, Jay **134**
Boekelheide, Todd **7**
Boen, Earl 154
Bogarde, Dirk 37, 38, 144
Bogart, Humphrey: *African Queen* 3, 123, 150, 186, 202, 245; *Barefoot Contessa* 14; *Caine Mutiny* 203; *Casablanca* 27, 198; *Key Largo* 86; *Sabrina* 138; *Treasure of the Sierra Madre* 164
Bogdanovich, Peter 90, 100, 120, 211, 241
"Bojangles of Harlem" 152
Boland, Mary 126
Bold and the Brave, The (1956) 204
Bolero, The (1973) 233
Boles, John 87
Boleslawski, Richard 241
Bolger, Ray 68, 71, 176
Bolkan, Florinda 80
Bologna, Joseph 176
Bolt, Robert **43**, **98**
Bonacelli, Paolo 102
Bond, Rudy 150
Bond, Ward 72, 81, 83, 105, 129
Bondarchuk, Sergei 171
Bondi, Beulah 143, 172, 194, 195
Bonfire of the Vanities (1990) 249
Bonnet, Frank Olivier 129
Bonney, Lawrence A. 142
Bonnie and Clyde (1967) **19–20**, 23, 80, 156, 188, 209, 239
Bonnot, Francoise **181**
Boone, Richard 4
Boorman, John 134, 211, 218, 239, 240, 246, 247, 250, 251
Booth, Charles G. **74**
Booth, Margaret 257
Booth, Shirley **32**, 186, 202
Borden, Eddie 44
Borders, Gloria S. **154**
Bored of Education (1936) 226
Boren, Charles 257
Borgnine, Ernest 42, 55, **99**, 125, 186, 203
"Born Free" 20
Born Free (1966) **20**, 224
Born on the Fourth of July (1989) **20**, 191, 219, 239
Born Yesterday (1950) **20**, 185, 201, 239, 245
Borzage, Frank: *Bad Girl* 14, 183, 193, 239; *Farewell to Arms* 51, 240; *Flirtation Walk* 240; *Seventh Heaven* **140**, 183, 192, 242; *Street Angel* 150
Bosco, Philip 177
Bostonians, The (1984) 217, 246
Bottin, Rob **163**
Bottoms, Sam 11, 90
Bottoms, Timothy 90, 119, 120
Boulle, Pierre **22**
Boulting, Roy 140⁻

Bound for Glory (1976) **20**, 213, 239
Bounty, The (1984) 249
Bourgoin, Jean **95**
Bourguignon, Serge 151
Boushel, Joy 53
Bovasso, Julie 106
Bow, Clara 175
Bowden, Dorris 66
Bowens, Malick 118
Bowie, Les **152**
Bowman, Lee 34
Box, John **43**, **91**, **111**, **115**
Box, Muriel and Sydney **140**
Box, The (1967) 232
Boxer, Nat **11**
box-office revenues 238–243
Boy and His Dog, A (1946) 228
Boyar, Sully 44
Boyd, Stephen 16, 51
Boyd, William 166
Boyens, Phyllis 31
Boyer, Charles 58, 173, 195, 198, 206, 254
Boyle, Edward G. **11**
Boyle, Peter 26
Boys and Girls (1983) 235
Boys from Brazil, The (1978) 214
Boys' Town (1938) **20–21**, 131, 184, 195, 196, 222, 239
Boy with Green Hair, The (1948) 249
Boyz 'N The Hood (1991) 220, 246
Bozman, Ron **142**
Bozzuffi, Marcel 55
Brabin, Charles 22
Bracco, Lorraine 65, 219
Brackett, Charles **95**, **151**, **160**, 222, 256
Bradbury, Lane 4
Bradford, Richard 102, 165, 168
Brady, Alice 58, 63, **79**, 116, 184, 195
Braga, Sonia 88, 102
Braine, John 136
Bram Stoker's Dracula (1992) **21**
Branagh, Kenneth 72, 219, 250
Brancia, Armando 8
Brand, Neville 147
Brandauer, Klaus Maria 101, 118, 217
Brando, Marlon: *Apocalypse Now* 11; *Dry White Season* 219; *Godfather* **61–62**, 121*n*, 131, 188, 211, 222; *Julius Caesar* 85, 202; *Last Tango in Paris* 212; *Sayonara* 139, 204; *Street Car Named Desire* 150, 202; *Superman* 152; *Viva Zapata!* 170, 202; *On the Waterfront* **117**, 131, 186, 203, 222, 244
Brandon, Michael 96
Brandt, Carlo 79
Brasselle, Keefe 124
Braugher, Andre 61
Brave One, The (1956) **21**
Brazil (1985) 246
Brazzi, Rossano 14, 94, 146, 159
Breakfast at Tiffany's (1961) **21**, 206, 225
Breaking Away (1979) **21**, 214, 215, 239

Breaking the Sound Barrier (1952) **21–22**
Breen, Joseph I. 256
Breen, Richard **160**, 222
Brendel, Frank 46
Brennan, Eileen 90, 149, 215
Brennan, Walter: *Come and Get It* **32**, 184, 194, 222, 244; *Cowboy and the Lady* 34; *Kentucky* **86**, 184, 195, 222; *Pride of the Yankees* 126; *Sergeant York* 140, 197; *Westerner* **172**, 184, 196, 222
Brenner, David **20**
Brenon, Herbert 90, 192
Brent, Evelyn 89, 167
Brent, George 67, 82, 131
Brent, Romney 2
Breslau, Susan 60
Bressart, Felix 19
Brest, Martin 139, 220, 242, 250
Bretherton, David **25**
Brett, Jeremy 109
Bretton, Raphael **72**
Brevig, Eric **163**
Brian, David 73
Brice, Fanny 68
Brickman, Marshall **9**
Bricusse, Leslie **43**, **169**
Bridge, Joan **98**
Bridge of San Luis Rey, The (1928/29) **22**, 223
Bridge on the River Kwai, The (1957) **22**, 186, 204, 205, 221, 239, 258
Bridges, Alan 251
Bridges, Beau 112
Bridges, James 120, 246
Bridges, Jeff 53, 87, 90, 211, 212, 217
Bridges, Lloyd 74, 125
Bridges at Toko-Ri, The (1955) **22**
Bridge Too Far, A (1977) 249
Brief Encounter (1946) 199, 200, 246
Briers, Richard 72
Bright, John **136**
Bright Victory (1951) 202
Briley, John **57**
Brimley, Wilford 32, 153
Bringing Up Baby (1938) 249
Brink, Gary **6**
British Ministry of Information 254
Broadbent, Jim 34
Broadcast News (1987) 218, 239, 246
Broadway Danny Rose (1984) 217, 246
Broadway Melody, The (1928/29) **22–23**, 175, 183, 192, 239
Broadway Melody of 1936, The (1935) **23**, 53, 194, 239
Broccoli, Albert R. 252
Brochet, Anne 35
Brocksmith, Roy 163
Broderick, Helen 152
Broderick, Matthew 61
Broidy, Steve 252
Broken Arrow (1950) 36, 201
Broken Lance (1954) **23**, 203
Broken Rainbow (1985) 236
Bromberg, J. Edward 122

Bromfield, Louis 131
Bron, Eleanor 177
Bronson, Charles 42, 138
Bronte, Emily 177
Brook, Clive 27, 141, 167
Brook, Albert 218
Brooks, Dean R. 116
Brooks, Hazel 19
Brooks, James L. **154**, 190, 216, 239, 242, 246
Brooks, Joseph **180**
Brooks, Mel **127**, 246, 250, 251
Brooks, Phyllis 79
Brooks, Richard **46**, 47, 152, 205, 209, 239, 246, 247
Brophy, Edward S. 45, 177
Brothers Karamazov, The (1958) 205
Brown, Bernard B. **173**
Brown, Christy 109
Brown, Clarence: *Anna Christie* 193, 246; *Free Soul* 54, 193, 250; *Human Comedy* 77, 198, 240; *Intruder in the Dust* 250; *National Velvet* 110, 199; *Plymouth Adventure* 125; *Rains Came* 131; *Romance* 193; *Yearling* 179, 200, 243
Brown, David 252
Brown, Eleanora 166
Brown, Francis Yeats 94
Brown, Harry **123**
Brown, Hilyard **30**
Brown, James 62
Brown, Jim 260
Brown, Joe E. 102, 144
Brown, John Mack 33, 50
Brown, John W. **26**
Brown, Malcolm F. **144**, 223
Brown, Pamela 31, 97
Brown, Timothy 110
Brown, Tom 79
Brown, Tregoweth **67**
Brown, Vanessa 72, 106
Browne, Cicely 52
Browne, Irene 27
Browne, Leslie 214
Browne, Roscoe Lee 95
Browning, Todd 249, 250
Browning Version, The (1951) 249
Brox Sisters, The (musical group) 87
Bruce, Nigel 27, 55, 93, 131, 132, 152, 157
Bruce, Virginia 68
Bruckner, Jane 42
Bruhl, Linda 119
Brunelle, Tom 104
Bruno, John **1**
Brute Force (1947) 249
Bryan, John **67**
Bryant, Adam 53
Brynner, Yul 9, **86–87**, 96, 108, 153, 186, 204
Buchanan, Edgar 141
Buchman, Sidney **73**
Buck, Pearl 65
Buckley, Betty 153
"Buddy" 175
Buddy Holly Story, The (1978) **23**, 214
Bugsy (1991) **23–24**, 220, 239

Bujold, Genevieve 9, 46, 210, 260
Bull, Peter 3, 43
Bulldog Drummond (1929/30) 44, 192
Bullitt (1968) **24**
Bumstead, Henry **149**, **161**
Buñuel, Luis 42
Buono, Victor 173, 207
Burgess, Anthony 129
Burgess, Dorothy 79
Burke, Billie 176, 195
Burke, Edwin **14**
Burke, Johnny **62**, 225
Burke, Michele **21**, **129**
Burke, Paul 158
Burkley, Dennis 100
Burks, Robert **161**
Burmester, Leo 1
Burnett, Carol 260
Burns, Bob 171, 259
Burns, Cathy 210
Burns, George 36, 45, **151**, 189, 213
Burns, Ralph **6**, **25**
Burr, Raymond 124
Burstyn, Ellen 260; *Alice Doesn't Live Here Anymore* **4**, 189, 212, 245; *Exorcist* 49, 212; *Harry and Tonto* 71; *Last Picture Show* 90, 211; *Resurrection* 215; *Same Time, Next Year* 214
Burton, Frederick 116
Burton, Norman 118
Burton, Richard: *Anne of the Thousand Days* 9, 174*n*, 210; *Becket* 15, 174*n*, 208; *Cleopatra* 31; *Equus* 174*n*, 213; *Longest Day* 95; *My Cousin Rachel* 174*n*, 202; *Night of the Iguana* 112; *Robe* 135, 174*n*, 202; *Sandpiper* 138; *Spy Who Came In from the Cold* 174*n*, 208; *V.I.P.s* 169; *Who's Afraid of Virginia Woolf?* 174, 208
Burton, Tim 14, 15, 246, 247
Burton, Willie D. **17**
Burtt Jr., Benjamin **48**, **78**, **130**, **148**
Busey, Gary 23, 148, 214
Bush, Billy Green 4, 134
Bushell, Anthony 42
Bus Stop (1956) 204
Busy Little Bears (1939) 227
Butch Cassidy and the Sundance Kid (1969) **24**, 29, 101, 210, 239
Butler, David 25, 86, 140
Butler, Frank **62**
Butler, Lawrence **156**
Butterfield 8 (1960) **24**, 174*n*, 187, 206
Butterflies Are Free (1972) **24**, 188, 211
Butterworth, Charles 157
Buttons, Red 125, **139**, 156, 186, 204
"Buttons and Bows" **119**
Buzzell, Edward 111
Byington, Spring 180, 195
Byrd, Richard E. 175
Byrd, William D. 29
Byrne, David **89**
Byrne, Michael 78
Byron, Walter 54

C

Caan, James 61, 103, 104, 211
Cabaret (1972) **25**, 188, 211, 221, 239
Cabot, Sebastian 159
Cacoyannis, Michael 181, 208, 243
Cactus Flower (1969) **25**, 188, 210
Cadell, Jean 128
Caesar, Adolph 217
Caesar, Arthur **98**
Caesar, Sid 81
Cage, Nicolas 106
Caged (1950) 80, 201
Caglione Jr., John **41**
Cagney, James: *Angels with Dirty Faces* 195; *Blood on the Sun* 19; *Come Fill the Cup* 156; *Love Me or Leave Me* 96, 203; *Midsummer Night's Dream* 102; *Mister Roberts* 105; *Yankee Doodle Dandy* **179**, 184, 197
Cahn, Sammy **74**, **84**, **119**, **159**, 225
Cain, James M. 173
Caine, Michael 260; *Alfie* 208; *California Suite* 25–26; *Educating Rita* 153, 216; *Hannah and Her Sisters* **70**, 190, 218; *Sleuth* 211
Caine Mutiny, The (1954) 3, 203, 239, 246
Calamity Jane (1953) **25**, 225
Calhern, Louis 9, 201
Calhoun, Rory 175
California Suite (1978) **25–26**, 108n, 189, 214, 222
Callahan, Gene **8**, **77**
Callan, Michael 27
Calleia, Joseph 26, 54
"Call Me Irresponsible" **119**, 225
Call Me Madam (1953) **26**, 224, 225
Call Northside 777 (1948) 249
Callow, Simon 8, 136
Camelot (1967) **26**, 225
Cameron, James 1, 5, 154
Camille (1937) 195
Camille Claudel (1989) 219
Campbell, Bill 21
Campbell, Charles L. **13**, **48**, **174**
Campbell, Cheryl 28
Campbell, Glen 165, 260
Camus, Marcel 18
Candidate, The (1972) **26**
Cannom, Greg **21**
Cannon, Dyan 72, 210, 214
Cannon, J. D. 33
Canonero, Milena **14**, **27**
Cantamessa, Gene **48**
Cantinflas 12
Cantor, Eddie 256
Canutt, Yakima 257
Capaldi, Peter 37
Cape Fear (1991) 220, 246
Capolicchio, Lino 58
Capone, Al 168
Capote, Truman 21
Capra, Frank 259; *Here Comes the Groom* 73; *Hole in the Head* 74; *It Happened One Night* **81**, 183, 194, 221, 240; *It's a Wonderful Life* 200, 240, 247; *Lady for a Day* 241, 247; *Lost Horizon* 95, 241; *Mr. Deeds Goes to Town* **107**, 184, 193, 195, 221, 241; *Mr. Smith Goes to Washington* 108, 196, 241; *State of the Union* 251; *You Can't Take It With You* **180**, 184, 196, 221, 243
Capshaw, Kate 78
Captain Blood (1935) 2, 92, 194, 239
Captain Carey, U.S.A. (1950) 26
Captain Newman, M.D. (1963) 207
Captains Courageous (1937) 20, **26**, 131, 184, 195, 222, 239
Capucine, 144
Cara, Irene 50, **53**
Cardenas, Elsa 21
Cardiff, Jack **18**, 39, 133, 145, 206, 242
Cardinal, Tantoo 36
Cardinal, The (1963) 207
Cardinale, Claudia 46, 260
Carey, Harry 3, 196
Carey Jr., Harry 100, 141
Carey, Joyce 19
Carey, Leslie I. **61**
Carey, Philip 25, 105
Carfagno, Edward **13**, **16**, **85**, 223
Carhart, Timothy 156
Cariou, Len 94
Carlin, Lynn 210
Carlisi, Olimpia 52
Carlson, Karen 26
Carlson, Les 53
Carlson, Richard 87
Carmen, Julie 102
Carmen Jones (1954) 203
Carmet, Jean 18
Carmichael, Hoagy 17, **73**, 225
Carminati, Tullio 116
Carnal Knowledge (1971) 211
Carney, Art **71**, 189, 212
Carnovsky, Morris 35
Caron, Leslie 8, 37, 51, 61, 92, 93, 203, 207
Carpenter, John 251
Carradine, David 20
Carradine, John 4, 19, 26, 66, 77, 146
Carradine, Keith **110**
Carradine, Robert 33
Carrere, Edward **26**
Carrie (1976) 213
Carrillo, Leo 98, 122, 169
Carroll, Diahann 125, 212, 260
Carroll, Joan 16
Carroll, John 89
Carroll, Leo G. 75, 146, 178
Carroll, Lisa Hart 154
Carroll, Madeleine 112, 113
Carroll, Nancy 192
Carroll, Pat 93, 94
Carson, Jack 102, 103, 126
Carson, Johnny 259, 260
Carson, Robert **147**
Carter Jr., Frank 29
Carter, Helena Bonham 76, 136
Carter, John **82**
cartoons 226–237
Cartwright, Veronica 5, 134
Caruso, David 114

Casablanca (1943) 3, **26–27**, 144, 184, 185, 198, 239
Casals Conducts: 1964 (1964) 231
Cascio, Salvatore 30
"Casey Junior" 45
Cass, Peggy 205
Cassavetes, John 42, 137, 209, 212
Cassel, Jean-Pierre 42, 108
Cassel, Seymour 209
Cassidy, Joanna 174
Castaway (1987) 249
Castellano, Richard 61, 96
Castillo, Antonio **111**
Castle, John 93
Cat Ballou (1965) **27**, 187, 208
Cat Concerto, The (1946) 228
Catlett, Walter 123
Cat on a Hot Tin Roof (1958) 32, 205, 239, 246
Caton-Jones, Michael 250
Cavalcade (1932/33) **27**, 183, 193, 239
Cavalcanti, Alberto 249
Cavett, Frank **62**, **66**
Cazale, John 39, 44, 62
Cederna, Giuseppe 100
Celi, Adolfo 159
Cerney, Karel **7**
Cesari, Bruno **89**
Chagall (1963) 231
Chakiris, George **172–173**, 187, 206
Chaliapin, Feodor 106
Chalk Garden, The (1964) 208
Chamberlain, Richard 164
Chambers, John 257
Champ, The (1931/32) **27**, 45, 183, 193, 239
Champ, The (1979) 102
Champion (1949) **27**, 171, 201
Champion, Michael 163
Chance to Live, A (1949) 228
Chandler, Jeff 201
Chaney, Lon 17, 90
Chaney Jr., Lon 40, 74
Channing, Carol 158, 209
Chaplin (1992) 220, 246
Chaplin, Charlie 257; *Circus* 89, 192, 253; *City Lights* 249; *Great Dictator* 196, 240, 247; *Limelight* 93; *Modern Times* 249, 250
Chaplin, Geraldine 43, 110
Chaplin, Saul **8**, **140**, **172**, 225
Chaplin, Sydney 93
Chapter Two (1979) 214
Charade (1984) 235
Charge of Light Brigade, The (1936) **27**
Chariots of Fire (1981) **27–28**, 58, 130, 189, 215, 216, 239
Charles, Josh 38
Charleson, Ian 28, 58
Charly (1968) **28**, 188, 209
Charman, Roy **130**
Chartoff, Robert **135**
Chase, Chevy 260, 261
Chase, Ilka 113
Chatterton, Ruth 44, 192
Chayefsky, Paddy **74**, **99**, **111**, 222
Chekhov, Michael 152, 199
Chen, Joan 90

Cher 100, **105–106**, 190, 216, 218
Chevalier, Maurice 53, 61, 101, 192, 256
Chew, Richard **148**
Chiang, Doug **39**
Chiao, Roy 78
Chicken, The (1965) 232
Children of a Lesser God (1986) **28–29**, 190, 217, 218, 239
Children's Hour, The (1961) 206
Chiles, Lois 39, 67, 172
Chilvers, Colin **152**
"Chim Chim Cher-ee" 99
China Syndrome, The (1979) 214, 246
Chinatown (1974) **29**, 71, 212, 239
Chong, Rae Dawn 129
Christian, Linda 169
Christian, Roger **148**
Christie, Agatha 39, 108
Christie, Audrey 146
Christie, Julie **37–38**, 43, 71, 141, 145, 187, 208, 211
Christmas Carol, A (1972) 174, 226, 233
Christopher, Dennis 21
Churchill, Berton 146
Churchill, Frank **45**
Churchill's Island (1941) 227, 254
Chuvalo, George 53
Ciannelli, Eduardo 88
Cilento, Diane 162, 207
Cimarron (1930/31) **29**, 36, 167, 183, 193, 239
Cimino, Michael **39**, 189, 214, 239
Cincinnati Kid, The (1965) 249
Cinderella Liberty (1973) 212
Cinema Paradiso (1989) **29–30**, 100n
cinematography 222–223 see also personal names (e.g., Rittenberg, Joseph)
Cioffi, Charles 88, 104, 141
Ciolli, Augusta 99
Circus, The (1927/28) 89, 192, 253
Citadel, The (1938) 195, 196, 239
Citizen Kane (1941) 6, 10, **30**, 76, 133, 178, 197, 239
City Lights (1931) 249
City of Wax (1934) 226
City Slickers (1991) **30**, 191, 220
City Streets (1931) 249
Clancy, Tom 77
Clanton, Ralph 35
Clark, Candy 212
Clark, Fred 143, 151
Clark, Jim **86**
Clark, Oliver 148
Clark, Petula 260
Clarke, T. E. B. **90**
Clatworthy, Robert **142**
Claudine (1974) 212
Clayburgh, Jill 214
Clayton, Jack 67, 136, 206, 242, 250, 251
Cleese, John 52, 53
Clements, Ron 3, 93
Clennon, David 16, 104
Cleopatra (1934) **30**, 193, 239
Cleopatra (1963) 18, **30–31**, 207, 222, 223, 239

Clift, Montgomery 55, 72, 84, 123, 124, 139, 200, 202, 206
Climbing the Matterborn (1947) 228
Cline, Georgia Ann 29
Cline, Patsy 31
Clockwork Orange, A (1971) 211, 239, 246
Cloquet, Ghislain **155**
Close, Glenn 37, 133, 134, 216, 217, 218
Closed Mondays (1974) 233
Close Encounters of the Third Kind (1977) 1, **31**, 214
Close Harmony (1981) 235
Closely Watched Trains (1967) 31
Cluzet, Francois 137
Coal Miner's Daughter (1980) **31**, 189, 215, 239
Coates, Anne **91**
Cobanoglu, Necmettin 84
Cobb, Irvin S. 259
Cobb, Lee J. 9, 48, 49, 76, 117, 144, 159, 203, 205
Cobbs, Bill 32
Coburn, Charles **106**, 126, 175, 185, 197, 198, 199
Cochran, Steve 177
Cocker, Joe 114
Coco, James 215
Cocoon (1985) **31–32**, 190, 217
Coe, Fred 158, 242
Coe, George 88
Coen, Joel 246, 249, 250
Cohan, George M. 179
Cohn, Harry **81**
Colasanto, Nicholas 130
Colbert, Claudette 11, 30, **81**, 116, 143, 183, 194, 198
Cole, George 31
Cole, Nat King 26, 27
Coleman, Dabney 117, 162
Colette 61
Colicos, John 9
Collector, The (1965) 208
Collier, Constance 36
Collier Jr., William 29
Collin, John 155
Collinge, Patricia 197
Collings, Pierre **149**
Collins, Pauline 219
Collins, Ray 13, 30, 44, 72, 92, 143
Collins, Russell 47
Collodi, Carlo 123
Colman, Ronald **44**, 95, 185, 192, 197, 200, 245
Colonel Redl (1985) 114
Color of Money, The (1986) **32**, 77, 190, 217, 218, 245
Color Purple, The (1985) 118, 217, 239, 246
Coltrane, Robbie 72
Columbus, Chris 247
Come and Get It (1936) **32**, 184, 194, 222, 244
Come Back, Little Sheba (1952) **32**, 186, 202
Come Fill the Cup (1951) 156, 202
Comegys, Kathleen 103
Comer, Sam 55, **137, 138, 151**
Comes a Horseman (1978) 214

"Come Tell Me What's Your Answer" 109
Come to the Stable (1949) 201
Coming Home (1978) **32–33**, 189, 214, 221, 239
Comingore, Dorothy 30
Commitments, The (1991) 246
Common Threads: Stories from the Quilt (1989) 236
Compson, Betty 192
Conant, Oliver 150
Condemned (1929/30) 192
Cong Su **89**
Conklin, William 42
Conn, DiDi 180
Connelly, Sean 63, 77, 78, 108, 159, **168**, 190, 218
Connolly, Walter 65, 81
Conquest (1937) 195
Conrad, Con **58**
Conrad, Michael 156
Conrad, Scott **135**
Conrad, William 19
Constant Nymph, The (1943) 198
Conte, Richard 62, 78
Conti, Bill **134**
Conti, Gino 150
Conti, Tom 153, 216
Conti, Ugo 100
Contreras, Patricio 114
Conversation, The (1974) 212, 239, 246
Conway, Jack 169, 241, 242, 243
Coogan, Jackie 84
Coogan, Robert 143
Cook, Donald 170
Cook Jr., Elisha 30, 141
Cook, Gordon Henry 253
Cook, the Thief, His Wife and Her Lover, The (1990) 249
Cool Hand Luke (1967) 32, **33**, 188, 209
Coolidge, Martha 248
Coolidge, Philip 81
Cooney, Kevin 165
Coop, Denys **152**
Cooper, Ben 137
Cooper, Gary 256; *Cowboy and the Lady* 34; *Farewell to Arms* 51; *High Noon* **73–74**, 131, 186, 202, 222, 245; *Lives of a Bengal Lancer* 94; *Mr. Deeds Goes to Town* 107, 194; *Northwest Mounted Police* 112–113; *Pride of the Yankees* 126, 197; *Sergeant York* 131, **140**, 184, 197, 222; *Westerner* 172; *For Whom the Bell Tolls* 54, 198; *Wings* 175
Cooper, Gladys: *Bishop's Wife* 18; *Kitty Foyle* 88; *My Fair Lady* 109, 208; *Now, Voyager* 113, 198; *Princess O'Rourke* 126; *Rebecca* 132; *Separate Tables* 140; *Song of Bernadette* 144, 198; *That Hamilton Woman* 155; *This Above All* 157
Cooper, Jackie 27, 143, 152, 193
Cooper, James Fenimore 90
Cooper, Melville 2
Cooper, Merian C. 250, 255
Copeman, Michael 53
Copland, Aaron **72**

Coppola, Carmine **62**, 164
Coppola, Francis Ford: *Apocalypse Now* 11, 215, 238; *Bram Stoker's Dracula* 21; *Conversation* 239, 246; *Cotton Club* 246; *Godfather* **61–62**, 117, 211, 222, 240; *Godfather Part II* **62**, 117, 164, 189, 212, 222, 240; *Godfather Part III* 219, 240, 247; *Patton* **121**, 222; *Tucker: The Man and His Dream* 248
"Coquette"(1928/29) 33
Coquette (1928/29) **33**, 183, 192
Corby, Ellen 200
Corcoran, James P. **145**, 224
Cording, Harry 121
Corduner, Allan 179
Corey, Wendell 139
Corman, Roger 251
Corn Is Green, The (1945) 199
Cornthwaite, Bob 171
Corrigan, Lloyd 35
Cortese, Valentina 14, 38, 212
Corti, Jesse 15
Cosby, Bill 26
Cossart, Ernest 88, 139
Costa-Gavras 98, **104**, 181, 210, 241, 243, 247
Costello, Dolores 157
Coster, Nicolas 133
Costner, Kevin **36**, 82, 168, 191, 219, 239
costume design 223 see also personal names (e.g., Head, Edith)
Cotten, Joseph 30, 51, 58, 125, 143, 157, 163
Cotton Club, The (1984) 246
Coulouris, George 30, 112, 172
Coulson, Bernie 2
Country (1984) 217
Country Cousin (1936) 226
Country Girl, The (1954) **33**, 103, 186, 203, 239
Courcel, Nicole 151
Courtenay, Tom 43, 153, 208, 216
Court Jester, The (1956) 249
Cousin, Cousine (1976) 213
Cover Girl (1944) **33–34**
Cowan, Jerome 67, 103
Coward, Noel 19, 27, 139, 240, 254
Cowboy and Lady, The (1938) **34**
Cowling, Bruce 149
Cox, Joel **167**
Cox, John **91**
Cox, Ronny 20, 135, 163
Coyote, Peter 48
Crac (1981) 235
Craig, Helen 143
Craig, James 6, 77, 88
Craig, Stuart **37, 57**
Crain, Jeanne 84, 149, 201
Crane, Norma 52
Crash Dive (1943) **34**
Crashing the Water Babies (1956) 230
Crawford, Broderick **6**, 20, 94, 185, 201
Crawford, Joan: *Grand Hotel* 65; *Mildred Pierce* **102–103**, 185, 199; *Possessed* 51, 200; *Sudden*

Fear 30, 202; *What Ever Happened to Baby Jane?* 173
Crawford, Michael 56, 72
Creature Comforts (1990) 237
Cregar, Laird 18, 19, 72
Crenna, Richard 99
Crichton, Charles 52, 53, 91, 219, 249, 250
Cries and Whispers (1973) **34**, 212, 239
Crimes and Misdemeanors (1989) 219, 246
Crimes of the Heart (1986) 217, 218
Crino, Isa 93
Crisp, Donald: *Charge of the Light Brigade* 27; *How Green Was My Valley* **76**, 184, 197, 245; *Jezebel* 82; *Life of Emile Zola* 92; *Mutiny on the Bounty* 108; *National Velvet* 110; *Wuthering Heights* 178
Cristiani, Gabriella **89**
Critic, The (1963) 231
Croghan, Declan 109
Cromwell (1970) **34**
Cromwell, John 9, 143, 242, 248, 259
Cromwell, Richard 94, 95
Cronenberg, David 53, 249, 250
Cronyn, Hume 31, 32, 198
Crosby, Bing: *Bells of St. Mary's* 16, 199; *Country Girl* 33, 203; *Going My Way* **62**, 175, 185, 198; *Here Comes the Groom* 73; *Holiday Inn* 74; *King of Jazz* 87; *Waikiki Wedding* 171
Crosby, Floyd **153**
Crosby, Percy 143
Crosman, Henrietta 37
Cross, Ben 28
Cross, Christopher **12**
Cross, Hugh 140
Cross Creek (1983) 216, 246
Crosse, Rupert 210
Crossfire (1947) 59, 80, 200, 239, 246
Crouse, Lindsay 124, 217
Crowd, The (1927/28) 192
Cruel Sea, The (1953) 91
Cruickshank, Art **51**
Cruise, Tom 20, 32, 131, 163, 219
Crunch Bird, The (1971) 233
Cry Freedom (1987) 218, 246
Crying Game, The (1992) **34**, 220, 239
Cry in the Dark, A (1988) 145, 218, 246
Crystal, Billy 30, 259, 261
Cserhalmi, Gyorgy 101
Cugat, Xavier 111
Cukor, George 244; *Born Yesterday* 20, 201, 239, 245; *David Copperfield* 239, 246; *Dinner at Eight* 249; *Double Life* 44, 200, 245; *Gaslight* 58, 240, 245; *Les Girls* 92; *Little Women* 94, 193, 241; *My Fair Lady* **109**, 187, 208, 241, 245; *Philadelphia Story* 122, 197, 241, 245; *Romeo and Juliet* 242; *Song Without End* 144; *Star Is Born* 248; *Travels With My Aunt* 164; *Women* 251

Cul-de-Sac (1966) 249
Culver, Michael 121
Culver, Roland 161, 169
Cummings, Constance 19
Cummings, Irving 79, 109, 192, 243
Cummings, Quinn 64, 214
Cummings, Robert 126
Cunningham, Cecil 12
Cuny, Alain 44
Curram, Roland 38
Curreri, Lee 50
Currie, Finlay 16, 67
Currier, Frank 153
Curry, Tim 77
Curtis, Donald 146
Curtis, Jamie Lee 52, 53
Curtis, Tony 40, 67, 144, 146, 205, 260
Curtiz, Michael: *Adventures of Robin Hood* 2, 238; *Angels With Dirty Faces* 196; *Captain Blood* 239; *Casablanca* 26–27, 185, 198, 239; *Charge of the Light Brigade* 27; *Four Daughters* 196, 240; *Life With Father* 247; *Mildred Pierce* 103, 241; *Private Lives of Elizabeth and Essex* 248; *Sea Hawk* 248; *This Is the Army* 157; *Yankee Doodle Dandy* 179, 198, 243
Cusack, Joan 177, 218
Cushing, Peter 148
Cyphers, Charles 33
Cyrano de Bergerac (1950) 34–35, 71, 84, 185, 201
Cyrano de Bergerac (1990) 35, 219
Czechoslovakia 1968 (1969) 232

D

Da Costa, Morton 108, 239, 241
Dafoe, Willem 20, 104, 105, 125, 218
Dailey, Dan 106, 200
Dale, Virginia 74
Dali, Salvador 146
Dall, John 199
Dalrymple, Ian **128**
Dalton, Audrey 140, 160
Dalton, Phyllis **43, 72**
Dalton, Timothy 34, 93
Damage (1992) 109, 220
Damita, Lily 22
Damsel in Distress, A (1937) **36**
Dances With Wolves (1990) 29, **36**, 167, 191, 219, 224, 239
Dandridge, Dorothy 125, 203
Dane, Clemence **169**
Dane, Patricia 84
D'Angelo, Beverly 31
Dangerous (1935) 36–37, 184, 194, 221
Dangerous Liaisons (1988) **37**, 218, 219, 239
Dangerous Moves (1984) **37**
Daniel, Gordon **65**
Daniell, Henry 92, 97, 172
Daniels, Anthony 47, 133, 148
Daniels, Jeff 154
Daniels, William 65, **110**, 158
Danova, Cesare 31
Dante, Joe 79

Dantine, Helmut 26
Danton, Ray 78
D'Antoni, Philip **54**
Darby, Ken **26, 87, 125,** 225
Darby, Kim 165
D'Arcy, Alexander 12
Darien, Frank 14
Darin, Bobby 207
Dark Angel, The (1935) **37**, 194, 223
Dark at the Top of the Stairs, The (1960) 206
Dark Eyes (1987) 218
Dark Victory (1939) 196, 239, 246
Darling (1965) 37–38, 145, 187, 208, 239
Darling, William S. **9, 27, 144,** 223
Darnell, Linda 9, 19, 92
Darren, James 69
Darro, Frankie 123
Darrow, Tony 65
Darwell, Jane 6, **66,** 100, 131, 184, 197, 245
Das Boot (1982) 216, 246
da Silva, Howard 96
Dassin, Jules 110, 111, 163, 206, 249
Dauphin, Claude 98
Davalos, Richard 46
Davenport, Doris 172
Davenport, Harry 13, 34, 51, 81, 126
Davenport, Nigel 28, 98
Daves, Delmer 251
Davey, Allen 253
David, Hal **24**
David, Keith 17
David, Thayer 135, 138
David and Lisa (1962) 207
David Copperfield (1935) 194, 239, 246
Davidson, Jaye 34, 220
Davies, Marion 50
Davies, Terence 249
Davies, Valentine **103**
Davis, Bette: *All About Eve* 5, 201; *Dangerous* 36–37, 184, 194, 221; *Dark Victory* 196; *Death on the Nile* 39; *Great Lie* 67; *Jezebel* **82,** 184, 195, 221, 244; *Letter* 196, 244; *Little Foxes* 197; *Mr. Skeffington* 198; *Now, Voyager* 113, 197; *Star* 202; *Watch on the Rhine* 172; *What Ever Happened to Baby Jane?* 173, 207
Davis, Brad 101, 102
Davis, Geena 1, 15, 53, 156, 162, 190, 218, 220
Davis, George W. **40, 135,** 223
Davis, Harry 8
Davis, Judy 109, 120, 121, 217, 220
Davis Jr., Sammy 125, 260
Davison, Bruce 219
Dawn, Jeff **154**
Dawn, Marpessa 18
Dawn Patrol, The (1930/31) **38**
Dawson, Ralph **2, 10, 102,** 223, 224
Day, Doris 25, 96, 99, 123, 205
Day, Laraine 73

Day, Morris 127
Day, Richard 37, **43, 76, 109,** **117, 150, 157,** 223
Daybreak in Udi (1949) 229
Day for Night (1973) **38**, 59, 78n, 212
Day-Lewis, Daniel 45, 90, **109,** 136, 191, 219
Day of the Locust, The (1975) 213
Day of the Painter (1960) 231
Days of Heaven (1978) **38**
Days of Waiting (1990) 237
"Days of Wine and Roses" **38,** 225
Days of Wine and Roses (1962) **38,** 207, 225
Day the Earth Stood Still, The (1951) 249
Dead, The (1987) 246
Dead End (1937) 178, 195, 239, 246
Deadly Deception: General Electric, Nuclear Weapons and Our Environment (1991) 237
Dead of Night (1945) 249
Dead Poets Society (1989) 38–39, 219, 239
Dead Ringers (1988) 249
"Deadwood Stage, The" 25
Dean, James 46, 60, 144, 203, 204
Dean, Laura 50
Dean, Quentin 80
Dear, William 71
Dearden, Basil 249
Death Becomes Her (1992) **39**
Death of a Salesman (1951) 202, 246
Death on the Nile (1978) **39**
De Banzie, Brenda 99
De Camp, Rosemary 19, 157, 179
De Carlo, Yvonne 153
December 7th (1943) 226, 227
Decision Before Dawn (1951) 201, 239
Declaration of Independence (1938) 227
De Concini, Ennio **43**
De Cordova, Arturo 54, 55
De Corsia, Ted 84, 110, 111, 166
DeCuir, John **30, 72, 86,** 223
Dee, Frances **94**
Deeley, Michael **39**
Deer Hunter, The (1978) 32, 39–40, 71, 124, 189, 214, 239
De Fas, Boris 153
Defiant Ones, The (1958) **40,** 205, 239
DeFore, Don 50, 157
De Forest, Lee 256
Degnan, Martina 60
De Guzman, Hermino 179
De Havilland, Olivia: *Adventures of Robin Hood* 2; *Anthony Adverse* 10; *Charge of the Light Brigade* 27; *Gone With the Wind* 64, 196; *Heiress* **72,** 185, 201, 221, 244; *Hold Back the Dawn* 197; *Midsummer Night's Dream* 102; *Princess O'Rourke* 126; *Snake Pit* 143, 200; *To Each His Own* **161,** 185, 199, 221
Dehn, Paul **140**

De Keyser, David 179
Dekker, Albert 46, 59
De Lacey, Philippe 172
Delerue, Georges **94**
Del Hoyo, Pablo 161
De Lint, Derek 12
Deliverance (1972) 211, 239, 246
Del Ruth, Roy 23, 53, 239
Demarest, William 67, 84, 199
Dembo, Richard 37
DeMille, Cecil B. 252, 255; *Cleopatra* 30, 239; *Greatest Show on Earth* 66, 74, 202, 240; *Northwest Mounted Police* 112–113; *Plainsman* 251; *Reap the Wild Wind* 132; *Samson and Delilah* 138; *Ten Commandments* 113, 153, 242
DeMille, William C. 259
Demme, Jonathan 101, **142,** 191, 220, 242, 251
De Mornay, Rebecca 165
Dench, Judi 73, 136
Deneuve, Catherine 79, 220
De Niro, Robert: *Awakenings* 219; *Cape Fear* 220; *Deer Hunter* 39, 214; *Godfather Part II* **62,** 189, 212, 222; *Goodfellas* 65; *Mission* 104; *Raging Bull* **130,** 189, 215, 222, 245; *Taxi Driver* 213; *Untouchables* 168
Denner, Charles 181
Dennis, Nick 150
Dennis, Sandy **174,** 188, 209
Denny, Reginald 132
De Oliveira, Lourdes 18
DePalma, Brian 168, 249
Depardieu, Gerard 35, 59, 219
De Pasquale, Frederic 55
DePatie, Edmond L. 252
De Re, Michel 151
Derek, John 6, 48, 153
Der Fuehrer's Face (1942) 227
Dern, Bruce 32, 33, 67, 156, 214
Dern, Laura 100, 220
Derr, Richard 173
Dershowitz, Alan 133
Dersu Uzala (1975) **40,** 132
De Santis, Pasqualino **136**
Desert Victory (1943) 227
De Sica, Vittorio 58, 166, 180, 204
Desideri, Osvaldo **89**
Design for Death (1947) 228
Designing Woman (1957) **40**
Desny, Ivan 145
Destination Moon (1950) **40,** 159
Detective Story (1951) 80, 202, 246
Deutsch, Adolph **9, 114, 140**
Deutsch, Ernst 157
Devil and Miss Jones, The (1941) 197
Devil's Holiday, The (1929/30) 192
Devine, Andy 79, 146, 147
De Vinna, Clyde **173**
DeVito, Danny 154, 247, 251
Dewaere, Patrick 59
De Wilde, Brandon 76, 141, 203
DeWolfe, Billy 26
Diamantidou, Despo 111
Diamond, Donald 115
Diamond, I. A. L. **10,** 222

269

Diary of a Mad Housewife (1970) 210

Diary of Anne Frank, The (1959) **40–41**, 121, 187, 205, 222, 223, 239

Dick, Phillip K. 163

Dickens, Charles 67, 115, 174, 226

Dickinson, Angie 260

Dick Tracy (1990) **41**, 139, 219

Dieterle, William: *All That Money Can Buy* 6; *Hunchback of Notre Dame* 247; *Life of Emile Zola* 12, 92, 195, 241; *Midsummer Night's Dream* 102, 241; *Portrait of Jennie* 125; *Story of Louis Pasteur* 149, 242

Dietrich, Marlene 84, 141, 193

Digges, Dudley 108

Dighton, John 135*n*

Digirolamo, Don **48**

Dillaway, Donald 103

Dilley, Leslie **130**, **148**

Dillinger, John 98

Dillman, Bradford 172

Dillon, Carmen **70**, 72*n*

Dillon, Kevin 125

Dillon, Melinda 20, 31, 71, 214, 215

Diner (1982) 247

Dinesen, Isak 13, 118

Dinner at Eight (1933) 249

direction 183–220 *see also* personal names (e.g., Wyler, William)

Dirty Dancing (1987) **41–42**

Dirty Dozen, The (1967) **42**, 209

Dirty Harry (1971) 249

Discreet Charm of the Bourgeoisie, The (1972) **42**, 59, 78*n*

Disney, Walt 45, 226, 252, 253, 254

Disney Studios **165**

Disraeli (1929/30) **42**, 92, 183, 192, 239

Disraeli, Benjamin 42

Distant Voices, Still Lives (1989) 249

Dith Pran 86

Divine Lady, The (1928/29) **42**, 183, 192

Divorcee, The (1929/30) **42–43**, 183, 192, 193, 239

Divorce Italian Style (1962) **43**, 207

Dix, Richard 29, 193

Dixon, Ivan 121

Dixon, Vernon **14**, **111**, **115**

Dmytryk, Edward 23, 200, 239, 246, 249

Doctor Dolittle (1967) **43**, 209, 239

Doctor Zhivago (1965) **43**, 121, 137, 223, 224, 239

documentary and short subjects 226–237

Dodsworth (1936) **43–44**, 194, 195, 223, 239

Dog Day Afternoon (1975) **44**, 139, 212, 213, 239

Doll, Dora 18

Dollar Bottom, The (1980) 235

Dominici, Arturo 80

Donald, James 22, 97

Donaldson, Roger 249

Donaldson, Ted 165

Donat, Robert **64–65**, 126, 184, 195, 196

Donath, Ludwig 84

Donati, Danilo **51**, **136**

Donen, Stanley 117, 140, 242, 248

Donlevy, Brian 67, 79, 81, 196

Donner, Richard 115, 152

Donovan, King 40

Don't (1974) 233

Don't Look Now (1973) 249

"Don't Rain on My Parade" 56

Doody, Alison 78

Dooley, Paul 21

Doors, The (1991) 249

DoQui, Robert 110, 135

Doran, Mary 23

Dorian, Angela 137

Dot and the Line, The (1965) 232

Do the Right Thing (1989) 219, 247

Dotrice, Karen 100

Dotrice, Roy 8

Double Indemnity (1944) 198, 199, 239, 247

Double Life, A (1947) **44**, 185, 200, 224, 245

Douglas, Kirk: *Bad and the Beautiful* 13, 171, 202; *Champion* 27, 171, 201; *Letter to Three Wives* 92; *Lust for Life* 96–97, 171, 204; *Spartacus* 146; *20,000 Leagues under the Sea* 165

Douglas, Lloyd C. 135

Douglas, Melvyn 260; *Being There* **15–16**, 189, 214–215, 222; *Captains Courageous* 26; *Hud* **76**, 187, 207, 222; *I Never Sang for My Father* 210

Douglas, Michael **171**, 190, 218

Douglas, Mike **116**

Douglas, Nathan E. **40**

Douglas, Paul 92, 119, 143, 259

Douglas, Robert 2

Douglass, Robyn 21

Dourif, Brad 105, 116, 213

Dove, The (1927/28) **44**, 153

Dow, Peggy 71

Dowd, Nancy **32**

Dowling, Doris 96

Down, Lesley-Ann 94

Down And Out In America (1986) 236

Down and Out in Beverly Hills (1986) 249

Downey Jr., Robert 220

Dr. Ehrlich's Magic Bullet (1940) 149

Dr. Jekyll and Mr. Hyde (1931/32) 27, **45**, 131, 183, 193, 222

Dr. Strangelove (1964) 207, 208, 239, 247

Dr. Zhivago (1965) 208

Dracula (1931) 249

Drag (1928/29) 192

Drago, Billy 168

Dragon, Carmen **33**

Dragon Seed (1944) 199

Drake, Charles 3, 61, 71

Draughtsman's Contract, The (1983) 247

Dreier, Hans **55**, **138**, **151**

Dresser, Louise 140, 192

Dresser, The (1983) 153, 216, 239, 247

Dressler, Marie 42, **103**, 183, 193

Drexler, Doug **41**

Dreyfuss, Richard 31, **64**, 82, 189, 213

Driscoll, Bobby 144, 255

Drivas, Robert 33

Driving Miss Daisy (1989) **44–45**, 151, 190, 191, 219, 239

Drugstore Cowboy (1989) 249

"Drum Crazy" 46

Drums Along the Mohawk (1939) 196

Dry White Season, A (1989) 219

Duberg, Axel 169

Dubin, Al **62**, 225

Duel in the Sun (1946) 199

Duff, Howard 88, 110

Dufilho, Jacques 18

Dukakis, Olympia **105–106**, 106, 190, 218

Duke, Patty **103**, 187, 207

Dukes, David 94

Dullea, Keir 166

Du Maurier, Daphne 55, 132

Dumbo (1941) **45**, 93

Dumbrille, Douglas 86, 107, 110

Dumke, Ralph 143

Dun, Dennis 90

Dunaway, Faye: *Bonnie and Clyde* 19–20, 209; *Chinatown* 29, 212; *Network* **111**, 189, 213, 245; *Thomas Crown Affair* 158; *Towering Inferno* 164

Dunbar, Adrian 34

Duncan, Mary 106

Dunn, James 14, **164–165**, 185, 199, 244

Dunn, Lindwood G. 253

Dunn, Michael 142, 208

Dunn, Nora 177

Dunn, Stephen **16**, **157**

Dunne, Griffin 8

Dunne, Irene 9, 12, 29, 173, 193, 194, 195, 196, 200

Dunning, John D. **16**

Dunnock, Mildred 24, 152, 170, 202, 204

Duprez, June 112, 157

Dupuis, Stephan **53**

Durante, Jimmy 81

Durbin, Deanna 116, 253

Durning, Charles 149, 162, 216

Duryea, Dan 126

Duvall, Robert: *Apocalypse Now* 11, 215; *Bullitt* 24; *Godfather* 61, 211; *Godfather Part II* 62; *Great Santini* 215; *M*A*S*H* 100; *Network* 111; *Tender Mercies* **153–154**, 190, 216; *True Grit* 165

Duvall, Shelley 10, 110

Duvivier, Julien 68

Dwan, Allan 28

Dwyer, William 28

Dyall, Franklin 126

Dykstra, John **148**

Dylan, Bob 32

Dylan Thomas (1962) 231

Dysart, Richard 15, 100, 171

Dresser, Louise 140, 192

Dzundza, George 40

E

Eagels, Jeanne 192

Eagler, Paul **125**

Earthquake (1974) **46**

Easdale, Brian **132–133**

"Easter Parade" 4

Easter Parade (1948) **46**, 225

East Lynne (1930/31) 193, 239

Eastman Kodak 258

East of Eden (1955) **46**, 186, 203, 204, 244

Eastwood, Clint 17, **167–168**, 191, 220, 243, 250, 251, 260

Easy Rider (1969) 210, 247

Eaton, Shirley 63

Ebersole, Christine 8

Ebsen, Buddy 21, 23

Eddy, Nelson 110, 122

Edemann, Louis L. **174**

Eden, Barbara 17

Edens, Roger **9**, **46**, **117**, 225

editing 223–224

Edlund, Richard **47**, **130**, **133**, **148**

Edouart, Farciot **81**, **132**

Edson, Richard 125

Educating Peter (1992) 237

Educating Rita (1983) 70, 153, 216, 247

Edward, My Son (1949) 201

Edwards, Anthony 163

Edwards, Blake 21, 38, 67, 169

Edwards, Cliff 45, 123, 143

Edwards, James 138

Edwards, Paddi 94

Edwards, Vince 159

Edward Scissorhands (1990) 247

Edzard, Christine 247

Egg and I, The (1947) 200

Eggar, Samantha 43, 208

Eginton, Margaret 139

8 1/2 (1963) 8, 8*n*, 46, 100*n*, 112, 207

Eight Men Out (1988) 249

84 Charing Cross Road (1987) 249

Eikenberry, Jill 12

Eilbacher, Lisa 114

Eilers, Sally 14

Ekberg, Anita 44

El Cid (1961) 247

Eldredge, John 37

Eldridge, Florence 43

Eleanor Roosevelt Story, The (1965) 232

Elek, Zoltan **100**

Elephant Man, The (1980) 215, 239, 246, 247

Elg, Taina 92

Elias, Hal 258

El-Kadi, Nameer 129

Ellenshaw, Peter **99**

Elliot, Stephen 12

Elliott, Denholm 22, 78, 131, 136, 218

Elliott, Sam 100

Elliott, Stephen 74

Elliott, Walter G. **81**

Ellis, Evelyn 80

Elmer Gantry (1960) **46–47**, 187, 206, 239

270

Elsom, Isobel 96
Elwes, Cary 21, 61
Emerson, Hope 201
Emert, Oliver **161**
Emery, John 19, 73, 146
Emigrants, The (1972) 211, 239
Emma (1931/32) 193
Empire of the Sun (1987) 247
Empire Strikes Back, The (1980) **47**
Enchanted April (1992) 109, 220, 247
End of the Game, The (1975) 234
Enemies: A Love Story (1989) 219, 247
Enemy Below, The (1957) **47**
Entertainer, The (1960) 206
Epstein, Julius J. and Philip G. **26**
Equus (1977) 174n, 213, 214
Erdman, Richard 147
Erickson, Leif 143
Ericson, John 15
Erikson, Leif 171
Ermey, R. Lee 105
Ersatz (The Substitute) (1961) 231
Erwin, Stuart 32, 170, 194
Escape Me Never (1935) 194
Eskimo (1934) **47**
Estabrook, Howard **29**
E.T. *The Extra-Terrestrial* (1982) **48**, 162, 216, 224, 239
Eureka (1984) 249
Evans, Edith 162, 207, 208, 209
Evans, Josh 20
Evans, Maurice 137
Evans, Ray **26**, **98**, **119**
"Evergreen" **147–148**
Every Child (1979) 234
Executive Suite (1954) 203, 247
Exodus (1960) **48**, 206
Exorcist, The (1973) **49**, 149, 212, 239
Eythe, William 75, 144

F

Fabulous Baker Boys, The (1989) 102, 219, 247
Face in the Crowd, A (1957) 249
Face of Lincoln, The (1955) 230
Faces (1968) 210
Face to Face (1976) 213
Facing Your Danger (1946) 228
Facts of Life, The (1960) **50**, 223
Fahrenheit 451 (1966) 249
Fain, Sammy **25**, **96**, 225
Fairbanks, Douglas 254, 259
Fairbanks Jr., Douglas 38, 106
Fair Co-ed, The (1927/28) **50**, 90, 153
Faison, Frankie 143
Falana, Lola 260
Falk, Peter 67, 81, 206
Falk, Rosella 46
Fallen Idol, The (1949) 115, 201, 247
"Fame" **50**
Fame (1980) **50**
Fancy Free (ballet) 117
Fanny (1961) 206, 240
Fanny and Alexander (1983) **50–51**, 216
Fantasia 254

Fantastic Voyage (1967) **51**, 79
Fapp, Daniel L. **172**
Farewell, My Lovely (1944) 249
Farewell, My Lovely (1975) 213
Farewell to Arms, A (1932/33) **51**, 193, 240
Farewell to Arms, A (1957) 204
Farley, Walter 18
Farmer, Frances 32
Farmer's Daughter, The (1947) **51**, 185, 200
Farnham, Joseph **50**, **90**, **153**
Farr, Glenn **134**
Farrar, David 18
Farrar, Jane 122
Farrar, Scott **31**
Farrell, Charles 140, 150
Farrell, Glenda 63, 84
Farrell, Nicholas 28
Farrow, John **11**, 198, 243, 248, 249
Farrow, Mia 39, 67, 70, 137
"Fascinating Rhythm" 89
Fast, Howard 146
Fatal Attraction (1987) 218, 240, 247
Fat City (1972) 211
Father Goose (1964) **51**
Father of the Bride (1950) 201, 240, 247
Faulkner, Carl **86**
Faust (play by Goethe) 101
Fawcett, George 153
Fawcett-Majors, Farrah 95
Faye, Alice 4, 72, 79, 160
Faylen, Frank 96
Fazan, Adrienne **61**
Fedora (1978) 249
Fegte, Ernst 40, **55**
Feld, Fritz 173
Felix, Seymour **68**
Fell, Norman 24
Fellini, Federico 8n, 258; *Amarcord* 8, 112, 213; *8 1/2* 8, 8n, 46, 112, 207; *Fellini Satyricon* 8n, 211; *Fellini's Casanova* 8n, 51–52; *I Vitelloni* 8n; *La Dolce Vita* 8n, 44, 206; *La Strada* 8, 8n, 112, 149; *Nights of Cabiria* 8, 112; *Open City* 8n; *Paisan* 8n
Fellini Satyricon (1970) 8n, 211
Fellini's Casanova (1976) 8n, **51–52**
Felton, Verna 45
Fenton, Leslie 21
Ferber, Edna 29, 32, 60
Ferdinand the Bull (1938) 227
Fernandez Muro, Marta 161
Ferrándis, Antonio 161
Ferrari, William **58**, 223
Ferrer, Jose: *Cyrano the Bergerac* **34–35**, 71, 185, 201; *Joan of Arc* 83, 200; *Lawrence of Arabia* 91; *Moulin Rouge* 106–107, 202; *Ship of Fools* 142
Ferrer, Mel 92, 93
Ferrer, Miguel 135
Ferrier, Noel 179
Few Good Men, A (1992) 220, 240, 247
Fiddler on the Roof (1971) **52**, 211, 240

Field, Betty 123
Field, Roy 152
Field, Sally 112, **124**, 189, 190, 214, 217, 221
Field, The (1990) 219, 247
Fielding, Henry 162
Fielding, Marjorie 91
Field of Dreams (1989) 219, 240, 247
Fields, A. Roland **19**
Fields, Dorothy **152**
Fields, Verna **82**
Fields, W. C. 17
Fighting Lady, The (1944) 227
Fillmore, Clyde 106
film *see* specific title (e.g., *Ben-Hur*)
Finch, Jon 39
Finch, Peter **111**, 189, 211, 213, 245
Finlay, Frank 34, 208
Finlayson, James 38
Finn, John 61
Finney, Albert 71, 108, 153, 162, 207, 212, 216, 217
First a Girl (1936) 169
First Steps (1947) 228
Firth, Peter 77, 155, 214
Fishburne, Larry 11
Fish Called Wanda, A (1988) **52–53**, 190, 218, 219
Fisher, Carrie 47, 70, 133, 141, 148
Fisher, Eddie 24
Fisher, Frances 168
Fisher King, The (1991) **53**, 191, 220
Fitzgerald, Barry: *Going My Way* 16, **62**, 90, 185, 198; *How Green Was My Valley* 76; *Naked City* 110; *None But the Lonely Heart* 112; *Quiet Man* 129
Fitzgerald, Cissy 90
Fitzgerald, Geraldine 12, 71, 172, 175, 178, 196
Fitzgerald, Scott 67
Five Easy Pieces (1970) 210, 240, 247
Five Fingers (1952) 202
Five Star Final (1931/32) 193, 240
Fixer, The (1968) 209
Flaherty, Robert 153
Flaiano, Ennio 8n
Flamenco at 5:15 (1983) 235
Flannery, William **122**
Flashdance (1983) 50n, **53**
"Flashdance...What a Feeling" 50n, **53**
Flash Gordon (1936) 148
Fleischer, Charles 174
Fleischer, Richard 43, 51, 163, 165, 239
Fleming, Rhonda 146
Fleming, Victor: *Captains Courageous* 26, 239; *Gone With the Wind* 63–64, 184, 196, 240; *Joan of Arc* 70, 83; *Test Pilot* 242; *Way of All Flesh* 172, 243; *Wizard of Oz* 176, 243
Fletcher, Louise **116**, 189, 213
Flick, Stephen **135**

Flight of the Gossamer Condor, The (1978) 234
Flight of the Phoenix (1965) 208
Flirtation Walk (1934) 193, 240
Flon, Suzanne 107
Flowers, A. D. **125**, **163**
Flowers and Trees (1931/32) 226
Fly, The (1980) 235
Fly, The (1986) **53**
Flynn, Errol 2, 27
Foch, Nina 8, 146, 153, 203
"Foggy Day in London Town, A" 36
Foldi, Erzsebet 6
Folies Bergere (1935) 23, **53–54**
Fonda, Henry 258; *Grapes of Wrath* 66, 196; *How the West Was Won* 76; *Jezebel* 82; *Longest Day* 95; *Mister Roberts* 105; *On Golden Pond* 116–117, 189, 215
Fonda, Jane 260, 261; *California Suite* 25–26; *Cat Ballou* 27; *China Syndrome* 214; *Coming Home* 32–33, 189, 214, 221; *On Golden Pond* 117, 215; *Julia* 85, 214; *Klute* 88, 188, 211, 221; *Morning After* 217; *They Shoot Horses, Don't They?* 156, 210
Fontaine, Joan: *Constant Nymph* 198; *Damsel in Distress* 36; *Frenchman's Creek* 55; *Rebecca* 132, 196; *Suspicion* 152, 184, 197; *This Above All* 157
Fontanne, Lynne 193
Foote, Horton **153**, **161**, 165
"Footloose" 50n
Footloose (1984) 50n
"For All We Know" **96**
Foran, Dick 37
Forbes, Ralph 55
Forbidden Games (1951) 255
Forbstein, Leo **10**
Force in Readiness, A 256
Ford, Francis 129
Ford, Glenn 80, 152
Ford, Harrison: *Apocalypse Now* 11; *Empire Strikes Back* 47; *Indiana Jones and the Last Crusade* 78; *Indiana Jones and the Temple of Doom* 78; *Raiders of the Lost Ark* 130; *Return of the Jedi* 133; *Star Wars* 148; *Witness* 175–176, 217; *Working Girl* 177
Ford, John: *Arrowsmith* 239; *Battle of Midway* 226; *December 7th* 226; *Grapes of Wrath* 66, 184, 197, 221, 240, 245; *How Green Was My Valley* 76, 184, 197, 221, 240, 245; *How the West Was Won* 76, 240; *Hurricane* 77; *Informer* **79**, 184, 194, 221, 240, 245; *Last Hurrah* 250; *Long Voyage Home* 241, 247; *Man Who Shot Liberty Valance* 247; *Mister Roberts* 105, 241, 244, 245; *My Darling Clementine* 250; *Quiet Man* **129**, 186, 202, 221, 242; *Searchers* 251; *Seven Women* 251; *She Wore a Yellow Ribbon* 141; *Stagecoach* 146, 196, 242, 245; *Sun Shines Bright* 251; *Wagonmaster* 251

Ford, Michael **130**
Ford, Paul 108
Ford, Wallace 19, 79, 121
Foreign Correspondent (1940) 152, 196, 240, 247
Foreman, Carl 22n, 74
Forester, C. S. 3
Forman, Milos: *Amadeus* **7**, 190, 217, 238; *One Flew Over the Cuckoo's Nest* **116**, 189, 213, 241; *Ragtime* 248
Forrest, Frederic 11, 215
For Scent-imental Reasons (1949) 228
Forsey, Keith **53**
Forster, E. M. 75, 121, 136
Forsyth, Bill 250
Forsyth, Bruce 15
Forsythe, William 41
For the Boys (1991) 220
Fortune Cookie, The (1966) **54**, 188, 209
Forty Ninth Parallel (1942) See *Invaders, The*
Forty-Second Street (1932/33) 92, 193, 240, 247
For Whom the Bell Tolls (1943) **54**, 185, 198, 240
Fosse, Bob: *All That Jazz* 6, 215, 238; *Cabaret* **25**, 188, 211, 239; *Lenny* 212, 241, 247
Foster, Barry 137
Foster, Harve 144
Foster, Jodie: *Accused* **2**, 190, 218, 221; *Alice Doesn't Live Here Anymore* 4; *Silence of the Lambs* **142**, 191, 220, 221; *Taxi Driver* 213
Foster, Lewis R. **107**
Foster, Preston 71, 79, 112, 113
Foster, Susanna 122
Foundas, George 111, 181
Four Daughters (1938) 195, 196, 240
Four Feathers, The (1939) 249
Four Seasons, The (musical group) 42
1492: Conquest of Paradise (1992) 249
Fowler, Hugh S. **121**
Fowley, Douglas 102
Fox, Earle 164
Fox, Edward 58
Fox, James 121, 158
Fox, Michael J. 13
Fox, Paul S. **31**, **86**, **135**
Fox Studio **151**
Frances (1982) 216
Franceschi, Antonia 50
Franciosa, Anthony 204
Francis, Anne 56
Francis, Freddie **61**, **145**
Francis, Kay 116
Franciscus, James 99
Frank, Anne 40
Frank, Frederic M. **66**
Frank Jr., Harriet 112
Frank, Melvin 50, 164, 243, 249
Frankenheimer, John 65, 66, 247
Frankenstein (1931) 250
Frankeur, Paul 42
Frank Film (1973) 233
Franklin, Aretha 32

Franklin, Pamela 126
Franklin, Sidney 37, 65, **107**, 195, 239, 240, 242, 252
Frankovich, M. J. 252
Franz, Eduard 66
Fraser, Elisabeth 121
Frawley, William 103, 106
Frayne, John G. 253
Freaks (1933) 250
Frears, Stephen 37, 220, 239, 247, 250, 251
Frederici, Blanche 51
Freed, Arthur **8**, **60**, 252, 257
Freeman, Charles **125**
Freeman, Jonathan 3
Freeman, Mona 106
Freeman, Morgan 44, 45, 61, 167, 168, 218, 219
Freeman, Paul 130
Freeman, Y. Frank 252, 257
Free Soul, A (1930/31) **54**, 183, 193
Fregis, Lucien 105
French Connection, The (1971) **54–55**, 130, 168, 188, 211, 222, 240
French Lieutenant's Woman, The (1981) 145, 215, 240
Frenchman's Creek (1945) **55**
Fresholtz, Les **7**, **17**
Freund, Karl **65**, 250
Frey, Leonard 52, 211
Fricker, Brenda **109**, 191, 219
Fried Green Tomatoes at the Whistle Stop Cafe (1991) 220, 247
Friedhofer, Hugo **17**
Friedkin, William 49, **54–55**, 188, 211, 212, 239, 240
"Friend Like Me" 50n
Friendly Persuasion (1956) 204, 240, 247
Frobe, Gert 63
Froeling, Ewa 51
Froeschel, George **107**
From Here to Eternity (1953) 5n, **55**, 114, 135n, 141, 186, 202, 203, 221, 240, 245
From Mao to Mozart: Isaac Stern in China (1980) 235
Front Page, The (1930/31) 143, 193, 240, 247
Front Page, The (1975) 250
Frost, Sadie 21
Fruchtman, Lisa **134**
Frye, Sean 48
Fuchs, Daniel **96**
Fugard, Athol 58, 86
Full Metal Jacket (1987) 247
Fulton, Jessie Lee 120
Fulton, John **153**, **177**
"Fun House" **36**
Funke, Alex **163**
Funny Girl (1968) **55–56**, 93, 147, 188, 209, 210, 240, 244
Funny Thing Happened on the Way to the Forum, A (1966) 56
Furlong, Edward 154
Furneaux, Yvonne 44
Furness, Betty 152
Furse, Judith 65
Furse, Margaret **9**
Furse, Roger K. **70**
Furst, Anton **14**

G
Gable, Clark: *Free Soul* 54; *Gone With the Wind* 64, 196; *It Happened One Night* **81**, 183, 194; *Manhattan Melodrama* 98; *Mutiny on the Bounty* 108, 194; *San Francisco* 138; *Teacher's Pet* 156
Gabor, Eva 61
Gabor, Zsa Zsa 93, 107
Gaby—A True Story (1987) 218
Gaines, George **7**, **71**
Gaines, Richard 106
Gallo, Mario 130
Gam, Rita 88
Gammon, James 102
Gandhi (1982) 36, 48, **57–58**, 162, 190, 216, 221, 240
Gangelin, Victor A. **172**
Gann, Ernest 73
Garber, Matthew 100
Garbo, Greta 65, 110, 193, 195, 196, 256
Garci, José Luis 161
Garcia, Andy 168, 219
Garcia, Lea 18
Gardenia, Vincent 105, 106, 212, 218
Garden of Allah, The 253
Garden of the Finzi-Continis, The (1971) **58**, 100n
Gardiner, Reginald 36
Gardner, Ava 14, 46, 112, 203
Gardner, Herb 158
Garfield, Allen 26, 110
Garfield, John 3, 19, 59, 195, 200
Gargan, William 196
Garity, William 254
Garland, Beverly 84
Garland, Judy 254; *Easter Parade* 46; *Harvey Girls* 71; *Judgment at Nuremberg* 84, 206; *Star Is Born* 147, 203; *Strike Up the Band* 150; *Wizard of Oz* 176
Garmes, Lee **141**
Garner, James 65, 66, 139, 169, 217
Garner, Peggy Ann 165, 254
Garnett, Tay 116, 251
Garr, Teri 18, 31, 162, 216
Garrett, Betty 111, 117
Garrick, Beulah 44
Garson, Greer: *Blossoms in the Dust* 19, 197; *Goodbye, Mr. Chips* 64–65, 196; *Madame Curie* 198; *Mrs. Miniver* **107**, 184, 197, 244; *Mrs. Parkington* 198; *Pride and Prejudice* 126; *Sunrise at Campobello* 206; *Valley of Decision* 199
Gary, Lorraine 82
Gaslight (1944) 9, 25n, **58**, 108n, 185, 198, 199, 221, 223, 240, 245
Gassner, Dennis **23**
Gate of Hell (1954) **58**, 256
Gates, Larry 80
Gaudio, Tony **10**
Gausman, Russell A. **122**, **146**
Gavin, John 146, 158
Gay Divorcee, The (1934) **58**, 193, 194, 240
Gaynes, George 162

Gaynor, Janet 257, 260; *Seventh Heaven* **140**, 183, 192; *Star Is Born* 147, 195; *Street Angel* **150**, 183, 192; *Sunrise* **151**, 183, 192
Gaynor, Mitzi 84, 92, 146
Gazzo, Michael V. 62, 212
Gehrig, Lou 126
Gelin, Daniel 99
General Died at Dawn, The (1936) 32, 194
Genn, Leo 125, 143, 202
Genocide (1981) 235
Gentleman's Agreement (1947) 51, **58–59**, 162, 185, 200, 221, 240, 244
George, Dan 71
George, Gladys 194
George, William **79**
Georgeson, Tom 53
Georgy Girl (1966) 208, 209
Gerald McBoing-Boing (1950) 229
Gere, Richard 38, 114
Geret, Georges 181
Germi, Pietro 43, **43**, 207
Gerroll, Daniel 28
Gershe, Leonard 24
Gershwin, George 36, 125
Gershwin, Ira 34
Gerstad, Harry 27, **73**
Get Out Your Handkerchiefs (1978) **59**, 78n
Getty, Estelle 100
Getz, John 53
Gherardi, Piero **44**, **46**
Ghost (1990) **60**, 93, 114, 191, 219, 240
Ghostbusters (1984) 247
Giallelis, Stathis 8
Giannetti, Alfredo **43**
Giannini, Giancarlo 213
Giant (1956) **60**, 186, 204, 240
Gibbons, Cedric 223; *American in Paris* **8**, 223; *Bad and the Beautiful* **13**, 223; *Blossoms in the Dust* **19**, 223; *Bridge of San Luis Rey* **22**, 223; *Gaslight* **58**, 223; *Julius Caesar* **85**, 223; *Little Women* **94**, 223; *Merry Widow* **101**, 223; *Pride and Prejudice* **125**, 223; *Somebody Up There Likes Me* **144**, 223; *Yearling* **179**, 223
Gibbons, Floyd 175
Gibbs, George **78**, **174**
Gibney, Sheridan **149**
Gibson, Henry 110
Gibson, Mel 134, 179
Gibson, Virginia 140
Gibson, William 103
Gielgud, John 215; *Arthur* **12**, 190, 215; *Becket* 15, 208; *Chariots of Fire* 28; *Gandhi* 58; *Julius Caesar* 85; *Murder on the Orient Express* 108
Giger, H. R. **4**
"Gigi" **61**
Gigi (1958) **60–61**, 89, 144, 186, 187, 205, 221, 222, 225, 240
Giglio, Sandra 171
Gilbert, Billy 116
Gilbert, Lewis 238, 246, 247, 248
Gilbert, Lou 170
Gilbert, Ray **144**

Gilchrist, Connie 92
Gilda (1946) 250
Gilford, Jack 32, 56, 138, 212
Gilks, Alfred **8**
Gillespie, A. Arnold **16, 68, 125, 157**
Gillette, Anita 106
Gilliam, Terry 53, 246
Gilliat, Sidney 251
Gilmore, Lowell 87, 123
Gilmore, Virginia 126
Gilpin, Jack 134
Gilroy, Frank 150
Gimbel, Norman **112**
Gingold, Hermione 61, 94, 108
Ginty, Robert 33
Gish, Lillian 125, 199, 257
Giuffre, Aldo 180
Giuseppina (1960) 231
"Give a Little Whistle" 123
Give 'Em Hell, Harry (1975) 213
Give Me Liberty (1936) 226
"Give My Regards to Broadway" 22, 179
Glass (1959) 231
Glass, Ned 119
Glass, Robert **48**
Glasser, Michael 24
Glass Menagerie, The (1987) 250
Glazer, Benjamin **11, 140**
Gleason, Jackie 77, 119, 206
Gleason, James 18, 34, 54, 73, 109, 165, 197
Gleason, Keogh **8, 13, 61, 144**
Gleason, Paul 154
Gleason, Russell 6
Glengarry Glen Ross (1992) 139, 220
Glenn Sr., Roy E. 68
Glenn, Scott 77, 110, 134, 142
Glenn Miller Story, The (1954) 23, **61**
Glenville, Peter 15, 208, 239
Gloria (1980) 215
Glory (1989) **61**, 93, 114, 191, 219
Glover, Brian 8
Glover, Crispin 13
Glover, Danny 124, 176
Glover, John 173
Glover, Julian 78
Glynn, Carlin 165
Gner, Yasar 84
Go-Between, The (1971) 211
Goddard, Paulette 112, 113, 132, 198
Godden, Rumer 18
Godfather, The (1972) **61–62**, 117, 121*n*, 131, 139, 188, 211, 212, 222, 240
Godfather, Part II, The (1974) **62**, 71, 117, 130, 139, 164, 189, 212, 222, 240
Godfather, Part III, The (1990) 219, 240, 247
Godunov, Alexander 176
Going My Way (1944) 16, **62**, 90, 175, 185, 198, 199, 225, 240
Gold, Ernest **48**
Goldberg, Whoopi 60, 93, 114, 191, 217, 219
Goldblum, Jeff 53, 110, 155

Gold Diggers of 1935 (1935) **62–63**, 225
Golden Fish, The (1959) 230
Goldfinger (1964) **63**
Goldman, Bo **100, 116**
Goldman, Emma 133
Goldman, James **93**
Goldman, William **7, 24**, 104
Goldoni, Lelia 4
Goldsmith, Jerry **115**
Goldstein, Jenette 5
Goldwyn, Samuel **17**, 252
Goldwyn, Tony 60
Golino, Valeria 131
Golitzen, Alexander **122, 146, 161**
Gombell, Minna 14, 68
Gomez, Thomas 86, 200
Goncalves, Milton 88
Gone With the Wind (1939) 5*n*, 55, 60, **63–64**, 89, 108, 184, 196, 221, 223, 240, 254
Gonzalez, Agustin 161
Good, Jack 51
Goodbye, Miss Turlock (1947) 228
Goodbye, Mr. Chips (1939) 64, **64–65**, 184, 196
Goodbye, Mr. Chips (1969) 210
Goodbye Girl, The (1977) **64**, 189, 213, 214, 240
Goodbye to Berlin (Christopher Isherwood) 25
Good Earth, The (1937) **65**, 184, 195, 212, 221, 222, 240
Goodfellas (1990) **65**, 191, 219, 220, 240, 245
Goodman, John B. **122**
Good Morning, Vietnam (1987) 218, 247
Goodwin, Bill 84, 161
Goodwin, Laurel 119
Goosson, Stephen **95**
Gordon, Barry 158
Gordon, Dexter 137, 217
Gordon, Don 24
Gordon, Grant 150
Gordon, Harold 170
Gordon, Mack **72**, 225
Gordon, Michael 35, 123
Gordon, Ruth **137**, 188, 208, 210
Gordon, Steve 12
Gore, Michael **50**
Gorgeous Hussy, The (1936) 194, 195
Gorillas in the Mist (1988) 82*n*, 218, 247
Goring, Marius 14, 133
Goring, Ruth 179
Gorman, Cliff 6
Gorman, Robert 2
Goss, Walter **80**
Gossett Jr., Louis 61, 93, **114**, 164, 190, 216
Gottfried, Gilbert 3
Gottlieb, Carl 82
Goudge, Elizabeth 68
Gough, Michael 14, 118, 177
Gould, Chester 41
Gould, David **23, 53**
Gould, Elliott 24, 100, 210, 260
Gould, Harold 149

Goulding, Edmund 45, 65, 67, 132, 239, 240, 242, 246
Gozzi, Patricia 151
Grable, Betty 106, 160
Grace, Henry **61**
Graduate, The (1967) **65**, 80, 88, 188, 209, 240
Graff, Todd 1
Graham, Angelo **62**
Grahame, Gloria 13, 66, 115, 186, 200, 202
Grahame, Margot 79
Gran, Albert 140
Granath, Bjorn 122
Grand Canyon (1958) 230
Grand Canyon (1991) 247
Granddad of Races (1950) 229
Grand Hotel (1931/32) 45, **65**, 73, 169, 183, 193, 240
Grand Prix (1966) **65–66**
Granger, Stewart 87
Grant, Cary 257; *Awful Truth* 12; *Bachelor and the Bobby-Soxer* 13; *Bishop's Wife* 18; *To Catch a Thief* 161; *Father Goose* 51; *None But the Lonely Heart* 112, 198; *Penny Serenade* 197; *Philadelphia Story* 122; *Suspicion* 152
Grant, Lawrence 141, 259
Grant, Lee 80, 99, **141**, 189, 202, 211, 213
Grant, Richard E. 21
Grant, Rodney A. 36
Granville, Bonita 113, 195
Grapes of Wrath, The (1940) **66**, 184, 196, 197, 221, 240, 245
Grapewin, Charley 26, 65, 66, 176
Grass, Gunter 160
Grauman, Sid 255
Graves, Peter 147
Graves, Rupert 137
Gravet, Fernand 68
Gravity Is My Enemy (1977) 234
Gray, Dolores 40
Gray, Dorian 112
Gray, Nadia 44
Gray, Spalding 86
Grayson, Kathryn 9
Graziano, Rocky 144
Grease (1978) 155
Great (1975) 234
Great American Cowboy, The (1973) 233
Great Caruso, The (1951) **66**, 224
Great Dictator, The (1940) 196, 240, 247
Greatest Show on Earth, The (1952) **66**, 74, 186, 202, 240
Great Expectations (1947) **67**, 200, 240
Great Gatsby, The (1974) **67**
Great Lie, The (1941) **67**, 184, 197
Great McGinty, The (1940) **67**
Great Race, The (1965) **67**
Great Santini, The (1980) 215
Great Waldo Pepper, The (1975) 250
Great Waltz, The (1938) **68**, 144, 196, 222
Great White Hope, The (1970) 210
Great Ziegfeld, The (1936) 65, **68**, 107, 184, 194, 195, 221, 240

Greco, Jose 142
Greek Tragedy, A (1986) 236
Green, Alfred E. 37, 42, 84, 239
Green, Guy 67, 121
Green, Johnny **8, 46, 115, 172**, 224, 225
Green, Mitzi 143
Greenaway, Peter 249
Greenberg, Jerry **54**
Green Card (1990) 247
Green Dolphin Street (1947) **68**
Greene, Clarence **123**
Greene, Graham 36, 157, 164, 219
Greene, Lorne 46
Greene, Richard 86
Greene, W. Howard **122, 147**, 253
Green Goddess, The (1929/30) 192
Greenham, Vivian C. **69**
Greenlaw, Verina 51
Greenstreet, Sydney 27, 197
Greenwood, Charlotte 115
Greenwood, Joan 162
Green Years, The (1946) 199
Gregg, Virginia 96
Gregory's Girl (1982) 250
Gregson, John 91
Grenzbach, Charles "Bud" **124**
Gretler, Heinrich 99
Grey, Jennifer 42
Grey, Joel **25**, 188, 211
Greystoke: The Legend of Tarzan, Lord of the Apes (1984) 217, 247
Grief, Robert 54
Griem, Helmut 25
Griffin, Eleanore **20**
Griffith, Corinne 42, 119
Griffith, D(avid) W(ark) 253
Griffith, Hugh **16**, 48, 115, 162, 187, 205, 207, 244
Griffith, Melanie 102, 177, 218
Griffith, Raymond 6
Grifters, The (1990) 219, 220, 247
Griggs, Loyal **141**
Grimes, Gary 150
Grimes, Stephen **118**
Grodin, Charles 72, 87, 176
Groesse, Paul **94, 125, 179**, 223
Grosbard, Ulu 150
Group, The (1966) 250
Groves, George R. **109, 139**
Grusin, Dave **102**
Gryff, Stefan 173
Guard, Christopher 94
Guardsman, The (1931/32) 193
Guerra, Tonino 8*n*
Guess Who's Coming to Dinner (1967) **68**, 106, 117, 188, 209, 221, 240
Guest, Judith 118
Guetary, Georges 8
Guffey, Burnett **19, 55**
Guffey, Cary 31
Guffroy, Pierre **155**
Guillermin, John 39, 87, 164, 243
Guinness, Alec 257; *Bridge on the River Kwai* 22, 186, 204; *Cromwell* 34; *Doctor Zhivago* 43; *Empire Strikes Back* 47; *Great Expectations* 67; *Lavender Hill Mob* 90–91, 202; *Lawrence of Ara-*

273

bia 91; *Little Dorrit* 218; *Passage to India* 121; *Star Wars* 148, 214
Guittard, Laurence 94
Gulager, Clu 90
Gunga Din (1939) 250
Gunn, Moses 141
Guns of Navarone, The (1961) **69**, 206, 240
Guss, Louis 106
Guthrie, Woody 20
Guttenberg, Steve 32
Guve, Bertil 51
Gwenn, Edmund 10, 68, **103**, 126, 185, 200, 201
Gwynne, Fred 109

H

Haas, Hugo 87
Haas, Lukas 175, 176
Hackett, Buddy 81, 94, 108
Hackett, Joan 215
Hackford, Taylor 114, 173
Hackman, Gene: *Bonnie and Clyde* 20, 209; *French Connection* **54–55**, 130, 188, 211, 222; *Marooned* 99; *Mississippi Burning* 104–105, 218; *Poseidon Adventure* 125; *Superman* 152; *Unforgiven* **167–168**, 191, 220, 222
Hadjidakis, Manos **111**
Haffenden, Elizabeth **16, 98**
Hageman, Richard 66, **146**
Hagen, Jean 202
Hagen, Uta 134
Haggard, H. Rider 87
Hagman, Larry 71
Haigh, Kenneth 31
Haigh, Nancy **23**
Hail the Conquering Hero (1944) 67
Haines, Randa 28, 239
Haines, William 153
Haker, Gabrielle 137
Hale, Alan 2, 81, 157
Haley, Jack 4, 176
Haley, Jackie Earle 21
Hall, Albert 11
Hall, Alexander 73, 197, 240
Hall, Cecilia **77**
Hall, Conrad **24**
Hall, Grayson 112, 208
Hall, Jerry 14
Hall, Jon 77
Hall, Juanita 146
Hall, Kevin Peter 71
Hall, Porter 103
Hall Jr., William 45
Hallelujah (1929/30) 193
Haller, Ernest **64**
Halliday, John 37, 122, 164
Hallstrom, Lasse 218
Halmer, Gunter Maria 58
Halsey, Richard **135**
Halton, Charles 172
Hamer, Robert 249, 250
Hamill, Mark 47, 133, 148
Hamilton, Gay (actor) 14
Hamilton, Guy (director) 63
Hamilton, Hale 27
Hamilton, Linda 154
Hamilton, Margaret 176
Hamilton, Murray 65, 77, 82, 172

Hamilton, Neil 38, 121, 143
Hamilton, Suzanna 118
Hamilton, William 155
Hamlet (1948) 58, **70**, 162, 185, 200, 201, 240
Hamlet (1990) 247
Hamlisch, Marvin **149**, 155, **172**
Hammerstein II, Oscar 87, **89**, 114, 145, 146, **148**
Hammett, Dashiell 85
Hammond, Kay 19
Hampden, Walter 138
Hampton, Christopher **37**
Han, Maggie 90
Hancock, Herbie **137**
Handford, Peter **118**
Handful of Dust, A (1988) 247
Handy, James 17
Haney, Kevin **44**
Hanks, Tom 218
Hannah, Daryl 171
Hannah and Her Sisters (1986) **70**, 190, 217, 218, 240
Hansen, E. H. **131, 175**
Hansen, Gale 38
Hanson, Peter 173
Happy Anniversary (1962) 231
Happy Ending, The (1969) 210
Harada, Mieko 132
Harburg, E. Y. **176**
Hardin, Jerry 104
Harding, Ann 193
Harding, Lyn 65
Hardwicke, Cedric 152, 153, 175
Hardy, Oliver 226
Hardy, Thomas 155
Hare, Lumsden 54
Harlan County, U.S.A. (1976) 234
Harline, Leigh **123**
Harling, Franke **146**
Harlow, Jean 79
Harnick, Sheldon 52
Harper, Tess 153, 218
Harris, Barbara 110, 158, 211
Harris, Ed 1, 124, 134
Harris, Joel Chandler 144
Harris, Julie (actress) 46, 202
Harris, Julie (costume designer) **37**
Harris, Julius 87
Harris, Lara 53
Harris, Phil 73
Harris, Richard 26, 34, 168, 207, 219
Harrison, George 92
Harrison, Noel 158
Harrison, Rex: *Anna and the King of Siam* 9; *Blithe Spirit* 19; *Cleopatra* 31, 207; *Doctor Doolittle* 43; *My Fair Lady* 108, **109**, 187, 207, 245
Harry and the Hendersons (1987) **70–71**
Harry and Tonto (1974) **71**, 189, 212
Harryhausen, Ray 253
Hart, Dorothy 110
Hart, Emma 155
Hart, Moss 180
Hart, Richard 68
Hartman, Elizabeth 121, 208
Harvey (1950) **71**, 122, 186, 201

Harvey, Anthony 93, 210, 241
Harvey, Laurence 3–4, 24, 37, 38, 136, 177, 205
Harvey Girls, The (1946) **71**, 225
Hasegawa, Kazuo 58
Haskin, Byron 171
Hasso, Signe 44, 75
Hasty Heart, The (1949) 201
Hatfield, Hurd 123
Hathaway, Henry 75, 76, 94, 165, 194, 240, 241, 247, 249
Hatten, Yankton 124
Hauben, Lawrence **116**
Havana (1990) 102
Havelkova, Libuse 31
"Have Nothing" 50n
Haver, Phyllis 172
Havers, Nigel 28, 121
Havlick, Gene **95**
Havoc, June 59, 72
Havrilla, Joann 45
Hawaii (1966) 209
Hawke, Ethan 38
Hawkins, Jack 16, 22, 91, 112
Hawkins, John N. A. 254
Hawks, Howard 257; *Big Sleep* 249; *Bring Up Baby* 249; *Come and Get It* 32, 244; *Dawn Patrol* 38; *To Have and Have Not* 251; *His Girl Friday* 250; *Red River* 248; *Rio Bravo* 251, 257; *Scarface* 251; *Sergeant York* 140, 197, 242; *Viva Villa!* 169
Hawn, Goldie 24, **25**, 39, 141, 188, 210, 215, 260
Haworth, Ted **139**
Hayakawa, Sessue 22, 204
Hayareet, Haya 16
Hayden, Sterling 61
Haydn, Richard 145
Haydon, Julie 139
Hayes, Helen 260; *Airport* **3**, 25n, 108n, 188, 211, 221; *Anastasia* 9; *Farewell to Arms* 51; *Sin of Madelon Claudet* 25n, 108n, **143**, 183, 193, 221
Hayes, Isaac **141**
Hayes, Patricia 17
Haymes, Dick 149
Hayton, Lennie **72**, **117**
Hayward, David 110
Hayward, Louis 10
Hayward, Susan: *I'll Cry Tomorrow* 78, 81, 203; *I Want to Live* **81**, 187, 205; *My Foolish Heart* 81, 201; *Reap the Wild Wind* 132; *Smash-Up, the Story of a Woman* 51, 81, 200; *With a Song in My Heart* 175, 202
Hayworth, Rita 19, 33, 34, 109, 139
Head, Edith **50**, **72**, **123**, **135**, **138**, **149**, 223
Headly, Glenne 41
Heald, Anthony 142
Heard, John 102, 165
Hearn, Ann 2
Hearst, William Randolph 30
Heartbreak Kid, The (1972) 211
Heart Is a Lonely Hunter, The (1968) 209, 210, 247

Hearts and Minds (1974) 234
Heat and Dust (1983) 250
Heather, Jean 62
Heaven Can Wait (1943) 73, 198, 240
Heaven Can Wait (1978) 10n, **71–72**, 102, 214, 240
Heaven Knows, Mr. Allison (1957) 204
Heavenly Music (1943) 227
Hecht, Ben **139**, **167**
Hecht, Harold **99**
Heckart, Eileen **24**, 144, 188, 204, 211
Heckroth, Hein **132**
Hedda (1975) 213
Hedison, Al 47, 53
Heerman, Victor **94**
Heffner, Kyle T. 53, 176
Heflin, Van 3, 68, **83–84**, 141, 184, 197
Heim, Alan **6**
Heindorf, Ray **108**, **157**, **179**
Heineman, Laurie 138
Heiress, The (1949) **72**, 161, 185, 201, 221, 223, 240, 244
Helen Keller in Her Story (1955) 230
Hell in the Pacific (1968) 250
Hellman, Jerome **101**
Hellman, Lillian 85, 171
Hello, Dolly! (1969) **72**, 210, 240
Hello Frisco, Hello (1943) **72**, 225
Hellstrom Chronicle, The (1971) 233
Helm, Levon 31
Helmore, Tom 40, 159
Helpmann, Robert 133
He Makes Me Feel Like Dancin' (1983) 235
Heman, Roger **34**, **82**
Hemingway, Ernest 51, 54, 115
Hemingway, Mariel 215
Hemmings, David 26
Hemphill, Doug **90**
Hemsley, Estelle 8
Hendricks, William L. 256
Hendrix, Wanda 26
Henn, Carrie 5
Hennesy, Dale **51**
Henning, Pat 117
Henreid, Paul 27, 65, 113
Henry, Buck 71, 72, 214, 240
Henry, Justin 88, 215
Henry and June (1990) 134
Henry V (1946) 70n, 72n, 199, 240, 247, 254
Henry V (1989) **72–73**, 219
Henson, Basil 38
Hepburn, Audrey 253; *Breakfast at Tiffany's* 21, 206; *My Fair Lady* 99, 109; *Nun's Story* 205; *Roman Holiday* **135–136**, 186, 203, 244; *Sabrina* 138, 203; *Wait Until Dark* 209, 253
Hepburn, Katharine 221; *African Queen* 3, 202; *Alice Adams* 194; *On Golden Pond* 106, **116–117**, 190, 215, 221; *Guess Who's Coming to Dinner* **68**, 106, 188, 209, 221; *Lion in Winter* 56, **93**, 106, 188, 209, 221; *Little Women* 94;

Long Day's Journey Into Night 207; *Morning Glory* **106**, 183, 193, 221; *Philadelphia Story* 122, 196; *Rainmaker* 204; *Suddenly, Last Summer* 205; *Summertime* 203; *Woman of the Year* 176, 197
Herald, Heinz **92**
Herb Alpert and The Tijuana Brass Double Feature (1966) 232
Herbert, Holmes 45
Herbert, Hugh 68, 102
Herbert, Victor 110
Herczeg, Geza **92**
Here Comes Mr. Jordan (1941) 71, **73**, 197, 240
Here Comes the Groom (1951) **73**, 225
Here Comes the Navy (1934) 92, 194, 240
Herlie, Eileen 70
Hero (1992) 250
Heron, Julia **146**
Herrmann, Bernard **6**
Herrmann, Edward 120, 133
Hershey, Barbara 70, 134, 261
Hersholt, Jean 4, 65, 143, 164, 255
Hersholt Humanitarian Award, Jean 252–253
Hester Street (1975) 213
Heston, Charlton 252, 260; *Ben-Hur* **16**, 187, 205, 244; *Big Country* 17; *Earthquake* 46; *Greatest Show on Earth* 66; *Ten Commandments* 153
Hewitt, Alan 38
Heydt, Louis Jean 67
Heyes, Herbert 124
Heyman, John 121
Hickey, William 127, 217
Hickman, Dwayne 27
Hickson, Joan 140
Hidden Agenda (1990) 250
"Hi-Diddle-Dee-Dee" 123
Higgins, Michael 18
High and the Mighty, The (1954) **73**, 147, 203, 224
High Anxiety (1977) 250
"High Hopes" **74**, 225
High Noon (1952) 29, **73–74**, 131, 140, 186, 202, 222, 224, 240, 245
"High Noon" ("Do Not Forsake Me, Oh My Darlin'") **73–74**
High Sierra (1941) 250
High Society (1956) 247
Hildyard, David **25**, **52**
Hildyard, Jack **22**
"Hi Lili, Hi Lo" 93
Hill, Arthur 94
Hill, George 17, 103, 239
Hill, George Roy: *Butch Cassidy and the Sundance Kid* 24, 210, 239; *Great Waldo Pepper* 250; *Little Romance* 94; *Slaughterhouse Five* 251; *Sting* **149**, 189, 212, 242; *Thoroughly Modern Millie* 158
Hill, James 20
Hill, Steven 179
Hill, The (1965) 250
Hill, Thelma 50
Hiller, Arthur 74, 96, 211, 241

Hiller, Wendy: *Man for All Seasons* 98, 209; *Murder on the Orient Express* 108; *Pygmalion* 128, 195; *Separate Tables* **139–140**, 187, 205; *Sons and Lovers* 145
Hillerman, John 29, 120
Hiltermann, Bob 29
Hilton, James 64, 95, **107**
Hindenburg, The (1975) **74**
Hinds, Samuel S. 19, 180
Hines, Gregory 173
Hingle, Pat 14, 112, 146
Hirsch, Judd 118, 215
Hirsch, Paul **148**
Hirschhorn, Joel **125**, **164**
His Girl Friday (1940) 250
Hitchcock, Alfred 252; *To Catch a Thief* 161; *Foreign Correspondent* 240, 247; *I Confess* 250; *Lady Vanishes* 250; *Lifeboat* 199; *Man Who Knew Too Much* 99; *Marnie* 250; *North by Northwest* 248; *Notorious* 248; *Psycho* 6, 206, 248; *Rear Window* 203, 248; *Rebecca* 132, 197, 242; *Spellbound* 146, 199, 242; *Suspicion* 152, 242; *Thirty-Nine Steps* 251; *Trouble with Harry* 251; *Vertigo* 34, 248; *Wrong Man* 251
Hitler Lives? (1945) 228
Hobart, Rose 45, 51
Hobbes, Halliwell 45
Hobson, Valerie 67
Hobson's Choice (1954) 250
Hoch, Winton C. **82**, 107, **129**, **141**, 223
Hodiak, John 14, 71
Hoerbiger, Paul 157
Hoffa (1992) 247
Hoffman, Dustin: *All the President's Men* 7; *Graduate* 65, 209; *Kramer vs. Kramer* 6, 15, **88**, 189, 214, 222; *Lenny* 71, 212; *Midnight Cowboy* 101, 210; *Rain Man* **131**, 190, 218, 222; *Tootsie* 162, 216
Hoffman, Philip S. 139
Hogan, Louanne 149
Hogan, Paul 260
Holbrook, Hal 7, 85, 171
Hold Back the Dawn (1941) 197, 240
Holden, Fay 19
Holden, Gloria 92
Holden, William: *Born Yesterday* 20; *Bridge on the River Kwai* 22; *Bridges at Toko-ri* 22; *Country Girl* 33; *I Wanted Wings* 81; *Love Is a Many Splendored Thing* 96; *Network* 111, 213; *Picnic* 122; *Sabrina* 138; *Stalag 17* 85, **147**, 186, 202; *Sunset Boulevard* 151, 201; *Towering Inferno* 164
Hole, The (1962) 231
Hole in the Head, A (1959) **74**, 225
Holiday (1930/31) 193
Holiday, Hope 81
Holiday Inn (1942) **74**
Holliday, Judy **20**, 143, 185, 201, 245
Holliman, Earl 23

Holloway, Stanley 90, 91, 109, 208
Holloway, Sterling 45
Holly, Martin 142
Hollywood Revue (1928/29) 192, 240
Holm, Celeste 5, **58–59**, 92, 143, 185, 200, 201, 244
Holm, Ian 5, 28, 72, 215
Holmes, Philip 29
Holmes, William **140**
Holt, Jack 138
Holt, Tim 146, 164
Hombre (1967) 112, 250
Home Alone (1990) 247
Homicide (1991) 250
Homolka, Oscar 177, 200
Hondo (1953) 165, 203
honorary awards 252–258
Hood, Don 134
Hooper, Tobe 248
Hoosiers (1986) 218
Hope, Bob 17, 50, 119, 252, 254, 256, 257, 259, 260
Hope, Frederic **101**, 223
Hope, William 5
Hope and Glory (1987) 134, 218, 240, 247
"Hopelessly Devoted to You" 155
Hopkins, Anthony: *Bram Stoker's Dracula* 21; *Howards End* 75–76; *Lion in Winter* 93; *Silence of the Lambs* 23, **142**, 191, 220
Hopkins, Bo 102
Hopkins, George James 72, **109**, **150**, **174**
Hopkins, Miriam 45, 72, 194
Hoppe, Rolf 101
Hopper, Dennis 11, 60, 165, 218, 247
Hordern, Michael 9, 56
Horn, Camilla 153
Hornbeck, William **123**
Horne, Geoffrey 22
Horne, Victoria 71
Horner, Harry 72, **77**
Horning, William A. **16**, **60**
Horse with the Flying Tail, The (1960) 231
Horton, Edward Everett 58, 73, 95, 101
Horton, Helen 5
Hoskins, Bob 174, 217
Hospital, The (1971) **74**, 211, 222
hosts and presenters 259–260
Hotel Terminus: The Life and Times of Klaus Barbie (1988) 236
Houghton, Katharine 68
House I Live In, The (1945) 254
Houseman, John **119–120**, 188, 212
House of Games (1987) 250
House of Rothschild, The (1934) 194, 240
House of Strangers (1949) 23
House on 92nd Street, The (1945) **74–75**
Houser, Jerry 150
Houston, Donald 136
Howard, Andrea 155
Howard, Cy 96
Howard, Joan 95

Howard, John 122
Howard, Leslie 54, 64, 80, 128, 193, 195, 242
Howard, Ron 32, 248
Howard, Sidney **63**
Howard, Thomas **19**, **162**
Howard, Trevor 51, 58, 137, 145, 152, 157, 206
Howard, William K. 164
Howards End (1992) **75–76**, 191, 220, 240
Howe, James Wong **76**, **137**
Howell, Tom 48
How Green Was My Valley (1941) **76**, 184, 197, 221, 222, 223, 240, 245
How the West Was Won (1963) 29, **76**, 207, 240
How to Sleep (1935) 226
Hoyos, Pablo 161
Hoyos, Rodolfo 21
Hoyt, John 173
Hoyt, Robert **82**
Hubbard, Allan 153
Hubbard, Lucien **175**
Huber, Gusti 41
Hud (1963) 32, **76**, 112, 187, 207, 222
Huddleston, Michael 176
Hudson, Hugh 28, 216, 239, 247
Hudson, Rock 60, 123, 177, 204, 260
Hue and Cry (1947) 250
Hughes, Barnard 74, 101
Hughes, Frank E. **9**
Hughes, Howard 100
Hughes, Ken 34
Hughes, Teresa 33
Hulce, Tom 7, 217
Huldschinsky, Paul **58**
Hull, Henry 21, 68, 125
Hull, Josephine **71**, 186, 201
Human Comedy, The (1943) **76–77**, 198, 240
Human Desire (1954) 250
Humberstone, Bruce 72, 177
Hunchback of Notre Dame, The (1939) 247
Hunnicutt, Arthur 71, 202
Hunt, Hugh **16**, **85**
Hunt, Linda **179**, 190, 216
Hunt, Marsha **19**, 77
Hunt, Martita 9, 15, 67, 145
Hunter, Holly 218
Hunter, Ian 2, 102
Hunter, Ian McLellan **135**, 135n
Hunter, Kim **150**, 186, 202, 244
Hunt for Red October, The (1990) **77**
Hurricane, The (1937) **77**, 195
Hurst, Paul 172
Hurt, John 5, 98, 101, 102, 214, 215
Hurt, William 1–2, 28, **87–88**, 190, 217, 218
Husbands and Wives (1992) 109, 220, 247
Hush...Hush, Sweet Charlotte (1964) 208
Hussey, Olivia 39, 136
Hussey, Ruth 50, 122, 197

Hustler, The (1961) 32, **77**, 206, 240

Huston, Anjelica **126–127**, 190, 217, 219, 245, 261

Huston, John 260; *African Queen* 3, 202, 245; *Asphalt Jungle* 201, 246; *Beat the Devil* 249; *Cardinal* 207, 245, 260; *Chinatown* 29; *Dead* 246; *Key Largo* 86, 245; *Maltese Falcon* 241, 247; *Misfits* 250; *Moulin Rouge* 107, 202, 241; *Night of the Iguana* 112; *Prizzi's Honor* 127, 217, 242, 245; *Red Badge of Courage* 251; *Treasure of the Sierra Madre* 164, 185, 200, 243, 245; *Under the Volcano* 248

Huston, Walter: *All That Money Can Buy* 6, 197; *Dodsworth* 43–44, 194; *Treasure of the Sierra Madre* 127, **164**, 185, 200, 245; *Yankee Doodle Dandy* 179, 197

Hutchinson, Josephine 149

Hutshing, Joe **20**, **82**

Hutton, Betty 9, 66

Hutton, Timothy **118**, 189, 215

Hvenegaard, Pelle 122

Hyams, Leila 17

Hyams, Peter 248

Hyde-White, Wilfrid 109, 157

Hyer, Martha 138, 205

Hymer, Warren 116

Hymns, Richard **78**

Hynes, Fred **3**, **114**, **145**, **172**, 224, 253

I

I Am a Fugitive from a Chain Gang (1932/33) 92, 193, 240, 247

I Confess (1953) 250

If I Were King (1938) 195

If You Love This Planet (1982) 235

Ihnen, Wiard **19**, **175**

"I Just Blew In from the Windy City" 25

"I Just Called to Say I Love You" **176**

"I Left My Heart at the Stage Door Canteen" 157

I'll Cry Tomorrow (1955) **78**, 81, 203

I'll Find a Way (1977) 234

"I'm Easy" **110**

Imitation of Life (1934) 194, 240

Imitation of Life (1959) 205

In a Lonely Place (1950) 250

In Cold Blood (1967) 209, 247

Incredible Shrinking Man, The (1957) 250

Indiana Jones and the Last Crusade (1989) **78**

Indiana Jones and the Temple of Doom (1984) **78**

Indochine (1992) **78–79**, 100n, 220

Inescort, Frieda 37, 126

I Never Sang for My Father (1970) 210

Informer, The (1935) **79**, 108, 143, 183, 184, 194, 221, 224, 240, 245

Inge, William 32, **146**

Ingram, Rex 157

Ingrassia, Ciccio 8

Inherit the Wind (1960) 206, 247

Innerspace (1987) **79**

Innocents, The (1961) 250

Inn of The Sixth Happiness, The (1958) 205

In Old Arizona (1928/29) 29, **79**, 183, 192, 240

In Old Chicago (1937) **79**, 184, 195, 240

Inside Daisy Clover (1965) 208

Inside Moves (1980) 215

Interiors (1978) 165, 214, 247

Interrupted Melody (1955) **80**, 203

Interviews with My Lai Veterans (1970) 233

"In the Cool, Cool, Cool of the Evening" **73**, 225

In the Heat of the Night (1967) **80**, 188, 209, 240

In the Region of Ice (1976) 234

In the Shadow of the Stars (1991) 237

Intruder in the Dust (1949) 250

Invaders, The (1942) **80**, 197, 240

Invasion of the Body Snatchers (1956) 250

Invasion of the Body Snatchers (1978) 250

Investigation of a Citizen Above Suspicion (1970) **80**, 100n

Invisible Man, The (1933) 250

In Which We Serve (1943) 198, 240, 254

Ireland, John 6, 201

I Remember Mama (1948) 200

Irma La Douce (1963) **80–81**, 154, 207, 225

Irons, Jeremy 104, **133–134**, 191, 219

Ironside, Michael 163

Ironweed (1987) 145, 218, 247

Irving, Amy 179, 216

Isadora (1968) 209

Isedal, Tor 169

Isherwood, Christopher 25

Ishioka, Eiko **21**

Is It Always Right to Be Right? (1970) 233

"It Goes Like It Goes" **112**

It Happened One Night (1934) 64, **81**, 116, 142, 183, 194, 221, 240

"It Might as Well Be Spring" **148–149**

It's a Mad, Mad, Mad, Mad World (1963) **81**

It's a Wonderful Life (1946) 122, 199, 200, 240, 247

It's Tough to Be a Bird (1969) 232

Iturbi, Jose 9

Ivan, Rosalind 83

Ivanhoe (1952) 202, 240

"I've Got a Feeling You're Fooling" **23**

"I've Had the Time of My Life" **41–42**

Ivernel, Daniel 151

Ives, Burl **17**, 46, 187, 205, 244

Ivey, Judith 176

Ivory, James 76, 136, 218, 220, 240, 242, 246, 247, 250

I Vitelloni (1957) 8n

I Wanted Wings (1941) **81**

I Want to Live (1958) 78, **81**, 187, 205

I Won't Play (1944) 227

J

Jabara, Paul **155**

Jabbour, Gabriel 98

Jackson, Glenda: *Hedda* 213; *Sunday, Bloody Sunday* 211; *Touch of Class* 76, **163–164**, 188, 212, 221; *Women in Love* **176–177**, 188, 210, 221

Jackson, Gordon 126

Jackson, Wilfred 144

Jacobi, Derek 72

Jacobi, Lou 41, 81, 145

Jaeckel, Richard 32, 42, 211

Jaffe, Leo 252

Jaffe, Sam 15, 16, 95, 201

Jaffe, Stanley R. **88**

Jaffrey, Saeed 58

Jagged Edge (1985) 217

Jagger, Dean 47, 135, **165**, 185, 201

Jahan, Marine 53

Jahraus, Donald **157**

James, Arthur **96**

James, Clifton 33

James, Gennie 124

James, Geraldine 58

James, Gerard **37**

James, Henry 72

James, Sidney 90, 91

Janda, Krystyna 101

Jandl, Ivan 139, 255

Janis, Conrad 23

Janney, Leon 28

Janney, William 33, 38

Jannings, Emil **89**, 121, **172**, 183, 192

Janssen, David 99

Janssen, Elsa 126

Jarman Jr., Claude 179, 255

Jarre, Maurice **43**, **91**, **120–121**, 224

Jarrott, Charles 9, 238

Jarvis, Graham 104

Jaws (1975) 31, **82**, 212, 224, 240

Jayston, Michael 111

Jazz Singer, The 253

Jeakins, Dorothy **82–83**, **112**, **138**, 223

Jeans, Isabel 61, 152

Jeffries, Lionel 26, 251

Jenkins, Allen 160, 177

Jenkins, Chris **90**, **118**

Jenkins, George **7**

Jenney, Lucinda 131, 156

Jennings, Brent 176

Jennings, DeWitt 103, 166

Jennings, Gordon **81**, **132**

Jennings, Will 114

Jenssen, Eloise **138**, 223

Jerome, Helen 126

Jessel, George 252, 259

Jessel, Patricia 56

Jessup, Harley **79**

Jeter, Michael 53

Jewell, Isabel 95

Jewison, Norman: *Cincinnati Kid* 249; *Fiddler on the Roof* 52, 211, 240; *In the Heat of the Night* 80, 209, 240; *Moonstruck* 106, 218, 241; *Russians Are Coming, the Russians Are Coming* 242; *Soldier's Story* 242; *Thomas Crown Affair* 158

Jezebel (1938) **82**, 184, 195, 221, 240, 244

JFK (1991) **82**, 220, 240

Jhabvala, Ruth Prawer 75, **136**

Joan of Arc (1948) 70, **82–83**, 200, 223, 255

Joffe, Charles H. **9**

Joffe, Roland 86, 104, 217, 218, 240, 241

Johann Mouse (1952) 229

Johar, I. S. 39

Johnny Belinda (1948) **83**, 143, 185, 200, 201, 240

Johnny Eager (1942) **83–84**, 184, 197

Johns, Arthur W. **177**

Johns, Glynis 80, 100, 119, 169, 206

Johnson, Ben **90**, 102, 141, 188, 211

Johnson, Brian **4**, **47**

Johnson, Celia 126, 199

Johnson, J. McMillan **125**

Johnson, Mark **131**

Johnson Jr., Mel 163

Johnson, Nunnally 159

Johnson, P. J. 120

Johnson, Reggie 125

Johnson, Rita 73

Johnson, Sunny 53

Johnson, Tom **154**

Johnson, Van 14, 77, 125, 157

Johnston, Amy 23

Johnston, Joe **130**

Johnstown Flood, The (1989) 236

Joker Is Wild, The (1957) **84**, 225

Jolson, Al 84

Jolson Story, The (1946) **84**, 199

Jones, Barry 125, 140

Jones, Carolyn 74, 204

Jones, Christopher 137

Jones, David 249

Jones, Dickie 123

Jones, Edward **174**

Jones, Henry 24

Jones, James Earl 47, 77, 133, 210, 260

Jones, Jeffrey 8

Jones, Jennifer: *Duel in the Sun* 199; *Love Is a Many Splendored Thing* 96, 203; *Love Letters* 199; *Portrait of Jennie* 125; *Since You Went Away* 143, 199; *Song of Bernadette* **144**, 185, 198; *Towering Inferno* 164

Jones, Jill 128

Jones, Robert C. **32**

Jones, Shirley **46–47**, 108, 115, 187, 206, 260

Jones, Tommy Lee 31, 82, 220

Joplin, Scott 149

Jordan, Dorothy 103

Jordan, Neil **34**, 220, 239, 247

Jordan, Richard 77, 95

Jordan, William 23

Jorgensen, Morten 122

Jory, Victor 102, 103
Josephson, Erland 34, 51
Josiane 99
Joslyn, Allyn 67, 160
Jourdan, Louis 61, 159, 169
Journey Into Self (1968) 232
Journey of Hope (1990) 35, **84–85**
Joyce, Brenda 131
Juarez (1939) 149, 196
Judels, Charles 123
Judgment at Nuremberg (1961) 84, 187, 206, 240
Julia (1977) **85**, 189, 213, 214, 222, 240, 245
Julia, Raul 87–88
Julius Caesar (1953) **85**, 202, 223, 240
Junge, Alfred **18**
Jungle Fever (1991) 250
Junior Bonner (1972) 250
Jurado, Katy 23, 74, 203
Juraga, Boris **30**
Juran, Nathan **76**, 223
Jurgens, Curt 47, 95
Just Another Missing Kid (1982) 235
Justice, James Robertson 69
Justin, John 22, 157

K

Kadar, Jan 142
Kaestner, Erich 253
Kagemusha (1980) 106
Kahane, B. B. 256
Kahn, Madeline 120, 212
Kahn, Michael **130**
Kaminska, Ida 142, 208
Kane, Bob 14
Kane, Carol 10, 213
Kane, Eddie 23
Kanin, Garson 20
Kanin, Michael **176**
Kaper, Bronislau **92–93**
Kaplan, Jonathan 2
Karabarsos, Ron 53
Karam, Elena 8
Karas, Anton 157
Karate Kid, The (1984) 217
Karin, Rita 145
Karinska **82–83**
Karlatos, Olga 127
Karl Hess: Toward Liberty (1980) 235
Karlin, Fred **96**
Karns, Roscoe 81
Karras, Alex 169
Kasdan, Lawrence 2, 238, 239, 246, 247, 248
Kasha, Al **125, 164**
Kasznar, Kurt 93
Kath, Katherine 107
Kato, Kazuo 13
Katselas, Milton 24
Kaufman, Boris **117**
Kaufman, George S. 180
Kaufman, Philip 134, 242, 248, 250
Kava, Caroline 20
Kay, Charles 8
Kaye, Danny 177, 252, 256, 259
Kaye, Lila 8

Kaye, Simon **90, 124**
Kaye, Stubby 27, 174
Kazan, Elia 244; *America, America* 8, 207, 238; *Baby Doll* 246; *East of Eden* 46, 204, 244; *Face in the Crowd* 249; *Gentleman's Agreement* 58–59, 185, 200, 240, 244; *On the Waterfront* 117, 186, 203, 241, 244; *Panic in the Streets* 119; *Splendor in the Grass* 146; *Streetcar Named Desire* 150, 202, 242, 244; *Tree Grows in Brooklyn* 165, 244; *Viva Zapata!* 170, 244; *Wild River* 251
Kazan, Lainie 71
Keaton, Buster 56, 93, 256
Keaton, Diane **9–10**, 62, 133, 189, 214, 215
Keaton, Michael 14, 15
Kedrova, Lila **181**, 187, 208
Keel, Howard 9, 25, 140
Keen, Geoffrey 20
Keene, Christopher J. 60
Kehoe, Jack 101, 168
Ke Huy Quan 78
Keighley, William 2, 238
Keitel, Harvey 24, 156, 220
Keith, David 114
Keith, Donald 172
Keith, Ian 42, 166
Keith, Robert 73, 96, 177
Kellaway, Cecil 55, 68, 71, 80, 125, 178, 200, 209
Keller, Frank P. **24**
Keller, Helen 103
Keller, Jerry 180
Kellerman, Sally 94, 100, 211, 260
Kelley, Barry 84
Kelley, William **175**
Kelly, Emmett 66
Kelly, Gene 255, 260; *American in Paris* 8; *Anchors Aweigh* 9, 199; *Cover Girl* 33–34; *Hello, Dolly!* 72; *Les Girls* 92; *Singin' in the Rain* 248; *On the Town* 117
Kelly, Grace 22, **33**, 74, 161, 186, 203
Kelly, Nancy 204
Kelly, Patsy 34, 137
Kelly, Paul 73
Kempson, Rachel 118
Kendall, Kay 92
Kennedy, Arthur: *Airport* 3; *Bright Victory* 202; *Champion* 27, 201; *Elmer Gantry* 47; *Fantastic Voyage* 51; *Lawrence of Arabia* 91; *Peyton Place* 204; *Some Came Running* 205; *Trial* 203
Kennedy, George 3, **33**, 39, 42, 46, 188, 209
Kennedy, Jihmi 61
Kentucky (1938) **86**, 184, 195, 222
Kern, Hal C. **64**
Kern, Jerome 34, **89, 152**, 225
Kern, Robert J. **110**
Kerr, Deborah: *Black Narcissus* 18; *Edward, My Son* 201, 204, 206; *Heaven Knows, Mr. Allison* 204; *From Here to Eternity* 55, 203; *King and I* 87, 204; *King Solomon's Mines* 87; *Night of the*

Iguana 112; *Separate Tables* 139, 205; *Sundowners* 206
Kerr, John 146
Kershner, Irvin 47
Keyes, Evelyn 73, 84
Key Largo (1948) **86**, 185, 200, 245
Keys of the Kingdom, The (1945) 161, 199
Khouri, Callie **156**
Kibbee, Guy 108
Kidder, Margot 152
Kidnappers, The (1953) 256
Kiebach, Jurgen **25**
Kilburn, Terry 65
Killers, The (1946) 200, 247
Killing, The (1956) 250
Killing Fields, The (1984) **86**, 104, 190, 216, 217, 240
Kilmer, Val 163
Kind Hearts and Coronets (1948) 250
Kindt, Jean-Michel 129
King, Alan 260
King, Betty R. 154
King, Charles 22, 23
King, Henry: *Alexander's Ragtime Band* 4, 238; *Black Swan* 19; *Love is a Many Splendored Thing* 96, 240; *In Old Chicago* 79, 240; *Song of Bernadette* 144, 198, 242; *State Fair* 242, 248; *Twelve O'Clock High* 165, 243; *Wilson* 175, 199, 243
King, Stephen 104
King and I, The (1956) 9, **86–87**, 97, 108, 186, 204, 223, 225, 240
King Kong (1933) 102, 250
King Kong (1976) **87**
King of Comedy, The (1983) 250
King of Jazz (1929/30) **87**
Kingsley, Ben 24, **57–58**, 190, 216, 220
King Solomon's Mines (1950) **87**, 201, 223, 240
Kings Row (1942) 107, 197, 198, 241, 247
Kinski, Nastassia 155
Kinugasa, Teinosuke 58
Kinyanjui, Stephen 118
Kipling, Rudyard 26
Kirby, Bruno 30
Kirkland, Sally 82, 218
Kirsten, Dorothy 66
Kish, Joseph **142**
Kiss Me Deadly (1955) 250
Kiss of Death (1947) 200, 247
Kiss of the Spider Woman (1985) **87–88**, 190, 217, 241
"Kiss the Girl" 50n
Kitchen, Michael 118
Kitty Foyle (1940) **88**, 184, 196, 197, 241
Kjer, Bodil 13
Klane, Robert 155
Kline, Kevin **52–53**, 145, 190, 218
Klos, Elmar 142
Kloves, Steve 247
Klugman, Jack 38
Klute (1971) **88**, 188, 211, 221
Knight, Darrin **39**
Knight, Eric 157
Knight, Esmond 18

Knight, Fuzzy 34
Knight, June 23
Knight, Shirley 152, 206, 207
Knighty Knight Bugs (1958) 230
Knowles, Patric 27
Knox, Alexander 175, 198
Knudson, Robert 25, 48, **49**
Koch, Howard (screenwriter) **26**
Koch, Howard W. (producer/director) 253
Koch, Norma **173**
Koenekamp, Fred **164**
Kohler, Fred 167, 172
Kohner, Susan 205
Kokoda Front Line (1942) 227
Kolker, Henry 33, 34
Koller, Xavier 84
Kon-Tiki (1951) 229
Kopelson, Arnold **124**
Korda, Alexander 126, 155, 169, 242
Korda, Vincent **156**
Korda, Zoltan 249
Korjus, Miliza 68, 196
Korngold, Erich Wolfgang 2, 10n
Korsmo, Charlie 41
Korvin, Charles 142
Kosa Jr., Emil **31**
Kosinski, Jerzy 15, 133
Kostal, Irwin **145, 172**, 225
Koster, Henry 18, 71, 116, 135, 200, 239, 241, 242, 243
Kotch (1971) 211
Kotero, Apollonia 127
Kotto, Yaphet 5, 158
Kovic, Ron 20
Kraaykamp, John 12
Krakatoa (1932/33) 226
Kraly, Hans **121**
Kramer, Stanley 252; *Defiant Ones* 40, 205, 239; *Guess Who's Coming to Dinner* 68, 209, 240; *Inherit the Wind* 247; *It's a Mad, Mad, Mad, Mad World* 81; *Judgment at Nuremberg* 84, 206, 240; *Ship of Fools* 142, 242
Kramer vs. Kramer (1979) 6, 11, 15, 25n, **88**, 108n, 124, 145, 189, 214, 215, 222, 241
Krams, Arthur **137**
Krasker, Robert **157**
Krasna, Norman **126**
Krasner, Milton **159**
Kress, Carl **164**
Kress, Harold F. **76, 164**
Kreuger, Kurt 47
Krige, Alice 28
Krim, Arthur B. 252
Kristofferson, Kris 4, 148
Kroner, Josef 142
Kruger, Hardy 14, 151
Kruger, Otto 34, 74
Krupa, Gene 61
Kruschen, Jack 11, 206
Kubrick, Stanley: *Barry Lyndon* 14, 213, 239; *Clockwork Orange* 211, 239, 246; *Dr. Strangelove* 208, 239, 247; *Full Metal Jacket* 247; *Paths of Glory* 250; *Shining* 251; *Spartacus* 146; *2001: A Space Odyssey* **166**, 166, 210

Kudelski, Stefan 253
Kukan (1941) 254
Kulle, Jarl 13
Kulp, Nancy 159
Kuri, Emile **72, 165**
Kurokawa, Yataro 58
Kurosawa, Akira 40, 106, 131, 132, 217, 258
Kurtz, Swoosie 37
Kussman, Dylan 38
Kyo, Machiko 58

L

La Cage Aux Folles (1979) 215
LaCava, Gregory 195, 242, 247
Lacey, Ronald 130
Laclos, Choderlos de 37
La Cucaracha (1934) 226
Ladd, Alan 26, 141
Ladd, Diane 4, 29, 212, 219, 220
La Dolce Vita (1961) 8n, **44**, 206
Lady Be Good (1941) **89**
Lady for a Day (1932/33) 193, 241, 247
Lady from Shanghai, The (1948) 250
Lady Hamilton (1941) 155
Ladykillers, The (1956) 91
Lady Sings the Blues (1972) 211
Lady Vanishes, The (1938) 250
Laemmle Jr., Carl **5**
Lafont, Jean-Philippe 13
LaGarde, Jocelyn 209
La Grande Illusion (1938) 195, 240
Lagrange, Valerie 98
Lahr, Bert 176
Lahti, Christine 217
Lai, Francis **96**, 98
Laing, Bob **57**
Lake, Veronica 81
Lally, James 177
Lamarr, Hedy 138
Lamorisse, Albert **132**, 132
Lamorisse, Pascal 132
La Motta, Jake 130
Lamour, Dorothy 17, 66, 77
Lancaster, Burt 260; *Airport* 3; *Atlantic City* 215; *Birdman of Alcatraz* 207; *Come Back, Little Sheba* 32; *Elmer Gantry* **46–47**, 187, 206; *From Here to Eternity* 55, 202; *Judgment at Nuremberg* 84; *Rose Tattoo* 137; *Separate Tables* 140
Lanchester, Elsa 18, 100, 110, 126, 132, 201, 204
Landaker, Gregg **47, 130**
Landau, Martin 218, 219
Landicho, Domingo 179
Landis, Carole 109
Landis, Jessie Royce 161
Landis, John 8, 248, 249
Landlord, The (1970) 211
Landsburg, Valerie 155
Lane, Diane 94
Lang Jr., Charles B. **51**
Lang, Fritz 14, 249, 250, 251
Lang, Walter 26, 87, 106, 149, 160, 175, 204, 240
Langan, Glenn 143
Lange, Hope 205

Lange, Jessica: *All That Jazz* 6; *Country* 217; *Frances* 82n, 216; *King Kong* 87; *Music Box* 219; *Sweet Dreams* 217; *Tootsie* 82n, **162**, 190, 216
Langlois, Henry 257
Langrick, Margaret 71
Lanovoi, Vasily 171
Lansbury, Angela 15, 39, 58, 71, 110, 123, 138, 199, 207
Lansing, Joi 21
Lanteau, William 117
Lantz, Walter 257
Lanza, Mario 66
La Porte, Steve **15**
Lardner Jr., Ring **100, 176**
Larkin, Bryan 20
Larkin, Linda 3
Larner, Jeremy **26**
Larsen, Tambi **137**
La Rue, Jack 51
LaShelle, Joseph **90**
Lassally, Walter **181**
Lassick, Sydney 116
Last Angry Man, The (1959) 205
Last Command, The (1927/28) **89**, 172, 175, 183, 192, 241
"Last Dance" **155**
Last Detail, The (1973) 212
Last Emperor, The (1987) 37, **89–90**, 190, 218, 221, 223, 241
Last Hurrah, The (1958) 250
Last Metro, The 106
Last of the Mohicans, The (1992) **90**
Last Picture Show, The (1971) **90**, 188, 211, 241
La Strada (1956) 8, 8n, 100n, 112, **149**
Last Summer (1969) 210
Last Tango in Paris (1973) 212, 247
Last Temptation of Christ, The (1988) 219, 247
"Last Time I Felt Like This, The" 155
"Last Time I Saw Paris, The" **89**
Laszlo, Ernest **142**
Latimore, Frank 132
Lau, Wesley 81
Laugh, Clown, Laugh (1927/28) 50, **90**, 153
Laughton, Charles: *Mutiny on the Bounty* 108, 194; *Night of the Hunter* 249, 250; *Private Life of Henry VIII* **126**, 183, 193; *Spartacus* 146; *This Land Is Mine* 157; *Witness for the Prosecution* 204
Launder, Frank 251
Laura (1944) **90**, 198, 199
Laure, Carole 59
Laurel, Stan 226, 256
Laurie, Piper 29, 77, 206, 213, 218
Lavender Hill Mob, The (1952) 52, **90–91**, 202
Lawford, Peter 46, 48, 94, 95, 123
Lawrence, Barbara 92
Lawrence, D. H. 145, 176
Lawrence, Marjorie 80
Lawrence, Stanley 60

Lawrence of Arabia (1962) **91**, 95, 121, 137, 187, 206, 207, 221, 223, 224, 241
Lawson, Arthur **132**
Lawson, Leigh 155
Lawson, Wilfrid 128
Leach, Rosemary 137
Leachman, Cloris **90**, 188, 211
Lean, David: *Blithe Spirit* 19; *Breaking the Sound Barrier* 21–22; *Bridge on the River Kwai* 22, 186, 205, 239; *Brief Encounter* 200, 246; *Doctor Zhivago* 43, 208, 239; *Great Expectations* 67, 200, 240; *Hobson's Choice* 250; *Lawrence of Arabia* 91, 187, 207, 241; *Oliver Twist* 250; *Passage to India* 120–121, 217, 241; *Ryan's Daughter* 137; *Summertime* 204, 248; *In Which We Serve* 240
Léaud, Jean-Pierre 38
Leave Her to Heaven (1945) 18, **91–92**, 199, 222
Leavitt, Sam **40**
LeBaron, William **29**
LeBlanc, Paul **7**
Le Brock, Kelly 176
Lederer, Francis 26
Lee, Anna 76, 173
Lee, Bernard 63, 157, 159
Lee, Canada 19
Lee, Danny **15**
Lee, Gwen 90
Lee, Harper 161
Lee, Peggy 204
Lee, Spike 247, 250
Leeds, Andrea 32, 195
Leeds, Peter 80
Le Gallienne, Eva 215
Legrand, Michel **150, 158, 179**
Lehman, Ernest 240
Lehne, John 20
Leiber, Fritz 149
Leibman, Ron 112
Leigh, Janet 94, 152, 206
Leigh, Mike 250
Leigh, Vivien: *Gone With the Wind* 63–64, 184, 196, 221; *Ship of Fools* 142; *Streetcar Named Desire* 123, **150**, 186, 202, 221, 244; *That Hamilton Woman* 155
Leighton, Lillian 50
Leighton, Margaret 211
Leipold, John **146**
Leisen, Mitchell 11, 17, 26, 55, 81, 161, 169, 240, 250
Leisure (1976) 234
Leitch, Donovan 61
Leland, David 251
Lelouch, Claude **98**, 209
LeMaire, Charles **96, 135**, 223
LeMat, Paul 100, 101
Lembeck, Harvey 147
Lemmon, Jack 259, 260; *Apartment* 11, 206; *China Syndrome* 214; *Days of Wine and Roses* 38, 207; *Fortune Cookie* 54; *Great Race* 67; *Irma La Douce* 81; *Missing* 104, 216; *Mister Roberts* **105**, 130, 186, 203, 222, 245; *Save the Tiger* 130, **138**, 188, 212, 222;

Some Like It Hot 144, 205; *Tribute* 215
Lemmons, Kasi 142
Lend a Paw (1941) 227
Lennon, John 92
Lenny (1974) 71, 88, 212, 241, 247
Le Noire, Rosetta 151
Lenya, Lotte 206
Lenz, Rick 25
Leonard, Robert Sean 38
Leonard, Robert Z. 42, 68, 126, 193, 195, 239, 240
Leonardi, Mario 30
Leone, Sergio 250
Le Parmentier, Richard 174
Lerner, Alan Jay **8**, 26, **60**
Lerner, Michael 220
LeRoux, Gaston 122
LeRoy, Mervyn 252; *Anthony Adverse* 10, 238; *Blossoms in the Dust* 19, 239; *Five Star Final* 240; *House I Live In* 254; *I Am a Fugitive from a Chain Gang* 240, 247; *Johnny Eager* 84; *Little Women* 94, 241; *Madame Curie* 241, 247; *Mister Roberts* 105, 244; *Quo Vadis* 246, 248; *Random Harvest* 198, 242, 248; *They Won't Forget* 251; *Thirty Seconds Over Tokyo* 157; *Waterloo Bridge* 248
Les Girls (1957) **92**
Leslie, Joan 140, 157, 179
Les Miserables (1935) 178, 194, 241
Lesser, Sol 252
Lester, Richard 56
Let It Be (1970) **92**
"Let's Hear It for the Boy" 50n
Letter, The (1928/29) 192
Letter, The (1940) 196, 197, 241, 247
Letter from an Unknown Woman (1948) 250
Letter to Three Wives, A (1949) **92**, 185, 201, 241
"Let the River Run" **177**
Lettieri, Al 62
Levant, Oscar 8
Leven, Boris **172**
Levene, Sam 40
Levien, Sonya **80**
Levin, Henry 177
Levine, Jerry 20
Levine, Ted 142
Levinson, Barry: *Avalon* 246; *Bugsy* 24, 220, 239; *Diner* 247; *Good Morning, Vietnam* 247; *Natural* 247; *Rain Man* 88, **131**, 190, 219, 242; *Tin Men* 251
Levinson, Nathan **179**, 254
Lewgoy, Jose 88
Lewin, Albert **108**, 123
Lewis, Cecil **128**
Lewis, David 11
Lewis, E. M. (Al) 258
Lewis, Fiona 79
Lewis, Harold C. **51**
Lewis, Jerry 259, 260
Lewis, Juliette 220
Lewis, Sinclair 46, 47
Libeled Lady (1936) 194, 241
Lieven, Albert 141

Life and Death of Colonel Blimp, The (1943) 250
Lifeboat (1944) 132, 199
Life Is Sweet (1991) 250
Life of Emile Zola, The (1937) 12, **92**, 149, 184, 195, 241
Life with Father (1947) 200, 247
Light in the Window (1952) 229
Light of Day, The (Eric Ambler) 163
Liguisos, Mitsos 111
Lili (1953) **92–93**, 203
Lilies of the Field (1963) **93**, 114, 187, 207, 241
Lillie, Beatrice 158
Limelight (1952) **93**
Limnidis, John 29
Lindblom, Gunnel 169
Linden, Jennie 176, 177
Linder, Cec 164
Linder, Stewart **65**
Lindfors, Viveca 2, 172
Lindon, Lionel **11**
Lindsay, Margaret 37, 82
Lindsay-Hogg, Michael 92
Lindtberg, Leopold 99
Linh Dan Pham 79
Linley, Betty 72
Linow, Ivan 79
Lion in Winter, The (1968) 56, **93**, 106, 117, 188, 209, 210, 221, 224, 241
Liotta, Ray 65
Lipscomb, W. P. **128**
Liszt, Franz 144
Litel, John 82, 92
Lithgow, John 71, 154, 216
Little, Thomas A. **9, 76, 109, 144, 157, 175**
Little Dorrit (1988) 218, 247
Little Foxes, The (1941) 76, 197, 241, 246, 247
Little Kidnappers, The (1953) 256
Little Mermaid, The (1989) 50n, **93–94**, 224, 225
Little Night Music, A (1977) **94**
Little Orphan, The (1948) 228
Little Romance, A (1979) **94**
Little Shop of Horrors, The (1986) 247
Little Women (1932/33) **94**, 193, 241
Little Women (1949) **94**, 223
Litvak, Anatole 9, 143, 157, 201, 238, 239, 242
Livadary, John P. **55, 84**
Lives of a Bengal Lancer (1935) **94–95**, 194, 241
Living Desert, The (1953) 226, 229
Livingston, Jay **26, 98, 119**
Livingston, Margaret 151
Llewellyn, Richard 76, 112
Lloyd, Christopher 13, 174
Lloyd, Doris 42
Lloyd, Emily 135
Lloyd, Frank: *Blood on the Sun* 19; *Cavalcade* **27**, 183, 193, 239; *Divine Lady* 42, 183, 192; *Drag* 192; *East Lynne* 239; *Mutiny on the Bounty* 108, 194, 241; *Weary River* 192
Lloyd, Harold 255

Lloyd, John Bedford 1
Lloyd, Norman 39, 93
Loach, Ken 250
LoBianco, Tony 55
Local Hero (1983) 250
Locke, Sondra 210
Lockhart, Gene 6, 75, 83, 92, 103, 195
Lockwood, Gary 166
Loden, Barbara 146
Loder, John 76, 113
Loeb, Philip 44
Loesser, Frank **110–111**
Loewe, Frederick 26, **61**
Loff, Jeanette 87
Loftin, Cary 121
Lofting, Hugh 43
Logan, Joshua 26, 122, 139, 146, 204, 205, 240, 241, 242
Logan's Run (1976) **95**
Loggia, Robert 114, 127, 217
Lohr, Marie 128
Lojodice, Adele Angela 52
Lom, Herbert 141
Lombard, Carole 194
Lombard, Michael 127
Lombardi, Paul 53
London Films Sound Department **21**
Lone, John 90
Lonely Are the Brave (1962) 250
Lonelyhearts (1958) 205
"Long Ago and Far Away" 34
Long Day's Journey Into Night (1962) 207
Longest Day, The (1962) **95**, 206, 241
Long Hot Summer, The (1958) 112
Longtime Companion (1990) 219
Long Voyage Home, The (1940) 178, 196, 241, 247
Lonow, Mark 155
"Looking for a Needle in a Haystack" 58
Looking for Mr. Goodbar (1977) 214
Lopez, Perry 29
Lopez Vasquez, Jose Luis 164
Lord, Robert **116**
Loren, Sophia **166**, 180, 187, 206, 208, 258
Lorenzo's Oil (1992) 220, 247
Lorre, Peter 27, 165
Lorring, Joan 199
Lory, Milo **16**
Losch, Tillie 65
Losey, Joseph 249, 251
Lost Horizon (1937) **95**, 195, 241
Lost Weekend, The (1945) **95–96**, 185, 199, 222, 241
Louis, Jean **143**
Louise, Anita · 10, 149
Love, Bessie 22, 23, 192
Love Affair (1939) 196, 241, 247
Love Field (1992) 220
"Love Is a Many Splendored Thing" **96**, 225
Love Is a Many-Splendored Thing (1955) **96**, 203, 225, 241
Love Letters (1945) 199
Love Me or Leave Me (1955) **96**, 203

Love Me Tonight (1932) 250
Love Parade, The (1929/30) 192, 193, 241, 247
Lovers and Other Strangers (1970) **96**
Love Story (1970) **96**, 210, 211, 241
Love with the Proper Stranger (1963) 207
Lovsky, Celia 26
Lowe, Edmund 79, 164
Loy, Myrna 13, 17, 68, 98, 131, 164, 258, 260
L-Shaped Room, The (1963) 207
Lubin, Arthur 122
Lubitsch, Ernst 169, 255; *Bluebeard's Eighth Wife* 249; *Heaven Can Wait* 198, 240; *Love Parade* 193, 241, 247; *Merry Widow* 101; *Ninotchka* 241, 247; *One Hour with You* 241; *Patriot* 121, 192, 241; *Smiling Lieutenant* 242; *Trouble in Paradise* 251
Lucas, George 78, 148, 212, 214, 238, 242, 252
Lucas, Marcia **148**
Lucas, William 145
Luck of the Irish, The (1948) 200
Ludwig, William **80**
Luedtke, Kurt 118
Lukas, Paul 44, 94, 165, **171–172**, 172, 184, 198
"Lullaby of Broadway" **62–63**, 225
Lumet, Sidney: *Dog Day Afternoon* 44, 213, 239; *Hill* 250; *Murder on the Orient Express* 108, 245; *Network* 74, 111, 213, 241, 245; *Running on Empty* 248; *Twelve Angry Men* 205, 243, 248; *Verdict* 216, 243, 248
Lunch Date, The (1990) 237
Lund, John 161
Lunghi, Cherie 104
Lunt, Alfred 193
LuPone, Patti 45, 176
Luske, Hamilton 99, 123
Lust for Life (1956) **96–97**, 171, 186, 204, 222
Lusty Men, The (1952) 250
Lycett, Eustace **15, 99**
Lynch, Becky Jo 134
Lynch, David 215, 218, 239, 246, 247, 248
Lynch, Helen 167
Lyne, Adrian 53, 218, 240, 247
Lynley, Carol 125
Lynn, Jeffrey 92
Lynn, Jonathan 109
Lynn, Loretta 31
Lyon, Francis **19**
Lyon, Sue 112
Lyon, William A. **55, 122**

M

MacArthur, Charles **139**
MacAvin, Josie **118**
Macchio, Ralph 109
MacCorkindale, Simon 39
MacDonald, Gordon 157
MacDonald, J. Farrell 79, 151

MacDonald, Jeanette 101, 110, 138
MacDonald, Joe 119
MacDonald, Robert **16, 95**
MacDougall, Don **148**
MacGinnis, Niall 80, 97
MacGowran, Jack 49
MacGraw, Ali 96, 210, 260, 261
Mackendrick, Alexander 251
MacLaine, Shirley 260; *Apartment* 11, 206; *Around the World in Eighty Days* 12; *Being There* 15; *Irma La Douce* 80–81, 207; *Some Came Running* 205; *Terms of Endearment* **154**, 190, 216; *Turning Point* 214
MacLane, Barton 164
MacLean, Alistair 69
Maclean, Norman 134
MacLiam, Eanna 109
MacMahon, Aline 116, 139, 199
MacMillan, David **134**
MacMurray, Fred 11
MacNaughton, Robert 48
MacNicol, Peter 145
MacRae, Gordon 115
Madame Curie (1943) 198, 241, 247
Madame Rosa (1977) 59, 78n, **98**
Madame X (1928/29) 143, 192
Madery, Earl **82**
Madigan, Amy 124, 217
Madonna 41
Madsen, Michael 156
Magee, Patrick 14, 34
Maggio, Pupella 8, 30
Magic (1978) 250
Magic Machines, The (1969) 232
Magidson, Herb **58**
Magnani, Anna 78, **137**, 186, 203, 204
Magnificent Ambersons, The (1942) 107, 197, 198, 241, 247
Magnificent Obsession (1954) 203
Magnificent Seven, The (1960) 48, 158
Magnificent Yankee, The (1950) 201
Magnoli, Albert 127
Mahin, John Lee 47
Mahoney, John 106
Maia, Nuno Leal 88
Main, Marjorie 71, 200
Main Street on the March (1941) 227
Major Barbara (1941) 250
Major Dundee (1965) 250
Mako 209
Mala 47
Malcolm X (1992) 220, 247
Malden, Karl 76, 117, 121, **150**, 186, 202, 203, 244
Maley, Alan **15**
Malick, Terrence 38
Malkovich, John 37, 86, 124, 217
Malle, Louis 13, 216, 239, 246
Malleson, Miles 157
Mallett, Tania 63
Malmsjo, Jan 51
Malone, Dorothy **177**, 186, 204
Maltese Falcon, The (1941) 76, 197, 241, 247

Malyon, Eily 62
Mamet, David 250
"Mammy" 84
Mamoulian, Rouben 19, 45, 249, 250, 251
Manahan, Sheila 140
Man and a Woman, A (1966) 78*n*, **98**, 208, 209
Manchurian Candidate, The (1962) 207, 247
Mancini, Henry 21, **38**, **169**, 225
Mandel, Johnny **138**, 225
Mandell, Daniel **11**, **17**, **126**, 223, 224
Mander, Miles 126
Man for All Seasons, A (1966) **98**, 187, 188, 208, 209, 241, 245
Manhattan (1979) 215, 247
Manhattan Melodrama (1934) **98**
"Maniac" 50*n*, 53
Man in the Glass Booth, The (1975) 213
Manipulation (1991) 237
Mankiewicz, Herman J. **30**
Mankiewicz, Joseph L.: *All About Eve* **5**, 186, 201, 238; *Barefoot Contessa* 14; *Cleopatra* 31, 239; *Five Fingers* 202; *House of Strangers* 23; *Julius Caesar* 240; *Letter to Three Wives* 92, 185, 201, 241; *People Will Talk* 250; *Sleuth* 212, 248; *Suddenly, Last Summer* 248
Mann, Abby **84**
Mann, Anthony 61, 247, 251
Mann, Daniel 24, 32, 137, 242
Mann, Delbert **99**, 139, 186, 204, 241, 242
Mann, Lisa 93
Mann, Michael 90
Mann, Paul 52
Manning, Irene 179
Manoff, Dinah 118
Man of Iron (1980) 101
Mantegna, Joe 24
Mantell, Joe 99, 203
"Man That Got Away, The" 147
Man Who Knew Too Much, The (1956) **98–99**
Man Who Planted Trees, The (1987) 236
Man Who Shot Liberty Valance, The (1962) 247
Man Who Skied Down Everest, The (1975) 234
Man with the Golden Arm, The (1955) 203
Manz, Linda 38
Marathon Man (1976) 213
March, Fredric: *Anthony Adverse* 10; *Best Years of Our Lives* **17**, 131, 185, 199, 222, 244; *Bridges at Toko-ri* 22; *Dark Angel* 37; *Death of a Salesman* 202; *Dr. Jekyll and Mr. Hyde* 27, **45**, 131, 183, 193, 222; *Royal Family of Broadway* 193; *Star is Born* 147, 195
Marchal, Arlette 175
Marchand, Colette 107, 202
Marchand, Nancy 74
March of Time, The 253
Margo 78, 95, 170

Margolin, Janet 10
Margolin, Stuart 38
Marie, Dominique 105
Marie Antoinette (1938) 195
Marie-Louise (1945) **99**
Marin, Jason 94
Marion, Frances **17**, **27**
Marion, George F. 17
Marjoe (1972) 233
Mark, The (1961) 206
Markham, David 155
Markowitz, Donald **41**
Marley, John 61, 96, 260
Marlowe, Hugh 5, 165
Marnie (1964) 161, 250
Marooned (1969) **99**
Marquand, Richard 133
Marrakesh Express (1989) 100
Marriage Italian-Style (1964) 208
Married to the Mob (1988) 218
Mars, Kenneth 127
Marsh, Oliver 253
Marsh, Terence **115**
Marsh, Terry **43**
Marshall, Connie 106
Marshall, E. G. 163
Marshall, Garry 248
Marshall, George 76, 119, 240
Marshall, Herbert 37, 132
Marshall, Penny 239, 246
Marshman Jr., D. M. **151**, 222
Marteau, Henri 79
Martel, K. C. 48
Martin, Dean 3, 106
Martin, Lewis 171
Martin, Rosemary 155
Martin, Strother 24, 33, 165
Martinelli, Elsa 169
Marton, Andrew 87, 95, 240, 241
Marty (1955) 74, **99**, 186, 203, 204, 222, 241
Marvin, Lee **27**, 42, 142, 187, 208
Marx, Groucho 257
Mary, Queen of Scots (1971) 211
Mary Poppins (1964) **99–100**, 145, 187, 207, 208, 241
Marzi, Franca 112
*M*A*S*H* (1970) **100**, 210, 211, 241
Masina, Giulietta 112, 149
Mask (1985) **100**
Mask of Dimitrios, The (1944) 250
Maslow, Steve **47**, **130**
Mason, James 71, 85, 140, 141, 147, 165, 203, 209, 216
Mason, Marsha 64, 212, 214, 215
Mason, Sarah Y. **94**
Massey, Daniel 210
Massey, Raymond 46, 77, 80, 132, 196
Massine, Leonide 133
Masterson, Peter 165
Mastrantonio, Mary Elizabeth 1, 32, 218
Mastroianni, Marcello 43, 44, 46, 180, 207, 214, 218
Matchmaker, The (Thornton Wilder play) 72
Mate, Rudoph 173
Mateos, Antonio **121**
Matheson, Murray 96
Mating Season, The (1951) 202

Matkosky, Dennis 53
Matlin, Marlee **28**, 190, 217
Matter of Life and Death, A (1946) 250
Matthau, Walter 260; *Cactus Flower* 25; *California Suite* 25–26; *Fortune Cookie* **54**, 188, 209; *Hello Dolly* 72; *Kotch* 211; *Sunshine Boys* 151, 213
Matthews, Jessie 162, 169
Mature, Victor 109, 135, 138
Maugham, W. Somerset 132
Maumont, Jacques **95**
Max, Edwin 32
Maxsted, Jack A. **111**
Maxwell, Marilyn 27
May, Elaine 26
May, Johdi 90
Mayer, Louis B. 255
Mayhew, Peter 47, 133, 148
Mayo, Archie 34
Mayo, Virginia 17, 177
Mayron, Melanie 104, 180
Mazurki, Mike 111
Mazursky, Paul 71, 148, 243, 247, 248, 249
McAlister, Michael **78**
McAnally, Ray 104, 109
McCabe, Ruth 109
McCabe and Mrs. Miller (1971) 211
McCallum, Gordon K. **52**
McCambridge, Mercedes **6**, 60, 185, 201, 204
McCarey, Leo: *Awful Truth* **12**, 184, 195, 239; *Bells of St. Mary's* 16, 199, 239; *Going My Way* **62**, 185, 199, 240; *Love Affair* 241, 247; *Ruggles of Red Gap* 242
McCarthy, Frank 121
McCarthy, Kevin 79, 202
McCarthy, Tom C. **21**
McCartney, Paul 92
McCaughey, William **39**
McCleary, Urie 19, **121**, 223
McClure, Marc 13
McClurg, Edie 135
McCormack, Patty 204
McCormick, Myron 77
McCowen, Alec 72, 164
McCrane, Paul 50
McCrea, Joel 32, 106
McCready, Keith 32
McCune, Grant **148**
McDaniel, Hattie 60, **63–64**, 67, 93, 143, 144, 184, 196
McDermott, Hugh 141
McDiarmid, Ian 133
McDonald, Christopher 156
McDonnell, Mary 36, 219, 220
McDormand, Frances 105, 219
McDowall, Roddy 15, 31, 76, 125
McEnery, John 136
McEnroe, Annie 15
McGill, Everett 129
McGillis, Kelly 2, 163, 175, 176
McGinley, John C. 125
McGiver, John 21, 101
McGovern, Elizabeth 118, 216
McGovern, Tim **163**
McGraw, Charles 22, 40
McGuire, Biff 158

McGuire, Dorothy 51, 59, 159, 165, 200
McGuire, Michael 17
McHugh, Frank 63, 102, 116
McIntire, John 47
McKay, Scott 157
McKee, Lonette 137
McKenna, Breffini 34
McKenna, Siobhan 43
McKenna, Virginia 20
McKeon, Doug 117
McKern, Leo 98, 116, 137
McLaglen, Victor **79**, 108, 129, 141, 183, 194, 202, 245
McLean, Barbara 195
McLeod, Norman Z. 89, 119
McLerie, Allyn 25
McNair, Barbara 260
McNally, Stephen 83
McNamara, J. Patrick 31
McNamara, Maggie 159, 203
McQuarrie, Ralph **31**
McQueen, Steve 24, 158, 164, 208, 260
McTiernan, John 77
Means, Russell 90
Medal for Benny, A (1945) 199
Meddings, Derek **152**
Medford, Kay 56, 210
Mediterraneo (1991) 79, **100**
Medley, Bill 42
Medoff, Mark 28
Meehan, John 72, **151**, **165**
Meek, Donald 146, 149, 180
Meet Me in St. Louis (1944) 247
Meet Whiplash Willie (1966) 54
Megna, John 162
Mello, Breno 18
Mellor, William C. **40**, **123**
Melvin and Howard (1980) **100–101**, 189, 215
Member of the Wedding, The (1952) 202
memorial awards 252–258
Memphis Belle (1990) 250
Men Against the Arctic (1955) 230
Menendez, Ramon 248
Menges, Chris **86**, **104**, 251
Menjou, Adolphe 51, 63, 106, 116, 147, 193
Menken, Alan **3**, **14–15**, **93**, 224, 225
Menken, Robert 155
Menshov, Vladimir 106
Menzel, Jiri 31
Menzies, William Cameron **44**, **64**, **153**, 251, 254
Mephisto (1981) **101**
Mercer, Beryl 27
Mercer, Johnny **21**, **38**, **71**, **73**, 225
Merchant, Vivien 209
Mercouri, Melina 111, 163, 206
Mercurio, Micole 100
Meredith, Burgess 74, 135, 213
Meredith, Lee 151
Merkel, Una 23, 101, 157, 175, 206
Merkerson, S. Epatha 154
Merman, Ethel 4, 26, 81
Merrill, Barbara 173
Merrill, Dina 24

Merrill, Gary 5, 165
Merrily We Live (1938) 196
Merritt, Theresa 64
Merrow, Jane 93
Merry Christmas, Mr. Lawrence (1983) 250
Merry Widow, The (1934) **101**, 223
Merry Wives of Windsor Overture, The (1953) 229
Mesenkop, Louis **81**, **132**
Metcalf, Laurie 82
Metcalfe Sr., Melvin **46**
Mete, Hseyin 84
Metro-Goldwyn-Mayer Studio 254
Metropolis (1927) 14
Metty, Russell **146**
Metzler, Fred L. 256
Meyer, Emile 141
Michael, Gertrude 30
Michael, Pierre 37
Michener, James A. 22, 146
Midler, Bette 104, 214, 220
Midnight (1939) 250
Midnight Cowboy (1969) 88, **101**, 188, 210, 241
Midnight Express (1978) 20, **101–102**, 214, 241
Midnight Run (1988) 250
Midsummer Night's Dream, A (1935) 70n, 92, **102**, 194, 224, 241
Mielziner, Jo **122**
Mifune, Toshiro 66
Mighty Joe Young (1949) **102**
Mihashi, Tatsuya 163
Milagro Beanfield War, The (1988) **102**
Mildred Pierce (1945) **102–103**, 185, 199, 241
Miles, Bernard 67, 99, 162
Miles, Sarah 137, 210, 260
Miles, Sylvia 101, 171, 210, 213
Milestone, Lewis: *All Quiet on the Western Front* **5–6**, 183, 193, 238; *Front Page* 143, 193, 240, 247; *Of Mice and Men* 241, 248; *Mutiny On the Bounty* 241, 247; *Racket* 242; *Two Arabian Knights* 140, **166**, 183, 192; *Walk in the Sun* 251
Milford, Gene **95, 117**
Milford, Penelope 33, 214
Milky Way, The (1940) 227
Milland, Ray 11, 81, **95–96**, 96, 132, 185, 199
Millard, Helene 43
Miller, Ann 46, 117, 180
Miller, Arthur 9, **76, 144**, 222
Miller, Barry 50
Miller, David 250
Miller, George 247
Miller, Glenn 61
Miller, Jason 49, 212
Miller, Robert Ellis 247
Miller, Seton I. **73**
Miller's Crossing (1990) 250
Mills, Hayley 256
Mills, John 58, 65, 67, **137**, 188
Milner, Martin 105
Milner, Victor **30**
Milo, Sandra 46

Milton, Franklin E. **16, 65, 76**
Mimieux, Yvette 159
Min and Bill (1930/31) **103**, 183, 193
Minciotti, Esther 99
Mineo, Sal 48, 144, 204, 206
Minkler, Bob **148**
Minnelli, Liza 12, **25**, 188, 210, 211, 260
Minnelli, Vincente: *American in Paris* 8, 202, 238; *Bad and the Beautiful* 13; *Band Wagon* 246; *Designing Woman* 40; *Father of the Bride* 240, 247; *Gigi* **60–61**, 187, 205, 240; *Lust for Life* 97; *Meet Me in St. Louis* 247; *Sandpiper* 138
Miracle, Irene 102
Miracle of Morgan's Creek, The (1944) 67
Miracle on 34th Street (1947) **103**, 185, 200, 241
Miracle Worker, The (1962) **103**, 187, 207
Mirisch, Walter **80**, 252
Mirren, Helen 173
Misery (1990) **103–104**, 191, 219
Misfits, The (1961) 250
Missing (1982) **104**, 216, 241
Mission, The (1986) **104**, 217, 218, 241
Mississippi Burning (1988) **104–105**, 218, 219, 241
Mister 880 (1950) 201
Mister Magoo's Puddle Jumper (1956) 230
Mister Roberts (1955) 99, **105**, 130, 138, 186, 203, 222, 241, 245
Mitchell, Cameron 96
Mitchell, George Alfred 255
Mitchell, Grant 67
Mitchell, Gwenn 141
Mitchell, Millard 44, 165
Mitchell, Thomas: *Black Swan* 19; *Gone With the Wind* 64; *High Noon* 74; *Hurricane* 77, 195; *Mr. Smith Goes to Washington* 108; *Stagecoach* **146**, 184, 196, 245; *This Above All* 157; *Wilson* 175
Mitchum, Robert 47, 95, 137, 157, 199
Mittelman, Rachel 15
Miyazaki, Yoshiko 132
Mizrahi, Moshe 98
Modern Times (1936) 249, 250
Mogambo (1953) 203
Mohr, Hal **102, 122**
Molen, Jerry 131
Molina, Alfred 131
Molinaro, Edouard 215
Mollo, John **57, 148**
Molly's Pilgrim (1985) 235
"Mona Lisa" **26**
Mona Lisa (1986) 217, 247
Mona Lisa Descending a Staircase (1992) 237
Mon Oncle (1958) 78n, **105**
Monroe, Marilyn 5, 144
Monsieur Vincent (1948) 255
Montalban, Ricardo 14, 110, 111, 260
Montand, Yves 65, 66, 181

Montgomery, Douglass 94
Montgomery, Robert 17, 43, 73, 195, 197, 259
Monzani, Sarah **129**
Moody, Ron 115, 209
Moonbird (1959) 230
Moon Is Blue, The (1953) 203
"Moon River" **21**, 225
Moonstruck (1987) **105–106**, 190, 218, 241
Moore, Constance 81
Moore, Demi 60
Moore, Dudley 12, 215, 260
Moore, Grace 116, 194
Moore, Jack D. **94**
Moore, Juanita 205
Moore, Mary Tyler 118, 158, 215
Moore, Matt 33
Moore, Robert 250
Moore, Roger 80
Moore, Ted **98**
Moore, Terry 32, 102, 202
Moore, Victor 152
Moorehead, Agnes 30, 83, 143, 149, 198, 199, 200, 208, 259
Moran, Lois 164
Moran, Polly 153
Moravia, Alberto 166
More, Kenneth 95
Moreau, Jeanne 260
Morell, Andre 22, 140
Moreno, Rita 87, **172–173**, 187, 206
More the Merrier, The (1943) **106**, 185, 198, 241
Morgan: A Suitable Case for Treatment (1966) 209
Morgan, Dennis 88
Morgan, Frank 68, 77, 110, 149, 176, 194, 198
Morgan, Henry 34, 61
Moriarty, Cathy 130, 215
Morier-Genoud, Philippe 35
Morison, Patricia 144
Morita, Noriyuki "Pat" 217
Moritzen, Henning 34
Morley, Christopher 88
Morley, Karen 86
Morley, Robert 3, 34, 163, 195
"Morning After, The" **125**
Morning After, The (1986) 217
Morning Glory (1932/33) **106**, 117, 183, 193, 221
Morocco (1930/31) 143, 193, 247
Moroder, Giorgio **53, 101, 163**
Moross, Jerome 17
Morris, Chester 17, 42, 192
Morris, Desmond 129
Morris, Oswald **52**, 106
Morris, Wayne 81
Morrow, Barry **131**
Morrow, Douglas **149**
Morton, Clive 91
Morton, Joe 154
Moscow Does Not Believe In Tears (1980) **106**
Moscow Strikes Back (1942) 227
Mosquini, Marie 140
Mosquito Coast, The (1986) 250
Moss, Arnold 170
Mostel, Josh 30, 145
Mostel, Zero 56, 119, 127

Mother Wore Tights (1947) **106**, 224
Motion Picture and Television Engineers, Society of 256
Motion Picture Relief Fund 254
Mott, Bradley 2
Moulin Rouge (1952) **106–107**, 202, 241
Moulton, Thomas T. **34, 77, 143, 165**
Mourning Becomes Electra (1947) 51, 200
Mouse Trouble (1944) 227
Mowbray, Alan 155
Moyer, Ray **31, 138, 151**
Mr. and Mrs. Bridge (1990) 219, 247
Mr. Deeds Goes to Town (1936) 81, 107, **107**, 184, 194, 195, 221, 241
Mr. Saturday Night (1992) 220
Mr. Skeffington (1944) 198
Mr. Smith Goes to Washington (1939) **107–108**, 122, 196, 241
Mrs. Miniver (1942) 82n, **107**, 143, 144, 184, 197, 198, 221, 222, 241, 244
Mrs. Parkington (1944) 198, 199
Muggleston, Ken **115**
Muir, Jean 102
Mulligan, Robert 150, 162, 207, 243
Mummy, The (1933) 250
Mundin, Herbert 27, 108
Mungle, Matthew W. **21**
Muni, Paul: *Good Earth* 65; *I Am a Fugitive from a Chain Gang* 193; *Last Angry Man* 205; *Life of Emile Zola* 92, 195; *Story of Louis Pasteur* 149, 184, 194; *Valiant* 192
Munro (1960) 231
Munshin, Jules 46, 117
Munzuk, Maxim 40
Murawjova, Irina 106
Murch, Walter **11**
Murder by Death (1976) 250
Murder, Inc. (1960) 206
Murder on the Orient Express (1974) 9, 25n, 39, 71, **108**, 189, 212, 221, 245
Murdock, Jack 131
Murdock, Tim 157
Muren, Dennis **1, 47, 48, 78, 79, 133, 154**
Murnau, F. W. 151, 153
Murphy, George 14, 157, 255
Murphy, Michael 110, 179
Murphy, Rosemary 85, 162
Murphy's Romance (1985) 217
Murray, Bill 162
Murray, Don 204
Muse, Clarence 18
Museum of Modern Art 257
Museum of Modern Art Film Library 253
music 224–225 *see also* composers (e.g., Williams, John)
Music Box (1989) 219, 247
Music Box, The (1931/32) 226
Music Man, The (1962) **108**, 207, 241
Musker, John 3, 93

Mutiny on the Bounty (1935) **108**, 183, 194, 241
Mutiny on the Bounty (1962) 207, 241, 247
My Cousin Rachel (1952) 174*n*, 202
My Cousin Vinny (1992) **108–109**, 191, 220
My Darling Clementine (1946) 250
Myers, Harry 44
My Fair Lady (1964) 99, 108, **109**, 128, 187, 207, 208, 221, 225, 241, 245
My Favorite Year (1982) 216
My Foolish Heart (1949) 81, 201
My Gal Sal (1942) **109**, 223
My Left Foot (1989) 45, **109**, 191, 219, 241
My Life as a Dog (1987) 218
My Man Godfrey (1936) 32, 194, 195, 247
My Own Private Idaho (1991) 250
My Sister Eileen (1942) 197

N

Nagel, Conrad 43, 259
Naish, J. Carrol 9, 19, 83, 198, 199
Naismith, Laurence 26
Nakadai, Tatsuya 132
Naked City, The (1948) **110**
Naked Gun, The (1988) 250
Naked Lunch, The (1991) 250
Name of the Rose, The (1986) 250
Nash, Mary 131
Nashville (1975) **110**, 212, 213, 241
Nathan, Stephen 180
National Endowment for the Arts 258
National Film Board of Canada 258
National Velvet (1945) **110**, 185, 199
Natural, The (1984) 217, 247
Nature's Half Acre (1951) 229
Natwick, Mildred 37, 129, 142, 209
Naughton, David 8
Naughton, James 120
Naughty Marietta (1935) **110**, 194, 224, 241
Navarro, Carlos 21
Nazimova, Alla 19
Nazzari, Amadeo 112
Neal, Patricia 21, **76**, 150, 187, 207, 209
Neal, Paul **116**
Neame, Ronald 125, 126
Neckar, Vaclav 31
Neeson, Liam 104
Negulesco, Jean 83, 159, 160, 201, 240, 242, 250
Neighbors (1952) 229
Neil, Hildegard 164
Neill, Sam 77
Neill, Ve **15**
Nelligan, Kate 220
Nelson, Barry 3
Nelson, Charles **122**
Nelson, Craig T. 86
Nelson, Gene 115

Nelson, George R. **62**
Nelson, Horatio 155
Nelson, Ralph 28, 51, 93, 241
Nelson, Ruth 165, 175
Neptune's Daughter (1949) **110–111**
Nero, Franco 26
Nervig, Conrad A. **47, 87**
Nesbitt, Cathleen 140
Network (1976) 74, **111**, 189, 213, 222, 241, 245
Neumann, Kurt 53
Neuwirth, Bebe 24
"Never on Sunday" **111**
Never on Sunday (1960) **111**, 206
Newcom, James E. **64**
Newcombe, Warren **68, 157**
Newell, Mike 247
Newley, Anthony 43
Newman, Alfred **4, 26, 87, 96, 106, 144, 160, 175**, 224
Newman, Chris **7, 49**
Newman, Lionel **72**
Newman, Paul 258; *Absence of Malice* 215; *Butch Cassidy and the Sundance Kid* 24; *Cat On a Hot Tin Roof* 205; *Color of Money* **32**, 190, 217, 245; *Cool Hand Luke* 33, 209; *Exodus* 48; *Glass Menagerie* 250; *Hud* 76, 207; *Hustler* 77, 206; *Rachel, Rachel* 242; *Somebody Up There Likes Me* 144; *Sting* 149; *Sweet Bird of Youth* 152; *Towering Inferno* 164; *Verdict* 216
Newman, Stephen D. 145
Newton, Robert 12, 73
Nexo, Martin Andersen 122
Ney, Richard 107
Nezu, Jinpachi 132
Ngor, Haing S. **86**, 190, 217
"Nice Work If You Can Get It" 36
Nicholas and Alexandra (1971) **111–112**, 211, 241
Nicholls, Allan 110
Nichols, Dudley **79**
Nichols, Mike: *Graduate* **65**, 188, 209, 240; *Postcards From the Edge* 248; *Silkwood* 216, 248; *Who's Afraid of Virginia Woolf?* 174, 209, 243; *Working Girl* 177, 219, 243
Nicholson, Bruce **47, 130**
Nicholson, Jack: *Batman* 14; *Chinatown* 29, 71, 212; *Easy Rider* 210; *Few Good Men* 220; *Five Easy Pieces* 210; *Ironweed* 218; *Last Detail* 212; *One Flew Over the Cuckoo's Nest* **116**, 130, 189, 213, 222; *Prizzi's Honor* 126–127, 217; *Reds* 133, 215; *Terms of Endearment* 130, **154**, 190, 216, 222
Nicola, John **41**
"Night and Day" 58
Night Must Fall (1937) 195
Night of the Hunter (1955) 249, 250
Night of the Iguana, The (1964) **112**, 208

Nights of Cabiria, The (1957) 8, 100*n*, **112**
Ninchi, Annibale 44
Nine from Little Rock (1964) 231
Ninotchka (1939) 196, 241, 247
Nissen, Greta 164
Nitzsche, Jack **114**
Niven, David 259, 260; *Around the World in Eighty Days* 11–12; *Bishop's Wife* 18; *Charge of the Light Brigade* 27; *Death on the Nile* 39; *Dodsworth* 39; *Guns of Navarone* 69; *Separate Tables* **139–140**, 186, 205; *Wuthering Heights* 178
Niver, Kemp R. **256**
Noble, Ray 36
Noble, Roderic 112
Noble, Thom **175**
Noel, Magali 8, 44
Noiret, Philippe 30
Nolan, Lloyd 3, 70, 75, 165
Nollier, Claude 107
Nolte, Nick 220
nominees 192–220
None But the Lonely Heart (1944) **112**, 185, 198, 199
Noose, The (1927/28) 89, 192
Norman, Maidie 173
Norman Rockwell's World...An American Dream (1972) 233
Norma Rae (1979) **112**, 124, 189, 214, 221, 241
Norris, Edward 21
North, Alex 258
North, Edmund H. **121**, 222
North by Northwest (1959) 248
Northwest Mounted Police (1940) **112–113**
Norton, Edgar 45
Nothing Sacred (1937) 250
Notorious (1946) 152, 199, 248
Nouri, Michael 53
Novak, Kim 122, 123
Novarese, Vittorio Nino **31, 34**, 223
Novotna, Jarmila 66, 139
Now, Voyager (1942) **113**, 143, 197, 198, 224
Number Our Days (1976) 234
Nunn, Larry 150
Nunn, Terri 155
Nun's Story, The (1959) 205, 206, 241, 246, 248
Nuyen, France 146
Nyby, Christian 251
Nye, Louis 50
Nykvist, Sven **34, 50**
Nype, Russell 96

O

Oakie, Jack 72, 160, 196
Oakland, Simon 24, 81
Oates, Warren 80
Ober, Philip 32, 50, 55
Oberon, Merle 34, 37, 53, 126, 177, 178, 194, 260
O'Brian, Hugh 23
O'Brien, Edmond **14**, 44, 51, 186, 203, 208
O'Brien, George 151

O'Brien, Margaret 94, 254
O'Brien, Pat 144
O'Brien, Tom 2
O'Brien, Virginia 71, 89
O'Brien, Willis **102**
O'Brien-Moore, Erin 40, 92
Obsession (1976) 6
Occurrence at Owl Creek Bridge, An (1963) 231
O'Connell, Arthur 51, 67, 122, 123, 143, 204, 205
O'Connor, Donald 26, 259
O'Connor, Hugh 109
O'Connor, Una 27, 79, 158
Odd Couple, The (1968) 248
Odd Man Out (1947) 248
Odets, Clifford 33, 112
O'Donnell, Cathy 16, 17
O'Donnell, Chris 139
O'Donnell, Michael Donovan 41
O'Donovan, Edwin **71**
Officer and a Gentleman, An (1982) 61, 93, **114**, 190, 216
Official Story, The (1985) **114**
Of Human Bondage (1934) 37
Of Human Hearts (1938) 195
O'Flaherty, Liam 79
Of Mice and Men (1939) 196, 241, 248
Of Mice and Men (1992) 250
Of Pups and Puzzles (1941) 227
Ogier, Bulle 42
Ogilvy, Ian 39
O'Hara, Catherine 15
O'Hara, John 24
O'Hara, Maureen 19, 76, 103, 129, 157
O'Hara, Paige 15
O'Herlihy, Daniel 135, 203
"Oh, How I Hate to Get Up in the Morning" 157
"Oh, What a Beautiful Mornin'" 114
Okay, Yaman 84
O'Keefe, Dennis 11
O'Keefe, Michael 215
Oklahoma! (1955) **114–115**, 224
Oland, Warner 141
Olbrychski, Daniel 37, 160
Oldman, Gary 21, 82
Old Man and the Sea, The (1958) 17, **115**, 205, 224
Old Mill, The (1937) 226
Olin, Lena 219
Oliver! (1968) 28, 58, **115**, 188, 209, 210, 225, 241, 257
Oliver, Edna May 94, 126, 196
Oliver, Rochelle 139
Oliver Twist (1948) 250
Olivier, Laurence 257, 260; *Boys From Brazil* 214; *Entertainer* 206; *Hamlet* **70**, 185, 200, 201, 240; *Henry V* 70*n*, 72*n*, 199, 240, 247, 254; *Invaders* 80; *Little Romance* 94; *Marathon Man* 213; *Nicholas and Alexandra* 112; *Othello* 208; *Pride and Prejudice* 126; *Rebecca* 132, 152, 196; *Richard III* 204; *Sleuth* 211; *Spartacus* 146; *That Hamilton Woman* 155; *Wuthering Heights* 177–178, 196
Olmos, Edward James 218

282

Olsen, Moroni 86, 103
Olson, Nancy 151, 201
O Lucky Man (1972) 250
Omen, The (1976) **115–116**
O'Mitchell, Donald **61**
Omnibus (1992) 237
Once and Future King, The (book by T. H. White) 26
Once Is Not Enough (1975) 213
Once Upon a Time in America (1984) 250
O'Neal, Patrick 172
O'Neal, Ryan 14, 96, 120, 210, 260
O'Neal, Tatum **120**, 189, 212
One-Eyed Men Are Kings (1974) 233
One Flew Over the Cuckoo's Nest (1975) 10, 81, 82, **116**, 130, 142, 171, 189, 213, 222, 241
One Foot in Heaven (1941) 197, 241
One Hour with You (1931/32) 193, 241
One Hundred Men and a Girl (1937) **116**, 195, 241
O'Neil, Barbara 173, 197
O'Neil, Nance 29
O'Neill, Henry 82, 92, 149
O'Neill, Jennifer 150
One Night of Love (1934) **116**, 194, 241
One Way Passage (1932/33) **116**
On Golden Pond (1981) 66, 102, 106, **116–117**, 189, 190, 215, 216, 221, 241
Only When I Laugh (1981) 215
"On the Atchison, Topeka and Santa Fe" **71**, 225
"On the Banks of the Wabash" 109
On the Town (1949) **117**
On the Waterfront (1954) 73, **117**, 131, 186, 203, 221, 222, 223, 241, 244
Open City (1970) 8n
Ophüls, Max 250
Orbach, Jerry 15, 42
Orbom, Eric **146**
Ordinary People (1980) 36, **117– 118**, 189, 215, 241
Orfei, Nandino 8
Orloff, Lee **154**
Orry-Kelly **8, 92, 144**, 223
Osborne, John **162**
O'Shea, Milo 136
Oshima, Nagisa 250
Osmond, Cliff 54
O'Sullivan, Maureen 70, 126
Othello (1965) 208
Other Half of the Sky, The: A China Memoir (1975) 154
O'Toole, Peter: *Becket* 15, 207; *Goodbye, Mr. Chips* 210; *Last Emperor* 90; *Lawrence of Arabia* 91, 207; *Lion in Winter* 93, 209; *My Favorite Year* 210, 216; *Ruling Class* 211; *Stunt Man* 215
Otto, Frank 20
Oumansky, Andre 151
Our Man in Havana (1960) 250
Our Town (1940) 196, 241

Ouspenskaya, Maria 44, 131, 195, 196
Outcast of the Islands (1952) 250
"Out Here On My Own" 50
Out of Africa (1985) **118**, 145, 176, 190, 217, 224, 241
Overman, Lynne 17, 113, 132
"Over the Rainbow" **176**
"Over There" 179
Overton, Frank 162
Owen, Patricia 139
Owen, Reginald 68, 107, 176
Owens, Harry **171**
Ox-Bow Incident, The (1943) 29, 198, 241
Oz, Frank 47, 133, 247

P

Paaske, Erik 122
Pacino, Al: *Dick Tracy* 41, 219; *Dog Day Afternoon* 44, 213; *Glengarry Glen Ross* 220; *Godfather* 61, 211; *Godfather, Part II* 62, 71, 212; *And Justice for All* 214; *Scent of a Woman* **139**, 191, 220; *Serpico* 212
Page, Anita 22, 23, 153
Page, Genevieve 144
Page, Geraldine: *Hondo* 203; *Interiors* 214; *Pete 'n' Tillie* 211; *Pope of Greenwich Village* 217; *Summer and Smoke* 206; *Sweet Bird of Youth* 152, 207; *Trip to Bountiful* 165, 190, 217; *White Nights* 173; *You're a Big Boy Now* 209
Page, Maurice 15
Page, Patti 47
Paget, Debra 153
Paisan (1949) 8n
Pakula, Alan J. 7, 88, 145, 213, 238
Pal, George **40**, 159, 162, 171, 173, 177, 254
Palance, Jack 14, **30**, 119, 141, 191, 202, 203, 220
Paleface, The (1948) **119**
Pale Rider (1985) 250
Palin, Michael 53
Pallette, Eugene 2, 108, 116, 141
Palm Beach Story (1942) 250
Palmer, Betsy 105
Palmer, Ernest **19**
Palmer, Geoffrey 53
Palmer, Leland 6
Palmer, Lili 19
Palmer, Tom 38
Paluzzi, Luciana 159
Pan, Hermes **36**
Panama, Norman 249
Panama Deception, The (1992) 237
Panic in the Streets (1950) **119**
"Papa, Can You Hear Me?" 50n
Papas, Irene 9, 69, 181
Papa's Delicate Condition (1963) **119**, 225
Paper Chase, The (1973) **119–120**, 188, 212
Paper Moon (1973) **120**, 189, 212
Paradine Case, The (1947) 152, 200
Paramount Studios **171, 173**, 253
Pardon Mon Affaire 176

Parenthood (1989) 219, 248
Paris, Jerry 99
Paris, Simone 98
Paris, Texas (1984) 250
Parker, Alan 50, 102, 104, 105, 214, 219, 241, 246, 249
Parker, Charlie "Yardbird" 17
Parker, Eleanor 74, 80, 145, 201, 202, 203
Parker, Jean 94
Parks, Gordon 141
Parks, Larry 84, 199
Parrish, Robert **19**
Parrondo, Gil **111, 121**
Parsons, Estelle **19–20**, 188, 209, 210
Pascal, Christine 137
Pascal, Gabriel 250
Paso, Encarna 161
Passage to India, A (1984) **120– 121**, 190, 216, 217, 224, 241
Passenger, The (1975) 250
Passgard, Lars 159
Passion Fish (1992) 220
Passport to Pimlico (1949) 91
Pasternak, Boris 43
Pasteur, Louis 149
Pastorelli, Robert 36
Patch of Blue, A (1965) **121**, 187, 208, 222
Patent Leather Kid, The (1927/28) 89, 192
Paterson, Bill 86
Paterson, Neil **136**
Paths of Glory (1957) 250
Patinkin, Mandy 179
Patrick, Lee 103, 113, 143
Patrick, Nigel 22
Patrick, Robert 154
Patriot, The (1928/29) **121**, 192, 241
Patten, Luanna 144
Patterson, James 80
Patterson, Neva 143
Patton (1970) **121**, 188, 210, 211, 222, 241
Paulin, Scott 134
Paul Robeson: Tribute to an Artist (1979) 234
Pavan, Marisa 137, 204
Pawley, William 14
Pawnbroker, The (1965) 208
Paxinou, Katina **54**, 185, 198
Paxton, Bill 5
Paymer, David 220
Payne, James **149**
Payne, John 72, 103, 132, 160
Pazes, Felipe 115
Pearson, Richard 155
Peck, Gregory 252, 260; *Big Country* 17; *Designing Woman* 40; *Gentleman's Agreement* 58– 59, 200; *Guns of Navarone* 69; *How the West Was Won* 76; *Keys of the Kingdom* 199; *Marooned* 99; *Omen* 115; *Roman Holiday* 136; *Spellbound* 146; *To Kill a Mockingbird* 108, **161–162**, 187, 207; *Twelve O'Clock High* 165, 201; *Yearling* 179, 199
Peckinpah, Sam 248, 250
Peel, Dave 110

"Peggy Sue" 23
Peggy Sue Got Married (1986) 217
Pelle the Conqueror (1988) **121– 122**, 218
Pelling, Maurice **30**
Pemberton, Antonia 121
Pendleton, Austin 109
Pendleton, Nat 68, 98
Penn, Arthur 20, 103, 207, 209, 210, 239
Penny Serenade (1941) 197
Penny Wisdom (1937) 227
"People Will Say We're in Love" 114
People Will Talk (1951) 250
Peploe, Mark **89**
Peppard, George 21, 76
Percy, Eileen 153
Pereira, Hal **137**
Pereira, William L. **132**
Perelman, S. J. **11**
Perez, Vincent 35, 79
Perfect Strangers (1946) 169
Performance (1970) 250
Perier, Francois 112, 181
Perinal, Georges **156**
Perisic, Zoran **152**
Perkins, Anthony 108, 204
Perkins, Jeffrey **36**
Perkins, Millie 41
Perlman, Ron 129
Perrin, Jacques 30, 181
Perrine, Valerie 152, 212
Perry, Frank 207
Persoff, Nehemiah 144, 179
Pesci, Joe **65**, 82, 108, 109, 130, 191, 215, 219, 245
Pete Kelly's Blues (1955) 204
Pete 'n' Tillie (1972) 165, 211
Peters, Brock 125, 162
Peters, Jean 23, 159, 170
Peters, Susan 198
Petersen, Wolfgang 216, 246
Peter's Friends (1992) 250
Peterson, Lorne **78**
Pete Smith Specialties (1953) 256
Petri, Elio 80
Petrie, Howard 140
Pettersson, Birgitta 169
Peverall, John **39**
Pevney, Joseph 19
Peyton Place (1957) 204, 205, 241
Pfeiffer, Michelle 37, 219, 220
Pflug, Jo Ann 100
Phantom of the Opera, The (1943) **122**
Philadelphia Story, The (1940) **122**, 184, 196, 197, 241, 245
Philips, Mary 51, 92
Phillips, Leslie 92
Phillips, Michael and Julia **149**
Phoenix, River 78, 218
Photopoulos, Vassilis **181**
Piantadosi, Arthur **7**
Picardo, Robert 79
Piccoli, Michel 37
Pichel, Irving 40, 242
Pickford, Mary **33**, 183, 192, 257
Pickup, Ronald 104
Pickup on South Street (1953) 203
Picnic (1955) 99, **122–123**, 203, 204, 241

Picon, Molly 52
Picture of Dorian Gray, The (1945) **123**, 199
Pidgeon, Walter 13, 19, 56, 76, 107, 197, 198
Pied Piper, The (1942) 197, 242
Pierce, David 53
Pierce, Ronald **46**
Pierson, Frank **44**, 148
Pigott, Tempe 27
Pigskin Parade (1936) 32, 194
Pileggi, Nicholas 65
Pillow Talk (1959) **123**, 205
Pinelli, Tullio **8**n
Pink Phink, The (1964) 231
Pinky (1949) 201
Pinocchio (1940) **123**
Pires, Miriam 88
Pirosh, Robert **14**
Pistek, Theodor **7**
Pitchford, Dean **50**
Pitt, Brad 135, 156
Place in the Sun, A (1951) **123–124**, 186, 201, 202, 223, 242
Places in the Heart (1984) **124**, 190, 216, 217, 221, 242
Place to Stand, A (1967) 232
Plainsman, The (1936) 251
Plana, Tony 114
Planet of the Apes (1968) 257
Platoon (1986) 20, 39, **124–125**, 190, 217, 218, 242
Platt, Louise 146
Platt, Oliver 177
Player, The (1992) 220, 248
Pleasence, Donald 51
Plowright, Joan 109, 220
Plummer, Amanda 53
Plummer, Christopher 145
Plunkett, Walter **8**, 223
Plymouth Adventure (1952) **125**
Pocketful of Miracles (1961) 206
Poe, James **11**
Point Blank (1967) 251
Poitier, Sydney 260; *Defiant Ones* 40, 205; *Guess Who's Coming to Dinner* 68; *In the Heat of the Night* 80; *Lilies of the Field* **93**, 114, 187, 207; *Patch of Blue* 121; *Porgy and Bess* 125
Polanski, Roman 29, 137, 155, 212, 215, 239, 242, 249
Pollack, Sydney: *Out of Africa* **118**, 176, 190, 217, 241; *They Shoot Horses, Don't They?* 156, 210; *Tootsie* 162, 216, 243; *Way We Were* 172
Pollard, Michael J. 20, 101, 209
Pollyanna 256
Poltergeist (1982) 248
Pomeroy, Roy **175**
Pontecorvo, Gillo 210
Poore, Vern **17**
Pope of Greenwich Village, The (1984) 165, 217
Porgy and Bess (1959) **125**, 225
Porter, Cole 225
Porter, Don 26
Porter, Katherine Anne 142
Portis, Charles 165
Portman, Eric 80
Portman, Richard **39**

Portrait of Jennie (1948) **125**
Poseidon Adventure, The (1972) **125**, 211
Pospisil, John **135**
Possessed (1947) 51, 200
Postcards from the Edge (1990) 145, 219, 248
Postman Always Rings Twice, The (1946) 251
Potter, H. C. 34, 51
Potter, Jerry 104
Powell, Anthony **39**, **155**, **164**
Powell, Bud 137
Powell, Dick 13, 47, 62, 63, 102, 259
Powell, Eleanor 23, 89
Powell, Jane 140
Powell, Michael 18, 80, 133, 157, 240, 242, 250, 251
Powell, William 68, 89, 98, 105, 116, 194, 200
Power, Hartley 136
Power, Tyrone 4, 18, 19, 34, 79, 131, 132, 157
Powers, Mala 35
Powers, Tom 40
Poyner, John **42**
Precious Images (1986) 236
Preisser, June 150
Prelude to War (1942) 227
Preminger, Otto 48, 90, 125, 147, 199, 207, 238, 246, 249
Prentiss, Paula 260
presentation see hosts and presenters
Pressburger, Emeric 18, **80**, 133, 242, 250, 251
Pressman, Lawrence 141
Preston, Robert 76, 108, 112, 113, 132, 169, 216
"Pretty Girl Is Like a Melody, A" 4, 68
Pretty Woman (1990) 219, 248
Previn, Andre 61, **80**, **109**, **125**, 224, 225
Previn, Charles **116**
Previte, Franke **41**
Prevost, Marie 143
Price, Lonny **42**
Price, Vincent 53, 90, 92, 144, 153, 175
Prick Up Your Ears (1987) 251
Pride and Prejudice (1940) **125–126**, 223
Pride of the Yankees, The (1942) 82n, **126**, 197, 224, 242
Priestley, Robert 122, **139**
Prime of Miss Jean Brodie, The (1969) 25n, 108n, **126**, 188, 210, 222
Primrose Path (1940) 197
Prince (musician) **127**
Prince, Andrew 103
Prince, Hal 94
Prince, William 35
Prince of Tides, The (1991) 220, 242, 248
Princess O'Rourke (1943) **126**
Princeton: A Search for Answers (1973) 233
Prisoner of Zenda, The (1937) 248
Private Benjamin (1980) 215

Private Life of Henry VIII, The (1932/33) **126**, 183, 193, 242
Private Life of Sherlock Holmes, The (1970) 251
Private Life of the Gannets (1937) 226
Private Lives of Elizabeth and Essex, The (1939) 248
Private Worlds (1935) 194
Prizzi's Honor (1985) **126–127**, 190, 217, 242, 245
Producers, The (1968) **127**, 210
production 183–220 see also personal names (e.g., *Zanuck, Darryl F.*)
Professionals, The (1966) 209
Project Hope (1961) 231
Prouty, Jed 23
Prowse, David 47, 133, 148
Pryor, Richard 25, 26, 260
Psycho (1960) 6, 132, 152, 206, 248
Public Pays, The (1936) 226
Puenzo, Luis 114
Puig, Manuel 87
Pullman, Bill 2
Pumpkin Eater, The (1964) 208
Purcell, Dick 11
Purcell, Noel 97
Puri, Amrish 78
Purple Rain (1984) **127–128**
Purple Rose of Cairo, The (1985) 248
Puttnam, David **27**, 104
Pu Yi 89
Puzo, Mario **61**, **62**, 222
Pygmalion (1938) **128**, 195, 242

Q

Quaid, Dennis 21, 79, 134
Quaid, Randy 20, 102, 212
Qualen, John 121
Quaranta, Gianni **136**
Quayle, Anthony 9, 69, 91, 210
"Que Sera, Sera" **98–99**
Quest for Fire (1982) **129**
Quicker 'N a Wink (1940) 227
Quiet Man, The (1952) 107, **129**, 186, 202, 221, 223, 242
Quiet Please (1945) 228
Quillan, Eddie 108
Quine, Richard 143
Quinn, Aidan 104
Quinn, Anthony: *Black Swan* 19; *Blood and Sand* 19; *Guns of Navarone* 69; *La Strada* 149; *Lawrence of Arabia* 91; *Lust for Life* **96–97**, 186, 204, 222; *Viva Zapata!* **170**, 186, 202, 222, 244; *Wild Is the Wind* 204; *Zorba the Greek* 181, 207
Quinn, Francesco 125
Quinn, J. C. 1
Quo Vadis (1951) 201, 202, 242, 246, 248

R

Rabagliati, Alberto 150
Rachel, Rachel (1968) 209, 210, 242
Racket, The (1927/28) 175, 192, 242
Rademakers, Fons 12

Radio Days (1987) 248
Radner, Gilda 176
Rafelson, Bob 240, 247
Raft, George 144
Raging Bull (1980) **130**, 189, 215, 222, 242, 245
Ragtime (1981) 215, 216, 248
Raiders of the Lost Ark (1981) 78, **130**, 215, 216, 242
Railway Children, The (1970) 251
Rain, Douglas 166
Rainbow, The (1989) 251
"Raindrops Keep Fallin' On My Head" 24
Raine, Norman Reilly **92**
Rainer, Luise **65**, **68**, 68, 184, 194, 195, 221
Raines, Christina 110
Rainger, Ralph **17**
Rainmaker, The (1956) 204
Rain Man (1988) 88, **131**, 190, 218, 219, 222, 242
Rains, Claude: *Adventures of Robin Hood* 2; *Anthony Adverse* 10; *Casablanca* 27, 198; *Here Comes Mr. Jordan* 73; *Lawrence of Arabia* 91; *Mr. Skeffington* 198; *Mr. Smith Goes to Washington* 108, 196; *Notorious* 152, 199; *Now, Voyager* 113; *Phantom of the Opera* 122
Rains Came, The (1939) **131**
Raintree County (1957) 204
Rake's Progress, The (1945) 251
Rall, Tommy 140
Ralph, Jessie 65, 116, 138
Ralston, Esther 160
Ralston, Jobyna 175
Ralston, Ken **31**, **39**, **133**, **174**
Rambaldi, Carlo **4**, **48**, **87**
Rambeau, Marjorie 103, 197, 203
Rambling Rose (1991) 220, 248
Ramin, Sid **172**, 225
Ramirez, Anthony 82
Ramsey, Anne 218
Ran (1985) **131–132**, 217
Randall, Tony 123, 260
Randolph, John 87, 127
Random Harvest (1942) 44, 107, 197, 198, 242, 248
Randone, Salvo 80
Rapf, Harry **22**
Raphael, Frederic **37**
Rappeneau, Jean-Paul 35
Rapper, Irving 21, 113, 241
Rasch, Raymond **93**
Rash, Steve 23
Rashomon (1951) 131, 255
Rathbone, Basil 2, 32, 55, 194, 195
Rattigan, Terence 139, 169
Ravetch, Irving 112
Rawlings, Margaret 136
Rawlings, Marjorie Kinnan 179
Ray, Gene Anthony 50
Ray, Joey 115
Ray, Michael 21
Ray, Nicholas 248, 250
Ray, Satyajit 258
Raye, Martha 17, 171, 252
Ray's Male Heterosexual Dance Hall (1987) 236

Razor's Edge, The (1946) **132**, 185, 199, 242

RCA Manufacturing Company 254

Rea, Stephen 34, 220

Reap the Wild Wind (1942) **132**

Rear Window (1954) 132, 203, 248

Reaves-Phillips, Sandra 137

Rebecca (1940) **132**, 152, 184, 196, 197, 242

Rebel Without a Cause (1955) 204, 248

Rebhorn, James 139

Red Badge of Courage, The (1951) 251

Red Balloon, The (1956) **132**

Redding, Otis 42

Redfield, William 51, 116

Redford, Robert: *All the President's Men* 7; *Butch Cassidy and the Sundance Kid* 24; *Candidate* 26; *Great Gatsby* 67; *Milagro Beanfield War* 102; *Ordinary People* 36, **117–118**, 189, 215, 241; *Out of Africa* 118; *River Runs Through It* 134–135; *Sting* 149, 212; *Way We Were* 172

Redgrave, Lynn 208

Redgrave, Michael 200

Redgrave, Vanessa: *Bostonians* 217; *Camelot* 26; *Howards End* 76, 220; *Isadora* 209; *Julia* **85**, 189, 214, 245; *Mary, Queen of Scots* 211; *Morgan* 208; *Murder on the Orient Express* 108

Redman, Joyce 162, 207, 208

Red River (1948) 248

Reds (1981) 10n, 28, 36, **133**, 190, 215, 216, 223, 242

Red Shoes, The (1948) **132–133**, 200, 242

Redwoods, The (1967) 232

Ree, Max **29**

Reed, Alan 170

Reed, Carol: *Fallen Idol* 201, 247; *Odd Man Out* 248; *Oliver!* **115**, 188, 210, 241; *Outcast of the Islands* 250; *Third Man* 157, 201

Reed, Donna **55**, 68, 77, 123, 186, 203, 245

Reed, John 133

Reed, Oliver 115, 176, 177

Reed, Pamela 101, 134

Reeve, Christopher 152

Reeves, Keanu 21, 37

Reeves, Lisa 180

Reid, Carl Benton 66

Reiner, Rob 104, 240, 247, 248

Reinhardt, Max 102, 241

Reinking, Ann 6

Reis, Irving 13

Reisch, Walter **160**, 222

Reiser, Paul 5

Reisner, Charles 240

Reiss, Stuart A. **40, 51**

Reisz, Karel 247, 251

Reitman, Ivan 247

Reivers, The (1969) 210

Remick, Lee 38, 115, 207

Remsen, Bert 110

Renaldo, Duncan 22

Renie 31, 223

Rennahan, Ray **19, 64**

Rennie, Michael 135

Reno, Kelly 18

Renoir, Jean 157, 199, 240, 257

Renzetti, Joe **23**

Reservoir Dogs (1992) 251

Resurrection (1980) 215

Resurrection of Broncho Billy, The (1970) 233

Return of the Jedi (1983) **133**

Reuben, Reuben (1983) 153, 216

Revere, Anne 19, 59, **110**, 124, 185, 198, 199, 200

Reversal of Fortune (1990) **133–134**, 191, 219, 220

Rey, Fernando 42, 55

Reynolds, Burt 260

Reynolds, Debbie 76, 208

Reynolds, Gene 33

Reynolds, Kevin 248

Reynolds, Marjorie 74

Reynolds, Norman **130, 148**

Reynolds, William **145, 149**

Rhoades, Barbara 64

Rhodes, Cynthia 42

Rhodes, Erik 58

Rhodes, Leah **2**

Rhys-Davies, John 78, 131, 169

Rhythm Boys, The (musical group) 87

Rice, Tim **3**, 225

Rich, Irene 27

Rich, Robert **21**

Rich, Ron 54

Richard III (1956) 204

Richards, Addison 21

Richards, Beah 68, 209

Richards, Jeff 140

Richardson, John **5**

Richardson, Lee 127

Richardson, Miranda 34, 109, 220

Richardson, Ralph 22, 43, 48, 72, 201, 217

Richardson, Robert **82**

Richardson, Tony **162**, 187, 207, 243

Richie, Lionel **173**

Richlin, Maurice **123**

Richter, Daniel 166

Richwine, Maria 23

Riddle, Nelson **67**

Ride the Pink Horse (1947) 200

Ridgely, John **3**

Ridges, Stanley 139, 140

Ridolfi, Giovanni 180

Riel, Louis 112

Rigg, Diana 74, 94

Right Stuff, The (1983) **134**, 216, 242

Rinker, Al 87

Rio Bravo (1959) 251

Riot in Cell Block 11 (1954) 251

Riquelme, Carlos 102

Riskin, Robert **81**

Ritchie, Michael 26

Riton 59

Ritt, Martin 76, 112, 207, 241, 242, 246, 248, 250

Ritter, Thelma: *All About Eve* 5, 201; *Birdman of Alcatraz* 207; *Hole in the Head* 74; *Letter to Three Wives* 92; *Mating Season*

202; *Pickup on South Street* 203; *Pillow Talk* 123, 205; *Titanic* 160; *With a Song in My Heart* 175, 202

Rivas, Carlos 87

River, The (1984) **134**, 217

Rivera, Fermin 21

River Runs Through It, A (1992) **134–135**

Rjasanova, Raissa 106

Roach, Bert 153

Roach, Hal 258

Roaring Twenties, The (1939) 251

Robards, Jason: *All the President's Men* 7, 189, 213, 222; *Julia* **85**, 189, 214, 222, 245; *Melvin and Howard* 100–101, 215; *Thousand Clowns* 158; *Tora! Tora! Tora!* 163

Robbins, Jerome **172–173**, 187, 206, 243, 256

Robbins, Tim 249

Robe, The (1953) **135**, 174n, 202, 223, 242

Robert Frost: A Lover's Quarrel with the World (1963) 231

Robert Kennedy Remembered (1968) 232

Roberts, Eric 217

Roberts, Julia 219

Roberts, Michael D. 131

Roberts, Rachel 108, 207

Roberts, Tony 10

Robertson, Cliff **28**, 123, 188, 209, 260

Robertson, Willard 143

Robin, Leo **17**

Robin Hood: Prince of Thieves (1991) 248

Robinson, Ann 171

Robinson, Edward G. 74, 86, 153, 257

Robinson, Glen 46, 74, **87, 95**

Robinson, Jay 135, 141

Robinson, Phil Alden 240, 247

Robinson, Robbie **99**

Robocop (1987) **135**, 135n

Robson, Flora 18, 178, 199

Robson, Mark 22, 27, 46, 205, 241

Robson, May 147, 193

Rocca, Daniella 43

Rocchetti, Manlio **44**

Rochin, Aaron **39**

Rocket, Charles 36

Rocky (1976) 10, **135**, 189, 213, 242

Roco, Bembol 179

Rodgers, Richard 87, 114, 145, 146, **148**

Roeg, Nicolas 249, 250, 251

Roemheld, Heinz **179**

Rogers, Charles (Buddy) 175, 253

Rogers, Ginger 58, **88**, 152, 184, 196

Rogers, Richard **124**

Rogers, Will 259

Rogue Song, The (1929/30) 192

Roland, Gilbert 44

Rolf, Tom **134**

Rolle, Esther 45

Rollins Jr., Howard E. 215

Roman, Ruth 27

Romance (1929/30) 193

Roman Holiday (1953) 135n, **135–136**, 186, 202, 203, 223, 242, 244

Roman Spring of Mrs. Stone, The (1961) 206

Romeo and Juliet (1936) 32, 70n, 194, 242

Romeo and Juliet (1968) 70n, **136**, 209, 210, 242

Rondi, Brunello 8n

Ronettes, The (musical group) 42

Rooker, Michael 82, 105

Room at the Top (1959) **136**, 187, 205, 206, 242

Room with a View, A (1986) 75, **136–137**, 217, 218, 242

Rooney, Mickey 253, 258; *Babes in Arms* 196; *Black Stallion* 18, 215; *Bold and the Brave* 204; *Boys' Town* 20; *Breakfast at Tiffany's* 21; *Bridges at Toko-Ri* 22; *Captains Courageous* 26; *Human Comedy* 76–77, 198; *It's a Mad, Mad, Mad, Mad World* 81; *Midsummer Night's Dream* 102; *National Velvet* 110; *Strike Up the Band* 150

Rose, Helen **13, 78**

Rose, Kay **134**

Rose, William **68**

Rose, The (1979) 214, 215, 248

Rosemary's Baby (1968) **137**, 188, 210

Rosenberg, Philip **6**

Rosenberg, Stuart 33

Rosenblatt, Marc 145

Rosenman, Leonard **14, 20**

Rose Tattoo, The (1955) 78, 99, **137**, 186, 203, 204, 242

Rosher, Charles **151, 179**

Ross, Anthony 33

Ross, Diana 211, 260

Ross, Herbert 26, 64, 151, 214, 240, 243, 246, 248

Ross, Katharine 24, 65, 209, 260

Ross, Shirley 17, 171

Ross, Ted 12, 53

Rosse, Herman **87**

Rossellini, Isabella 39, 173

Rossellini, Roberto 8n

Rossen, Robert **6**, 19, 32, 77, 201, 206, 238, 240

Rossi, Leo 2

Rossi, Luigi 8

Rossi, Walter **47**

Rossing, Bodil 151

Rossiter, Leonard 166

Rosson, Harold 253

Rostand, Edmond 35

Rota, Nino **62**

Rotter, Stephen A. **134**

'Round Midnight (1986) **137**, 217

Roundtree, Richard 46, 141

Rouse, Russell **123**

Rousselot, Philippe **134**

Rouvel, Catherine 18

Rovena, Marcella 149

Rowe, Bill **89**

Rowlands, Gena 212, 215

Roxanne (1987) 251

Royal Family of Broadway, The (1930/31) 193

Rozakis, Gregory 8

Rozsa, Miklos **16**, **44**, **146**, 224
Rub, Christian 123
Rubes, Jan 176
Rubin, Joel **60**
Rubinek, Saul 168
Rucker, Joseph T. **175**
Ruddy, Albert S. **61**
Rudloff, Gregg C. **61**
Rudoy, Joshua 71
Ruehl, Mercedes **53**, 191, 220
Ruggiero, Allelon 39
Ruggiero, Gene **11**
Ruggles, Charles 119
Ruggles, Wesley 29, 193, 239
Ruggles of Red Gap (1935) 194, 242
Ruiz, Chela 114
Ruling Class, The (1972) 211
Ruman, Sig 68, 147
Runaway Train (1985) 217
Running on Empty (1988) 218, 248
"Run to You" *50n*
Rush, Barbara 173
Rush, Richard 215, 248
Russell, Harold **17**, 86, 185, 199, 244, 254
Russell, Jane 119
Russell, Ken 177, 211, 251
Russell, Larry **93**
Russell, Rosalind 51, 122, 197, 199, 200, 205, 252, 259, 260
Russians Are Coming, The Russians Are Coming, The (1966) 208, 242
Ruth, Babe 126
Rutherford, Ann 2, 126
Rutherford, Margaret 19, 162, **169**, 187, 207
Rutledge, Robert **13**
Ruttenberg, Joseph **60**, **68**, **107**, **144**, 222
Ryan, Kathleen 18
Ryan, Meg 79
Ryan, Robert 42, 95, 200
Ryan's Daughter (1970) **137**, 188, 210, 223
Rydell, Chris 117
Rydell, Mark 117, 134, 216, 241, 248
Ryder, Alfred 165
Ryder, Winona 21
Rydstrom, Gary **154**
Ryu, Daisuke 132

S
Sabatini, Rafael 18
Sabato, Antonio 65, 66
Sabrina (1954) **138**, 203, 223
Sabu 18, 157
Sadie Thompson (1927/28) 140, 192
Sager, Carole Bayer **12**
Sahara (1943) 198
Sahl, Mort 260
Sainpolis, John 33
Saint, Eva Marie 48, 66, **117**, 138, 186, 203, 244, 260
St. John, Christopher 141
St. John, Howard 20
St. John, Theodore **66**
St. Valentine's Day Massacre (1967) 251
Sainte-Marie, Buffy 114
Sakall, S. Z. 27, 177, 179

Sakamoto, Ryuichi **89**, 90
Sakata, Harold 63
Saks, Gene 25, 158, 248
Saldana, Theresa 130
Salt, Waldo **32**, **101**
Salvador (1986) 217, 248
Salvatores, Gabriele 100
Salvatori, Renato 166
Same Time, Next Year (1978) 155, 214
Samson and Delilah (1950) **138**, 223
Samurai (1955) 256
Sanda, Dominique 58
Sand Castle (1977) 234
Sanders, George 134; *All About Eve* **5**, 185, 201; *Black Swan* 18–19; *Call Me Madam* 26; *Picture of Dorian Gray* 123; *Rebecca* 132; *Samson and Delilah* 138; *This Land Is Mine* 158
Sanders, Jay O. **82**
Sanders brothers 226
Sanderson, William 31
Sand Pebbles, The (1966) 208, 209, 242
Sandpiper, The (1965) **138**, 225
Sandrelli, Stefania 43
Sandrich, Mark 58, 74, 240, 243, 248
Sands, Edward 121
Sands, Julian 86, 136
Sands of Iwo Jima (1949) 165, 201, 248
Sanford, Erskine 30
San Francisco (1936) 46, **138**, 194, 195, 224, 242
Santiago, Emile **135**
Santillo, Frank **65**
Santopietro, George 127
Santuccio, Gianni 80
Saraband for Dead Lovers (1949) 91
Sarafian, Richard 24
Sarah and Son (1929/30) 193
Sarandon, Chris 213
Sarandon, Susan 156, 215, 220
Saratoga Trunk (1946) 199
Sargent, Alvin **85**, **118**
Saroyan, William **76**
Sarrazin, Michael 156
Sartain, Gailard 105
Saturday Night and Sunday Morning (1960) 251
Saturday Night Fever (1977) 214
Satyricon (1970) 211
Saunders, John Monk **38**
Saunders, Terry 87
Savage, John 39
Savalas, Telly 42, 207
Savegar, Brian **136**
Savelyeva, Ludmila 171
Save the Tiger (1973) 130, **138**, 188, 212, 222
Saville, Victor 68
Savino, Joe 34
Sawyer, Gordon E. **3**, **18**, **172**, 224
Sawyer Award, The Gordon E. 253
Saxon, Don 150
Saxon, Edward **142**
Sayles, John 249

Sayonara (1957) **139**, 186, 204, 205, 242
"Say You, Say Me" *50n*, **173**
Scala, Gia 69
Scales, Prunella 76
Scalia, Pietro **82**
Scared Straight (1978) 234
Scarface (1932) 251
Scarfiotti, Ferdinando **89**
Scarlet Empress, The (1934) 251
Scarlet Street (1945) 251
Scarwid, Diana 215
Scent of a Woman (1992) **139**, 191, 220, 242
Schaal, Wendy 79
Schaffner, Franklin J. 111, **121**, 188, 211, 241
Schanberg, Sydney 86
Schary, Dore **20**
Scheider, Roy 6, 55, 82, 88, 211, 214
Schell, Maximilian **84**, 85, 163, 187, 206, 213, 214
Schenck, Joseph M. **255**
Schepisi, Fred 246, 251
Schertzinger, Victor 116, 194, 241
Schildkraut, Joseph 30, 41, **92**, 131, 170, 184, 195
Schlesinger, John: *Darling* 38, 145, 208, 239; *Midnight Cowboy* **101**, 188, 210, 241; *Sunday Bloody Sunday* 211, 248
Schlondorff, Volker 160
Schmidt, Arthur **174**
Schnee, Charles **13**
Schoedsack, Ernest B. 102, 250
Schollin, Christina 51
Schoonmaker, Thelma **130**
Schroeder, Barbet 134, 220
Schulberg, Budd **117**
Schulman, Tom **38**
Schwartz, Gary 129
Schwary, Ronald L. **117**
Schwarzenegger, Arnold 154, 163
Schweig, Eric 90
Schweizer, Armin 99
Schweizer, Richard **99**, **139**
Sciorra, Annabella 134
Scofield, Paul 73, **98**, 188, 208, 245
Scorsese, Martin: *After Hours* 249; *Alice Doesn't Live Here Anymore* 4, 245; *Cape Fear* 246; *Color of Money* 32, 77, 245; *Goodfellas* 65, 219, 240, 245; *King of Comedy* 250; *Last Temptation of Christ* 219, 247; *Raging Bull* 130, 215, 242, 245; *Taxi Driver* 242, 248
Scott, Alex 38
Scott, George C. 74, 77, **121**, 188, 205, 206, 210, 211
Scott, Jesse 27
Scott, Kimberly 1
Scott, Leslie 125
Scott, Martha 16, 139, 153, 196
Scott, Rey 254
Scott, Ridley 5, 156, 220, 246, 249
Scott, Tom **7**, **134**
Scott, Tony 163
Scott, Walter M. **31**, **40**, **51**, **72**, **86**, **135**

Scott, Zachary 102, 103
Scoundrel, The (1935) **139**
screenwriting 222 see also personal names (e.g., Wilder, Billy)
Sea Around Us, The (1952) 229
Sea Hawk, The (1940) 248
Seale, Douglas 3
Seal Island (1948) 228
Seance on a Wet Afternoon (1964) 208
Search, The (1948) **139**, 200, 201, 255
Searchers, The (1956) 251
Searl, Jackie 119, 143
Sears, Heather 136, 145
Seaton, George 3, **33**, **103**, 203, 238, 239, 241, 252
Seawards the Great Ships (1961) 231
Seberg, Jean 3
Secombe, Harry 115
Secret Land, The (1948) 228
"Secret Love" **25**, 225
Sedgwick, Kyra 20
Seeds of Destiny (1946) 228
Segal, George 142, 164, 174, 209, 260
Segall, Harry **73**
Seirton, Michael **57**
Selig, William N. **255**
Selleck, Tom 261
Sellers, Peter 15, 162, 207, 214
Selwyn, Edgar 143
Selznick, David O. 13, **63**, **132**, 143, 252
Sembello, Michael 53
Semler, Dean **36**
Semon, Larry 167
Sennett, Mack 253
Sentinels of Silence (1971) 233
"Separate Lives" *50n*, 173
Separate Tables (1958) **139–140**, 186, 187, 205, 242
September (1987) 251
Serengeti Shall Not Die (1959) 231
Sergeant York (1941) 131, **140**, 184, 197, 222, 242
Serpico (1973) **139**, 212
Serrault, Michel 59
Sersen, Fred **34**, **131**
Servant, The (1964) 251
Session Man (1991) 237
Sessions, John 72
Seth, Roshan 78
Set-Up, The (1949) 251
Seven Beauties (1976) 213
Seven Brides for Seven Brothers (1954) **140**, 203, 242
Seven Days in May (1964) 208
Seven Days to Noon (1951) **140**
7 *Faces of Dr. Lao* 257
Seventh Cross, The (1944) 198
Seventh Heaven (1927/28) **140**, 150, 151, 175, 183, 192, 242
Seventh Veil, The (1946) **140–141**
Seven Women (1966) 251
Sex, Lies and Videotape (1989) 248
Seymour, Ralph 131
Seyrig, Delphine 42
"Shadow of Your Smile, The" **138**, 225
Shadows and Fog (1992) 251

Shaffer, Peter **7**
Shaft (1971) **141**
Shakespeare, William 70, 72, 85, 102, 131, 136, 172
"Shakin' the Blues Away" 46
Shampoo (1975) **141**, 189, 213
Shamroy, Leon **18**, **30**, **91**, **175**, 222
Shane (1953) 29, 30, **141**, 202, 203, 242
Shanghai Express (1931/32) **141**, 193, 242
Shanley, John Patrick **105**
Shapiro, Stanley **123**
Sharaff, Irene **8**, **31**, **86**, **172**, **174**, 223
Sharif, Omar 43, 56, 91, 207
Sharpe, Albert 125
Sharpe, Don **5**
Sharpsteen, Ben 45, 123
Sharrock, Ivan **89**
Shaughnessy, Mickey 40, 55
Shaver, Helen 32
Shaw, Fiona 109
Shaw, George Bernard 109, **128**
Shaw, Robert 82, 98, 149, 209, 260
Shaw, Sebastian 133
Shawlee, Joan 11, 81, 144
Shawn, Dick 81, 127
Shawn, Michael 64
Shayne, Tamara 84
Shea, John 104
Shearer, Douglas **17**, **66**, **68**, **110**, **138**, **150**, **157**, 224
Shearer, Moira 133
Shearer, Norma **42–43**, 54, 183, 193, 194, 195
Shearman, Russell **125**
She Done Him Wrong (1932/33) 193, 242
Sheehan, Winfield **27**
Sheen, Charlie 124, 125, 171
Sheen, Martin 11, 58, 150, 171
Sheffer, Craig 135
Sheldon, Sidney **13**
Shellen, Stephen 135
Sheltering Sky, The (1990) 251
Shepard, Sam 38, 134, 216
Shepherd, Cybill 90
Shepperton Studios Sound Department **115**
Sheridan, Dinah 22
Sheridan, Jim 109, 219, 241, 247
Sheriff, Paul 72*n*, **106**
Sherman, Hiram 143
Sherman, Lowell 106, 242
Sherman, Richard M. and Robert B. **99**, 141
Sherman, Vincent 2
Sherwood, Madeleine 152
Sherwood, Robert E. **17**
She Wore a Yellow Ribbon (1949) **141–142**, 223
Shingleton, Wilfred **67**
Shining, The (1980) 251
Ship Comes In, A (1927/28) 140, 192
Ship of Fools (1965) **142**, 208, 242
Shire, David **112**
Shire, Talia 62, 135, 212, 213
Shirley, Anne 6, 195

Shirley Valentine (1989) 219, 248
Shocking Accident, A (1982) 235
Shoe Shine 255
Shooting Party, The (1985) 251
Shop Around the Corner, The (1940) 251
Shop on Main Street, The (1966) **142**, 208
Short, Martin 79
Short, Robert **15**
short subjects see documentary and short subjects
Showboat (1936) 251
Shuftan, Eugene **77**
Shuken, Leo **146**
Shultis, Jackie 38
Shumlin, Herman 172, 243
Sidney, George 9, 71, 238
Sidney, Sylvia 19, 212
Siegel, Bernard 90
Siegel, Bugsy 23
Siegel, Don 249, 250, 251
Signoret, Simone 98, **136**, 142, 187, 205, 208
Silence of the Lambs, The (1991) 2, 23, 116, **142–143**, 191, 220, 221, 242
Silent Movie (1976) 251
Silent World, The (1956) 230
Silk Stockings (1957) 251
Silkwood (1983) 145, 216, 248
Silliphant, Stirling **80**
Silvana, Aldo 112, 149
Silver, Joe 180
Silver, Ron 134
Silverado (1985) 248
Silvers, Louis **116**
Silvers, Phil 34, 56, 81, 109
Silverstein, Elliott 27
Simmons, Jean 17, 18, 46–47, 67, 70, 135, 146, 200, 210
Simon, Carly **177**
Simon, Neil 25, 64
Simon, Paul 10
Simon, Simone 6
Simoni, Dario **43**, **91**
Simpson, Claire **124**
Simpson, Ivan 42
Simpson, O. J. 164
Simpson, Rick **41**
Simpson, Russell 66
Sinatra, Frank 252, 260; *Anchors Aweigh* 9; *From Here to Eternity* **55**, 186, 203, 245; *Hole in the Head* 74; *House I Live In* 254; *Joker Is Wild* 84; *Man with the Golden Arm* 203; *On the Town* 117
Since You Went Away (1944) **143**, 198, 199, 224, 242
Singer, Isaac Bashevis 179
Singin' in the Rain (1952) 202, 248
Singleton, John 220, 246
Sinise, Gary 250
Sin of Madelon Claudet, The (1931/32) 3, 25*n*, 108*n*, **143**, 183, 193, 221
Siodmak, Robert 200, 247, 248
Sipperly, Ralph 151
Sirk, Douglas 177
Sister Kenny (1946) 199
Sitting Pretty (1948) 200

Sivas, Emin 84
Sivero, Frank 65
Skala, Lilia 28, 53, 93, 207
Skall, William V. **82**, 223
Skelton, Red 89, 110, 111
Skerritt, Tom 5, 100, 135, 163
Skippy (1930/31) **143**, 183, 193, 242
Skipworth, Alison 37
Skolimowski, Jerzy 173
Skotak, Dennis **1**
Skotak, Robert **5**, **154**
Sky Above and Mud Below, The (1961) 231
Slate, Jeremy 165
Slater, Helen 30
Slaughterhouse Five (1972) 251
Sleeper, Martha 16, 139
Sleuth (1972) 70, 211, 212, 248
Slezak, Walter 158, 177
Slifer, Clarence **125**
Slivkova, Hans 142
Sloane, Everett 30, 97, 144
Sloane, Olive 140
Small Back Room, The (1948) 251
Smash-Up, the Story of a Woman (1947) 51, 81, 200
Smiles of a Summer Night (1955) 94
Smiling Lieutenant, The (1931/32) 193, 242
Smilin' Through (1932/33) 193, 242
Smith, Albert E. 255
Smith, Alexis 73
Smith, Betty 165
Smith, C. Aubrey 77, 94, 95, 106, 132
Smith, Charles Martin 23, 168
Smith, Dick **7**
Smith, Harold Jacob 40
Smith, Jack Martin **30**, **51**, **72**
Smith, Kenneth F. **48**, **79**
Smith, Kent 158
Smith, Kurtwood 135
Smith, Lane 109, 124
Smith, Leonard **179**
Smith, Maggie 260; *California Suite* **25–26**, 108*n*, 189, 214, 222; *Death on the Nile* 39; *Othello* 208; *Prime of Miss Jean Brodie* 25*n*, 108*n*, **126**, 188, 210, 222; *Room With a View* 136, 218; *Travels With My Aunt* 164, 211; *V.I.P.s* 169
Smith, Mark **90**
Smith, Muriel 107
Smith, Patricia 138
Smith, Paul J. **123**
Smith, Pete 256
Smith, Stanley 87
Smythe, Doug **39**
Snake Pit, The (1948) **143**, 200, 201, 242
Snodgrass, Carrie 210
Snow White and the Seven Dwarfs (1938) 253
Soderbergh, Steven 248
Soderlund, Ulla-Britt **14**
Sokoloff, Vladimir 54
Solari, Laura 136
Soldier Blue (1970) 36

Soldier's Story, A (1984) 216, 217, 242, 248
Solid Gold Cadillac, The (1956) **143**
Solomin, Yuri 40
Solomon, Jack **72**
Somebody Up There Likes Me (1956) **144**, 222, 223
Some Came Running (1958) 154, 205
Some Like It Hot (1959) **144**, 162, 205, 206
Something Wicked This Way Comes (1983) 251
Something Wild (1986) 251
Sometimes a Great Notion (1971) 211
Sommer (Somr), Josef 31, 176
So Much for So Little (1949) 228
Sondergaard, Gale 9, **10**, 92, 184, 195, 200
Sondheim, Stephen **41**, 94
Song of Bernadette, The (1943) **144**, 185, 198, 222, 242
Song of the South (1947) **144**
Song to Remember, A (1945) 199
Song Without End (1960) **144–145**
songwriting 225 see also song titles (e.g., *All the Way*); lyricists (e.g., Cahn, Sammy)
Sons and Lovers (1960) 61, **145**, 206, 242
Sons of Liberty (1939) 227
"Sooner or Later" ("I Always Get My Man") 41
Sophie's Choice (1982) 25*n*, 108*n*, **145**, 190, 216, 222
So Proudly We Hail (1943) 198
Sorrell and Son (1927/28) 192
Sorry, Wrong Number (1948) 200
Sorvino, Paul 65, 133, 164
Sothern, Ann 54, 89, 92, 218
So This Is Harris (1932/33) 226
Sound Barrier, The (1952) 21
Sounder (1972) 211, 242
Sound of Music, The (1965) **145**, 146, 187, 208, 224, 242
sound recording 224
Soussanin, Nicholas 89
Southerner, The (1945) 199
South Pacific (1958) **145–146**, 224
Spacek, Sissy: *Carrie* 213; *Coal Miner's Daughter* **31**, 189, 215; *Crimes of the Heart* 217; *JFK* 82; *Missing* 104, 216; *River* 134, 217
Spark, Muriel 126
Sparke, Pip 51
Sparks, Billy 128
Spartacus (1960) **146**, 187, 206
Spawn of the North (1938) 254
Speaking of Animals and Their Families (1942) 227
Special Day, A (1977) 214
Special Delivery (1978) 234
Speedy (1927/28) 192
Speedy Gonzales (1955) 230
Spellbound (1945) 132, **146**, 152, 199, 224, 242
Sperber, Wendie Jo 13
Spiegel, Sam **22**, **91**, **117**, 221, 252
Spielberg, Steven 252; *Close Encounters of the Third Kind* 31, 214;

Color Purple 118, 239, 246; *Empire of the Sun* 247; *E.T. The Extraterrestrial* 48, 216, 239; *Indiana Jones and the Last Crusade* 78; *Indiana Jones and the Temple of Doom* 78; *Jaws* 82, 240; *Raiders of the Lost Ark* 130, 216, 242
Spiesser, Jacques 18
Spikings, Barry **39**
Spiral Staircase, The (1946) 199, 248
Spivak, Murray **72**
Splendor in the Grass (1961) **146**, 206
Splet, Alan **18**
Spoor, George K. 255
Spradlin, G. D. 11
Springer, Gary 44
Spy Who Came In from the Cold, The (1965) 174n, 208, 248
Squarciapino, Franca **35**
Stack, Robert 73, 168, 177, 204
Stagecoach (1939) 29, **146**, 184, 196, 242, 245
Stage Door (1937) 195, 242
Stahl, John M. 92, 173, 240
Stairway to Light (1945) 228
Stalag 17 (1953) 85, **147**, 186, 202, 203
Stallone, Sylvester 135, 213
Stamp, Terence 171, 207
Stand and Deliver (1988) 218, 248
Stander, Lionel 107, 147
Standing, Guy 95
Stanford, Thomas **172**
Stanger, Hugo 15
Stanitsin, Viktor 171
Stanley, Kim 134, 208, 216
Stanton, Harry Dean 5
Stanwyck, Barbara 160, 195, 197, 198, 200, 258
Stapleton, Maureen 3, 32, **133**, 190, 205, 211, 214, 216
Star! (1968) 210
Star, The (1952) 202
Stardust Memories (1980) 251
Star in the Night (1945) 228
Star Is Born, A (1937) **147**, 195, 242, 253
Star Is Born, A (1954) 203, 248
Star Is Born, A (1976) **147–148**
Stark, Graham 169
Stark, Ray 252
Starman (1984) 217
Starr, Mike 65
Starr, Ringo 92
"Stars Shine in Your Eyes" 149
Starting Over (1979) 214, 215
Star Wars (1977) 31, 47, **148**, 213, 214, 224, 242
State Fair (1932/33) 193, 242, 248
State Fair (1945) **148–149**
State of the Union (1948) 251
Stears, John **148**, **159**
Steele, Barbara 46
Steele, Gile **72**, **138**, 223
Steele, Karen 99
Steel Magnolias (1989) 219
Steenburgen, Mary **100–101**, 189, 215
Steiger, Rod: *Doctor Zhivago* 43; *In the Heat of the Night* **80**, 188,

209; *Longest Day* 95; *Oklahoma!* 114–115; *On the Waterfront* 117, 203; *Pawnbroker* 208
Stein, Jules 252
Steinbeck, John 46, 66, 170
Steiner, Max 64, **79**, **113**, **143**, 224
Steinkamp, Frederic **65**
Steinore, Michael **68**
Stella Dallas (1937) 195
Stensgaard, Hanne 13
Stensvold, Larry **118**
Stephens, Harvey 116
Stephens, Robert 72, 126, 164
Stephenson, Henry 27, 94, 108, 157
Stephenson, James 196
Sterile Cuckoo, The (1969) 210
Sterling, Jan 73, 83, 203
Sterling, Robert 84
Stern, Daniel 21, 30, 70
Sternhagen, Frances 104
Stevens, Fisher 134
Stevens, George 252; *Alice Adams* 238; *Damsel in Distress* 36; *Diary of Anne Frank* 41, 205, 239; *Giant* **60**, 186, 204, 240; *Gunga Din* 250; *More the Merrier* 106, 198, 241; *Place in the Sun* **123–124**, 186, 202, 242; *Shane* 141, 203, 242; *Swing Time* 152; *Talk of the Town* 242; *Woman of the Year* 176
Stevens, Jack **155**
Stevens, Mark 143
Stevens, Onslow 173
Stevens, Rise 62
Stevens, Stella 125
Stevenson, Edward **50**, 223
Stevenson, Robert 15, 100, 208, 241
Stevenson, Robert Louis 45
Stewart, Donald Ogden **104**, **122**
Stewart, Douglas **134**
Stewart, Edward **6**
Stewart, James 258, 259; *Anatomy of a Murder* 205; *Glenn Miller Story* 61; *Greatest Show on Earth* 66; *Harvey* 71, 201; *How the West Was Won* 76; *It's a Wonderful Life* 199; *Man Who Knew Too Much* 99; *Mr. Smith Goes to Washington* 107–108, 196; *Philadelphia Story* **122**, 184, 196, 245; *Stratton Story* 149; *You Can't Take It With You* 180
Stewart, James G. 125
Stewart, Paul 27, 30, 165
Stiers, David Ogden 2, 15
Sting, The (1973) **149**, 188, 189, 212, 223, 242
Stockwell, Dean 9, 145, 218
Stockwell, John 163
Stokowski, Leopold 116, 254
Stoleru, Josiane 35
Stoll, Georgie **9**
Stoll, John **91**
Stoloff, Morris **33**, **84**, **144**
Stoltz, Eric 100
Stone, David E. **21**
Stone, Fred 172
Stone, George E. 29, 170

Stone, Harold J. 144
Stone, Lewis 17, 65, 121, 143, 192
Stone, Oliver: *Born on the Fourth of July* **20**, 191, 219, 239; *Doors* 249; *JFK* 82, 220, 240; *Midnight Express* **101**; *Platoon* **124–125**, 190, 218, 242; *Salvador* 248; *Talk Radio* 249; *Wall Street* 171
Stone, Peter **51**
Stone, Philip 78
Stone, Sharon 163
Stone Carvers, The (1984) 235
Stong, Philip 148
Storaro, Vittorio **11**, **89**, **133**, 223
Storke, Adam 39
Story of Adele H., The (1975) 213
Story of G.I. Joe, The (1945) 199, 248
Story of Louis Pasteur, The (1936) 92, **149**, 184, 194, 242
Stossel, Ludwig 126
Stothart, Herbert 64, **176**
Stout, Archie 107, **129**, 223
Stowe, Madeleine 90
Strabl, Herbert **25**
Stradling, Harry **109**, **123**
Straight, Beatrice **111**, 189, 213, 245
Strangers on a Train (1951) 161
Strasberg, Lee 62, 212
Strasberg, Susan 123
Stratton Story, The (1949) **149**
Strauss, Johann 68
Strauss, Robert 22, 147, 203
"Straw Hat" 53
Streep, Meryl: *Cry in the Dark* 218; *Death Becomes Her* 39; *Deer Hunter* 39, 214; *French Lieutenant's Woman* 215; *Ironweed* 218, 219; *Kramer vs. Kramer* 25n, **88**, 189, 215, 222; *Out of Africa* 118, 217; *Postcards from the Edge* 219; *Silkwood* 216; *Sophie's Choice* 25n, **145**, 190, 216, 222
Street Angel (1927/28) 140, **150**, 151, 183, 192
Streetcar Named Desire, A (1951) 111, 123, **150**, 186, 202, 221, 223, 242, 244
Street Smart (1987) 218
Streisand, Barbra: *Funny Girl* **55–56**, 93, 188, 209, 244; *Hello, Dolly!* 72; *Prince of Tides* 242, 248; *Star Is Born* 147, 147–148; *Way We Were* 172, 212; *Yentl* 179
Strickland, Gail 20, 112
Strike Up the Band (1940) **150**, 224
Strobye, Axel 122
Stromberg, Hunt **68**
Strong, Michael 121
Stroud, Don 23
Strudwick, Shepperd 6, 124
Struss, Karl **151**
Stuart, Gloria 62, 63
Studi, Wes 90
Stunt Man, The (1980) 215, 248
Sturges, John 99, 115, 204, 246
Sturges, Preston **67**, 100, 250, 251
Sturridge, Charles 247
Styne, Jule **159**, 225

Styron, William 145
Subject Was Roses, The (1968) **150**, 188, 209
Suchet, David 71
Sudden Fear (1952) 30, 202
Suddenly, Last Summer (1959) 205, 248
Sugerman, Alvin M. 45
Sukman, Harry **144**
Sullivan, Margaret 195
Sullivan, Annie 103
Sullivan, Barry 13
Sullivan, Brad 168
Sullivan, Francis L. 67, 83
Sullivan, Jack **27**
Sullivan's Travels (1942) 251
Summer, Donna 155
Summer and Smoke (1961) 165, 206
Summer of '42 (1971) **150**
Summers, Gary **154**
Summertime (1955) 203, 204, 248
Summerville, Slim 6
Summer Wishes, Winter Dreams (1973) 212
Sundae in New York (1983) 235
Sunday Bloody Sunday (1971) 211, 248
Sundays and Cybele (1962) 78n, **150–151**
Sundberg, Clinton 46
Sunderland, Scott 128
Sundowners, The (1960) 206, 242
Sunrise (1927/28) 140, 150, **151**, 183, 192
Sunrise at Campobello (1960) 206
Sunset Boulevard (1950) **151**, 201, 222, 242
Sunshine Boys, The (1975) 45, **151**, 189, 213
Sun Shines Bright, The (1953) 251
Superman (1978) **152**
supporting actors/actresses *see* acting; personal names (e.g., Winters, Shelley)
Surer, Nur 84
"Surrey with the Fringe on Top, The" 114
Surtees, Robert L. **13**, **16**, **87**, 223
Survival City (1955) 230
Suspicion (1941) **152**, 184, 197, 242
Sutherland, Donald 42, 52, 88, 100, 118
Sutton, John 109
Sutton, Peter **47**
Suzman, Janet 111, 211
"Swanee" 84
Swanson, Gloria 140, 151, 192, 193, 201
Swayze, Patrick 42, 60, 261
Sweeney, Birdie 34
Sweet Bird of Youth (1962) **152**, 165, 187, 207
Sweet Charity (1969) 112
Sweet Dreams (1985) 217
Sweethearts 253
"Sweet Leilani" 171
Sweet Smell of Success, The (1957) 251
Swenson, Inga 103

288

"Swinging on a Star" **62**, 225
Swing Shift (1984) 217
Swing Time (1936) **152**
Sydney, Basil 70
Sylbert, Paul **71**
Sylbert, Richard **41**, **174**
Sylvester, Harold 114
Sylvester, William 166
Sylwan, Kari 34
Symphony of a City (1948) 228
Szabo, Istvan 101

T

Tabu (1930/31) **153**
Taka, Miiko 139
"Take My Breath Away" **163**
Talbot, Lyle 116
Tale of Two Cities, A (1936) 194, 242
Talk of the Town, The (1942) 107, 197, 242
Talk Radio (1988) 251
"Talk to the Animals" **43**
Tally, Ted **142**
Talmadge, Norma 44
Tamblyn, Russ 140, 162, 173, 204
Tamiroff, Akim 9, 10, 32, 54, 67, 113, 163, 194, 198
Tamura, Takahiro 163
Tandy, Jessica 32, **44–45**, 151, 191, 219, 220
Tango (1982) 235
Taradash, Daniel **55**, 135*n*
Tarantino, Quentin 251
Target for Tonight 254
Tarloff, Frank **51**
Tati, Jacques 105
Taurog, Norman 20, **143**, 183, 193, 196, 239, 242
Tavernier, Bertrand 137
Tavoularis, Dean **62**
Taxi Driver (1976) 2, 213, 242, 248
Taylor, Don 78, 110, 147
Taylor, Elizabeth 253, 260; *Butterfield 8* **24**, 174*n*, 187, 206; *Cat on a Hot Tin Roof* 205; *Cleopatra* 31; *Giant* 60; *Little Night Music* 94; *Little Women* 94; *National Velvet* 110; *Place in the Sun* 123–124; *Raintree County* 204; *Sandpiper* 138; *Suddenly, Last Summer* 205, 209; *V.I.P.s* 169; *Who's Afraid of Virginia Woolf?* **174**, 188, 209
Taylor, Estelle 29
Taylor, Peter **22**
Taylor, Robert 23, 83, 84
Taylor, Rod 140, 159, 169
Taylor, Ronnie **57**
Taylor, Sam 33, 153
Taylor, Samuel 138
Teacher's Pet (1958) 156, 205
Technicolor Company 254
Teddy, The Rough Rider (1940) 227
Teefy, Maureen 50
Teenage Father (1978) 234
Te Kanawa, Kiri 136
Telling the World (1927/28) 50, 90, **153**
Tempest, The (1927/28) 44, **153**

Temple, Shirley 13, 143, 253
Ten Commandments, The (1956) 113, **153**, 158, 204, 242
Ten Days That Shook the World (book by John Reed) 133
Tender Mercies (1983) **153–154**, 190, 216, 242
Ten-Year Lunch, The: The Wit and Legend of the Algonquin Round Table (1987) 236
Terao, Akira 132
Terminator 2: Judgment Day (1991) **154**
Terms of Endearment (1983) 130, **154**, 190, 216, 222, 242
Terry, Nigel 93
Terry, Philip 96, 161
Terry-Thomas 81, 162
Teshigahara, Hiroshi 208
Tesich, Steve **21**
Tess (1980) **155**, 215, 242
Testament (1983) 216
Testi, Fabio 58
Test Pilot (1938) 195, 242
Tevis, Walter 77
Thalbach, Katharina 160
Thalberg, Irving **108**
Thalberg Memorial Award, Irving G. 252
Thank God It's Friday (1978) **155**
"Thanks for the Memory" **17**
Thatcher, Torin 96, 138
That Hamilton Woman (1941) **155**
"That'll Be the Day" 23
That Mothers Might Live (1938) 227
"That's Amore!" 106
Thaxter, Phyllis 152, 157
"The Continental" **58**
Their Own Desire (1929/30) 193
Thelma and Louise (1991) **156**, 220
"Theme from Shaft" 141
Theodora Goes Wild (1936) 194
These Three (1936) 195
Thevenet, Pierre-Louis **121**
They Knew What They Wanted (1940) 196
They Shoot Horses, Don't They? (1969) **156**, 188, 210
They Won't Forget (1937) 251
Thiaka, Joseph 118
Thief of Baghdad, The (1940) **156–157**
Thing, The (1951) 251
Thing, The (1982) 251
Things to Come (1936) 251
Thin Man, The (1934) 194, 242, 248
Thinnes, Roy 74
Third Man, The (1950) 115, **157**, 201
Thirty-Nine Steps, The (1935) 251
Thirty Seconds Over Tokyo (1944) **157**
This Above All (1942) **157**, 223
This Gun for Hire (1942) 251
This Is The Army (1943) **157**
This Land Is Mine (1943) **157–158**
This Mechanical Age (1954) 230
This Sporting Life (1963) 207
This Tiny World (1972) 233
Thom, Randy **134**

Thomas, Bill **146**
Thomas, Henry 48
Thomas, Jameson 81
Thomas, Jeremy **89**
Thomas Crown Affair, The (1968) **158**
Thompson, Emma 73, **75–76**, 191, 220
Thompson, Ernest **116**
Thompson, J. Lee 69, 206, 240
Thompson, Kenneth 23
Thompson, Lea 13
Thompson, Marshall 14
Thompson, Rex 87
Thomson, Anna 168
Thorburn, June 162
Thorne, Ken **56**
Thoroughly Modern Millie (1967) **158**, 209
Thorpe, Richard 66, 240
Thousand Clowns, A (1965) **158**, 187, 208, 242
"Three Coins in the Fountain" **159**, 225
Three Coins in the Fountain (1954) **159**, 203, 225, 242
Three Comrades (1938) 195
Three Faces of Eve, The (1957) **159**, 186, 204
Three Little Pigs, The (1932/33) 226
Three Men and a Cradle (1985) 114
Three Orphan Kittens (1935) 226
Three Smart Girls (1936) 194, 243
3:10 to Yuma (1957) 251
Through a Glass Darkly (1961) 50, **159**
Throw Momma from the Train (1987) 218
Thulin, Ingrid 34
Thunderball (1965) **159**
Thunderbolt (1928/29) 192
Thunderbolt and Lightfoot (1974) 212
Thurman, Uma 37
Thursday's Children (1954) 230
Tibbett, Lawrence 192
Ticotin, Rachel 163
Tidyman, Ernest **54**
Tierney, Gene 90, 91, 92, 125, 132, 199
Tierney, Lawrence 127
Tikhonov, Vyacheslav 171
Tilly, Meg 217
Tilvern, Alan 174
Time Machine, The (1960) **159**
Time Out of War, A (1954) 226, 230
Times of Harvey Milk, The (1984) 235
Tin Drum, The (1979) **160**
Tin Men (1987) 251
Tin Pan Alley (1940) **160**, 224
Tin Toy (1988) 236
Tiomkin, Dimitri 17, **73**, **73–74**, **115**, 224
Tippett, Phil **133**
Titan, The: Story of Michelangelo (1950) 229
Titanic (1953) **160**, 222
To Be Alive! (1965) 232

To Begin Again (Volver a Empezar) (1982) **160–161**
To Be or Not To Be (1983) 216
Tobias, George 3, 61, 103, 140, 157, 179
Tobolowsky, Stephen 105, 156
To Catch a Thief (1955) **161**
Todd, Ann 22, 140, 141, 169
Todd, Mabel 34
Todd, Michael **11**
Todd, Richard 95, 201
To Each His Own (1946) **161**, 185, 199, 221
To Have and Have Not (1944) 251
To Kill a Mockingbird (1962) 108, 158, **161–162**, 187, 207, 243
Tolan, Michael 6
Toland, Gregg 30, **177–178**
Toldy, John S. **11**
Tolkan, James 134
Tolstoy, Leo 171
Tomei, Marisa **108–109**, 191, 220
Tomelty, Joseph 22
Tom Jones (1963) 58, **162**, 187, 207, 243
Tomlin, Lily 110, 213, 261
Tomlinson, David 15, 100
Tommy (1975) 213
Tom Thumb (1958) 159, **162**
Tone, Franchot 37, 73, 94, 108, 194
Toot, Whistle, Plunk and Boom (1953) 229
Tootsie (1982) 88, **162**, 190, 216, 243
top-grossing films *see* box-office revenues
Top Gun (1986) **163**
Top Hat (1935) 194, 243, 248
Topkapi (1964) **163**, 187, 208
Topol 52, 211
Topper (1937) 195
Tora! Tora! Tora! (1970) **163**
Torch Song (1953) 203
Torn, Rip 152, 216
Tornatore, Giuseppe 29
Tornqvist, Kristina 122
Torrence, David 42
Torrence, Ernest 22
Torres, Fernando 88
Torres, Raquel 22, 174
Tortilla Flat (1942) 198
Tortoise and the Hare, The (1934) 226
Torture Money (1937) 227
Total Recall (1990) **163**
Touch of Class, A (1973) 76, **163–164**, 188, 212, 221, 243
Touch of Evil (1958) 251
Toulouse-Lautrec, Henri de 106
Toward Independence (1948) 228
Towering Inferno, The (1974) **164**, 212, 243
Towne, Robert **29**
Tracy, Lee 208
Tracy, Spencer: *Bad Day at Black Rock* 203; *Boys' Town* **20–21**, 131, 184, 195, 222; *Broken Lance* 23; *Captains Courageous* **26**, 131, 184, 195, 222; *Father of the Bride* 201; *Guess Who's Coming to Dinner* 68, 209; *Inherit the Wind*

206; *It's a Mad, Mad, Mad, Mad World* 81; *Judgment at Nuremberg* 84, 206; *Old Man and the Sea* 115, 205; *Plymouth Adventure* 125; *San Francisco* 138, 194; *Thirty Seconds Over Tokyo* 157; *Woman of the Year* 176
Tracy, William 150
Trader Horn (1930/31) 193, 243
Trading Places (1983) 248
"Tramp, Tramp, Tramp" 110
Transatlantic (1931/32) **164**
Trauner, Alexander **11**
Travels with My Aunt (1972) **164**, 211
Travers, Bill 20
Travers, Henry 16, 107, 198
Travers, P. L. 99
Travis, Neil **36**
Travolta, John 214
Treasure of the Sierra Madre, The (1948) 127, **164**, 185, 200, 243, 245
Tree, David 128
Tree, Lady 126
Tree Grows in Brooklyn, A (1945) **164–165**, 185, 199, 244
Tremayne, Les 171
Trento, Guido 150
Trespasser, The (1929/30) 193
Trevor, Claire 73, **86**, 146, 185, 195, 200, 203, 245
Trial (1955) 203
Tribute (1980) 215
Trieste, Leopoldo 43
Trintignant, Jean-Louis 98, 181
Trip to Bountiful, The (1985) **165**, 190, 217
Tristan, Dorothy 88
Troell, Jan 211, 239
Trotti, Lamar **175**
Trouble in Paradise (1932) 251
Trouble with Harry, The (1956) 251
Troughton, Patrick 116
Trousdale, Gary 15
Trovajoli, Armando 180
True Glory, The (1945) 228
True Grit (1969) **165**, 188, 210
True Story of the Civil War, The (1956) 230
Truffaut, Francois 31, 38, 106, 212, 249
Trumbo, Dalton 21*n*, 88, 135*n*
Truscott, John **26**
Tucker, Forrest 172
Tucker: The Man and His Dream (1988) 218, 248
Tully, Tom 96, 203
Tunick, Jonathan **94**
Turken, Greta 145
Turné (1990) 100
Turner, Kathleen 1–2, 126, 127, 174, 217
Turner, Lana 13, 68, 83, 84, 204
Turning Point, The (1977) 154, 213, 214, 243, 246, 248
Turturro, John 32
Tushingham, Rita 43
Tutin, Dorothy 34
Tuttle, Frank 171, 251
Tuttle, Lurene 54
Tuttle, William 256

Tweetie Pie (1947) 228
Twelve Angry Men (1957) 204, 205, 243, 248
Twelve O'Clock High (1949) 162, **165**, 185, 201, 243
20th Century-Fox Film Corporation 256
20,000 Leagues Under the Sea (1954) 1, **165–166**
Twice in a Lifetime (1985) 217
Twilight of Honor (1963) 207
Two Arabian Knights (1927/28) 140, **166**, 183, 192
Two Mouseketeers (1951) 229
2001: A Space Odyssey (1968) **166**, 210, 248
Two Women (1961) **166**, 187, 206
Tyler, Walter **138**
Tyrrell, Susan 211
Tyson, Cicely 211
Tyson, Elliot **61**

U

Ugly Duckling, The (1939) 227
Uhry, Alfred **44**
Ullmann, Liv 34, 37, 211, 213
Umeki, Miyoshi **139**, 186, 205
Unbearable Lightness of Being, The (1988) 248
"Under the Sea" 50*n*, **93**, 225
Under the Volcano (1984) 217, 248
Underwood, Ron 30
Underworld (1927/28) **167**
Unforgiven (1992) 29, 130, **167–168**, 191, 220, 222, 243
Unmarried Woman, An (1978) 214, 243, 248
Unsinkable Molly Brown, The (1964) 208
Unsworth, Geoffrey **25**, **155**
Untouchables, The (1987) **168**, 190, 218
Up (1984) 235
"Up Where We Belong" 114
Ure, Mary 145, 206
Uris, Leon 48
Ustinov, Peter 39, 95, **146**, **163**, 187, 202, 206, 208
Utt, Kenneth **142**
Uytterhoeven, Pierre **98**

V

Vacation From Marriage (1946) **169**
Vaccaro, Brenda 101, 213
Valberg, Birgitta 169
Valenta, Vladimir 31
Valentine, Joseph **82**, 223
Valiant, The (1928/29) 192
Valiant Is the Word for Carrie (1936) 194
Vallee, Rudy 13
Valles **146**
Valley of Decision, The (1945) 199
Valli, Alida 157
Valli, Frankie 42
Valli, Romolo 58
Vallone, Raf 166
Vance, Vivian 67
Van Der Lubbe, Huub 12
Van Der Molen, Ina 12

Van Der Veer, Frank **87**
Van Der Veer, Willard **175**
Van De Ven, Monique 12
Vandis, Tito 111
Van Druten, John 25
Van Dyke, Dick 100
Van Dyke II, W. S.: *Eskimo* 47; *Manhattan Melodrama* 98; *Naughty Marietta* 110, 241; *San Francisco* 138, 195, 242; *Thin Man* 194, 242, 248; *Trader Horn* 243; *White Shadows in the South Seas* 174
Vanel, Charles 161
Van Fleet, Jo 33, **46**, 78, 137, 186, 204, 244
Vangelis **27**
Van Gogh (1949) 228
Van Gogh, Vincent 96
Van Heusen, James **62**, **74**, **84**, **119**, 225
Vanishing Prairie, The (1954) 226, 230
Van Nutter, Rik 159
Van Patton, Dick 28
Van Sant Jr., Gus 249, 250
Van Uchelen, Marc 12
Varconi, Victor 42
Varney, Bill **47**, **130**
Varsi, Diane 205
Vaughn, Robert 24, 164, 205
Vavitch, Michael 166
Veidt, Conrad 27, 157
Venable, Evelyn 123
Vennera, Chick 155
Venora, Diane 17
Venture, Richard 104, 139
Venturini, Lidia 149
Vera-Ellen 26, 117, 177
Verdict, The (1982) 32, 216, 243, 248
Verdon, Gwen 32
Vereen, Ben 6
Verhoeven, Paul 135, 163, 246
Verne, Jules 11, 165
Vertes, Marcel 96
Vertigo (1958) 34, 248
Vertinskaya, Anastasia 171
Victor/Victoria (1982) **169**, 216
Vidor, Charles 34, 84, 96, 144, 250
Vidor, Florence 121
Vidor, King 27, 192, 193, 196, 204, 239, 257
Villa, Pancho 169, 170
Villafane, Chunchuna 114
Villalonga, Jose-Luis de 37
Villaume, Astrid 122
Vince, Pruitt Taylor 105
Vincent, Frank 65, 130
Vincent, Virginia 81
Ving, Lee 53
Violet (1981) 235
V.I.P.s, The (1963) 162, **169**, 187, 207
Virgin Spring, The (1960) 50, **169**
Visaroff, Michael 89
Vitte, Ray 155
Viva Villa! (1934) **169–170**, 194, 243
Viva Zapata! (1952) **170**, 186, 202, 222, 244

Vogel, Paul C. **14**
Voight, Jon **32–33**, 101, 189, 210, 214, 217, 260
Volonte, Gian Maria 80
Volter, Philippe 35
Von Brandenstein, Patrizia **7**
Von Bulow, Claus 133
Von Dohlen, Lenny 153
Von Sternberg, Josef: *Blue Angel* 249; *Last Command* 89, 241; *Morocco* 143, 193, 247; *Scarlet Empress* 251; *Shanghai Express* 141, 242; *Underworld* 167
Von Stroheim, Erich 151, 201
Von Sydow, Max 49, 70, 122, 159, 169, 218
Voronina, Vera 121
Vortman, Frans 12
Vos, Marik **50**
Voyage of the Damned (1976) 213

W

Wada, Emi **131**
Wada, Sanzo **58**
Waddington, Steven 90
Wager, Anthony 67
Wagner, Lindsay 119, 120
Wagner, Robert 95, 160, 164, 175
Wagonmaster (1950) 251
Waikiki Wedding (1937) **171**
Waits, Tom 21
Wait Until Dark (1967) 209
Wajda 101
Wake Island (1942) 107, 197, 198, 243, 248
Wakeling, Gwen **138**, 223
Walas, Chris **53**
Walbrook, Anton 80, 133
Walburn, Raymond 107
Wald, Jerry 252
Walken, Christopher **39–40**, 102, 189, 214
Walker, Joseph B. 253
Walker, Robert 143, 157
Walker, Roy **106**
Walk in the Sun, A (1946) 251
Walk on the Wild Side, A (1962) 158
Wallace, Dee 48
Wallace, Lew 16
Wallace, Oliver **45**
Wallace, Pamela and Earl W. **175**
Wallach, Eli 76
Wallgren, Gunn 51
Wallis, Hal B. **26**, 252
Wallis, Shani 115
Walls of Malapaga, The 255
Wall Street (1987) **171**, 190, 218
Walsh, M. Emmet 71, 118
Walsh, Raoul 79, 240, 248, 250, 251
Walston, Ray 11, 146, 149
Walter, Jessica 66
Walter, Tracey 14
Walters, Charles 46, 93, 203, 247
Walters, Julie 216
Walthall, Henry B. 22, 170
Walton, Tony **6**
Walton, William 72*n*
Wanger, Walter 254, 255, 259
Wanstall, Norman **63**

War and Peace (1956) 204
War and Peace (1968) **171**
Warburton, Cotton **99**
Ward, David S. **149**
Ward, Fred 134
Ward, James 112
Warden, Jack 7, 15, 39, 71, 141, 213, 214
War Game, The (1966) 232
Wargnier, Regis 79
Warner, David 116
Warner, Frank **31**
Warner, H. B. 42, 95, 107, 180, 195
Warner, Harry M. 253
Warner, Jack L. **109**, 252
Warner Brothers 253
Warnes, Jennifer 42, 114
War of the Roses, The (1989) 251
War of the Worlds, The (1953) 159, **171**
Warren, Gene **159**
Warren Jr., Gene **154**
Warren, Harry 62, 71, 72, 225
Warren, Lesley Ann 169, 216
Warren, Mike 24
Warren, Robert Penn 6
Warrick, Ruth 30, 144
Warrington, Bill **69**
Washington, Denzel **61**, 93, 114, 191, 218, 219, 220
Washington, Ned **73**, **123**
"Washington Square" (novel by Henry James) 72
Wasserman, Lew 252
Wassiliev, Juri 106
Watch on the Rhine (1943) **171–172**, 184, 198, 243
Water Birds (1952) 229
Waterloo Bridge (1940) 248
Waters, Ethel 201
Waters, John **169**
Waterston, Sam 67, 70, 86, 217
Watkin, David **118**
Watkins, Greg **36**
Watson, Lucile 67, 94, 132, 144, 172, 198
Watson, Minor 176
Watson, Robert 119
Watters II, George **77**
Waxman, Franz **123**, **151**
"Way He Makes Me Feel, The" **50n**
Wayne, David 125, 159
Wayne, John 260; *Alamo* 3, 238; *High and the Mighty* 73; *How the West Was Won* 76; *Longest Day* 95; *Quiet Man* 129; *Reap the Wild Wind* 132; *Sands of Iwo Jima* 201; *She Wore a Yellow Ribbon* 141; *Stagecoach* 146; *True Grit* **165**, 188, 210
Way of All Flesh, The (1927-28) 89, **172**, 175, 183, 192, 243
"Way We Were, The" **172**
Way We Were, The (1973) **172**, 212
"Way You Look Tonight, The" **152**
Weary River (1928/29) 192
Weathers, Carl 135
Weatherwax, Paul **11**, **110**

Weaver, Sigourney 5, 82n, 177, 179, 217, 218, 219
Webb, Clifton 90, 132, 159, 160, 198, 199, 200
Webb, Elven **30**
Webb, Ira **122**
Webb, Jack 151
Webb, James R. **76**
Webb, Jim **7**
Webb, Robert **79**
Webber, Robert **138**
Weber, Fritz 25
Weber, Jacques 35
Webster, Paul Francis **25**, **96**, **138**, 225
We Can't Have Everything (1918) 113
Wechsler, David **139**
"Wedding of the Painted Doll" 22
Weingarten, Lawrence 252
Weinger, Scott 3
Weir, Peter: *Dead Poets Society* 38, 219, 239; *Green Card* 247; *Mosquito Coast* 250; *Witness* 175–176, 217, 243; *Year of Living Dangerously* 179
Welch, Raquel 51, 260
Weld, Tuesday 214
Welker, Frank 3
Welland, Colin **27**
Weller, Elly 12
Weller, Peter 135
Welles, Gwen 110
Welles, Orson 257; *Citizen Kane* 6, 10, **30**, 133, 197, 239; *Lady from Shanghai* 250; *Magnificent Ambersons* 241, 247; *Man for All Seasons* 98; *Third Man* 157; *Touch of Evil* 251; *V.I.P.s* 169
Wellman, William A.: *Battleground* 14, 147, 201, 239; *High and the Mighty* 73, 147, 203; *Nothing Sacred* 250; *Ox-Bow Incident* 241; *Star is Born* 147, 195, 242; *Story of G.I. Joe* 248; *Wings* 45, 175, 243
Wells, Claudia 13
Wells, George **40**
Wells, H. G. 159, 171
Wells, Veron 79
"We May Never Love Like This Again" **164**
Wenders, Wim 250
"We're a Couple of Swells" 46
Werker, Alfred 240
Werner, Oskar 142, 208
Wertmuller, Lina 213
Wesson, Dick 25, 40
West, Claudine **107**
West, Judi 54
West, Kit **130**
West, Ray **148**
West, Roland 44, 238
West, Samuel 76
West, Timothy 112
Westcott, Helen 175
Westerman, Floyd Red Crow 36
Westerner, The (1940) **172**, 184, 196, 222, 244
Westley, Helen 4
Westman, Nydia 116, 173
Westmore, Michael **100**

Weston, Jack 25, 42, 158
West Side Story (1961) 77, 89, **172–173**, 187, 206, 221, 223, 224, 225, 243, 256
Wetback Hound, The (1957) 230
Wettig, Patricia 30
Wexler, Haskell **20**, **174**
Weyl, Carl 2
Whale, James 250, 251
Whales of August, The (1987) 218
Whaley, Frank 20
What Ever Happened to Baby Jane? (1962) **173**, 207
Wheeler, Lyle R. **9**, **40**, **64**, **86**, **135**, 223
Whelan, Alison 109
Whelan, Tim 157
When Harry Met Sally (1989) 248
"When I See an Elephant Fly" 45
When Magoo Flew (1954) 229
When My Baby Smiles at Me (1948) 200
When Tomorrow Comes (1939) **173**
When Worlds Collide (1951) 159, **173**
"When You Wish Upon a Star" **123**
Whisperers, The (1967) 209
Whitaker, Forest 17, 34, 125
White, Jesse 40, 71
White, Onna **115**, 257
White, Richard 15
White, Ruth 101, 162
White, T. H. 26
White Banners (1938) 82n, 195
"White Christmas" **74**
White Heat (1949) 248
White Hunter, Black Heart (1990) 251
Whitelaw, Billie 116
Whitely, Jon 256
Whiteman, Paul 150
White Nights (1985) 50n, **173**
White Parade, The (1934) 194, 243
White Shadows in the South Seas (1928/29) **173–174**
White Wilderness (1958) 230
Whitfield, Mitchell 109
Whitford, Bradley 139
Whiting, Leonard 136
Whitlock, Albert **46**, **74**
Whitlock, Tom **163**
Whitman, Stuart 206
Whitmore, James 115, 163, 201, 213
Whitney, Jack **155**, **156**
Whitney Sr., John H. 258
Whittaker, Ian **75**
Whitty, May 34, 58, 68, 107, 152, 195, 198
Robin 3, 38, 53, 218, 219, 220, 260
Who Are the Debolts? And Where Did They Get Nineteen Kids? (1977) 234
Who Framed Roger Rabbit? (1988) **174**, 258
Who Is Harry Kellerman? (1971) 211
"Whole New World" 3, 50n, 225
Whorf, Richard 179
Who's Afraid of Virginia Woolf? (1966) 5n, **174**, 188, 208, 209, 223, 243

Who's Who in Animal Land (1944) 227
Why Korea? (1950) 229
Why Man Creates (1968) 232
Wicki, Bernard 95, 241
Widmark, Richard 3, 23, 76, 84, 108, 119, 200
Wiest, Dianne **70**, 190, 218, 219
Wilby, James 76
Wilcoxon, Henry 30, 107, 138, 155
Wild, Jack 115, 210
Wild at Heart (1990) 219, 248
Wild Bunch, The (1969) 248
Wilde, Cornel 66, 92, 199
Wilde, Oscar 123
Wilde, Ted 192
Wilder, Billy 223, 252; *Apartment* **10–11**, 187, 206, 222, 238; *Double Indemnity* 199, 239, 247; *Fedora* 249; *Fortune Cookie* 54; *Front Page* 250; *Irma La Douce* 80–81; *Lost Weekend* **95–96**, 185, 199, 222, 241; *Private Life of Sherlock Holmes* 251; *Sabrina* 138, 203; *Some Like It Hot* 144, 206; *Stalag 17* 147, 203; *Sunset Boulevard* **151**, 201, 222, 242; *Witness for the Prosecution* 205, 243, 248
Wilder, Gene 127, 176, 210
Wilder, Thornton 22, 72
Wild Is the Wind (1957) 204
Wild One, The (1953) 251
Wild River (1960) 251
Wild Wings (1966) 232
Wiles, Gordon **164**
Wilke, Robert J. 38, 165. 177
Wilkey, Jim 41
Wilkinson, John K. **124**
William, Warren 30
Williams, Bill 149
Williams, Billy **57**
Williams, Billy Dee 14, 47, 133
Williams, Cara 205
Williams, Cindy 164
Williams III, Clarence 128
Williams, Douglas **121**
Williams, Elaine 150
Williams, Elmo **73**
Williams, Esther 110, 111
Williams, Grant 177
Williams, Harcourt 136
Williams, Hugh 178
Williams, Jobeth 88
Williams, John 48, **52**, **82**, 138, 143, **148**, 161, 224
Williams, Paul **147**
Williams, Rhys 51
Williams, Richard **174**, 226, 258
Williams, Robin 3, 38, 53, 218, 219, 220, 260
Williams II, Russell **36**, **61**
Williams, Tennessee 112, 137, 150, 152
Williams, Vaughan 80
Willis, Bruce 39
Willis, Edwin B. **8**, **13**, **19**, **58**, **85**, **94**, **144**, **179**
Wills, Chill 60, 172, 179, 206
Wills, Mary **177**
Wilson (1944) 18, **175**, 198, 199, 222, 243

291

Wilson, Elizabeth 65
Wilson, Jim 36
Wilson, Michael 22n, **123**
Wilson, Richard 121
Wilson, Robb **96**
Wilson, Scott 67
Wilson, Thomas F. 13
Wimperis, Arthur **107**
Winchester 73 (1950) 251
"Windmills of Your Mind, The"
158
Winfield, Paul 211
Winfrey, Oprah 217
Wing, Paul **94**
Winger, Debra 114, 154, 216
Wings (1927/28) 45, **175**, 183,
192, 243
Wings Over Mt. Everest (1935) 226
Winkler, Angela 160
Winkler, Irwin **135**
Winn, Kitty 49
winners 183–191
*Winnie the Pooh and the Blustery
Day* (1968) 232
Winninger, Charles 149
Winston, Stan **5**, **154**
Winter, Margrit 99
Winter, Vincent 256
Winters, Jonathan 81
Winters, Ralph E. **16**, **87**
Winters, Shelley: *Diary of Anne
Frank* **40–41**, 187, 205, 222;
Double Life 44; *Patch of Blue*
121, 187, 208, 222; *Place in the
Sun* 123–124, 202; *Poseidon Ad-
venture* 125, 211
Winton, Jane 50
Winwood, Estelle 127
Wise, Kirk 15
Wise, Ray 135
Wise, Robert 252; *Day the Earth
Stood Still* 249; *Executive Suite*
247; *Hindenburg* 74; *I Want to
Live* 81, 205; *Sand Pebbles* 242;
Set-Up 251; *Somebody Up There
Likes Me* 144; *Sound of Music*
145, 187, 208, 242; *West Side
Story* **172–173**, 187, 206, 243
Wise Guy (book by Nicholas
Pileggi) 65
Wiseman, Joseph 170
Wish You Were Here (1987) 251
Witches, The (1990) 251
With a Song in My Heart (1952)
81, **175**, 202, 224
With Byrd at the South Pole
(1929/30) **175**
Withers, Jane 60
With the Marines at Tarawa (1944)
227
Witness (1985) **175–176**, 217, 243
Witness for the Prosecution (1957)
204, 205, 243, 248
*Witness to War: Dr. Charlie Clem-
ents* (1985) 236
Wivesson, Gudmar 13
Wizard of Oz, The (1939) 64, **176**,
196, 243
Wolfe, Tom 134
Wolff, Frank 8

Wolfit, Donald 15, 91, 136
Wolheim, Louis 6, 153, 166
Wolper, David L. 253
Wolsky, Albert **6**, **23**
Woman in Red, The (1984) **176**
Woman of the Dunes (1965) 208
Woman of the Year (1942) 40, **176**,
197
Woman Under the Influence, A
(1974) 212
Women, The (1939) 251
*Women—For America, For the
World* (1986) 236
Women in Love (1970) 163, **176–
177**, 188, 210, 211, 221
Wonder, Stevie **176**
*Wonderful World of the Brothers
Grimm, The* (1962) **177**
Wonder Man (1945) **177**
Wong, Anna May 141
Wong, Victor 90
Wood, Natalie 260; *Great Race*
67; *Love with the Proper Stranger*
207; *Miracle on 34th Street* 103;
Rebel Without a Cause 204, 207;
Splendor in the Grass 146, 206;
West Side Story 172–173
Wood, Peggy 145, 208
Wood, Sam: *Fair Co-ed* 50; *Good-
bye, Mr. Chips* 65, 196; *Kings Row*
198, 241, 247; *Kitty Foyle* 88,
197, 241; *Our Town* 241; *Pride of
the Yankees* 126, 242; *Stratton
Story* 149; *Telling the World* 153;
For Whom the Bell Tolls 54, 240
Woodard, Alfre 216
Woodruff, Tom **39**
Woods, Donald 10, 149, 172
Woods, James 217
Woodstock (1970) 233
Woodvine, John 8
Woodward, Joanne **159**, 186,
204, 209, 212, 219
Wooland, Norman 70
Woolf, John **115**
Woollcott, Alexander 139
Woolley, Monty 18, 143, 197, 199
Woolvett, Jaimz 167, 168
"Words of Love" 23
Work Experience (1989) 236
Working Girl (1988) 82n, **177**,
218, 219, 243
World According to Garp, The
(1982) 216
World Apart, A (1988) 251
World of Kids (1951) 229
World Without Sun (1964) 232
Wottitz, Walter **95**
Wray, Fay 169
Wray, John 6
Wrentz, Lawrence T. 142
Wrestling Swordfish (1931/32) 226
Wright, Amy 2, 21
Wright, Joseph C. **109**, **157**, 223
Wright, Samuel E. 17, 93
Wright, Teresa 17, 82n, **107**,
126, 184, 197, 198, 244
Written on the Wind (1956) **177**,
186, 204
Wrong Man, The (1957) 251

Wrubel, Allie **144**
Wuhl, Robert 14
Wuthering Heights (1939) **177–
178**, 196, 243
Wyatt, Jane 59, 95, 112
Wycherly, Margaret 140, 197
Wyler, William 252; *Ben-Hur*
16, 187, 205, 221, 239; *Best Years
of Our Lives* **17**, 185, 200, 221,
239; *Big Country* 17; *Collector*
208; *Come and Get It* 32; *Dead
End* 239, 246; *Detective Story*
202, 246; *Dodsworth* 44, 195,
239; *Friendly Persuasion* 204, 240,
247; *Funny Girl* 56, 240; *Heiress*
72, 201, 240; *Jezebel* 82, 240; *Letter* 197, 241, 247; *Little Foxes*
197, 241, 247; *Mrs. Miniver* **107**,
184, 198, 221, 241; *Roman Holiday* 136, 203, 242; *Westerner*
172; *Wuthering Heights* 178, 196,
243
Wyman, Jane: *Blue Veil* 202; *Here
Comes the Groom* 73; *Johnny
Belinda* **83**, 143, 185, 200; *Lost
Weekend* 96; *Magnificent Obsession* 203; *Princess O'Rourke* 126;
Yearling 179, 199
Wymark, Patrick 34
Wynn, Ed 41, 100, 205
Wynn, Keenan 9, 67, 74, 110, 111
Wynter, Dana 3
Wynyard, Diana 27, 193

Y

Yamagata, Isao 58
Yamamura, Soh 163
"Yankee Doodle Boy" 179
Yankee Doodle Dandy (1942) 96,
107, **179**, 184, 197, 198, 243
Yankee Doodle Mouse (1943) 227
Yanne, Jean 79
Yarnell, Bruce 81
Yates, Peter 21, 24, 215, 216,
239, 247
Yeager, Chuck 134
Yearling, The (1946) 161, **179**,
199, 200, 223, 243
Year of Living Dangerously, The
(1983) **179**, 190, 216
Year Toward Tomorrow, A (1966)
232
Yeatman, Hoyt **1**
Yentl (1983) 50n, **179**, 216
Yesterday, Today and Tomorrow
(1964) 100n, **180**
Ying Ruocheng 90
Yip, David 78
Yordan, Philip **23**
York, Michael 25, 95, 108, 136
York, Susannah 98, 152, 156,
162, 210
You Can't Take It With You (1938)
81, **180**, 184, 195, 196, 221, 243
You Don't Have to Die (1988) 236
"You Light Up My Life" **180**
You Light Up My Life (1977) **180**
"You'll Never Know" **72**, 225
Young, Alan 159, 162
Young, Burt 135, 213

Young, Carleton 166
Young, Freddie A. **43**, **91**, **137**,
223
Young, Gig 260; *Air Force* 3;
Come Fill the Cup 202; *Hinden-
burg* 74; *Lovers and Other Strang-
ers* 96; *Teacher's Pet* 205; *They
Shoot Horses, Don't They?* **156**,
188, 210
Young, Lester 137
Young, Loretta 18, **51**, 86, 90,
185, 200, 201
Young, Peter **14**
Young, Ric 90
Young, Robert 89, 143
Young, Roland 122, 195
Young, Sean 171
Young, Stephen 121
Young, Terence 159
Young, Victor **11–12**
Young at Heart (1987) 236
Young Philadelphians, The (1959)
205
You Only Live Once (1937) 251
You're a Big Boy Now (1966) 165,
209
"You Were Meant for Me" 22
Yuricich, Matthew **95**

Z

Z (1969) 104, **181**, 210, 243
Zaentz, Saul **7**, **116**, 171
Zanuck, Darryl F. **5**, **58**, **76**, 95,
221, 252
Zanuck, Lili Fini **44**
Zanuck, Richard D. **44**, 252
Zapata, Emiliano 170
Zapponi, Bernadino 8n
Zaslow, Michael 180
Zavitz, Lee **40**
Zeffirelli, Franco 70n, 136, 210,
242, 247
Zehetbauer, Rolf **25**
Zelig (1983) 248
Zelniker, Michael 17
Zemeckis, Robert 13, 39, 174
Zimbalist, Sam **16**
Zinnemann, Fred 245; *From Here
to Eternity* **55**, 186, 203, 240;
High Noon 74, 202, 240; *Julia*
85, 214; *Man For All Seasons* **98**,
188, 209, 241; *Nun's Story* 206,
241, 246, 248; *Oklahoma!* 115;
Search 139, 201; *Sundowners*
206, 242
Zinner, Peter **39**
"Zip-a-Dee-Doo-Dah" **144**
Zola, Jean-Pierre 105
Zorba the Greek (1964) **181**, 187,
207, 208, 243
Zsigmond, Vilmos **31**, 134
Zucco, George 11, 19
Zucker, David 250
Zucker, Jerry 60, 240
Zukor, Adolph 255
Zvarik, Frantisek 142
Zvarikova, Helen 142
Zwerling, Darrell 29
Zwick, Edward 61